WITHDRAWN
UTSA LIBRARIES

INDEX TO BRITISH
LITERARY BIBLIOGRAPHY

V

BRITISH BIBLIOGRAPHY AND TEXTUAL CRITICISM

A BIBLIOGRAPHY
(AUTHORS)

T. H. HOWARD-HILL

CLARENDON PRESS · OXFORD
1979

Oxford University Press, Walton Street, Oxford OX2 6DP
OXFORD LONDON GLASGOW
NEW YORK TORONTO MELBOURNE WELLINGTON
NAIROBI DAR ES SALAAM CAPE TOWN
KUALA LUMPUR SINGAPORE JAKARTA HONG KONG TOKYO
DELHI BOMBAY CALCUTTA MADRAS KARACHI

© *T. H. Howard-Hill 1979*

All rights reserved. No part of this publication may be reproduced, stored in a retrieval system, or transmitted, in any form or by any means, electronic, mechanical, photocopying, recording, or otherwise, without the prior permission of Oxford University Press

British Library Cataloguing in Publication Data

Howard-Hill, Trevor Howard
   British bibliography and textual criticism, a bibliography.–
   (Index to British literary bibliography; 4, 5).
   1. Publishers and publishing – Great Britain –
   Bibliography   2. English literature – Criticism,
   Textual – Bibliography   3. English literature – Bibliography
   I. Title   II. Series
   016.0705'73'0941   Z324   77-30735
   ISBN 0-19-818163-9

LIBRARY
The University of Texas
At San Antonio

Text set in 10/11 pt Photon Baskerville, printed and bound in Great Britain at The Pitman Press, Bath

TABLE OF ABBREVIATIONS

Aber.   Aberdeenshire
Abr.   Abroad
Abstr   Abstract/s
Acad   Academy/ia
A.D.   Anno Domini
Afric   Africa/n
Ag   August
Ala.   Alabama
Am   America/n
Ann   Annals; Annual/s
Angl   Anglia; Anglaises
anr.   another
Antiqu   Antiquarian; Antiquities
Ap   April
Archæol   Archæology/ical
Architect   Architectural
Archiv   Archivists
archbp.   archbishop
Assn   Association/s
Asst   Assistant
Atlan   Atlantic
attrib.   attributed
Auc   Auction
AUMLA   Australasian Universities' Language and Literature Association Journal
Austral   Australasian
Autogr   Autograph/s
Ayr   Ayrshire

b.   born
BBC   British Broadcasting Corporation
B.C.   British Columbia; Before Christ
Beds.   Bedfordshire
Beibl   Beiblatt
Berks.   Berkshire
Bib   Bibliography/ical
Bibliogr. descr.   bibliographical description (Index)
bibliogr/s.   bibliographical/y/ies
Biblioph   Bibliophile/s
Biblioth   Bibliotheck
Bibs.   bibliographies (Index)
Biog   Biography/ical

Bkbndng   Bookbinding
Bkbndr   Bookbinder
Bk/s   Book/s
Bkmkr   Bookmaker
Bkmn/s   Bookman/'s
Bksllng.   bookselling (Index)
Bksllr   Bookseller
B.M.   British Museum
Bndng.   bookbinding (Index)
Bod   Bodleian
bp.   bishop
Brecon.   Breconshire
Brit   Britain; British
Bucks.   Buckinghamshire
Bull   Bulletin/s

c.   circa (about)
Caith.   Caithness-shire
Calif.   California
Cambs.   Cambridgeshire
card.   cardinal
Cards.   Cardiganshire
Carms.   Carmarthenshire
Carnarvs.   Carnarvonshire
Cath   Catholic
CBEL   Cambridge Bibliography of English Literature
cent.   century
chapt.   chapter
Ches.   Cheshire
Chron   Chronicle
chronol.   chronological
Circ   Circular
cm.   centimetre/s
co.   County/county; Company
col.   coloured; column/s
Coll   Collector/'s/ion; College
Collns.   collections (Index)
Coloph   Colophon
Comm   Communication/s
Comp   Comparée
comp.   compiled/er/s
Congreg   Congregational

Conn.   Connecticut
Connoiss   Connoisseur
Contemp   Contemporary
contrib/s.   contribution/s
Cornw.   Cornwall
Crit   Criticism/ical
Cumb.   Cumberland
C.U.P.   Cambridge University Press

d.   died
D   December
Denbigh.   Denbighshire
Dept.   Department
Derbys.   Derbyshire
descr/s.   description/s
Devon.   Devonshire
diagr/s.   diagram/s
Doc   Documentation
Dumf.   Dumfriesshire

Econ   Economic/s
ed.   edited; edition/s; editor/s
Educ   Education/al
Eng   English
Engl   Englische
enl.   enlarged
est.   established
extr.   extract/ed

F   February; folio/s
facsim/s.   facsimile/s
f/ff.   following
Fict   Fiction
Fifes.   Fifeshire
fl.   *floruit* (flourished)
fold.   folded
Forfars.   Forfarshire
Fortn   Fortnightly

Gaz   Gazette
Gen   General
Gent   Gentleman's
Geogr   Geography/ical
Geol   Geological
Germ   German/ic
Glam.   Glamorganshire
Glos.   Gloucestershire
Graph   Graphic
Grol   Grolier

Guildh   Guildhall

Hants.   Hampshire
Herefs.   Herefordshire
Herts.   Hertfordshire
hft   heft
Hisp   Hispanic
Hist   History/ical
H.M.S.O.   His/Her Majesty's Stationery Office
Hndbk   Handbook
Hunts.   Huntingdonshire

ib.   *ibidem* (in the same place)
Ill.   Illinois
illus.   illustration/s; illustrated
Illus.   illustration (*Index*)
Ind.   Indiana
Inst   Institute/ion
Int   International
I.O.W.   Isle of Wight
Ital   Italian

J   Journal
Ja   January
Jahrb   Jahrbuch
Je   June
Jl   July

Keats-Sh   Keats-Shelley

l.   leaf/leaves; line/s
Lanark.   Lanarkshire
Lancs.   Lancashire
Lang   Language/s; Langues
ld.   lord
Leics.   Leicestershire
Let   Letters
Lib/s   Library/ies
Libn   Librarian
Librnshp   Librarianship
Librs.   library/ies (*Index*)
Lincs.   Lincolnshire
Lit   Literary; Literature
Litt   Littérature
Lond   London
ltd.   limited

Mag   Magazine
Mar   Mariner's

Mass. Massachusetts
Med Medieval; Medicine/al
Merc Mercury
Merion. Merionethshire
Midloth. Midlothian
Mirr Mirror
Misc Miscellany
Miss. Mississippi
M.I.T. Massachusetts Institute of Technology
Mkr Maker
Mnthly Monthly
Mod Modern/es
Mons. Monmouthshire
Mr March
ms/s. manuscript/s
Mss. manuscript/s (*Index*)
Mus Music/al; Museum
My May

N Note/s; News; November
N&Q Notes and Queries
Nat National; Natural
N.C. North Carolina
NCBEL New Cambridge Bibliography of
    English Literature
n.d. no date
Neb. Nebraska
Neophilol Neophilologus
Newsl Newsletter
News-sh News-sheet
Ninet Nineteenth
N.J. New Jersey
no/s. Number/s; numero/s, etc.
Norf. Norfolk
Northants. Northamptonshire
Notebk Notebook
Notts. Nottinghamshire
n.p. no place
nr Nummer
Nth North
Nthmb. Northumberland
N.Y. New York
N.Z. New Zealand

Oc October
Occas Occasional
O.E.D. Oxford English Dictionary
Opp Opportunities
O.U.P. Oxford University Press

Oxon. Oxfordshire

p. page/s
Pa Paper/s; Pennsylvania
Pam/s Pamphlet/s
Paper. papermaking (*Index*)
Pemb. Pembrokeshire
Perth. Perthshire
Philobib Philobiblon
Philol Philology/ical
Philos Philosophy/ical
port/s. portrait/s
pr. press
Print Printer/s
Priv Private
Proc Proceedings
Prod Production
pseud. pseudonym
pt/s. part/s
ptd. printed
ptg. printing
Ptg Printing; printing (*Index*)
ptr/s. printer/s
pub. published
Pub/s Public; Publication/s; Publisher/s'
Publ. Publication (*Index*)

Q Quarterly; quarto/s
quasifacsim. quasifacsimile

R Review/s; Revue
Rec Record/s
Recus Recusant
refs. references
Renaiss Renaissance
Renfrew. Renfrewshire
repr. reprint/ed
Repub Republic
Res Research
Restor Restoration
rev. revised
Rev: Review/s
rf. refer
R.I. Rhode Island
Roxb. Roxburghshire
Roy Royal

S September
Sat Saturday

Sci   Science/s
Scot/t   Scotland; Scottish
SD   stagedirection/s
Sec   Section
ser   series
Sevent   Seventeenth
Sh   Shakespeare/'s/ian
Shrop.   Shropshire
sig/s.   signature/s
Signat   Signature
Soc   Society/ies
Som.   Somerset
SP   speechprefix/es
Staffs.   Staffordshire
Statesmn   Statesman
STC   Short Title Catalogue
Sth/ly   South/erly
Stud   Study/ies; Studien
Suff.   Suffolk
Suppl   Supplement
Surv   Survey

Tech   Technical
Text.   text (*Index*)
Theat   Theatre/ical
Theol   Theology/ical
TLS   Times Literary Supplement

TP   title-page
trans.   translated/ion/s
Trans   Transactions
transcr/s.   transcription/s
Transit   Transition
Typogr   Typography/ica/ical

Univ   University
U.P.   University Press

v.   volume/s
Va.   Virginia
Vict   Victorian

Warws.   Warwickshire
Westm.   Westmorland
Wilts.   Wiltshire
Wk   Work
Wkly   Weekly
Worcs.   Worcestershire

Yorks.   Yorkshire
Yrs   Year's

4°   quarto
8°   octavo
12°   duodecimo

AUTHORS

À BECKETT, GILBERT ABBOTT, 1811–56

8222 **Argus book shop.** À Beckett: Comic history of Rome. [Distinction of 1st ed.]. Bib N&Q 2no2:2 F '36.

ADDISON, JOSEPH, 1672–1719

8223 **Reed, Edward B.** Two notes on Addison. Mod Philol 6no2:181–9 Oc '08.

'The text of Addison' (p. 181–6)

8224 **Guthkelch, Adolph C. L.** Cogan's edition of Addison's Miscellaneous works. N&Q ser11 11:88 Ja '15.

8225 **Bloodworth, Hubert.** Addison's Works in 12mo. [1726]. (Notes, queries and answers). Bkmns J new ser 9no29:184–5 F '24.

8226 **Sherburn, George.** [A bibliographical note on the 1726 ed. of Addison's Works]. Mod Philol 23no3:361 F '26. [Sg.: G. S.]

8227 **Heilman, Lee W.** Addison's The drummer. TLS 1 Oc '31:754.

8228 **Anderson, Paul B.** Addison's Letter from Italy. Mod Lang N 47no5:318 My '32.

8229 **Bradner, Leicester.** The composition and publication of Addison's Latin poems. Mod Philol 35no4:359–67 My '38.

8230 **Atkins, Stuart.** Addison's Cato, I.i.47–53. Philol Q 21no4:430–3 Oc '42.

8231 **Horn, Robert D.** The early editions of Addison's Campaign. Stud Bib 3:256–61 '50/1.

8232 **Reinert, Otto.** Addison poems. N&Q 196:83 F '51.

8233 **Crum, Margaret C.** A manuscript of essays by Addison. Bod Lib Rec 5no2:98–103 Oc '54.

8234 **Campbell, Hilbert H.** The sale catalogue of Addison's library. Eng Lang N 4no4:269–73 Je '67.

Æ., *pseud. of* GEORGE WILLIAM RUSSELL, 1867–1935

8235 **McAnally, sir Henry.** An Æ curiosity. [Poems attrib. to S. J. O'Grady, 1929]. Bk Coll Q 3:67–9 Je '31.

8236 **O'Hegarty, Patrick S.** A. E. The hero in man, 1909. (Bibliographical notes). Dublin Mag new ser 22no3:60 Jl/S '47.

8237 **Kindilien, Carlin T.** George William Russell ('Æ') and the Colby collection. Colby Lib Q ser4 2:21–4 My '55. port.

AINSWORTH, WILLIAM HARRISON, 1805–82

8238 **Wise, Charles.** Jack Sheppard. N&Q ser9 3:249 Ap '99.

8239 **D., R.** Ainsworth the novelist. N&Q ser9 9:409 My '02; H. B. Clayton *ib.* 10:11 Jl '02; J. T. Page 10:56–7 Jl '02.

8240 **Weaver, H. F.** Ainsworth's Auriol. [First edition in book form]. Bkmns J 1no5:121 D '19; Editor of Book prices current *ib.* 1no7:141 D '19.

8241 **Ainsworth** and Egan. (Notes on sales). TLS 10 Ag '22:524.

8242 **Randall, David A.** Ainsworth: Nell Gwynn, 1850. [Am. ed.]. Bib N&Q 2no3:6 Ap '36. [Sg.: D. R.]

8243 **William** Harrison Ainsworth. [Acquisition of ms. of Beatrice Tyldesley]. Princeton Univ Lib Chron 12no3:162–3 '51.

AKENSIDE, MARK, 1721–70

8244 **Chapman, Robert W.** A note on the first edition of The pleasures of the imagination. R Eng Stud 1no3:346–8 Jl '25; 3no11:349 '27.

8245 **Foxon, David F.** Akenside's The pleasures of imagination. (Note no.62). Bk Coll 5no1:77–8 '56.

ALEXANDER, SIR WILLIAM, EARL OF STIRLING, 1567?–1640

8246 **Wiles, A. G. D.** The date of publication and composition of sir William Alexander's Supplement to Sidney's Arcadia. Pa Bib Soc Am 50:387–92 '56.

8247 **Mitchell, Alison** and **Katharine Foster.** Sir William Alexander's Supplement to book III of Sidney's Arcadia. Library ser5 24no3:234–41 S '69. facsims., tables.

ALEYN, CHARLES, fl.1638

8248 **Lowe, G. Burnham** [*i.e.* Burman]. Aleyn's The historie of that wise prince Henrie the seventh. 8°. T. Cotes for W. Cooke, 1638. (STC 353). [Distinction of ptgs.]. (Query 80). Bk Coll 6no2:181 '57.

ALFRED, KING OF THE WEST-SAXONS, 849–901

8249 **Sparke, Archibald.** The works of king Alfred the great. N&Q ser12 3:249 Mr '17.

ALLESTREE, RICHARD, 1619–81

8250 **Jonas, Alfred C.** The Whole duty of man. N&Q ser9 2:536 D '98; Harriet McIlquhan *ib.* 3:72 Ja '99; Q. V. 3:118 F '99.

8251 **Jaggard, William.** Literary secrets: authorship of the Whole duty of man and cognate writings, 1658–84. Bkmn 81no481:66–9 Oc '31. facsim.

8252 **N.** The Whole duty of man. N&Q 175:190 S '38; W. Jaggard *ib.* 175:231 S '38.

8253 **Elmen, Paul.** Richard Allestree and The whole duty of man. Library ser5 6no1:19–27 Je '51.

ALLIN, RALPH, fl.1585

8254 **Williams, Franklin B.** The Hauen of hope. (Bibliographical notes). TLS 25 Ap '35:276.

ALLINGHAM, WILLIAM, 1824–89

8255 **White, H. O.** An Allingham pamphlet. [Flower pieces, 1887]. TLS 17 Ag '56:487.

ALLOTT, ROBERT, fl.1600

8256 **Crawford, Charles.** England's Parnassus, 1600. N&Q ser10 9:341–3, 401–3 My '08; S. L. Petty *ib.* 9:403 My '08; C. Crawford 10:4–6, 84–5, 102–3, 262–3, 362–3, 444–5 Jl–D '08; 11:4–5, 123–4, 204–5, 283–5, 383–4, 443–5, 502–3 Ja–Je '09; 12:235 S '09.

AMORY, THOMAS, 1691?–1788

8257 **Roberts, M. A. M.** The life of John Buncle, by Thomas Amory. N&Q 195:370 Ag '50.

AMPHLETT, JAMES, 1776–1860

8258 **Axon, William E. A.** James Amphlett and Samuel Taylor Coleridge. [The newspaper press, 1860]. Library ser3 2no5:34–9 Ja '11.

ANDREWES, BP. LANCELOT, 1555–1626

8259 **Barker, Francis E.** Crashaw and Andrewes. [XCVI sermons, 1631]. TLS 21 Ag '37:618; K. N. Colvile *ib.* 28 Ag '37:624.

ANDREWS, JOHN, b.1583?

8260 **D., H. W.** John Andrews. [A subpoena, 1623]. TLS 31 Jl '30:628.

ANSTEY, CHRISTOPHER, 1724–1805

8261 **Williams, Iolo A.** Bibliographical notes and news. [Includes Anstey collations]. London Merc 11no64:413–17 F '25; 11no65:525–9 Mr '25; 11no66:641–5 Ap '25; 12no68:193–7 Je '25; 12no69:298–302 Jl '25.

8262 **Munby, Alan N. L.** Anstey's Election ball and the Epistle to Bampfylde. Bk Coll Q 16:19–23 Oc/D '34.

ANWYL, LEWIS, d.1776.

8263 **Davies, sir William L.** Lewis Anwyl (?–1776). (Biographica et bibliographica). Nat Lib Wales J 4no1/2:96 '45.

ARBUTHNOT, JOHN, 1667–1735

8264 **Griffith, Reginald H.** Memoirs of Scriblerus. N&Q ser11 6:167–8 Ag '12; J. F. Palmer *ib.* 6:278 Oc '12; T. Bayne 6:336–7 Oc '12.

8265 **Brouckmans, Aloys.** Arbuthnot's Laws of chance, third edition. [1692]. N&Q 178:100 F '40.

ARCHER, MICHAEL, fl.1634

8266 **Shaaber, Matthias A.** Michael Archer's Dream of bounden duty. Lib Chron Univ Pennsylvania 32no2:89–100 '66.

ARGYLE, ARCHIBALD CAMPBELL, 9TH EARL OF, d.1685 *see* Campbell, Archibald, 9th earl of Argyle, d.1685.

ARLEN, MICHAEL, 1895–1956

8267 **Chaundy, Leslie.** The first edition of Arlen's London venture. Bkmns J new ser 11no38:93–4 N '24.

8268 **James, Harold E.** Michael Arlen: The London venture. [Issues]. Bib N&Q 1no3:4 Ag '35.

ARMSTRONG, JOHN, d.1758

8269 **Eddy, Donald D.** Missing: John Armstrong's History of the island of Minorca, 1756. Cornell Lib J 2:83–4 '67.

ARNOLD, MATTHEW, 1822–88

8270 **Prideaux, William F.** The bibliography of Matthew Arnold. [The strayed reveller, 1849]. N&Q ser8 1:313–14 Ap '92.

8271 **Hutchinson, Thomas.** Matthew Arnold's Poems of Wordsworth. Athenæum 3661:836 D '97.

8272 **Kempling, William B.** Matthew Arnold's Horatian echo. N&Q ser10 3:6 Ja '05.

8273 **Ellerton, F. G.** The Scholar-gipsy. TLS 20 S '23:620; F. J. Hall; C. C. Bell *ib.* 27 S '23:636; sir H. S. Milford 4 Oc '23:652; F. G. Ellerton 11 Oc '23:670.

8274 **Dr.** and Matthew Arnold volumes; . . . . (Books in the sale rooms). Bkmns J new ser 9no29:179 F '24.

8275 **Keogh, Andrew.** Letters of Matthew Arnold [purchased for Library]. Yale Univ Lib Gaz 6no1:14 Jl '31.

8276 **Motter, Thomas H. V.** A check list of Matthew Arnold's letters. Stud Philol 31no4:600–5 Oc '34.

8277 **Brown, Edward K.** Studies in the text of Matthew Arnold's prose works. Paris, P. André, 1935. ii,139p. 25cm.

Rev: H. F. Lowry Mod Lang N 52:536–7 '37.

8278 **Goodspeed, George T.** Arnold: Empedocles on Etna, 1852. Bib N&Q 2no9:2 Ja '38; A. Pforzheimer; J. H. Pershing *ib.* 2no11:4 N '38. [Sg.: G. G.]

8279 —— Arnold: The strayed reveller, 1849. [Suppression]. Bib N&Q 2no9:2 Ja '38. [Sg: G. G.]

8280 **Munsterberg, Margaret.** First editions of Matthew Arnold. More Bks Boston Pub Lib Bull 13no5:200–1 My '38. [Sg.: M. M.]

8281 **Ruff, William.** An exhibition of the writings of Matthew Arnold. Yale Univ Lib Gaz 13no4:95–8 Ap '39.

8282 **Gill, W. W.** A line in The scholar gypsy. N&Q 177:423 D '39; L. R. M. Strachan *ib*. 177:482 D '39; F. Page 178:51 Ja '40; W. W. Gill 178:68 Ja '40.

8283 **Mainwaring, Marion.** Notes towards a Matthew Arnold bibliography. Mod Philol 49no3:189–94 F '52.

8284 **[Weber, Carl J.].** An Arnold-Forman-Wise item, with a letter from Tom Wise. [Alaric at Rome]. Colby Lib Q ser3 8:114–47 N '52; Two corrections *ib*. 11:184 Ag '53.

8285 **Davis, Arthur K.** Arnold's letters. Vict News Letter 3:2–4 Ap '53.

8286 **Buckler, William E.** An American edition of Matthew Arnold's Poems. [1878]. Pub Mod Lang Assn 69no3:678–80 Je '54.

8287 **Townsend, Francis G.** A neglected edition of Arnold's St. Paul and protestantism. R Eng Stud new ser 5no17:66–9 Ja '54.

8288 **Lowe, Robert L.** Matthew Arnold and Percy William Bunting, some new letters, 1884–1887. Stud Bib 7:199–207 '55.

8289 **Super, Robert H.** The authenticity of the first edition of Arnold's Alaric at Rome, 1840. (Notes and documents). Huntington Lib Q 19no3:306–9 My '56.

8290 **Neiman, Fraser.** Some newly attributed contributions of Matthew Arnold to the Pall Mall gazette. Mod Philol 55no2:84–92 N '57. table.

8291 **Allott, Kenneth.** Matthew Arnold's original version of The river. [Ms.]. TLS 28 Mr '58:172; 11 Ap '58:195; A. Harris *ib*. 18 Ap '58:209.

8292 **Buckler, William E.** Matthew Arnold's books: toward a publishing diary. Geneva, E. Droz; Paris, Minard, 1958. 182p. 25cm.

    Rev: TLS 22 Ag '58:472; W. A. Madden Vict Stud 2:173–5 '59; A. D. Culler J Eng Germ Philol 58:140–2 '59; K. Allott Mod Lang R 54:267–8 '59; F. Neiman Mod Philol 56:215–16 '59; R. L. Brooks Mod Lang Q 20:385–7 '59.

8293 **Brooks, Roger L.** Matthew Arnold and his contemporaries; a check list of unpublished and published letters. Stud Philol 56no4:647–53 Oc '59.

8294 —— Matthew Arnold in private collections. (Query 111). Bk Coll 8no1:73 '59.

8295 —— A census of Matthew Arnold's Poems, 1853. Pa Bib Soc Am 54:184–6 '60.

8296 —— Matthew Arnold and the Pall Mall gazette. Mod Philol 58no3:202–3 F '61.

8297 —— A neglected edition of Matthew Arnold's poetry, and a bibliographical correction. [Poems, 1856]. Pa Bib Soc Am 55:140–1 '61.

8298 —— An unrecorded American edition of the Selected poems of Matthew Arnold. [1878]. Library ser5 16no3:213–14 S '61.

8299 **Super, Robert H.** The first publication of Thyrsis. [1866]. N&Q 206:229 Je '61.

8300 **Polhemus, George W.** An additional variation in Arnold's The terrace at Berne. [Ms.]. N&Q 207:299 Ag '62.

8301 **Brooks, Roger L.** The Strayed reveller myth. Library ser5 18no1:57–60 Mr '63.

Census of copies (p. 58–60)

8302 **Brown, T. Julian.** The autograph of Arnold's Sohrab and Rustum. (Note 209). Bk Coll 12no4:494 '63.

8303 —— Matthew Arnold, 1822–88. (English literary autographs, XLVI). Bk Coll 12no2:195 '63. facsim.

8304 **Brooks, Roger L.** Matthew Arnold and Ticknor & Fields. Am Lit 35no4:514–19 Ja '64.

8305 —— The Story manuscript of Matthew Arnold's New Rome. Pa Bib Soc Am 58:295–7 '64. table.

8306 —— Letters of Matthew Arnold, a supplementary checklist. Stud Philol 63no1:93–8 Ja '66.

8307 **Super, Robert H.** American piracies of Matthew Arnold. Am Lit 38no1:123–5 Mr '66.

8308 **Davis, Arthur K.** Matthew Arnold's letters, a descriptive checklist. Charlottesville, Published for the Bibliographical society of Virginia by the U.P. of Virginia [1968]. xlv,429p. port. 23cm.

Introduction.–Part I: The letters listed and described in chronological order.–Part II: The letters arranged under the names of correspondents.–Appendices . . .: A. Table of correspondents, with the number of letters addressed to each. B. The holders of autograph letters, with the number of letters held by each.

Rev: Pa Bib Soc Am 63:61 '69; A. D. Culler Vict Prose 7:77–8 '69; S. M. B. Coulling Vict Stud 13:100–1 '69.

8309 **Carter, John W.** The Death of Balder. TLS 31 Jl '69:859.

ARTHUR, LEGENDARY KING OF BRITAIN, fl.520

8310 **Nitze, William A.** The Newberry collection of Arthuriana. Mod Philol 30no1:1–4 Ag '32. facsim.

ASCHAM, ROGER, 1515–68

8311 **Chapman, Robert W.** Bennet's Ascham. [1761]. R Eng Stud 5no17:69–70 Ja '29.

8312 **Parks, George B.** The first draft of Ascham's Scholemaster. Huntington Lib Q 1no3:313–27 Ap '38. table.

> 1. The occasion.–2. The date.–3. General comparison of the two versions of book 1.–4. Specific material in R.–5. Conclusion.

ASHBEE, HENRY SPENCER, 1834–1900

8313 **Bookhunter, A,** *pseud.* Mr. Henry Spencer Ashbee. (Bookworms of yesterday and to-day). Bkworm 2no21:257–61 Ag '89.

8314 **Thomas, Ralph.** The late H. S. Ashbee. N&Q ser9 6:121–2 Ag '00; F. Marcham *ib.* 6:358 N '00; W. Roberts 7:347 My '01.

8315 **Bensly, Edward.** H. S. Ashbee: Pisanus Fraxi. N&Q ser11 8:365 N '13.

ASTELL, MARY, 1666?–1731

8316 **Halsband, Robert.** Two facts about Mary Astell. (Note 163). Bk Coll 10no1:334 '61.

8317 **Todd, William B.** Mary Astell's Serious proposal to the ladies, 1694. (Note 164). Bk Coll 10no3:334–5 '61.

AUBREY, JOHN, 1626–97

8318 **Gunther, R. T.** The library of John Aubrey, F.R.S. Bod Q Rec 6no69:230–6 '31.

8319 **Powell, Anthony.** John Aubrey. [His Wiltshire collections]. TLS 2 Mr '46:103.

8320 **John** Aubrey's books. TLS 13 Ja '50:32; 20 Ja '50:48.

AUDEN, WYSTAN HUGH, 1907–73

8321 **Beach, Joseph W.** The making of the Auden canon. [Minneapolis] University of Minnesota pr. [1957]. viii,315p. 23cm.

> 1. In time of war: revisions in the commentary.–2. Certain peculiarities of Auden's method.–3. Further significant verbal alterations.–4. Passages eliminated for ideological reasons.–5. Passages eliminated for reasons less clear.–6. Poems eliminated for ideological reasons.–7. The Orators: poems discarded and poems retained.–8. Light verse, including the three jolly ballads.–9. Uncollected poems of serious ideological import.–10. More un-

collected poems.–11. Letters from Iceland.–12. Paid on both sides and The dance of death.–13. The Dog beneath the skin.–14. Prothalamion and the vicar's sermon.–15. The Ascent of F6 and On the frontier.–16. Opera librettos.–17. The three long poems.–18. Collected shorter poems.–19. A summary of findings and conclusions.–20. W. H. Auden, the question of identity.–Supplementary notes.–Appendixes: I. Auden's juvenilia.–II. Poems in the 1930 volume replaced by others in 1933.–III. Check list of poems in the Collected poetry.–IV. Poems of Auden not reprinted in the Collected poetry.

Rev: L. D. Lerner Mod Lang R 54:107 '59; A. J. Farmer Étude Angl 12:362 '59; J. M. Ferguson New Mexico Q 29:124–5 59; M. Marcus J Eng Germ Philol 58:315–18 '59.

8322 **Bloomfield, Barry C.** W. H. Auden's first book. [Poems, 1928]. Library ser5 17no2:152–4 Je '62.

8323 **Tolley, A. Trevor.** The printing of Auden's Poems, 1928, and Spender's Nine experiments. Library ser5 22no2:149–50 Je '67.

AUNGERVILLE, RICHARD (RICHARD DE BURY), BP., 1287–1342? *see* Richard de Bury (Richard Aungerville), bp., 1287–1342?

AUSTEN, JANE, 1775–1817

8324 **A., G. E. P.** Jane Austen's Persuasion. N&Q ser12 1:466 Je '16.

8325 **Keynes, sir Geoffrey L.** The text of Mansfield Park. TLS 30 Ag '23:572; R. W. Chapman *ib.* 3 S '23:604.

8326 **Meyerstein, Edward H. W.** The first passage in Persuasion. TLS 28 Je '23:440; F. D. M. *ib.* 5 Jl '23:456; E. R. Faraday 26 Jl '23:504.

8327 **Marsh, sir Edward.** Some notes on miss Austen's novels. [Emendations]. (Correspondence). London Merc 10no56:189–93 Je '24.

8328 **Sampson, John.** Jane Austen's Sanditon. [Text]. TLS 16 Ap '25:268; N. W. H. *ib.* 30 Ap '25:300; R. W. Chapman 14 My '25:335.

8329 **Chapman, Robert W.** A Jane Austen collection. [Mss.]. TLS 14 Ja '26:27. [Sg.: R. W. C.]

8330 **Flower, Robin E. W.** The first draft of Jane Austen's Persuasion. Brit Mus Q 1no1:15–17 My '26. facsim. [Sg.: R. F.]

8331 **Jane** Austen documents. (Notes on sales). TLS 28 Ja '26:68.

8332 **Chapman, Robert W.** Jane Austen and her publishers. [Thomas Egerton; John Murray]. London Merc 22no130:337–42 Ag '30; 22no133:66 N '30.

8333 —— Jane Austen's Camilla. Bod Q Rec 6no67:162–3 '30.

8334 **Nonesuch press.** Jane Austen bibliography. [Errata leaf for Keynes, 1929]. TLS 16 Jl '31:564.

8335 **Winterich, John T.** Pride and prejudice. (Romantic stories of books, second series, XXIII). Pub Wkly 120no3:250–4 Jl '31. port., facsims.

8336 **Chapman, Robert W.** Jane Austen's books. [Her library]. Bk Coll Q 9:92–5 Ja/Mr '33.

8337 —— Jane Austen's library. Bk Coll Q 11:28–32 Jl/S '33.

8338 **Bell, sir Harold I.** A reposit of Jane Austen manuscripts. Brit Mus Q 11no1:27–8 Oc '36.

8339 **Chapman, Robert W.** Contrive or continue. [In Pride and prejudice]. TLS 10 Ap '37:275.

8340 —— Jane Austen's text; authoritative manuscript corrections. TLS 13 F '37:116.

8341 **Sadleir, Michael T. H.** Austen, Jane: The first collected edition. Bib N&Q 2no12:6–7 My '39.

8342 **Hogan, Charles B.** [Bibliogr. note on Emma, American ed., 1816]. Pa Bib Soc Am 34:89–90 '40.

8343 **Chapman, Robert W.** 'XI. Jane Austen and her publishers' *in* Jane Austen; facts and problems. Oxford [1948]. (Repr. 1949+). p. 154–7.

8344 **Gilson, E. P.** Jane Austen mss. [Love and friendship]. N&Q 194:84 F '49. [Sg.: E. P. G.]

8345 **Southam, Brian C.** The text of Sanditon. [Ms.]. N&Q 206:23–4 Ja '61.

8346 —— The manuscript of Jane Austen's Volume the first. Library ser5 17no3:231–7 S '62.

8347 —— A note on Jane Austen's Volume the first. N&Q 207:422 N '62.

8348 —— Jane Austen documents. TLS 12 D '63:1031.

8349 **Morkam, R. C.** Austen editions. TLS 18 N '65:1023.

8350 **Gilson, D. J.** The first American editions of Jane Austen. (Query 218). Bk Coll 16no4:512 '67.

8351 **Parrish, Morris L.** Jane Austen from the collection of Charles Beecher Hogan. Grolier Club Gaz new ser 6:28 F '68 [Sg.: M. P.]

8352 **Gilson, D. J.** The early American editions of Jane Austen. Bk Coll 18no4:340–52 '69. facsims., tables.

8353 ——— Jane Austen bibliography. TLS 17 Ap '69:415.

AYLETT, ROBERT, c.1583–1655

8354 **Padelford, Frederick M.** Robert Aylett. Huntington Lib Bull 10:1–48 Oc '36; A supplement *ib.* 2no4:471–8 Jl '39.

AYRES, PHILIP, 1638–1712

8355 **Thomas, sir Henry.** The Emblemata amatoria of Philip Ayres. [1683]. Library ser3 1no1:73–95 Ja '10. facsims.

AYTOUN, SIR ROBERT, 1570–1638

8356 **Gullans, Charles B.** Ralegh and Ayton, the disputed authorship of Wrong not sweete empress of my heart. Stud Bib 13:191–8 '60.

8357 **Roberts, William.** The Rogers editions of sir Robert Aytoun. Pa Bib Soc Am 58:32–4 '64.

BACON, ANNE (COOKE), LADY, 1528–1610

8358 **Hughey, Ruth.** Lady Anne Bacon's translations. R Eng Stud 10no38:211 Ap '34.

BACON, FRANCIS, BARON VERULAM AND VISCOUNT ST. ALBANS, 1561–1626

8359 **Thorpe, W. G.** A survival of Bacon's Twickenham scrivenery. Acad 47:316 Ap '95.

8360 **X.** The Tate central library [containing the Durning-Lawrence Baconiana]. (Bookmen's libraries, no.2). Bkmns J 3no67:255 F '21.

8361 **Gibson, Reginald W.** Lost Bacon editions. [Essays]. TLS 30 My '42:271; E. N. Adler *ib.* 20 Je '42:312.

8362 **Bacon** mss. TLS 13 F '43:79.

8363 **Dunkin, Paul S.** The 1613 editions of Bacon's Essays. Library ser5 3no2:122–4 S '48.

8364 **Willoughby, Edwin E.** Bacon's copy of a Douai-Reims Bible. Library ser5 3no1:54–6 Je '48.

8365 **Adams, Thomas R.** Unrecorded Francis Bacon. [A brief discourse touching the happy union, 1702]. (Library notes). Lib Chron Univ Pennsylvania 17no2:129 '51.

8366 **Willoughby, Edwin E.** Francis Bacon and the King's printer. [Robert Barker]. Lib Q 22no3:285–7 Jl '52.

8367 **Gibson, Reginald W.** A new-found discourse on Bacon. [By William Griffith]. TLS 16 Mr '56:165.

8368 **Rickert, Corinne.** An addition to the canon of Bacon's writings. [A letter written out of England, 1599]. Mod Lang R 51no1:71–2 Ja '56.

8369 **Wrigley, Elizabeth S.** The Bacon collection in the Francis Bacon library. Claremont Q 9no2:43–7 '62.

8369a **Pirie, Robert S.** Fine paper copies of Bacon's Essays, 1625. (Note 263). Bk Coll 14no4:545 '65.

8369b **Brown, T. Julian.** Francis Bacon, 1561–1626. (English scientific autographs, VIII). Bk Coll 15no2:185 '66. facsim.

BACON, SIR JAMES, 1798–1895

8370 **Bridge, Alexander.** Sir James Bacon and Byron. [Memoirs of Byron, by George Clinton, *pseud.*, 1825]. TLS 16 Mr '51:165.

BACON, NATHANAEL, fl.1669.

8371 **Cooper, Thomson.** A journal of meditations. N&Q ser8 10:254 S '96.

BAGEHOT, WALTER, 1826–77

8372 **Chapman, Robert W.** The text of Bagehot's Constitution. Philol Q 31no4:446–7 Oc '52.

BAILEY, NATHANIEL, d. 1742

8373 **Roberts, William.** Bailey's Dictionary. Bkworm 2no19:201–4 Je '89. [Sg.: W. R.]

8374 **Gove, Philip B.** Bailey's folio dictionary, a supplementary note. Oxford Bib Soc Pub new ser 1pt1:45–6 '47.

BAILEY, PHILIP JAMES, 1816–1902

8375 **Peckham, Morse.** A Bailey collection [presented to Princeton]. Princeton Univ Lib Chron 7no4:149–54 Je '46.

8376 —— American editions of Festus, a preliminary study. Princeton Univ Lib Chron 8no4:177–84 Je '47.

'A check-list of American editions of Festus' (p. 180–4).

BAILEY, WALTER c.1529–92

8377 **Power, sir D'Arcy.** Prof. Walter Baily's books. N&Q ser10 6:507–8 D '06; B. Walker *ib.* 7:96 F '07.

8378 —— Dr. Walter Bayley and his works, 1529–1592. Library ser2 8no32:370–407 Oc '07. facsims.

'Bibliography' (p. 378–86)

8379 **Smith, L. Graham H. Horton-.** Dr. Walter Bayley (Baily), physician to queen Elizabeth. N&Q 191:191 N '46.

BAILLIE, JOANNA, 1762–1851

8380 **Newton, E. E.** Poems edited by Joanna Baillie. [A collection of poems, 1823]. N&Q 158:313–14 My '30.

BAILY, WALTER, c.1529–92 *see* Bailey, Walter, c.1529–92.

BAKER, DAVID ERSKINE, d.1782

8381 **Powell, Lawrence F.** George Steevens and Isaac Reed's Biographia dramatica. R Eng Stud 5no19:288–93 Jl '29; Further notes *ib.* 6no22:186 Ap '30.

8382 **Perkinson, Richard H.** Walpole and the Biographia dramatica. R Eng Stud 15no58:204–6 Ap '39.

BAKER, HENRY, 1698–1774

8383 **Potter, George R.** Mss. of Henry Baker, F.R.S. N&Q 158:9 Ja '30. [Sg.: G. R. P.]

8384 —— Henry Baker, F.R.S., 1698–1774. Mod Philol 29no3:301–21 F '32.

I. The date of Baker's The universe.–II. Baker's debt to James Thomson and Pope . . .–III. Henry Baker's personal copy of The universal spectator.–IV. History of the Dawson Turner collection of Baker mss.–V. Baker's account of his courtship of Sophia Defoe.–VI. John Hill through the eyes of Baker and Arderon.–VII. Two hitherto unnoticed works of Baker.

BALDWIN, WILLIAM. fl.1547–71

8385 **Willoughby, Edwin E.** Baldwin's Treatise of morall philosophie. N&Q 174:188 Mr '38.

BALE, BP. JOHN, 1495–1563

8386 **Cason, Clarence E.** Additional lines for Bales's Kynge Johan. J Eng Germ Philol 27no1:42–50 Ja '28.

8387 **Pafford, John H. P.** Bale's King John. J Eng Germ Philol 30no2:176–8 Ap '31. table.

8388 **McCusker, Honor.** Books and manuscripts formerly in the possession of John Bale. Library ser4 16no2:144–65 S '35.

8389 **Garrett, Christine.** The Resurreccion of the masse by Hugh Hilarie—or John Bale (?). [Ptd. abroad by Hugh Singleton]. Library ser4 21no2:143–59 S '40. facsims.

8390 **Pafford, John H. P.** Two notes on Bale's King John. Mod Lang R 56no4:553–5 Oc '61.

8391 **Pineas, Rainer.** The authorship of The resurreccion of the masse. Library ser5 16no3:210–13 S '61.

BALES, PETER, 1547–1610?

8392 **Matthews, William.** Peter Bales, Timothy Bright and William Shakespeare. [The writing schoolmaster, 1590]. J Eng Germ Philol 34no3:483–510 Oc '35. facsims., tables.

'Appendix: The table for orthographie and for the references of words to the table of brachygraphie' (p. 498–9)

8393 **Hoppe, Henry R.** The third, 1600, edition of Bales's Brachygraphy. J Eng Germ Philol 37no3:537–41 Oc '38. table.

BALLARD, GEORGE, fl.1638

8394 **Mundy, Percy D.** George Ballard: The history of Susannah. [1638]. N&Q ser11 10:6–7 Jl '14.

BANKES, THOMAS, fl.1790

8395 **Wright, G. W.** The rev. Thomas Bankes's System of universal geography. N&Q ser12 11:191 S '22.

BANKS, JOHN, fl.1650–1700

8396 **Lumiansky, R. M.** A note on Blair's edition of The unhappy favorite. [1682]. Mod Lang N 56no4:280–2 Ap '41.

8397 **Bowers, Fredson T.** The variant sheets in John Banks's Cyrus the great, 1696. Stud Bib 4:174–82 '51/2.

BARBER, MARY, 1690?–1757

8398 **Gay, Ernest L.** Mrs. Barber's A true tale. N&Q ser11 12:23–4 Jl '15.

8399 **Carpenter, Andrew Isdell-.** On a manuscript of poems catalogued as by Mary Barber in the library of TCD. [Not by her]. Hermathena 109:54–64 '69.

BARBOUR, JOHN, 1316?–95

8400 **McKinlay, Robert.** Barbour's Bruce. Glasgow Bib Soc Rec 6:20–38 '20.

I. The manuscripts.–II. The popular editions.–III. The critical editions.–IV. Barbour and his imitators.–Bibliography.

BARCLAY, ALEXANDER, 1475?–1552

8401 **White, Beatrice.** A note on Alexander Barclay. Mod Lang R 26no2:169–70 Ap '31.

BARCLAY, JOHN, 1582–1621

8402 **Smedley, Constance.** Barclay's Argenis. Bkmn 81no484:238–40 Ja '32. facsim.

BARHAM, RICHARD HARRIS, 1788–1845 *see* Ingoldsby, Thomas, *pseud.*

BARING, MAURICE, 1874–1945

8403 **Goodspeed, George T.** Maurice Baring: C., London, 1924. [TP errata slip]. Bib N&Q 2no2:3 F '36; T. Warburton *ib.* 2no4/5:4 My '36. [Sg.: G. G.]

BARKER, MRS. JANE, fl.1688–1736

8404 **Lincoln's inn,** *pseud.* Mrs. Jane Barker, novelist. N&Q ser9 10:87 Ag '02; J. Phillips *ib.* 10:171 Ag '02.

8405 **McBurney, William H.** Edmund Curll, mrs. Jane Barker, and the English novel. Philol Q 37no4:385–99 Oc '58.

BARLAS, JOHN, 1860–1914

8406 **Looker, Samuel J.** Eight little books of a Scottish poet. Bkmns J new ser 5no5:155–7 F '22.

BARNES, ROBERT, 1495–1540

8407 **Chester, Allan G.** Robert Barnes and the burning of books. Huntington Lib Q 14no3:211–21 My '51.

8408 **Thompson, W. D. J. Cargill.** The sixteenth-century editions of A supplication unto king Henry the eighth, by Robert Barnes, D. D.: a footnote to the history of the royal supremacy. Cambridge Bib Soc Trans 3pt2:133–42 '60.

BARRET, JOHN, d.1580?

8409 **Sledd, James H.** Nugae academicae: some remarks on the Alvearie of John Barret. Lib Chron Univ Texas 1no1:19–26 '44.

BARRETT, EATON STANNARD, 1786–1820

8409a **Mendenhall, John C.** An old discovery. [Barrett's letters to his bookseller]. Univ Pennsylvania Gen Mag 30:10–14 '27.

BARRIE, SIR JAMES MATTHEW, 1860–1937

8410 **Garland, Herbert.** The collector's interest in sir James Barrie. Bkmns J new ser 10no34:117–18 Jl '24.

8411 **Barrie's** Twelve-pound look. [Ms.]. (Notes on sales). TLS 2 My '29:368.

8412 **Brett, Oliver S. B., 3d viscount Esher.** Barrie: Courage. [Issues]. Bib N&Q 1no1:4–5 Ja '35; G. G[oodspeed]; M. L. Parrish *ib* 1no2:4–5 Ap '35. [Sg.: Esher.]

8413 **Goodspeed, George T.** Barrie: Auld licht idylls, London, 1888. [Dedication leaf removed]. Bib N&Q 2no2:3 F '36. [Sg.: G. G.]

8414 **Kaplan, Israel B.** A Scot in America. [Collecting]. Coloph new ser 1no3:358–66 F '36.

8415 **Muir, Percival H.** Barrie and Doyle: Jane Annie, 1893. [Issues]. Bib N&Q 2no4/5:6–7 My '36.

8416 **Warburton, Thomas.** Barrie: The superfluous man. [Book publication]. Bib N&Q 2no3:7 Ap '36.

8417 **Sir** James Barrie's library. (Notes on sales). TLS 25 D '37:984.

8418 **Brett, Oliver S. B., 3d viscount Esher.** Barrie: Dear Brutus. [Date]. Bib N&Q 2no9:2 Ja '38; T. Warburton *ib.* 2no10:4 Ap '38. [Sg.: Esher.]

8419 **Olybrius,** *pseud.* Barrie's Tillyloss scandal: date of first edition. [1893]. N&Q 179:208 S '40.

8420 **Parrish, Morris L.** J. M. Barrie's first book, Better dead. Pub Wkly 138no22:2030–2 N '40. facsims.

8421 **Wynne, Marjorie G.** The James Matthew Barrie collection. Yale Univ Lib Gaz 23no4:184–8 Ap '49. facsim.

8422 **Barrie's** The wedding guest. Princeton Univ Lib Chron 12no3:163–4 '51.

8423 **Beinecke, Walter.** Barrie in the Parrish collection. [Princeton university]. Princeton Univ Lib Chron 17no2:96–8 '56.

8424 **Mott, Howard S.** The Walter Beinecke, jr. J. M. Barrie collection. Yale Univ Lib Gaz 39no4:163–7 Ap '65. facsim.

BARTHOLOMEW ANGLICUS, fl.1230–50

8425 **Hanford, James H.** De proprietatibus rerum of Bartholomaeus Anglicus. Princeton Univ Lib Chron 23no3:126–30 '62. facsim.

BASSE, WILLIAM, d.1653?

8426 **Bond, Richard W.** William Basse's Polyhymnia. [Ms.]. N&Q ser8 2:7 Jl '92.

BASTARD, THOMAS, 1566–1618

8427 **Sanderson, James L.** Thomas Bastard's disclaimer of an Oxford libel. [Jenkin why man?]. Library ser5 17no2:145–9 Je '62.

BAXTER, RICHARD, 1615–91

8428 **Dearing, Vinton A.** Baxter's Saint's everlasting rest. [Sheets of 2d ed. ptd. for insertion in 1st ed.]. (Notes). Harvard Lib Bull 2no2:252–3 '48.

8428a **Nuttall, Geoffrey F.** A transcript of Richard Baxter's library catalogue. J Ecclesiological Hist 2:206–21 '51; 3:74–100 '52.

   'A catalogue of the library . . .' (p. 209–21,74–100)

8429 —— The manuscript of the Reliquiae Baxterianae. London, Dr. Williams's trust, 1954. [8]p. 20cm. Covertitle. (Dr. Williams's library. Occasional paper, 1)

8430 **Thomas, Roger.** The Baxter treatises: a catalogue of the Richard Baxter papers other than the letters in dr. Williams's library. London, Dr. Williams's trust, 1959. 31p. 20cm. Covertitle. (Dr. Williams's library. Occasional paper, no.8)

   BAYLEY, WALTER, c.1529–92 *see* Bailey, Walter, c.1529–92.

   BAYLY, B.P. LEWIS, d.1631

8431 **H., C. E.** The Practice of piety. N&Q 178:29–30 Ja '40; W. Jaggard *ib*. 178:69 Ja '40.

BEARDSLEY, AUBREY VINCENT, 1872–98

8432 **Walker, Rainforth A.** Aubrey Beardsley and The yellow book. TLS 2 Oc '24:612; W. A. Hutchinson *ib.* 16 Oc '24:651.

8433 —— Le Mort darthur. TLS 31 Mr '45:156.

8434 —— Le Morte darthur with Beardsley illustrations, a bibliographical essay. Bedford, 1945. 24p. 18cm.

8435 —— How to detect Beardsley forgeries. Bedford, 1950. 31p. facsims. 23cm.

8436 **Aubrey** Beardsley. [Additions to the Library's collections]. Princeton Univ Lib Chron 12no3:163 '51.

8437 **Additions** to the Beardsley collection. Princeton Univ Lib Chron 19no2:104–5 '58. illus.

8438 **Bush, Alfred L.** Beardsley in London. [Victoria and Albert museum exhibition]. Princeton Univ Lib Chron 28no1:55–6 '66. [Sg.: A. L. B.]

BEATTIE, JAMES, 1735–1803

8439 **Gordon, James.** James Beattie's Poems. [1760 ed. ptd. in Aberdeen]. Scott N&Q 5no4:61 S '91; G. B. C. *ib.* 5no5:75 Oc '91.

8440 **Sinclair, William.** The bibliography of James Beattie. Glasgow Bib Soc Rec 7:27–35 '23.

8441 **Allardyce, Mabel D.** Beattie mss. and letters. Aberdeen Univ Lib Bull 7no38:101–12 Ja '29.

8442 **Tave, Stuart M.** Some essays by James Beattie in the London magazine, 1771. N&Q 197:534–7 D '52.

BEAUMONT, FRANCIS, 1584–1616, and JOHN FLETCHER, 1579–1625
see also Fletcher, John, 1579–1625

8443 **Leonhardt, Benno.** Die Textvarianten von Beaumont und Fletchers Philaster, or Love lies a-Bleeding, nebst einer Zusammenstellung der Ausgaben und Litteratur ihrer Werke. Anglia 19:34–74 Oc '96; 19:509–41 Ag '97.

8444 —— [Same]: III. Bonduca. *ib.* 20:421–51 Je '98.

8445 —— [Same]: IV. The maid's tragedy. *ib.* 23:14–66 F '00.

8446 —— [Same]: V. Rule a wife and have a wife. *ib.* 24:311–40 Jl '00.

8447 —— [Same]: VI. A king and no king. [VII. Thierry and Theodoret] *ib.* 26:313–63 Je '03.

8448 **Brereton, J. LeGay.** Notes on some plays of Beaumont and Fletcher. Eng Studien 38no2:278–85 '07.

8449 —— [Same]: Eng Studien 43no1:52–66 D '10.

8450 —— Notes on the text of Beaumont and Fletcher. Eng Studien 47no2:209–18 D '13.

8451 **Greg, sir Walter W.** Notes on old books. The printing of the Beaumont and Fletcher folio of 1647. Library ser4 2no2:109–15 S '21.

8452 **Loomis, John T.** Beaumont and Fletcher: corrected copy of 1647 edition. N&Q 148:135–6 F '25.

8453 **Greg, sir Walter W.** Nathan Field and the Beaumont and Fletcher folio of 1679. R Eng Stud 3no11:337–8 Jl '27.

8454 **McKeitham, D. M.** Bullen's Beaumont and Fletcher. TLS 7 F '35:76.

8455 **Bald, R. Cecil.** Bibliographical studies in the Beaumont & Fletcher folio of 1647. [Oxford] Ptd. at the O.U.P. for the Bibliographical society, 1938. vi,114p. illus., facsims. 22cm. (Bib Soc Trans Suppl 13)

Part I: The folio of 1647: 1. The collection of the copy.–2. The book itself.–3. The printers.–4. The printing of the folio.–Appendix to part I.–Part II: The five manuscripts: 1. The manuscripts.–2. Censorship.–3. Stage directions.–4. Textual confusion, revision, &c.–5. Problems of transmission.–Part III: The nature of the copy.

8456 **Battle, Guy A.** A bibliographical note from the Beaumont and Fletcher first folio. [Box-rules]. Stud Bib 1:187–8 '48.

8457 —— The case of the altered C; a bibliographical problem in the Beaumont and Fletcher first folio. Pa Bib Soc Am 42:66–70 '48. table.

8458 **Gerritsen, Johan.** The printing of the Beaumont and Fletcher folio of 1647. Library ser5 3no4:233–64 Mr '49. facsims., tables.

8459 **Savage, J. E.** The gaping wounds in the text of Philaster. Philol Q 28no4:443–57 Oc '49.

8460 **Simpson, Percy.** Francis Beaumont's verse-letter to Ben Jonson: The sun, which doth the greatest comfort bring. . . . Mod Lang R 46no3/4:435–6 Jl/Oc '51.

8461 **Sturman, Berta.** The second quarto of A king and no king, 1625. [Quartos as prompt books]. Stud Bib 4:166–70 '51/2.

8462 Greg, sir Walter W. [and] **C. J. Sisson.** [Correspondence on Bonduca and Edward Knight]. Mod Lang R 48no2:195 Ap '53.

8463 Hoy, Cyrus. The shares of Fletcher and his collaborators in the Beaumont and Fletcher canon, I. Stud Bib 8:129–46 '56. tables.

Repr. in Zitner, Sheldon P., *ed.* The practice of modern literary scholarship. Glenview, Ill., 1966. p .[58]–73.

8464 —— [**Same**]: II. [Fletcher and Massinger]. Stud Bib 9:143–62 '57. tables.

Barnavelt.–The custom of the country.–The double marriage.–The elder brother.–The falseone,–The little French lawyer.–The lovers' progress.–The prophetess.–The sea voyage.–The Spanish curate.–A very woman.

8465 Turner, Robert K. The relationship of The maid's tragedy, Q1 and Q2. Pa Bib Soc Am 51:322–7 '57. tables.

8466 Hoy, Cyrus. The shares of Fletcher and his collaborators in the Beaumont and Fletcher canon, III. Stud Bib 11:84–106 '58. tables.

Beggars' bush. [With Massinger].–The coxcomb.–Cupid's revenge.–A king and no king.–The knight of the burning pestle. [By Beaumont].–Love's pilgrimage.–The maid's tragedy.–The noble gentleman.–Philaster.–The scornful lady.–Thierry and Theodoret.[With Massinger].–The woman hater.

8467 —— [**Same**]: IV. Stud Bib 12:91–116 '59. tables.

Four plays in one. [Fletcher and Field].–The knight of Malta. [Fletcher, Field, and Massinger].–The queen of Corinth. [Fletcher, Field, and Massinger].–The honest man's fortune. [Fletcher, Field, and Massinger].–The night walker. [Fletcher and Shirley].–Wit without money. [Fletcher].

8468 —— [**Same**]: V. Stud Bib 13:77–108 '60. tables.

Wit at several weapons. [Middleton and Rowley].–The nice valour. [Fletcher and Middleton].–The maid in the mill. [Fletcher and Rowley].–The laws of Candy. [Ford].

8469 Turner, Robert K. The printing of Beaumont and Fletcher's The maid's tragedy, Q1, 1619. Stud Bib 13:199–220 '60. tables.

8470 —— The printing of Philaster, Q1 and Q2. Library ser5 15no1:21–32 Mr '60. tables.

8471 Hoy, Cyrus. The shares of Fletcher and his collaborators in the Beaumont and Fletcher canon, VI. Stud Bib 14:45–67 '61. tables.

The captain.–Love's cure. [With Massinger].–Rollo, duke of Normandy. [Chapman, Fletcher, Jonson, Massinger].

8472 Turner, Robert K. Notes on the text of Thierry and Theodoret, Q1. [And proofsheet]. Stud Bib 14:218–31 '61. facsim., tables.

8473 **Hoy, Cyrus.** The shares of Fletcher and his collaborators in the Beaumont and Fletcher canon, VII. Stud Bib 15:72–90 '62. tables.

The two noble kinsmen. [Fletcher and Shakespeare].–Henry VIII. [Fletcher and Shakespeare].

8474 **Turner, Robert K.** The printing of A king and no king, Q1. Stud Bib 18:255–61 '65. tables.

8475 **Norland, Howard B.** The text of The maid's tragedy. Pa Bib Soc Am 61:173–200 '67.

8476 **Turner, Robert K.** The printers and the Beaumont and Fletcher folio of 1647, section 2. Stud Bib 20:35–59 '67. tables.

8477 **Henning, Standish.** The printers and the Beaumont and Fletcher folio of 1647, sections 4 and 8D-F. Stud Bib 22:165–78 '69. tables.

BECKETT, SAMUEL BARCLAY, 1906–

8477a **Freeman, Elsie T.** Beckett on the Mississippi. [Washington university, St. Louis, colln., with papers of Alexander Trocchi]. (Collectors and collections). Manuscripts 20no1:48–50 '68.

BECKFORD, WILLIAM, 1759–1844

8478 **Hodgkin, John E.** The Nonesuch Vathek. TLS 26 D '29:1097; G. Chapman ib. 2 Ja '30:12; H. B. Grimsditch; J. E. Hodgkin 9 Ja '30:28; G.Chapman 16 Ja '30:44; J. E. Hodgkin 23 Ja '30:60.

8478a **Hunter, A. O.** Le Vathek de William Beckford: historique des éditions françaises. R Litt Comparée 15no1:119–26 Ja/Mr '35.

8479 **Chapman, Guy.** Beckford and Al Raoui. TLS 31 Oc '36:887.

8480 **Carter, John W.** The Lausanne edition of Beckford's Vathek. [1787]. Library ser4 17no4:369–94 Mr '37.

8481 —— Two Beckford collections. [Rowland Burdon-Muller; James T. Babb]. Coloph new graphic ser 1:[8p.] Mr '39. facsims.

8481a **Parreaux, André.** Un Vathek ignoré. [Lausanne ed. with new TP: Londres, 1791]. Bull Bibliophile 5:176–9 '57.

8482 —— Beckford's Vathek, Londres, 1791. (Note 99). Bk Coll 7no3:297–9 '58. facsim.

8483 **Hobson, Anthony R. A.** Beckfordiana. (Query 120). Bk Coll 8no4:432 '59.

8484 **Chapman, Guy.** The story of Al Raoui. TLS 25 N '60:759.

8485 **William** Beckford at Yale. [Exhibition]. TLS 28 Oc '60:699.

8486 **Hobson, Anthony R. A.** 'William Beckford's binders' *in* Festschrift Ernst Kyriss. Stuttgart [1961]. p. 375–81. illus.

8487 **Beckford's** letters to George Clarke. TLS 16 F '62:112.

8488 **Marlow, Harriet.** Beckford's Vathek, 'Londres, 1791.' (Note 99). Bk Coll 11no2:211 '62.

8489 **Carter, John W.** Beckford and Vathek; Ged and stereotype. Library ser5 18no4:308–9 D '63.

8489a **Rosebery, Eva.** Books from Beckford's library now at Barnbougle. [Scottish libr. of 5th earl of Rosebery]. Bk Coll 14no3:324–34 '65.

'Concordance' (p. 333–4)

8490 **Babb, James T.** William Beckford of Fonthill. Yale Univ Lib Gaz 41no2:60–9 Oc '66.

'Note [acquisition of books from Beckford's library]' (p. 67–9)

8491 **William** Beckford in the saleroom. TLS 20 Oc '66; R. J. Gemmett *ib.* 17 N '66:1056.

8492 **Gemmett, Robert J.** The caliph Vathek from England and the continent to America. Am Bk Coll 18no9:12–19 My '68. illus., port., facsims.

BEDE, THE VENERABLE, 673–735

8493 **A., E. H.** John and George Smith, editors of Bede. N&Q ser8 12:124–5 Ag '97.

8494 **Colgrave, Bertram** and **I. Masson.** The editio princeps of Bede's prose life of St. Cuthbert, and its printer's XIIth century copy. Library ser4 19no3:289–303 D '38. facsims.

8495 **Brown, T. Julian.** English literary autograph number one. (Note 107). Bk Coll 8no2:180 '59.

BEDE, CUTHBERT, *pseud. of* **EDWARD BRADLEY, 1827–89**

8496 **Robinson, John.** First Christmas card. N&Q ser9 9:56 Ja '02.

BEERBOHM, SIR HENRY MAXIMILIAN, 1872–1956

8497 **Wade, Allan.** Mr. Beerbohm's Works. [Corrections to bibliogr.]. (Correspondence). London Merc 2no8:206 Je '20.

8498 **Talbot, William.** The Happy hypocrite. [1896]. TLS 15 Jl '26:480.

8499 **Smith, Simon H. Nowell-.** Max at Charterhouse. TLS 16 D '44:611.

8500 **Evans, Charles.** A note on Carmen becceriense. [1890]. Bk Coll 1no4:215–16 '52. fold. facsim.

8501 **Bond, William H.** The Gallatin-Oliver Bibliography of Max Beerbohm. [And bibliogr. description]. Library ser5 9no1:56–8 Mr '54.

8502 **Ewing, Majl.** On collecting Max Beerbohm: grazie per tutto. Bk Club California Q Newsl 28no3:52–9 '63.

BEHN, APHRA (AMIS), 1640–89

8503 **Bennett, R. E.** A bibliographical correction. [The emperor of the moon, 1687]. R Eng Stud 3no12:450–1 Oc '27.

8504 **Gregory, K.** Behn, Aphra: Lycidus. [Issues]. Bib N&Q 2no7:3 Oc '36.

BELLENDEN, JOHN, fl.1533–87

8505 **Warner, George F.** Bellenden's Scots translation of Livy. [Ms.]. Athenæum 3898:64 Jl '02.

8506 **Seton, Walter W.** Manuscripts of Bellenden. TLS 22 Ja '20:52.

BELLOC, HILAIRE, 1870–1953

8507 **Belloc:** Cautionary tales. [Issues]. Bib N&Q 1no2:9 Ap '35.

8508 **Brett, Oliver S. B., 3d viscount Esher.** Belloc: Pongo and the bull. [Issues]. Bib N&Q 2no2:3 F '36. [Sg.: Esher.]

BENNETT, ENOCH ARNOLD, 1867–1931

8509 **Arnold** Bennett's library. (Notes on sales). TLS 6 Ag '31:612.

8510 **Hopkinson, Cecil.** Mr. Arnold Bennett's works. [His bibliogr.]. TLS 29 Ja '31:79.

8511 **Nicholls, Norah.** Arnold Bennett; some bibliographical points. Bkmn 80no476:128–9 My '31.

8512 **Arnold** Bennett mss. (Notes on sales). TLS 30 My '36:464.

8513 **Hepburn, James G.** Arnold Bennett manuscripts and rare books, a list of holdings. Eng Fict Transit 1no2:23–9 '58.

8514 **Codlock, Roger.** An unusual form of dating quires. [Riceyman steps, 1923]. (Query 143). Bk Coll 10no2:202 '61.

BENTHAM, JEREMY, 1748–1832

8515 **Siegwart, Alfred.** Benthams Werke und ihre Publikation. Bern, K. J. Wyss, 1910. 119p. 19cm.

'*Separatabdruck aus dem* Politischen Jahrbuch der Schweizer, 1910'.

8516 **Muirhead, Arnold M.** A Jeremy Bentham collection. Library ser5 1no1:6–27 Je '46. facsims.

8517 **Bowyer, Tony H.** Bentham's publications on evidence. [An introductory view of the rationale of evidence]. Library ser5 9no3:205–7 S '54.

BENTLEY, JOHN, fl.1588–95

8518 **Bond, William H.** 'The Cornwallis-Lysons manuscript and the poems of John Bentley' *in* McManaway, James G., G. E. Dawson, and E. E. Willoughby, *ed*. Joseph Quincy Adams memorial studies. Washington, 1948. p. 683–93.

'Index of first lines of poems in Folger ms. 1.112' (p. 691–3)

BENTLEY, RICHARD, 1662–1742

8519 **Bentley** versus Boyle, the bookseller's view. Bkworm 2no14:55–7 Ja '89.

8520 **Hillhouse, James T.** 'Bentley's Milton and Theobald's Shakespeare' *in* The Grub-street journal. Durham, N.C., 1928. p. 84–104.

8521 **Fox, Adam.** John Mill and Richard Bentley, a study of the textual criticism of the New testament, 1675–1729. Oxford, B. Blackwell, 1954. xii,168p. port. 22cm. (Aularian series, III)

BERKELEY, BP. GEORGE, 1685–1753

8522 **Dowden, Edward.** A pamphlet by bishop Berkeley, hitherto undescribed. [Queries relating to a national bank, 1737]. Mod Lang R 1no4:286–9 Jl '06.

8523 **Meyerstein, Edward H. W.** The first London edition of The querist. TLS 20 My '26:339.

8524 **The Berkeley** exhibition. Yale Univ Lib Gaz 3no4:79–80 Ap '29.

8525 **Hone, J. M.** A manuscript of bishop Berkeley. [The Irish patriot]. TLS 13 Mr '30:211; 3 Ap '30:295.

8526 **Aaron, R. I.** A catalogue of Berkeley's library. Mind 41no164:465–75 Oc '32.

8527 **Keogh, Andrew.** Bishop Berkeley's gift of books in 1733. Yale Univ Lib Gaz 8no1:1–41 Jl '33. facsims. [Sg.: A. K.]

'The Berkeley gift in classified order' (p. 9–26); 'Letters of bishop Berkeley in the Yale university library' (p. 26–41)

8528 **Cadbury, Henry J.** Bishop Berkeley's gifts to the Harvard library. Harvard Lib Bull 7no1:73–87 '53; 7no2:196–207 '53.

I. Gifts in 1733 and earlier.–II. A further gift in 1748.

8529 **Fuller, Henry M.** Bishop Berkeley as a benefactor of Yale. Yale Univ Lib Gaz 28no1:1–18 Jl '53.

8530 **Luce, A. A.** The original title and the first edition of Siris. Hermathena 84:45–58 N '54.

8531 **Furlong, E. J.** How much of Steele's Guardian no. 39 did Berkeley write? Hermathena 89:76–88 My '57.

'Bibliographical note' (p. 87–8)

8532 **Brown, T. Julian.** George Berkeley, 1685–1753; David Hume, 1711–1776. (English literary autographs, XXVI). Bk Coll 7no2:181 '58. facsims.

8533 **Howell, Wilbur S.** A misprint in Berkeley. [The querist]. TLS 13 Oc '61:683.

BERKELEY, SIR WILLIAM, 1609–77

8534 **Bald, R. Cecil.** Sir William Berkeley's The lost lady. Library ser4 17no4:395–426 Mr '37. facsims., table.

'List of corrections in the Folger copy of the first edition of The lost lady' (p. 423–6)

BERNERS, JULIANA, b.1388?

8535 **Wynne, Marjorie G.** The Boke of St. Albans. Yale Univ Lib Gaz 26no1:33–6 Jl '51.

BETJEMAN, SIR JOHN, 1906–

8536 **Carter, John W.** Betjemaniana. (Note 140). Bk Coll 9no2:199 '60; 9no4:452 '60.

BETTERTON, THOMAS, 1635?–1710

8537 **Bowers, Fredson T.** A bibliographical history of the Fletcher-Betterton play, The prophetess, 1690. Library ser5 16no3:169–75 S '61. tables.

BEWICK, THOMAS, 1753–1828 *see under* Book production and distribution–Printers, publishers, etc.

BICKHAM, GEORGE, d.1769

8538 **Muir, Percival H.** The Bickhams and their Universal penman. Library ser4 25no3/4:162–84 D/Mr '44/5. table, facsims.

'Summary of the dates in the various numbers of the first and second (or first complete) edition' (p. 173); 'Analysis of the make-up of six variants of The universal penman' (p. 174–84)

8539 **Ø.** [On The Bickhams and their Universal penman]. Library ser4 26no2/3:196 S/D '45.

8540 **Muir, Percival H.** Bickham's Universal penman. Library ser5 1no3/4:247–8 D/Mr '46/7.

BILSON, THOMAS, 1547–1616

8541 **Thompson, W. D. J. Cargill.** The two editions of Thomas Bilson's True difference between Christian subjection and unchristian rebellion. [1585]. Cambridge Bib Soc Trans 2pt2:199–203 '55.

BIRKHEAD, HENRY, 1617?–96

8542 **Wagner, Bernard M.** Annals of English drama. [Birkhead's The female rebellion]. TLS 22 Oc '64:966; S. Schoenbaum *ib.* 12 N '64:1026.

BISHOP, JOHN, 1665–1737

8543 **Frost, Maurice.** John Bishop, 1665–1737. (Query no.15). Bk Coll 1no3:195 '52.

BLACKBURN, CHARLES FRANCIS, 1828–96

8544 **Thomas, Ralph.** Charles Francis Blackburn. [Ed. of English catalogue]. N&Q ser8 12:242–3 S '97; 12:303–4 Oc '97.

BLACKBURNE, HARRIOTT ELIZABETH, fl.1881

8545 **Anderton, Henry P. J. Ince-.** Ireland Blackburn[e]: author of Hale hall. N&Q 168:335 My '35; R. S. B.; A. J. H. *ib.* 168:372 My '35; H. I. A. 168:411 Je '35. [Sg.: H. I. A.]

BLACKMORE, RICHARD DODDRIDGE, 1825–1900

8546 **Manuscripts** of R. D. Blackmore. (News and notes). TLS 1 Oc '38:621.

8547 **Etherington, J. R. M.** R. D. Blackmore and his illustrators. N&Q 188: 199–21 Mr '45.

8548 **Seybolt, Paul S.** Blackmore's Poems by Melanter. New Coloph 2pt8:380–1 F '50.

8549 **Carter, John A.** Supplement to Blackmore bibliography. [Kit and Kitty, 1889]. N&Q 207:305 Ag '62.

8550 **Todd, William B.** Blackmore, Fringilla, 1895. (Query 239). Bk Coll 18no2:226 '69.

BLACKSTONE, SIR WILLIAM, 1723–80

8551 **Thomas, Ralph.** Sir W. Blackstone's works. N&Q ser8 7:407 My '95.

8552 **Prideaux, W. R. B.** Blackstone's Commentaries: first edition. N&Q ser10 12:385–6 N '09; Q. V. *ib.* ser11 3:98 F '11; 12:58 Jl '15.

8553 **H., W. B.** Sir William Blackstone, 1723–80. N&Q ser12 6:209 My '20; A. Sparke *ib.* 6:320 Je '20.

8554 **Harlan, Robert D.** Sales of and profits on some early editions of sir William Blackstone's Commentaries. [Ptd. by Strahan]. Pa Bib Soc Am 58:156–63 '64. tables.

BLADES, WILLIAM, 1824–90 *see* Book production and distribution–
   Printers, publishers, etc.

BLAIR, HUGH, 1718–1800

8555 **Chapman, Robert W.** Blair on Ossian. [Ms. of A critical dissertation on the poems of Ossian, 1763]. R Eng Stud 7no25:80–3 Ja '31.

8556 **Jiriczek, Otto L.** Zur Bibliographie und Textgeschichte von Hugh Blair's Critical dissertation on the poems of Ossian. Eng Studien 70no1:181–9 Ap '35.

8557 **Schmitz, Robert M.** Dr. Johnson and Blair's sermons. [And A. Kincaid, ptr.]. Mod Lang N 60no4:268–70 Ap '45.

8558 **Corbett, Edward P. J.** Hugh Blair's three(?) critical dissertations. N&Q 199:478–80 N '54.

BLAKE, WILLIAM, 1757–1827

8559 **Thomas, Ralph.** William Blake. N&Q ser8 11:302–3 Ap '97; ser9 1:454–5 Je '98.

8560 **A., B. C.** William Blake. [Sale of works, 1902]. N&Q ser9 11:285 Ap '03.

8561 **Binyon, Lawrence.** A famous Blake collection. [Monckton Milnes]. Bibliographer 2no4:234–9 Ap '03.

8562 **Thomas, Ralph.** William Blake [as engraver]. N&Q ser10 5:86 F '06.

8563 **Sampson, John.** Blake's Songs; an early private reprint. N&Q ser10 6:421–2 N '06; S. Butterworth *ib.* 6:473 D '06; 7:56 Ja '07.

8564 **Melville, Lewis,** *pseud. of* **L. S. Benjamin.** Blake as book-illustrator. Bk-Lover's Mag 6pt6:238–43 '07. illus.

8565 **Keynes, sir Geoffrey L.** William Blake's Laughing song, a new version. [Ms.]. N&Q ser11 2:241–2 S '10.

8566 **Discovery** of a lost work by Blake; illustrations of Gray's Poems. Bkmns J 1no3:55 N '19.

8567 **Grierson, sir Herbert J. C.** A textual point in Blake. [Poetical sketches]. TLS 9 Oc '19:548; J. Sampson *ib.* 16 Oc '19:572; sir G. L. Keynes; G. B. 23 Oc '19:591; T. J. Wise 30 Oc '19:611; sir G. L. Keynes 12 F '19:105–6.

8568 **Sampson, John.** On a manuscript poem attributed to William Blake. [Hayley's Genesis, copied by Blake]. TLS 23 Mr '22:195.

8569 **Keynes, sir Geoffrey L.** Blake's Milton. [1804]. TLS 13 D '23:875.

8570 —— The MacGeorge Blakes. TLS 26 Je '24:403.

8571 **The MacGeorge** Blakes. (Notes on sales). TLS 10 Jl '24:440.

8572 **Plowman, Max.** Blake's Bible of hell. [And The four Zoas]. TLS 6 N '24:710.

8573 —— A text of Blake. TLS 16 Oc '24:651; sir G. L. Keynes *ib.* 23 Oc '24:667–8.

8574 **Damon, S. Foster.** A note on the discovery of a new page of poetry in William Blake's Milton. Boston, Ptd. for the Club of odd volumes, The Merrymount pr., 1925. 14p. 29cm.

8575 **Mabbott, Thomas O.** Blake's designs for Blair's Grave: American edition. N&Q 148:98 F '25.

8576 **Plowman, Max.** The incomplete Marriage of heaven and hell. TLS 22 Oc '25:693.

8577 **Binyon, R. Laurence.** The engraved designs of William Blake. London, E. Benn; New York, C. Scribner's [1926]. xiv,140p. + 82 plates. illus., facsims. 29cm.

I. The line-engravings.—II. The invention of 'illuminated printing'.—III. The year of experiments.—IV. 'White-line' design and wood engraving.—V. The beautiful book.—VI. Myth and symbol.—VII. The later prophetic books.—Catalogue of Blake's engraved designs.

Rev: TLS 3 F '27:71; Saturday R Lit 17 Mr '28:68.

8578 **Blake,** Cromek and Hoppner. (Notes on sales). TLS 7 Oc '26:680.

8579 **Plowman, Max.** Blake's Infant sorrow. TLS 18 N '26:819.

8580 **Wallis, J. P. R.** Blake's Milton. TLS 11 Mr '26:182.

8581 **Plowman, Max.** Blake: a textual point. ['Rossetti ms.']. TLS 29 Mr '28:243.

8582 **Blake's** Songs of innocence and of experience. (Notes on sales). TLS 13 Ag '31:624; W. Cater *ib.* 3 S '31:664.

8583 **Plowman, Max.** Blake: binds not bends. [He who binds to himself a joy]. TLS 11 Je '31:467.

8584 **Binyon, R. Laurence.** Blake's Songs of innocence and experience. Brit Mus Q 7no3:65–6 D '32. [Sg.: L. B.]

8585 **Mabbott, Thomas O.** More American references to Blake before 1863. Mod Lang N 47no2:87–8 F '32.

8586 —— More early American publications of Blake. N&Q 165:279 Oc '33.

8587 —— The text of Blake's A fairy stepd upon my knee. N&Q 164:388–9 Je '33; sir G. L. Keynes *ib.* 165:302 Oc '33. [Sg.: T. O. M.]

8588 Cancelled.

8589 **Lowery, Margaret R.** A census of copies of William Blake's Poetical sketches, 1783. Library ser4 17no3:354–60 D '36.

8590 **Popham, A. E.** Proofs of William Blake's Europe. Brit Mus Q 11no4:184–5 S '37.

8591 **Brown, Allan R.** Unrecorded engravings of Blake. (Notes and queries). Coloph new ser 3no3:457–8 S '38.

8592 **E., J.** Blake's engravings for Night thoughts. More Bks Boston Pub Lib Bull 15no2:64 F '40.

8593 —— Blake's illustrations for the Book of Job. More Bks Boston Pub Lib Bull 15no7:290 S '40.

8594 **Hind, Arthur M.** Wood-blocks by William Blake. Brit Mus Q 14:37 Je '40.

8595 [**Madan, Falconer**]. Two works of Blake. [Songs of innocence; Illustrations of the book of Job]. Bod Lib Rec 1no11:178–9 Oc '40.

8596 **Keynes, sir Geoffrey L.** Blake's copper-plates. TLS 24 Ja '42:48.

Surviving plates.–Electrotypes found.

Repr. in Blake studies. London, 1949. (2d ed. 1971). p. [105]–9. (*See nos.*8605, 8645)

8597 —— and **R. Todd.** William Blake's catalogue, a new discovery. TLS 12 S '42:456.

A printed leaf.–Blake's prejudices.–A census.

Repr. in Blake studies. London, 1949. (2d ed. 1971). p. [76]–83. (*See nos.*8605, 8645)

8598 —— New Blake documents; history of the Job engravings. TLS 9 Ja '43:24.

Accounts and receipts.–Agreement with Linnell.–Linnell's generosity.–Mr. Lahee.

Repr. in Blake studies. London, 1949. (2d ed. 1971). p. [119]–34. (*See nos.*8605, 8645)

8599 —— New lines from Blake's Jerusalem. TLS 10 Jl '43:336.

Repr. in Blake studies. London, 1949. (2d ed. 1971). p. [110]–18. (*See nos.*8605, 8645)

8600 **Wolf, Edwin.** The Blake-Linnell accounts in the library of Yale university. Pa Bib Soc Am 37:1–22 '43. tables.

8601 **Keynes, sir Geoffrey L.** Blake's Poetical sketches. TLS 10 Mr '45:120; 17 Mr '45:132.

I. Blake and Flaxman.–The typography.–Blake's punctuation.–Blake's corrections.–Further corrections.–II. Census of copies.

Repr. in Blake studies. London, 1949. (2d ed. 1971). p. [22]–39. (*See nos.*8605, 8645)

8602 —— Blake, Tulk, and Garth Wilkinson. [Ptg. of Songs of innocence and experience]. Library ser4 26no2/3:190–2 S/D '45.

8603 **Stone, M. W.** William Blake and the juvenile drama. Theat Notebk 1no4:41 Jl '46.

8604 **Todd, Ruthven.** William Blake's illuminated printing. Print 6no1:53–64 '48. facsims.

8605 **Keynes, sir Geoffrey L.** Blake studies; notes on his life and works in seventeen chapters. London, R. Hart-Davis, 1949. (Repr. New York, Haskell, 1971; 2d ed. 1971). xiii,208p. + 49 plates, illus., facsims. 26cm.

Includes, rev. and enl. from 1st pub.: II. Blake's notebook.–III. Poetical sketches.–IV. The engraver's apprentice.–V. Engravers called Blake.–VI. Blake's illustrations to Young's Night thoughts.–VIII. A Descriptive catalogue [of Blake's exhibition, with rev. census of copies].–X. Blake's copper-plates.–XI. New lines from Jerusalem [with census].–XII. The history of the Job designs.–XIII. The Blake-Linnell documents.–XV. Thornton's Virgil.–Bibliography of writings by Geoffrey Keynes on Blake.

8606 **Tinker, Chauncey B.** The Book of Thel [acquired]. Yale Univ Lib Gaz 26no1:38 Jl '51.

8607 **Jugaku, Bunshō.** A bibliographical study of William Blake's note-book. Tokyo, Hokuseido pr., 1953; New York, Perkins, 1954. (Repr. New York, Haskell, 1971). xii,175p. facsims. 27cm.

I. Introductory.–II. General.–III. Descriptive.–IV. Analytical.–V. Concluding.–Transcription of the Note-book. . . .

Rev: TLS 21 My '54:336; *rf.* B. Jugaku *ib.* 30 Jl '54:487; H. Adams Mod Lang Q 15:375–6 '55; H. M. Margoliouth R Eng Stud new ser 6:92–4 '55.

8608 **The Blake** exhibition at Cambridge. TLS 19 F '54:128.

8609 **Brown, T. Julian.** William Blake, 1757–1827. (English literary autographs, XI). Bk Coll 3no3:219 '54. facsims.

8610 **Carter, John W.** The Stirling copy of Jerusalem. TLS 7 My '54:304; K. Preston *ib.* 14 My '54:319.

8611 **Margoliouth, Herschel M.** Blake's drawings for Young's Night thoughts. R Eng Stud 5no17:46–54 Ja '54.

8612 **Bentley, Gerald E., jr.** Blake and Percy's Reliques. N&Q 201:352–3 Ag '56.

8613 —— The date of Blake's Vala or The four zoas. Mod Lang N 71no7:487–91 N '56.

8614 —— William Blake as a private publisher. N.Y. Pub Lib Bull 61no11:539–60 N '57.

8615 **Blake** bicentenary in America. [Exhibition]. TLS 17 My '57:312.

8616 **Keynes, sir Geoffrey L.** Blake's copy of Dante's Inferno. TLS 3 My '57:277.

'Blake's annotations to Boyd's translation of Dante's Inferno, Dublin, 1785.'

Repr. in Blake studies. 2d ed. Oxford. 1971. p. [147]–54. (*See no.*8645)

8617 **Wark, Robert R.** A minor Blake conundrum. [Young's Night thoughts, 1797, and ptg. on vellum]. Huntington Lib Q 21no1:83–6 N '57.

8618 **Wolf, Edwin.** Blake exhibitions in America. Bk Coll 6no4:378–85 '57.

8619 **Bentley, Gerald E., jr.** Blake's engravings and his friendship with Flaxman. Stud Bib 12:161–88 '59. port., facsims.

8620 **Keynes, sir Geoffrey L.** Blake's library. TLS 6 N '59:648.

Repr. in Blake studies. 2d ed. Oxford, 1971. p. [155]–62. (*See no.*8645)

8621 **Wright, Cyril E.** William Blake's notebook. [Rossetti ms.]. Brit Mus Q 21no4:88–90 Oc '59.

8622 **Bentley, Gerald E., jr.** Additions to Blake's library. [Keynes]. N.Y. Pub Lib Bull 64no11:595–605 N '60.

8623 **Keynes, sir Geoffrey L.** Blake's Holy Thursday in Anne and Jane Taylor's City scenes. (Note 128). Bk Coll 9no1:75–6 '60.

8624 **Ryskamp, Charles.** A Blake collection for Princeton. [Presented by mrs. Gerard B. Lambert]. Princeton Univ Lib Chron 21no3:172–5 '60.

8625 **Sewter, A. C.** William Blake and the art of the book. Manchester R 8:360–73 '60. facsims.

8625a **Bentley, Gerald E., jr.** The promotion of Blake's Grave designs. [And R. H. Cromek]. Univ Toronto Q 31no3:339–53 Ap '62. facsims.

8626 **Keynes, sir Geoffrey L.** A Blake engraving in Bonnycastle's Mensuration, 1782. (Note 197). Bk Coll 12no2:205–6 '63. facsims.

8627 **Erdman, David V.** The binding, et cetera of Vala. Library ser5 19:112–29 '64.

8628 —— The suppressed and altered passages in Blake's Jerusalem. Stud Bib 17:1–54 '64. facsims., tables.

'Addenda: list of copies' (p. 41–3)

8629 **Keynes, sir Geoffrey L.** On editing Blake. Eng Stud Today ser3:137–53 '64.

8630 **Preston, Kerrison.** Blake's America. [Facsimile]. TLS 5 Mr '64:195; sir G. L. Keynes *ib.* 19 Mr '64:238.

8631 **Bentley, Gerald E., jr.** Blake's Hesiod. Library ser5 20no4:315–20 D '65. tables.

8632 **Bogen, Nancy.** Blake's Book of Thel. N&Q 210:464 D '65.

8633 **Erdman, David V.** Blake's Jerusalem: plate 3 fully restored. Stud Bib 18:281–2 '65.

8634 **Keynes, sir Geoffrey L.** A study of the illuminated books of William Blake, poet, printer, prophet. London, Methuen; New York, Orion pr. [1964]; Paris, Trianon pr. [1965]. 89p. + 7 plates. facsims. 32cm.

Covertitle: William Blake, poet, printer, prophet, *enl. ed. of* An exhibition of the illuminated books.

Rev: TLS 2 D '65:1104; K. Garlick Mod Lang R 61:503–4 '66.

8635 **Bentley, Gerald E., jr.** The date of Blake's Pickering manuscript, or the way of a poet with paper. Stud Bib 19:232–43 '66.

8636 —— The printing of Blake's America. Stud Romanticism 6no1:46–57 '66. facsims., tables.

8637 **Bogen, Nancy.** An early listing of William Blake's Poetical sketches. Eng Lang N 3no3:194–6 Mr '66.

8638 **Erdman, David B.** Blake's transcript of Bisset's Lines written on hearing the surrender of Copenhagen. N.Y. Pub Lib Bull 72no8:518–21 Oc '68.

8639 **Halloran, William F.** William Blake's The French revolution: a note on the text and a possible emendation. N.Y. Pub Lib Bull 72no1:3–18 Ja '68.

8639a **Howell, John.** An early hand-made facsimile of the Songs of innocence and of experience. [c.1821]. (Queries). Blake Newsl 1no4:10–11 Mr '68.

8640 **Keynes, sir Geoffrey L.** Blake's Little Tom the sailor. Bk Coll 17no4:421–7 '68. facsims.

8641 **Ryskamp, Charles.** Songs of innocence and of experience and miss Caroline Newton's Blake collection. Princeton Univ Lib Chron 29no2:150–5 '68. facsims.

8642 **Todd, Ruthven.** Blake's Dante plates. TLS 29 Ag '68:928; J. Evenden *ib.* 12 S '68:1032; R. Todd 26 S '68:1090.

8643 —— Blake's Dante plates: revised version. Bk Coll & Lib Mnthly 6:164–71 Oc '68.

Rev. from TLS 29 Ag '68:928; 26 S '68:1090.

8644 —— Blake's Dante plates. [London, 1968]. 12p. 21cm. Covertitle.

Repr. with adds. from Bk Coll & Lib Mnthly 6:164–71 Oc '68.

8645 **Keynes, sir Geoffrey L.** Blake studies; essays on his life and work. 2d ed. Oxford, Clarendon pr., 1971. (First pub. 1949). xii,263p. illus., facsims. 26cm.

Additions to contents of 1st ed.: XIX. Remember me! [Christmas annual, 1825].–XX. Blake's copy of Dante's Inferno.–XXI. Blake's library.–XXII. The Pilgrim's progress.

BLAKEWAY, JOHN BRICKDALE, 1756–1826

8646 **Whitfield, A. Stanton.** Rev. J. B. Blakeway: bibliography. N&Q ser11 11:231 Mr '15; H. T. Beddows; A. Sparke *ib*. 11:286–7 Ap '15.

8647 **Ogilvy, Murray.** Blakeway's mss.: Godolphin Edwards. N&Q 176:367 My '39; A. L. Humphreys *ib*. 176:412 Je '39.

BLISS, PHILIP, 1787–1857

8648 **Gibson, Strickland** and **C. J. Hindle.** Philip Bliss, 1787–1857, editor and bibliographer. Oxford Bib Soc Proc 3pt2:173–260 '32; Additions and corrections *ib*. 3pt3:367–8 '33; [Additions and corrections] Oxford Bib Soc Pub new ser 1pt1:40–2 '47.

Rev: TLS 29 Je '33:452.

BLOOMFIELD, ROBERT, 1766–1823

8649 **Bridge, Alexander.** Bloomfield's Rural tales, 1802. (Query 119). Bk Coll 8no4:431–2 '59; C. S. Bliss *ib*. 9no2:199 '60.

8650 **Sparrow, John H. A.** Robert Bloomfield . . . addenda. (Note 116). Bk Coll 8no3:299 '59.

8651 **Bloomfield, Barry C.** Bloomfield's Rural tales, 1802. (Note 188). Bk Coll 11no4:482 '62.

8652 **Clements, Jeff.** Early editions of Bloomfield's poems. (Note 179). Bk Coll 11no2:216–17 '62.

BOASE, GEORGE CLEMENT, 1829–97

8653 **Courtney, William P.** Boase, George Clement. N&Q ser8 12:301–2 Oc '97.

BOBBIN, TIM, *pseud. of* JOHN COLLIER, 1708–86

8654 **Briscoe, J. Potter.** Tim Bobbin, Lancashire humorist: a bibliographical note. Library 10no118:308–9 Oc '98.

8655 **Gordon, R. J.** John Collier: the man and his work. Lib Assn Rec 15no3:130–7 Mr '13.

BOECE, HECTOR, 1465?–1536

8656 **Watson, George.** A manuscript of Hector Boece. [History of Scotland]. Edinburgh Bib Soc Trans 2pt4:392–3 '46.

8657 **Mitchell, William S.** Hector Boece's copy of Galen's Thegni. Aberdeen Univ R 33no1:34–5 '49.

BOLINGBROKE, HENRY ST. JOHN, 1ST VISCOUNT, 1678–1751 *see* St. John, Henry, 1st viscount Bolingbroke, 1678–1751.

BOLTON, EDMUND, 1575?–1633?

8658 **Blackburn, Thomas H.** The date and evolution of Edmund Bolton's Hypercritica. [Ms.]. Stud Philol 63no2:196–202 Ap '66.

BORDE, ANDREW, 1490?–1549

8659 **Duff, E. Gordon.** The printer of Borde's Introduction to knowledge. [Copland or Middleton, 1548]. Library ser2 8no29:30–3 Ja '07.

8660 **Bühler, Curt F.** Some remarks on a nineteenth-century reprint. [Borde's First book of the introduction of knowledge, ed. by W. Upcott, 1814]. Pa Bib Soc Am 41:53–9 '47.

Repr. in Early books and manuscripts. New York, 1973. p. [115]–20.·

8661 **Thornton, John L.** Andrew Boorde's Dyetary of helth and its attribution to Thomas Linacre. Library ser5 2no2/3:172–3 S/D '47.

BORROW, GEORGE HENRY, 1803–81

8662 **Shorter, Clement.** Translation of Klinger's Faustus. N&Q ser11 7:207 Mr '13.

8663 George Borrow and his Lavengro. [Proof sheets]. (Marginalia). Bkmns J ser3 15no5:274–5 '28.

8664 **Borrow, George:** The death of Balder, London, Jarrold, 1889. [Date]. Bib N&Q 2no11:7 N '38.

8665 George Borrow's strange experiences in Man; one of his manuscripts secured for the museum. [His library, and Dust and ashes]. Manx Mus J 4no59:115–18 Je '39. facsim.

8666 **Jones, Evan D.** George Borrow mss. [in Library]. (News and notes). Nat Lib Wales J 1no3:145 '40.

8667 **Enquirer,** *pseud.* Borrow: The death of Balder. London, Jarrold, 1889. (Query no.6). Bk Coll 1no1:56 '52; E. Schlengemann *ib.* 1no2:129 '52; J. P. W. Gaskell 1no4:266–7 '52; J. Rubinstein 4no1:78–81 '55.

8668 **Borrow, K. T.** George Borrow's The Zincali. [Ms.]. (Note no.58). Bk Coll 5no1:75 '56.

8669 **Park, Julian.** Tales of the wild and wonderful, 1825. (Query 104). Bk Coll 7no4:417 '58.

8670 **Todd, William B.** Borrow's Lavengro and Faustus. (Note 153). Bk Coll 10no1:70 '61.

8671 **Carter, John W.** and **H. G. Pollard.** The mystery of The death of Balder. Oxford, Distributed for the authors by B. H. Blackwell, 1969. 21p. facsims. 22cm. (Working paper, no.3)

'Appendix: The 1886 proofs and the '1889' edition of The death of Balder' (p. 18–21)

Rev: TLS 3 Jl '69:736.

BOSWELL, JAMES, 1740–95

8672 **Fitzgerald, Percy H.** Editing a la mode; an examination of dr. Birkbeck Hill's new edition of Boswell's Life of Johnson. Enl. from an article in Time. London, Ward & Downey [1891]. 50,16,36p. 22cm.

8672a **Collinson, Joseph.** The proof-sheets of Boswell's Life. N&Q ser8 5:488 Je '94.

8673 **Hill, G. Birkbeck N.** Boswell's proof sheets. Atlantic Mnthly 74no445:657–68 N '94.

8674 —— 'Boswell's proof-sheets' *in* Johnson club, London. Johnson club papers by various hands. London; New York, 1899. p. 51–80.

8675 **B., G. L.** James Boswell and The shrubs of Parnassus. [1760 miscellany attrib. to]. N&Q ser10 7:429 Je '07.

8676 **Chapman, Robert W.** Birkbeck Hill's Johnson. [Boswell's Life, 1887]. TLS 26 Jl '23:504.

8677 —— Boswell's Tour to the Hebrides. TLS 9 Ag '23:533; W. M. L. Hutchinson *ib.* 23 Ag '23:556; R. W. Chapman 13 S '23:604; W. M. L. Hutchinson 27 S '23:636.

8678 **Pottle, Frederick A.** Boswelliana: two attributions. [Observations on The minor, 1760; View of the Edinburgh theatre, 1760]. N&Q 147:281 Oc '24; 147:375 N '24.

8679 **Proofsheets** of Boswell's Johnson. (Notes on sales). TLS 17 Ja '24:44.

8680 **Chapman, Robert W.** Cancels in Boswell's Hebrides. Bod Q Rec 4no42:124 Jl '24; 4no47:257 N '25.

8681 **Pierpont, Robert.** Boswell's Life of Johnson; first edition. N&Q 148:458 Je '25; J. Tregaskis; L. F. Powell; G. A. Gibbs; E. Bensly *ib.* 149:34 Jl '25.

8682 **Pottle, Frederick A.** Boswellian notes. II. A lost publication by Boswell: Verses in the character of a Corsican . . . 1769. N&Q 149:131–2 Ag '25.

8683 —— Boswellian notes. III. The Letters of lady Jane Douglas, 1767. N&Q 149:184–6 S '25.

8684 —— Boswellian notes. IV. The Irish editions of Corsica. N&Q 149:222 S '25.

8685 —— Boswell's Observations on The minor. N.Y. Pub Lib Bull 29no1:3–6 Ja '25.

8686 **Chapman, Robert W.** Boswell's proof sheets. London Merc 15no85:50–8 N '26; 15no86:171–80 D '26.

1. Boswell and his printer.–2. Various corrections.–3. Alteration of Johnson's words.–4. Cancel pages.

Repr. in Johnson and Boswell revised by themselves and others. Oxford, 1928. p. 19–50.

8687 **The Boswell** papers. (Notes on sales). TLS 22 S '27:652.

8688 **How** many issues are there of the first edition of Boswell's Life of Johnson? N.Y. Pub Lib Bull 31no10:826–7 Oc '27.

8689 **Pottle, Frederick A.** Boswell's Corsica. Yale Univ Lib Gaz 1no2:21–2 Oc '27.

8690 **Powell, Lawrence F.** 'The revision of dr. Birkbeck Hill's Boswell' *in* Johnson and Boswell revised by themselves and others. Oxford, 1928. p. 51–66.

8691 **Boswell** and Shakespeare problems. [Cancel in the Life]. (Notes on sales). TLS 16 My '29:408.

8692 **Pottle, Frederick A.** The Hodgson extra-illustrated Boswell. Yale Univ Lib Gaz 3no4:71–6 Ap '29.

8693 **Grolier club,** NEW YORK. Catalogue of an exhibition of the private papers of James Boswell from Malahide castle held at the Grolier club, New York. . . . [New York, 1930]. 1v.(unpaged) 24cm.

Also issued with title: The private papers. . . .

I. Journals of James Boswell.–II. Letters by James Boswell.–III. Manuscripts by James Boswell not journals or letters.–IV. Letters received by James Boswell and other manuscripts not written by him.–V. Books, broadsides, prints, etc.

8694 **McKinlay, Robert.** Boswell's fugitive pieces. Glasgow Bib Soc Rec 8:64–80 '30. facsim.

'Bibliography' (p. 78–80)

8695 **Chapman, Robert W.** Boswell's archives. [Library]. Essays & Stud 17:33–43 '31.

8696 **Denton, E. K. Willing-.** Boswell and the copyright of the Life. TLS 1 D '32:923.

8697 **Abbott, Claude C.** A catalogue of papers relating to Boswell, Johnson & sir William Forbes, found at Fettercairn house . . . 1930–1931. Oxford, Clarendon pr.; New York, O.U.P., 1936. xxvii,257p. 23cm.

Rev: TLS 16 Ja '37:38; B. Dobrée Spectator 1 Ja '37:22; J. T. Winterich Saturday R Lit 15:21 '37; sir H. H. Williams R Eng Stud 14:230–1 '38; R. L. Greene Mod Lang N 53:384–7 '38.

8698 **Pottle, Frederick A. [and others].** Index to the private papers of James Boswell from Malahide castle in the collection of 1t.–colonel Ralph Heyward Isham. Oxford, O.U.P.; London, H. Milford, O.U.P., 1937. (Repr. 1958). xx,359p. 23cm.

Corrigenda: vols. I–XVIII of the Boswell papers.–The catalogue to the Boswell papers.–Index.–Key to the meetings and conversations between Johnson and Boswell. . . .

Rev: R. L. Greene Mod Lang N 53:384–7 '38.

8699 **Powell, Lawrence F.** Boswell's original journal of his tour to the Hebrides and the printed version. Essays & Stud 23:58–69 '37.

8700 **Boswell** papers. [Report of judgement in Fettercairn house claim]. (Notes and news). Bull John Rylands Lib 22no2:314–16 Oc '38.

8701 **Hazen, Allen T.** Boswell's cancels in the Tour to the Hebrides. Bib N&Q 2no11:7 N '38.

8702 **Murray, John.** Notes on Johnson's movements in Scotland; suggested attributions to Boswell in the Caledonian mercury. N&Q 178:3–5 Ja '40.

8703 —— Boswell and the Caledonian mercury; further suggested attributions to him in this journal, January 1772–March 1774. N&Q 178:182–5 Mr '40.

8704 **The Malahide** and Fettercairn papers. TLS 18 D '48:720; R. W. Hunt *ib.* 8 Ja '49:25.

8705 **The Boswell** papers. TLS 12 Ag '49:528.

8706 **Chapman, Robert W.** Johnsonian and other essays and reviews. Oxford, Clarendon pr., 1953. 243p. 20cm.

Includes The making of the Life of Johnson.–Textual criticism.

8707 **Thompson, Karl F.** An anonymous Epistle to James Boswell. [1790]. N&Q 194:162–3 Ap '49.

8708 **The Boswell** papers (Isham collection). [Purchased by Yale university]. New Rambler 16:2–3 Ja '50.

8709 **Horne, Colin J.** Boswell and literary property. N&Q 195:296–8 Jl '50.

8710 **The Isham** collection at Yale. New Rambler 17:2–3 Jl '50.

8711 **Henderson, Robert W.** Extra-illustrated edition. [Boswell's Life of Samuel Johnson, 1885]. N.Y. Pub Lib Bull 55no2:95 F '51.

8712 **Turner, J. W.** Boswell's crest. [Ptd. on final leaf of E. Raffald's The experienced English housekeeper, 1799]. (Query no.23). Bk Coll 1no4:268 '52.

8713 **Fifer, C. N.** Editing Boswell, a search for letters; an editor explains the many problems faced in compiling and editing a complete correspondence. Manuscripts 6no1:2–5 '53. facsim.

8714 **Adams, Sarah F.** Boswell's Life of Johnson [with uncancelled leaves]. Yale Univ Lib Gaz 29no1:35–6 Jl '54.

8715 **Lonsdale, Roger.** Dr. Burney and the integrity of Boswell's quotations. Pa Bib Soc Am 53:327–31 '59.

8716 **Hamilton, Harlan W.** Boswell's suppression of a paragraph in Rambler 60. [Life]. Mod Lang N 76no4:218–20 Mr '61.

8717 **Liebert, Herman W.** Boswell's Life of Johnson, 1791. [Points]. Am N&Q 1no1:6–7 S '62.

8718 **Rae, Thomas I.** and **W. Beattie.** 'Boswell and the Advocates' library' *in* Johnson, Boswell and their circle; essays presented to Lawrence Fitzroy Powell. . . . Oxford, 1965. p. [254]–67.

'Appendix: Some books in the National library of Scotland formerly owned by James Boswell' (p. 266–7)

8719 **Cole, Richard C.** James Boswell and the Irish press, 1767–1795. N.Y. Pub Lib Bull 73no9:581–98 N '69. facsims.

BOYCE, SAMUEL, d.1775

8720 **Williams, Iolo A.** Samuel Boyce's Poems on several occasions, 1757; a postscript [to The elusive dr. Johnson *ib.* v.7]. Bk Coll Q 14:73–6 Ap/Je '34.

BOYD, MARK ALEXANDER, 1563–1601

8721 **Fergusson, James.** The text of Boyd's Sonet. TLS 12 My '50:293.

BOYD, ZACHARY, 1585?–1653

8722 **Weir, John L.** Bibliographical notices of The last battell of the soule in death, 1628–29. N&Q 195:535–7 D '50; 196:76–9 F '51.

BOYLE, JOHN, 5TH EARL OF CORK, AND ORRERY, 1707–62

8723 **Korshin, Paul J.** The earl of Orrery and Swift's early reputation. [Annotated, interleaved copies of Remarks on the life of Swift, 1752]. Harvard Lib Bull 16no2:167–7 Ap '68.

BOYLE, ROBERT, 1627–91

8724 **S., G. W.** Robert Boyle; mss. wanted. N&Q 157:172 S '29; J. Ardagh *ib.* 157:215 S '29.

8725 **Kirkpatrick, T. Percy C.** Boyle's Sceptical chymist, an advertisement. [1680]. Irish Bk Lover 23no1:12–13 Ja/F '35.

8726 **McKie, D.** Boyle's library. (Three historical notes). Nature 163no4147: 627–8 Ap '49.

8727 **Bühler, Curt F.** A projected but unpublished edition of the Life and works of Robert Boyle. [By William Wotton]. Chymia 4:79–83 '53.

 Repr. in Early books and manuscripts; forty years of research. New York, 1973. p. [490]–4.

8728 **Neill, Desmond G.** The cancel title in Boyle's Tracts, 1675. Bod Lib Rec 6no1:386–8 Oc '57.

8729 **Maddison, R. E. W.** Robert Boyle and the Irish Bible. [Tr. by W. Bedell; ptd. in Gaelic]. Bull John Rylands Lib 41no1:81–101 S '58. facsims.

8730 —— A tentative index of the correspondence of the honourable Robert Boyle, F.R.S. Roy Soc London N & Rec 13no2:128–201 N '58.

8731 **Osborne, Eric A.** Cancellandum R2 in Boyle's Sceptical chymist 1661. (Note 176). Bk Coll 11no2:215 '62.

8732 **Brown, T. Julian.** Robert Boyle, 1627–1691. (English scientific autographs, II). Bk Coll 13no4:487 '64. facsim.

BOYLE, ROGER, 1ST EARL OF ORRERY, 1621–79

8733 **Clark, William S.** Notes on two Orrery manuscripts. [The general; Zoroastres]. Mod Lang N 44no1:1–6 Ja '29.

8734 —— Lost stage directions in Orrery's plays. Mod Lang N 47no4:240–3 Ap '32.

BOYS, JOHN, 1571–1625

8735 **Hummel, Ray O.** Seventeenth-century publishing economy. [An exposition of the last psalm, 1613, ptd. by F. Kingston]. Mod Lang N 56no1:61–2 Ja '41.

BRADDON, MARY ELIZABETH (MRS. JOHN MAXWELL), 1837–1915

8736 **Sadleir, Michael T. H.** Notes on Lady Audley's secret. TLS 11 My '40:236; 1 Je '40:272.

8737 **Summers, A. Montague J-M. A.** Miss Braddon. (Bibliography and sales). TLS 29 Ag '42:432; sir I. MacAlister; A. M. J-M. A. Summers ib. 26 S '42:480; M. H. T. Sadleir 10 Oc '42:504; A. M. J-M. A. Summers 24 Oc '42:528; 15 Ap '44:192; 16 S '44:456.

8738 —— Miss Braddon's Black band. TLS 24 Ap '43:204; Maud Wyndham 15 My '43:235.

The critics.–The Black band.–Piracies.

8739 —— Mr. Babington White. [Circe, by mrs. Braddon, 1867]. TLS 30 S '44:480; F. B. Evans ib. 21 Oc '44:511; A. M. J-M. A. Summers 25 N '44:576; F. B. Evans 23 D '44:621.

Mystery letter.–A Dutch advertisement.–Ada Buisson.

8740 —— The Black band scandal. TLS 17 F '45:84.

Opening the attack.–Old novels as new.–G. A. Sala's views.

BRADLEY, EDWARD, 1827–89 *see* Bede, Cuthbert, *pseud.*

BRADSHAWE, NICHOLAS, d.1655

8741 **Bloxam, R. N.** Nicholas Bradshawe. [Canticum evangelicum, 1635]. N&Q 190:121–2 Mr '46; H. W. Edwards ib. 190:195 My '46.

BRATHWAITE, RICHARD, 1588?–1673

8742 **Roberts, William.** Brathwait's The good wife, 1618. Athenæum 3657:751 N '97; 3658:787 D '97; 3659:822 D '97.

8743 **Prideaux, William F.** Brathwait's Shepherds' tales. Athenæum 4079:896–7 D '05.

8744 **Tate, W. E.** Scott and Drunken Barnaby. N&Q 193:298–9 Jl '48; J. C. Corson *ib.* 193:391–3 S '48.

BRETON, NICHOLAS, 1545?–1626?

8745 Cancelled.

8746 **Williams, Franklin B.** An unrecognised edition of Nicholas Breton. [A flourish upon fancy, n.d.]. Mod Lang R 32no2:81–2 Ja '37.

8747 **Robertson, Jean.** The passions of the spirit, 1599, and Nicholas Breton. Huntington Lib Q 3no1:69–75 Oc '39.

8748 Cancelled.

8749 **Sullivan, Frank.** [Bibliogr. note on Breton's A post with a packet of mad letters, 1606, 1607]. Pa Bib Soc Am 37:233 '43.

8750 **Robertson, Jean.** Nicholas Breton's collections of proverbs. Huntington Lib Q 7no3:307–15 My '44.

8751 —— Nicholas Breton's poems. [The soul's heavenly exercise, 1601]. TLS 20 Mr '48:163.

8752 **Crow, John.** Poems of Nicholas Breton. [And definition of bibliogr.]. TLS 3 Oc '52:645; Reviewer *ib.* 17 Oc '52:684.

8753 **Wilson, Frank P.** Nicholas Breton's I would and would not, 1619. Library ser5 12no4:273–4 D '57.

BRIDGES, ROBERT SEYMOUR, 1844–1930

8754 **Jackson, Holbrook.** Robert Bridges, George Moore, Bernard Shaw and printing. Fleuron 4:43–53 '25.

8755 **Milford, sir Humphrey S.** Bridge's Shorter poems. TLS 2 Jl '31:528.

8756 **Wilkinson, Cyril H.** Bibliography of Robert Bridges. TLS 28 D '33:924.

8757 **Trevanion, Michael,** *pseud.* Bridges: Shorter poems, 1890. [Issues]. Bib N&Q 2no7:3 Oc '36.

8758 **Smith, Simon H. Nowell-.** Bridges: Poems, 1873. [Date of suppression]. Bib N&Q 2no8:5 F '37; D. M[assey?] *ib.* 2no11:3 N '38.

8759 **Adams, Charles M.** Robert Bridges first edition. [Poems, 1873]. Am N&Q 1no3:40–1 Je '41.

8760 **Fleming, Thomas P.** [Bibliogr. note on Bridges' A case of thickening of the cranial bones, 1879]. Pa Bib Soc Am 35:161 '41.

8761 **Tindall, William Y.** The Robert Bridges collection. Columbia Univ Q 33:154–8 Ap '41.

8762 **Smith, Simon H. Nowell-.** The phonotypes of Robert Bridges. Alphabet & Image 5:30–42 S '47. facsims.

8763 —— 'A poet in Walton street' *in* Essays mainly on the nineteenth century presented to sir Humphrey Milford. London, 1948. p. [58]–71.

8764 **Brown, T. Julian.** Robert Bridges, 1844–1930. (English literary autographs, XX). Bk Coll 5no4:369 '56. facsim.

8765 **Smith, Simon H. Nowell-.** Bridges, Hopkins and dr. Daniel. TLS 13 D '57:764.

8766 —— Mosher and Bridges. (Note 189). Bk Coll 11no4:482–3 '62.

BRIDIE, JAMES, *pseud. of* **OSBORNE HENRY MAVOR, 1888–1951**

8767 **Sadleir, Michael T. H.** How variants happen, a curious example from contemporary bibliography. [Collations and bibliogr. discussion of six Bridie items]. Bk Coll Q 10:54–65 Ap/Je '33.

BRIGHT, TIMOTHY, 1550–1615

8768 Cancelled.

8769 **Doran, Madeleine.** Manuscript notes in the Bodleian copy of Bright's Characterie. Library ser4 16no4:418–24 Mr '36. facsims.

8770 **Keynes, sir Geoffrey L.** Bright's Characterie. TLS 29 Ap '60:273; W. J. Carlton *ib.* 10 Je '60:369.

8771 **Carlton, William J.** An unrecorded manuscript by dr. Timothy Bright. N&Q 209:463–5 D '64.

BRODRIBB-IRVING, SIR JOHN HENRY, 1838–1905 *see* Irving, sir John Henry Brodribb-, 1835–1905.

8772 Cancelled.

BROME, RICHARD, d.1652?

8773 **Fried, Harvey.** The early quartos of Brome's Northern lasse. Pa Bib Soc Am 54:179–81 '60.

BRONTË FAMILY

8774 **Bibliographical** notes. [First ed. of Poems by Currer, Ellis and Acton Bell, 1846, with list of pirated modern ed.]. Bkmn (N.Y.) 1no6:427–8 Jl '95. facsim.

8775 **Wood, Butler.** Some bibliographical notes on the Brontë literature. Brontë Soc Trans 4pt21:189–98 '11.

8776 **First** editions of Jane Eyre and Wuthering Heights. Brontë Soc Trans 5pt27:188 '17.

8777 **Cook, T. Davidson.** Brontë manuscripts in the Law collection. Bkmn 69no410:100–4 N '25.

8778 **Brontë** treasures returned to England. [Bonnell gift to Brontë society]. (Marginalia). Bkmns J ser3 17no9:46–7 '29.

8779 **DeL., P.** Brontë books and mss. [lent by Wise]. Lib Assn Rec ser3 1no11:388 N '31.

8780 **Brontë:** Poems, 1846, 2nd issue. Bib N&Q 1no2:9 Ap '35.

8781 **Christian, Mildred G.** A census of Brontë manuscripts in the United States. Trollopian 2no3:177–99 D '47; 2no4:241–59 Mr '48; 3no1:55–72 Je '48; 3no2:133–54 S '48; 3no3:215–33 D '48.

8782 **Marchand, Leslie A.** An addition to the census of Brontë manuscripts. [Rutgers university acquisition of The history of Angria with Symington colln.]. (Notes and queries). Trollopian 2no1:81–4 Je '49.

8783 **Bentley, Phyllis.** A German Brontë forgery. [Rockingham or the younger brother, by Acton and Currer Bell, 1851, by count de Jarnac]. Brontë Soc Trans 12no1:30–4 '52.

8784 **Foxon, David F.** Binding variants in the Brontës' Poems. (Note no.25). Bk Coll 2no3:219–21 '53.

8785 **Brown, T. Julian.** The Brontës. (English literary autographs, XVII). Bk Coll 5no1:55–6 '56. facsims.

8786 **Hayward, John D.** The first American edition of the Brontës' poems. (Query 121). Bk Coll 8no4:432 '59; D. A. Randall ib. 9no2:199–201 '60; S. Adelman 9no2:201–2 '60.

8787 **Smith, Simon H. Nowell-.** More Wise reprints. [Brontë Poems, 1846]. TLS
      3 F '66:92; H. Marley *ib.* 17 F '66:132.

8788 **Hargreaves, G. D.** The publishing of Poems by Currer, Ellis and Acton
      Bell. Brontë Soc Trans 15no4:294–300 '69.

BRONTË, ANNE, 1820–49

8789 Cancelled.

8790 **Taylor, Robert.** Anne Brontë's The tenant of Wildfell hall. New Coloph
      1pt2:194–5,196 Ap '48.

8791 **Pacey, Desmond.** The Narrow way. TLS 18 Ag '66:743.

BRONTË, CHARLOTTE (MRS. A. B. NICHOLLS), 1816–55

8792 **Hatfield, C. W.** The early manuscripts of Charlotte Brontë, a bibliography.
      Brontë Soc Trans 6pt32:97–111 '22; 6pt33:153–65 '23; 6pt34:220–35 '24.

8793 **Wise, Thomas J.** A warning. [Forged Charlotte Brontë inscription]. TLS 13
      Je '29:474.

8794 **Partington, Wilfred G.** The forging of manuscripts. TLS 28 My '31:427;
      J. Malham-Dembleby *ib.* 15 Oc '31:802.

8795 **Brontë** juvenilia. (Notes on sales). TLS 6 Ap '33:252.

8796 **Warburton, Thomas.** Brontë: Shirley. [Issues]. Bib N&Q 2no4/5:7 My '36;
      Harriet Marlow; D. Flower *ib.* 2no6:3 Jl '36; M. L. Parrish 2no7:2 Oc '36.

8797 **Edgerley, C. M.** A Charlotte Brontë manuscript. [Young gentleman's
      magazine ser2 no4]. Brontë Soc Trans 10no2:69–70 '41.

8798 **Brooks, Roger L.** Unrecorded newspaper reviews of Charlotte Brontë's
      Shirley and Villette. Pa Bib Soc Am 53:270–1 '59.

8799 **Brammer, M. M.** The manuscript of The professor. R Eng Stud new ser
      11no42:157–70 My '60.

      I. Alterations in the manuscript.–II. The first edition.

8800 **Todd, William B.** An early state of Charlotte Brontë's Shirley, 1849. (Note
      204). Bk Coll 12no3:355–6 '63.

BRONTË, EMILY, 1818–48

8801 **Blakiston, H. E. D.** Emily Brontë's Poems. TLS 19 Ja '11:22.

8802 **Mince, H. A.** An account of the ms. of Emily Brontë's poems in the collection of mr. A. J. Law, Honresfeld, Littleborough. Rochdale Lit & Scientific Soc Trans 12:93–102 '16. facsim.

'List of pieces in the Honresfeld ms.' (p. 97)

8803 **McGovern, John B.** A Brontë poem. [Hologr. of 'There let thy bleeding branch atone']. N&Q ser12 8:247 Mr '21.

8804 **Shorter, Clement** and **C. W. Hatfield.** The text of Emily Brontë. TLS 20 Mr '24:176; Your reviewer *ib.* 27 Mr '24:192; C. Shorter; C. W. Hatfield 3 Ap '24:208.

8804a **Hatfield, C. W.** Brontë poems. [Selections from poems by Ellis Bell, 1850]. TLS 21 Je '34:443; M. Robertson *ib.* 28 Je '34:460.

8805 **Henderson, Philip.** Emily Brontë's poems. TLS 29 Ja '49:73; L. R. Chambers *ib.* 12 Mr '49:169; P. Henderson 23 Ap '49:270.

8806 —— Emily Brontë's poems. TLS 30 N '51:765; Helen Brown *ib.* 21 D '51:821.

8807 **Kite, J. E.** Wuthering Heights. [Author's copy]. TLS 16 Mr '51:165.

8808 **A first** edition of Wuthering Heights. [With ms. corrections attrib. to Emily]. Brontë Soc Trans 14no4:50 '64.

8809 **Hewish, John.** Emily Brontë's missing novel. TLS 10 Mr '66:197; C. Lemon *ib.* 17 Mr '66:223.

BROOKE, SIR FULKE GREVILLE, 1ST BARON, 1554–1628 *see* Greville, sir Fulke, 1st baron Brooke, 1554–1628.

BROOKE, HENRY, 1703–83

8810 **Chapman, Robert W.** Brooke's Gustavus Vasa. R Eng Stud 1no4:460–1 Oc '25; 2no5:99 Ja '26.

BROOKE, RUPERT, 1887–1915

8811 **Bookshop** buys Rupert Brooke's library. [Brick row bookshop, N.Y.]. Pub Wkly 120no2:173 Jl '31.

8812 **Hockett, Byrne.** Rupert Brooke's library. [To Dartmouth college]. TLS 22 Oc '31:820.

8813 **Early** writings of Rupert Brooke. [Arthur Eckersley's library]. (Notes on sales). TLS 28 Mr '36:284.

8814 **Haines, J. W.** Rupert Brooke: Letters from America. [Variant date on label]. Bib N&Q 2no1:2 Ja '36; 2no2:1 F '36; D. A. Randall; O. S. B. Brett, 3d viscount Esher *ib.* 2no3:3 Ap '36.

8815 **Randall, David A.** [Bibliogr. note on Brooke's Collected poems, 1915]. Pa Bib Soc Am 36:68 '42.

8816 **Platnauer, Maurice.** Variants in the manuscripts of the poems of Rupert Brooke and A. E. Housman. R Eng Stud 19no76:386–94 Oc '43.

8817 **Keynes, sir Geoffrey L.** A bibliography of Rupert Brooke. TLS 10 S '54:573.

8817a **Randall, David A.** The first American edition of 1914 and other poems. (Query 185). Bk Coll 13no3:359 '64; sir G. L. Keynes *ib.* 13no4:503 '64.

BROOME, WILLIAM, 1689–1745

8818 **Forshaw, Charles F.** Rev. William Broome, Ll.D. N&Q ser8 12:348 Oc '97; W. F. Prideaux; C. Green; W. E. A. Axon; R Pierpoint *ib.* 12:513 14 D '97.

BROUGHTON, HUGH, 1549–1612

8819 **Hill, Trevor H. Howard-.** Hugh Broughton and some Elizabethan printers. N&Q 202:286–8 Jl '57.

BROWN, JOHN, 1715–76

8820 **Roberts, sir Sydney C.** Bibliography of Estimate Brown. [Addenda]. (Note 157). Bk Coll 10no2:198 '61.

BROWN, JOHN, 1722–87

8821 **Hulton, Blanche.** Brown's superb Bible. [1812]. N&Q ser10 3:228 Mr '05.

BROWN, THOMAS, 1663–1704

8822 **Mason, Alexandra.** A cautionary tale for young bibliographers. [The weesils, 1691, and half-sheet imposition]. Bks & Libs Univ Kansas 2no6:11–13 Mr '65.

BROWNE, SIR THOMAS, 1605–82

8823 **Starkey, James S.** Author's emendation in the Religio medici. Athenæum 3974:858 D '03.

8824 **Osler, sir William.** The Religio medici. Library ser2 7no25:1–31 Ja '06. port., facsims.

8825 **Thomas, P. G.** Drummond and Browne. [Religio medici]. Mod Lang R 7no2:241–2 Ap '12.

8826 **Letts, Malcolm H. I.** Sir Thomas Browne and his books. N&Q ser11 10:321–3,342–4 Oc '14; 10:361–2 N '14; Harmatopegos, *pseud., ib.* 10:397 N '14.

8827 **H., W. B.** Sir Thomas Browne's Religio medici. [Ed. by G. B. M., 1894]. N&Q ser12 9:11 Jl '21.

8828 **Monro, T. K.** The early editions of sir Thomas Browne. Glasgow Bib Soc Rec 7:44–61 '23.

8829 **Pearson, Karl.** A missing edition of sir Thomas Browne's Religio medici, folio 1663. TLS 25 Ja '23:60.

8830 **Keynes, sir Geoffrey L.** An unrecorded edition of Browne's Christian morals. [1723]. Library ser4 10no4:419–20 Mr '30. facsim.

8831 **Browne's** Religio medici. [Presented to Library]. Yale Univ Lib Gaz 6no1:22 Jl '31.

8832 **Carter, John W.** Sir Thomas Browne. [Appeal for copies of Hydriotaphia with hologr. corrs.]. (Correspondence). London Merc 24no142:361 Ag '31.

8833 —— Sir Thomas Browne. [Books with ms. corrections]. TLS 16 Jl '31:564.

8834 —— The iniquity of oblivion foil'd. [The text of Urn burial and The garden of Cyrus with ms. corrections]. Coloph [4]pt13:[10p.] '33. facsims.

8835 **Cawley, R. R.** Sir Thomas Browne and his reading. Pub Mod Lang Assn 48:426–70 Je '33.

8836 **Carter, John W.** Browne's Urne buriall. [With hologr. corrs.]. (Bibliographical notes). TLS 22 Ag '35:528.

8837 **Finch, Jeremiah S.** Musæum clausum. TLS 13 N '37:871.

8838 **De Beer, Esmond S.** The correspondence between sir Thomas Browne and John Evelyn. Library ser4 19no1:103–6 Je '38.

8839 **Finch, Jeremiah S.** A newly discovered Urn burial. [With authorial corrs.]. Library ser4 19no3:347–53 D '38. facsims.

8840 **Keynes, sir Geoffrey L.** Browne's Letter to a friend. [1690]. (Antiquarian notes). TLS 19 N '38:748.

8841 **Carter, John W.** Sir Thomas Browne's autograph corrections. [Urn burial]. Library ser4 19no4:492–3 Mr '39.

8842 **Finch, Jeremiah S.** An author-corrected Urne burial. TLS 16 Mr '40:140; J. W. Carter *ib.* 11 My '40:236.

8843 —— Early drafts of The garden of Cyrus. Pub Mod Lang Assn 55no3:742–7 S '40. facsims.

8844 **Carter, John W.** Urne buriall. [With census of 10 copies with author's corrections]. TLS 27 F '43:108.

8845 —— Browne's Urn burial. Library ser5 2no2/3:191–2 S/D '47. facsims.

8846 **Cook, Elizabeth.** The first edition of Religio medici. Harvard Lib Bull 2no1:22–31 '48.

8847 **Finch, Jeremiah S.** Sir Thomas Browne; early biographical notices, and the disposition of his library and manuscripts. Stud Bib 2:196–201 '49/50.

8848 —— The Norfolk persuaders of sir Thomas Browne; a variant copy of the 1742 Posthumous works. Princeton Univ Lib Chron 11no4:199–201 '50. facsims.

8849 **Keynes, sir Geoffrey L.** Sir Thomas Browne's Religio medici. TLS 18 Ap '52:265.

8850 **Carter, John W.** Browne's Urne buriall. [Author corrected copies]. TLS 7 Je '57:349; *ib.* 30 Ag '57:519.

8851 **The T. K.** Monro collection of the works of sir Thomas Browne [presented to Glasgow university library]. Biblioth 1no3:45–6 '58.

8852 **Endicott, N. J.** Sir Thomas Browne, Montpellier, and the tract 'of languages'. [Ms.]. TLS 24 Ag '62:645; D. E. Rhodes *ib.* 7 S '62:679.

8853 **Carter, John W.** Works of sir Thomas Browne. TLS 15 Ap '65:293; C. Gordon *ib.* 6 My '65:356.

8853a **Carter, John W.** The iniquity of oblivion foil'd. [With census of 12 author-corr. copies of Hydriotaphia]. (Collector's piece, II). Bk Coll 15no3:279–82 '66. facsims.

8854 **Shaaber, Matthias A.** A crux in Religio medici. Eng Lang N 3no4:263–5 Je '66.

8855 **Finch, Jeremiah S.** Browne index. [Browne's library]. TLS 15 Je '67:548.

BROWNE, WILLIAM, 1591–1643

8856 **Cox, Edwin M.** The first edition of Browne's Britannia's pastorals. N&Q ser11 9:3 Ja '14.

8857 **Candy, Hugh C. H.** Notes on old books. Britannia's pastorals. Library ser3 9no36:248–50 Oc '18.

8858 —— Britannia's pastorals. [Emendations]. TLS 6 Mr '19:126; E. M. Cox ib. 13 Mr '19:138; W. Jaggard; C. E. Mathews 20 Mr '19:153; H. C. H. Candy 3 Ap '19:184.

8859 **Loane, George G.** Britannia's pastorals. [Emendations]. TLS 14 S '22:584; A. R. Ropes ib. 21 S '22:601; G. G. Loane 12 Oc '22:648.

8860 **Tillotson, Geoffrey.** Towards a text of Browne's Britannia's pastorals. Library ser4 11no2:193–202 S '30.

8861 **Cutts, John P.** Original music to Browne's Inner temple masque, and other Jacobean masque music. N&Q 199:194–5 My '54.

8862 **Grundy, Joan.** A new manuscript of the Countess of Pembroke's Epitaph. N&Q 205:63–4 F '60.

BROWNING, ELIZABETH (BARRETT), 1806–61 *see also under* Browning, Robert, 1812–89.

8863 **Mrs.** Browning's early poem, The battle of Marathon. Athenæum 3341:618–19 N '91; *rf.* 3345:763 D '91.

8864 **The Battle** of marathon. [Scarcity of copies]. Bkworm 5no50:38 Ja '92.

8865 **Curtis, Myra.** The Browning letters. TLS 20 N '30:991; Hibernicus ib. 4 D '30:1042.

8866 **Carter, John W.** Sonnets by E. B. B. TLS 23 F '33:127.

8867 **Gaylord, Harriet.** Gosse and the Reading sonnets. [And T. J. Wise]. TLS 8 N '34:775; J. W. Carter; Clotilda Marson ib. 15 N '34:795; J. W. Carter 22 N '34:840.

8868 **Wise, Thomas J.** Mrs. Browning's Sonnets, 1847. (Bibliographical notes). TLS 24 My '34:380; M. B. Forman; H. G. Pollard ib. 31 My '34:396.

8869 **Corkey, E.** A Browning misprint. [In Letters]. TLS 16 N '35:746.

8870 **Honeyman, R. B.** Mrs. Browning: Sonnets from the Portuguese. [Date of 1st separate ed.]. Bib N&Q 1no2:9 Ap '35; D. A. Randall ib. 1no3:2 Ag '35; N. A. Hall 1no4:7 Oc '35.

8871 **Carter, John W.** Mrs. Browning's poems, 1850. TLS 30 My '36:464.

8872 **Davidson, Gustav.** The first edition of The sonnets from the Portuguese. [Boston, Ticknor, 1886]. Pub Wkly 136no22:1976–7 N '39.

8873 Cancelled.

8874 **Taylor, Clyde R. H.** Marginalia by E. B. B.; Milton's prose works. Turnbull Lib Rec 2:5–6 Jl '40. [Sg.: C. R. H. T.]

8875 **Harlan, Aurelia E. B.** Not by Elizabeth Barrett Browning. [To Robert Lytton]. Pub Mod Lang Assn 57no2:582–5 Je '42.

8876 **Sonnets** from the Portuguese. [Ms.]. TLS 21 Je '47:316.

8877 **Hagedorn, Ralph.** Edmund Gosse and the Sonnets from the Portuguese. [1906]. Pa Bib Soc Am 46:67–70 '52.

8878 **Pettit, Kenneth I.** By Elizabeth Barrett Browning. [Donation of mss.]. Yale Univ Lib Gaz 34no1:34–7 Jl '59.

8879 **Brown, T. Julian.** Elizabeth Barrett Browning, 1806–1861 and Robert Browning, 1812–1889. (English literary autographs, XXXV). Bk Coll 9no3:317 '60. facsims.

8880 **E. B. B.** [Exhibition]. TLS 2 Je '61:348.

8881 **Singer, George C.** A unique copy of The runaway slave, 1849. [Wise forgery]. (Note 191). Bk Coll 12no1:68–71 '63; J. W. Carter *ib.* 12no2:202–3 '63.

8882 Cancelled.

8883 **Kelley, Philip.** Collection: Moulton-Barrett papers in the New York public library. Browning Newsl 2:10–12 Ap '69. [Sg.: Philip Kelly.]

8884 —— Response to a query by Warner Barnes [on On a poem by E. B. B.: not by her]. (Notes and queries). Browning Newsl 2:30 Ap '69.

BROWNING, ROBERT, 1812–89

8885 **Furnivall, Frederick J.** The line-numbering in Browning's Ring and the book. Acad 37:47 Ja '90.

8886 **Livingston, Luther S.** Robert and Elizabeth Barrett Browning. (The first books of some English authors, I). Bkmn (N.Y.) 10no1:76–81 S '99. facsims.

8887 **Hudson, C. M.** Browning's text. N&Q ser10 1:208 Mr '04.

8888 **Armstrong, A. Joseph.** Baylor university's Browning collection and other Browning interests. Waco, Tex., Baylor university, 1927. (2d ed. 1928). 51p. illus., port., facsim. 23cm.

Repr. from Baylor Bull 30no4:1–51 D '27.

8889 —— [**Same**]: [2d ed.]. Waco, Tex., Baylor university, 1928. (First pub. 1927). 43p. illus., port., facsims. 24cm.

How the Browning collection came into existence.–The Browning collection: the books.–The home of the collection.–Letters in manuscript.–Personalia and gifts.–Donations.–The real worth of the collection.–Browning in foreign languages.–Queries.–Odds and ends.–The Browning pilgrimage.

8890 **DeVane, William C.** The new Browning letters [purchased for Library]. Yale Univ Lib Gaz 7no2:39–41 Oc '32.

8891 **Phelps, William L.** Notes on Browning's Pauline. Mod Lang N 47no5:292–9 My '32.

8892 **Budd, Ruth.** Baylor university's Browning collection. Lib J 60no18:789–90 Oc '35.

8893 **Brett, Oliver S. B., 3d viscount Esher.** Browning: Fifine at the fair. [Issues]. Bib N&Q 2no1:2 Ja '36. [Sg.: Esher.]

8894 —— Browning: Prince Hohenstiel-Schwangau. [Binding variants]. Bib N&Q 2no2:4 F '36. [Sg.: Esher.]

8895 **O'Hegarty, Patrick S.** Browning, Robert: Helen's tower. Bib N&Q 2no11:7 N '38.

8896 **Brett, Oliver S. B., 3d viscount Esher.** Browning: Pacchiarotto. [Issues]. Bib N&Q 2no7:3 Oc '36; A. Pforzheimer *ib.* 2no8:4 F '37; P. S. O'Hegarty 2no12:1 My '39. [Sg.: Esher.]

8897 **Fox, Bernice.** Revision in Browning's Paracelsus. Mod Lang N 55no3:195–7 Mr '40.

8898 **Munsterberg, Margaret.** Browning's copy of La Légende des siècles. [By V. Hugo]. More Bks Boston Pub Lib Bull 16no7:335–6 S '41. [Sg.: M. M.]

8899 **Bayford, E. G.** Poem by Browning. [Lines to the memory of his parents]. N&Q 193:248–9 Je '48.

8900 **Altick, Richard D.** Robert Browning rides the Chicago and Alton. [American ed. of Poems ptd. in railway timetable]. New Coloph 3:78–81 '50. facsim.

8901 **Joseph, D. C.** A Browning book. [Browning's library]. TLS 3 Ap '53:221.

8902 **Archibald, Raymond C.** Musical settings of Robert Browning's poetry and drama. N&Q 199:270 Je '54.

8903 **A Browning** exhibit in the Treasure room. Boston Pub Lib Q 11no1:50–2 Ja '59.

8904 **Sanders, Steven.** A supplement to A calendar of letters. Baylor Browning Interests 18:11–20 My '61.

8905 **Barnes, Warner.** The Browning collection. Lib Chron Univ Texas 7no3:12–13 '63.

8906 **Honan, Park.** The texts of fifteen fugitives by Robert Browning. [Impromptu verse]. Vict Poet 5no3:157–69 '67.

8907 **Baker, Ronald.** Collection: The University of Texas at Austin; recent acquisitions. Browning Newsl 1:7–8 Oc '68.

8908 **The Ohio** university press edition: The complete works of Robert Browning, with variant readings, annotated. Browning Newsl 1:9–13 Oc '68.

8909 **Herring, Jack W.** Willie Macready's drawings for The cardinal and the dog [in Baylor Browning library]. (Notes and queries). Browning Newsl 3:42 '69.

8910 **Ewing, Douglas C.** Collection: The Browning collection of the Pierpont Morgan library. Browning Newsl 3:23–5 '69.

8910a **Jack, Ian.** '1848' edition of Browning's Poems. (Notes and queries). Browning Newsl 2:30–1 Ap '69; J. W. Herring Further note ib. 2:31–2 Ap '69.

8911 **King, Roma A.** A new last edition of Robert Browning's poetry. [1889 ed.]. (Notes and queries). Browning Newsl 3:37–8 '69.

8912 **McNally, James.** Revision of Home-thoughts, from the sea. (Notes and queries). Browning Newsl 2:32–3 Ap '69.

8913 **Raymond, William O.** Holographs of Browning letters in University of Toronto library. (Notes and queries). Browning Newsl 3:38–40 '69.

BRUCE, GEORGE, fl.1775–1820

8914 **Webb, W. L.** George Bruce. N&Q ser9 3:348 Mr '99.

BUC, SIR GEORGE, d.1623

8915 **Bald, R. Cecil.** A Revels office entry. [Buc's ms. Commentary upon the new roll of Winchester]. TLS 17 Mr '27:193.

8916 **Greg, sir Walter W.** Three manuscript notes by sir George Buc. Library ser4 12no3:307–21 D '31. facsims.

Repr. in Maxwell, James C., *ed.* Collected papers. Oxford, 1966. p. [226]–38.

8917 **Tannenbaum, Samuel A.** 'A forgery in a copy of Buck's Daphnis polustephanos' *in* Shaksperian scraps and other Elizabethan fragments. New York, 1933. p. 51–74.

8918 **Bald, R. Cecil.** The Locrine and George-a-Greene title-page inscriptions. [By Buc]. Library ser4 15no3:295–305 D '34. facsims.

*See also no.*10961.

8919 —— A manuscript work by sir George Buc. [A commentary upon the new roll of Winchester]. Mod Lang R 30no1:1–12 Ja '35.

8920 **Schwartz, Elias.** Sir George Buc's authority as licenser for the press. [And Chapman]. Sh Q 12no4:467–8 '61.

BUCHAN, JOHN, BARON TWEEDSMUIR, 1875–1940

8921 **Goodspeed, George T.** Buchan: Huntingtower, London, 1922. [Variant states]. Bib N&Q 2no2:4 F '36. [Sg.: G. G.]

8922 **Hanna, Archibald.** A John Buchan collection. Yale Univ Lib Gaz 37no1:25–9 Jl '62.

BUCHANAN, GEORGE, 1506–82

8923 **Bayne, William.** 'Appendix III: A. List of books presented by Buchanan to the University of St. Andrews; B. List of books presented to the University of Glasgow' *in* Millar, David A., *ed.* George Buchanan, a memorial, 1506–1906. St. Andrews; London [1907]. p. 407–9.

8924 **Finlayson, C. P.** An unpublished commentary by George Buchanan on Virgil. Edinburgh Bib Soc Trans 3pt4:269–88 '57.

8925 **McFarlane, I. D.** George Buchanan's Latin poems from script to print: a preliminary survey. Library ser5 24no4:277–332 D '69. facsims.

A. The formative years.–B. Bordeaux and the third sojourn in Paris.–C. Coimbra.–D. Paris, 1552–1560.–E. The search for material towards publication.–G. Editions of the poetry until the Edinburgh edition of 1615.

BUCK, SIR GEORGE, d.1623 *see* Buc, sir George, d.1623.

BUCKLER, EDWARD, 1610–1706

8926 **Moore, C. A.** Midnights meditations, 1646: a bibliographical puzzle. Mod Lang N 41no4:220–6 Ap '26.

8927 **Buckler, W. H.** Edward Buckler, 1610–1706, poet and preacher. Library ser4 17no3:349–53 D '36.

8928 **Mead, Herman R.** Three issues of A buckler against the fear of death. Library ser4 21no2:199–206 S '40.

BULWER-LYTTON, EDWARD, GEORGE EARLE LYTTON, 1ST BARON LYTTON, 1803–73 *see* Lytton, Edward George Earle Lytton Bulwer-, 1803–73.

BUNYAN, JOHN, 1628–88

8929 **Early** editions of the Pilgrim's progress. Bkworm 1no6:201–3 My '88. facsim.

8930 **Early** illustrated editions of Pilgrim's progress. Bkworm 1no10:346–9 S '88. facsims.

8931 **Muir, John.** The spurious second part of The pilgrim's progress. N&Q ser8 5:425 Je '94; Dollar, *pseud., ib.* 6:217 S '94; I. C. Gould 6:258 S '94.

8932 **King, Charles.** The Pilgrim's progress; early edition in French. N&Q ser9 7:167–8 Mr '01.

8933 **£1,475** for a first edition of Pilgrim's progress. Pub Circ 74no1820:559 My '01.

8934 **Stock, Elliot.** The first edition of The pilgrim's progress. Athenæum 3831:404 Mr '01.

8935 **Foster, John C.** An unrecorded first edition of Bunyan. [Barren fig-tree, 1673]. Baptist Hist Soc Trans 1:92–9 '08/9. facsims.

8936 **Hill, N. W.** Pilgrim's progress, second edition, 1678: suppressed passage. N&Q ser11 4:25 Jl '11; 4:239 S '11.

8937 **Plomer, Henry R.** A lawsuit as to an early edition of the Pilgrim's progress. [Braddill v. Ponder, and copyright]. Library ser3 5no17:60–9 Ja '14.

8938 **M., J. G.** A lawsuit about the Pilgrim's progress. TLS 24 Jl '19:401; H. R. Plomer *ib.* 31 Jl '19:413; J. G. M. 7 Ag '19:425.

8939 **Bunyan's** Pilgrim's progress. (Notes on sales). TLS 13 Oc '21:668; A. Birrell; G. C. Williamson *ib.* 20 Oc '21:680; Writer of Notes on sales [i.e. W. Roberts] 27 Oc '21:704; 8 Je '22:384; 29 Je '22:432.

8940 **Pilgrim's** progress, Welsh and English. Baptist Q new ser 1no1:39–42 Ja '22.

8941 **Bunyan's** Pilgrim's progress. (Notes on sales). TLS 15 Jl '26:484.

8942 **Greg, sir Walter W.** The 'issues' of The pilgrim's progress. [And bibliogr. terminology]. TLS 19 Ag '26:549.

8943 **Hodgson, J. E.** Bunyan's Book for boys and girls. [1686]. TLS 4 N '26:770.

8944 **Pilgrim's** progress and others. (Notes on sales). TLS 5 Ag '26:528.

8945 **Waterston, David.** A 'unique' Bunyan. [A discourse of the building, 1688]. TLS 5 My '27:318; I. G. M. Shelley *ib.* 26 My '27:380.

8946 **First** editions of John Bunyan's Pilgrim's progress. Pub Wkly (N.Y.) 114no20:2063–5 N '28. facsim.

8947 **Harris, J. Rendel.** A further note on the fictitious Bunyan books. Bull John Rylands Lib 13no1:123–7 Ja '29.

8948 **Whitley, William T.** T. S. and his publishers. [Author of Second part of The pilgrim's progress; T. Malthus, ptr.]. Bull John Rylands Lib 13no2:231–3 Jl '29.

8949 **Troxell, Gilbert McC.** An unrecorded Pilgrim's progress. Coloph [1]pt1:[7p.] '30. facsims.

8950 **Thomas, sir Henry.** Bunyan's Pilgrim's progress, 1684. Brit Mus Q 8no2:37 Jl '33. [Sg.: H. T.]

8951 **Harrison, F. Mott.** Some illustrators of The pilgrim's progress, part one: John Bunyan. Library ser4 17no3:241–63 D '36. illus.

8952 —— The Pilgrim's progress. [Reported Catholic version]. TLS 23 Ja '37:60; W. Kent *ib.* 30 Ja '37:76.

8953 —— Editions of The pilgrim's progress. Library ser4 22no1:73–81 Je '41.

8954 —— Notes on the early editions of Grace abounding. Baptist Q 11no4/7:160–4 Ja/D '43. facsims.

8955 —— Repudiable Bunyan writings. Baptist Q 11no10/11:277–81 Oc/D '44.

8956 **Prices** for Pilgrim's progress. TLS 1 F '47:71.

8957 **Silver, Louis H.** Bunyan's Barren fig tree, 1670. [i.e. 1673]. Library ser5 5no1:61 Je '50.

8958 **Kaufman, Paul.** Bunyan signatures in a copy of the Bible. (Note 120). Bk Coll 8no4:427–8 '59. facsim.

8959 **Brown, T. Julian.** John Bunyan. (English literary autographs, XXXIII). Bk Coll 9no1:53–5 '60. facsims.

8960 **Tibbutt, H. G.** Bunyan libraries. Assn Brit Theol & Philos Libs Bull 16:3–8 Mr '62.

8961 **Griffin, Gillett G.** Adaptations of The pilgrim's progress for children, an addendum. [American ed.]. Princeton Univ Lib Chron 26no1:25–6 '64.

8962 **Smith, David E.** Illustrations of American editions of The pilgrim's progress to 1870. Princeton Univ Lib Chron 26no1:16–25 '64. facsims.

English prototypes.–Early American Pilgrim's progresses.–The 1790's: Anderson.–Garret Lansing, William Mason, George Gilbert.–Later innovations and experiments.

8963 **Kaufman, Paul.** Bunyan's popularity in eighteenth century Wales. [Welsh tr., ptd. by J. Ross, Carmarthen]. Bedfordshire Mag 10no76:146–8 '66.

BURGON, JOHN WILLIAM, 1831–88

8964 **Barker, Nicolas J.** A very famous line. [Apparent plagiarism from Samuel Rogers' Italy 1822 (1823) and 1828 in Burgon's Petra, 1845]. TLS 26 Jl '63:578–9; R. P. C. Mutter *ib.* 9 Ag '63:615.

BURKE, EDMUND, 1729–97

8965 **Bradley, Henry.** A misprint in Burke. [Third letter on a regicide peace]. Acad 42:390 Oc '92.

8966 **Pottle, Frederick A.** Burke On the sublime and beautiful. N&Q 148:80 Ja '25; E. Bensly; T. Prince *ib.* 148:140 F '25.

8967 **Drew, Helen L.** The date of Burke's Sublime and beautiful. [1757]. Mod Lang N 50no1:29–31 Ja '35.

8968 **Hardy, Robert E. Gathorne-.** Burke: French revolution. [Variants in 1790 ed.]. Bib N&Q 1no1:9–10 Ja '35; 1no2:8 Ap '35; 1no3:2 Ag '35. [Sg.: R. E. G-H.]

8969 **Copeland, Thomas W.** Burke's Vindication of natural society. Library ser4 18no4:461–2 Mr '38.

8970 —— Burke and Dodsley's Annual register. Pub Mod Lang Assn 54no1:223–45 Mr '39.

8971 —— Edmund Burke and the book reviews in Dodsley's Annual register. Pub Mod Lang Assn 57no2:446–68 Je '42.

8972 **Gwynn, Aubrey.** A presentation copy from Edmund Burke to Mary Shackleton. [Mr. Burke's speech on . . . the Nabob of Arcot's private debts, 1785]. Irish Bk Lover 29no4:84–5 Mr '45.

8973 **Cone, Carl B.** Edmund Burke's library. Pa Bib Soc Am 44:153–72 '50.

8974 **Todd, William B.** The bibliographical history of Burke's Reflections on the revolution in France. Library ser5 6no2:100–8 S '51. tables.

A. Differentiation of copy.–B. Press figures.

8975 **Fields, J. E.** An eighteenth century best-seller. [A philosophical enquiry into the origin of our ideas]. Autogr Coll J 5no2:34–7 '53. facsims.

8976 **Sarason, Bertram D.** Edmund Burke and the two Annual registers. Pub Mod Lang Assn 68no3:496–508 Je '53.

8977 **Cambray, Philip G.** Towards an abridgment of the English history. TLS 27 My '55:285.

8978 **Todd, William B.** Burke's Reflections on the revolution in France. [Horne Tooke's commentary on]. (Query no.58). Bk Coll 4no1:81 '55.

8979 **Weston, John C.** Burke's authorship of the historical articles in Dodsley's Annual register. Pa Bib Soc Am 51:244–9 '57.

8980 —— An essay by Burke. [An abridgement of the English history not by Burke]. TLS 17 My '57:305; W. B. Todd *ib.* 14 Je '57:365; J. C. Weston 19 Jl '57:441.

8981 **Love, Walter D.** Edmund Burke, Charles Vallancey, and the Sebright manuscripts. [In Trinity college, Dublin]. Hermathena 95:21–35 Jl '61.

8982 **Brown, T. Julian.** Edmund Burke, 1729–97. (English literary autographs, XLIV). Bk Coll 11no4:467 '62. facsims.

8983 **Copeland, Thomas W.** Edmund Burke's friends and The annual register. Library ser5 18no1:29–39 Mr '63. table.

BURKE, BP. THOMAS, 1710?–76

8984 [**Crone, John S.**]. Hibernia Dominicana. Irish Bk Lover 9no11/12:121–3 Je/Jl '18.

8985 **Dix, Ernest R. McC.** Who printed Hibernia Dominicana? [Edmund Finn; Michael Butler]. Irish Bk Lover 14no9/10:116–17 S/Oc '24.

8986 **Ó Casaide, Séamus.** Hibernia Dominicana. Irish Bk Lover 16no4/6:117 Jl/D '28; 17no1:9 Ja/F '29. [Sg.: S. OC.]

8987 **Bourke, Francis S.** Hibernia Dominicana. [Canicopolis imprint, 1762]. Bib N&Q 1no1:12 Ja '35.

8988 [**Ó Lochlainn**], **Colm.** Hibernia Dominicana. Irish Bk Lover 27no5:259 N '40.

BURLEY, WALTER, d.1345?

8989 **Bühler, Curt F.** [Bibliogr. note on Burley's De vita et moribus philosophorum, 1490]. Pa Bib Soc Am 37:75 '43.

8990 —— Literary research and bibliographical training. Pa Bib Soc Am 51:303–11 '57. tables.

Repr. in Early books and manuscripts. New York, 1973. p. [266]–73.

BURNET, BP. GILBERT, 1643–1715

8991 **Foxcroft, Helen C.** Burnet manuscripts. N&Q ser9 5:314 Ap '00.

8992 **Mogg, William Rees-.** Some reflections on the bibliography of Gilbert Burnet. Library ser5 4no2:100–13 S '49. facsim.

8993 **Dobell, R. J.** The bibliography of Gilbert Burnet. Library ser5 5no1:61–3 Je '50. table.

8994 **Masson, David I.** The bibliography of Gilbert Burnet. Library ser5 5no2:151 S '50; J. H. P. Pafford *ib.* 6no2:126 S '51.

8995 Cancelled.

BURNET, SIR THOMAS, 1694–1753

8996 **Jones, Thomas L.** A Second tale of a tub: a bibliographical puzzle. N&Q 153:9 Jl '27; E. Bensly *ib.* 153:68 Jl '27.

BURNEY, CHARLES, 1726–1814

8997 **Marchant, Francis P.** Burney's History of music. N&Q ser10 10:9 Jl '08; 10:57 Jl '08; P. Robson *ib.* 12:494–5 D '09.

8998 **Willetts, Pamela J.** The Memoirs of dr. Burney. [Ms.]. Brit Mus Q 19no4:72–3 D '54.

BURNEY, FRANCES (MRS. D'ARBLAY), 1752–1840

8999 **Eaves, Thomas C. D.** Edward Burney's illustrations to Evelina. Pub Mod Lang Assn 62no1:995–9 D '47. facsim.

9000 **Munby, Alan N. L.** The publication of Camilla. (Note no.23). Bk Coll 2no3:219 '53.

9001 **Hemlow, Joyce.** Preparing a catalogue of the Burney family correspondence, 1749–1878. N.Y. Pub Lib Bull 71no8:486–95 Oc '67.

The provenance of the Burney-d'Arblay manuscripts.–Barrett collection.–The Comyn and the Osborn collections.

BURNEY, SOPHIA ELIZABETH, fl.1780–1828

9002 **Mendenhall, John** C. Sophia Burney mss. Univ Pennsylvania Lib Chron 3no1:9–13 Mr '35.

BURNS, ROBERT, 1759–96

9003 **The first** edition of Burns. Bkworm 1no6:210–11 My '88.

9004 **Brown, William.** List of documentary relics of Robert Burns. Edinburgh Bib Soc Pub 1pt2:1–2 Oc '92. facsims.

9005 **Pickford, John.** First edition of Burns's Poems. N&Q ser8 2:163–4 Ag '92; B. W. S. *ib.* 2:199 S '92; W. E. Wilson 2:210 S '92; ser9 1:185–6 Mr '98.

9006 **Aitken, George A.** A collection of Burns manuscripts. [Sold by Puttick and Simpson, 2 My 1861]. Burnsiana 5:31 '95.

9007 **Hope, Henry G.** Burns and his love of books. [Use of subscription libraries]. N&Q ser8 10:42–3 Jl '96.

9008 **Scott, H. D. Colvill-.** The Burns mss. at the Glasgow exhibition, 1896. J Soc Archivists & Autogr Coll 2:8–9 Ag '96.

9009 **Burnsiana.** [Sale of Edinburgh commonplace book]. Scott N&Q 11no4:59 Oc '97.

9010 **Burns's** Poems. [Philadelphia, 1788]. (Book sales). Scott N&Q 11no1:11 Je '97.

9011 **Inglis, George S.** Burns and Scott forgeries. (Expertiana). J Soc Archivists 3:1–5 Ag '97. facsims.

9012 **The original** manuscript of Auld lang syne. Scott N&Q 11no9:131 Mr '98.

Report of article by Cuyler Reynolds: no.9013.

9013 **Reynolds, Cuyler.** The manuscript of Auld lang syne. Century Mag 55no4:585–9 F '98. port., facsims.

9014 **Young, Harold E.** Burns's Auld Lang syne. Athenæum 3789:721 Je '00; C. A. Ward *ib.* 3790:753 Je '00; H. E. Young 3792:816 Je '00; H. E. Young; J. Dick 3797:153 Ag '00; J. Dick 3800:250 Ag '00.

9015 **Murdoch, Robert.** A Kilmarnock Burns sold for £1000. Scott N&Q ser2 5no3:33 S '03.

9016 —— Burnsiana. [Ms. of The cottar's Saturday night, and others]. Scott N&Q ser2 6no5:65 N '04; 6no6:81 D '04.

9017 —— Burnsiana. [Sales]. Scott N&Q ser2 6no4:41 S '04; 6no5:65 N '04; 6no6:81 D '04.

9018 —— Sale of a Burns letter. [Dated 21 January, 1784]. Scott N&Q ser2 6no1:9 Jl '04.

9019 —— Gordon subscribers to the 1787 Edinburgh edition of Burns' Poems. Scott N&Q ser2 7no6:91 D '05.

9020 **Bayne, Thomas.** Burns's Bonnie Lesley. [Text]. N&Q ser10 5:345–6 My '06.

9021 —— Anonymous song attributed to Burns. [Braw lads of Galla water]. N&Q ser10 8:305–6 Oc '07.

9022 **Facsimile** of the first edition of Burns' Poems. Aberdeen J N&Q 2:242 '09.

9023 **McNaught, Duncan.** Volume annotated by Burns (Observer, vol. IX, MDCCLXXXVIII.). Ann Burns Chron 25:13–16 Ja '16. [Sg.: Editor.]

9024 **Ewing, James C.** Robert Burns's Letters addressed to Clarinda: a history of its publication and interdiction, with a bibliography. Edinburgh Bib Soc Pub 11pt2:87–112 Oc '21. facsims.

'Bibliography' (p. 107–12)

9025 **Cook, T. Davidson.** Annotations of Scottish songs by Burns: an essential supplement to Cromek and Dick. Ann Burns Chron 31:1–21 Ja '22.

9026 **MacDougall, Ian,** *pseud.* The Dunfermline manuscripts, for the guidance of Burns collectors. [Not by Burns]. Ann Burns Chron 32:85–7 Ja '23.

1. Letter to Clarinda.–2. Polworth on the green.–3. Elegy on Stella.

9027 **Marsh, George L.** 'The text of Burns' *in* Manly anniversary studies in language and literature. Chicago, Ill., 1923. p. 219–28.

9028 **Black, George F.** The Glenriddell manuscripts of Robert Burns. N.Y. Pub Lib Bull 28no10:733–5 Oc '24.

9029 **Clarinda's** copy of Burns's Poems. Burns Chron ser2 1:108–9 '26.

9030 **Cook, T. Davidson.** Unpublished manuscripts of Burns: mr. A. J. Law's collection. Burns Chron ser2 1:60–9 '26; 2:14–27 '27; 3:11–17 '28. facsims.

9031 **Thomson, James.** A Burns manuscript. [As I walk'd by mysel, transcr. by Burns]. Burns Chron ser2 1:103–4 '26. facsim.

9032 **Black, George F.** The earliest American editions of Burns's Poems. Burns Chron ser2 2:141–3 '27.

9033 **Glenriddell-Burns** manuscripts, handed over to Scottish national library. [Donated by J. Gribbel]. Burns Chron ser2 2:85–6 '27.

9034 **The Jolly** beggars, an unrecorded edition. [1816]. Burns Chron ser2 2:144 '27. facsim.

9035 **Carlton, William N. C.** The Kilmarnock Burns. Am Coll 5no5:208–11 F '28. facsim.

9036 **Dewar, R.** Two Burns relics. [From his library]. TLS 25 Oc '28:783; T. D. Cook *ib.* 8 N '28:834.

9037 **Ferguson, J. DeLancey.** Canceled passages in the letters of Robert Burns to George Thomson. Pub Mod Lang Assn 43no4:1110–20 D '28.

Repr. in Burns Chron ser2 4:90–103 '29.

9038 **[Ewing, James C.].** Burns in the auction-room; record of the more important sales during 1927–1928 of Burns manuscripts and of books with Burns associations. Burns Chron ser2 4:17–18 '29.

9039 —— Burns in the auction-room; record of the more important sales during 1928–1929 of Burns manuscripts and printed books. Burns Chron ser2 5:23–6 '30. [Sg.: J. C. E.]

9040 —— Burns's Poems, 1786: the dedication copy to Gavin Hamilton. Burns Chron ser2 5:32–6 '30. [Sg.: J. C. E.]

9041 **Ferguson, J. DeLancey.** The text of Burns's Passion's cry. [Ms.]. Mod Lang N 45no2:99–102 F '30.

9042 **Bronson, Bertrand H.** The Caledonian muse. Pub Mod Lang Assn 46no4:1202–20 D '31.

9043 **[Ewing, James C.].** Burns in the auction-room: record of the more important sales during 1929–1930 of Burns manuscripts and printed books. Burns Chron ser2 6:14–15 '31.

9044 **Averill, Esther C.** The authenticity of Burns' When first I saw fair Jeannie's face. Mod Lang N 47no5:303–5 My '32.

9045 **[Ewing, James C.].** Burns in the auction-room; record of the more important sales during 1930–1931 of Burns manuscripts and printed songs. Burns Chron ser2 7:6–9 '32.

9046 —— Poor Mailie's elegy, an early manuscript. Burns Chron ser2 7:25–7 '32. facsim.

9047 **Ferguson, J. DeLancey.** The suppressed poems of Burns. Mod Philol 30no1:53–60 Ag '32.

9048 **Painter, Anna M.** American editions of the Poems of Burns before 1800. Library ser4 12no4:434–56 Mr '32.

9049 **Ewing, James C.** Burns in the auction-room: record of the more important sales during 1931–1932 of Burns manuscripts and printed books. Burns Chron ser2 8:12 '33. [Sg.: J. C. E.]

9050 **The Kilmarnock** Burns. (Notes on sales). TLS 13 Jl '33:484.

9051 **Ross, John D.** The story of the Kilmarnock Burns. Stirling, E. MacKay [1933]. 96p. facsims. 22cm.

> In the beginning.–Publication, reception, contents and preface.–Reviews and notices.–Copies of the Kilmarnock still to the fore.–The binding.–Dr. Blacklock's appreciation.–Record of prices.–Concerning a Kilmarnock Burns.–The centenary of publication, 1886.–Adventures of a Kilmarnock Burns.–Wilson's printing press.–Notes on Burns's first volume, by Franklyn Bliss Snyder.–A copy that was stolen.–Poems chiefly in the Scottish dialect.

> *Rev:* TLS 27 Jl '33:514; C. C. Spectator 152:826–8 '34.

9052 **Ewing, James C.** Burns in the auction-room; record of the more important sales during 1932–1933 of Burns manuscripts and printed books. Burns Chron ser2 9:11 '34. [Sg.: J. C. E.]

9053 —— A guide to Burns literature; catalogue of the Robert Burns collection in the Mitchell library, Glasgow. Burns Chron ser2 9:23–6 '34.

9054 **Ferguson, J. DeLancey.** Burns's journal of his border tour. [Ms.]. Pub Mod Lang Assn 49no4:1107–15 D '34.

9055 **Ewing, James C.** Burns in the auction-room; record of the more important sales during 1933–1934 of Burns manuscripts and printed books. Burns Chron ser2 10:12–13 '35. [Sg.: J. C. E.]

9056 **Besterman, Theodore D. N.** Burns documents. [Cadell and Davies]. (Bibliographical notes). TLS 7 Mr '36:208.

9057 **Ewing, James C.** Burns in the auction-room, 1934–1935; record of the more important sales during 1934–35 of Burns manuscripts and printed books. Burns Chron ser2 11:6–7 '36. [Sg.: J. C. E.]

9058 [——]. The Lament. [First illus. of a Burns poem]. Burns Chron ser2 4:43 '36. facsim.

9059 —— The Stair Burns manuscript. Burns Chron ser2 11:44–8 '36. [Sg.: J. C. E.]

9060 —— John Gribbel. [Burns collector and patron]. Burns Chron ser2 12:43–7 '37. port. [Sg.: J. C. E.]

9061 **Watt, Lauchlan M.** A plea for the true text. Burns Chron ser2 12:48–53 '37.

9062 **Cook, T. Davidson.** The fame of Burns; evidence of the auction room. TLS 30 Ap '38:xi. illus.

Lives of Burns.–Manuscript prices.–Bibliographies.

9063 **Ewing, James C.** Burns in the auction-room; record of the more important sales during 1936–37 of Burns manuscripts and printed books. Burns Chron ser2 13:85–7 '38. [Sg.: J. C. E.]

9064 —— An edition of Burns's Works, published at London, by William Clark, in 1831. Burns Chron ser2 13:79–80 '38. [Sg.: J. C. E.]

9065 **Munsterberg, Margaret.** The Poems of Robert Burns. More Bks Boston Pub Lib Bull 13no8:373–4 Oc '38. [Sg.: M. M.]

9066 **Ewing, James C.** Burns in the auction-room; record of the more important sales during 1937–38 of Burns manuscripts and printed books. Burns Chron ser2 14:102 '39. [Sg.: J. C. E.]

9067 **Fitzhugh, Robert T.** An American edition of Burns. [Poems]. TLS 26 Ag '39:508; J. C. Ewing ib. 30 S '39:563.

9068 **Angus, W. Craibe.** Burns and the Della Cruscans: unpublished marginalia. [The British album]. Burns Chron ser2 15:12–16 '40. facsim.

9069 **Ewing, James C.** Alleged commonplace books of Burns, not the poet's composition or holograph. Burns Chron ser2 15:24–8 '40. [Sg.: J. C. E.]

9070 —— Burns in the auction-room; record of the more important sales during 1938–39 of Burns manuscripts and printed books. Burns Chron ser2 15:65–6 '40. [Sg.: J. C. E.]

9071 —— The Glenriddell Burns manuscripts: a romantic history. Burns Chron ser2 15:13–53 '40. [Sg.: J. C. E.]

Rev. from Glasgow herald, 1920.

Robert Riddell.–History of the manuscripts.–The manuscripts at Liverpool.–Their return to Scotland, via America [J. Gribbel].

9072 [——]. An unknown edition of Burns's Poems a yankee mare's-nest. Burns Chron ser2 15:59–61 '40.

Repr. from TLS 30 S '39:563; *See no.*9067.

9073 **Munsterberg, Margaret.** Poems and letters of Burns. [An inventory, 1799?; Letters addressed to Clarinda, 1802.] More Bks Boston Pub Lib Bull 15no4:157 Ap '40. [Sg.: M. M.]

9074 [**Ewing, James C.**]. Burns in the auction-room. Burns Chron ser2 16:59 '41.

9075 —— A book from Burns's library. [Poetical remains of James the first, 1783]. Burns Chron ser2 17:14 '42. [Sg.: J. C. E.]

9076 —— Burns in the auction-room. Burns Chron ser2 17:45 '42. [Sg.: J. C. E.]

9077 **Fynmore, A. H. W.** Relic of Robert Burns. [From his library]. N&Q 183:45 Jl '42.

9078 **Augus, W. Craibe.** Burns and the circulating library: lord Lytton's tribute. Burns Chron ser2 18:26–8 '43.

9079 [**Ewing, James C.**]. Books from Burns's library [now in Glasgow university library]. Burns Chron ser2 19:23 '44.

9080 —— Some missing Burns manuscripts; the auction sales of 1861–1862. Burns Chron ser2 20:15–19 '45. [Sg.: J. C. E.]

Burn's letters to mrs. Dunlop in the 1862 sale.–Other documents in the 1862 sale.

9081 —— Burns in the auction-room, 1945–6. Burns Chron ser2 22:43 '47. [Sg.: J. C. E.]

Letter from Burns to mrs. Dunlop.–Ms. of the Lass o' Ballochmyle.

9082 **Wolf, Edwin.** 'Skinking' or 'Stinking'? A bibliographical study of the 1787 Edinburgh edition of Burns' Poems. Lib Chron Univ Pennsylvania 14no1:3–14 Ap '47. facsims., table.

Burns' evidence. The bibliographical evidence.

9083 **Robert** Burns and The Scots musical museum. New Coloph 1pt2:190–3 Ap '48.

Variant title-pages and prefaces.–Variant indexes, and attributions of authorship in the text.

9084 **Ewing, James C.** Stothard's illustrations of Burns: lost portraits and views. [And R. H. Cromek]. Burns Chron ser2 22:46–50 '47; 24:29–34 '49. [Sg.: J. C. E.]

9085 —— Burns in the auction-room, 1947. Burns Chron ser2 23:58 '48. [Sg.: J. C. E.]

9086 **Ewing, James C.** The copyright of Burns's Poems, 1786–1787. Burns Chron ser2 23:23–5 '48. [Sg.: J. C. E.]

9087 —— The Murison Burns collection, library and museum. Burns Chron ser2 23:52–3 '48. [Sg.: J. C. E.]

9088 [——]. Burns letter sold for £17. Burns Chron 24:48 '49.

9089 [——]. Burns mss. for cottage museum. [Burns cottage museum, Ayr]. Burns Chron ser2 24:54 '49.

9090 [——]. £30 for Edinburgh edition. [1787]. Burns Chron ser2 24:23 '49.

9091 **Burns** books on show; a noteworthy exhibition [at Signet library]. Burns Chron ser3 1:71–4 '52.

9092 **The Kilmarnock** Burns; copy sold for £750. Burns Chron ser3 1:54–5 '52.

9093 **C., N. H.** The catalogue of the Murison Burns collection. Burns Chron ser3 2:70–1 '53.

9094 **The Murison** Burns collection. TLS 9 Ja '53:32.

9095 **Sale** of another Kilmarnock Burns. Burns Chron ser3 2:25 '53.

9096 **Burns** exhibition in Edinburgh; mss. and letters on view. [Edinburgh district Burns clubs association and Edinburgh public libraries committee exhibition, 1953]. Burns Chron ser3 3:63–4 '54.

9097 **Gillis, William.** Burns' copy of Fergusson's Poems. Burns Chron ser3 5:1–2 '56.

9098 **Lyons, John O.** The Dartmouth Burns collection and the Burns business. [Davidson Cook collection]. Dartmouth Coll Lib Bull new ser 1no2:25–31 '58.

9099 **£580** for Kilmarnock edition. Burns Chron ser3 7:40 '58.

9100 **Brown, T. Julian.** Robert Burns, 1759–1796. (English literary autographs, XXX). Bk Coll 8no2:169 '59. facsims.

9101 **Kinsley, James.** Editing Burns. Burns Chron ser3 8:7–11 '59.

9102 —— The subscription list for the first Edinburgh edition, 1787. Burns Chron ser3 8:26–37 '59; 10:38–56 '61; 11:11–43 '62; 12:58–70 '63; Supplement, by Arthur G. Hepburn *ib.* 12:71–8 '63.

Introduction by Kinsley; 'Annotated list of subscribers' by J. W. Egerer.

9103 **Bi-centenary** exhibitions. Burns Chron ser3 4:82–93 '60.

Burns's work on show at National library of Scotland [article by W. Park, repr. from The Scotsman].–Mauchline.–Henry E. Huntington library, San Marino, California.–Exhibition of Burns translations, by G. M. Mackley.

9104 **Weston, John C.** The text of Burns' The jolly beggars. Stud Bib 13:239–47 '60.

9105 **Werkmeister, Lucyle.** Some account of Robert Burns and the London newspapers, with special reference to the spurious Star, 1789. N.Y. Pub Lib Bull 65no8:483–504 Oc '61.

9106 **Egerer, Joel W.** Thomas Stewart, Robert Burns, and the law. Pa Bib Soc Am 56:46–55 '62.

9107 **Werkmeister, Lucyle.** An early version of Burns's song, Their groves of sweet myrtle. N&Q 207:460 D '62.

9108 **Roy, G. Ross.** French translations of Robert Burns to 1893. R Litt Comparée 37no2:279–97 Av/Juin '63; 37no3:437–53 Jui/S '63.

Repr. in Burns Chron ser3 14:58–80 '65; 15:56–76 '66.

9109 **£600** for Burns ms. [Lament for James earl of Glencairn]. Burns Chron ser3 13:26 '64.

9110 **Namba, Toshio.** Robert Burns in Japan. Stud Scot Lit 1no4:253–8 Ap '64.

The Meiji era, 1868–1911.–The Taisho era, 1912–1926.–The Showa era, 1926.

9111 **£5500** for a Burns work. [Annotated The Scots musical museum]. Burns Chron ser3 14:86–9 '65.

Repr. from Ayr Advertiser 12 Mr '64.

9112 **Kinsley, James.** Burns and The merry muses. Renaiss & Mod Stud 9:5–21 '65.

9113 **Roy, G. Ross.** The Merry muses of Caledonia. Stud Scot Lit 2no3:211–12 Ja '65.

9114 **High** price for a copy of the Kilmarnock edition. [£6,000]. Burns Chron ser3 15:76 '66.

9115 **Parks, Stephen.** Justice to William Creech. Pa Bib Soc Am 60:453–64 '66.

9116 **Roy, G. Ross.** Robert Burns and William Creech, a reply [to S. Parks]. Pa Bib Soc Am 61:357–9 '67.

BURROW, EDWARD, fl.1774

9116g **Knott, David H.** Unpublished second volume of Edward Burrow's A new and compleat book of rates, 1774. [The rates of his majesty's customs, n.d.]. Bk Coll 16no3:375–7 '67.

BURTON, SIR RICHARD FRANCIS, 1821–90

9117 **Burton, Isabel, lady.** Sir R. F. Burton's works. Acad 40:538 D '91.

9118 —— The story of one of sir R. Burton's mss. Bkworm 4no45:285–7 Ag '91; *cf.* The burned Burton ms. *ib.* 4no46:319 S '91.

9119 R. Burton's Scented garden. [Ms.]. N&Q ser10 7:449 Je '07.

9120 **Sermones,** *pseud.* Mr. Herbert Jones; new stories of Richard Burton. (Books and the man, no.20). Bkmns J 3no65:211 Ja '21.

> Burton as a philistine.–An annotated copy of The nights.–Bernard Quaritch's biggest mistake.–False economy.

9121 X. Camberwell. [Burton collection]. (Bookmen's libraries, no.1). Bkmns J new ser 3no66:236 Ja '21.

BURTON, ROBERT, 1557–1640

9122 **Bensly, Edward.** Burton's Anatomy of melancholy; presentation copy of the first edition. N&Q ser10 8:326–7 Oc '07; 11:65 Ja '09.

9123 —— Robert Burton and Jacques Ferrand's Melancholie erotique. N&Q ser10 11:286 Ap '09.

9124 **Osler, sir William.** The library of Robert Burton. Bib Soc News-sh 1–3 D '09.

> *Report of paper read* 15 N '09.

9125 —— [**Same**]: The library of Robert Burton. Bib Soc Trans 11pt1:4–7 '09/10.

> *Summary of paper read* 15 N '09.

9126 **Bensly, Edward.** Robert Burton and Joannes Pitseus. [And A. Vincent]. N&Q ser11 1:325–6 Ap '10.

9127 —— Robert Burton's library. N&Q ser11 4:44 Jl '11; 5:125–6 F '12.

9128 —— A book that belonged to Robert Burton. N&Q ser11 8:346 N '13.

9129 **Madan, Falconer.** Burtoniana. The anatomy of melancholy, 5th edition, 1638. Bod Q Rec 2no16:101–2 Ja '18.

> *Report of paper read by* E. G. Duff *to Edinburgh Bib Soc; see no.*9131.

9130 **Burton's** Anatomy. (Notes on sales). TLS 28 Ap '21:280.

9131 **Duff, E. Gordon.** The fifth edition of Burton's Anatomy of melancholy. [1638]. Library ser4 4no2:81–101 S '23.

9132 **Bensly, Edward.** Some alterations and errors in successive editions of The anatomy of melancholy. Oxford Bib Soc Proc 1pt3:198–215 '25.

See also no.9135.

9133 **Madan, Falconer and S. Gibson.** Lists of Burton's library. Oxford Bib Soc Proc 1pt3:222–46 '25. facsims.

a. Bodleian list.–b. Christ Church list.—a. The volumes received by the Bodleian library, under Burton's will.—b. The volumes received by the Christ Church library, under Burton's will.

9134 **Osler, sir William.** Robert Burton, the man, his book, his library. Oxford Bib Soc Proc 1pt3:163–90 '25.

'Burton's library' (p. [182]–90)

9135 **Bensly, Edward.** Burtoniana. [Corrections to *no.*9132]. TLS 3 F '27:76.

9136 **Hill, R. H.** Robert Burton's copy of Breydenbach. [Peregrinatio, 1486]. Bod Q Rec 5no58:285 D '28.

9137 **Hiscock, Walter G.** Burton's Anatomy. [1624 proofs]. TLS 18 My '33:348.

9138 **Kimmelman, Elaine.** A first edition of The anatomy of melancholy. Boston Pub Lib Q 2no1:89–91 Ja '50.

9139 **Hunter, Richard A. and Ida MacAlpine.** Alexander Boswell's copies of The anatomy of melancholy, 1621 and 1624. (Note 88). Bk Coll 6no4:406–7 '57.

9140 **Donovan, Dennis G.** A note on the text of The anatomy of melancholy. Pa Bib Soc Am 60:85–6 '66.

9140a —— Two corrected-forme readings in the 1632 The anatomy of melancholy. (Note 276). Bk Coll 15no3:353–4 '66

9141 **Heventhal Charles.** Robert Burton's Anatomy of melancholy in early America. Pa Bib Soc Am 63:157–75 '69.

'A check list of seventeenth-century quarto and folio editions . . . available in the United States in . . . 1964' (p. 174–5)

BURTON, WILLIAM, d.1616

9142 **Cate, Chester M.** Works of William Burton; collected edition, 1602. N&Q ser12 11:532 D '22.

BURY, RICHARD DE, (RICHARD AUNGERVILLE), BP., 1287–1342? *see*
Richard de Bury (Richard Aungerville), bp., 1287–1342?

BUTLER, HENRY MONTAGU, 1833–1918

9143 **Collins, Rowland L.** How rare are Montagu Butler's translations of Tennyson? [Crossing the bar and a few other translations, 1890]. (Query 162). Bk Coll 12no1:72–3 '63; C. S. Bliss *ib.* 12no3:356 '63.

BUTLER, SAMUEL, 1612–80

9144 **Smith, Wood.** The first illustrators to Hudibras, a discovery and a suggestion. N&Q ser8 10:229–30 S '96; F. G. Stephens *ib.* 10:277–8 Oc '96; W. Smith 10:337–8 Oc '96; A. D. 10:404 N '96. facsims.

9145 **Robbins, Alfred F.** Hudibras: earliest pirated edition. [1662]. N&Q ser11 2:142–3 Ag '10.

9146 **Hindle, Christopher J.** A broadside by Samuel Butler. [A true and perfect copy of the lord Roos his answer, 1660]. TLS 21 Mr '36:244.

9147 **Richards, Gertrude R. B.** Butler's Hudibras. More Bks Boston Pub Lib Bull 18no9:407–10 N '43.

9148 **Bentley, Norma E.** Another Butler manuscript. [Hudibras]. Mod Philol 46no2:132–5 N '48.

9149 **Thorson, James L.** The publication of Hudibras. Pa Bib Soc Am 60:418–38 '66. facsims.

'A bibliography of editions of Hudibras published during the lifetime of Samuel Butler' (p. 426–38)

9150 **Steininger, Franz.** Samuel Butlers Hudibras and die Illustrationen der Dichtung durch William Hogarth. Biblos 17hft1/2:62–75 '68. facsims.

9151 **De Quehen, A. H.** Hudibrastic drafts. TLS 9 Ja '69:39.

BUTLER, SAMUEL, 1835–1902

9152 **Eckel, John C.** Butler's The way of all flesh: scarcity of the first editions. Bkmns J 3no64:193 Ja '21.

9153 **Jones, Henry F.** Mr. Yeats' prose. [Misquotation from mistranscription of Butler's ms.]. TLS 29 My '24:340.

9154 **Hoppé, Alfred J.** If mr. Higgs came to Bond street; the first editions of Samuel Butler. Bkmns J new ser 12no44:74–5 My '25.

9155 ... **More** high Samuel Butler prices among the modern firsts. (Books in the sale rooms). Bkmns J new ser 12no45:122–3 Je '25.

9156 **Keynes, sir Geoffrey L.** and **B. Hill.** Distribution of Samuel Butler's manuscripts; new gift to the British museum. TLS 23 N '35:764.

9157 **Lowry, K. B.** Butler: Way of all flesh. [Issues]. Bib N&Q 1no4:8 Oc '35.

9158 **Bell, sir Harold I.** Manuscripts of Samuel Butler. Brit Mus Q 10no3:111–12 Mr '36.

9159 **Holt, Lee E.** Samuel Butler's revisions of Erewhon. Pa Bib Soc Am 38:22–38 '44.

9160 —— The note-books of Samuel Butler. [And H. F. Jones]. Pub Mod Lang Assn 60no4:1165–79 D '45.

9161 **Swarthout, Glendon.** The Way of all flesh. [Ms.]. TLS 3 Ag '51:485.

9162 **Davies, David W.** The Samuel Butler collection of the Honnold library. Claremont Q 7no4:59–62 '60.

BYRD, WILLIAM, 1538?–1623

9163 **Backus, Edythe N.** and **Lucyle Hook.** Byrd's Parthenia. TLS 26 Oc '46:521.

9164 **Hook, Lucyle.** William Byrd. [Parthenia]. N&Q 201:226 My '56.

9165 **Andrews, H. K.** Printed sources of William Byrd's Psalmes, sonets and songs. Music & Letters 44no1:5–20 Ja '63. facsims.

> Table I: Source list.–Table II: Title-pages.–Table III: Errata notice (on the last page of the preface).–Table IV: Time-signatures.–Appendix: Evidence concerning the date of edition B.

9166 —— The printed part-books of Byrd's vocal music. Library ser5 19:1–10 '64. facsims.

> The relationship of bibliography and musical scholarship.–The Cantiones sacrae of Tallis and Byrd, 1575.–The 1588 Psalmes, sonets and songs.–Songs of sundrie natures, 1589.–The masses.–Gradualia, book I.–Gradualia, book II.–Psalmes, songs and sonnets, 1611.

9167 **Clulow, Peter.** Publication dates for Byrd's Latin masses. Music & Letters 47no1:1–9 Ja '66.

> Table I: (a) Mass for three voices.–(b) Mass for four voices.–(c) Mass for five voices.–Table II: Condition of capitals relative to first editions of masses.–Table III: Condition of capitals relative to second editions of masses.

BYRON, GEORGE GORDON DE LUNA, *pseud.*, fl.1809–52

9168 **Ehrsam, Theodore G.** Major Byron, the incredible career of a literary forger. New York, C. S. Boesan; London, J. Murray, 1951. 217p. facsims. 24cm.

> The life of major Byron.–A study of manuscripts and books.–The sources for the forgeries.–Influence of G. Byron and his forgeries on biography.–Conclusions.–Bibliography.–Watermarks of papers used in forgeries by G. Byron.–Forgeries of Byron letters by G. Byron chronologically arranged.

> *Rev*: J. Bakeless Pa Bib Soc Am 45:272; J. D. Hayward Sunday Times 29 Jl '51:3; TLS 10 Ag '51:498; K. N. Cameron Philol Q 31:125 '52; T. G. Ehrsam *ib.* 32:217–19 '53.

9169 —— Major Byron. (Note no.31). Bk Coll 3no1:69–71 '54.

9170 **Brown, T. Julian.** Some Shelley forgeries by major Byron. Keats-Sh Mem Bull 14:47–54 '63. facsims.

BYRON, GEORGE GORDON, afterwards NOËL, BARON BYRON OF ROCHDALE, 1788–1824

9171 **Campbell, James D.** English bards and Scotch reviewers. Athenæum 3471:578–9 My '94; J. R. Bagguley *ib.* 3472:614 My '94; B. Dobell; Rosa-Spina; T. F. A. Webb 3473:646 My '94; J. Murray; S. Lane-Poole; J. Bromley 3474:680 My '94; J. D. C[ampbell]; T. C. S. Corey; W. Brown; E. H. Bates 3474:710–11 Je '94; J. Murray; J. R. Bagguley; R. Griffin; B. Dobell; R. J. A. Shelley 3476:741–2 Je '94; J. D. C[ampbell]; J. Bromley 3477:774 Je '94; A Surrey lad, *pseud.*; W. T. Spencer 3478:804–5 Je '94; E. M. Barry; J. Schonberg; H. R. Yorke 3480:32 Jl '94. [Sg.: J. D. C.]

9172 **Wake, Henry T.** Byroniana. [Mss.]. N&Q ser8 6:144–5 Ag '94; R. Edgcumbe *ib.* 6:355 N '94; 6:515–16 D '94; J. Pickford 6:516 D '94.

9173 **Edgcumbe, Richard.** Omitted stanza in Childe Harold. N&Q ser8 8:101 Ag '95; E. H. Coleman *ib.* 8:336 Oc '95.

9174 **Redgrave, Gilbert R.** The first four editions of English bards and Scotch reviewers. Library ser2 1no1:18–25 D '99.

9175 **Forman, H. Buxton.** Early poems by Byron authenticated. [Mss.]. Athenæum 3998:752 Je '04.

9176 **H., W. B.** Byroniana. [A sequel to Don Juan, n.d.]. N&Q ser10 1:488 Je '04.

9177 **Forman, H. Buxton.** Some Byron crumbs: The Irish avatar again. [1821]. Athenæum 4261:756–7 Je '09.

9178 **Herz, N.** Byron's Bride of Abydos. N&Q ser10 11:445 Je '09.

9179 **McGovern, John B.** Byron and the Hobhouse ms. [English seminar library, University, Erlangen, Bavaria]. N&Q ser11 7:509 Je '13; 8:51 Jl '13; A. R. Bayley; W. Douglas *ib.* 8:51 Jl '13.

9180 **Northup, Clark S.** Byron and Gray. [Byron's Beauties of English poets, 1852]. Mod Lang N 32no5:310–12 My '17.

9181 **Andrews, J. T.** Byron's Don Juan, cantos 17 and 18. N&Q ser12 5:179 Jl '19; H. C. Roe; W. B. H. *ib.* 5:240–1 S '19.

9182 **Chew, Samuel C.** The Byron apocrypha. N&Q ser12 5:113–15 My '19.

9183 **Roe, Herbert C.** The rare quarto edition of lord Byron's Fugitive pieces described. Nottingham, Ptd. for private circulation, 1919. 30p. port., facsims. 24cm.

9184 **Hale, C. P.** Continuation of Don Juan. N&Q ser12 7:49 Jl '20; W. J. M. *ib.* 7:97 Jl '20.

9185 **Murray, John.** Two passages in Childe Harold. TLS 25 Ag '21:548; sir G. G. Greenwood *ib.* 1 S '21:564.

9186 **Marsh, sir Edward.** The new Byron letters. [Textual notes]. (Correspondence). London Merc 6no31:83 My '22.

9187 **Maples, A. K.** Byron's Hours of idleness. N&Q 146:326 My '24.

9188 **Marchetti, Ernest.** The binding of Byron's Works, 1832. Bkmns J new ser 9no30:197 Mr '24.

9189 **Smith, Harry B.** Byron, his books and autographs. Scribner's Mag 76no3:237–50 S '24. facsims.

9190 **White, G. H.** Byron's Armenian translations. N&Q 146:250 Ap '24; S. F. *ib.* 146:292 Ap '24.

9191 **Forsythe, Robert S.** Byron's lines on Hoppner. TLS 5 Mr '25:156.

9192 **G., D. M.** Byron's Hebrew melodies. [Whereabouts of ms.]. TLS 19 Mr '25:200; A. M. Friedlander *ib.* 2 Ap '25:240; C. H. Bertie 2 Jl '25:448.

9193 **McCarthy. William H.** The printing of canto IV of Byron's Childe Harold: a bibliographical study. Yale Univ Lib Gaz 1no3:39–41 Ja '27. diagr. [Sg.: W. H. M.]

9194 **Ryan, Michael J.** The adventures of lord Byron's Prefaces; additional notes to the bibliography of the poet. [Manfred; Werner]. Bkmns J ser3 16no8:419–30 '28.

9195 **Byron** and Coleridge. [James Gillman's library]. (Notes on sales). TLS 27 Je '29:520.

9196 **Byron** manuscripts. (Notes on sales). TLS 20 N '30:996.

9197 **Lovelace, Edith, countess.** A missing Byron manuscript. [Beppo]. TLS 23 Ja '30:60.

9198 **Butterwick, J. C.** A note on the first editions of Manfred. Bk Coll Q 3:39–42 Je '31.

9199 **Byron** and Murray. [And Smith, Elder and company]. (Notes on sales). TLS 23 Jl '31:588.

9200 **Byron's** Ode to Napoleon. [Ms.]. (Notes on sales). TLS 19 N '31:920.

9201 **Kessel, Marcel.** A Byron inscription. [His library]. TLS 23 Jl '31:583.

9202 **Low, D. M.** The text of Byron's letters. TLS 10 D '31:1006.

9203 **Doane, Gilbert H.** Byron bibliography. [Childe Harold, 4th canto]. (Notes on sales). TLS 17 N '32:864; T. J. Wise *ib.* 1 D '32:928.

9204 **Thomas, sir Henry.** Byron's Sketch from private life. [1816]. Brit Mus Q 7no2:41 S '32. [Sg.: H. T.]

9205 **Carter, John W.** Notes on the bibliography of Byron. TLS 27 Ap '33:300; 4 My '33:316.

9206 **Kessel, Marcel,** *ed.* 'Bibliographical notes' *in* Byron, George G. N., baron Byron. Fugitive pieces. ... New York, 1933. (Repr. Norwood, Pa., Norwood editions, 1976). p. [1–4] at beginning.

9207 **Jones, Claude E.** An American Lara, 1814. N&Q 167:276 Oc '34.

9208 **Seymour, W. Douglas.** Byron's juvenilia. [Fugitive pieces]. TLS 28 D '33:924; M. Kessel; S. R. *ib.* 15 F '34:112.

9209 **Doane, Gilbert H.** Byron's Letter to the editor of my grand-mother's review, 1819. Bib N&Q 1no1:8 Ja '35.

9210 **Rendall, Vernon.** Byron, an emendation. [Churchill's grave]. TLS 21 D '35:879.

9211 **McCarthy, William H.** The first edition of Byron's Corsair. Coloph new ser 2no1:51–9 Oc '36.

9212 **Smith, Francis P.** Byron's Memoirs. [Ms.]. N&Q 171:405 D '36.

9213 **Basler, Roy P.** The publication date and source of Byron's Translation of a Romaic love song. [1813]. Mod Lang N 52no7:503 N '37.

9214 **Cook, T. Davidson.** Byron's Fare thee well; unrecorded editions. [1816]. TLS 18 S '37:680.

9215 **Pollard, H. Graham.** Pirated collections of Byron. TLS 16 Oc '37:764.

9216 **Chew, S. P.** Notes on some false Byrons. N&Q 175:132–3 Ag '38.

9217 **Eaves, T. C. Duncan.** A note on lord Byron's Select works, 1823. Library ser5 1no1:70–2 Je '46.

9218 **Greenberg, Herbert.** Two versions of Byron's poem, Ossian's address to the sun. N&Q 190:256–7 Je '46.

9219 **Steffan, T. Guy.** Autograph letters and documents of the Byron circle at the library of the University of Texas. Univ Texas Stud Eng 1945–6:177–99 '46.

9220 —— Byron autograph letters in the library of the University of Texas. Stud Philol 43no4:682–99 Oc '46.

'Descriptive survey of the autograph letters and documents of lord Byron . . .' (p. 687–99)

9221 **Daghlian, Philip B.** Byron's Observations on an article in Blackwood's magazine. R Eng Stud 23no90:123–30 Ap '47.

9222 **Steffan, T. Guy.** Byron at work on canto I of Don Juan. [Ms.]. Mod Philol 44no3:141–64 F '47. table.

9223 —— The Byron poetry manuscripts in the library of the University of Texas. Mod Lang Q 8no2:194–210 Je '47.

9224 **Texas. University. Library.** Lord Byron and his circle; a calendar of manuscripts in the University of Texas library. Comp. by Willis W. Pratt. Austin, Tex., 1947. 60p. 22cm.

Family letters and documents, 1642–1811.–George Gordon, lord Byron.–Lady Anne Isabella Byron.–Sir Ralph Noel, lady Noel, lady Byron, Ada Byron.–The hon. Augusta Leigh.–Countess Teresa Guiccioli.–Miscellaneous Byroniana.

Rev: F. H. Ristine Mod Lang Q 10:411–12 '49.

9225 **Bandy, W. T.** Lord Byron and lady Blessington, a bibliographical note. ['When I asked for a verse . . .' 1827]. Philol Q 27no2:186–7 Ap '48.

9226 **Steffan, T. Guy.** Don Juan. [Mss.]. TLS 12 Je '48:331

9227 —— Don Juan mss. N&Q 193:215 My '48.

9228 **Bandy, W. T.** The first printing of Byron's stanzas on the death of the duke of Dorset. [1824]. Mod Lang R 44no1:93–4 Ja '49.

9229 **Kimmelman, Elaine.** First editions of Byron. Boston Pub Lib Q 1no2:169–72 Oc '49.

9230 **Steffan, T. Guy.** The extent of ms. revision of canto I of Don Juan. Stud Philol 46no3:440–52 Jl '49.

9231 **Pafford, Ward.** The date of Hours of idleness. N&Q 196:339–40 Ag '51; 196:476–7 Oc '51.

9232 **Simkins, Thomas M.** The Byron collection in the rare book room of Duke university library. Lib N Duke Univ Lib 25:14–22 Ja '51.

9233 **Zall, Paul M.** Lord Eldon's censorship. Pub Mod Lang Assn 68no3:436–43 Je '53.

9234 **Pratt, Willis W.** Lord Byron and his circle: recent manuscript acquisitions. Lib Chron Univ Texas 5no4:16–25 '56.

9235 **Rutherford, Andrew.** An early ms. of English bards and Scotch reviewers. Keats-Sh Mem Bull 7:11–13 '56. facsim.

9235a **Hofman, Alois.** Manuscrits de Jean-Jacques Rousseau et de G. G. Byron à Prague. [Part of Prologue of Prophesy of Dante, and sonnet dedicated to countess Guiccioli, in National museum]. Philologica [Suppl to Časopis pro moderní filologii] 9:20–9 '57. facsims.

9236 **Bridge, Alexander.** Byron's The corsair, 1814. (Note 98). Bk Coll 7no2:191 '58.

9237 **Marchand, Leslie A.** John Hunt as Byron's publisher. Keats-Sh J 8pt2:119–32 '59.

9238 **Elwin, Malcolm.** The Lovelace papers. TLS 4 Ag '61:481; lord Lytton *ib.* 22 S '61:629; C. H. Gibbs-Smith 29 S '61:645; lord Lytton 6 Oc '61:663; Doris L. Moore 13 Oc '61:683; M. Elwin 20 Oc '61:753; Doris L. Moore 27 Oc '61:771; Reviewer 3 N '61:789.

9239 **Brown, T. Julian.** Lord Byron, 1788–1824. (English literary autographs, XLII). Bk Coll 11no2:205 '62. facsim.

9239a **Oldham, Ellen M.** Lord Byron and mr. Coolidge of Boston. [Presentation copy]. (Note 221). Bk Coll 13no2:211–13 '64.

9240 **Luke, Hugh J.** The publishing of Byron's Don Juan. Pub Mod Lang Assn 80no3:199–209 Je '65.

9241 **Steffan, T. Guy.** Byron's dramas. [Mss.]. N&Q 210:278 Jl '65.

9242 **Steffan, T. Guy.** Byron's dramas: three untraced mss. (Query 191). Bk Coll 14no3:367 '65.

9243 —— A Byron facsimile. [Letter, 1819]. Lib Chron Univ Texas 8no2:2–7 '66; A postscript *ib.* 8no3:19–21 '67. facsim.

9244 **Marshall, William H.** The Byron collection in memory of Meyer Davis, jr. Lib Chron Univ Pennsylvania 33no1:8–29 '67. facsims.

9245 —— The catalogue for the sale of Byron's books. Lib Chron Univ Pennsylvania 34no1:24–50 '68. facsims.

9246 **Manners, G. S.** Byron on Job. [In H. S. Shepherd's Poetical remains, 1835]. TLS 2 Oc '69:1132.

9247 **Marshall, William H.** The Davis collection of Byroniana [at the University of Pennsylvania]. Keats-Sh J 18:9–11 '69.

9248 **Mortenson, Robert.** The copyright of Byron's Cain. Pa Bib Soc Am 63:5–13 '69.

BYSSHE, EDWARD, fl.1712

9249 **Culler, A. Dwight.** Edward Bysshe and the poet's handbook. [Art of English poetry, 1702]. Pub Mod Lang Assn 63no3:858–85 S '48.

I. Publication and reception of the Art of English poetry.–II. Rhyming dictionaries.–III. Poetical commonplace books.–IV. Bysshe's rules for making English verse.–V. Influence of Bysshe on eighteenth century prosodical criticism.

CALVERLEY, CHARLES STUART formerly BLAYDS, 1831–84

9250 **King, Hilda D.** A descriptive catalogue of the Calverley material in Toronto university library. N&Q 199:450–3 Oc '54; 199:536–9 D '54.

CAMDEN, WILLIAM, 1551–1623

9251 **Mount, C. B.** Camden's Annals of Elizabeth: translations. N&Q ser8 9:43–4 Ja '96.

9252 **Norman, William.** Camden's Remaines concerning Britaine. [1637]. N&Q ser10 9:408–9 My '08.

9253 **W., R. F.** Camden's Britannia: editions wanted. N&Q 163:332 N '32; R. S. B.; W. Jaggard *ib.* 163:376–7 N '32.

9254 **Birch, J. G.** Camden's Britain, 1610. [Maps]. Library ser5 23no3:253 S '68.

9255 **Dunham, William H.** William Camden's commonplace book. Yale Univ Lib Gaz 43no3:139–56 Ja '69.

CAMPBELL, ARCHIBALD, 9TH EARL OF ARGYLE, d.1685

9256 **Brown, William.** Notes on Argyle's Declaration printed at Campbeltown, 1685. Edinburgh Bib Soc Pub 3pt3:149–51 Mr '99.

CAMPBELL, THOMAS, 1733–95

9257 **Woolley, David.** Dr. Campbell's Diary, 1775. N&Q 193:517–19 N '48.

CAMPBELL, THOMAS, 1777–1844

9258 **Martin, Stapleton.** Lochiel's warning, by Thomas Campbell. [Ms.]. N&Q ser10 4:127 Ag '05.

9259 **Gowans, Adam L.** The Soldier's dream. TLS 30 Ag '23:572.

9260 **McGovern, John B.** The Exile of Erin: question of copyright. N&Q ser13 1:489 D '23. [Sg.: J. B. M.]

CAMPION, THOMAS, d.1619.

9261 **Simpson, Percy.** Thomas Campiani poemata, 1595. N&Q ser8 10:270–1 Oc '96.

CAPELL, ARTHUR, EARL OF ESSEX, 1631–83

9262 **Tillotson, Geoffrey.** The commonplace book of Arthur Capell. Mod Lang R 27no4:381–91 Oc '32. tables.

CAPELL, EDWARD, 1713–81

9263 **Taylor, George C.** The date of Edward Capell's Notes and various readings to Shakespeare, volume II. [1780]. R Eng Stud 5no19:317–19 Jl '29.

CAREW, BAMFYLDE MOORE, 1693–1770?

9264 **H., W. S. B.** Bamfylde Moore Carew. [Life, and R. Goadby]. N&Q ser12 8:248–9 Mr '21.

9265 **Collins, Ralph L.** An early edition of B. M. Carew. [The accomplished vagabond, 1745]. Mod Lang N 48no4:249–51 Ap '33.

CAREW, RICHARD, 1555–1620

9266 **Dodge, R. E. Neil.** The text of the Gerusalemme liberata in the versions of Carew and Fairfax. Pub Mod Lang Assn 44no2:681–95 Je '29.

9267 **Bullock, Walter L.** Carew's text of the Gerusalemme liberata. Pub Mod Lang Assn 45no1:330–5 Mr '30.

CAREW, SIR RICHARD, d.1643?

9268 **Curry, John T.** A seventeenth-century plagiary. [The excellency of the English tongue and Vindex anglicus, 1644]. N&Q ser9 8:457–9 D '01; O. O. H. *ib.* 9:112–13 F '02.

CAREW, THOMAS, 1598?–1639?

9269 **Powell, C. L.** New material on Thomas Carew. Mod Lang R 11no3:285–97 Jl '16.

I. The present texts.–II. Doubtful poems.–III. New poems.

CAREY, HENRY, d.1743

9270 **Prosser, R. B.** Henry Carey as a librarian. Lib Assn Rec 3no1:28–9 Ja '01.

9271 **Wood, Frederick T.** A Learned dissertation on old women, 1720. [Attrib. to]. N&Q 166:349–50 My '34.

CARION, JOHANN, 1499–1537

9272 **Richards, Gertrude R. B.** John Carion's Thre bokes of cronicles. More Bks Boston Pub Lib Bull 19no9:370–1 N '44. [Sg.: G. R. B. R.]

CARLELL, LODOWICK, fl.1629–64

9273 **Ruoff, James E.** A lost manuscript of Lodowick Carlell's Arviragus and Philicia. N&Q 200:21–2 Ja '55.

CARLYLE, THOMAS, 1795–1881

9274 **Cade, R.** Carlyle's Lectures on literature; a note respecting the various manuscripts. Library 4no43/5:225–7 Jl/S '92.

9275 **Muir, John.** Addition to Carlyle bibliography. N&Q ser8 4:246 S '93.

9276 **Carlyle's house memorial trust.** Carlyle's house: illustrated descriptive catalogue of books, manuscripts . . . exhibited therein. London, 1897. (5th ed. 1907; 6th ed. 1914). vi,118p. illus., ports. 16cm.

9277 —— Illustrated memorial volume of Carlyle's house purchase fund committee, with catalogue of Carlyle's books, manuscripts . . . exhibited therein. [London, 1897]. vi,160p. illus., ports. 17cm.

9278 **H., S.** Essay by Carlyle. [By John Leaf]. N&Q ser9 1:368 My '98; D. Patrick *ib.* 2:10 Jl '98.

9279 **Harrison, Frederic,** *ed.* Carlyle and the London library; account of its foundation. ... London, Chapman & Hall, 1907. x,111p. illus., facsims. 18cm.

Origin of the library.–London society interested.–Unpublished letters of Carlyle.–Public meeting.–Carlyle's one speech.–Library in full work.

Rev: TLS 22 Mr '07:90.

9280 **Johnston, T. Ruddiman.** Carlyle and a bookseller. [John Menzies]. N&Q ser12 9:88 Jl '21.

9281 **Gilson, J. P.** Carlyle's Past and present. [Ms.]. Brit Mus Q 3no3:75–6 D '28. [Sg.: J. P. G.]

9282 **Calder, Grace J.** Carlyle's Past and present. [Holographic printer's copy]. Yale Univ Lib Gaz 6no2:33–5 Oc '31.

9283 **Mabbott, Thomas O.** Carlyle: a bibliographical item. [Report of unpublished lectures on the revolutions of modern Europe]. N&Q 160:114 F '31.

9284 **Coffin, Edward F.** American first editions of Carlyle; why not greater catholicity in selecting American firsts. Am Bk Coll 4no5:236–7 N '33.

9285 **Barrett, James A. S.** Two note books of Thomas Carlyle. [Text]. N&Q 166:164–5 Mr '34.

9286 **Brooks, Richard.** Manuscripts pertaining to Carlyle's Frederick the great. Yale Univ Lib Gaz 9no2:38–41 Oc '34.

9287 **Hirst, W. A.** The manuscript of Carlyle's French revolution. Ninet Cent 123no731:93–8 Ja '38.

9288 **Calder, Grace J.** The writing of Past and present; a study of Carlyle's manuscripts. New Haven, Yale U.P.; London, G. Cumberlege, O.U.P., 1949. xii,216p. facsim. 25cm. (Yale Stud Eng 112)

I. The inception of Past and present.–II. The manuscripts described.–III. The historical sources of book II.–IV. The composition of books I, III, and IV.–V. The development of Carlyle's style.–Appendices.

Rev: R. H. Saturday R Lit 9 Jl '49:10; W. D. Templeman Mod Philol 47:266 '51; S. K. Winther Mod Lang Q 13:106 '51; M. M. Bevington South Atlan Q 49:118–19 '51; L. Davidson Mod Lang N 66:350–1 '51; H. V. Routh R Eng Stud new ser 2:195–6 '51.

9289 **Sanders, Charles R.** Carlyle's letters to Ruskin: a finding list with some unpublished letters and comments. Bull John Rylands Lib 4no1:208–38 S '58.

9290 **Calder, Grace J.** Carlyle manuscript. [Reminiscences of my Irish journey, 1882]. N&Q 207:30 Ja '62.

9291 **Brown, T. Julian.** Thomas Carlyle, 1795–1881. (English literary autographs, XLVII). Bk Coll 12no3:339 '63. facsims.

9292 **Sharples, Edward.** A missing ms. section of Carlyle's Reminiscences. (Query 173). Bk Coll 12no4:496 '63.

9293 **Sanders, Charles R.** 'Editing the Carlyle letters: problems and opportunities' in Robson, John M., ed. Editing nineteenth century texts; papers. . . . [Toronto, 1967]. p. [77]–95.

9294 **Eichler, Udi** and **A. Osler,** A Carlyle ms. [Memorandum in support of L. Hunt's pension]. TLS 8 F '68:141; D. G. Wilson ib. 15 F '68:157.

CARNIE, ALFRED, d.1898

9295 **Lawrance, Robert Murdoch-.** Aberdeen bibliography: Alfred Carnie. Aberdeen J N&Q 2:17 '09.

CARPENTER, WILLIAM, fl.1625–1710

9296 **Jenson, John R.** The author of Jura cleri. Pa Bib Soc Am 62:241–5 '68. table.

CARR, RALPH, fl.1594–1600

9297 **Randall, Dale B. J.** The Troublesome and hard adventures in love: an English addition to the bibliography of Diana. [By Carr, not Codrington]. (Notes). Hispanic Stud Bull 38:154–8 '61.

CARROLL, LEWIS, *pseud. of* **CHARLES LUTWIDGE DODGSON, 1832–98**

9298 **Roberts, William.** Alice's adventures in Wonderland. Athenæum 3798:186–7 Ag '00.

9299 **Leigh, Geoffrey H.** A Lewis Carroll query. [The first edition of The hunting of the snark]. Bkmns J 1no4:80 N '19; G. Pryce ib. 1no5:100 N '19.

9300 **Williams, Sidney H.** Some rare Carrolliana. London, Ptd. for private circulation only, 1924. 23p. illus., facsims. 27cm.

9301 **Pennell, Joseph.** . . .The four issues of the 1866 Alice. . . . (Marginalia). Bkmns J new ser 12no44:71–2 My '25.

9302 **Alice** in Wonderland. [Library of mrs. A. P. Hargreaves]. (Notes on sales). TLS 29 Mr '28:248; 12 Ap '28:276.

9303 **Vail, Robert W. G.** Alice in Wonderland; the manuscript and its story. N.Y. Pub Lib Bull 32no12:783–5 D '28. facsims.

9304 **Harrison, E.** Carrolliana. [Through the looking glass]. TLS 24 Mr '32:217.

9305 **Ayres, Harry M.** Carroll's withdrawal of the 1865 Alice. Huntington Lib Bull 6:153–63 N '34.

9306 **[Haraszti, Zoltán].** The other works of Lewis Carroll. More Bks Boston Pub Lib Bull 10no4:136–7 Ap '35.

9307 **Heron, Flodden W.** Carroll: Alice in Wonderland. [Original ms.]. Bib N&Q 1no4:8 Oc '35; R. W. G. Vail; A. M. Grew *ib.* 2no2:1 F '36; M.; M. L. Parrish 2no3:2 Ap '36; R. W. G. Vail 2no6:1–2 Jl '36.

9308 **Alice** in Wonderland. (The sale room). TLS 15 F '36:144.

9309 **Heron, Flodden W.** The 1866 Appleton Alice. Coloph new ser 1no3:422–7 F '36. facsims.

9310 **Wilson, Oliver.** Alice's adventures in Wonderland; a survey of the most important editions and issues of one of the outstanding book rarities of nineteenth century literature. Rara Libri 1:1–41 '37.

9311 **Hiscock, Walter G.** A Dodgson attribution. [Endowment of the Greek professorship, 1861]. (Antiquarian notes). TLS 16 Jl '38:484.

9312 **[Muir, Percival H.].** Carroll: Nursery Alice, 1889–90. Bib N&Q 2no10:6–8 Ap '38; A. Rogers *ib.* 2no11:6 N '38.

9313 **Naumburg, Edward.** Early American editions of Lewis Carroll. Bib N&Q 2no10:8 Ap '38.

9314 **Carroll**: Alice, 1866. [Signatures]. Bib N&Q 2no12:7 My '39.

9315 **Williams, Sidney H.** The 1865 Alice. (Bibliographical notes). TLS 29 Jl '39:460.

9316 **Ayres, Harry M.** Lewis Carroll and The garland of Rachel. [Daniel pr. proofsheets]. Huntington Lib Q 5no1:141–5 Oc '41. facsim.

9317 **Green, Roger L.** Lewis Carroll and the St. James's gazette. N&Q 188:134–5 Ap '45.

9318 **An unbirthday** present. [Ms. of Alice's adventures under ground]. TLS 20 N '48:660.

9319 **Weaver, Warren.** Alice's adventures in Wonderland, its origin and its author. Princeton Univ Lib Chron 13no1:1–17 '51. illus., facsim.

9320 **Hayward, John D.** Alice, 1865. (Note no.6). Bk Coll 1no2:127 '52.

9321 **Lyde, R. G.** The Harmsworth Alice. [1865]. Brit Mus Q 17no4:77–9 D '52.

9322 **Black, Duncan.** Discovery of Lewis Carroll documents. N&Q 198:77–9 F '53.

9323 **Dustin, Thomas E.** Alice in Wonderland collection. [Lall G. Montgomery]. Hobbies 57no11:126–9 Ja '53.

9324 **Green, Roger L.** Lewis Carroll's fugitive pieces. TLS 31 Jl '53:500.

9325 **Kinard, Betty V.** The 1865 Alice. Yale Univ Lib Gaz 27no3:126–7 Ja '53.

9326 **Weaver, Warren.** The mathematical manuscripts of Lewis Carroll. Princeton Univ Lib Chron 16no1:1–9 '54. facsims.

Also pub. in Am Philos Soc Proc 98no5:377–81 Oc '54.

9327 **Bond, William H.** The publication of Alice's adventures in Wonderland. Harvard Lib Bull 10no3:306–24 '56. facsims.

Appendix A: The 1865 Alice: the page proof and the variants.–Appendix B: The variant titles of the 1866 Appleton issue.

Repr. in Targ, William, *ed.* Bibliophile in the nursery, a bookman's treasury of collector's lore on old and rare children's books. Cleveland [1957]. (Repr. Metuchen, N.J., 1969). p. 392–416. facsims.

9328 **Weaver, Warren.** The Parrish collection of Carrolliana. Princeton Univ Lib Chron 17no2:85–91 '56. table.

9329 **Bond, William H.** Alice in Wonderland: proof illustrations. (Query 79). Bk Coll 6no2:181 '57.

9330 **Green, Roger L.** Lewis Carroll's first publication. TLS 13 S '57:552; Dorothy Wormald *ib.* 11 Oc '57:609.

9331 **Godman, Stanley.** Lewis Carroll's final corrections to Alice. [1897]. TLS 2 My '58:248.

9332 **Berol, Alfred C.** Lanrick, a game for two players, by Lewis Carroll. Pa Bib Soc Am 53:74 '59.

9333 **Nathanson, H.** The first edition of Carroll's Phantasmagoria, 1869. (Query 116). Bk Coll 8no2:184 '59; J. M. Shaw; R. L. Green *ib.* 8no3:309 '59.

9334 **Green, Roger L.** Bibliographer in Wonderland. Priv Lib 4no4:62–5 Oc '62.

9335 **Hiscock, Walter G.** The lost Christ Church Alice. [Alice's adventures in Wonderland, 1865]. TLS 7 My '64:402.

9336 **Evans, Luther H.** The return of Alice's adventures under ground. Columbia Lib Columns 15no1:28–35 N '65. illus., facsim.

9337 **Weaver, Warren.** The India Alice. Priv Lib 6no1:1–7 Ja '65.

9338 **Cohen, Morton N.** and **R. L. Green.** The search for Lewis Carroll's letters. Manuscripts 20no2:4–15 '68. facsims.

9339 **Geach, Peter.** Symbolic logic. [Proofs]. TLS 26 D '68:1455.

CARTWRIGHT, WILLIAM, 1611–43

9340 **Evans, Gwynne B.** Comedies, tragi-comedies, with other poems by mr. William Cartwright, 1651; a bibliographical study. Library ser4 23no1:12–22 Je '42.

CARY, ARTHUR JOYCE LUNEL, 1888–1957

9341 **Meriwether, James B.** A note on Verse, Joyce Cary's first book. Lib Chron Univ Texas 6no4:13–16 '60. facsim.

9342 **Wright, Andrew.** An authoritative text of The horse's mouth. Pa Bib Soc Am 61:100–9 '67.

CARY, HENRY FRANCIS, 1772–1844

9343 **Marlow, Harriet.** Cary: Dante. [Variant imprint]. Bib N&Q 2no12:7 My '39.

9344 ——— Cary: Dante. (Query no.1). Bk Coll 1no1:54 '52; S. Roscoe *ib.* 1no2:127–8 '52.

CARYLL, JOHN, 1625–1711

9345 **Bowers, Fredson T.** Bibliographical evidence from a resetting in Caryll's Sir Salomon, 1691. Library ser5 3no2:134–7 S '48.

CASE, JOHN, d.1600

9346 **Ringler, William.** The Praise of musicke, by John Case. Pa Bib Soc Am 54:119–21 '60; D. G. Neill *ib.* 54:293 '60.

CATZIUS, JOSIAS, fl.1647

9347 **Solomons, Israel.** Josias Catzius. [Doomsday, 1647]. N&Q ser10 4:10 Jl '05; L. L. K. *ib.* 4:77–8 Jl '05.

CAVENDISH, GEORGE, 1500–61?

9348 **Sylvester, Richard S.** [Mss. of Cavendish's Life of Wolsey]. (Query no.54). Bk Coll 3no4:310 '54.

CAVENDISH, GEORGIANA, DUCHESS OF DEVONSHIRE, 1757–1806

9349 **The duchess** and The sylph. [1799]. (Notes on sales). TLS 15 Ag '18:384; H. Stokes *ib.* 22 Ag '18:393.

CAVENDISH, HENRY, 1731–1810

9349a **Brown, T. Julian.** Henry Cavendish, 1731–1810. (English scientific autographs, V). Bk Coll 14no3:349 '65. facsim.

CENTLIVRE, SUSANNA (FREEMAN), 1667?–1723

9350 **McKillop, Alan D.** Mrs. Centlivre's The wonder, a variant imprint. (Note 93). Bk Coll 7no1:79–80 '58.

9351 **Neill, Desmond G.** A poem by mrs. Centlivre. [To the army, 1715]. (Note 95). Bk Coll 7no2:189–90 '58.

9352 **Faure, Jacqueline.** Two poems by Susanna Centlivre. (Note 151). Bk Coll 10no1:68–9 '61.

CHALMERS, GEORGE, fl.1620

9353 **Anderson, Peter J.** George Chalmers's Sylva. [And J. Leech, Musæ priores, 1620]. N&Q ser11 1:226 Mr '10; W. Scott *ib.* 1:337 Ap '10; P. J. Anderson 1:435 My '10.

CHAPMAN, GEORGE, 1559?–1634

9354 **Parrott, Thomas M.** Chapman's All fools. N&Q ser10 5:347–8 My '06.

9355 **Brereton, J. LeGay.** Notes on the text of Chapman's plays. Mod Lang R 3no1:56–68 Oc '07.

9356 **Parrott, Thomas M.** Notes on the text of Bussy d'Ambois. Eng Studien 38no3:359–95 '07.

9357 —— Notes on the text of Chapman's plays. Anglia 30:349–79 Jl '07; 30:501–22 Oc '07.

A. Alphonso, emperor of Germany.–B. Caesar and Pompey.

9358 —— The text of Chapman's Conspiracy and tragedy of Charles duke of Byron. Mod Lang R 4no1:40–64 Oc '08.

9359 **Brettle, Robert E.** Eastward ho, 1605, by Chapman, Jonson, and Marston: bibliography, and circumstances of production. Library ser4 9no3:287–302 D '28. table.

9360 **Greg, sir Walter W.** Eastward ho, 1605. Library ser4 9no3:303–4 D '28.

9361 **Samuel, Howard.** Chapman's Iliad. [1598]. TLS 31 Mr '32:229.

9362 **Tannenbaum, Samuel A.** 'George Chapman autographs and forgeries' *in* Shaksperian scraps and other Elizabethan fragments. New York, 1933. p. 142–52.

9363 **Carson, Alice M.** George Chapman. [Her proposed bibliogr.]. TLS 2 Ag '34:541.

9364 **Loane, George G.** The text of Chapman's Homer. TLS 18 Ap '36:336.

9365 **Greg, sir Walter W.** A proof-sheet of 1606. [Monsieur D'Olive, 1606]. Library ser4 17no4:454–7 Mr '37.

9366 **Loane, George G.** Misprints in Chapman's Homer. N&Q 173:398–402, 453–5 D '37; 174:367 My '38; 175:331–2 N '38.

  I. The Odyssey.–II. The Iliad.–The Odyssey: addenda.–The Iliad: addenda.

9367 —— Notes on Chapman's plays. Mod Lang R 33no2:248–54 Ap '38.

9368 **Robertson, Jean.** Some additional poems by George Chapman. Library ser4 22no2/3:168–76 S/D '41. facsims.

9369 **Loane, George G.** More notes on Chapman's plays. [Text]. Mod Lang R 38no4:340–7 Oc '43.

9370 **Dunkin, Paul S.** [Bibliogr. note on Chapman's Homer, 1616?]. Pa Bib Soc Am 40:230–1 '46.

9371 **Sturman, Berta.** The 1641 edition of Chapman's Bussy d'Ambois. Huntington Lib Q 14no2:171–201 F '51.

9372 **Elsley, Ralph C.** The Masque of the twelve months. [Ms., and Collier]. N&Q 197:229–32 My '52; 197:329 Jl '52.

9373 **Fay, H. C.** Chapman's text corrections in his Iliads. Library ser5 7no4:275–81 D '52.

9374 **Ure, Peter.** The date of the revision of Chapman's The tragedy of Bussy d'Ambois. N&Q 197:1–2 Ja '52.

9375 **Fay, H. C.** Critical marks in a copy of Chapman's Twelve books of Homer's Iliades. [And Jonson]. Library ser5 8no2:117–21 Je '53.

9376 **Ure, Peter.** Chapman's Tragedy of Bussy d'Ambois; problems of the revised quarto. Mod Lang R 48no3:257–69 Jl '53.

9377 —— Chapman's Tragedy of Byron, 4.ii.291–5. Mod Lang R 54no4:557–8 Oc '59.

9378 **Yamada, Akihiro.** Bibliographical studies of George Chapman's Monsieur d'Olive, 1606, printed by Thomas Creede. Stud Eng Lit (Tokyo) 1–48 '63. facsims.

I. The nature of the printer's copy.–II. Press variants in Q (1606).–III. Compositorial analysis.–IV. The characteristics of the compositors.

9379 —— Bibliographical studies of George Chapman's The gentleman usher, 1606, printed by Valentine Simmes. Sh Stud (Tokyo) 2:82–113 '63. tables.

I. The nature of the printer's copy.–II. Press variants in Q (1606).–III. The compositorial analysis.–IV. The characteristics of the compositor.

9380 **Gabel, John B.** Some notable errors in Parrott's edition of Chapman's Byron plays. Pa Bib Soc Am 58:465–8 '64.

9381 **Yamada, Akihiro.** Bibliographical studies of George Chapman's All fools, 1605, printed by George Eld. Sh Stud (Tokyo) 3:73–99 '64. facsims., tables.

I. The nature of the printer's copy.–II. Press variants in Q (1605).–III. The compositorial analysis. IV. The characteristics of the compositors.

9382 —— Bibliographical studies of George Chapman's May-day, 1611, printed by William Stansby. Faculty Liberal Arts & Science Shinshu Univ J 1no15:13–34 '65. (Not seen)

9383 —— Bibliographical studies of George Chapman's The widow's tears, 1612, printed by Richard Bradock. Sh Stud (Tokyo) 4:57–83 '65/6. tables.

I. The nature of the printer's copy.–II. Press-variants in Q, 1612.–III. The compositorial analysis.–IV. The characteristics of the compositors.

9384 —— A proof-sheet in An humorous day's mirth, 1599, printed by Valentine Simmes. Library ser5 21no2:155–7 Je '66. facsims.

9385 —— Bibliographical studies of George Chapman's An humorous day's mirth, 1599, printed by Valentine Simmes. Sh Stud (Tokyo) 5:119–49 '66/7. tables.

I. The nature of the printer's copy.–II. Press-variants in Q, 1599.–III. The compositorial analysis.–IV. The characteristics of the compositor.–Appendix: Errors in the Malone society reprint.

9386 —— Bibliographical studies of George Chapman's The blind beggar of Alexandria, 1598. Sh Stud (Tokyo) 6:147–65 '67/8.

> The nature of the printer's copy.–II. Press-variants in Q (1598).–III. The compositorial analysis.–IV. The characteristics of the compositors.– Appendix: Errors in the Malone society reprint.

9387 —— Bibliographical studies of George Chapman's The memorable mask of the Middle temple and Lincoln's inn, 1613, printed by George Eld. Sh Stud (Tokyo) 7:81–111 '68/9. fold. table.

> I. The nature of the printer's copy.–II. Press-variants in Q1–3, 1613 and variants between Q1–2.–III. The compositorial analysis.–IV. The characteristics of the compositors.

CHARLES I, KING OF GREAT BRITAIN AND IRELAND, 1600–49

9388 **Almack, Edward.** The bibliography of Eikon basilike. Bib Soc Trans 2pt1:14–15 '94.

> *Report of paper read* 21 My '94; *also in* Bib Soc News-sh 5:18–19 Je '94.

9389 —— Eikon basilike. N&Q ser8 8:123–4 Ag '95.

9390 **Medley, J. B.** Notes on the Eikon basilike. . . with a reference to some French translations. Huguenot Soc London Proc 6no1:24–38 '98.

9391 **Davenport, Cyril J. H.** King Charles I's embroidered Bible. Library ser2 1no4:373–7 S '00.

9391a **Murdoch, W. G.** Blaikie. King Charles the first as a book-lover. Bk-Lover's Mag 6pt3:113–15 '06.

9391b **Petheridge, M.** Charles I's books. N&Q ser10 8:449 D '07; Fabia Rousby *ib.* 9:55 Ja '08.

9392 **Bühler, Curt F.** A footnote to the bibliographies of the Eikon basilike, the Eikonoklastes and the Eikonaklastos. Libri 2no1/2:27–30 '52

9393 **Madan, Francis F.** Lord Anglesey and the Eikon basilike. TLS 31 Ag '56:511.

9393a **Gerritsen, Johan.** 'The Eikon in Holland [publishing history]' *in* [Woude, S. van der], *ed.* Studia bibliographica in honorem Herman de la Fontaine Verwey. Amstelodami, 1966 [i.e 1968]. p. 129–43.

CHARLES, THOMAS, 1755–1814

9394 **Roberts, Gomer M.** Rhai o lyfrau Thomas Charles. Welsh Bib Soc J 8no4:221–2 Jl '57; I. Lewis *ib.* 9no1:55 Jl '58.

CHATTERTON, THOMAS, 1752–70

9395 **Clarke, sir Ernest.** New lights on Chatterton. Bib Soc Trans 13pt2:219–51 '14/15.

9396 —— [Same]: Bib Soc News-sh 1–3 Ja '15.
Report of paper read 21 D '14.

9397 **Mabbott, Thomas O.** A new poem by Thomas Chatterton. [Elegy Oct. 29; ms.]. Mod Lang N 39no4:226–9 Ap '24.

9398 **Powell, Lawrence F.** Thomas Tyrwhitt and the Rowley poems. R Eng Stud 7no27:314–26 Jl '31.

9399 **Mabbott, Thomas O.** Chatterton's Execution of sir Charles Bawdin. [1772: copies with 2 TPs]. Bib N&Q 1no1:9 Ja '35; R. W. Chapman *ib.* 1no2:8 Ap '35.

9400 —— Chatterton and Milton; a question of forgery. N&Q 177:314 Oc '39.

9401 **Meyerstein, Edward H. W.** The forged letter from Peele to Marlowe. TLS 29 Je '40:315; E. St.J. Brooks *ib.* 20 Jl '40:351.

9402 **Gordon, Ian A.** An unrecorded copy of Chatterton. [3d ed. of Rowley Poems, with ms. adds. by George Catcott]. Turnbull Lib Rec 4:6–9 Jl/D '41.

9403 **Muir, Percival H.** A Chatterton edition. [Execution of sir Charles Bawdin, 1772]. TLS 5 Ap '41:172.

9404 **Meyerstein, Edward H. W.** A Chatterton manuscript. [To Clayfield]. TLS 27 D '47:675.

9405 —— Chattertoniana. [The merry tricks of Lamingtown: ms.]. TLS 6 Ja '50:9.

9406 **Bequest** from E. H. W. Meyerstein. [Chatterton's Heccar and Gaira ms. and J. Earle's Microcosmography ms.]. Bod Lib Rec 4no5:235–6 S '53.

9407 **Brown, T. Julian.** Thomas Chatterton, 1752–1770. (English literary autographs, X). Bk Coll 3no2:137 '54. facsims.

9408 **Guthke, Karl S.** The Rowley myth in eighteenth-century Germany. Pa Bib Soc Am 51:238–41 '57.

9409 **Taylor, Donald S.** The authenticity of Chatterton's Miscellanies in prose and verse. Pa Bib Soc Am 55:289–96 '61.

9410 **Werkmeister, Lucyle.** The first publication of Chatterton's verses to miss C./ on hearing her play on the harpsicord. N&Q 207:270–1 Jl '62.

CHAUCER, GEOFFREY, 1340?–1400

9411 **Wheatley, Henry B.** The bibliography of Chaucer. Bib Soc Trans 2pt1:11–13 '94.

Report of paper read 19 Mr '94; *repr. from* Bib Soc News-sh 3:10–11 Ap '94.

9412 —— The bibliography of Chaucer. Bkworm 7no78:167–8 My '94.

Summary of paper read to Bibliographical society, by Alfred W. Pollard.

9413 **Furnivall, Frederick J.** Entick's proposed edition of Chaucer. [Proposals for printing . . . , 1736]. N&Q ser8 7:126 F '95.

9414 **Speight, E. E.** The Speght editions of Chaucer. Athenæum 4023:766 D '04.

9415 **Hammond, Eleanor P.** The need of bibliographies in literary history. Pa Bib Soc Am 1no1:65–70 '04/5.

9416 —— On the order of the Canterbury tales: Caxton's two editions. Mod Philol 3no2:159–78 Oc '05. tables.

9417 **Peach, Harry H.** Kynaston's translation of Chaucer. [Ms. of Troilus in Latin]. N&Q ser10 4:109 Ag '05.

9418 **Abel, Rose.** Cumberland's edition of Chaucer. [c.1828]. Mod Lang N 24no5:159 My '09.

9419 **Skeat, Walter W.** Chaucer: a curious misplacement. [Canterbury tales]. N&Q ser11 1:201–2 Mr '10.

9419a **Amy, Ernest F.** The text of Chaucer's Legend of good women. Princeton, Princeton U.P., 1918. (Repr. New York, Haskell house, 1965). ix,109p. diagrs. 23cm.

I. Description of the manuscripts.–II. The relationship of the manuscripts.–III. The Skeat [1894] and Globe [1898] texts.–Appendix. 1. Kunz's genealogical tree. 2. Bilderbeck's classification of the mss. 3. Some corrections of the Chaucer society prints of the mss. of the Legend of good women.

9420 **Greg, sir Walter W.** Early printed editions of the Canterbury tales. [Text]. Pub Mod Lang Assn 39no4:737–61 D '24. tables.

9421 —— [and] **Margaret Kilgour.** The ms. source of Caxton's second edition of the Canterbury tales. Pub Mod Lang Assn 44no4:1251–3 D '29.

9422 **Rickert, Edith.** Are there more Chaucer manuscripts? TLS 17 D '31:1028.

9423 **Bühler, Curt F.** Chaucer's House of fame; another Caxton variant. Pa Bib Soc Am 42:140–3 '48.

9424 **Pace, George B.** The text of Chaucer's Purse. Stud Bib 1:105–21 '48.

9425 **Hench, Atcheson L.** Printer's copy for Tyrwhitt's Chaucer. [1775–8]. Stud Bib 3:265–6 '50/1.

9426 **Pace, George B.** Chaucer's Lak of stedfastnesse. [Ms.]. Stud Bib 4:105–22 '51/2. diagrs.

9427 **Chewning, Harris.** The text of the Envoy to Alison. Stud Bib 5:33–42 '52/3. diagrs.

9428 **Marston, Thomas E.** The first illustrated edition of The Canterbury tales. [1484]. Yale Univ Lib Gaz 28no4:150–2 Ap '54. facsim.

9429 **Pace, George B.** The Chaucerian Proverbs. [Ms.]. Stud Bib 18:41–8 '65. diagrs.

9430 **Heyworth, Peter L.** The earliest black-letter editions of Jack Upland. Huntington Lib Q 30no4:307–14 Ag '67.

9431 **Pace, George B.** Speght's Chaucer and ms. Gg.4.27. Stud Bib 21:225–35 '68. diagr.

CHERBURY, EDWARD HERBERT, 1ST BARON HERBERT OF, 1583–1648 *see* Herbert, Edward, 1st baron Herbert of Cherbury, 1583–1648.

CHESTERFIELD, PHILIP DORMER STANHOPE, 4TII EARL OF, 1694–1773 *see* Stanhope, Philip Dormer, 4th earl of Chesterfield, 1694–1773.

CHESTERTON, GILBERT KEITH, 1874–1936

9432 **Sullivan, J. J.** The trials of bibliography. Manchester R 8:331–8 '59.

CHETTLE, HENRY, 1560?–1607? *see also* Book production and distribution–Printers, publishers, etc.

9433 **Peery, William W.** Notes on Bang's edition of The blind-beggar of Bednalgreen. [1902]. Eng Stud 27no5:152–5 Oc '46.

9434 **Hummel, Ray O.** Henry Chettle, Englandes mourning garment, 1603. Library ser5no3/4:246 D/Mr '46/7.

9435 **Peery, William W.** Correction at press in The blind-beggar of Bednalgreen. Pa Bib Soc Am 41:140–4 '47. tables.

9436 **Schlochauer, Ernst J.** A note on variants in the dedication of Chettle's Tragedy of Hoffman. Pa Bib Soc Am 42:307–12 '48.

9437 **Jenkins, Harold.** The 1631 quarto of The tragedy of Hoffman. Library ser5 6no2:88–99 S '51.

9438 **Thomas, Sidney.** The printing of Greenes groatsworth of witte and Kindharts dreame. Stud Bib 19:196–7 '66.

CHETWOOD, WILLIAM RUFUS, d.1766

9439 **Seeber, Edward D.** The authenticity of The voyage of Richard Castleman, 1726. Pa Bib Soc Am 37:261–74 '43. table.

CHEYNE, GEORGE, 1671–1743

9440 **Bulloch, J. Malcolm.** An Aberdeen Falstaff: dr. George Cheyne, our double M.D. Aberdeen Univ Lib Bull 7no41:393–411 Je '30.

CHEYNELL, FRANCIS, 1608–65

9441 **Mead, Herman R.** [Bibliogr. note on Cheynell's The man of honour, 1645]. Pa Bib Soc Am 35:203 '41.

CHEYNEY, PETER, 1891–1951

9441f **Woolf, Cecil.** Peter Cheyney's Poems of love and war and To Corona and other poems. [1916; 1917, sought]. (Query 192). Bk Coll 14no3:367 '65.

CHILD, SIR JOSIAH, 1630–99

9442 **Bowyer, Tony H.** The published forms of sir Josiah Child's A new discourse of trade. Library ser5 11no2:95–102 Je '56.

'Appendix [i.e. checklist]' (p. 97–102)

CHRISTOPHERSON, BP. JOHN, d.1558

9443 **Wagner, Bernard M.** The tragedy of Iephte. [Anglo-Latin play ms.]. TLS 26 D '29:1097; F. S. Boas *ib.* 30 Ja '30:78.

CHURCHILL, SIR WINSTON LEONARD SPENCER, 1874–1965

9444 **Churchill,** Winston Spencer: Savrola, 1900. Bib N&Q 2no12:7 My '39.

9445 **Woods, Frederick W.** Sir Winston Churchill's writings. TLS 20 Je '58:345.

9446 —— Two first editions of sir Winston Churchill. [Savrola; The second world war]. Am Bk Coll 9no5:17–19 Ja '59.

9447 **Churchill** on sale. TLS 27 Oc '66:988.

CHURCHYARD, THOMAS, 1520?–1604

9448 **Byrne, Muriel St.C.** Thomas Churchyard's spelling. Library ser4 5no3: 243–8 D '24.

9449 **Chester, Allan G.** Notes on the bibliography of Thomas Churchyard. Mod Lang N 52no3:180–3 Mr '37.

CHUTE, ANTHONY, d.1595?

9450 **Kane, Robert J.** Anthony Chute, Thomas Nashe, and the first English work on tobacco. [The transformation of . . . Panachaea and . . . tobacco, 1595]. R Eng Stud 7no26:151–9 Ap '31.

CIBBER, COLLEY, 1671–1757

9451 **MacMillan, W. Dougald.** The text of Love's last shift. Mod Lang N 46no8:518–19 D '31.

9452 **Peterson, William M.** The text of Cibber's She wou'd and she wou'd not. Mod Lang N 71no4:258–62 Ap '56.

CLARE, JOHN, 1793–1864

9453 **Warren, William.** John Clare's library. Athenæum 3898:64 Jl '02.

9454 **Blunden, Edmund C.** Manuscripts of John Clare. London Merc 2no9:316–26 Jl '20.

9455 **Brown, Reginald W.** John Clare's library. Northamptonshire Nat Hist Soc & Field Club J 25no199:57–64 S '29. port.

9456 **Tibble, J. W.** and **Anne Tibble.** The manuscripts of John Clare. TLS 20 Ap '51:245.

9457 **Brown, T. Julian.** John Clare, 1793–1864. (English literary autographs, XIV). Bk Coll 4no2:147 '55. facsims.

9458 **Chapple, John A. V.** Some unpublished manuscripts of John Clare. Yale Univ Lib Gaz 31no1:34–48 Jl '56.

9459 **Tibble, J. W.** and **Anne Tibble.** John Clare. TLS 11 My '56:283; Reviewer *ib.* 25 My '56:313.

9460 **Tibble, Anne.** Problems of John Clare's manuscripts. TLS 18 Oc '57:625; J. A. V. Chapple 17 Ja '58:31.

9461 —— Clare's Ha'penny ballads. TLS 7 Ag '59:459.

9462 **Summerfield, Geoffrey** and **E. Robinson.** John Clare: Moments of forgetfulness. TLS 3 N '61:793; D. Powell *ib.* 10 N '61:805; I. Jack 17 N '61:823; G. Summerfield and E. Robinson 22 D '61:913; Anne Tibble 2 F '62:73.

9463 **Robinson, Eric** and **G. Summerfield.** John Taylor's editing of Clare's The shepherd's calendar. R Eng Stud new ser 14no56:359–69 N '63. tables.

9464 **Grainger, Margaret.** John Clare, collector of ballads. Peterborough, Peterborough museum, 1964. 23p. music. 22cm. (Peterborough museum society. Occasional papers, 3)

9465 **Tibble, J. W.** and **Anne Tibble.** John Clare's manuscripts. TLS 11 Je '64:516; E. Robinson and G. Summerfield *ib.* 2 Jl '64:571.

CLARENDON, EDWARD HYDE, EARL OF, 1609–74 *see* Hyde, Edward, earl of Clarendon, 1609–74.

CLARK, JAMES, 1660–1724

9466 **Couper, William J.** The writings and controversies of James Clark, minister at Glasgow, 1702–1724. Glasgow Bib Soc Rec 11:73–95 '33.

CLARKE, ADAM, 1762?–1832

9467 **Cordasco, Francesco G. M.** Adam Clarke's Bibliographical dictionary, 1802–1806. Stud Bib 4:188–91 '51/2.

CLARKE, SAMUEL DACRE, fl.1856 *see under* Book production and distribution–Printers, publishers, etc.

CLAVERING, MOLLY ('MARY'), 1900–

9468 **J., C. P.** [and **P. H. Muir**]. Susan Ferrier and The lairds of Fife. [By miss Clavering?]. Bib N&Q 2no2:5 F '36. [Sg.: Ed.]

CLELAND, JOHN, 1709–89

9469 **Nicholls, Edmund.** Block versus Sadleir; some interesting speculations on the early editions of Fanny Hill. Plain Dealer 1no1:19–23 S '33.

9470 **Thompson, Ralph.** Deathless lady. [Memoirs of Fanny Hill]. Coloph new ser 1no2:207–20 Oc '35. facsims.

9471 **Dingwall, E. J.** Fanny Hill. TLS 16 S '55:541.

9472 **Foxon, David F.** John Cleland and the publication of the Memoirs of a woman of pleasure. [Fanny Hill]. Bk Coll 12no4:476–87 '63. illus., facsims.

Repr. in Libertine literature in England, 1660–1745. London, 1964; New York, 1965. p. 52–63.

9473 **Mann, Phyllis G.** The first of Fanny. TLS 23 Ja '64; C. Staal ib. 6 F '64:113.

9473a **Foxon, David F.** The reappearance of two lost black sheep. [Venus in the cloister, Curll, 1725; Memoirs of Fanny Hill, 1841]. (Note 239). Bk Coll 14no1:75–6 '65.

CLERK, SIR JOHN, 1684–1755

9474 **G., J. M.** Pamphlets by sir John Clerk. N&Q ser8 2:108 Ag '92.

CLEVELAND, JOHN, 1613–58

9475 **Hanson, Laurence W.** Points in the bibliographies of John Cleveland and Alexander Brome. R Eng Stud 18no71:321–2 Jl '42.

9476 **Turner, Alberta.** The university miscellanies; some neglected early texts of Cleveland and Cowley. Mod Lang N 64no6:423–4 Je '49.

9477 **Morris, Brian R.** The editions of Cleveland's poems, 1647–1687. Library ser5 19:90–111 '64. facsims., diagrs., tables.

9478 **Woodward, Daniel H.** Notes on the canon of John Cleveland's poetry. N.Y. Pub Lib Bull 68no8:517–24 Oc '64.

CLOUGH, ARTHUR HUGH, 1819–61

9479 **Norrington, sir Arthur L. P.** 'Say not, the struggle nought availeth [Ms.]' in Essays mainly on the nineteenth century presented to sir Humphrey Milford. London, 1948. p. [29]–41.

9480 **Robertson, D. A.** Clough's Say not in ms. N&Q 196:499–500 N '51.

9481 **Townsend, Francis G.** Clough's The struggle; the text, title, and date of publication. Pub Mod Lang Assn 67no4:1191–2 D '52.

9482 **Gift** of manuscripts of poetical works of A. H. Clough. Bod Lib Rec 4no6:289–10 D '53.

9483 **Gollin, Richard M.** The 1951 edition of Clough's Poems; a critical re-examination. Mod Philol 60no2:120–7 N '62.

9484 **Borrie, M. A. F.** Three poems of Arthur Hugh Clough. Brit Mus Q 27no1/2:9–11 '63.

9485 **Barish, Evelyn.** A new Clough manuscript. [Solvitur aeris hiems]. R Eng Stud new ser 15no58:168–74 My '64.

9485a **Randall, David A.** Variant binding of Clough's Poems. [1849]. (Note 257). Bk Coll 14no4:542 '65.

9485b **Harris, Wendell V.** The curious provenience of Clough's The longest day. N&Q 212:379–80 Oc '67.

COBBETT, WILLIAM, 1762–1835

9486 **Lavington, Margaret.** Cobbett bibliography. [The life of William Cobbett by himself, 1816]. N&Q ser11 8:36 Jl '13; W. Jerrold *ib.* 8:137 Ag '13.

9487 **Freeman, John.** The Poor man's Bible. [Mss.]. (Correspondence). London Merc 3no17:538 Mr '21.

9488 **Cleverdon, Douglas.** Cobbett: Three letters. [1812]. Bib N&Q 1no1:12 Ja '35; A. M. Muirhead *ib.* 2no1:1 Ja '36.

9489 **[Muir, Percival H.].** Cobbett: Rural rides, 1830. [Collation]. Bib N&Q 2no10:8–9 Ap '38; A. M. M[uirhead] *ib.* 2no12:3 My '39.

9490 **Muirhead, Arnold M.** An introduction to a bibliography of William Cobbett. Library ser4 20no1:1–40 Je '39. facsims.

9491 **Davis, C. Rexford.** Cobbett letters in the library. [With checklist]. J Rutgers Univ Lib 17no2:50–7 Je '54.

9492 —— Cobbett and Gillray. J Rutgers Univ Lib 19no1:1–5 '55. facsims.

9493 **Osborne, John W.** Recent acquisitions of the William Cobbett collection in the Rutgers university library. J Rutgers Univ Lib 26no2:60–4 Je '63.

9494 **Tyson, Jon W.** Cobbett abroad. TLS 29 Oc '64:986; W. F. Parrish *ib.* 29 Oc '64:986.

9495 **Osborne, John W.** William Cobbett's Grammar and its purchasers. J Rutgers Univ Lib 30no1:8–11 D '66.

COBDEN, RICHARD, 1804–65

9496 **Unwin, T. Fisher.** Cobden pamphlet. [Incorporate your borough]. N&Q ser9 12:469 D '03.

9497 **Hales, G. T.** The papers of Richard Cobden. Brit Mus Q 8no3:100–2 F '34.

COCKBURN, JOHN, 1652–1729

9498 **Menzies, Walter.** Bibliotheca universalis and the rev. John Cockburn. Scott N&Q ser3 8no3:50–1 Mr '30.

COCKER, EDWARD, 1631–75

9499 **D., T. F.** Cocker's Arithmetic, the first edition. N&Q ser12 3:352–4 Jl '17.

9500 **Cocker's** Arithmetic. (Notes on sales). TLS 7 S '22:572; D. Salmon *ib.* 14 S '22:585.

9501 **Salmon, David.** Cocker's Arithmetick. N&Q 155:460 D '28; H. M. Cashmore *ib.* 156:32 Ja '29; sir A. Heal 156:82–5 F '29; 156:100–3 F '29; W. R. Power 156:122 F '29; E. E. Newton 156:214–15 Mr '29.

'A list of the editions of Cocker's Arithmetick and the publishers' (p. 100–3)

9502 **Noyes, Gertrude E.** Edward Cocker and Cocker's English dictionary. [1704]. N&Q 182:298–300 My '42.

9503 **Mitchell, Stephen O.** Johnson and Cocker's Arithmetic. Pa Bib Soc Am 56:107–9 '62.

COKAYNE, SIR ASTON, 1608–84

9504 **Cockaine's** Chaine of golden poems. Bkworm 4no44:247–8 Jl '91.

9505 **Smith, G. Barnett.** Sir Aston Cokain's works. Athenæum 3885:468 Ap '02; H. C. H. Candy *ib.* 3886:499 Ap '02.

COKAYNE, SIR THOMAS, 1519?–92

9506 **Cockaine's** Treatise of hunting. (Notes on sales). TLS 1 Jl '26:452.

COLEMAN, THOMAS, 1598–1647

9507 **Mead, Herman R.** [Bibliogr. note on Coleman's Hopes deferred, 1645]. Pa Bib Soc Am 35:204 '41.

COLERIDGE, SAMUEL TAYLOR, 1772–1834

9508 **Campbell, James D.** The prospectus of Coleridge's Watchman. [1796]. Athenæum 3450:808 D '93. [Sg.: J. D. C.]

9509 **Shepherd, Richard H.** The bibliography of Coleridge. N&Q ser8 7:361–3, 401–3,443–5,482–3,502–3 My,Je '95.

9510 **Roberts, William.** Coleridge mss. N&Q ser8 9:285 Ap '96.

9511 **Hutchinson, Thomas.** Coleridge and the poet Young. [Mss.]. N&Q ser9 4:42–3 Jl '99.

9512 **Garnett, Richard.** Emendations of Coleridge and Milton. Athenæum 3870:878 D '01.

9513 **Haney, John L.** Coleridge bibliography. N&Q ser9 10:167 Ag '02; E. H. Coleman; W. G. Boswell-Stone *ib.* 10:231 S '02; W. F. Prideaux 10:310 Oc '02; ser10 2:81–2 Jl '04; 2:245–6 S '04.

9514 **T., H.** Coleridge's Christabel. N&Q ser9 10:326 Oc '02; T Hutchinson; W. F. Prideaux *ib.* ser9 10:389–90,429–30 N '02; 10:489–90 D '02; 11:30–1 Ja '03; T. Hutchinson 11:116–17,170–2 F '03; W. F. Prideaux 11:269–72 Ap '03.

9515 **Axon, William E. A.** Coleridge marginalia. [Libr.]. N&Q ser9 12:61–2 Jl '03.

9516 **Jerrold, Walter.** Coleridge's The wandering of Cain. N&Q ser10 6:386 N '06.

9517 **Axon, William E. A.** Coleridge's Epitaphium testamentarium. N&Q ser10 7:387 My '07.

9518 **Shawcross, J.** Coleridge's Dejection; a mispunctuation. N&Q ser10 7:45 Ja '07; T. Bayne *ib.* 7:95 F '07.

9519 **Rees, J. Rogers.** Coleridge items. N&Q ser10 9:63–4 Ja '08; R. A. Potts; S. Butterworth *ib.* 9:133–5 F '08.

9520 **Case, R. H.** Coleridge's first printed poem. [Absence, 1793]. TLS 12 F '20:105.

9521 **Lehman, B. H.** A paragraph deleted by Coleridge. [The friend, 1818]. Mod Lang N 39no1:58–9 Ja '24.

9522 **Raysor, Thomas M.** Coleridge's manuscript lectures. Mod Philol 22no1:17–25 Ag '24.

9523 **Vogt, George McG.** Coleridge and Wordsworth. Harvard Lib N [2no]14:31–3 Mr '25.

9524 **Winship, George P.** Coleridge bibliography. [Prospectus of The watchman, 1796]. TLS 19 Mr '25:199.

9525 **Lowes, John L.** Sibylline leaves. TLS 29 Ap '26:323.

9526 **Snyder, Alice D.** Books borrowed by Coleridge from the library of the University of Göttingen, 1799. Mod Philol 25no3:377–80 F '28.

9527 **Gibbs, Warren E.** Unpublished variants in S. T. Coleridge's poetry. [Poems, 1797]. Mod Lang N 46no4:239–40 Ap '31.

9528 **Patton, Lewis.** Coleridge's The watchman. [Ms.]. TLS 8 Oc '31:778.

9529 **Elmen, Paul.** Editorial revisions of Coleridge's marginalia. [And H. N. Coleridge]. Mod Lang N 67no1:32–7 Ja '32.

9530 **Griggs, Earl L.** Coleridge, De Quincey, and nineteenth century editing. Mod Lang N 47no2:88–90 F '32.

9531 **Patton, Cornelius H.** Important Coleridge and Wordsworth manuscripts acquired by Yale. Yale Univ Lib Gaz 9no2:42–5 Oc '34. facsim.

9532 **Snyder, Alice D.** The manuscript of Kubla Khan. TLS 2 Ag '34:541.

9533 **Evans, Benjamin I., baron Evans of Hungershall.** Coleridge's copy of Fears in solitude. TLS 18 Ap '35:255.

9534 **Scribblings** and marginalia. [Books from Coleridge's library, at Harvard]. Harvard Lib N 3no4:132–5 Je '36.

'Coleridgeana' (p. 133–5)

9535 **Van Patten, Nathan.** A presentation copy of Coleridge's Sibylline leaves, with manuscript notes, altered readings, and deletions by the author. Library ser4 17no2:221–4 S '36.

9536 **Griggs, Earl L.** The Friend: 1809 and 1818 editions. Mod Philol 35no4:369–73 My '38.

9537 **Wells, John E.** Printer's bills for Coleridge's Friend, and Wordsworth's Cintra. [C. & R. Baldwin, 1809]. Stud Philol 36no3:521–3 Jl '39.

9538 **Snyder, Alice D.** Coleridge and the encyclopedists. [Encyclopædia metropolitana]. Mod Philol 38no2:173–91 N '40. facsims.

The minutes.–The prospectus.

9539 **[Haraszti, Zoltán].** Coleridge's Christabel [and other Coleridge accessions]. More Bks Boston Pub Lib Bull 17no2:71–2 F '42.

9540 **Brinkley, R. Florence.** Poems by S. T. Coleridge, esq. [c.1808–12]. Pa Bib Soc Am 39:163–7 '45.

9541 —— Some notes concerning Coleridge material at the Huntington library. Huntington Lib Q 8no3:312–20 My '45.

9542 **Bandy, W. T.** Coleridge's friend Joseph Hardman; a bibliographical note. J Eng Germ Philol 47no4:395–7 Oc '48.

9543 **Brinkley, R. Florence.** Coleridge transcribed. [Mss.]. R Eng Stud 24no95:219–26 Jl '48.

9544 **Rooke, Barbara E.** Coleridge: The friend. N&Q 193:17–18 Ja '48.

9545 **The dispersal** of Coleridge's books. TLS 28 Oc '49:704; 9 D '49:809.

James Gillman's library.–J. H. Green's library.

9546 **Meyerstein, Edward H. W.** A manuscript of Kubla Khan. TLS 12 Ja '51:21; B. R. Davis *ib*. 26 Ja '51:53; E. H. W. Meyerstein 9 F '51:85.

9547 **Horrocks, Sidney.** The Coleridge collection. (Special collections in the Reference library, 1). Manchester R 6:255 '52. [Sg.: S. H.]

9548 **Skeat, Theodore C.** Note-books and Marginalia of S. T. Coleridge. [Association copies]. Brit Mus Q 16no4:91–3 Ja '52.

9549 **Brown, T. Julian.** Samuel Taylor Coleridge, 1772–1834. (English literary autographs, XII). Bk Coll 3no4:301 '54. facsims.

9550 **Griggs, Earl L.** Notes concerning poems by Samuel Taylor Coleridge. Mod Lang N 69no1:27–31 Ja '54.

9551 **Watson, George G.** The text of Biographia literaria. N&Q 199:262–3 Je '54.

9552 **Fynmore, A. H. W.** Coleridge mss. N&Q 201:134 Mr '56.

9553 **Coburn, Kathleen.** Original versions of two Coleridge couplets. [Mss.]. N&Q 203:225–6 My '58.

9554 **Erdman, David V.** Unrecorded Coleridge variants. Stud Bib 11:143–62 '58.

'Chronology of variants' (p. 147–62); *see also no*.9556.

9555 **Robinson, A. M. Lewin.** A Coleridge poem. [God omnipresent, 1832]. TLS 31 Jl '59:447.

9556 **Erdman, David V., Lucyle Werkmeister,** and **R. S. Woof.** Unrecorded Coleridge variants; additions and corrections [to *no*.9554]. Stud Bib 14:236–45 '61.

9557 **Whalley, George.** Samuel Taylor Coleridge, 1772–1834. (Portrait of a bibliophile, VII). Bk Coll 10no3:275–90 '61.

'Appendix: Note on identification of Coleridge's marked books' (p. 288–90)

9558 **Woodring, Carl R.** Two prompt copies of Coleridge's Remorse. N.Y. Pub Bull 65no4:229–35 Ap '61. facsim.

9559 **Ms.** of Kubla Khan. TLS 16 F '62:112; M. Bishop *ib.* 23 F '62:121.

9560 **Skeat, Theodore C.** Kubla Khan. [Ms. acquired]. Brit Mus Q 26no3/4:77–83 '63.

9561 **Sultana, Donald.** Coleridge autographs. TLS 15 F '63:116.

9562 **Collinson, Robert L.** New light on Coleridge and the Metropolitana. Progress Lib Sci 1966:152–61 '66.

9563 **Whalley, George.** Coleridge's poetical canon: selection and arrangement. R Eng Lit 7no1:9–24 Ja '66.

9564 **Woof, R. S.** A Coleridge-Wordsworth manuscript and Sarah Hutchinson's poets. Stud Bib 19:226–31 '66.

9565 **Martin, C. G.** Coleridge's Lines to Thelwall: a corrected text and a first version. Stud Bib 20:254–7 '67.

9566 **Zall, Paul M.** Coleridge and Sonnets from various authors. Cornell Lib J 2:49–62 '67. facsims.

9567 —— Coleridge's unpublished revisions to Osorio. [= Remorse]. N.Y. Pub Lib Bull 71no8:516–23 Oc '67.

9568 **Whalley, George.** Coleridge marginalia lost. Bk Coll 17no4:428–42 '68. facsims.

'Unlocated books with ms. notes by Coleridge' (p. 431–42)

COLES, ELISHA, fl.1641–88

9569 **Mander, Gerald.** The identity of Elisha Coles. Library ser3 10no37:34–44 Ja '19. port.

COLLIER, JOHN, 1708–86 *see* Bobbin, Tim, *pseud.*

COLLIER, JOHN PAYNE, 1789–1883

9570 **Greg, sir Walter W.** Henslowe, Collier and the latest German criticism. Library ser2 5no19:293–304 Jl '04.

9571 **Parrott, Thomas M.** Chapman's All fooles and J. P. Collier. Athenæum 4209:789 Je '08.

9572 **Greg, sir Walter W.** A Collier mystification. [G. Peele mss.]. R Eng Stud 1no4:452–4 Oc '25.

9573 **Spencer, Hazelton.** The forger at work; a new case against Collier. [Mss.]. Philol Q 6no1:32–8 Ja '27.

9574 **Tannenbaum, Samuel A.** Shakspere forgeries in the Revels accounts. New York, Columbia U.P., 1928. (Repr. Port Washington, N.Y., Kennikat pr., 1966). 109p. 36cm.

> *Rev*: Sir W. W. Greg R Eng Stud 5:344–58 '29; C. T. Brooke Saturday R Lit 5:1000 '29; S. A. Tannenbaum *ib*. 5:1085 '29; A. Brandl Archiv 155:127–8 '29; TLS 7 Mr '29:179; W. J. Lawrence *ib*. 7 Mr '29:186; A. E. Stamp 21 Mr '29:221; R. B. McKerrow Mod Lang N 46:120–4 '31; R. A. Law J Eng Germ Philol 30:119–21 '31.

9575 **Baldwin, Thomas W.** The Revels books of 1604–5, and 1611–12. [And Collier fabrications]. Library ser4 10no3:327–38 D '29.

9576 **Tannenbaum, Samuel A.** Another Shakspere forgery. [Collier in Stationers' register]. Mod Lang N 44no1:13–15 Ja '29.

9577 **Greg, sir Walter W.** Macdobeth. [In Stationers' register]. Mod Lang N 45no3:141–2 Mr '30.

9578 **Tannenbaum, Samuel A.** More about the forged Revels accounts. New York [Tenny pr.] 1932. 37p. 25cm. Covertitle. (Shakspere studies, no.3)

9579 —— 'Forged memoranda in George-a-Greene' *in* Shaksperian scraps and other Elizabethan fragments. New York 1933. p. 42–50.

9580 —— 'A Locrine forgery' *in* Shaksperian scraps and other Elizabethan fragments. New York, 1933. p. 36–41.

9581 R. J. Payne Collier's fabrications. N&Q 169:173 S '35.

9582 **McPharlin, Paul.** The Collier-Cruikshank Punch and Judy. Coloph new ser 1no3:371–87 F '36; Addendum *ib*. 1no4:613 Je '36. facsims.

9583 **Tillotson, Kathleen.** Another Collier forgery. [Drayton's Idea, 1593]. TLS 11 Jl '36:576.

9584 **Ringler, William.** Another Collier forgery. [Gosson's Pleasant quips for . . . gentlewomen, 1595]. TLS 29 Oc '38:693–4.

9585 **Gorrell, Robert M.** John Payne Collier and The murder of Iohn Brewen. Mod Lang N 57no6:441–4 Je '42.

9586 **Ashby, A. W.** John Payne Collier. TLS 27 My '49:347.

9587 **Race, Sydney.** John Payne Collier. [And William Percy]. N&Q 194:347 Ag '49; Madeleine H. Dodds *ib*. 194:458–9 Oc '49; S. R[ace] 195:21 Ja '50. [Sg.: S. R.]

9588 —— Collier's History of English dramatic poetry. [1831]. N&Q 195:33–5 Ja '50.

9589 —— J. P. Collier and the Dulwich papers. N&Q 195:112–14 Mr '50.

9590 **Schrickx, W.** Notes on the so-called Collier forgery of the dedication to Chapman's All fools. R Belge de Philol et d'Histoire 28:142–6 '50.

9591 **Race, Sydney.** J. P. Collier's fabrications. N&Q 195:345–6 Ag '50; 195:480–1 Oc '50; 195:501–2 N '50; sir W. Foster ib. 195:414–15 S '50; S. Race 197:54–6 F '52; K. Muir 197:150 Mr '52; S. Race 197:281–3 Je '52.

9592 **Bowers, Robert H.** The Masque of the four seasons (Egerton ms. 2623). [And Collier]. N&Q 197:96–7 Mr '52.

9593 **Race, Sydney.** The masques of the twelve months and the four seasons. N&Q 197:347–9 Ag '52; 197:525 N '52; R. C. Els[l]ey ib. 197:402 S '52.

9594 —— J. P. Collier and his fabrications: early poetical miscellanies and Shakespeare papers. N&Q 198:391–5 S '53; 198:531–4 D '53.

9595 **Speaight, George V.** Payne Collier and Punch and Judy. N&Q 199:31–2 Ja '54.

9596 **Race, Sydney.** John Payne Collier and the Stationers' registers. N&Q 200:492–5 N '55; 201:120–22 Mr '56.

9597 —— John Payne Collier and his Essex papers. N&Q 201:218–19 My '56.

9598 —— John Payne Collier and his fabrications. N&Q 202:309–12 Jl '57.

9599 —— John Payne Collier and the Percy society. N&Q 202:395–7 S '57; L. G. Matthews ib. 202:458 Oc '57; H. E. Rollins 203:182 Ap '58.

9600 —— Manningham and Marston. N&Q 202:147 Ap '57.

9601 **Dickey, Franklin.** The old man at work: forgeries in the Stationers' registers. Sh Q 11no1:39–47 '60.

9602 **Cutts, John P.** A John Payne Collier unfabricated 'fabrication'. [And John Wilson]. N&Q 204:104–6 Mr '59; F. W. Sternfeld ib. 207:152 Ap '62.

9603 **Griffiths, G. Milwyn.** Echoes of a Shakespearean controversy. [J. Mostyn papers concerning Collier, acquired by Library]. (News and notes). Nat Lib Wales J 12no3:298 '62.

9604 **Schoenbaum, Samuel.** The crimes and repentance of John Payne Collier. TLS 26 Je '69:709; 3 Jl '69:731; Rosalie Mander ib. 3 Jl '69:731. facsim.

COLLIER, WILLIAM, fl.1835–68

9605 **Hebb, John.** A forgotten dramatic author. N&Q ser9 4:457–8 D '99.

COLLINS, WILLIAM, 1721–59

9606 **Latham, Edward.** Poem in one sentence. [Ode to evening]. N&Q ser10 5:148 F '06; T. Bayne *ib.* 5:217 Mr '06.

9607 **Mabbott, Thomas O.** William Collins. [Epistle to sir Thomas Hanmer, 1771]. N&Q ser12 9:208 S '21.

9608 **McKillop, Alan D.** A bibliographical note on Collins. [Written on paper]. Mod Lang N 38no3:184–5 Mr '23.

9609 **Garrod, H. W.** Errors in the text of Collins. TLS 15 Mr '28:188; J. R. Macphail; A. Macdonald *ib.* 22 Mr '28:221; Margaret Bourke 29 Mr '28:243; H. O. White 5 Ap '28:257; J. H. A. Sparrow 12 Ap '28:272.

9610 **McKillop, Alan D.** A lost poem by Collins. [An epistle to the editor of Fairfax, 1750]. TLS 6 D '28:965.

9611 **Addington, Marion H.** Some notes about the essays intended for the Collins-Cooper publication. [The friendly examiner, or Letters of Polémon and Philéthus]. London Merc 22no130:351–2 Ag '30.

9612 **Wilmshurst, W. L.** Signatures of Collins. TLS 9 F '33:92.

9613 **Olybrius,** *pseud.* History of the revival of learning; The Christian magazine. Bib N&Q 1no1:9 Ja '35.

9614 **McKillop, Alan D.** Collins's Ode to the passions. TLS 7 Mr '36:204.

9615 **Todd, William B.** William Collins's Odes, 1747. (Query no.17). Bk Coll 1no3:195 '52.

9616 **Francis, T. R.** The plate in Collins's Odes. (Query no.17). Bk Coll 2no2:157 '53.

9617 **Collins** at Winchester. [Exhibition]. TLS 3 Jl '59:404.

COLLINS, WILLIAM WILKIE, 1824–89

9618 **Parrish, Morris L.** Wilkie Collins and The world. [Identification of journal]. Bib N&Q 1no3:4 Ag '35.

9619 —— Collins, Wilkie. Bib N&Q 2no4/5:9 My '36.

9620 —— Wilkie Collins queries. TLS 6 Je '36:484.

9621 **The manuscript** of Wilkie Collins' Poor miss Finch. Princeton Univ Lib Chron 15no3:164–5 '54.

9622 **Ashley, Robert P.** The Wilkie Collins collection. Princeton Univ Lib Chron 17no2:81–4 '56.

9623 **Manuscripts** of Wilkie Collins. [The fallen leaves and Blind love]. Princeton Univ Lib Chron 18no2:85 '57.

COLLOP, JOHN, fl.1660

9624 **Dr.** Collop's poems. (Notes on sales). TLS 30 D '20:896.

CONGREVE, WILLIAM, 1670–1729

9625 **Gosse, sir Edmund W.** A note on Congreve. [An impossible thing, 1720]. London Merc 3no18:638–43 Ap '21.

  Repr. in Aspects and impressions. London, 1922. (2d ed. 1928). p. 77–86.

9626 **Lawrence, William J.** A Congreve holograph. R Eng Stud 2no7:345 Jl '26.

9627 **Haraszti, Zoltán.** Early editions of Congreve's plays. More Bks Boston Pub Lib Bull 9no3:81–95 Mr '34. facsim.

9628 **Isaacs, J.** Congreve's library. Library ser4 20no1:41–2 Je '39.

9629 **Munsterberg, Margaret.** Congreve's Aristophanes. [Libr.]. More Bks Boston Pub Lib Bull 17no9:437–8 N '42. [Sg.: M. M.]

9630 **Bowers, Fredson T.** The cancel leaf in Congreve's Double dealer, 1694. Pa Bib Soc Am 43:78–82 '49. diagr., tables.

9631 **Hodges, John C.** Congreve's library. TLS 12 Ag '49:521; J. Isaacs *ib.* 2 S '49:569.

9632 **Van Lennep, William.** The Chetwyn manuscript of The school for scandal. [Licenser's copy, now at Yale]. Theat Notebk 6no1:10–12 Oc/D '51.

9633 **Hodges, John C.** The library of William Congreve. New York, New York public library, 1955. 118p. facsims. 25cm.

  Repr. from N.Y. Pub Lib Bull 58:367–85, 436–54, 478–88, 535–50, 579–91 Ag–D '54; 59:16–35, 82–97 Ja–F '55.

9634 **Brown, T. Julian.** William Congreve, 1670–1729. (English literary autographs, XXI). Bk Coll 6no1:61 '57. facsim.

CONRAD, JOSEPH, *pseud. of* TEODOR JÓZEF KONRAD KORZENIOWSKI, 1857–1924.

9635 **Conrad's** Chance: the real first edition and the fakes. Bkmns J 3no57:77 N '20; 3no59:109–10 D '20; T. J. Wise *ib*. 3no62:160 D '30; Correction 3no63:177 Ja '21.

The 1913 and 1914 issues compared.–Faked first issues.

9636 **Conrad** on his writings, a tribute to mr. Thomas Wise [by E. W. Gosse in The Sunday times]. Bkmns J 3no63:177 Ja '21.

9637 **Early** Conrad first editions, by an occasional contributor. Bkmns J 4no90:189–90 Jl '21.

9638 **More** frauds of the book forger: Conrad's A set of six, two issues of the first edition. Bkmns J 3no63:177 Ja '21; T. J. Wise *ib*. 3no63:177 Ja '21.

9639 **Conrad collector, A.** New discoveries in the bibliography of Chance. Bkmns J new ser 5no3:81–2 D '21; [Correction] *ib*. 5no4:141 Ja '22; *cf*. 5no5:175 F '22.

9640 **Conrad** manuscripts. (Notes on sales). TLS 22 N '23:796.

9641 **The Conrad** mss. [in Quinn sale]. (Men and matters). Bkmns J new ser 9no27:114–15 D '23.

9642 **... Joseph** Conrad mss. [in William F. Gable collection] .... (American notes). Bkmns J new ser 9no27:105 D '23.

9643 **Sargent, George H.** Conrad manuscripts in America. [Purchasers and prices at Quinn sale]. Bkmns J new ser 9no28:137–9 Ja '24. facsim. [Sg.: G. H. S.]

9644 **Conrad** books and manuscripts. [From his library]. (Notes on sales). TLS 26 F '25:144.

9645 **Conrad, Jessie G.** Conrad's share in The nature of a crime and his Congo diary. Bkmns J new ser 12no46:135–6 Jl '25.

9646 —— The romance of The rescue. Bkmns J new ser 12no43:19–20 Ap '25.

9647 **The bibliography** of Joseph Conrad. Bkmns J ser3 15no3:163–4 '27; T. J. Wise *ib*. 15no4:226–7 '27.

9648 **A Conrad** collection. [Richard Curle's library]. (Notes on sales). TLS 12 My '27:340.

9649 **Hopkins, Frederick M.** Curle sale of Conradiana. [And Wise on trial books]. Pub Wkly 111:2186–8 Je '27.

9650 **The Richard** Curle Conrad collection. (Books in the sale rooms). Bkmns J ser3 15no2:106–13 '27.

9651 **Conrad, Jessie G.** The manuscript of Almayer's folly. Bkmns J ser3 18no13:1–3 '30.

9652 **Whiting, George W.** Conrad's revision of six of his short stories. Pub Mod Lang Assn 48no2:552–7 Je '33.

9653 **Randall, David A.** Conrad: Some reminiscences, 1908. Bib N&Q 2no4/5:9 My '36. [Sg.: D. R.]

9654 **Tomkins, D.** Conrad: The rover. [Distinction of ed.]. Bib N&Q 1no2:9–10 Ap '35; T. Warburton *ib*. 1no4:7–8 Oc '35; J. T. Babb 2no1:1 Ja '36; T. Warburton 2no3:2 Ap '36; J. T. Babb 2no6:1 Jl '36.

9655 **Babb, James T.** Conrad's Chance, 1913. [First issue]. Yale Univ Lib Gaz 11no4:96 Ap '37.

9656 **Gee, John A.** The Conrad memorial library of mr. George T. Keating. Yale Univ Lib Gaz 13no1:16–28 Jl '38. port., facsims.

9657 —— The final typescript of book III of Conrad's Nostromo. Yale Univ Lib Gaz 16no4:80 Ap '42.

9658 **Johnson, Fred B.** [Bibliogr. note on Conrad's Suspense, 1925]. Pa Bib Soc Am 40:237–8 '46.

9659 **Bruccoli, Matthew J.** and **C. A. Rheault.** Imposition figures and plate gangs in The rescue. Stud Bib 14:258–62 '61. diagrs.

9659a **Randall, David A.** Copies of Conrad's Chance, dated 1913. (Query 198). Bk Coll 15no1:68 '66; G. Sims *ib*. 15no2:213–14 '66.

9659b **Turner, Michael L.** Conrad and T. J. Wise. [Notebook in Bodleian with entries for privately-ptd. pamphlets and mss.]. (Note 272). Bk Coll 15no3:350–1 '66.

9660 **Cagle, William R.** The publication of Joseph Conrad's Chance. Bk Coll 16no3:305–22 '67. illus., facsims.

9661 **Ault, Patricia.** Conradiana on display. [Exhib. at McMurry college, Abilene, Texas]. Conradiana 2no1:94 '69.

9662 **Bishop, Morchard.** Nostromo. ['fractious' for 'factious' in pt3 chapter 9]. TLS 2 Oc '69:1132; J. S. Lewis *ib*. 23 Oc '69:1235.

9663 **John** D. Gordan bequest: a notable Conrad archive. N.Y. Pub Lib Bull 73no3:145–6 Mr '69.

9664 **Lindstrand, Gordon.** Conrad's literary manuscripts: John Quinn and the New York public library. Conradiana 2no1:85–8 '69.

9665 **Maxwell, James C.** Victory. TLS 4 D '69:1405.

9666 **Welsh, David.** Conrad's copy of the Fredro memoirs. Conradiana [1no2]:36 ['69].

9666a **Lindstrand, Gordon.** A bibliographical survey of the literary manuscripts of Joseph Conrad. Conradiana 2no1:23–32 '69; 2no2:105–14 '69/70; 2no3:153–62 '69/70.

9667 —— An unknown Conrad manuscript and a record price for Conrad typescripts. [Notes on siege and fall of Paris, 1870–1; Almayer's folly and Chance]. Conradiana 2no3:152 '69/70.

CONSTABLE, HENRY, 1562–1613

9668 **Muir, Kenneth.** The order of Constable's sonnets. [Mss.]. N&Q 199:424–5 Oc '54.

CONWAY, SIR JOHN, d.1603

9669 **Stopes, Charlotte C.** Sir John Conway. [And Henry Wykes, ptr.]. N&Q ser8 10:89 Ag '96.

COOK, JAMES, 1728–79

9670 **Ray, F. R.** Capt. Cook's voyages. N&Q ser10 10:69 Jl '08.

9671 **Captain** Cook's manuscripts. (Notes on sales). TLS 14 D '22:848.

9672 **Captain** Cook manuscripts. (Notes on sales). TLS 29 Mr '23:220.

9673 **Holmes, sir Maurice G.** Captain Cook's Voyages. [1776]. TLS 5 N '31:866.

9674 —— Collecting captain Cook. Bk Coll 1no3:166–73 '52. illus.

COOKE, THOMAS, 1703–56

9675 **Shipley, John B.** Thomas Cooke. [Mss.]. N&Q 205:190 My '60.

COOPER, ANTHONY ASHLEY, 3D EARL OF SHAFTESBURY, 1671–1713

9676 **Whitaker, S. F.** The first edition of Shaftesbury's Moralists. Library ser5 7no4:235–41 D '52.

9677 **Alderman, William E.** English editions of Shaftesbury's Characteristics. Pa Bib Soc Am 61:315–34 '67.

'Authenticated English editions' (p. 332–4)

COOPER, SAMUEL, 1609–72

9678 **Long, B. S.** A manuscript by Samuel Cooper and a side-light on John Hoskins. N&Q ser12 9:1–2 Jl '21.

COPLAND, ROBERT, fl.1508–47 see Book production and distribution–Printers, publishers, etc.

COPLESTON, BP. EDWARD, 1776–1849

9679 **Sparrow, John H. A.** Copleston: Advice to a young reviewer, 1807. [Issues]. Bib N&Q 2no8:6 F '37.

9680 **Todd, William B.** Copleston. Advice to a young reviewer. (Note 85). Bk Coll 6no3:293 '57.

COPPARD, ALFRED EDGAR, 1878–1957

9681 **Saul, George B.** Cherry ripe. TLS 29 F '36:188; V. Stuart *ib.* 7 Mr '36:208.

CORBETT, BP. RICHARD, 1582–1635

9682 **Drury, George Thorn-.** Bishop Corbet's poems. [1647]. N&Q ser10 6:126 Ag '06.

CORK, JOHN BOYLE, 5TH EARL OF, 1707–62 see Boyle, John, 5th earl of Cork, and Orrery, 1707–62.

CORNWALLIS, SIR WILLIAM, d.1631?

9683 **Bennett, R. E.** The publication of Cornwallis's Essayes and paradoxes. R Eng Stud 9no34:197–8 Ap '33.

CORVO, BARON, *pseud. of* **FREDERICK ROLFE, 1860–1913** see Rolfe, Frederick William Serafino Austin Lewis Mary ('baron Corvo'), 1860–1913.

CORY, WILLIAM JOHNSON, 1823–92

9684 **Bushnell, George H.** 'On the bibliography of Ionica' *in* From bricks to books. London, 1949. p. 37–40.

CORYATE, THOMAS, 1577?–1617

9685 **Gibbs, Henry H., baron Aldenham** and **J. Pickford.** Coryate's Crudities. N&Q ser10 3:426 Je '05; C. G. Smithers *ib.* 3:494 Je '05. [Sg.: Aldenham.]

COSIN, BP. JOHN, 1594–1672

9686 **Hanson, Laurence W.** John Cosin's Collection of private devotions, 1627. Library ser5 13no4:282–7 D '58.

COTTESFORD, THOMAS, d.1555

9687 **Horst, Irvin B.** Thomas Cottesford's Two letters. [1589]. Library ser5 11no1:44–7 Mr '56.

COTTON, CHARLES, 1630–87

9688 **Jessel, Frederic.** Charles Cotton's Compleat gamester. N&Q ser12 2:514 D '16.

9689 **Turner, Ernest M.** Cotton's poems. [Mss.]. TLS 22 Ja '38:60; J. Beresford *ib.* 29 Ja '38:76.

9690 **Hussey, Richard.** The text of Cotton's poems. N&Q 186:87–8 F '44.

9691 **Parks, Stephen.** A Contentation of anglers. [Ms. in Library]. Yale Univ Lib Gaz 43no3:157–64 Ja '69. facsim.

COTTON, SIR ROBERT BRUCE, 1571–1631

9692 **Jackson, William A.** Sir Robert Bruce Cotton's A short view of the long life and raigne of Henry the third. Harvard Lib Bull 4no1:28–38 '50. facsims.

'Appendix: Table of variant readings in editions of sir Robert Cotton's Short view . . .' (p. 38)

9693 **Mirrlees, Hope.** 'The famous jewel-house' *in* A fly in amber, being an extravagant biography of the romantic antiquary, sir Robert Bruce Cotton. London [1962]. p. 56–70.

COWLEY, ABRAHAM, 1618–67

9694 **L., E.** Cowley's Poems set to music. [By William King]. N&Q ser9 8:16 Jl '01; J. Marshall *ib.* 8:67 Jl '01.

9695 **Sparrow, John H. A.** The text of Cowley's Mistress. R Eng Stud 3no9:22–7 Ja '27.

9696 —— Cowley's Plantarum libri duo, a presentation copy. London Merc 20no118:398–9 Ag '29.

9697 —— The text of Cowley's satire The puritan and the papist. Anglia 58:78–102 Ja '34.

9698 **Wiley, Autrey N.** The prologue and epilogue to the Guardian. [And F. Cole]. R Eng Stud 10no40:443–7 Oc '34.

9699 **Mead, Herman R.** [Bibliogr. note on Cowley's Verses, 1663]. Pa Bib Soc Am 35:68 '41.

9700 —— Two issues of Cowley's Vision. Pa Bib Soc Am 45:77–81 '51. facsims.

9700a **Miller, Clarence H.** The order of stanzas in Cowley and Crashaw's On hope. Stud Philol 61no1:64–73 Ja '64.

9700b **Williams, George W.** The order of stanzas in Cowley and Crashaw's On hope. Stud Bib 22:207–10 '69.

COWLEY, HANNAH (PARKHOUSE), 1743–1809

9701 **Rhodes, Raymond C.** The Belle's stratagem. R Eng Stud 5no18:129–42 Ap '29.

9702 **Todd, William B.** Hannah Cowley: re-impressions, not reissues. (Note 102). Bk Coll 7no3:301 '58.

COWPER, WILLIAM, 1731–1800

9703 **Roberts, William.** Cowper and the Times. [Verse contributions]. N&Q ser9 9:47 Ja '02.

9704 **Bates, Madison C.** Cowper bibliography. N&Q ser10 12:508 D '09.

9705 **Lynn, W. T.** Cowper misprint. [To the immortal memory of the halibut]. N&Q ser10 11:506 Je '09; J. F. Palmer; J. T. Greenslade *ib.* 12:77 Jl '09.

9706 **Povey, Kenneth.** The text of Cowper's letters. Mod Lang R 22no1:22–7 Ja '27. table.

9707 **Kirby, H. T.** John Gilpin in picture; some illustrators of Cowper's famous poem. Bkmn 81no483:198–200 D '31.

9708 **Nicholls, Norah.** Early editions of William Cowper. Bkmn 80no477:174 Je '31.

9709 **Povey, Kenneth.** Notes for a bibliography of Cowper's letters. R Eng Stud 7no26:182–7 Ap '31.

9710 —— Further notes for a bibliography of Cowper's letters. R Eng Stud 8no31:316–19 Jl '32.

9711 **Y., E. E.** Illustrated editions of John Gilpin. N&Q 167:457 D '34; E. Syers *ib.* 168:32 Ja '35; A. M. Coleman 168:86 F '35.

9712 **Weiss, Harry B.** William Cowper's frolic in rhyme, The diverting history of John Gilpin. [Illus.]. N.Y. Pub Lib Bull 41no9:675–80 S '37. facsims.

9713 **Chapman, Robert W.** A book from Cowper's library. N&Q 186:291 Je '44. [Sg.: R. W. C.]

9714 **Brooks, Elmer L.** Cowper's periodical contributions. TLS 17 Ag '56:487.

9715 **Keynes, sir Geoffrey L.** The library of William Cowper. [With catalogue]. Cambridge Bib Soc Trans 3pt1:47–69 '59; Addendum 3pt2:167 '60.

   See also no.9717.

9716 **Ryskamp, Charles.** Cowper on the king's sea-bathing. Library ser5 15no3:208–9 S '60.

9717 **Russell, Norma H. H.** Addenda to The library of William Cowper. Cambridge Bib Soc Trans 3pt3:225–31 '61.

   See also no.9715.

9718 **Brown, T. Julian.** William Cowper, 1731–1800. (English literary autographs, XLIII). Bk Coll 11no3:331 '62. facsim.

9719 **Ryskamp, Charles.** William Cowper and his circle; a study of the Hannay collection. Princeton Univ Lib Chron 24no1:3–26 '62. facsims.

9720 **Tompkins, A. D. R.** A nursery version of John Gilpin. N&Q 207:460–1 D '62.

9721 **Zall, Paul M.** A variant version of Cowper's The rose. [Ms.]. Huntington Lib Q 25no3:253–6 My '62.

9722 **Povey, Kenneth.** Hand-list of manuscripts in the Cowper and Newton museum, Olney, Bucks. Cambridge Bib Soc Trans 4pt2:107–27 '65.

9723 **Russell, Norma H. H.** Of text and type. TLS 5 My '66:396.

9724 **Westcott, I. M.** A full set of Cowper's Poems in parts. [1814]. N&Q 211:467–9 D '66. table.

9725 **Baird, John D.** Mss. by or relating to William Cowper. (Query 214). Bk Coll 17no2:217 '68.

COX, WALTER, c.1770–1837

9726 **Bourke, Francis S.** Watty Cox and his publications, by Seamus O'Casaide. [Observations on a pamphlet, entitled An appeal]. Irish Bk Lover 32no5:104 Jl '56.

CRABBE, GEORGE, 1754–1832

9727 **Huchon, René.** Crabbe's mss. N&Q ser9 12:7 Jl '03.

9728 **Waller, A. R.** Crabbe bibliography. N&Q ser10 1:86 Ja '04.

9729 **Looker, Samuel J.** Unpublished poems by George Crabbe. [Mss.]. N&Q 156:192 Mr '29.

9730 **Sparrow, John H. A.** Crabbe's Works, 1823. [Labels and issues]. Bib N&Q 2no1:3 Ja '36.

9731 **Batdorf, Franklin P.** George Crabbe. [Tales]. N&Q 194:481 Oc '49.

9732 —— An unrecorded edition of Crabbe. [The village, 1838]. Pa Bib Soc Am 43:349–50 '49.

9733 —— Notes on three editions of George Crabbe's Tales. Pa Bib Soc Am 44:276–9 '50.

9734 —— An unrecorded early anthology of Crabbe. [The tales and miscellaneous poems, 1847]. Stud Bib 3:266–7 '50/1.

9735 **Todd, William B.** Two issues of Crabbe's Works, 1823. Pa Bib Soc Am 45:250–1 '51.

9736 **Batdorf, Franklin P.** The Murray imprints of George Crabbe; a publisher's record. Stud Bib 4:192–9 '51/2. tables.

9737 **Aillevard, Jean.** Crabbe's Inebriety, 1775. (Query no.53). Bk Coll 3no4:309–10 '54.

9738 **Crabbe** in Aldeburgh. [Exhibition]. TLS 2 Jl '54:431.

9739 **Pollard, H. Graham.** The early poems of George Crabbe and The lady's magazine. Bod Lib Rec 5no3:149–56 Jl '55.

CRAIG, EDWARD GORDON, 1872–1966

9740 **Rood, Arnold.** Private collections of Edward Gordon Craig in the United States. Theat Res 5no2:102–4 '63.

9741 **Sheren, Paul.** Gordon Craig's only American production. [Materials in Library]. Princeton Univ Lib Chron 29no3:163–92 '68. illus., facsims.

Dramatis personae.–The collaboration.–First readings.–Rehearsals.–Opening nights.–The critics.–Curtain.

CRAIK, DINAH MARIA (MULOCK), 1826–87

9742 **Dinah** Maria Mulock Craik and mrs. Browning. [Dedication copy of The head of the family]. Princeton Univ Lib Chron 16no3:153 '55.

CRANE, RALPH, fl.1575–1632

9743 **Wilson, Frank P.** Ralph Crane, scrivener to the King's players. Library ser4 7no2:194–215 S '26. facsims.

Repr. in Bentley, Gerald E., ed. The seventeenth-century stage, a collection of critical essays. Chicago, Ill.; London, 1968. p. 137–55.

9744 **Tannenbaum, Samuel A.** 'Ralph Crane and The winter's tale' in Shaksperian scraps and other Elizabethan fragments. New York, 1933. p. 75–86.

9745 **Partridge, Astley C.** 'The orthographical characteristics of Ralph Crane' in Orthography in Shakespeare and Elizabethan drama. London [1964]. p. [172]–4.

9746 **Hill, Trevor H. Howard-.** Ralph Crane's parentheses. N&Q 210:334–40 S '65. tables.

9747 —— 'Shakespeare, Crane and the computer' in 1965 International conference on computational linguistics. Proceedings. New York, 1965. 11p. (Duplicated typescript)

9748 **Nosworthy, James M.** 'The songs in The witch and Ralph Crane' in Shakespeare's occasional plays, their origin and transmission. London [1965]. p. [227]–31.

9749 **Hill, Trevor H. Howard-.** Knight, Crane, and the copy for the Folio Winter's tale. N&Q 211:139–40 Ap '66.

CRANMER, ARCHBP. THOMAS, 1489–1556

9750 **Burbidge, Edward.** Archbishop Cranmer's library and its recovery. Bkworm 4no43:209–14 Jl '91.

9751 —— Cranmer's and other missals. [Request for information]. Bkworm 4no47:351 Oc '91.

9752 **Prideaux, W. R. B.** Cranmer's library. N&Q ser10 3:24–5 Ja '05.

9753 **[Madan, Falconer].** Cranmer's library. Bod Lib Rec 1no4:57–8 F '39.

9754 **Selwyn, D. G.** A neglected edition of Cranmer's Catechism. [1548]. J Theol Stud new ser 15pt1:76–91 Ap '64.

'Additional note: The editions and date of the catechism' (p. 90–1)

CRASHAW, RICHARD, 1612?–49

9755 **Martin, Leonard C.** Crashaw's translation of Marino's La strage degli innocenti (Sospetto d'Herode). [Ms.]. Mod Lang R 10no3:378–80 Jl '15.

9756 **Candy, Hugh C. H.** Note on an adapted copy of Crashaw's Poems: Steps to the temple, The delights of the muses, and Carmen deo nostro, 1670. Library ser3 8no29:77–8 Ja '17.

9757 **Roberts, sir Sydney C.** Richard Crashaw. [Poemata et epigrammata, 1674]. (Correspondence). London Merc 8no44:187 Je '23.

9758 **F., R. O. L.** The editor of Crashaw's Steps to the temple. N&Q 175:263 Oc '38; J. Seton-Anderson *ib.* 175:305 Oc '38.

9759 **Williams, George W.** Textual revision in Crashaw's Vpon the bleeding crucifix. [Ms.]. Stud Bib 1:191–3 '48.

9760 **Maxwell, James C.** Steps to the temple; 1646 and 1648. Philol Q 29no2:216–20 Ap '50.

9761 **Martin, Leonard C.** An unedited Crashaw manuscript. [Hymn to saint Teresa]. TLS 18 Ap '52:272. facsim.

9762 **Williams, George W.** Richard Crashaw and the Little Gidding bookbinders. N&Q 201:9–10 Ja '56.

9763 **Yoklavich, John M.** A manuscript of Crashaw's poems from Loseley. Eng Lang N 2no2:92–7 D '64.

CRASHAWE, WILLIAM, 1572–1626

9764 **Wallis, Peter J.** William Crashaw, puritan divine, poet and bibliophile. N&Q 199:101–2 Mr '54.

9765 —— The library of William Crashawe. Cambridge Bib Soc Trans 2pt3:213–28 '56. illus.

CROKE, SIR GEORGE, 1560–1642

9766 **Spencer, Lois.** The printing of sir George Croke's Reports. [1657]. Stud Bib 11:231–46 '58.

CROMEK, ROBERT HARTLEY, 1770–1812

9767 **Ferguson, J. DeLancey.** In defence of R. H. Cromek. [And Burns]. Philol Q 9no3:239–48 Jl '30.

9768 **De Ternant, Andrew.** Cromek's Reliques of Robert Burns. N&Q 161:174 S '31.

9769 **French, Hannah D.** A slashed copy of Reliques of Robert Burns, 1808. [Cancels]. (Note 263). Bk Coll 15no1:67–8 '66.

CROMWELL, OLIVER, 1599–1658

9770 **Neilson, George.** Cromwell's library. N&Q ser9 2:465 D '98.

9771 **Williams, J. B.,** *pseud. of* **J. G. Muddiman.** Cromwelliana. N&Q ser11 4:262–4 S '11.

VI. A fraudulent version of Cromwell's prayer printed by Carlyle.

9772 **Clyde, William McC.** Towards a complete bibliography of Oliver Cromwell. N&Q 162:423–4 Je '32.

9773 **The Matthew** Cable collection on Oliver Cromwell. Turnbull Lib Rec 15:16 N '62.

CRONIN, ARCHIBALD JOSEPH, 1896–

9774 **Lowry, K. B.** [and] **Argus book shop.** Cronin: Hatter's castle. [Issues]. Bib N&Q 1no4:8 Oc '35; T. Warburton *ib.* 2no4/5:2 My '36.

CROSS, MARY ANN (EVANS), 1819–80 *see* Eliot, George, *pseud.*

CROSSE, HENRY, fl.1603

9775 **Hummel, Ray O.** Henry Crosse's Vertues commonwealth. Pa Bib Soc Am 43:196–9 '49.

CROWLEY, ROBERT, 1518?–88 *see* Book production and distribution–Printers, publishers, etc.

CRUDEN, ALEXANDER, 1701–70 *see* Book production and distribution–Printers, publishers, etc.

CULLEN, WILLIAM, 1710–90

9776 **Jolley, Leonard J.** Two inquiries about the bibliography of William Cullen. [First lines of the practice of physic]. Biblioth 1no1:28–9 '56.

CUNNINGHAM, ALLAN, 1784–1842

9777 **C., F. H.** Allan Cunningham's The King of the peak. N&Q ser10 5:208 Mr '06; R. A. Potts; W. B. H. *ib.* 5:271 Ap '06; J. Pickford 5:337 Ap '06; W. B. H. 5:352 My '06; J. Pickford 5:518–19 Je '06.

CUNNINGHAM, JOHN, 1729–73

9778 **Shaw, John M.** John Cunningham's Day, a pastoral: illustrator of 1854 edition. (Query 243). Bk Coll 18no4:521 '69.

CUNNINGHAM, PETER, 1816–69

9779 **Law, Ernest P. A.** Some supposed Shakespeare forgeries; an examination into the authenticity of certain documents affecting the dates of composition of several of the plays. [Peter Cunningham and the Revels accounts]. London, G. Bell, 1911. xv,80p. facsims. 21cm.

Rev: TLS 20 Ap '11:157; Athenæum 4362:638–9 '11; Audi alteram partem *ib.* 4369:101–2 '11 4370:130–1 '11; 4380:421–2 '11. *See also no.*9781.

9780 **S.** Peter Cunningham's vindication. [Rev. article on Law]. New Shakespeareana 10no3:93–103 Ag/Oc '11.

9781 **Law, Ernest P. A.** More about Shakespeare forgeries; a reply to certain articles in the Athenæum signed Audi alteram partem, controverting the arguments and conclusions set forth in some supposed Shakespeare forgeries. London, G. Bell, 1913. 70p. facsims. 21cm.

Reply to the articles . . .–Supplementary remarks in further reply to further articles.–Appendix.

Repr. from Athenæum 4376:297–9 S '11; 4377:324 S '11; 4379:388–9 S '11; 4406:390 Ap '12; 4409:470–1 Ap '12.

9782 **Stopes, Charlotte C.** The seventeenth century Revels books. [And Cunningham]. TLS 2 D '20:798; E. P. A. Law *ib.* 23 D '20:876; 30 D '20:891; 27 Ja '21:59–60; C. C. Stopes 24 F '21:127–8.

9783 **Thompson, sir Edward M.** Shaxberd [in Revels mss.]. TLS 10 F '21:91.

9784 **Lawrence, William J.** Was Peter Cunningham a forger? Mod Lang R 19no1:25–34 Ja '24.

I. The Revells booke. Anno 1605.–II. The Revels booke, 1611–12.–III. The King's men's court list, 1636.

9785 **Stopes, Charlotte C.** [and] **W. J. Lawrence.** Mr. W. J. Lawrence and Peter Cunningham. Mod Lang R 19no3:340–4 Jl '24.

9786 **The Malone** scrap. Bod Q Rec 4no44:178–9 Ja '25.

Account of Wood's *article (no.9787) with further evidence of association of sir William Musgrave and Malone.*

9787 **Wood, D. T. B.** The suspected Revels books. [And sir W. Musgrave]. R Eng Stud 1no2:166–72 Ap '25. illus.

9788 **Stamp, Alfred E.** Revels accounts. [And Cunningham]. TLS 21 Mr '29:241.

9789 —— The disputed Revels accounts reproduced ... with a paper read before the Shakespeare association. [London] Ptd. for the Shakespeare association at the O.U.P., 1930. 16p. + XXVI facsims. 35cm.

The authenticity of the disputed Revels accounts.–Bibliographical note.

Rev: W. J. Lawrence Mod Lang R 28:87–8 '32; TLS 5 Mr '31:173; W. Keller Sh Jahrb 67:89 '31; G. C. M. S[mith] Eng Hist R 49:743 '34.

DALLAS, ENEAS SWEETLAND, 1828–79

9790 **Roellinger, Francis X.** A note on Kettner's Book of the table. Mod Lang N 54no5:363–4 My '39.

DALRYMPLE, SIR DAVID, LD. HAILES, 1726–92

9791 **Carnie, Robert H.** Lord Hailes's contributions to contemporary magazines. Stud Bib 9:233–44 '57.

Annotated checklist (p. 238–44)

DALTON, JOHN, 1766–1844

9792 **Neville, Roy G.** An unrecorded Dalton prospectus, 1808. (Note 112). Bk Coll 8no3:295 '59.

9793 **Smyth, Albert L.** Some bibliographical aspects of the work of John Dalton. Manchester R 11:73–9 '66/7.

DANIEL, SAMUEL, 1562–1619

9794 **Prideaux, William F.** Daniel's Sonnets to Delia. [Selection, ed. by H. C. Beeching]. N&Q ser9 4:101–3 Ag '99; H. C. Beeching; C. C. B. *ib.* 4:170–1 Ag '99; W. F. Prideaux 4:209–10 S '99; A. E. Thistleton 4:293 Oc '99.

9795 **Greg, sir Walter W.** Hymen's triumph and the Drummond ms. Mod Lang Q 6no2:59–64 Ag '03.

9796 **Prideaux, William F.** Daniel's Delia, 1592. Athenæum 3952:126–7 Jl '03; Carolyn Shipman *ib.* 3975:18 Ja '04.

9797 —— Daniel's Civil wars, 1595. N&Q ser10 8:405–6 N '07.

9798 **Redgrave, Gilbert R.** Daniel and emblem literature. Bib Soc Trans 11pt1:39–58 '09/10.

9799 —— Daniel and the emblem literature. Bib Soc News-sh 1–3 Mr '10.
Report of paper read 21 F '10.

9800 **Prideaux, William F.** Daniel's Whole workes, 1623. N&Q ser11 4:344–5 Oc '11.

9801 **Sellers, Harry.** Samuel Daniel: additions to the text. Mod Lang R 11no1:28–32 Ja '16.

9802 **Hibernicus,** *pseud.* Daniell; stray notes on the text. N&Q 186:6–8 Ja '44.

9803 **McManaway, James G.** Some bibliographical notes on Samuel Daniel's Civil wars. Stud Bib 4:31–9 '51/2.

9804 **Seronsy, Cecil C.** Daniel's manuscript Civil wars with some previously unpublished stanzas. J Eng Germ Philol 52no2:153–60 Ap '53; Correction *ib.* 52no4:594 Oc '53.

9805 —— Daniel's Panegyrike and the earl of Hertford. [1603]. Philol Q 32no3:342–4 Jl '53.

9806 **Gottfried, Rudolf B.** The authorship of A breviary of the history of England. [And Raleigh]. Stud Philol 53no2:172–90 Ap '56.

9807 **Michel, Laurence.** Daniel's Civil wars. TLS 30 Oc '59:632.

9808 **Schaar, Claes.** A textual puzzle in Daniel's Delia. Eng Stud 40no5:382–5 Oc '59.

9809 **Godshalk, William L.** Daniel's History. J Eng Germ Philol 63no1:45–57 Ja '64.

9810 —— Samuel Daniel and sir Peter Leigh. [Civil wars, 1609]. N&Q 209:333–4 S '64.

9811 **Seronsy, Cecil C.** The case for Daniel's letter to Egerton reopened. [Forgery?] Huntington Lib Q 29no1:79–82 N '65.

9812 —— and **R. Krueger.** A manuscript of Daniel's Civil wars, book III. Stud Philol 63no2:157–62 Ap '66.

DANSKIN, HENRY, d.1625

9813 **Donaldson, Robert.** Henry Danskin's De remoris, a bio-bibliographical note. [And W. Drummond's library]. Biblioth 1no2:15–25 '57.

D'ARBLAY, FRANCES (BURNEY), 1752–1840 *see* Burney, Frances (mrs. D'Arblay), 1752–1840.

DARLEY, GEORGE, 1795–1846

9814 **Simmons, John S. G.** George Darley's Poems '[1890]' (Note 169). Bk Coll 10no4:449 '61.

9815 **Smith, Simon H. Nowell-.** Cancels in Darley's Sylvia, 1827. (Query 146). Bk Coll 10no3:337 '61.

DARWIN, CHARLES ROBERT, 1809–82

9816 **Victorius, Paul B.** A sketch of The origin of species. Coloph [3]pt9:[16p.] '32. facsims.

9817 **Darwin:** Origin of species, 1859. Bib N&Q 2no8:6 F '37.

9818 **West, Geoffrey.** The Darwins. [Two bibliogr. items by Charles Darwin]. TLS 21 Ag '37:608.

9819 **Charles** Darwin's Manual of geology, 1859. Yale Univ Lib Gaz 35no2:94 Oc '60.

9820 **Osborne, Eric A.** The first edition of On the origin of species. (Note 130). Bk Coll 9no1:77–8 '60.

9821 **Todd, William B.** Variant issues of On the Origin of species, 1859. (Note 131). Bk Coll 9no1:78 '60.

9822 **Appleton, D. and co.** Darwin's works in America. Acad 39:468 My '61.

9823 **Osborne, Eric A.** The first edition of On the origin of species. (Notes 130 & 131). Bk Coll 10no4:446 '61.

9824 **Freeman, Richard B.** Issues of the fifth edition of On the origin of species. [Binding variants]. (Note 225). Bk Coll 13no2:213–14 '64; 13no3:350 '64.

9825 —— On the Origin of species, 1859. Bk Coll 16no3:340–4 '67. illus.

9826 **Nethery, Wallace.** On the origin of species, 1859. (Note 297). Bk Coll 17no2:216 '68.

DAUNCE, EDWARD, fl.1585

9827 **Sargent, Ralph M.** The authorship of The prayse of nothing. [And sir Edward Dyer]. Library ser4 12no3:322–31 D '31.

DAVENANT, CHARLES, 1656–1714

9828 **Bird, E. S.** Davenant's Essays. [1704]. N&Q ser9 6:267 Oc '00.

9829 **Waddell, David.** The writings of Charles Davenant, 1656–1714. Library ser5 11no3:206–12 S '56.

D'AVENANT, SIR WILLIAM, 1606–68

9830 **Hooper, Edith S.** The authorship of Luminalia, with notes on some other poems of sir William D'Avenant. Mod Lang R 8no4:540–3 Oc '13.

9831 **Dowlin, Cornell M.** The first edition of Gondibert: quarto or octavo? Library 20no2:167–79 S '39.

9832 **McManaway, James G.** The 'lost' canto of Gondibert. Mod Lang Q 1no1:63–78 Mr '40.

9833 **Mead, Herman R.** [Bibliogr. note on D'Avenant's Gondibert, 1651]. Pa Bib Soc Am 35:68–9 '41.

9834 **Dust, Alvin I.** The Seventh and last canto of Gondibert and two dedicatory poems. [1685]. J Eng Germ Philol 60no2:282–5 Ap '61.

9835 **Woodward, Daniel H.** The manuscript corrections and printed variants in the quarto edition of Gondibert, 1651. Library ser5 20no4:298–309 D '65. tables.

9836 —— A note on the quarto edition of Gondibert, 1651. Library ser5 22no1:69–70 Mr '67. table.

DAVID AP GWILYM, 14th cent.

9837 **Parry, Thomas.** Barddoniaeth Dafydd ab Gwilym, 1789. Welsh Bib Soc J 8no4:189–99 Jl '57.

English summary (p. 224–5)

DAVIDSON, JOHN, 1857–1909

9838 **John** Davidson. [Mss. from Grant Richards' files]. Princeton Univ Lib Chron 12no1:42 '50.

9839 **Townsend, J. Benjamin.** The quest for John Davidson. Princeton Univ Lib Chron 13no3:123–42 '52. illus., port., facsim.

9840 **John** Davidson and Arthur Symons. [Adds. to collns.]. Princeton Univ Lib Chron 15no4:216–17 '54.

9841 **Lester, John A.** John Davidson. TLS 6 Ag '54:501.

DAVIES, JOHN, 1565?–1618

9842 **Ennis, Lambert.** Wit's bedlam of John Davies of Hereford. Huntington Lib Bull 11:13–21 Ap '37.

9843 **Sowerby, E. Millicent.** [Bibliogr. note on Davies' Wit's pilgrimage, 1605?]. Pa Bib Soc Am 36:63 '42.

9844 **Wilkes, G. A.** The Humours heav'n on earth of John Davies of Hereford, and a suppressed poem. N&Q 204:209–10 Je '59.

DAVIES, SIR JOHN, 1569–1626

9845 **Sparrow, John H. A.** Some later editions of sir John Davies's Nosce teipsum. Library ser5 1no2:136–42 S '46.

9846 **Perkinson, Richard H.** Additional observations on the later editions of Nosce teipsum. Library ser5 2no1:61–3 Je '47.

9847 **Eberle, Gerald J.** Sir John Davies' Nosce teipsum, 1599; a bibliographical puzzle. [Ptg.]. Stud Bib 1:135–48 '48. tables.

9848 **Bowers, Robert H.** An Elizabethan manuscript continuation of sir John Davies' Nosce teipsum. [R. Chambers' A Christian reformation of Nosce teipsum]. Mod Philol 58no1:11–19 Ag '60.

9849 **Wilkes, G. A.** William Ravenhill and Nosce teipsum. TLS 20 Oc '61:753.

9850 **Krueger, Robert.** Sir John Davies: Orchestra complete, Epigrams, unpublished poems. R Eng Stud new ser 13no49:17–29 F '62; 13no50: 113–24 My '62.

9851 **Kennedy, R. F.** Another Davies manuscript. R Eng Stud new ser 15no58:180 My '64.

DAVIES, JOHN, 1570?–1644

9852 **Willoughby, Edwin E.** Seeking a publisher in 1629. [Antiquæ linguæ ... dictionarium duplex, 1632]. Lib World 33no385:231–2 F '31.

9853 **Jones, Evan D.** The tercentenary of dr. John Davies, Mallwyd, 1570?–1644. [Exhibition of works]. (Biographica et bibliographica). Nat Lib Wales J 4no1/2:95 '45.

DAVIES, JOHN, 1627?–93

9854 **Fletcher, Ifan W. K.** John Davies. [Projected bibliogr.]. TLS 9 Jl '31:547.

9854a **Tucker, Joseph E.** The earliest English translation of La Rochefoucauld's Maximes. [Epictetus junior, 1670]. Mod Land N 64no6:413–15 Je '49.

9854b —— The earliest English translations of Scarron's Nouvelles. [By J. Davies]. R de Litt Comparée 24:557–63 D '50.

9855 —— John Davies of Kidwelly, 1627?–1693, translator from the French, with an annotated bibliography of his translations. Pa Bib Soc Am 44:119–52 '50.

'Bibliography of Davies' translations from the French' (p. 141–52)

DAVIES, MILES, 1662–1715?

9856 **Jones, J. J.** Myles Davies. Welsh Bib Soc J 6no5:249–53 Jl '48; E. R. Harries *ib.* 6no6:309 Jl '49.

DAVIES, WILLIAM HENRY, 1871–1940

9857 **Davies, W. H.:** New poems, 1907. [Issues]. Bib N&Q 2no12:8 My '39.

DAVIS, THOMAS OSBORNE, 1814–45

9858 **Noonan, J. D.** The library of Thomas Davis. Irish Bk Lover 5no3:37–9 Oc '13.

9859 **O'Hegarty, Patrick S.** Thomas Davis. The reform of the House of lords, 1837. (Bibliographical notes). Dublin Mag new ser 22no3:61 Jl/S '47.

DAY, JOHN, fl.1606

9860 **Day's** Ile of guls. (Notes on sales). TLS 3 Ag '22:512.

9861 **Greg, sir Walter W.** The two issues of Day's Isle of gulls, 1606. Library ser4 3no4:307–9 Mr '23. facsim.

9862 **Peery, William W.** Correction at press in the quarto of Law-trickes. Library ser5 2no2/3:186–90 S/D '47. tables.

DAY, JOHN, d.1640

9863 **Borish, M. E.** A second version of John Day's Peregrinatio scholastica. [Ms.]. Mod Lang N 55no1:35–9 Ja '40.

DAY, RICHARD, 1552–1607? *see* Book production and distribution– Printers, publishers, etc.

DEANE, EDMUND, 1572?–1640

9864 **Neville, Roy G.** Spadacrene Anglica. (Note no.47). Bk Coll 4no2:170–1 '55.

DE BEAU CHESNE, JOHN, fl.1571

9865 **Goff, Frederick R.** [Bibliogr. note on De Beau Chesne and Baildon's A book containing divers sorts of hands . . . 1531]. Pa Bib Soc Am 35:293 '41.

DEE, JOHN, 1527–1608

9866 **Prideaux, W. R. B.** Books from John Dee's library. N&Q ser9 8:137–8 Ag '01; ser10 1:241–2 Mr '04; [Same] *ib.* 146:170,234 Mr '24.

9867 **James, Montague R.** List of manuscripts formerly owned by dr. John Dee, with preface and identifications. [Oxford] Ptd. at the O.U.P for the Bibliographical society, 1921. 39[1]p. 23cm. (Bib Soc Trans Suppl 1)

'Additional note' (after p. 39)

9868 **Washburn, Wilcomb E.** A ms. by John Dee, 1581. [De modo evangeli Jesu Christi publicandi]. N&Q 199:406 S '54.

9869 **Watson, Andrew G.** An identification of some manuscripts owned by dr. John Dee and sir Simonds D'Ewes. Library ser5 13no3:194–8 S '58.

DEFOE, DANIEL, 1661?–1731

9870 **The first** edition of Robinson Crusoe. Bkworm 1no5:173–6 Ap '88. illus., facsim.

9871 **Aitken, George A.** Defoe and Mist's weekly journal. Athenæum 3435:287–8 Ag '93.

9872 **Bülbring, Karl D.** An autograph ms. of Defoe's in the British museum. [Of royal education]. Acad 46:280–1 Oc '94.

9873 **Aitken, George A.** Defoe's library. Athenæum 3527:706–7 Je '95; C. A. Ward *ib.* 3529:773 Je '95.

9874 **Layard, George S.** Robinson Crusoe and its illustrators. Bibliographica 2pt2:181–203 '96. illus.

9875 **Marshall, Edward H.** Robinson Crusoe. N&Q ser9 2:248 S '98.

9876 **Murdoch, Robert.** Record price for a book. [Robinson Crusoe, 1719]. Scott N&Q ser2 4no4:51 Oc '02.

9877 **Purves, W. Laidlaw.** The O edition of Robeson Cruso. Athenæum 3937:465–6 Ap '03; 3938:498 Ap '03.

9878 **Duff, E. Gordon.** Defoe's novels issued in parts. [A new voyage round the world]. N&Q ser10 7:389 My '07.

9879 **Prideaux, William F.** Defoe's Colonel Jacque. N&Q ser10 8:87 Ag '07; 8:411–12 N '07.

9880 **Davis, Andrew McF.** A bibliographical puzzle. [News from the moon, 1721, repr. of Defoe's Review, 1710]. Colonial Soc Massachusetts Trans 13:2–15 Ja '10/11.

9881 **Purves, W. Laidlaw.** The literary output of Daniel Defoe. Library ser3 3no11:333–5 Jl '12. table.

9882 **Pollard, Alfred W.** Robeson Cruso. Library ser3 4no14:204–20 Ap '13.

9883 **Purves, W. Laidlaw** [and] **A. W. Pollard.** Robeson Cruso, a rejoinder. Library ser3 4no15:338–52 Jl '13.

9884 **Williams, Aneurin.** Cassell's illustrated Robinson crusoe. [1860]. N&Q ser12 3:110 F '17; J Makeham, R. J. Parker; J: F. Palmer; J. B. Wainewright *ib.* 3:194 Mr '17; Cassell and co. 3:308 My '17.

9885 **A forgotten** satire of Defoe. [Parson Plaxton of Barwich ms.]. (Notes on sales). TLS 19 F '20:128.

9886 **Hutchins, Henry C.** Robinson Crusoe and its printing, 1719–1731; a bibliographical study. New York, Columbia U.P., 1925. xix,201p. facsims. 26cm.

Introduction.–I. A brief survey of the conditions of printing in England during the first quarter of the eighteenth century.–II. William Taylor, the publisher of Robinson Crusoe.–III. The first edition, part 1.–IV. The later editions of the first part of Robinson Crusoe: I. Bibliographical. II. The sequence of the Taylor editions and their issues.–V. The second part of Robinson Crusoe. I. The first edition. II. The later editions of Part II.–VI. The third part of Robinson Crusoe.–VII. The abridgments of Robinson Crusoe.–VIII. The 1719 pirated editions of the first part of Robinson Crusoe and its first serial publication. I. The Dublin piracy. II. The Amsterdam coffee house edition. III. The first serial Robinson Crusoe.–IX. The pirated editions of Robinson Crusoe, continued. The O edition.–Appendix I: The Taylor entries in the Stationers' register.–Appendix II: A list of readings by which a copy of the first edition of Robinson Crusoe (part I) can be checked.–Appendix III: A list of readings by which copies of The farther adventures of Robinson Crusoe can be checked.

Rev: TLS 22 Oc '25:695; T. Scott Saturday R Lit 2:339 '25; N&Q 149:467–8 '25; sir H. H. Williams Lib Assn Rec new ser 4:24–5 '26.

9887 **Hubbard, Lucius L.** Text changes in the Taylor editions of Robinson Crusoe, with remarks on the Cox edition. Pa Bib Soc Am 20pt1/2:1–76 '26. facsims., tables, diagr.

9888 **Dublin** edition of Robinson Crusoe. [1719]. (Notes on sales). TLS 29 S '27:672; E. R. McC. Dix *ib.* 13 Oc '27:715; 20 Oc '27:742.

9889 **Hutchins, Henry C.** Two hitherto unrecorded editions of Robinson Crusoe. Library ser4 8no1:58–72 Je '27.

9890 **Burch, Charles E.** Wodrow's list of Defoe's pamphlets on the Union. Mod Philol 28no1:99–100 Ag '30.

9891 **Haraszti, Zoltán.** A great Defoe library. [Boston public]. More Bks Boston Pub Lib Bull 6no1:1–14 Ja '31. facsims.

9892 **Nicholls, Norah.** Some early editions of Defoe. Bkmn 80no475:42–3 Ap '31. facsim.

9893 **Fletcher, Edward G.** Some University of Texas copies of Robinson Crusoe, part I. N&Q 164:4–5 Ja '33.

9894 **MacManus, Michael J.** The first Dublin Robinson Crusoe, a discovery. (Bibliographical notes). Dublin Mag new ser 8no3:66 Jl/S '33.

9895 **Bonner, Willard H.** Moll, Knapton, and Defoe; a note on early serial publication. R Eng Stud 10no39:320–3 Jl '34.

9896 **Fletcher, Edward G.** The London and Edinburgh printings of Defoe's Review, volume VI. Univ Texas Stud Eng 14:50–8 Jl '34. tables.

9897 —— Some notes on Defoe's Review. N&Q 166:218–21 Mr '34.

9898 **Friday,** *pseud. of* **Henry C. Hutchins.** The Yale Robinson Crusoe. Yale Univ Lib Gaz 8no3:85–94 Ja '34. facsims.

9899 —— Robinson Crusoe at Yale. Yale Univ Lib Gaz 11no2:17–37 Oc '36. facsims.

Editions of Robinson Crusoe in English.–Some piracies and abridgements.–Editions in French and some other translations.–Some imitations of Robinson Crusoe, called Robinsonades.

9900 **M., F. A.** German translations of Defoe. N&Q 171:421 D '36; T. P. A. *ib.* 172:11 Ja '37.

9901 **Secord, Arthur W.** Defoe's Review. (Antiquarian notes). TLS 11 Je '38:408; H. Bergholz *ib.* 18 Je '38:424; A. W. Secord 30 Jl '38:508.

9902 **Moore, John R.** Defoe and the eighteenth-century pamphlets on London. Philol Q 20no1:38–45 Ja '41.

9903 **Anderson, Paul B.** [and] **J. R. Moore.** A reply to John Robert Moore [on points of Defoe bibliography]. Philol Q 21no4:419–24 Oc '42.

9904 **Van Patten, Nathan.** An Eskimo translation of Defoe's Robinson Crusoe, Godthaab, Greenland, 1862–1865. Pa Bib Soc Am 36:56–8 '42. illus., facsim.

9905 **Burch, Charles E.** Defoe and his northern printers. Pub Mod Lang Assn 60no1:124–8 Mr '45.

9906 **Friday,** *pseud. of* **Henry C. Hutchins.** Defoe at Yale. Yale Univ Lib Gaz 22no4:99–115 Ap '48. facsims.

I. The Yale Defoe collection.–II. Defoeana and Defoe's library.

9907 —— On the completeness of a special collection [and Defoe studies]. Yale Univ Lib Gaz 23no3:149–50 Ja '49.

9908 **Payne, William L.** Another Defoe item. [Proposals for printing ... a Complete history of the Union, 1707 ?]. N&Q 194:326 Jl '49; G. H. Healey *ib.* 195:195 Ap '50.

9909 **Davies, Godfrey.** Daniel Defoe's A tour thro' the whole island of Great Britain. Mod Philol 48no1:21–36 Ag '50.

9910 **Friday,** *pseud. of* **Henry C. Hutchins.** The True-born Englishman at Yale. Yale Univ Lib Gaz 24no3:132–40 Ja '50.

9911 **Mornand, Pierre.** Les Robinson Crusoe. [Illus. ed.]. Portique 7:49–64 '50. illus.

9912 **Healey, George H.** Defoe's handwriting. TLS 19 D '52:837.

9913 **Maslen, Keith I. D.** The printers of Robinson Crusoe. Library ser5 7no2:124–31 Je '52. facsims., table.

9914 **Moore, John R.** Defoe's Essay upon projects: an unrecorded issue. N&Q 200:109–10 Mr '55.

9915 **Oldham, Ellen M.** Problems of a Defoe cataloger. Boston Pub Lib Q 7no4:192–206 Oc '55. facsim.

9916 **Moore, John R.** The canon of Defoe's writings. Library ser5 11no3:155–69 S '56.

9917 **Pafford, John H. P.** Defoe's Proposals for printing the History of the Union. Library ser5 11no3:202–6 S '56. facsim.

9918 **Peterson, Spiro.** A lost edition, 1745, of Defoe's Roxana. N&Q 201:44 Ja '56.

9919 **Robinson** Crusoe. [Acquisition of first ed.]. Princeton Univ Lib Chron 17no4:270–1 '56.

9920 **Brown, T. Julian.** Daniel Defoe, 1661?–1731. (English literary autographs, XXIV). Bk Coll 6no4:387 '57. facsims.

9921 **Peterson, Spiro.** A lost edition (1745) of Defoe's Roxana. (Query 99). Bk Coll 7no3:295 '58; W. R. Cagle *ib.* 11no4:483–4 '62.

9922 **O'Donovan, Anne.** Sale catalogue of Defoe's library. (Note 147). Bk Coll 9no4:454–5 '60.

9923 **Barber, Giles G.** French illustrations in English books of the romantic period. [Robinson Crusoe]. (Note 159). Bk Coll 10no2:200–1 '61.

9924 **Moore, John R.** Defoe acquisitions at the Huntington library. Huntington Lib Q 28no1:45–57 N '64.

9925 **Foxon, David F.** Defoe: a specimen of a catalogue of English verse, 1701–1750. [And bibliogr. descr.]. Library ser5 20no4:277–97 D '65.

9926 **Moore, John R.** Defoe's Some seasonable queries, a chapter concerning the humanities. Newberry Lib Bull 6no6:179–86 D '65.

9927 **Shipley, John B.** Daniel Defoe and Henry Baker: some of their correspondence again and its provenance. Bod Lib Rec 7no6:317–29 F '67.

9928 **Baine, Rodney M.** Chalmers' first bibliography of Daniel Defoe. Texas Stud Lit & Lang 10no4:547–68 '69.

9929 **Maslen, Keith I. D.** Edition quantities for Robinson Crusoe, 1719. Library ser5 24no2:145–50 Je '69.

DE GIBLER, (MAJOR BYRON), fl.1809–52 *see* Byron, George Gordon DeLuna, *pseud.*

DEHAN, RICHARD, *pseud. of* **CLOTILDA INEZ MARY GRAVES, 1863–1932**

9930 **Todd, William B.** Dehan's Dop doctor, a forgotten bestseller. Lib Chron Univ Texas 7no3:17–26 '63. tables.

1. Opinions of the press.–2. Bibliographical record.–3. Printing record.

DEKKER, THOMAS, 1570?–1641?

9931 **Hazlitt, W. Carew.** Dekker and Webster's Sir Thomas Wyatt, 1607. [Text]. Bkworm 7no84:367–8 Oc '94.

9932 **Sisson, Charles J.** Keep the widow waking, a lost play by Dekker. Library ser4 8no1:39–57 Je '27; 8no2:233–59 S '27. facsims.

9933 **Baird, Matthew.** The early editions of Thomas Dekker's The converted courtezan or The honest whore, part 1. Library ser4 10no1:52–60 Je '29; F. Marcham *ib.* 10no3:339 D '29. tables.

9934 **Greg, sir Walter W.** The Honest whore, or The converted courtezan. Library ser4 15no1:54–60 Jl '34.

9935 **Spencer, Hazelton.** The undated quarto of 1 Honest whore. Library ser4 16no2:241–2 S '35.

9936 **Bowers, Fredson T.** Bibliographical problems in Dekker's Magnificent entertainment. Library ser4 17no3:333–9 D '36. tables.

9937 —— Thomas Dekker: two textual notes. Library ser4 18no3:338–41 D '37. table.

    I. The roaring girle, 1611.–II. The honest whore, 1605.

9938 **Greg, sir Walter W.** Dekker's Magnificent entertainment. Library ser4 17no4:476–8 Mr '37.

9939 **McManaway, James G.** Thomas Dekker: further textual notes. [The roaring girl]. Library ser4 19no2:176–9 S '38.

    Repr. in Hosley, Richard, A. C. Kirsch [and] J. W. Velz, *ed.* Studies in Shakespeare, bibliography and theater. New York, 1969. p. [31]–3.

9940 **Halstead, W. L.** Note on the text of The famous history of sir Thomas Wyatt. Mod Lang N 54no8:585–9 D '39.

9941 **Bowers, Fredson T.** Thomas Dekker, Robert Wilson and The shoemakers holiday. [And J. P. Collier]. Mod Lang N 64no8:517–19 D '49.

9942 **George, J.** Four notes on the text of Dekker's Shoemaker's holiday. N&Q 194:192 Ap '49.

9943 **Bowers, Fredson T.** The Cambridge edition of Dekker. [And editing]. Library ser5 10no2:130–3 Je '55.

9944 **Freeman, Arthur.** An emendation in Dekker. [If this be not a good play]. N&Q 207:334 S '62.

9945 **Murray, Peter B.** The collaboration of Dekker and Webster in Northward ho and Westward ho. Pa Bib Soc Am 56:482–6 '62. tables.

9946 **Hoeniger, F. David.** Thomas Dekker, the restoration of St. Paul's and J. P. Collier, the forger. [Paul his temple triumphant]. Renaiss N 16no3:181–200 '63.

> The dedication and epistle.–The poem's date of composition.–Date and author of manuscript.–The restoration of St. Paul's and sir Paul Pindar.–Postscript.

9947 **Sturman, Berta.** A date and a printer for A looking glasse for London and England, Q4. [Ralph Blower]. Stud Bib 21:248–53 '68.

DELAFIELD, THOMAS, fl.1818

9948 **Delafield, John R.** Rev. Thomas Delafield's manuscripts. N&Q ser11 3:347 My '11; W. C. B. *ib.* 3:412 My '11.

DE LA MOTHE, GEORGE, fl.1595

9949 **Royster, James F.** The first edition of De La Mothe's French alphabeth and of Hollybrand's French schoolemaister. Philol Q 7no1:1–51 Ja '28.

DE LA RAMÉE, MARIE LOUISE, 1839–1908 *see* Ouida, *pseud.*

DENHAM, SIR JOHN, 1615–69

9950 **Banks, Theodore H.** Sir John Denham. [Holographs]. TLS 9 F '33:92.

9951 **ÓHehir, Brendan.** Lost, authorized, and pirated editions of John Denham's Cooper's Hill. Pub Mod Lang Assn 79no3:242–53 Je '64.

9952 —— The early acquaintance of Denham and Waller. N&Q 211:19–23 Ja '66.

DENNIS, JOHN, 1657–1734

9953 **Hooker, Edward N.** An unpublished autograph manuscript of John Dennis. [The causes of the decay and defects]. Eng Lit Hist 1no2:156–62 S '34.

DE QUINCEY, THOMAS, 1785–1859

9954 **Axon, William E. A.** The De Quincey collection at Moss Side. [Manchester]. Lib Assn Rec 2no8:410–24 Ag '00.

9955 **Kempling, William B.** De Quincey's editorship of the Westmorland gazette. N&Q ser10 2:101 Ag '04.

9956 **Axon, William E. A.** De Quincey and T. F. Dibdin. [The street companion and Dibdin's The library companion]. Library ser2 8no31:267–74 Jl '07.

9957 —— De Quincey's Opium-eater, 1853. N&Q ser11 4:466 D '11.

9958 **Meyerstein, Edward H. W.** De Quincey's copy of Chatterton's Miscellanies. TLS 8 My '30:394.

9959 **Jones, Claude E.** Some De Quincey manuscripts. Eng Lit Hist 8no3:216–25 S '41.

9960 **Grantham, Evelyn.** De Quincey to his publisher. [J. A. Hessey]. More Bks Boston Pub Lib Bull 20no10:440–1 D '45.

9961 **Musgrove, Sidney** and **M. K. Joseph.** A De Quincey manuscript. TLS 30 Mr '51:197.

9962 **Jack, Ian.** De Quincey revises his Confessions. Pub Mod Lang Assn 72no1:122–46 Mr '57.

9963 **Brown, T. Julian.** Thomas DeQuincey, 1785–1859. (English literary autographs, XXXIV). Bk Coll 9no2:179 '60. facsims.

DERBY, CHARLES STANLEY, 8TH EARL OF, fl.1669 *see* Stanley, Charles, 8th earl of Derby, fl.1669.

DERBY, WILLIAM STANLEY, 6TH EARL OF, c.1561–1642 *see* Stanley, William, 6th earl of Derby, c.1561–1642.

DE SAINLIENS, CLAUDE, fl.1568–97 *see* Holyband, Claude, *pseud*.

DE VALERA, EAMONN, 1882–1975

9964 **A De Valera** broadside. (Bibliographical notes). Irish Bk 1no3:78 '60/1.

DEVONSHIRE, GEORGIANA CAVENDISH, DUCHESS OF, 1757–1806 *see* Cavendish, Georgiana, duchess of Devonshire, 1757–1806.

DIBDIN, CHARLES, 1745–1814

9965 **Dibdin, Edward R.** Dibdin bibliography. N&Q ser11 12:47 Jl '15.

DIBDIN, THOMAS FROGNALL, 1776–1847

9966 **Abrahams, Aleck.** Thomas Frognal Dibdin. N&Q ser12 10:461–3 Je '22.

9967 **Kent, Henry W.** Another day; a retrospective note on Thomas Frognall Dibdin and the printers of the Shakespeare press. Coloph [1]pt2:[16p.] '30. port., facsims.

9968 **Woodhead, Margaret L.** T. F. Dibdin. TLS 4 Ap '52:237.

9969 **Dibdin** correspondence [recently acquired]. (Notes and news). Bull John Rylands Lib 42no2:261–2 Mr '60.

9970 **Hall, Ronald.** T. F. Dibdin, book-collector. Manchester R 9:193–210 '61.

9971 **O'Dwyer, Edward J.** Thomas Frognall Dibdin; bibliographer & bibliomaniac extraordinary, 1776–1847. Pinner, Private libraries association [1967]. 45p. port., facsims. 22cm.

'A check-list of T. F. Dibdin's bibliographical works' (p. 43–4)

Rev: L. F. Craik Lib R 21:148–9 '67; J. O'Riordan Lib World 69:109 '67.

DICKENS, CHARLES JOHN HUFFAM, 1817–70

9972 **Johnson, Charles P.** First editions. I. Charles Dickens. Bkworm 1no3:80–3 F '88; II. *ib.* 1no4:132–3 Mr '88.

9973 **Illustrations** to Dickens in the market. Bkworm 2no23:345–8 Oc '89.

9974 **Johnson, Charles P.** To be read at dusk, by Charles Dickens. [1852]. Athenæum 3316:636 My '91.

9975 **Sabin, Frank T.** Dickensiana. [Mr. Nightingale's diary, 1851]. Athenæum 3320:765 Je '91.

9976 **Kitton, Frederic G.** Dickens's Household words. N&Q ser8 9:327 Ap '96.

9977 **Fitzgerald, Percy H.** Pickwickiana. Gent Mag 282:178–202 F '97.

9978 **Kitton, Frederic G.** The novels of Charles Dickens, a bibliography and sketch. London, E. Stock, 1897. ix,245p. 18cm.

Bibliogr. remarks throughout, but no checklist.

9979 —— Pseudo-Dickens rarities. Athenæum 3646:355–6 S '97.

9980 —— A pseudo-Dickens item. N&Q ser9 1:144–5 F '98.

9981 **Axon, William E. A.** Dickens in Welsh. N&Q ser9 3:225 Mr '99.

9982 **Grego, Joseph.** Pictorial Pickwickiana; Charles Dickens and his illustrators ... Notes on contemporaneous illustrations and Pickwick artists. London, Chapman and Hall, 1899. 2v. illus., facsims. 19cm.

V.1: Universal popularity obtained by Pickwick at a bound.–Origin of the Pickwick club.–Robert Seymour.–Robert William Buss.–W. M. Thackeray's proposal to illustrate Pickwick, 1836.–John Leech.–Phiz–Hablôt Knight Browne.–William Heath, Pickwickian illustrations.–Alfred Crowquill (Alfred H. Forrester).–Thomas Onwyn; Samuel Weller's illustrations to The Pickwick club, 1837.–Thomas Onwyn.–F. W. Pailthorpe.–Thomas Sibson.–V.2: Pickwick characters, by Kenny Meadows.–Pickwick on the stage.–Illustrations; pictorial versions of Pickwick theatrical characters.–Pickwick piracies, plagiarisms, forgeries, imitations, and so-called continuations.–Pickwickiana.–Pickwick revived, by Charles Dickens, 1840.–First cheap edition, 1847.–The first library edition, 1858.–The household edition, 1874.–Extra illustrations, published by Robson and Kerslake, 1882.–H. M. Paget.–Christopher Coveny, Sydney, 1883.–American illustrators.

9983 **Kitton, Frederic G.** Dickens and his illustrators. . . . London, 1899. (Repr. Amsterdam, S. Emmering; New York, A. Schram, 1972). xvi,256p. illus., ports., facsims., tables. 28cm.

George Cruikshank.–Robert Seymour.–Robert W. Buss.–Hablôt K. Browne ('Phiz').–George Cattermole.–Illustrators of the Christmas books.–John Leech.–Richard Doyle.–Clarkson Stanfield, R.A.–Daniel Maclise, R.A.–Sir John Tenniel.–Frank Stone, A.R.A.–Sir Edwin Landseer, R.A.–Samuel Palmer.–F. W. Topham.–Marcus Stone, R.A.–Samuel Palmer.–F. W. Topham.–Marcus Stone, R.A.–Luke Fildes, R.A.–Appendix I. Illustrators of cheap editions.–II. Concerning extra illustrations.–III. Dickens in art.

9984 —— The minor writings of Charles Dickens, a bibliography and sketch. London, E. Stock; New York, A. C. Armstrong [1900]. xi,260p. 18cm.

Bibliogr. remarks throughout, but no checklist.

9985 **Spenser, W. T.** A lost play by Dickens. [Is she his wife, 1835]. Athenæum 3846:72 Jl '01; G. M. Fenn *ib.* 3847:104 Jl '01.

9986 **Welsh, Charles.** American edition of Dickens. N&Q ser9 9:387 My '02; F. G. Kitton *ib.* 10:96 Ag '02. [Sg.: C. W.]

9987 **Sewell, C. W. H.** Edwin Drood continued. N&Q ser9 12:389 N '03; J. T. Page *ib.* 12:510–11 D '03; W. C. B.; T. N. Brushfield ser10 1:37 Ja '04; H. S. Ward 1:331–2 Ap '04.

9988 **The manuscript** of the Battle of life. Dickensiana 1no5:122 My '05.

9989 **Matz, Bertram W.** Sketches by Boz; a bibliographical note. Dickensian 1no3:64–5 Mr '05. facsim.

9990 **Prideaux, William F.** Bibliographical notes on Dickens and Thackeray. N&Q ser10 3:22–3 Ja '05; R. E. Francillon; W. Jerrold *ib.* 3:72–3 Ja '05; W. F. Prideaux; E. R. Dibdin 3:131–2 F '05; W. H. Cummings 3:151 F '05; W. Jerrold; W. Douglas 3:196 Mr '05; S. J. A. F. 3:275 Ap '05; R. Pierpont 3:337–8 Ap '05; R. Walters 3:377 My '05.

9991 **Fitzgerald, Percy H.** Boz's publishers. Dickensian 3no1:10–14 Ja '07; 3no2:33–7 F '07; 3no3:70–3 Mr '07; 3no4:93 Ap '07; 3no5:126–9 My '07; 3no6:158–61 Je '07. facsims.

I. Macrone and others.–II. Richard Bentley and his Miscellany.–III. From Richard Bentley to Chapman and Hall.–V. Bradbury & Evans and some others.

9992 **How** Dickens corrected his proofs. Dickensian 3no11:297–8 N '07. facsims.

Excerpted from Emma S. Williamson's Glimpses of Dickens. (Not in Bodleian, B.M. or L.C. catalogues).

9993 **Matz, Bertram W.** An untraced article by Dickens. [Proof of The spirit of chivalry]. Athenæum 4158:15 Jl '07.

9994 **Wilkins, William G.** First and early American editions of the works of Dickens. Dickensian 3no7:186–8 Jl '07.

*Rev. as no.*9999.

9995 **Second** Dickensian exhibition. [New Dudley gallery, Piccadilly]. Dickensian 4no9:234–6 S '08. illus.

9996 **Wilkins, William G.** More about early American editions of the works of Dickens. Dickensian 4no7:190–1 Jl '08.

9997 —— First American edition of American notes. Dickensian 5no8:210–11 Ag '09.

9997a **Hammerton, sir John A.**, *ed.* The Dickens picture-book, a record of the Dickens illustrators. London, Educational book [1910]. viii,466p. illus., port. 19cm. (Charles Dickens library, v.17)

I. The artistic partnerships.–II. Phiz and his work.–III. Illustrators of the Christmas books.–IV. Mr. Marcus Stone, R.A.–Mr. Luke Fildes, R.A.–Samuel Palmer–F. W. Topham.–V. Illustrators of the later editions.–VI. The art of mr. Harry Furniss.–VII. Extra illustration.–VIII. Dickens in art.–IX. Sketches by Boz.–X. The Pickwick papers.–XI. Oliver Twist.–XII. Nicholas Nickleby.–XIII. The old curiosity shop.–XIV. Barnaby Rudge.–XV. Martin Chuzzlewit.–XVI. Dombey and son.–XVII. David Copperfield.–XVIII. Bleak house.–XIX. Little Dorrit.–XX. A tale of two cities.–XXI. The other novels.–XXII. Selected illustrations from the Christmas books.

9998 **T., O. S.** Edwin Drood continued. N&Q ser11 1:69 Ja '10; J. T. Page *ib.* 1:153 F '10; W. B. H. 1:394 My '10.

9999 **Wilkins, William G.** First and early American editions of the works of Charles Dickens. Cedar Rapids, Ia., Privately ptd., 1910. 51p. facsims. 25cm.

Rev. from Dickensian 3no7:186–8 Jl '07.

10000 —— First collected edition of Travelling letters written on the road. Dickensian 6no1:17 Ja '10.

10001 **B., C. C.** Pickwick papers: printers' errors in first edition. N&Q ser11 4:248 S '11; R. Pierpont; C. S. Burdon *ib.* 4:292–3 Oc '11; W. F. Prideaux; R. Austin; F. Verisopht 4:352–3 Oc '11.

10002 **Miller, William.** The Household words almanac. Dickensian 7no2:44 F '11.

10003 —— A unique Dickens item. [James Waterson's Lucie Manette, a dramatic overture]. Dickensian 7no4:94–6 Ap '11.

10004 **The Dickens** exhibition at the Victoria and Albert museum. Dickensian 8no5:131–2 My '12.

10005 **Southton, J. Y.** Authorised Leipzig edition of Dickens. [Tauchnitz]. Dickensian 8no7:181–3 Jl '12.

10006 **A unique** Pickwick. [Extra-illustrated copy owned by W. G. Wilkins]. Dickensiana 9no8:206–7 Ag '13.

10007 **Wilkins, William G.** Dickens and his first American publishers. Dickensian 9no10:257–61 Oc '13.

10008 **A Dickens** exhibition at Olympia. Dickens 10no5:122 My '14.

10009 **Exhibition** of Dickensiana [at Children's welfare exhibition, Olympia]. Dickensiana 10no4:94 Ap '14.

10010 **Matz, Bertram W.** Books presented by Dickens to Ainsworth and his daughter. Dickensian 12no6:157–8 Je '16. facsims.

10011 **Original** Dickens sale in New York; Pickwick fetches over £1000. Dickensian 12no6:156 Jl '16.

10012 **Dickens** rarities in America. Dickensian 13no2:46–7 F '17.

10013 **Miller, William** and **T. W. Hill.** Charles Dickens's manuscripts. Dickensian 13no7:181–5 Jl '17; 13no8:217–19 Ag '17. facsims.

Chronological table (p. 217–19) *showing locations of mss.*

10014 **New** auction record for Pickwick papers. Dickensian 13no7:192 Jl '17.

10015 **Ker, William P.** A misprint in Little Dorrit. TLS 19 S '18:441.

10016 **Wilkins, William G.** Variations in the Cruikshank plates to Oliver Twist. Dickensian 15no2:71–4 Ap '19. facsim.

10017 **Dickens's** Christmas carol. (Notes on sales). TLS 23 D '20:880.

10018 **L., S.** The first edition of Dombey and son. TLS 22 Ja '20:52; sir H. B. Poland; W. Sinclair *ib.* 29 Ja '20:68; W. J. Garnett 5 F '20:87.

10019 **Matz, Bertram W.** A notable Dickens collection. [R. T. Jupp]. Dickensian 16no4:198–200 Oc '20. facsim.

10020 **Secutor,** *pseud.* Early issues of first editions. Bkmns J 2no28:23 My '20; 2no29:41 My '20.

> Dickens' Christmas books.–A Christmas carol.–The chimes.–The cricket on the hearth.–The battle of life.–The haunted man.

10021–2 Cancelled.

10023 **Weaver, H. F.** Dickens, a bibliographical query. [Hunted down; The uncommercial traveller, Tauchnitz, 1860]. Bkmns J 2no42:248 Ag '20. [Sg.: H. F. W.]

10024 **The Wiener** Dickens collection . . . . Dickensian 16no2:83–5 Ap '20.

> *Repr. from* The Boston evening transcript.

10025 **Dartle, R.** Dickens: page-headings. N&Q ser12 9:208–9 S '21; T. W. Tyrrell *ib.* 9:515–16 D '21.

10026 **Pennell, Joseph.** The real first issue of A Christmas carol. Bkmns J 4no91:207–8 Jl '21; C. J. Sawyer; E. G. Sykes *ib.* 4no93:236 Ag '21; A. M. Cohn 4no94:252 Ag '21; J. Pennell 6no7:34 Ap '22.

10027 **Cohn, Albert M.** A Christmas carol. Bkmns J new ser 5no4:141 Ja '22; C. J. Sawyer *ib.* 5no5:170 F '22.

10028 **Dickens's** imitators. (Notes on sales). TLS 13 Ap '22:248.

10029 **Dickens's** manuscripts. (Notes on sales). TLS 1 Je '22:368.

10030 **Sargent, George H.** Dickensiana in America. Bkmns J new ser 6no7:23–4 Ap '22.

10031 **Christmas** books by Dickens and others. (Notes on sales). TLS 20 D '23:900.

10032 **Exhibition** of Dickensiana in America; a famous Pickwick [exhibited by Harry F. Marks, New York]. Dickensian 19no3:140–1 Jl '23.

10033 **Dickens's** Christmas numbers. (Notes on sales). TLS 25 D '24:888; R. Pierpont *ib.* 8 Ja '25:24.

10034 **Eckel, John C.** The reading edition of Dickens' Great expectations. Bkmns J new ser 11no38:93 N '24.

10035 **A Dickens** souvenir. [Presentation copy of A Christmas carol]. Harvard Lib N [2no]14:37–8 Mr '25.

10036 **Matz, Bertram W.** Writings wrongly attributed to Dickens. Dickensian 21no2:128–32 Ap '25.

10037 **Palmer, Cecil.** The B. W. Matz loan collection now at the Dickens house. Dickensian 21no4:193–5 Oc '25.

10038 **Hopkins, Albert A.** The George Barr McCutcheon sale. Dickensian 22no3:169–72 Jl/S '26. facsims.

10039 —— An important sale of Dickens manuscripts. [Newbury Frost Read, New York]. Dickensian 22no2:113–15 Ap/Je '26. facsims.

10040 **Where** the mss. of Dickens are. (Marginalia). Bkmns J ser3 15no4:221 '27.

10041 **Davis, George W.** The Posthumous papers of the Pickwick club; some new bibliographical discoveries. London, Marks, 1928. 20p. 21cm. Covertitle.

   Rev: TLS 13 D '28:996.

10042 **Gawthorp, Walter E.** Nicholas Nickleby; a strange misprint. N&Q 155:365 N '28.

10043 **Hopkins, Albert A.** Notes on the Thomas Hatton sale. Dickensian 24no206:116–18 Mr '28. facsims.

10044 **Miller, William.** First editions of the works written at 48 Doughty street, presented to the Dickens house by sir George Sutton, bart. Dickensian 24no206:101–2 Mr '28.

10045 **The minor** mystery of Edwin Drood. [Ms. with portions pasted over]. (Marginalia). Bkmns J ser3 16no7:393 '28.

10046 **Pickwick** and others. [Mss.]. (Notes on sales). TLS 20 D '28:1016.

10047 **Williams, Aneurin.** Kyd, illustrator of Dickens. [J. Clayton Clarke]. N&Q 154:138 F '28; T. W. Tyrrell; A. Sparke *ib.* 154:213 Mr '28; R. 154:249 Ap '28.

10048 **Dickens'** autographs. TLS 20 D '28:1016; J. P. Gilson *ib.* 3Ja '29:12.

10049 **Dickens** and others. (Notes on sales). TLS 20 Je '29:500.

10050 **The Penny** Pickwick. [Imitation pub. by E. Lloyd in parts]. (Notes on sales). TLS 19 D '29:1088.

10051 **Two** important sales. Dickensian 25no210:98–9 Mr '29.

I. The Jerome Kern sale, by A. A. Hopkins.–II. At Sotheby's, by W. Miller.

10052 **Rendall, Vernon.** Dickens: Pickwickiana. N&Q 158:96 F '30. [Sg.: V. R.]

10053 [**Sawyer, Charles J.** and **F. J. H. Darton**]. Dickens v. Barabbas, Forster intervening; a study based upon some hitherto unpublished letters. London, C. J. Sawyer, 1930. 79,4p. facsims. 22cm.

Mr. Dickens and mr. Bentley [a letter to The times, 7 D 1871, by George Bentley], 4p. *at end.*

10054 **Dexter, Walter,** *ed.* Dickens to his first publisher, John Macrone; some hitherto unpublished letters. [London, Privately ptd.] 1931. 9p. facsims. 25cm.

Repr. from Dickensian 28no221:33–9 D '31.

10055 **Osborne, Eric A.** The variants of The Christmas carol. Bkmn 81no483:192–4 D '31. illus.

10056 **Cutler, Bradley D.** The great Victorians come to America; Dickens made pertinent—and potent—remarks on the question of copyright while Carlyle quoted the scriptures. Pub Wkly 122no21:1927–30 N '32. ports.

10057 **Dickens** and his French publishers. [Hachette et cie, Paris]. Dickensian 29no225:7–10 D '32.

10058 **Hills, Gertrude.** Pursuing a perfect Pickwick in parts. Am Bk Coll 1no6:346–52 Je '32.

10059 **Hopkins, Albert A.** A notable Drood collection. [Howard Duffield]. Dickensian 28no223:231–4 Je '32. facsim.

10060 **Hughes, T. Cann.** The Picnic papers. N&Q 163:296 Oc '32; T. O. Mabbott *ib.* 163:463 D '32.

10061 **Pickwick** and A Christmas carol. (Notes on sales). TLS 14 Ja '32:32.

10062 **Suzannet, comte Alain de.** The original manuscript of The Pickwick papers. Dickensian 28no223:193–6 Je '32. facsims. [Sg.: A. S.]

10063 **Sadleir, Michael T. H.** A Christmas carol. TLS 28 Ja '32:60.

10064 **Mr.** T. Hatton's collection. TLS 9 Mr '33:172.

10065 **Read, Newbury F.** On the writing of Barnaby Rudge. Dickensian 30no229:53–7 D '33.

10066 **Miller, William** and **E. H. Strange.** The original Pickwick papers, the collation of a perfect first edition. Dickensian 29no228:303–9 S '33; 30no229:31–7 D '33; 30no230:121–4 Mr '34; 30no231:177–80 Je '34; 30no232:249–59 Ag '34; 31no233:35–40 D '34; 31no234:95–9 Mr '35; 31no235:219–22 Je '35; 31no236:284–6 Ag '35. facsims.

10067 **Unique** items in famous Dickens collections. Dickensian 30no229:63–7 D '33; 30no230:112–16 Mr '34; 30no231:204–6 Je '34; 30no232:292–6 Ag '34; 31no233:31–4 D '34; 31no234:91 Mr '35; 32no240:264–5 Ag '36.

I. The Pierpont Morgan library, New York.–2. The library of mr. W. M. Elkins, Philadelphia.–3. Count de Suzannet's library at La Petite Chardière, Lausanne.–4. The Henry E. Huntington library, San Marino, California.–5. The Dickens house, 48 Doughty street, London.–6. The Harry Elkins Widener library at Harvard university.–7. The Forster collection at the Victoria and Albert museum, London.–8. The late Chas. J. Sawyer collection.

10068 **Dexter, Walter,** *ed.* Dickens's first publisher; correspondence with John Macrone. [n.p., London] Privately ptd., 1934. 28p. facsim. 25cm.

10069 —— Dickens's first publisher; more correspondence with John Macrone hitherto unpublished. Dickensian 30no230:135–43 Mr '34; 30no231:163–72 Je '34.

10070 **Dickens** copyright awarded. [The life of our lord]. Pub Wkly 125no24:2206 Je '34.

10071 **Dickens** copyright problem. [The life of our lord]. Pub Wkly 125no12:1213 Mr '34.

10072 **Hayes, E. B.** Some notes on Hatton and Cleaver's bibliography of Dickens. Dickensian 30no231:193–6 Je '34.

10073 **Rubens, Charles.** The dummy library of Dickens at Gad's Hill place; recollections of a pilgrimage as narrated . . . to J. Christian Bay. [Chicago] Privately ptd., 1934. 20p. facsims. 24cm.

10074 **Stonehouse, John H.** Dickens's library. TLS 21 Je '34:443.

10075 **Suzannet, comte Alain de.** Dickens part issues. TLS 12 Ap '34:268.

10076 **Dexter, Walter.** Dickens's agreements with Bentley; important new facts. Dickensian 31no236:241–54 Ag '35. [Sg.: W. D.]

10077 —— The Pickwick dedications and prefaces. Dickensian 32no237:61–4 D '35. facsim.

10078 **Stonehouse, John H.,** *ed.* Catalogue of the library of Charles Dickens from Gadshill, reprinted from Sotheran's Price current of literature, nos. CLXXIV and CLXXV; catalogue of his pictures ...; catalogue of the library of W. M. Thackeray sold by messrs. Christie, Manson & Woods, March 18, 1864, and relics from his library. ... London, Piccadilly fountain pr., 1935. vii,182p. illus., facsim. 22cm.

Rev: TLS 18 Ap '35:260.

10079 **The agreement** to write Pickwick; some unpublished letters. [Chapman & Hall]. Dickensian 33no241:5–9 D '36.

10080 **Blood, J. K. Lloyd-.** A Christmas carol. (Bibliographical notes). TLS 12 D '36:1040.

10081 **Dickens:** Remarks on ventilation. [1875]. Bib N&Q 2no1:3 Ja '36.

10082 **Dickens's** instructions to Phiz for the Pickwick illustrations. Dickensian 32no240:266–8 Ag '36. facsims.

10083 **Miller, William.** The value of first editions. Dickensian 33no241:38–9 D '36.

10084 **Parrish, Morris L.** Dickens: Christmas carol. [1844]. Bib N&Q 2no6:6 Jl '36.

10085 **Pickwick** centenary exhibitions. (Bibliographical notes). TLS 4 Ap '36:304.

10086 **Strange, E. H.** Notes on the bibliography of Nicholas Nickleby. Dickensian 33no241:30–3 D '36.

10087 **Smith, Simon H. Nowell-.** Dickens: Oliver Twist, 1838. [Issues]. Bib N&Q 2no6:6 Jl '36; M. L. Parrish *ib.* 2no11:3 N '38.

10088 **The agreements** with Richard Bentley. Dickensian 33no243:199–204 Je '37.

10089 **Carter, Harry G.** The Nonesuch Dickens. TLS 28 Ag '37:628.

10090 **Dexter, Walter.** Bentley's miscellany. Dickensian 33no244:232–8 S '37. facsim.

10091 —— Macrone and the reissue of Sketches by Boz. Dickensian 33no243:173–6 Je '37. facsim.

10092 **Dickens's** letters at Hodgson's. (Sales and bibliography). TLS 27 N '37:916.

10093 **Maxwell, William.** Dickens: Great expectations. [Original ms. of sad ending]. Bib N&Q 2no8:7 F '37.

10094 **Miller, A. G. Schaw.** Dickens's The battle of life. TLS 31 Jl '37:564.

10095 **Nonesuch press,** LONDON. The Nonesuch Dickens: retrospectus and prospectus. Bloomsbury, Nonesuch pr., 1937. 128p. illus., facsims. 25cm. (Nonesuch Dickensiana)

> I. Charles Dickens and his illustrators, by Arthur Waugh.–II. A bibliographical list of the original illustrations to the works of Charles Dickens being those made under his supervision, now comp. for the first time by Thomas Hatton.–III. Retrospectus: editions of Dickens's works.–IV. Prospectus: The Nonesuch Dickens.

10096 **Osborne, Eric A.** A Christmas carol. (Bibliographical notes). TLS 30 Oc '37:808.

10097 —— The facts about A Christmas carol. London, Bradley pr., 1937. (Anr. issue, 1937). 26p. tables. 23cm.

> The history of the Carol.–The bibliography of the Carol.–Conjectures about the Carol.–Appendices: 1. Dickens' corrections in the proof copy. 2. Christmas carol account. 3. The various editions of the Carol. 4. Folding chart of textual variations. [*Fuller in limited issue*].

10098 **Rust, Sydney J.** At the Dickens house; legal documents relating to the piracy of A Christmas carol. Dickensian 34no245:41–4 D '37.

10099 **Strange, E. H.** The Memoirs of Grimaldi, a bibliographical note. Dickensian 33no244:239–40 S '37.

10100 **Bay, J. Christian.** The Pickwick papers; some bibliographical remarks; an address delivered before the Caxton club, January sixteenth, 1937. Chicago, Caxton club, 1938. 28p. facsims. 23cm.

10101 **C., M.** Dickens: Martin Chuzzlewit. [Wrapper]. Bib N&Q 2no9:3 Ja '38; G. W. *ib.* 2no11:4 N '38.

10102 **Dr. Duffield's Drood collection.** Dickensian 34no247:211 Je '38.

10103 **Letters** of Charles Dickens. [Dickens to Bentley from Suzannet colln.]. (Antiquarian notes). TLS 23 Jl '38:500.

10104 **Manuscripts** of Dickens [from Suzannet collection]. (News and notes). TLS 2 Jl '38:441.

10105 **Parrish, Morris L.** Dickens: David Copperfield. [American ed., 1849–50]. Bib N&Q 2no9:3 Ja '38.

10106 —— Dickens: Gabriel Vardon (Barnaby Rudge). [Macrone's ed.]. Bib N&Q 2no10:9 Ap '38.

10107 ——— Oliver Twist. (Antiquarian notes). TLS 14 My '38:344; J. Thomson *ib.* 11 Je '38:408.

10108 **Rolfe, Franklin P.** The Dickens letters in the Huntington library. Huntington Lib Q 1no3:335–63 Ap '38.

10109 **Adams, Elizabeth L.** First editions of Dickens. More Bks Boston Pub Lib Bull 14no10:457 D '39. [Sg.: E. L. A.]

10110 **Dickens's** Life of Christ. [Hologr. ms.]. (Bibliographical notes). TLS 29 Jl '39:460.

10111 **Haight, Anne L.** Charles Dickens tries to remain anonymous . . . notes on The loving ballad of lord Bateman. Coloph new graphic ser 1:[30p.] Mr '39. illus., facsims.

> Informal notes. Lord Bateman in America.–Bandy Tom the dustman.–The Pailthorpe note.–Thackeray A.L.S. to Cruikshank referring to his own copper-plates.–The Thackeray drawings.–The letters from Dickens to Cruikshank relating to Lord Bateman.–The Bell and Daldy 1870 edition and the further estrangement of Cruikshank and Dickens.–Bibliographical note.

10112 **Hill, T. W.** A catalogue of the Miller collection of Dickens music at the Dickens house. Dickensian 37no257:48–54 D '40.

10113 **Wilson, R. A.** Translations of the works of Charles Dickens. [Lady Dickens's collection]. Brit Mus Q 14no3:59–60 S '40.

10114 **The A. E.** Newton library. Dickensian 37no260:221–2 S '41.

10115 **Grubb, Gerald G.** On the serial publication of Oliver Twist. Mod Lang N 56no4:290–4 Ap '41.

10116 **Houtchens, Lawrence H.** Charles Dickens and international copyright. Am Lit 13no1:18–28 Mr '41.

10117 **Bromhill, Kentley.** Phiz's illustrations to Dombey and son. Dickensian 38no264:219–21 S '42; 39no265:48–51 S '42; 39no266:57–60 Mr '43. facsims.

10118 ——— Phiz's illustrations to David Copperfield. Dickensian 40no269:47–50 D '43; 40no270:83–6 Mr '44.

> I. The cover.–II. The plates.

10119 **Grubb, Gerald G.** Dickens' editorial methods. Stud Philol 40no1:79–100 Ja '43.

10120 ——— The editorial policies of Charles Dickens. Pub Mod Lang Assn 58no4:1110–24 D '43.

10121 **Kennethe, L. A.** The cheap edition. Dickensian 39no267:112–14 Je '43.

10122 —— The unique reading books. Dickensian 39no266:75–8 Mr '43. facsims.

10123 **Bromhill, Kentley.** Phiz's illustrations to Bleak house. Dickensian 40no271:146–50 Je '44; 40no272:192–5 S '44.

Monthly wrapper cover design.–Frontispiece.–Title vignette.–The plates.

10124 **Dexter, Walter** and **K. Bromhill.** The David Copperfield advertiser. Dickensian 41no273:21–5 D '44.

10125 **Dexter, Walter.** The Library, Peoples and Charles Dickens editions. Dickensian 40no272:186–7 S '44.

10126 —— A note on the payment for Pickwick. Dickensian 40no271:118–19 Je '44. facsim.

10127 **Fynmore, A. H. W.** A Dickens manuscript. [Our mutual friend]. N&Q 187:255 D '44.

10128 **Calhoun, Philo** and **H. J. Heaney.** Dickens' Christmas carol after a hundred years; a study in bibliographical evidence. Pa Bib Soc Am 39:271–317 '45. facsims., tables.

'Description of the first state of the first issue . . .' (p. 309); 'The known presentation copies . . . and a few dated copies of bibliographical interest' (p. 310–15); 'The first and second editions . . .' (p. 316–17)

10129 **Hennessy, dame Una Pope-.** The Gad's Hill library. Dickensian 41no274:60–4 Mr '45.

10130 **Gerould, Gordon H.** The Dickens collection [of M. L. Parrish]. Princeton Univ Lib Chron 8no1:21–3 N '46.

10131 **Randall, David A.** Charles Dickens and Richard Bentley. TLS 12 Oc '46:496; dame Una Pope-Hennessy ib. 2 N '46:535.

10132 **Calhoun, Philo** and **H. J. Heaney.** Dickensiana in the rough. Pa Bib Soc Am 41:293–320 '47.

A list of some sources to be consulted in compiling a bibliography of Dickensiana.–Some special sources of Dickensiana and Dickens bibliography. . . .

10133 **Gibson, Frank A.** Dickens's unique book, a bibliographical causerie. [Master Humphrey's clock]. Dickensian 44no285:44–8 D '47.

10134 **Mead, Herman R.** Some Dickens variations. [Sketches of young gentlemen, 1838]. Pa Bib Soc Am 41:344 '47.

10135 **Partington, Wilfred G.** Should a biographer tell? The story of Dickens's denunciation of Thomas Powell's forgeries. Dickensian 43no284:193–200 S '47; 44no285:14–23 D '47. port., facsim.

10136 **Suzannet, comte Alain de.** The original manuscript of Nicholas Nickleby. Dickensian 43no284:189–92 S '47. facsims.

10137 **Woodman, R. E. G.** Dickens and his publishers. TLS 25 Ja '47:51.

10138 **Carlton, William J.** Dickens in shorthand. Dickensian 44no288:205–8 S '48.

10139 **Gomme, G. J.** L. T. B. Aldrich and Household words. Pa Bib Soc Am 42:70–2 '48.

10140 **Calhoun, Philo.** Rarity of Great expectations. New Coloph 1pt4:402 Oc '48; *ib.* 2pt5:84–5 Ja '49; J. W. Carter 2pt7:278–9 S '49.

10141 **Bushnell, George H.** 'A famous Dickens library [the Jupp collection]' *in* From bricks to books. London, 1949. p.149–55.

10142 **Butt, John E.** Dickens's notes for his serial parts. Dickensian 45no291:129–38 Je '49. facsims.

10143 **Johnson, Edgar.** Dickens clashes with his publisher. Adapted from a forthcoming biography, Charles Dickens, his tragedy and triumph. [Bentley]. Dickensian 46no293:10–17 D '49; 46no294:76–83 Mr '50. port.

10144 **Buckler, William E.** Dickens's success with Household words. Dickensian 46no296:197–203 S '50. table.

10145 **Butt, John E.** David Copperfield; from manuscript to print. R Eng Stud new ser1no3:247–51 Jl '50.

10146 **Fielding, K. J.** A new article by Dickens; Scott and his publishers from The examiner, September 2nd 1838; with a note. Dickensian 46no295:122–7 Je '50.

10147 **Buckler, William E.** Household words in America. Pa Bib Soc Am 45:160–6 '51.

10148 **E., A. C.** Charles Green, R.I. [Illustr. of Dickens]. N&Q 196:392 '51; G. G. Grubb *ib.* 198:499 N '53.

10149 **Fielding, K. J.** The ms. of the Cricket on the hearth. N&Q 197:324–5 Jl '52.

10150 **Grubb, Gerald G.** The American edition of All the year round. Pa Bib Soc Am 47:301–4 '53.

10151 **House, Humphry.** A Dickens letter: a copy or a forgery? Dickensian 49no306:69–73 Mr '53. facsims.

10152 **Weitenkampf, Frank.** American illustrators of Dickens. Boston Pub Lib Q 5no4:189–94 Oc '53. facsim.

10153 **Brown, T. Julian.** Charles Dickens, 1812–1870. (English literary autographs, XV). Bk Coll 4no3:237 '55. facsims.

10154 **Fielding, K. J.** The piracy of Great expectations. N&Q 200:495–6 N '55.

10155 **Grubb, Gerald G.** Some unpublished correspondence of Dickens and Chapman and Hall, annotated. . . . (Notes and documents). Boston Univ Stud Eng 1no1/2:98–127 '55.

10156 **Muir, Percival H.** Dickens and Tauchnitz. (Note no.55). Bk Coll 4no4:329 '55.

10157 —— The Tauchnitz David Copperfield, 1849. (Note no.53). Bk Coll 4no3:253–4 '55.

10158 **Fielding, K. J.** Charles Reade and Dickens, a fight against piracy. Theat Notebk 10no4:106–11 Jl/S '56.

10159 **Gimbel, Richard.** Charles Dickens' A Christmas carol; three states of the first edition. [Princeton, 1956]. [8]p. tables. 16cm.

10160 **Rendall, Vernon.** An American Pickwick. [1840]. N&Q 202:123–4 Mr '57. [Sg.: V. R.]

10161 **Gimbel, Richard.** The earliest state of the first edition of Charles Dickens' A Christmas carol. Princeton Univ Lib Chron 19no2:82–6 '58. facsim.

10162 **Todd, William B.** Dickens, A tale of two cities, 1859. (Note 94). Bk Coll 7no1:80 '58.

10163 **Charles** Dickens. [First ed. presented to Library]. Princeton Univ Lib Chron 20no3:158–60 '59.

10164 **A Dickens** exhibit in the Treasure room. Boston Pub Lib Q 11no3:147–8 Jl '59.

10165 **Peyrouton, N. C.** A postscript on pirates. [Dickensiana in The Australasian, 1850]. Dickensian 56no332:179–81 S '60.

10166 **Butt, John E.** Dickens's instructions for Martin Chuzzlewit, plate XVIII. R Eng Lit 2no3:49–50 Jl '61. facsim.

10167 —— Editing a nineteenth-century novelist; proposals for an edition of Dickens. Eng Stud Today 2:187–95 '61.

10168 **Carlton, William J.** Dickens periodicals. TLS 22 S '61:629.

10169 **Collins, Philip A. W.** The significance of Dickens's periodicals. [All the year round; Household words]. R Eng Lit 2no3:55–64 Jl '61.

10170 **Harvey, Paul D. A.** Charles Dickens as playwright. [Mss. acquired]. Brit Mus Q 24no1/2:22–5 Ag '61.

10171 **Todd, William B.** Dickens's Christmas carol. [Ptg.]. (Note 170). Bk Coll 10no4:449–54 '61.

10172 **Butt, John E.** Dickens's manuscripts. Yale Univ Lib Gaz 36no4:149–61 Ap '62.

10173 **Dickens** exhibition. (Notes and news). Bull John Rylands Lib 45no1:7–9 S '62.

10174 **Tillotson, Kathleen.** Oliver Twist in three volumes. Library ser5 18no2:113–32 Je '63. tables.

10175 **Carter, John W.** The Battle of life: round three. [Distinction of 1st and forged ed.]. Antiqu Bkmn 33no20:2203–5 My '64; 33no21:2319 My '64. facsims.

10176 **Dickens'** Life of our lord. [Ms. in Philadelphia Free library]. Am Bk Coll 15no3:24 N '64. port.

10177 **Lohrli, Anne.** Household words and its Office book. Princeton Univ Lib Chron 26no1:27–47 '64.

10178 **The Nonesuch** Dickens. Serif 1no1:29–30 Ap '64.

10179 **Patten, Robert L.** The interpolated tales in Pickwick papers. Dickens Stud 1no2:86–9 My '65. facsims.

10180 **Schweitzer, Joan.** The chapter numbering in Oliver Twist. Pa Bib Soc Am 60:337–43 '66.

10181 **Todd, William B.** Dickens's Battle of life, round six. [Distinction of 1st and forged ed.]. Bk Coll 15no1:48–54 '66. facsims., table.

   1. Engraved title variants.–2. Proofs and other variants.–3. The title and the book.

10182 **Stott, R. Toole.** Boz's Memoirs of Joseph Grimaldi, 1838. (Note 277). Bk Coll 15no3:354–6 '66; W. J. Smith *ib.* 16no1:80 '67.

10183 **Levy, H. M.** and **W. Ruff.** The interpolated tales in Pickwick papers, a further note. Dickens Stud 3no2:122–5 Oc '67.

10184 **Smith, Simon H. Nowell-**. The cheap edition of Dickens's Works (first series) 1847–1852. Library ser5 22no3:245–51 S '67. facsims., table.

10185 **Stevens, Joan**. Woodcuts dropped into the text: the illustrations in The old curiosity shop and Barnaby Rudge. Stud Bib 20:113–34 '67. facsims., table.

10186 **Muir, Percival H**. A Curious dance round a curious tree. (Note 295). Bk Coll 17no1:80–1 '68.

10187 **Bracher, Peter**. The Lea & Blanchard edition of Dickens's American notes, 1842. Pa Bib Soc Am 63:296–300 '69. table.

10188 **Steig, Michael**. Dombey and son: chapter XXXI, plate 20. [Relation of illus. to text]. Eng Lang N 7no2:124–7 D '69.

DICKINSON, HENRY, fl.1682

10189 **Ward, Charles E**. Religio laici and father Simon's History. [And Tonson]. Mod Lang N 61no6:407–12 Je '46.

DICKSON, ALEXANDER, 1558–1604?

10190 **Durkan, John**. Alexander Dickson and S.T.C. 6823. [Alexandri Dicsoni Arelii de umbra, 1583]. Biblioth 3no5:183–90 '62.

DIGBY, EVERARD, fl.1590

10191 **Thomas, Ralph**. Translation of Digby's De arte natandi. [C. Middleton's A short introduction . . . to swim, 1595]. N&Q ser8 12:107 Ag '97; G. F. Barwick *ib*. ser9 2:397 N '98.

10192 **Wilks, John**. Theoria analytica. [1579]. TLS 28 My '54:345.

10193 —— Presentation-copies of Everard Digby's Theoria analytica. Library ser5 12no2:121–2 Je '57. facsims.

DIGBY, JOHN, fl.1722

10194 **Neville, Roy G**. Digby's Philosophical account of nature, 1722. (Note 92). Bk Coll 7no1:79 '58; C. A. Gordon *ib*. 7no2:189 '58.

DIGBY, SIR KENELM, 1603–65

10195 **Delisle, Léopold**. Sir Kenelm Digby and the ancient relations between the French libraries and Great Britain. Library 5no1/4:1–15 Ja/Ap '93.

10196 **Fulton, John F**. 'Bibliophile' *in* Sir Kenelm Digby, writer, bibliophile and protagonist of William Harvey. New York, 1937. p. 39–55. illus.

10197 **Schofield, B.** Manuscripts of sir Kenelm Digby. Nat Lib Wales J 1no2:89–90 '39. port., facsim.

10198 **Rhodes, Dennis E.** Sir Kenelm Digby and Siena. [Association copy]. Brit Mus Q 21no3:61–3 Je '58.

DIGGES, LEONARD, d.1571

10199 **Dygge's** Prognostication, 1555. Bkworm 1no8:293–5 Jl '88.

10200 **Johnson, Francis R.** and **S. V. Larkey.** Thomas Digges, the Copernican system, and the idea of the infinity of the universe in 1576. [Leonard Digges' Prognostication everlasting, 1576]. Huntington Lib Bull 5:69–117 Ap '34. diagr.

10201 **Friedman, Lee M.** A Leonard Digges autograph and a mystery. [Digges's signature in book from Royal library]. Autogr Coll J 5no1:34–5,37 '52. il-lus., facsim.

DIGGES, THOMAS, 1546?–95

10202 **Webb, Henry J.** Two additions to the military bibliography of Thomas Digges. Mod Lang Q 12no2:131–3 Je '51.

10203 **Johnson, Francis R.** Two treatises by Thomas Digges. R Eng Stud new ser 9no34:141–5 My '58.

DISRAELI, BENJAMIN, 1ST EARL OF BEACONSFIELD, 1804–81

10204 **The ms.** of Vivian Grey [sold at Sotheby's]. Bkworm 4no47:334 Oc '91.

10205 **Prideaux, William F.** Disraeli's juvenilia. N&Q ser11 9:125–6 F '14.

10206 **Sadleir, Michael T. H.** Disraeli queries. N&Q ser12 10:8 Ja '22. [Sg.: M. T. H. S.]

10207 **Stewart, R. W.** The publication and reception of Disraeli's Vivian Grey. Q R 298:409–17 Oc '60.

10208 **Jerman, B. R.** The production of Disraeli's trilogy. [By H. Colburn]. Pa Bib Soc Am 58:239–51 '64. tables.

    1. Coningsby.–2. Sybil.–3. Tancred.

D'ISRAELI, ISAAC, 1766–1848

10209 **Samuel, Wilfred S.** Isaac D'Israeli; first published writings. N&Q 194:192–3 Ap '49.

DOBSON, HENRY AUSTIN, 1840–1921

10210 **Murray, Francis E.** Mr. Austin Dobson's writings. Athenæum 3733:596 My '99.

10211 **Dobson, Alban T. A.** Austin Dobson; some of his books of association and others. London Merc 10no59:511–19 S '24.

DOCKWRA, WILL, fl.1682–1716

10212 **Muir, Percival H.** Will Dockwra. (Note no. 45).Bk Coll 4no2:168 '55.

DODDRIDGE, PHILIP, 1702–51

10213 **Letters** of dr. Philip Doddridge, 1702–51. (Notes and news). Bull John Rylands Lib 41no1:12 S '58.

DODGSON, CHARLES LUTWIDGE, 1832–98 *see* Carroll, Lewis, *pseud.*

DODINGTON, GEORGE BUBB, 1691–1762

10214 **Holworthy, Richard.** Dodington's Diaries. [Ms.]. N&Q ser12 7:269 Oc '20.

DODSLEY, ROBERT, 1703–64 *see under* Book production and distribution–Printers, publishers, etc.

DONLEVY, ANDREW, 1694?–1761?

10215 **Ó Casaide, Séamus.** Donlevy's Catechism. Irish Bk Lover 24no1:16 Ja/F '36.

DONNE, JOHN, 1573–1631

10216 **Norton, C. E.** The text of Donne's poems. Harvard Stud & N Philol & Lit 5:1–22 '96.

10217 **Prideaux, William F.** Donne's Poems, 1650. N&Q ser9 1:29 Ja '98; 1:255–6 Mr '98.

10218 **Grierson, sir Herbert J. C.** Donne's poems. [First and Second anniversary, 1612]. N&Q ser11 2:7–8 Jl '10; W. Scott *ib.* 2:75–6 Jl '10.

10219 —— Donniana. Mod Lang R 9no2:237–9 Ap '14.

10220 **Smith, Herbert F. B. Brett-.** A crux in the text of Donne. [Since she must go]. Mod Lang R 10no1:86–8 Ja '15.

10221 **Simpson, Evelyn M. S.** John Donne and sir Thomas Overbury's Characters. Mod Lang R 18no4:410–15 Oc '23.

10222 **Robbie, H. J. L.** An undescribed ms. of Donne's Poems. R Eng Stud 3no12:415–19 Oc '27. tables.

10223 **Simpson, Evelyn M. S.** Two manuscripts of Donne's Paradoxes and problems. R Eng Stud 3no10:129–45 Ap '27.

10224 **Robbie, H. J. L.** Two more undescribed mss. of John Donne's Poems. R Eng Stud 4no14:214–16 Ap '28.

10225 **Simpson, Evelyn M. S.** A note on Donne's punctuation. R Eng Stud 4no15:295–300 Jl '28.

10226 **Sisson, Charles J.** The Oxford Donne. [Donne's Satyres II, 11. 71–3]. TLS 20 F '30:142; sir H. J. C. Grierson *ib.* 6 Mr '30:190; C. J. Sisson 13 Mr '30:214.

10227 **Sparrow, John H. A.** John Donne and contemporary preachers; their preparation of sermons for delivery and for publication. Essays & Stud 16:144–78 '30.

    I. 1. Delivery and transcription.–2. Publication.–II. 1. Delivery and transcription.–2. The surviving texts.

10228 **Nicholls, Norah.** The early editions of John Donne. Bkmn (N.Y.) 79no474:370–1 Mr '31.

10229 **Shapiro, Isaac A.** The text of Donne's Letters to severall persons. [1651]. R Eng Stud 7no27:291–301 Jl '31.

10230 **Sparrow, John H. A.** A book from Donne's library. [Epigrammata et poematia vetera, ed. P. Pithou, 1590]. London Merc 25no146:171–80 D '31.

10231 **Williamson, George.** The Donne canon. [And licensing for the press]. TLS 18 Ag '32:581.

10232 **Bennett, R. E.** The addition to Donne's Catalogus librorum. [Ms.]. Mod Lang N 48no3:167–8 Mr '33.

10233 **Brown, Alex.** Some notes on scientific criticism, in connection with the Clarendon edition of Donne. Dublin Mag new ser 8no2:20–31 Ap/Je '33.

10234 **Coffin, Charles M.** Bibliography of Donne. [Keynes addenda]. TLS 2 Ag '34:541.

10235 **Simpson, Evelyn M. S.** More manuscripts of Donne's Paradoxes and problems. R Eng Stud 10no39:288–300 Jl '34; 10no40:412–16 Oc '34.

Dobell ms.–Burley and Westmoreland mss.–Bridgewater ms.–British museum mss.–Phillipps ms.–Stephens ms(s).–Trinity college mss.

10236 **Maxwell, Ian R.** John Donne's library. TLS 11 Jl '35:448.

10237 **Simpson, Percy.** A book from the library of John Donne. [Parkers' De antiquitate Britannicæ ecclesiae, 1605]. Oriel Rec 6no14:427–9 Ja '35.

10238 **French, J. Milton.** Bowman v. Donne. [Sermons]. TLS 12 D '36:1035.

10239 **Bennett, R. E.** Tracts from John Donne's library. R Eng Stud 13no51:333–5 Jl '37.

10240 **Keynes, sir Geoffrey L.** Death's duell. TLS 24 S '38:620; P. James *ib.* 15 Oc '38:668. illus.

Two sermons.–The stolen title.–Michell the bookseller.

10241 **[Madan, Falconer].** A book from Donne's library. Bod Lib Rec 1no9:147–8 Ap '40.

10242 **Simpson, Evelyn M. S.** The text of Donne's Divine poems. Essays & Stud 26:88–105 '40.

10243 **Williamson, George.** Textual difficulties in the interpretation of Donne's poetry. [And sir Herbert Grierson]. Mod Philol 38no1:37–72 Ag '40.

Repr. in Seventeenth century contexts. London, 1960. p. 78–119.

10244 **Simpson, Evelyn M. S.** A Donne manuscript in St. Paul's cathedral library. [Sermons]. Philol Q 21no2:237–9 Ap '42.

10245 —— Notes on Donne. R Eng Stud 20no79:224–7 Jl '44.

'III. Another undescribed manuscript of Donne's poems [Bodleian Rawl. ms. 117]'. (p. 225–7)

10246 **Potter, George R.** Hitherto undescribed manuscript versions of three sermons by Donne. J Eng Germ Philol 44no1:28–35 Ja '45.

10247 **Sparrow, John H. A.** Donne's Anniversaries. [Text]. TLS 29 Je '46:312; sir H. J. C. Grierson; H. W. Jones *ib.* 20 Jl '46:343.

10248 **Hayward, John D.** The Nonesuch Donne. [Text]. TLS 5 Jl '47:337.

10249 **Simpson, Evelyn M. S.** Donne's Sermons. [1661]. TLS 15 Mr '47:115.

10250 **Bald, R. Cecil.** A Spanish book of Donne's. N&Q 193:302 Jl '48.

10251 **Keynes, sir Geoffrey L.** Books from Donne's library. Cambridge Bib Soc Trans 1pt1:64–8 '49.

10252 **Pafford, John H. P.** John Donne's library. TLS 2 S '49:569; A. C. Powell *ib.* 23 S '49:617.

10253 **Husain, Itrat-.** Donne's Pseudo-martyr. [Copy presented to James I]. TLS 12 Je '53:381.

10254 **Potter, George R.** 'Problems in the editing of Donne's sermons' *in* California. University. University at Los Angeles. William Andrews Clark memorial library. Editing Donne and Pope; papers.... [Los Angeles, 1953]. p. 1–10.

10255 **Keynes, sir Geoffrey L.** John Donne's sermons. [Mss.]. TLS 28 My '54:351.

10256 **Elmen, Paul.** John Donne's dark lantern. [A litany]. Pa Bib Soc Am 49:181–6 '55.

10257 **Sparrow, John H. A.** Donne's books in the Middle temple. TLS 29 Jl '55:436; 5 Ag '55:451.

10258 **Hindle, Christopher J.** A poem by Donne. [Go and catch a falling star]. TLS 8 Je '56:345.

10259 **Sparrow, John H. A.** The text of Donne. TLS 21 D '56:765.

10260 **Hagspian, John V.** Some cruxes in Donne's poetry. N&Q 202:500–2 N '57.

10261 **Main, C. F.** New texts of John Donne. [Mss.]. Stud Bib 9:225–33 '57.

10262 **Keynes, sir Geoffrey L.** Dr. Donne and Scaliger. [Donne's library]. TLS 21 F '58:108; J. H. A. Sparrow *ib.* 28 F '58:115.

10263 **Gardner, dame Helen L.** Donne mss. for the Bodleian. TLS 11 Mr '60:168.

10264 **Williamson, George,** *ed.* 'Textual difficulties in Donne's poetry' *in* Seventeenth century contexts. London, 1960. p. 78–119.

10265 **Crum, Margaret C.** Notes on the physical characteristics of some manuscripts of the poems of Donne and of Henry King. Library ser5 16no2:121–32 Je '61. diagr.

10266 **Krueger, Robert.** The publication of John Donne's sermons. R Eng Stud new ser 15no58:151–60 My '64.

10267 **Bald, R. Cecil.** Dr. Donne and the booksellers. Stud Bib 18:69–80 '65.

10268 **Pirie, Robert S.** Fine paper copies of Donne's Biathanatos, ?1646. (Note 250). Bk Coll 14no3:362 '65.

10269 **Sparrow, John H. A.** Donne's books in Oxford. TLS 25 N '65:1060; L. Forster *ib.* 9 D '65:1159; J. Callard; R. S. Pirie 23 D '65:1204; C. Dobb 30 D '65:1213; J. H. A. Sparrow 6 Ja '66:9; sir G. L. Keynes 13 Ja '66:25; L. Forster 27 Ja '66:68.

10270 **Whitlock, Baird W.** A note on two Donne manuscripts. [P.R.O. State papers miscellaneous 9/51; Nat Lib Wales Peniarth 500B]. Renaiss News 18no1:9–11 '65.

10270a **Armitage, C. M.** Donne's poems in Huntington manuscript 198: new light on The funerall. Stud Philol 63no5:697–707 Oc '66.

10271 **Gardner, dame Helen L.** On editing Donne. TLS 24 Ag '67:772; M. Roberts *ib.* 7 S '67:804.

10272 **MacColl, Alan** [and] **M. Roberts.** The new edition of Donne's love poems. [Ed. by dame Helen Gardner]. Essays in Crit 17no2:258–78 Ap '67.

10272a **Nishiyama, Yoshio.** Some cruxes in the Paradoxes of John Donne. Essays & Stud Eng Lang & Lit (Tohuku Gakuin Univ Sendai) 51/2:217–36 '67. (Not seen: MLA Bib 1971:3490)

In Japanese.

10273 **Shawcross, John T.** John Donne and Drummond's manuscript. Am N&Q 5:104–5 '67.

10274 **Stanwood, P. G.** A Donne discovery. [Ms.]. TLS 19 Oc '67:984; C. Dionisotti *ib.* 2 N '67:1037.

10275 **Shawcross, John T.** An early-nineteenth century life of John Donne: an edition with notes and commentary. [Mark Noble]. J Rutgers Univ Lib 32no1:1–32 D '68. facsim.

DORSET, CATHERINE ANN (TURNER), 1750?–1817?

10276 **Smith, C. S.** The Peacock at home. N&Q ser8 7:188 Mr '95; F. G. S.; E. Marshall; C. W. Penny; Henrietta Cole *ib.* 7:249–50 Mr '95.

DORSET, CHARLES SACKVILLE, 6TH EARL OF, 1638–1706 *see* Sackville, Charles, 6th earl of Dorset, 1638–1706.

DORSET, THOMAS SACKVILLE, 1ST EARL OF, 1536–1608 *see* Sackville, Thomas, 1st earl of Dorset, 1536–1608.

DOUGHTY, CHARLES MONTAGU, 1843–1926

10277 **Fairley, Barker.** [Under arms, 1900]. (Correspondence). London Merc 4no22:411 Ag '21.

10278 **Flower, Robin E. W.** Doughty's Mansoul. [Ms.]. Brit Mus Q 1no2:51–2 S '26. [Sg.: R. F.]

10279 **Doughty's** Arabia deserta [dated 1887]. (Marginalia). Bkmns J ser3 17no9:48 '29.

10280 **Wright, C. Hagberg.** Doughty's Arabia deserta. TLS 28 Mr '29:260; B. Fairley *ib.* 2 My '29:362; sir S. C. Roberts 9 My '29:383.

DOUGLAS, BP. GAVIN, 1474?–1522

10281 **A copy** of Douglas' Eneados [acquired by McGill university]. Stud Scot Lit 3no3:176 Ja '66.

DOUGLAS, NORMAN, *pseud. of* GEORGE NORMAN DOUGLASS, 1868–1952

10282 **Stirling, Matthew.** Douglas, Norman: Limericks. Bib N&Q 2no9:3 Ja '38; J. D. Hayward *ib.* 2no10:2 Ap '38; 2no11:4 N '38.

10283 **Waynflete, George,** *pseud.* Douglas, Norman: Old Calabria, Secker, 1915. [Issues]. Bib N&Q 2no12:8 My '39.

10284 **Woolf, Cecil.** Norman Douglas. (Query no.34). Bk Coll 2no2:158 '53; H. E. James *ib.* 2no3:222 '53.

10285 —— The bibliography of Norman Douglas. [Woolf's bibliogr.] Library ser5 10no3:211 S '55.

10286 —— Notes on the bibliography of Norman Douglas. Edinburgh, Tragara pr., 1955. 8p. 19cm.

Repr. from Amat Bk Coll 4no3:1–2 Ja '54.

DOUGLASS, GEORGE NORMAN, 1868–1952 *see* Douglas, Norman, *pseud.*

DOWDALL, JOHN, fl.1693

10287 **G., J. W.** Dowdall's Traditionary anecdotes of Shakespeare. [Ms.]. N&Q ser10 1:128 F '04.

10288 **Jaggard, William.** Dowdall: Traditionary anecdotes of Shakespeare. [Ms.]. N&Q ser12 11:93 Jl '22.

DOWLAND, JOHN, 1563?–1626?

10289 **Dowling, Margaret.** The printing of John Dowland's Second book of songs or ayres. Library ser4 12no4:365–80 Mr '32.

'Discussion [by sir W. W. Greg]' (p. 379–80)

DOWSON, ERNEST CHRISTOPHER, 1867–1900

10290 **Wright, Cyril E.** Eight poems of Ernest Dowson. Brit Mus Q 12no3:87–90 Je '38.

DOYLE, SIR ARTHUR CONAN, 1859–1930

10291 **Bates, George.** Doyle: Adventures of Sherlock Holmes, 1892. [Faked copies]. Bib N&Q 1no1:12 Ja '35; H. W. Bell *ib.* 2no3:2 Ap '36.

10292 **W., C. A. and H. W. B.** Conan Doyle: A study in scarlet, London, 1888. [Issues]. Bib N&Q 2no8:5 6 F '37.

10293 **Stone, P. M.** Doyle, A. Conan: A plea for justice; An enquiry into the case of George Edalji, 1907. [Variant imprints]. Bib N&Q 2no9:3 Ja '38.

10294 **Randall, David A.** A study of A study in scarlet, London: Ward, Lock & co., 1888; or, A scandal in bibliography. Baker Street J 1no1:102–6 Ja '46. illus.

10295 —— The Valley of fear bibliographically considered, with a few notes on its sources and some textual problems. [1914–18]. (Bibliographical notes). Baker Street J 1no2:282–7 Ap '46.

10296 —— Bibliographical notes. [A Study in scarlet, 1895]. Baker Street J 2no1:104–5 Ja '47.

10297 —— A tentative enquiry into the earliest printings in book form of the first Sherlock Holmes short stories: A scandal in Bohemia; The red-headed league, A case of identity, and The Boscombe valley mystery; with a conclusion tending to prove . . . America first! (Bibliographical notes). Baker Street J 2no4:491–6 Oc '47.

10298 **Eccles, J. S.** Doyle's A study in scarlet. New Coloph 1pt4:401,403 Oc '48.

10299 **Bengis, Nathan L.** Bibliographical notes. [Souvenir ed., 1901–6]. Baker Street J 4no1:128–9 Ja '49; new ser 2no1:40–3 Ja '52.

10300 **Sterne, Madeleine B.** Sherlock Holmes, rare-book collector; a study in book detection. Pa Bib Soc Am 47:135–55 '53.

10301 **Walbridge, Earle F.** An additional note on The cardboard box. Pa Bib Soc Am 47:75–6 '53.

10302 **Bengis, Nathan L.** Why I collect Sherlockiana. Hobbies 59no1:126–30 Mr '54.

10303 **Brimmell, R. A.** Holmesiana. (Note 84). Bk Coll 6no2:183 '57.

10304 **Cameron, Mary S.** Bibliographical notes. [Adventures and memoirs of Sherlock Holmes and Sign of four, pub. by James Askew]. Baker Street J new ser 8no3:169–73 Jl '58.

10305 **Bengis, Nathan L.** Why I collect Sherlockiana. Am Bk Coll 9no9:15–19 My '59. illus., port.

   Rev. and enl. from no.10302.

10306 **Williams, Howard B.** Bibliographical notes. [An unlisted Study in scarlet? The case of the golden blonde]. Baker Street J Christmas Ann new ser 4:293–5 '59.

10307 **Dalliba, William S.** The manuscripts of the Sherlock Holmes stories. (Bibliographical notes). Baker Street J new ser 10no3:164–6 Jl '60.

10308 **Skeat, Theodore C.** 'The case of the missing three-quarter'. [Ms.]. Brit Mus Q 22no3/4:54–6 Ap '60.

10309 **Bengis, Nathan L.** Variety is the spice of Sherlockiana; a prolegomenon to a compendium of the various states of the 1902 American edition of The hound of the Baskervilles, published by McClure, Phillips & co. Baker Street Gasogene 1no4:37–46 Ap '62. facsims., port.

10310 **Bergman, Ted.** Bibliografiska noteringar. [Swedish ed. of Holmes stories]. Baker Street Cab Lantern 3:7–10 '64.

10311 **Bengis, Nathan L.** Signs of a bookman. [Sign of four]. Bkworm 1no8:10–12 D '67.

10312 —— 'Got any Beeton's today?', or, The byways of the Sherlockian game [Collecting]' *in* Kennedy, Bruce, *ed.* Four wheels to Baker street. [Fulton, Mo.], 1968. p. 7–18.

DRAKE, SIR FRANCIS, 1540?–96

10313 **Michigan. University. William L. Clements library.** Bigges: Drake's West Indian voyage. [Location of copies for a bibliogr.]. Bib N&Q 1no3:7–8 Ag '35; T. Warburton *ib.* 2no4/5:2 My '36; L. A. Brown 2no7:1 Oc '36.

10314 **Kraus, Hans P.** On book collecting; the story of my Drake library. [Minneapolis] Associates of the James Ford Bell library, 1969. 18p. 20cm. (James Ford Bell lectures, no.6)

DRAYTON, MICHAEL, 1563–1631

10315 **Bookhunter, A,** *pseud.* Drayton's Polyolbion. Bkworm 2no19:209–13 Je '89. facsim.

10316 **McKerrow, Ronald B.** The supposed calling-in of Drayton's Harmony of the church, 1591. Library ser3 1no4:348–50 Oc '10.

> *Repr. in* Immroth, John P., *ed.* Ronald Brunlees McKerrow, a selection of his essays. Metuchen, N.J., 1974. p. 39–44.

10317 **Hebel, John W.** The surreptitious edition of Michael Drayton's Peirs Gaueston. Library ser4 4no2:151–5 S '23.

10318 **White, Newport B.** Keats and Drayton. [Copy of Drayton's Endimion and Phœbe, in Marsh's library]. TLS 2 Ap '25:240; B. H. Newdigate *ib.* 9 Ap '25.259.

10319 **Tillotson, Kathleen.** Drayton and Richard II: 1597–1600. [Englands' heroical epistles, 1599–1600]. R Eng Stud 15no58:172–9 Ap '39.

10320 **Jensen, Bent Juel-.** Polyolbion, Poemes lyrick and pastorall, Poems, 1619, The owle, and a few other books by Michael Drayton. Library ser5 8no3:145–62 S '53. facsims.

> The portrait of prince Henry playing with a lance.–Contemporary bindings and prices.

10321 —— Michael Drayton's Owle, 1604. TLS 23 Jl '54:473.

10322 —— A Drayton collection. Bk Coll 4no2:133–43 '55. illus., facsim.

10323 —— Drayton and his patron. [Poems, 1619]. TLS 7 D '56:731.

10324 —— Three lost Drayton items. (Query 122). Bk Coll 9no1:78–9 '60.

10325 —— An Oxford variant of Drayton's Polyolbion. Library ser5 16no1:53–4 Mr '61. facsim.

10326 —— Fine and large-paper copies of S.T.C. books, and particularly of Drayton's Poems, 1619, and The battaile of Agincourt, 1627. Library ser5 19:226–30 '64. facsims.

> Poems, 1619 (S.T.C. 7222).–The battaile of Agincourt, 1627 (S.T.C. 7190). *See also no.* 10328.

10327 —— Michael Drayton and William Drummond of Hawthornden: a lost autograph letter rediscovered. Library ser5 21no4:328–30 D '66. facsim.

10328 —— Fine and large-paper copies of S.T.C. books: a further note. Library ser5 23no3:239–40 S '68.

DRINKWATER, JOHN, 1882–1937

10329 **Persuasion**: The privately printed edition of mr. Drinkwater's sonnets. Bkmns J new ser 5no4:139 Ja '22.

10330 **The Waterden** broadsheets. Bkmns J new ser 9no30:201 Mr '24.

DRUMMOND, WILLIAM, 1585–1649

10331 **Dent, Robert K.** A curious catalogue; some notes on the catalogue and library of William Drummond of Hawthornden. Lib Assn Rec 2no8:427–9 Ag '00.

10332 **Kastner, L. E.** Drummond of Hawthornden. N&Q ser11 4:487 D '11; W. Scott *ib.* 5:92–3 F '12; L. E. Kastner 5:230–1 Mr '12.

10333 **Simpson, Percy.** The genuineness of the Drummond Conversations. [And sir Robert Sibbald]. R Eng Stud 2no5:42–50 Ja '26.

10334 **MacDonald, Robert H.** William Drummond of Hawthornden. [Association copies sought]. (Query 187). Bk Coll 13no3:360 '64.

10335 —— William Drummond of Hawthornden. [Library]. N&Q 210:351 S '65.

10336 —— Amendments to L. E. Kastner's edition of Drummond's Poems. Stud Scot Lit 7no51/2:102–22 Jl/Oc '69.

DRYDEN, JOHN, 1631–1700

10337 **Gosse, sir Edmund W.** Dryden's Religio laici. Athenæum 3720:179 F '99; G. Neilson *ib.* 3722:241 F '99.

10338 **Noyes, George R.** An unnoticed edition of Dryden's Virgil. [1697]. Mod Lang N 19no5:125–7 My '04; 24no1:31 Ja '09.

10339 **Gosse, sir Edmund W.** Dryden's Art of painting. Athenæum 4059:208–9 Ag '05; H. B. Wheatley; W. J. Harvey; J. H. Swann *ib.* 4060:242 Ag '05; F. R. Ray; T. K. Abbott 4061:276 Ag '05; sir E. W. Gosse; F. R. Ray 4062:305 S '05.

10340 **Churchill, George B.** The relation of Dryden's State of innocence to Milton's Paradise lost and Wycherley's Plain dealer: an inquiry into dates. Mod Philol 4no2:381–8 Oc '06.

10341 **Bayne, Thomas.** Dryden's Alexander's feast: two readings. N&Q ser10 8:346 N '07.

10342 **Wheatley, Henry B.** Dryden's publishers. Bib Soc Trans 11pt1:17–38 '09/10.

'Appendix: Tonson's accounts with Dryden' (p. 36–8)

10343 —— [**Same**]: Bib Soc News-sh 2–4 Ja '10.

Report of paper read 20 D '09.

10344 **Strachan, Lionel R. M.** Dryden's Character of Polybius. N&Q ser11 9:103–5 F '14.

10345 **Dryden** and Drydeniana. (Notes on sales). TLS 12 Oc '22:652.

10346 **Strachan, Lionel R. M.** Reputed song by Dryden. N&Q ser12 11:341–2 Oc '22.

10347 **Doane, Gilbert H.** The first collation of an interesting Dryden item. [Miscellaneous essays by monsieur St. Evremont, with a character by mr. Dryden, 1692]. (Marginalia). Bkmns J new ser 12no46:163–4 Jl '25. facsim.

10348 **Low, D. M.** An error in Dryden. [Theodore and Honoria]. TLS 30 Ap '25:300.

10349 **Warmington, E. L.** A Dryden misprint. [All for love, 3.1.18]. (Correspondence). London Merc 14no80:188 Je '26; Gwendolen Murphy *ib.* 13no83:518 S '26.

10350 **Dryden** first editions. (Notes on sales). TLS 7 Ap '27:256.

10351 **Ham, Roswell G.** Uncollected verse by Dryden. TLS 27 D '28:1025.

10352 **Drury, George Thorn-.** Dryden's verses To the lady Castelmain upon her incouraging his first play. R Eng Stud 6no22:193–4 Ap '30.

10353 **Hiscock, Walter G.** A Dryden epilogue. [The epilogue spoken to the king, 1680]. TLS 5 Mr '31:178.

10354 **Nicholls, Norah.** Some early editions of John Dryden. Bkmn 80no479:266–7 Ag '31.

10355 **De Beer, Esmond S.** Mr. Montague Summers and Dryden's Essay of dramatic poesy. R Eng Stud 8no32:453–6 Oc '32.

10356 **Whiting, George W.** The Ellesmere ms. of The state of innocence. TLS 14 Ja '32:28.

10357 **Thorp, Willard.** A new manuscript version of Dryden's epilogue to Sir Fopling Flutter. R Eng Stud 9no34:198–9 Ap '33.

10358 **Ham, Roswell G.** Dryden's dedication for The music of the prophetesse, 1691. [And H. Purcell, The vocal music]. Pub Mod Lang Assn 50no4:1065–75 D '35.

10359 **Nettleton, George H.** Author's changes in Dryden's Conquest of Granada, part I. Mod Lang N 50no6:360–4 Je '35.

10360 **Hiscock, Walter G.** A poem attributed to Dryden. [The triumphs of levy, 1675]. TLS 18 Ap '36:340; 25 Ap '36:360; E. S. de Beer 16 My '36:420; W. G. Hiscock 23 My '36:440; E. S. de Beer 30 My '36:460.

10361 **Ward, Charles E.** Some notes on Dryden. [Tonson]. R Eng Stud 13no51:297–306 Jl '37.

The agreement for the Virgil (p. 301–3); An advertisement for the Virgil (p. 304–5).

10362 —— The publication and profits of Dryden's Virgil. Pub Mod Lang Assn 53no3:807–12 S '38. tables.

10363 **Ball, Alice D.** An emendation of Dryden's Conquest of Granada, part one. Eng Lit Hist 6no3:217–18 S '39.

10364 A Dryden collection. [Percy Dobell's library]. (News and notes). TLS 29 Jl '39:445.

10365 **Boys, Richard C.** Some problems of Dryden's Miscellany. Eng Lit Hist 7no2:130–43 Je '40.

10366 **Osborn, James M.** 'Books from Dryden's library' in John Dryden, some biographical facts and problems. New York, 1940. (Rev. ed. Gainesville, 1965). p. [225]–34.

His copies of Spenser.–Other books that belonged to Dryden.–A note on Dryden presentation copies.

10367 **Evans, Gwynne B.** Dryden's State of innocence. [Ms.]. TLS 21 Mr '42:144.

10368 **Hooker, Helene M.** Dryden's and Shadwell's Tempest. [Ms.]. Huntington Lib Q 6no2:224–8 F '43.

10369 **McManaway, James G.** Notes on A key . . . to . . . Absalom and Achitophel. [By C. Nesse]. N&Q 184:365–6 Je '43.

10370 **Bowers, Fredson T.** Variants in early editions of Dryden's plays. [Troilus and Cressida]. (Notes). Harvard Lib Bull 3no2:278–88 '49. facsims.

10371 **Dunkin, Paul S.** The Dryden Troilus and Cressida imprint; another theory. Stud Bib 2:185–9 '49. table.

10372 **Steck, James S.** Dryden's Indian emperour, the early editions and their relation to the text. Stud Bib 2:139–52 '49.

10373 **Bowers, Fredson T.** The first edition of Dryden's Wild gallant, 1669. Library ser5 5no1:51–4 Je '50.

10374 **Swedenberg, H. T.** 'On editing Dryden's early poems' in Essays critical and historical dedicated to Lily B. Campbell by members of the departments of English, University of California. Berkeley, 1950. p. 73–84.

10375 **Bowers, Fredson T.** The 1665 manuscript of Dryden's Indian emperor. Stud Philol 48no4:738–60 Oc '51.

History.–Textual relation of ms. and Q1.–The copy for ms. and Q1.

10376 **Adams, Henry H.** A prompt copy of Dryden's Tyrannic love. [Ptd. quarto used as promptbook]. Stud Bib 4:170–4 '51/2.

10377 **Brown, T. Julian.** John Dryden, 1631–1700. (English literary autographs, III). Bk Coll 1no3:180 '52. facsim.

10378 **Marshall, Arthur Calder-.** Dryden and the rise of modern publishing. Hist Today 11no9:641–5 S '52. ports., facsim.

10379 **Bowers, Fredson T.** The pirated quarto of Dryden's State of innocence. [c.1695]. Stud Bib 5:166–9 '52/3.

10380 **Hamilton, Marion H.** The early editions of Dryden's State of innocence. Stud Bib 5:163–6 '52/3. table.

10381 **Bowers, Fredson T.** Dryden as laureate; the cancel leaf in King Arthur. [1691]. TLS 10 Ap '53:244; K. Young ib. 8 My '53:301.

10382 **Cameron, William J.** An overlooked Dryden printing. [To you who live in chill degree]. N&Q 198:334 Ag '53.

10383 **Evans, Gwynne B.** The text of Dryden's Mac Flecknoe. Harvard Lib Bull 7no1:32–54 '53.

10384 **Hamilton, Marion H.** The manuscripts of Dryden's The state of innocence and the relation of the Harvard ms. to the first quarto. Stud Bib 6:237–47 '54. diagr.

10385 **Dearing, Vinton A.** Dryden's Mac Flecknoe: the case for authorial revision. [Mss.]. Stud Bib 7:85–102 '55.

10386 **Birrell, T. A.** Dryden's library. N&Q 203:409 S '58.

10387 **Browne, Ray B.** Dryden and Milton in nineteenth-century popular songbooks. Bull Bib 22no6:143–4 My/Ag '58.

10388 **Birrell, T. A.** John Dryden's purchases at two book auctions, 1680 and 1682. Eng Stud 42no4:193–217 Ag '61.

'Books purchased by Dryden at the Digby sale, ... 19 April 1680' (p. 197–209); '. . . at the Richard Smith sale, ... 15 May 1682' (p. 209–17)

10389 **Brown, David D.** John Tillotson's revisions and Dryden's Talent for English prose. R Eng Stud new ser 12:24–39 F '61.

10390 **Barnard, John.** Dryden, Tonson, and subscriptions for the 1697 Virgil. Pa Bib Soc Am 57:129–51 '63.

10391 **Stratman, Carl J.** John Dryden's All for love; unrecorded editions. Pa Bib Soc Am 57:77–9 '63.

10392 **Caracciolo, Peter.** Some unrecorded variants in the first edition of Dryden's All for love, 1678. (Note 232). Bk Coll 13no4:498–500 '64.

10393 **Crinò, Anna M.** Dryden ms. [Heroic stanzas on the death of Cromwell]. TLS 22 S '66:879.

DUCK, STEPHEN, 1705–56

10394 **Grant, Douglas.** Duck and the duchess of Newcastle. (Note no.14). Bk Coll 1no4:265 '52.

DUFF, WILLIAM, fl.1739–50

10395 **Mason, C.** William Duff. N&Q ser9 1:129 F '98.

DUGDALE, SIR WILLIAM, 1605–86

10396 **Jenkins, Herbert M.** Dr. Thomas's edition of sir William Dugdale's Antiquities of Warwickshire; an address ... 1930. Oxford, Ptd. for the Dugdale society by J. Johnson [O.U.P.] 1931. 20p. 23cm. (Dugdale Soc Occas Pa 3)

10397 **L., H. L. B-.** Dugdale's History of inbanking and draining. [1793]. N&Q 188:148 Ap '45.

DU MAURIER, GEORGE LOUIS PALMELIA BUSSON, 1834–96

10398 **Goodspeed, George T.** Du Maurier: Peter Ibbetson, London, 1892. [Binding variants]. Bib N&Q 1no4:8 Oc '35; J. W. Carter *ib.* 2no4/5:2 My '36. [Sg.: G. G.]

10399 **Feipel, Louis N.** The American issues of Trilby. Coloph new ser 2no4:537–49 Oc '37.

> I. Variant readings.–II. Variant word-usages.–III. Orthographic and typographic style-variants.

10400 **Whiteley, Derek P.** George du Maurier's illustrations for Once a week. Alphabet & Image 5:17–29 S '47.

DUNLOP, DURHAM, 1812–82

10401 **Bigger, Francis J.** Durham Dunlop, M.R.I.A. Irish Bk Lover 10no11/12:102–4 Je/Jl '19.

DUNSANY, EDWARD JOHN MORETON DRAX PLUNKETT, 18th BARON, 1878–1957 *see* Plunkett, Edward John Moreton Drax, 18th baron, 1878–1957.

DUNTON, ANNE, fl.1778

10402 **Whitebrook, J. C.** Mrs. Anne Dunton; authorship of B.M. 4255 aaaa 41. [A discourse on justification, 1778]. N&Q ser12 6:17 Ja '20.

DUNTON, WALTER THEODORE WATTS-, 1832–1914

10403 **Bayne, Thomas.** Aylwin. [1898]. N&Q ser9 3:124–5 F '99; A. R. Bayley *ib.* 3:174 Mr '99; St. Swithin, *pseud.* 3:256 Ap '99; W. F. Prideaux 3:428 Je '99.

10404 **Books** from The pines. [Watts-Dunton libr.]. (Antiquarian notes). TLS 1 Ap '39:196.

10405 **Marchand, Leslie A.** The Watts-Dunton letter books. [In Symington collection]. J Rutgers Univ Lib 17no1:7–19 D '53.

D'URFEY, THOMAS, 1653–1723

10406 **Bowers, Fredson T.** Thomas D'Urfey's Comical history of Don Quixote, 1694. Pa Bib Soc Am 43:191–5 '49.

10407 **Alden, John E.** and **T. R. Adams.** An unrecorded poem of Thomas D'Urfey. [Ode on the anniversary, 1690]. (Notes from the rare book collection). Lib Chron Univ Pennsylvania 16no2:93 '50.

10408 **Sanville, Donald W.** Thomas D'Urfey's Love for money, a bibliographical study. Lib Chron Univ Pennsylvania 17no1:71–7 '50.

10409 **Bowers, Fredson T.** The two issues of D'Urfey's Cynthia and Endymion. Princeton Univ Lib Chron 13no1:32–4 '51.

10410 **Biswanger, Raymond A.** Thomas D'Urfey's Richmond heiress, 1693, a bibliographical study. Stud Bib 5:169–78 '52/3. table.

DURRELL, LAWRENCE GEORGE, 1912–

10411 **Knerr, Anthony.** Regarding a checklist of Lawrence Durrell. Pa Bib Soc Am 55:142–52 '61.

DYER, SIR EDWARD, d.1607

10412 **Holyoake, George J.** Who has improved sir Edward Dyer. N&Q ser10 1:487–8 Je '04; W. B. Kingsford; J. B. Wainewright; E. Palmer; J. T. Page; R. A. Potts *ib.* 2:32–3 Jl '04.

DYER, JOHN, 1699–1758

10413 **Williams, Ralph M.** The publication of Dyer's Ruins of Rome. Mod Philol 44no2:97–101 Ag '46.

EARLE, BP. JOHN, 1601?–65

10414 **Jensen, Bent Juel-.** The 1628 editions of John Earle's Micro-cosmographie. Library ser5 21no3:231–4 S '66.

EBSWORTH, JOSEPH, 1788–1868

10415 **Harding, W. N. H.** Joseph W. Ebsworth's mss. N&Q ser12 3:209–10 Mr '17.

EDGEWORTH, MARIA, 1767–1849

10416 **Talbot, William.** Edgeworth's Castle Rackrent. TLS 2 Ja '30:12.

10417 **Palfrey, Thomas R.** Maria Edgeworth and Louise Swanton Belloc. N&Q 176:206–7 Mr '39.

10418 **Pollard, Mary.** The first Irish edition of Maria Edgeworth's Parents' assistant. Irish Bk 1no4:85–8 '62.

EDGEWORTH, RICHARD LOVELL, 1744–1817

10419 **Coolidge, Bertha** [*i.e.* **Bertha (Coolidge) Slade**]. Practical education. Coloph new ser 1no4:604–9 Je '36.

EGAN, PIERCE, 1772–1849

10420 **Marsh, George L.** Pierce Egan the elder. TLS 17 Jl '43:348; H. J. Norman *ib.* 7 Ag '43:384; A. Noakes; P. G. Cambray 21 Ag '43:408.

EGERTON, WILLIAM, *pseud. of* EDMUND CURLL, 1675–1747 *see under* Book production and distribution–Printers, publishers, etc.

ELIOT, GEORGE, *pseud. of* MARY ANN (EVANS) CROSS, 1819–80

10421 **The manuscripts** of George Eliot's works. Athenæum 3325:97–8 Jl '91.

10422 **Peet, William H.** George Eliot. N&Q ser8 1:72 Ja '92; O. W. Tancock *ib.* 1:135 F '92.

10423 **George** Eliot's Agatha. [Measurements]. (Marginalia). Bkmns J ser3 16no8:461 '28.

10424 **Purdy, Richard L.** Journals and letters of George Eliot. Yale Univ Lib Gaz 7no1:1–4 Jl '32.

10425 **Ignoramus,** *pseud.* George Eliot as reviewer. N&Q 173:443 D '37; L. R. M. Strachan 174:14 Ja '38.

10426 **Carter, John W.** Eliot, G.: Adam Bede, Blackwood, 1859. [Variant bindings]. Bib N&Q 2no12:9 My '39.

10427 **Haight, Gordon S.** The Tinker collection of George Eliot manuscripts. Yale Univ Lib Gaz 29no4:148–50 Ap '55.

10428 **Carter, John W.** George Eliot's Agatha, 1869 — and after. [Forgery]. Bk Coll 6no3:244–52 '57.

10429 **Haight, Gordon S.** The George Eliot and George Henry Lewes collection. Yale Univ Lib Gaz 35no4:170–1 Ap '61.

ELIOT, THOMAS STEARNS, 1888–1968

10430 **Hellman, Milton A.** Eliot, T. S.: The waste land. [Whereabouts of original ms.]. Bib N&Q 2no4/5:9 My '36.

10431 **Gallup, Donald C.** Exhibition of writings by T. S. Eliot. Yale Univ Lib Gaz 11no4:94–5 Ap '37. [Sg.: D. C. G.]

10432 **Warburton, Thomas.** T. S. Eliot: Sacred wood, London, Methuen, 1920. [States]. Bib N&Q 2no10:9 Ap '38.

10433 **Rosenfeld, Benjamin.** Eliot, T. S.: The waste land, first edition. [Binding variants]. Bib N&Q 2no11:8 N '38; E. Daniels *ib.* 2no12:5 My '39.

10434 **Marshall, William H.** The text of T. S. Eliot's Gerontion. Stud Bib 4:213–7 '51/2. table.

10435 **Beare, Robert L.** Notes on the text of T. S. Eliot: variants from Russell square. Stud Bib 9:21–49 '57. tables.

10436 **Walmsley, D. M.** An unrecorded article by T. S. Eliot. [Religious drama and the church, 1934]. (Note 139). Bk Coll 9no2:198–9 '60; B. C. Bloomfield *ib.* 11no3:350 '62.

10437 **Woodward, Daniel H.** John Quinn and T. S. Eliot's first book of criticism. [Ezra Pound, his metric and poetry, 1917]. Pa Bib Soc Am 56:259–65 '62.

10438 **T. S.** Eliot, a birthday tribute. [Exhibition]. Brit Mus Q News Suppl 5:5 Jl '63.

10439 **Woodward, Daniel H.** Notes on the publishing history and text of The waste land. Pa Bib Soc Am 58:252–69 '64.

10440 **Sackton, Alexander.** T. S. Eliot at Texas. Lib Chron Univ Texas 8no3:22–6 '67.

'Desiderata' (p. 26)

10441 **Gallup, Donald C.** The 'lost' manuscripts of T. S. Eliot. N.Y. Pub Lib Bull 72no10:641–52 D '68. facsims.

10442 —— The lost manuscripts of T. S. Eliot. TLS 7 N '68:1237–40; A. N. L. Munby *ib.* 14 N '68:1281; J. Seelye 5 D '68:1392.

The waste land.–The waste land: the miscellaneous sheets.–The notebook.–The notebook: the loose sheets.

ELIZABETH I, QUEEN OF ENGLAND AND IRELAND, 1533–1603

10443 **Queen** Elizabeth's New testament. Bkworm 1no1:10–11 D '87.

10444 **Queen** Elizabeth's prayer-book. Bkworm 6no68:246 Jl '93.

10445 **Hughey, Ruth.** A note on queen Elizabeth's Godly meditation. Library ser4 15no2:237–40 S '34.

10446 **Jackson, William A.** The funeral procession of queen Elizabeth. Library ser4 26no4:262–71 Mr '46.

'Appendix [of surviving pamphlets memorializing queen Elizabeth]' (p. 270–1)

Repr. in Bond, William H., *ed.* Records of a bibliographer. Cambridge, Mass., 1967. p. 95–105.

10447 **Riddehough, G. B.** Queen Elizabeth's translation of Boethius' De consolatione philosophiae. J Eng Germ Philol 45no1:88–94 Ja '46.

10448 **Lowther, Anthony W.** Elstrack's portrait of queen Elizabeth. [Injunctions given by the queen's majesty, 1559]. (Note 205). Bk Coll 12no4:490 '63.

ELLIOTT, EBENEZER, 1781–1849

10449 **Mabbott, Thomas O.** Contributions of Ebenezer Elliott to an American magazine. N&Q 166:385 Je '34. [Sg.: T. O. M.]

ELLWOOD, THOMAS, 1639–1713

10450 **Fischer, Walther.** Zur Textgeschichte von Thomas Ellwoods Davideis, 1712–1796. Anglia 55:84–100 F '31.

10451 **Brink, Andrew** and **Helen Brink.** Ellwood's Davideis: a newly discovered version? Friends' Hist Soc J 49no1:31–3 '59.

ELYOT, SIR THOMAS, 1490?–1546

10452 **Bouck, Constance W.** On the identity of Papyrius geminus eleates. [Hermathena, and Siberch]. Cambridge Bib Soc Trans 2pt5:352–8 '58.

ESSEX, ARTHUR CAPELL, EARL OF, 1631–83 *see* Capell, Arthur, earl of Essex, 1631–83.

ETHEREGE, SIR GEORGE, 1635?–91

10453 **Bracher, Frederick.** The letterbooks of sir George Etherege. Harvard Lib Bull 15no3:238–45 Jl '67.

EVANS, EDWARD, 1831–1901

10454 **O'Donoghue, David J.** Edward Evans. [With selective list of writings]. Irish Bk Lover 10no6/8:57–8 Ja/Mr '19. [Sg.: D. J. O'D.]

10455 **Lewis, Aneirin.** Ieuan Fardd a'r Gwaith o Gyhoeddi Hen Lenyddiaeth Cymru. [Evan Evans and the publication of Welsh mediæval texts and proposals]. Welsh Bib Soc J 8no3:120–47 Jl '56.

English summary (p. 168–70)

EVANS, JOHN, 1792–1827

10456 **Thomas, sir D. Lleufer.** Cyfieithydd Hanes Pleidiau y Byd Crist'nogol, 1808. [John and Thomas Evans]. Welsh Bib Soc J 3no8:323–37 Jl '31. facsims.

EVELYN, JOHN, 1655–99

10457 **Ellis, Frederick S.** The ms. life of mrs. Godolphin. Bkworm 7no76:110 Mr '94.

10458 **Robinson, John.** Discovery of John Evelyn's Memoirs. N&Q ser8 8:245–6 S '95; Hilda Gamlin *ib.* 8:317 Oc '95; W. F. Prideaux; Ayeahr, *pseud.* 8:458 D '95; Hilda Gamlin 8:495 D '95; W. F. Prideaux 9:95–6 F '96; Hilda Gamlin; Ayeahr, *pseud.*; H. B. Wheatley 9:218 Mr '96; Essington 9:317 Ap '96.

10459 **Redgrave, Gilbert R.** Evelyn's essays on Publick employment and an active life. Library ser2 2no8:349–52 Oc '01.

10460 **Keynes, sir Geoffrey L.** John Evelyn as a bibliophil. Library ser4 12no2:175–93 S '31. illus., facsims., table.

10461 **Lindsay, David A. E., 27th earl of Crawford and Balcarres.** Gabriel Naudé and John Evelyn, with some notes on the marazinades. [Instructions concerning erecting of a library, 1661]. Library ser4 12no4:382–408 Mr '32. facsims.

10462 **Miller, Clarence W.** Cowley and Evelyn's Kalendarium hortense. Mod Lang N 63no6:398–401 Je '48.

10463 **Hiscock, Walter G.** John Evelyn's library at Christ Church. TLS 6 Ap '51:220.

10464 **Fixler, Michael.** A note on John Evelyn's History of the three late famous imposters. Library ser5 9no4:267–8 D '54.

10465 **Hiscock, Walter G.** William Upcott and John Evelyn's papers. Library ser5 20no4:320–5 D '65.

FAIRFIELD, CICILY ISABEL, (MRS. H. M. ANDREWS), 1892– *see* West, dame Rebecca, *pseud.*

FALCONER, WILLIAM, 1732–69

10466 **Couchman, Gordon W.** Falconer's Nautical journal. [Ms.]. N&Q 193:369 Ag '48.

10467 —— Editions of Falconer's Shipwreck. N&Q 198:439–40 Oc '53.

FALKNER, PRISCILLA SUSAN, (MRS. EDWARD BURY), fl.1793–1867
see Bury, Priscilla Susan (Falkner), fl.1793–1867.

FANE, MILDMAY, 2D EARL OF WESTMORLAND, d.1666

10468 **Withington, Eleanor.** The fugitive poetry of Mildmay Fane. [Mss.]. Harvard Lib Bull 9no1:61–78 '55. facsims.

FANSHAWE, SIR RICHARD, 1606–66

10469 **Fanshawe, E.** Sir R. Fanshawe. [Presentation copies of Il pastor fido]. N&Q ser10 3:451 Je '05.

10470 **Fanshawe** books and manuscripts. (Notes on sales). TLS 14 Ag '24:504.

10471 **Vieira, Mildred.** An unrecorded reissue of Fanshawe's translation of the Lusiads, 1664. Library ser5 23no4:352–6 D '68. facsims., table.

10472 **Hamer, Douglas.** Fanshawe's Lusiads. Library ser5 24no3:250–1 S '69.

FARQUHAR, GEORGE, 1678–1707

10473 **Whiting, George W.** The date of the second edition of the Constant couple. Mod Lang N 47no3:147–8 Mr '32.

FAWKES, FRANCIS, 1720–77

10474 **Hadfield, John.** Francis Fawkes: The brown jug. (Query no.11). Bk Coll 1no1:58 '52; W. N. H. Harding ib. 1no2:130 '52. facsim.

FERGUSSON, ROBERT, 1750–74

10475 **Gillis, William.** Robert Fergusson's first printed work. N&Q 199:437–8 Oc '54.

10476 **Law, Alexander.** The inscribed copies of the first edition, 1773, of the Poems of Robert Fergusson. Edinburgh Bib Soc Trans 3pt2:125–35 '54.

FERRAR, NICHOLAS, 1592–1637 see Book production and distribution –Printers, publishers, etc.–Little Gidding bindery.

FIELD, JOHN, 1782–1837

10477 **Neighbour, Oliver W.** Early editions of John Field. Brit Mus Q 19no1:1–2 Je '54.

10478 **Hopkinson, Cecil.** Bibliography of John Field. TLS 18 My '62:364.

FIELD, NATHAN, 1587–1620

10479 **Peery, William W.** Note on a commonplace: the three souls. [Text of Amends for ladies]. Philol Q 25no4:382–3 Oc '46.

10480 —— The quarto of Field's Weather-cocke. Library ser5 1no1:62–4 Je '46. tables.

10481 —— Nineteenth-century editorial practice as illustrated in the descent of the text of Nathan Field. Stud Eng Univ Texas 1947:5–17 '47.

FIELDING, HENRY, 1707–54

10483 **Dobson, H. Austin.** Two English bookmen. II. Henry Fielding. Bibliographica 1pt2:163–73 '95.

10484 **Prideaux, William F.** Fielding's Journal of a voyage to Lisbon, 1755. N&Q ser10 6:61–2 Jl '06; St. Swithin, *pseud., ib.* 6:115 Ag '06.

10485 **M., H. C.** Henry Fielding's library. Academy 72no1815:164–5 F '07; H. A. Dobson *ib.* 72no1816:195 F '07; H. C. M. 72no1817:220 Mr '07. facsims.

10486 **Robbins, Alfred F.** Jonathan Wild bibliography. N&Q ser10 11:347 My '09; H. Bleackley *ib.* 11:435–6 My '09.

10487 **Wells, John E.** The Champion and some unclaimed essays by Henry Fielding. Eng Studien 46no3:355–66 Jl '13.

10488 **Dobson, H. Austin.** Fielding and Andrew Millar. Library ser3 7no27:177–90 Jl '16.

10489 **De Castro, J. Paul.** Henry Fielding's last voyage. Library ser3 8no30:145–59 Ap '17.

10490 **Dickson, Frederick S.** The early editions of Fielding's Voyage to Lisbon. Library ser3 8no29:24–35 Ja '17.

10491 **Pollard, Alfred W.** The two 1755 editions of Fielding's Journal of a voyage to Lisbon. (Notes on old books). Library ser3 8no29:75–7 Ja '17; 8no30:160–2 Ap '17.

10492 **Wells, John E.** Fielding's Miscellanies. Mod Lang R 13no4:481–82 Oc '18.

10493 —— Fielding's Champion; more notes. Mod Lang N 35no1:18–23 Ja '20.

10494 **De Castro, J. Paul.** The printing of Fielding's works. Library ser4 1no4:257–70 Mr '21.

10495 **Stonehill, Charles A.** Fielding's The miser. TLS 22 Oc '25:693.

10496 **Fielding's** Charge to the jury, 1745. (Notes on sales). TLS 4 Mr '26:168.

10497 **Cross, Wilbur L.** The Fielding collection [presented by F. S. Dickson]. Yale Univ Lib Gaz 1no3:31–4 Ja '27.

10498 **Digeon, A.** La condamnation de Tom Jones à Paris. [Censorship]. R Anglo-Am 4no6:529–31 Aout '27.

10499 **Fielding's** Miser. Huntington Lib Bull 1:211–13 My '31.

10500 **Seymour, Mabel.** Henry Fielding. [A complete history of the late rebellion]. (Correspondence). London Merc 24no140:160 Je '31.

10501 **Jensen, Gerald E.** Two recent additions to the Frederick S. Dickson Fielding collection. [Photographs of mss.]. Yale Univ Lib Gaz 10no2:42 Oc '35.

10502 **Coolidge, Archibald C.** A Fielding pamphlet? [Stultus versus Sapientem]. TLS 9 My '36:400.

10503 **Jensen, Gerard E.** Proposals for a definitive edition of Fielding's Tom Jones. Library ser4 18no3:314–30 D '37.

10504 **McCusker, Honor.** First editions of Fielding. More Bks Boston Pub Lib Bull 13no3:114 Mr '38. [Sg.: H. McC.]

10505 **Wallace, Robert M.** Fielding manuscripts. TLS 18 My '40:243; J. P. de Castro *ib.* 1 Je '40:267.

10506 **Mead, Herman R.** [Bibliogr. note on Fielding's Coffee-house politician, 1730]. Pa Bib Soc Am 35:69 '41.

10507 **Eaves, Thomas C. D.** The publication of the first translations of Fielding's Tom Jones. Library ser4 26no2/3:189–90 S/D '45.

10508 **Jarvis, Rupert C.** Fielding, Dodsley, Marchant and Ray: some fugitive histories of the '45. N&Q 189:90–2 S '45; 189:117–20 S '45; 189:138–41 Oc '45.

10509 **Shipley, John B.** Fielding and The plain truth, 1740. N&Q 196:561–2 D '51.

10510 **Masengill, Jeanne A.** Variant forms of Fielding's Coffee-house politican. Stud Bib 5:178–83 '52/3.

10511 **Todd, William B.** Three notes on Fielding. Pa Bib Soc Am 47:70–5 '53. tables.

1. An apology for . . . T.C., 1740.–2. A dialogue between a gentleman . . . and an honest alderman . . . , 1747.–3. Amelia, 1752.

10512 **Shepperson, Archibald B.** Additions and corrections to facts about Fielding. [Publication dates]. Mod Philol 51no4:217–24 My '54.

10513 **Shipley, John B.** Fielding's Champion and a publisher's quarrel. N&Q 200:25–8 Ja '55.

10514 **Foxon, David F.** Fielding's The modern husband, 1732. (Note no.61). Bk Coll 5no1:76–7 '56; W. B. Todd *ib.* 5no3:276 '56.

10515 **Jarvis, Rupert C.** Fielding and the forty-five. N&Q 201:391–4 S '56; 201:479–82 N '56; 202:19–24 Ja '57.

10516 **Shaw, E. P.** A note on the temporary suppression of Tom Jones in France. Mod Lang N 72no1:41 Ja '57.

10517 **Greason, A. LeRoy.** Fielding's The history of the present rebellion in Scotland. Philol Q 37no1:119–23 Ja '58.

10518 **Shipley, John B.** The Coronation, a poem, 1727. (Query 103). Bk Coll 7no4:417 '58.

10519 **Jones, B. P.** Was there a temporary suppression of Tom Jones in France? Mod Lang N 76no6:495–8 Je '61.

10520 **Miller, Henry K.** 'Circumstances of publication' *in* Essays on Fielding's Miscellanies, a commentary on volume one. Princeton, N.J.; London, 1961. p. 3–28.

10521 **Eddy, Donald D.** The printing of Fielding's Miscellanies, 1743. Stud Bib 15:247–56 '62. diagrs., tables.

10522 **Battestin, Martin C.** Fielding's revisions of Joseph Andrews. Stud Bib 16:81–117 '63.

'Textual notes' (p. 95–117)

10523 **Thomas, D. S.** The publication of Henry Fielding's Amelia. Library ser5 18no4:303–7 D '63.

10524 **Woods, Charles B.** The folio text of Fielding's The miser. Huntington Lib Q 28no1:59–61 N '64.

10525 **Amory, Hugh.** A preliminary census of Henry Fielding's legal manuscripts. Pa Bib Soc Am 62:587–601 '68.

FILMER, SIR ROBERT, 1588?–1669

10526 **L., T. P. R.** Sir Robert Filmer: editions and mss. N&Q 177:98 Ag '39.

FINCH, ANNE, COUNTESS OF WINCHILSEA, 1661–1720

10527 **Prideaux, William F.** The Progress of life. N&Q ser10 8:401–2 N '07.

10528 **Anderson, Paul B.** Mrs. Manley's texts of three of lady Winchilsea's poems. Mod Lang N 45no2:95–9 F '30.

10529 **Neill, Desmond G.** Lady Winchilsea ms. N&Q 196:83 F '51.

FIRBANK, ARTHUR ANNESLEY RONALD, 1886–1926

10530 **Benkovitz, Miriam J.** Ronald Firbank in periodicals. Pa Bib Soc Am 54:295–7 '60.

10531 **Horder, Thomas J., baron Horder.** More Ronald Firbank. [The new rhythum ms.]. TLS 14 Jl '61:440; Miriam J. Benkovitz ib. 18 Ag '61:549.

10532 **Alford, Norman W.** Seven notebooks of Ronald Firbank. [With material for Valmouth]. Lib Chron Univ Texas 8no3:33–9 '67. illus.

10533 **Davis, Robert M.** The text of Firbank's Vainglory. Pa Bib Soc Am 63:36–41 '69. tables.

FISHER, BP. JOHN, 1459–1535

10534 **Gray, George J.** Fisher's sermon against Luther. Library ser3 2no7:314–18 Jl '11.

10535 —— Fisher's sermons against Luther. Library ser3 3no9:55–63 Ja '12.

Sermon against Luther, Wynkyn de Worde [1521].–Sermon against Lutheranism [1526].

10536 —— Letters of bishop Fisher, 1521–3. [And R. Sharpe]. Library ser3 4no14:133–45 Ap '13.

10537 **Davidson, W. A. G. Doyle-.** John Fisher's English sermons. Mod Lang R 23no3:341–2 Jl '28.

FITCHETT, JOHN, 1776–1836

10538 **Pierpont, Robert.** King Alfred, by Fitchett: a long poem. N&Q ser9 5:101 F '00.

FITZGERALD, EDWARD, 1809–83

10539 **Prideaux, William F.** FitzGerald's Euphranor. [1851]. N&Q ser9 1:302–3 Ap '98.

10540 **Axon, William E. A.** Two of Edward FitzGerald's early poems. [And Edward Marlborough FitzGerald]. N&Q ser9 3:441–2 Je '99; W. F. Prideaux; C. C. B. *ib.* 4:15–16 Jl '99.

10541 **Allen, Edward Heron-.** The smallest book ever published. [FitzGerald's Rubáiyát, 1900]. N&Q ser9 8:120 Ag '01.

10542 **Prideaux, William F.** FitzGerald bibliography. N&Q ser10 2:141–2 Ag '04; W. E. Mozley *ib.* 2:214–15 S '04.

10543 **Allen, Edward Heron-.** Omar Khayyám: FitzGerald's first edition, 1859. N&Q ser10 4:105 Ag '05.

10544 **Willett, E. V. Anson.** FitzGerald's Omar Khayyám. N&Q ser10 6:388 N '06; R. L. Moreton *ib.* 6:453 D '06.

10545 **Penwick, George.** Illustrated editions of Rubáiyát of Omar Khayyám. Biblioph 2no7:22–6 S '08. illus., facsims.

10546 **Potter, Ambrose G.** Omar Khayyám bibliography. N&Q ser11 3:328 Oc '11; 3:358 Oc '11; 3:497 D '11; 5:295 Ap '12.

10547 —— Omar Khayyám's Rubáiyát. N&Q ser11 5:464–5 Je '12; W. F. Prideaux *ib.* 6:34–5 Jl '12.

10548 **Nicholls, Norah.** Some early editions of FitzGerald's Omar. Bkmn 79no473:320–1 F '31.

10549 **Allen, Edward Heron-.** An almost unrecorded edition of Salaman and Absal. [1871]. N&Q 176:350 My '39; 177:31–2 Jl '39.

10550 **Jones, Evan D.** Welsh printing in Mexico. [Trans. of FitzGerald's Omar, by T. Ifor Rees]. (News and notes). Nat Lib Wales J 2no1:37 '41.

10551 **Hanford, James H.** FitzGerald's Rubáiyát. [Presented to Library]. Princeton Univ Lib Chron 19no1:60–2 '57.

10552 **Horrox, Reginald.** The Rubáiyát after one hundred years. TLS 10 Ap '59:209.

10553 **Weber, Carl J.** Preparing for the centenary of FitzGerald's Rubáiyát. Colby Lib Q ser5 1:5–14 Mr '59.

10554 —— The 'discovery' of FitzGerald's Rubáiyát; three scholars discuss a Swinburne autograph in the Wrenn collection. Lib Chron Univ Texas 7no3:3–11 '63.

10555 **Bridge, Alexander.** Edward FitzGerald's Six dramas of Calderon; 1854 edition? (Query 229). Bk Coll 17no4:491 '68.

FITZHERBERT, SIR ANTHONY, 1470–1538

10556 **Clarke, sir Ernest.** Law books by or attributed to sir Anthony Fitzherbert. London, 1894. 28l. 30cm. (Duplicated typescript)

FLAHERTY, WILLIAM EDWARD, 1807–78

10557 **Wainewright, John B.** The Annals of England. N&Q ser11 2:289 Oc '10; J. Parker; F. W. Henkel; A. T. Everitt *ib.* 2:354–5 Oc '10.

FLAMSTEED, JOHN, 1646–1719

10558 **Flamsteed's** Historia cœlestis, 1712. Bod Lib Rec 6no1:343–4 Oc '57.

FLECKER, JAMES (formerly HERMAN) ELROY, 1884–1915

10559 **Roberts, Cecil M.** James Elroy Flecker. [And copyright]. TLS 5 Oc '16:477; sir J. C. Squire *ib.* 12 Oc '16:489; D. Goldring 26 Oc '16:513; E. Mathews 2 N '16:525; sir J. C. Squire 16 N '16:549; E. Mathews; J. M. Dent and sons 23 N '16:561; M. Secker 30 N '16:573; E. Mathews 7 D '16:589; J. M. Dent and sons 14 D '16:614.

FLETCHER, ANDREW, 1655–1716

10560 **Macfie, Robert A. S.** Fletcher of Saltoun. N&Q ser9 3:261 Ap '99.

FLETCHER, GILES, 1549?–1611

10561 **Berry, Lloyd E.** Giles Fletcher the elder's Licia. [Ptg.]. Library ser5 15no2:133–4 Je '60.

FLETCHER, GILES, 1588?–1623

10562 **Wasserman, Earl R.** Moses Browne and the 1783 edition of Giles and Phineas Fletcher. Mod Lang N 56no4:288–90 Ap '41.

FLETCHER, JOHN, 1579–1625 *see also* Beaumont, Francis, 1584–1616, and John Fletcher, 1579–1625.

10563 **Tannenbaum, Samuel A.** A hitherto unpublished John Fletcher autograph. J Eng Germ Philol 28no3:35–40 Ja '29. facsim.

10564 **Hiscock, Walter G.** Fletcher's The prophetess. [1690]. TLS 26 Mr '31:252.

10565 **Tannenbaum, Samuel A.** The John Fletcher holograph. Philol Q 13no4:401–4 Oc '34; sir W. W. Greg *ib.* 14no4:373 Oc '35; S. A. Tannenbaum 15no2:221 Ap '36.

10566 **Jump, John D.** Rollo, duke of Normandy; some bibliographical notes on the seventeenth-century editions. Library ser4 18no3:279–86 D '37.

FLETCHER, PHINEAS, 1582–1650

10567 **Seaton, Ethel.** Phineas Fletcher, a new ms. TLS 22 Mr '23:199; F. S. Boas *ib.* 29 Mr '23:216.

FORBES, JAMES, 1749–1819

10568 **Bullock, H.** James Forbes. N&Q 192:409 S '47; 193:382–3 S '48.

FORBES, JOHN, 1568?–1634

10569 **Willoughby, Edwin E.** [Bibliogr. note on Forbes' Four sermons, 1635]. Pa Bib Soc Am 34:85 '40.

FORBES, JOHN, d.1675

10570 **Anderson, Peter J.** Forbes's Cantus, 1662. TLS 27 N '24:798.

FORD, FORD MADOX, formerly HUEFFER, 1873–1939

10571 **Naumburg, Edward.** A collector looks at Ford Maddox Ford. Princeton Univ Lib Chron 9no3:105–18 Ap '48. facsims.

10572 **Ludwig, Richard M.** The manuscript of Ford's It was the nightingale. [Presented to Library]. Princeton Univ Lib Chron 22no4:190–1 '61.

10573 **Hoffman, Charles G.** Ford's manuscript revisions of The good soldier. Eng Lit Transit 9no3:145–52 '66.

FORD, JOHN, fl.1602–39

10574 **Lloyd, Bertram.** An inedited ms. of Ford's Fames memoriall. R Eng Stud 1no1:93–5 Ja '25.

10575 **Anderson, Donald K.** The date and handwriting of a manuscript copy of Ford's Perkin Warbeck. N&Q 208:340–1 S '63.

10576 **Crum, Margaret C.** A manuscript of Ford's Perkin Warbeck, an additional note. N&Q 210:104–5 Mr '65.

FORMAN, SIMON, 1552–1611

10577 **Klein, David.** The case of Forman's Bocke of plaies. [And Collier]. Philol Q 11no3:385–95 Oc '32.

10578 **Tannenbaum, Samuel A.** 'The Forman notes on Shakspere [and Collier]' *in* Shaksperian scraps and other Elizabethan fragments. New York, 1933. p. 1–35. facsim.

10579 **Eagle, Roderick L.** Simon Forman's ms. Booke of plaies and notes thereof. [And Collier]. N&Q 191:16 Jl '46.

10580 **Wilson, John D.** and **R. W. Hunt.** The authenticity of Simon Forman's Bocke of plaies. R Eng Stud 23no91:193–200 Jl '47.

10581 **Race, Sydney.** Simon Forman's Bocke of plaies: ms. Ashmole 208. [And Collier]. N&Q 197:116–17 Mr '52.

10582 —— Simon Forman's Bocke of plaies examined. [And Collier]. N&Q 203:9–14 Ja '58.

10583 **Pafford, John H. P.** Simon Forman's Bocke of plaies. R Eng Stud new ser 10no39:289–91 Ag '59.

FORRESTER, JAMES, fl.1734

10584 **Cordasco, Francesco G. M.** James Forrester's Polite philosopher, 1736; an addition to the bibliography of the Theophrastan character. N&Q 196:82 F '51.

FORSTER, EDWARD MORGAN, 1879–1970

10585 **Shipley, John B.** Additions to the E. M. Forster bibliography. Pa Bib Soc Am 60:224–5 '66.

FORSTER, JOHN, 1812–76

10586 **Super, Robert H.** Forster as Landor's literary executor. Mod Lang N 52no7:504–6 N '37.

10587 **Collins, Philip A. W.** John Forster's diary. TLS 30 N '62:937.

10588 **Lane, Lauriat.** The Mennen copy of Forster's Life of Dickens. [Extra-illustrated by E. J. Collings, with list of added material]. Cornell Lib J 8:21–34 '69. illus.

FOSTER, JOHN, BARON ORIEL, 1740–1828

10589 **Federer, Charles A.** John Foster. [Strictures on the address, 1825]. N&Q ser9 11:406–7 My '03; J. J. Foster *ib.* 11:451–2 Je '03.

FOWLER, HENRY WATSON, 1858–1933

10590 **Fowler** and his Modern English usage. TLS 30 My '58:302.

FOX, GEORGE, 1624–91

10591 **Sharp, Isaac.** The handwriting of George Fox. Friends' Hist Soc J
1no1:6–10 N '03; 1no2:61 My '04. facsims.

10592 **A grangerised** George Fox. [Biogr. by Thomas Hodgkin, 1896]. Friends'
Hist Soc J 20no1/2:58 '23.

10593 **Nickalls, John L.** George Fox's library. [With list]. Friends' Hist Soc J
28:2–21 '31. facsims.

10594 **Cadbury, Henry J.** George Fox's library: further identifications. Friends'
Hist Soc J 29:63–71 '32. facsims.

10595 —— George Fox's library again. Friends' Hist Soc J 30:9–19 '33. facsims.

> Titles identified.–Copies actually owned by George Fox.–Works not by Friends.–Other
> contents of the library.

FOXE, JOHN, 1516–87

10596 **Melville,** *pseud.* Information respecting book sought. [Foxe's Commen-
tarii rerum, 1554]. N&Q ser8 7:267 Ap '95; E. M. Borrajo; E. H.
Marshall *ib.* 7:311 Ap '95; E. Marshall 7:417 My '95.

10597 **Scholderer, J. Victor.** John Foxe's commonplace book [Locorum com-
munium tituli et ordines, 1557]; James I's speech on the gunpowder plot;
John Sharp's Cursus theologicus. Brit Mus Q 7no4:122–3 My '33. [Sg.:
V. S.]

10598 **Oliver, Leslie M.** The seventh edition of John Foxe's Acts and
monuments. [1632]. Pa Bib Soc Am 37:243–60 '43.

10599 —— Single-page imposition in Foxe's Acts and monuments, 1570.
Library ser5 1no1:49–56 Je '46.

10600 **Dunkin, Paul S.** Foxe's Acts and monuments, 1570, and single-page imposition. Library ser5 2no2/3:159–70 S/D '47. facsims.

FREETH, JOHN, 1731–1808

10601 **Horden, John R. B.** John Freeth, 1731–1808, the Birmingham poet.
Library ser5 18no4:309 D '63.

FREWEN, JOHN, 1558–1628

10602 **Gillett, Charles R.** John Frewen: title page of Certaine fruitful instructions. N&Q ser12 9:447 D '21.

FROUDE, JAMES ANTHONY, 1818–94

10603 **K., L. L.** Prof. Froude's Nemesis of faith. N&Q ser8 1:430 My '92; G. C. Boase *ib.* 1:452 Je '92; F. A. Blaydes 2:53 Jl '92; J. Pickford 2:324 Oc '92; E. L. H. Tew 2:472 D '92.

FULLER, THOMAS, 1608–61

10604 [**Madan, Falconer**]. Fuller's sermon in 1644. [Jacob's vow]. Bod Q Rec 2no21:208 Ap '19.

10605 **Wood, James.** Bibliography of Fuller's Worthies. N&Q 164:136 F '33.

10606 **Goodspeed, George T.** Fuller, Thomas: Worthies, 1662. [Copy with two TP]. Bib N&Q 2no7:4 Oc '36; D. M[assey] *ib.* 2no8:4 F '37.

10607 **Massey, Dudley.** Gibson: Bibliography of Fuller. [A sermon preached, 1643]. Bib N&Q 2no9:4 Ja '38. [Sg.: D. M.]

10608 **Woodward, Daniel H.** Thomas Fuller, the protestant divines, and plagiary yet speaking. [Abel redevivus, 1651]. Cambridge Bib Soc Trans 4pt3:201–24 '66.

10609 —— Thomas Fuller, William Dugard, and the pseudonymous Life of Sidney, 1655. Pa Bib Soc Am 62:501–10 '68.

GADDESDEN, JOHN OF, 1280?–1361 *see* John of Gaddesden, 1280?–1361.

GALBRAITH, ROBERT, d.1543

10610 **Menzies, Walter.** Robert Galbraith, 148- –1543. [Opus quadriperititum, 1510 with illus. of ptg. pr.]. Aberdeen Univ Lib Bull 7no39:205-13 Je '29. facsims.

GALSWORTHY, JOHN, 1867–1933

10611 **Flower, Robin E. W.** Mr. Galsworthy's Forsyte chronicles. Brit Mus Q 4no2:29–31 S '29. [Sg.: R. F.]

10612 **Bell, sir Harold I.** New Forsyte mss. Brit Mus Q 5no4:118 Mr '31. [Sg.: H. I. B.]

10613 **Adams, Frederick B.** Galsworthy: Justice. [Issues]. Bib N&Q 1no1:8 Ja '35; [P. H. Muir] *ib.* 1no2:6–7 Ap '35; F. B. Adams 1no3:2 Ag '35.

10614 **Davies, Sarah H.** Galsworthy the craftsman; studies in the original manuscripts of the Forsyte chronicles. Bkmn (Suppl) 85no505:18–20 Oc '33. facsims.

I. The man of property.–II. The plan of Robin Hill.–III. The Indian summer of a Forsyte.

10615 —— Galsworthy the craftsman; further studies in the original manuscripts of the Forsyte chronicles. *ib*. 86no512:12–16 Ap '34. facsim.

IV. In Chancery.–V. Awakening.–VI. To let.–VII. Note on the Forsyte family tree.

10616 —— Galsworthy the craftsman; studies in the original manuscripts of The white monkey and The silver spoon. *ib*. 87no517:27–31 Oc '34. facsim.

VIII. The white monkey.–IX. The silver spoon.

10617 —— Galsworthy the craftsman; final studies in the original manuscripts of the Forsyte [chronicle]. [n.p., Swansea?] Privately ptd. and published, 1935. 5p. facsim. 33cm. Covertitle.

X. Swan song.–XI. A silent wooing and Passers by.–XII. The short stories of On Forsyte 'change.–XIII. Conclusion.

10618 **James, Harold E.** Galsworthy: A bit o' love. [Issues]. Bib N&Q 1no3:5 Ag '35.

10619 **S.** Galsworthy: Man of property. [Issues]. Bib N&Q 1no2:10 Ap '35; F. B. Adams *ib*. 1no3:2 Ag '35.

10620 **Galsworthy**: Swan song. Bib N&Q 1no1:3 Ja '35; H. E. James *ib*. 1no3:1 Ag '35; E. B. M. 2no3:2 Ap '36; H. E. James 2no4/5:1 My '36; G. G[oodspeed] 2no6:1 Jl '36.

10621 **Fabes, Gilbert H.** The Forsyte saga. [Two issues]. Bk Hndbk 1no8:414 '49.

10622 **The Man** of property. TLS 22 Ja '49:64; H. S. Billing *ib*. 19 F '49:126.

10623 **Bennett, JoAnn W.** John Galsworthy and H. G. Wells. [Collections acquired by Library]. Yale Univ Lib Gaz 28no1:33–43 Je '53. facsim.

GALT, JOHN, 1779–1839

10624 **Roughead, William.** A Galt manuscript. [The Howdie]. TLS 19 Oc '22:666.

GAMBOLD, WILLIAM, 1672–1728

10625 **Owens, B. G.** The reverend William Gambold, 1672–1728. (Biographica et bibliographica). Nat Lib Wales J 1no4:228–9 '40.

GARRICK, DAVID, 1717–79

10626 **Evans, H. A.** Garrick's Jubilee. N&Q ser9 3:86 F '99; E. R. Dibdin *ib*. 3:329–30 Ap '99.

10627 **Sale** [of Garrick relics]. Athenæum 3794:67–8 Jl '00.

10628 **Two** Garrick collections. [G. E. Solly, Wimborne; mrs. Carew, Lustleigh]. (Notes on sales). TLS 7 Je '28:436; 28 Je '28:492.

10629 **Whibley, Leonard.** Garrick's verses to Gray. [And Strawberry Hill pr.]. (Bibliographical notes). TLS 12 F '38:112.

10630 **Martz, Louis L.** and **Edwine M. Martz.** Notes on some manuscripts relating to David Garrick. R Eng Stud 19no74:186–200 Ap '43.

10631 **Evans, Gwynne B.** Garrick's The fairies, 1755: two editions. N&Q 204:410–11 N '59.

GARTER, THOMAS, fl.1578

10632 **Evans, Benjamin I., baron Evans of Hungershall.** The lost 'commody' of Susanna. [1578]. TLS 2 My '36:372. facsim.

GASCOIGNE, GEORGE, 1525?–77

10633 **Greg, sir Walter W.** A Hundreth sundry flowers. Library ser4 7no3:269–82 D '26.

10634 —— A Hundreth sundrie flowers. Mod Lang R 22no4:441–2 Oc '27.

10635 **Ward, B. M.** A Hundreth sundrie flowers. Library ser4 8no1:123–30 Je '27.

'Dr. Greg's answer' (p. 127–30)

10636 **Bowers, Fredson T.** Notes on Gascoigne's A hundreth sundrie flowres and The posies. Harvard Stud & N Philol & Lit 16:13–35 '34.

'The publication of A hundreth sundrie flowres' (p. 27–35)

10637 **Prouty, Charles T.** and **Ruth Prouty.** 'George Gascoigne, The noble arte of venerie, and queen Elizabeth at Kenilworth' *in* McManaway, James G., G. E. Dawson, and E. E. Willoughby, *ed.* Joseph Quincy Adams memorial studies. Washington, 1948. p. 639–64. facsims.

I. The source.–II. The translation and the entertainment for queen Elizabeth.–III. The illustrations.

GASKELL, ELIZABETH CLEGHORN (STEVENSON), 1810–65

10638 [**Hatfield, C. W.**]. Suppressed passages: a collation of the earlier and later editions of mrs. Gaskell's Life of Charlotte Brontë. Brontë Soc Trans 6pt31:50–64 '21.

10639 **Lancaster, J. T.** Bibliography: Gaskell. [The half brothers]. N&Q ser12 11:289 Oc '22.

10640 **Hopkins, Annette B.** A uniquely illustrated Cranford. [Illus. by W. H. Drake after Hugh Thomson]. Ninet Cent Fict 4no4:299–314 Mr '50. illus.

See also no. 10642.

10641 **Horrocks, Sidney.** The Gaskell collection. (Special collections in the Reference library, V). Manchester R 6:483 '53. [Sg.: S. H.]

10642 **Lauterbach, Edward S.** A note on A uniquely illustrated Cranford. (Notes and queries). Ninet Cent Fict 8no3:232–4 D '53.

10643 **Sharps, John G.** Articles by mrs. Gaskell in The Pall Mall gazette, 1865. N&Q 210:301–2 Ag '65.

10644 **H., M. J.** Lizzie Leigh, a bibliographical inquiry. Manchester R 11:132–3 '67.

GAY, JOHN, 1685–1732

10645 **Peacock, Florence.** Gay's Fables. N&Q ser8 2:388 N '92; W. H. K. Wright; G. Y. Baldock *ib.* 2:454 D '92.

10646 **Brydges, E. T.** The Beggar's opera. [And copyright]. N&Q ser8 7:501–2 Je '95.

10647 **Gay, Ernest L.** Bibliography of John Gay. N&Q ser11 8:241–2 S '13.

10648 **Faber, Geoffrey C.** Gay's works. N&Q ser12 12:130–1 F '23; F. E. Ball; M. *ib.* 12:174 Mr '23; A. C. Potter 12:273 Ap '23; R. H. Griffith 12:375–6 My '23.

10649 **Schultz, William E.** The music of The beggar's opera in print, 1728–1923. [With list of ed.]. Nat Assn Music Teachers' Proc 87–99 '24.

10650 **Bryce, John C.** Addition to Gay's Fables. [A tale being a . . . , 1728]. TLS 4 Jl '35:432.

10651 **Sutherland, James R.** Polly among the pirates. [Copyright]. Mod Lang R 37no3:291–303 Jl '42.

10652 **Mack, Maynard.** Gay Augustan. [Gift of works]. Yale Univ Lib Gaz 21no1:6–10 Jl '46.

10653 **Knotts, Walter E.** Press numbers as a bibliographical tool; a study of Gay's The beggar's opera, 1728. Harvard Lib Bull 3no2:198–212 '49. table.

10654 **Osborn, James M.** 'That on Whiston' by John Gay. [Ode for music on the longitude, 1727, not by Gay; A true and faithful narrative, 1732, by him]. Pa Bib Soc Am 56:73–8 '62.

GIBBINGS, ROBERT JOHN, 1889–1958 *see* Book production and distribution–Printers, publishers, etc.–Golden cockerel press Waltham St.Lawrence, Berks., est. 1921.

GIBBON, EDWARD, 1737–94

10655 **Rae, W. Fraser.** Gibbon's library. Athenæum 3632:744–5 Je '97; R. Edgcumbe *ib.* 3636:36 Jl '97.

10656 **Edmunds, Albert J.** Gibbon's Decline and fall in America. [Sales]. N&Q ser10 4:405 N '05.

10657 **S.** Gibbon's ms. of The decline and fall. N&Q ser10 6:510 D '06.

10658 **Beatty, H. M.** Editions of Gibbon's History. N&Q ser11 5:189 Mr '12.

10659 —— The bibliography of Gibbon. TLS 15 Jl '20:456.

10660 **Gunther, R. T.** Some unedited accounts of Edward Gibbon. N&Q ser13 1:143–4 Ag '23; 1:163–5,183–5 S '23.

10661 **Harrison, E.** Errors in the text of Gibbon's Decline and fall. TLS 14 Jl '24:463–4; 31 Jl '24:477; 21 Ag '24:513.

10662 **Remnant** of Gibbon's library. (Notes on sales). TLS 27 D '34:924.

10663 **Books** from the library of Edward Gibbon ... left by him in Lausanne. ... Piccadilly N 14:11–13 '35.

10664 **Norton, Jane E.** Editions of Gibbon. [Her bibliogr.]. TLS 21 Mr '35:176.

10665 —— Gibbon bibliography. N&Q 168:154 Mı '35.

10666 **Parsons, Edward J. S.** Gibbon exhibition. Bod Q Rec 8:315–16 '37. [Sg.: E. J. S. P.]

10667 **Thompson, James W.** The library of Gibbon the historian. Lib Q 7no3:343–53 Jl '37.

10668 **Keynes, sir Geoffrey L.** The library of Edward Gibbon. Library ser4 19no2:155 S '38.

10669 **Davis, Rupert Hart-.** Gibbon's library. [Keynes' book]. TLS 29 Ap '39:250.

10670 **Keynes, sir Geoffrey L.** The library of Edward Gibbon, a catalogue of his books. London, J. Cape, 1940. (Reissued: Bibliographical society, 1950). 288p. port. 23cm.

Rev: TLS 4 My '40:224; J. E. N[orton] Library ser4 21:218–23 '40.

10671 —— Gibbon's library catalogue. TLS 22 S '45:456.

10672 **Boyce, George K.** The costs of publishing Gibbon's Vindication. Pa Bib Soc Am 43:335–9 '49. table.

10673 **Rea, Robert R.** Some notes on Edward Gibbon's Mémoire justificatif. Stud Bib 5:194–7 '52/3.

10674 **Fulton, John F.** Gibbon, the unprofitable undergraduate. [Gibbon's library and Magdalen college, Oxford]. ABA Ann 1953:13–18 '53.

10675 **Brown, T. Julian.** Edward Gibbon, 1737–1794. (English literary autographs, IX). Bk Coll 3no1:53 '54. facsims.

10676 **Barker, Nicolas J.** A note on the bibliography of Gibbon, 1776–1802. Library ser5 18no1:40–50 Mr '63. table.

10677 **Nickerson, Charles C.** Gibbon's copy of Steele's Dramatick works. (Note 217). Bk Coll 13no2:207 '64.

GIBBON, SKEFFINGTON, fl.1796–1831

10678 **Bourke, Francis S.** Bibliography of Skeffington Gibbon. [On the repeal of the Union, n.d.]. Irish Bk Lover 32no1:18 Je '52. [Sg.: F. S. B.]

10679 —— Skeffington Gibbon ... & bibliography. [On the repeal of the Union]. Irish Bk Lover 32no5:104–5 Jl '56.

Varies slightly from no.10678.

GIFFARD, HENRY, fl.1741

10680 **McKillop, Alan D.** Giffard's Pamela, a comedy. [Hitherto attrib. to J. Love]. (Note 148). Bk Coll 9no4:455–6 '60.

GIFFORD, WILLIAM, 1756–1826

10681 **William** Gifford. (Notes on sales). TLS 9 Jl '25:468.

10682 **Chapman, Guy:** Bibliography of William Gifford. [Locations of rare items]. Bib N&Q 2no6:5 Jl '36; Harriet Marlow *ib.* 2no8:3 F '37.

GILBERT, SIR WILLIAM SCHWENCK, 1836–1911

10683 **Sutcliffe, G. W.** Gilbert: More Bab ballads. [Issues]. Bib N&Q 1no3:5 Ag '35.

10684 **Savoyards** on 38th street. [Pierpont Morgan library exhibition]. TLS 9 F '51:92.

10685 **Allen, Reginald.** A Gilbert & Sullivan collection: owner of the largest G. & S. collection in America discusses autograph examples of the famous operetta team. Autogr Coll J 5no2:11–19 '53. facsims.

> Three collections in one.–The autographic material.–Letters reveal true character.–The mystery of the middle name.–Their earliest and latest letters.–Presentation copies.–Autograph manuscripts.

10686 **Pearson, Hesketh.** The private papers of W. S. Gilbert. Theat Arts 41no12:70–1,84–7 D '57.

10687 **Gransden, K. W.** and **P. J. Willetts.** Papers of W. S. Gilbert. Brit Mus Q 21no3:67–9 Je '58.

10688 **Randall, David A.** Gilbert and Sullivan's Princess Ida. Pa Bib Soc Am 59:322–6 '65.

10689 —— The Gondoliers. Pa Bib Soc Am 59:193–8 '65.

10690 **Jones, John B.** The printing of The grand duke: notes toward a Gilbert bibliography. Pa Bib Soc Am 61:335–42 '67; Correction *ib.* 62:264 '68.

GILDON, CHARLES, 1665–1724

10691 **The thing** about Wycherley. [Memoirs of the life of William Wycherley]. (Notes on sales). TLS 23 N '22:768.

10692 **Briscoe, John d'A.** Hypocrisie alamode. [The stage-beaux tossed]. TLS 15 Oc '31:802.

10693 **Moore, John R.** The Groans of Great Britain; an unassigned tract by Charles Gildon. [Les soupirs, or. . . .]. Pa Bib Soc Am 40no1:22–31 '46.

10694 **Anderson, G. L.** The authorship of Cato examin'd, 1713. Pa Bib Soc Am 51:84–90 '57.

GILPIN, WILLIAM, 1724–1804

10695 **Templeman, William D.** German translations of William Gilpin. N&Q 156:293–5 Ap '29.

10696 —— Gilpin's Essay upon prints. TLS 11 Ap '29:296.

10697 —— Three anonymous works by William Gilpin. N&Q 160:112–14 F '31.

10698 —— An 1811 publication of drawings by William Gilpin. [A practical illustration of Gilpin's day]. N&Q 184:39–40 Ja '43; M. W. Brockwell *ib.* 184:178 Mr '43; W. F. Perkins 184:235 Ap '43; W. D. Templeman 185:112 Ag '43.

10699 —— The engravings for Gilpin's works on picturesque beauty. [Aquatints]. N&Q 195:52–4 F '50.

GISSING, GEORGE ROBERT, 1857–1903

10700 **Leeds, H. E.** George Gissing. TLS 22 My '19:280.

10701 **Adams, George M.** How and why I collect George Gissing. Coloph [5]pt18:[1p.] '34.

10702 **Gissing**: Thyrza. Bib N&Q 1no1:8 Ja '35.

10703 **Richter, M. C.** Gissing: Human odds and ends. [Priority of 1897 and 1898 ed.]. Bib N&Q 1no1:7 Ja '35.

10704 **[Haraszti, Zoltán].** First editions of Gissing's works. More Bks Boston Pub Lib Bull 11no2:41–2 F '36.

10705 **Niebling, Richard F.** The Adams-Gissing collection [presented to Library]. Yale Univ Lib Gaz 16no2:47–50 Oc '41.

10706 **Wing, Donald G.** The Adams-Gissing collection. [Additions]. Yale Univ Lib Gaz 18no3:49 Ja '44. [Sg.: D. G. W.]

10707 **Coustillas, Pierre.** Gissing's writings on Dickens, a bio-bibliographical survey. Dickensian 6no347:168–79 S '65. port.

10708 —— Collecting George Gissing. Bk Coll & Lib Mnthly 1:9–13 My '68.

10709 —— The stormy publication of Gissing's Veranilda. N.Y. Pub Lib Bull 72no9:588–610 N '68.

10710 —— Gissing's writings on Dickens, a bio-bibliographical survey ... London, Enitharmon pr., 1969. 25p. 23cm. (Enitharmon press Gissing ser2)

   Rev. from no.10707.

10711 **Spiers, John** and **P. Coustillas.** A George Gissing bibliography. Bk Coll & Lib Mnthly 17:149–54 S '69; 18:183–7 Oc '69; 19:221–4 N '69.

GLADSTONE, WILLIAM EWART, 1809–98

10712 **Roberts, William.** The right hon. W. E. Gladstone, M.P. (Bookworms of yesterday and to-day). Bkworm 3no30:161–5 My '90.

10713 **Gladstone, William E.** Mr. Gladstone as a book collector. Acad 50:589 D '96.

10714 **McGovern, John B.** Gladstone as playwright. N&Q ser10 3:89–90 F '05.

10715 **Brown, J.** Rock of ages: Gladstone's Latin version. N&Q ser10 7:369 My '07; J. T. Page; J. Watson; E. A. *ib.* 7:458 Je '07; S. Waddington 8:17 Jl '07.

10716 **H., W. B.** Gladstoniana: Glynnese. [Contributions towards the Glynne language, 1851]. N&Q ser10 7:148 F '07.

10717 **Ballinger, sir John.** Gladstone's translation of Rock of ages. Library ser3 6no22:183–5 Ap '15. facsim.

10718 **[Gladstone, William E.].** Mr. Gladstone on book-collecting. (Marginalia). Bkmns J ser3 18no13:19–20 '30.

10719 **Bell, sir Harold I.** Gifts from mr. Gabriel Wells. [Gladstone's Locksley hall and the jubilee, 1887, and mss.]. Brit Mus Q 10no2:72–3 N '35.

GLANVILL, JOSEPH, 1636–80

10720 **J., H.** Glanvil: An essay concerning preaching. [His authorship]. Bib N&Q 1no4:8 Oc '35; T. Warburton *ib.* 2no4/5:3 My '36.

GLAPTHORNE, HENRY, fl.1639

10721 **Walter, J. H.** Wit in a constable; censorship and revision. Mod Lang R 34no1:9–20 Ja '39.

GLASSE, HANNAH, fl.1747

10722 **Hooper, Richard.** Mrs. Glasse's cookery book. Athenæum 3445:628 N '93; J. Humphreys *ib.* 3466:664–5 N '93; R. Hooper, W. F. Waller; G. Clulow 3448:733–4 N '93; R. Hooper 3450:809 D '93; 3477:774–5 Je '94.

10723 **Hayes, James.** Mrs. Glasse. N&Q ser9 11:147 F '03; Rachel E. Head; Matilda Pollard; E. H. Coleman *ib.* 11:231–2 Mr '03.

10724 **Heal, sir Ambrose.** Hannah Glasse and her Art of cookery. N&Q 174:401–3 Je '38; Madeleine H. Dodds *ib.* 174:461–2 Je '38; R. A. A[usten]-L[eigh] 175:49 Jl '38; Madeleine H. Dodds 175:68–9 Jl '38; V. H. 175:106 Ag '38; sir A. Heal 177:29–30 Jl '39.

GOAD, THOMAS, 1576–1638

10725 **Crow, John.** Thomas Goad and The dolefull euen-song: an editorial experiment. Cambridge Bib Soc Trans 1pt3:238–59 '51. diagr., facsims.

10726 **Freeman, Arthur.** The Fatal vesper and The doleful evensong: claim-jumping in 1623. [Goad's suppression of W. C.'s pamphlet]. Library ser5 22no2:128–35 Je '67.

GODWIN, BP. FRANCIS, 1562–1633

10727 **McColley, Grant.** The third edition of Francis Godwin's The man in the moone. [1686]. Library ser4 17no4:472–5 Mr '37.

GODWIN, WILLIAM, 1756–1836

10728 **Norman, Francis.** A Godwin pamphlet. [Letters of Verax, 1815]. TLS 25 Jl '42:367.

10729 **Liebert, Herman W.** The Swiss family Robinson, a bibliographical note. [Tr. by Godwin]. Yale Univ Lib Gaz 22no1:10–13 Jl '47.

GOGARTY, OLIVER ST.JOHN, 1878–1957

10730 **Hewson, Michael.** Gogarty's authorship of Blight. (Bibliographical notes). Irish Bk 1no1:19–20 '59. illus.

GOLDSMITH, OLIVER, 1728–74

10731 **Prideaux, William F.** Goldsmith and Newbery. N&Q ser8 3:221–2 Mr '93.

10732 **G., F.** Goldsmith's Deserted village. Athenæum 3582:810 Je '96; J. W. M. Gibbs *ib.* 3583:844 Je '96; A. H. Millar *ib.* 3589:193–4 Ag '96; J. S. Babb 3590:227 Ag '96.

10733 **Livingston, Luther S.** Goldsmith's Deserted village. Athenæum 3782:499–500 Ap '00. table.

10733a **Welsh, Charles.** Goldsmith's publishers. N&Q ser9 8:15 Jl '01; W. H. Peet *ib.* 8:68 Jl '01.

10734 **[Dobell, Bertram].** Explanation of the curious early form of The traveller. Bibliographer 1no6:231–2 Je '02.

Repr. from his ed. of A prospect of society, London, 1902.

10735 **England, George.** Goldsmith's Prospect of society. [Proof-sheets]. Library ser2 3no11:327–32 Jl '02.

10736 **F., S. J. A.** Goody two shoes. N&Q ser10 2:167 Ag '04; W. F. Prideaux; W. H. Peet; J. H. MacMichael; E. H. Coleman; R. Sanderson; H. G. Hope *ib.* 2:250–1 S '04.

10737 **Oliver,** *pseud.* Goldsmith: various readings in The traveller. N&Q ser10 5:167 Mr '06; T. White *ib.* 5:295 Ap '06; J. Curtis 5:397 My '06.

10738 **Pearson, J. Sidney.** Goldsmith's Traveller, 1764. Athenæum 4173:480 Oc '07.

10739 **Prideaux, William F.** Goldsmith's Deserted village. N&Q ser11 2:41-2 Jl '10; Diego, *pseud., ib.* 2:194 S '10.

10740 **Thiselton, Alfred E.** A Prospect of society. TLS 11 Ap '12:102.

10741 **Williams, Aneurin.** Illustrators of Goldsmith. N&Q ser11 12:160 Ag '15; J. T. Roby *ib.* ser12 1:394 My '16.

10742 **Goldsmith's** Memoirs of my lady B. (Notes on sales). TLS 19 D '18:648; J. F. Rotton *ib.* 2 Ja '19:12; *cf.* 16 Ja '19:36.

10743 **Williams, Iolo A.** [She stoops to conquer, 1773]. (Bibliographical notes & news). London Merc 11no61:82-6 N '24; R. B. McKerrow *ib.* 11no63:302-3 Ja '25.

10744 **Balderston, Katherine C.** A census of the manuscripts of Oliver Goldsmith. New York, Brickrow book shop, 1926. xii,73p. 19cm.

Letters.—Receipts, agreements, bills, etc.—Literary manuscripts.—Presentation books.—Items of undetermined authenticity.—Lost manuscripts.—Forged documents.—Addendum.

Rev: TLS 24 F '27:122; R. D. Havens Mod Lang N 42:494 '27; Saturday R Lit 3:687 '27; L. F. Powell R Eng Stud 4:484-5 '28.

10745 **Crane, Ronald S.** Goldsmith's Essays: dates of original publication. N&Q 153:153 Ag '27.

10746 **Bonner, Willard H.** Poems for young ladies, a bibliographical note. N&Q 155:129-32 Ag '28; E. E. Newton *ib.* 155:175 S '28.

10747 **Goldsmith** and chess. [Ms. trans. of Vida's Game of chess]. TLS 15 Mr '28:192.

10748 **Crone, John S.** Goldsmith autographs. Irish Bk Lover 17no6:136 N/D '29. [Sg.: J. S. C.]

10749 **Goldsmith** and Johnson manuscripts. (Notes on sales). TLS 24 Oc '29:852.

10750 **McCarthy, William H.** Goldsmith memorial exhibition. Yale Univ Lib Gaz 3no3:63-4 Ja '29. [Sg.: W. H. M.]

10751 **Balderston, Katherine C.** A manuscript version of She stoops to conquer. Mod Lang N 45no2:84-5 F '30.

10752 **Chapman, Robert W.** An unconsidered trifle. [Book mutilated for ptrs. copy for Goldsmith's History]. Coloph [1]pt3:[4p.] '30. facsim.

10753 **Crane, Ronald S.** The text of Goldsmith's Memoirs of m. de Voltaire. Mod Philol 28no2:212-19 N '30.

10754 **Impending** lawsuit over a 'Goldsmith' ms. [Verse trans. of Vida's The game of chess]. (Marginalia). Bkmns J ser3 18no13:19 '30.

10755 **Seitz, R. W.** Goldsmith and the English lives. Mod Philol 28no3:329–36 '30.

10756 —— Goldsmith and the Present state of the British empire. Mod Lang N 45no7:434–8 N '30.

10757 **A Goldsmith** agreement. [William Griffin]. (Notes on sales). TLS 5 Mr '31:184.

10758 **Nangle, Benjamin C.** Goldsmith accessions. Yale Univ Lib Gaz 5no3:51–3 Ja '31.

10759 **Kent, Elizabeth E.** Goldsmith and his booksellers. Ithaca, N.Y., Cornell U.P.; London, H. Milford, O.U.P., 1933. vii,119p. illus. 20cm. (Cornell Stud Eng XX)

I. Goldsmith's observations on the trade.–II. Ralph Griffiths.–III. Robert and James Dodsley.–IV. John Newbery.–V. Thomas Davies, William Griffin, Goldsmith's last years.

Rev: TLS 5 Oc '33:674; N&Q 165:180 '33; A. T. Mod Lang R 29:231 '34; R. W. Seitz Mod Philol 31:315–17 '34; C. F. Tupper J Eng Germ Philol 33:152–3 '34; R. S. Crane Mod Lang N 50:477–8 '35.

10760 **Kirby, H. T.** On collecting the Vicar of Wakefield. Bk Coll Q 12:61–9 Oc/D '33.

10761 **Chapman, Robert W.** Goldsmith: Works, 1801. [Cancels]. Bib N&Q 2no1:3 Ja '36.

10762 **Parsons, Coleman O.** Textual variations in a manuscript of She stoops to conquer. Mod Philol 40no1:57–69 Ag '42. diagr.

10763 **Knight, Douglas.** Two issues of Goldsmith's Bee. N&Q 187:276 D '44.

10764 **Thorpe, James.** Issues of the first edition of The vicar of Wakefield. Pa Bib Soc Am 42:312–15 '48.

10765 **Mundy, Percy D.** Illustrated edition of Goldsmith's Works. [1864–5]. N&Q 195:546 D '50. [Sg.: P. D. M.]

10766 **Todd, William B.** Goldsmith, The traveller, 1770. (Note no.13). Bk Coll 1no4:264–5 '52.

10767 **Friedman, Arthur.** The first edition of Essays by mr. Goldsmith, 1765. Stud Bib 5:190–3 '52/3. table.

10768 **Muir, Percival H.** Goldsmith's Millenium hall, 1762. [Publication date]. (Note no.15). Bk Coll 1no4:265–6 '52; T. G. Harmsen *ib.* 2no2:155–7 '53; W. B. Todd 2no1:72 '53.

10769 **Todd, William B.** The private issues of The deserted village. Stud Bib 6:25–44 '54. tables.

10770 —— Quadruple imposition: an account of Goldsmith's Traveller. Stud Bib 7:103–11 '55. tables.

*Repr. in no.*10772.

10771 **Friedman, Arthur.** Goldsmith's Essay on friendship: its first publication and the problem of authorship. Philol Q 35no3:346–9 Jl '56.

10772 **Todd, William B.** 'Bibliographical commentary' *in* A prospect of society, by Oliver Goldsmith, reconstructed from the earliest version of The traveller. Charlottesville, Va., 1956. p. [23]–30. tables.

Rev. from Stud Bib 7:103–11 '55.

10773 —— Goldsmith's The traveller. Library ser5 11no2:123–4 Je '56.

10774 **Friedman, Arthur.** The first edition of Goldsmith's Bee, no.1. Stud Bib 11:255–9 '58.

10775 **Todd, William B.** The first editions of The good natur'd man and She stoops to conquer. Stud Bib 11:133–42 '58. diagr., tables.

10776 **Brown, T. Julian.** Oliver Goldsmith, 1730?–1774. (English literary autographs, XXXII). Bk Coll 8no4:417 '59. facsims.

10777 **Friedman, Arthur.** The problem of indifferent readings in the eighteenth century, with a solution from The deserted village. Stud Bib 13:143–7 '60.

Repr. in Brack, O M and W. Barnes, *ed.* Bibliography and textual criticism. Chicago [1969]. p. 188–93.

10778 —— Two notes on Goldsmith. Stud Bib 13:232–35 '60. table.

'The first edition of Goldsmith's Life of Bolingbroke' (p. 232–4); 'The 1772 edition of Goldsmith's Traveller' (p. 234–5)

10779 **Kirby, H. T.** The Vicar of Wakefield, the pictorial evolution of a famous novel. Bks J Nat Bk League 355:179–85 S/Oc '64. facsims.

10780 **Roscoe, Sidney.** The History of Little goody two-shoes. [Pub. 1765?]. (Query 179). Bk Coll 13no2:214 '64; J. A. Birkbeck *ib.* 13no4:503 '64.

10781 **Goldy's** ballad. [Edwin and Angelina, 1765]. TLS 11 F '65:116.

10782 **Brack, O M.** Goldsmith's A survey of experimental philosophy, 1776. (Note 324). Bk Coll 18no4:519–20 '69.

GORDON, PATRICK, fl.1692–1700

10783 **Bulloch, J. Malcolm.** Rev. Patrick Gordon's Geography. N&Q ser11 4:188–9 S '11; C. C. B.; D. A. Burl *ib.* 4:237 S '11; W. Scott 5:16 Ja '12.

GORGES, SIR ARTHUR, d.1625

10784 **Bell, sir Harold I.** Early poems of sir Arthur Gorges. [Mss.]. Brit Mus Q 14no4:88–93 D '40.

10785 **Sandison, Helen E.** 'Manuscripts of the Island voyage and Notes on the Royal navy in relation to the printed versions in Purchas and in Ralegh's Judicious essays' *in* Essays and studies in honor of Carleton Brown. New York; London, 1940. p. [242]–52.

10786 ——— The Vanytes of sir Arthur Gorges youthe: Egerton ms. 3165, a preliminary report. Pub Mod Lang Assn 61no1:109–13 Mr '46.

GOSSE, SIR EDMUND WILLIAM, 1849–1928

10787 **Wheeler, Harold F. B.** The library of mr. Edmund Gosse, Ll.D. (Notable private libraries, no.2). Biblioph 3no14:76–82 Ap '09. illus., port., facsims.

10788 **Drinkwater, John.** 'The library of a man of letters' *in* A book for bookmen, being edited manuscripts & marginalia with essays on several occasions. London, 1926. p. 199–203.

10789 **Sir** E. Gosse's library. (Notes on sales). TLS 19 Jl '28:540.

10790 **Barker, Nicolas J.** So Gosse was in it after all? [Aromatic dealings with Wise]. (Note 235). Bk Coll 13no4:501–3 '64.

GOSSON, STEPHEN, 1554–1624

10791 **Kinney, Arthur F.** Two unique copies of Stephen Gosson's Schoole of abuse, 1579: criteria for judging nineteenth-century editing. Pa Bib Soc Am 59:425–9 '65.

GOTHER, JAMES, d.1704

10792 **Brockway, Duncan.** Some new editions from the reign of James II. Pa Bib Soc Am 55:118–30 '61. tables.

GOTT, SAMUEL, 1613–71

10793 **Jones, Stephen K.** The authorship of Nova solyma. Library ser3 1no3:225–38 Jl '10.

GOULD, JOHN, 1804–81

10794 **Haraszti, Zoltán.** John Gould, the British Audubon. More Bks Boston Pub Lib Bull 11no6:205–9 Je '36. [Sg.: Z. H.]

10795 **Sauer, Gordon C.** Gouldiana. Bks & Libs at Kansas 1no12:2–3 My '56.

GRAHAM, ROBERT BONTINE CUNNINGHAME, 1852–1936

10796 **Braun, Hildegarde.** A note on the George Matthew Adams collection of Cunninghame Graham. Quarto [Clements Lib Associates] 17:2–4 N '48.

'A checklist of the collection' (p. 3–4)

GRAHAME, JAMES, 1765–1811

10797 **Mabbott, Thomas O.** A suppressed anonymous work of James Grahame. [Fragments of a tour through the universe, 1814]. N&Q 169:438 D '35.

GRAHAME, KENNETH, 1859–1932

10798 **Green, Roger L.** Kenneth Grahame. TLS 5 Ag '44:384.

10799 **Bissell, E. E.** Grahamiana. [The wind in the willows, 1908]. (Query no.30). Bk Coll 2no1:79 '53.

GRAINGER, JAMES, 1721?–66

10800 Dr. Grainger's Sugar cane. [Ms.]. TLS 16 F '51:108; G. S. Alleman *ib.* 30 Mr '51:197.

GRANGER, JAMES, 1723–76

10801 **Abrahams, Aleck.** Granger annotated by Caulfield. [Biographical history, 1775]. N&Q ser10 7:65–6,223–5,323–5 Mr,Ap '07; J. Pickford *ib.* 7:225 Mr '07; A. Abrahams 7:464 Je '07.

10802 **Powell, Lawrence F.** Granger's Biographical history. [1769]. TLS 23 Ap '31:327.

GRANT, JAMES GREGOR, fl.1847

10803 **M., J. A.** Poems by J. G. Grant. [Madonna pia, 1847]. N&Q ser12 7:407 N '20.

GRANVILLE, GEORGE, BARON LANSDOWNE, 1666–1735

10804 **Cameron, William J.** George Granville and the Remaines of Aphra Behn. N&Q 204:88–92 Mr '59.

GRAVES, CLOTILDA INEZ MARY, 1863–1932 *see* Dehan, Richard, *pseud.*

GRAVES, JOHN WOODCOCK, 1795–1886

10805 **Partington, Wilfred G.** Do we ken John Peel? The author and his own version of the famous song. Coloph new ser 2no1:42–8 Oc '36.

GRAVES, ROBERT VON RANKE, 1895–

10806 **M., E. B.** Robert Graves's I Claudius. [Shared printing]. Bib N&Q 2no2:5 F '36.

10807 **Higginson, Fred H.** Graves recorded. [His bibliogr.]. TLS 8 D '66:1149.

GRAY, JOHN, 1724–1811

10808 **Hirsch, Lester.** A note on John Gray, 1724–1811. Pa Bib Soc Am 47:275–6 '52.

GRAY, JOHN, fl.1893

10809 **Smith, Simon H. Nowell-.** John Gray's Silverpoints, 1893. (Query 163). Bk Coll 12no1:73 '63.

GRAY, THOMAS, 1716–71

10810 **Murray, John.** Gray's Elegy. N&Q ser8 5:148 F '94; T. Auld; D. C. T.; C. K.; F. C. B. Terry *ib.* 5:237 Mr '94.

10811 **Gosse, sir Edmund W.** An undescribed edition of Gray's Elegy. Athenæum 3622:445 Ap '97.

10812 **Golver, Arnold.** A Gray ms. [Instructions to Dodsley on Gray's Poems]. Athenæum 3725:338 Mr '99.

10813 **Pomeroy, James S., 6th viscount Harberton.** Gray's Elegy [Text]. Athenæum 3756:557 Oc '99; P. A. Sillard *ib.* 3758:621 N '99; J. W. White 3759:655 N '99. [Sg.: Viscount Harberton.]

10814 **Beetenson, W. C.** Elegy imitating Gray's N&Q ser9 7:8 Ja '01.

10815 **Rickards, F. T.** Gray's Elegy in Latin. N&Q ser10 1:487 Je '04; W. C. B.; J. Pickford; E. Yardley; P. J. F. Gantillon *ib.* 2:92–3 Jl '04; R. Pierpont 2:175–6 Ag '04.

10816 **Prideaux, William F.** Gray's Poems, 1768. N&Q ser10 5:321–3 Ap '06; 5:406 My '06; J. Pickford *ib.* 5:406 My '06.

10817 **S., W.** Gray's Elegy in Russian. N&Q ser10 5:306 Ap '06; F. P. Marchant *ib.* 5:357 My '06.

10818 **Senga,** *pseud.* Gray's Elegy; its translations. N&Q ser10 5:428 Je '06; J. Oxberry *ib.* 5:477 Je '06; W. P. Courtney 5:511 Je '06.

10819 **Dowden, Edward.** The text of Gray's Poems. [1768]. Mod Lang R 2no2:165 Ja '07.

10820 **Aiguesparses, Christine.** Village blacksmith parodied. N&Q ser10 11:10 Ja '09; P. Jennings; W. Bradbrook *ib.* 11:193 Mr '09.

10821 **Northup, Clark S.** On some editions of Gray's Poems. Eng Studien 43no1:149–58 D '10.

10822 **Toynbee, Paget J.** A misprint in Gray. [Odes, 1757]. TLS 22 Ap '15:135.

10823 **Page, John T.** Gray: a book of squibs. [Ms.]. N&Q ser12 2:399 N '16.

10824 **Toynbee, Paget J.** Gray's Elegy. TLS 27 Ja '16:45; Miles, *pseud., ib.* 10 Ja '16:69; W. and R. Chambers, ltd. 24 F '16:94.

10825 **Northup, Clark S.** Gray's books and mss. [Libr.]. N&Q ser12 3:291–3 My '17; 3:326–8 Je '17; H. Maxwell *ib.* 3:363 Jl '17.

10826 **Gosse, sir Edmund W.** The text of Gray. TLS 23 My '18:245; P. J. Toynbee *ib.* 6 Je '18:264.

10827 **Toynbee, Paget J.** Garrick and Gray's Bard. [1757]. TLS 18 D '19:767.

10828 **Edwards, Howard.** American editions of Gray's Elegy. N&Q ser12 8:509 Jl '21; S. H. Walsh *ib.* 9:176 Ag '21.

10829 **McGovern, John B.** Variations in Gray's Elegy. [Text]. N&Q ser12 8:249–50 Mr '21; E. Bensly *ib.* 8:336 Ap '21.

10830 **Broadbent, Henry.** A literary discovery at Eton. [Gray's Elegy, 1751]. TLS 22 My '24:322.

10831 **Carlton, William N. C.** Thomas Gray's Elegy written in a country church yard; a bibliographical and descriptive note. [New York] Privately ptd. [for George D. Smith] 1925. 13p. facsim. 22cm.

10832 **Toynbee, Paget J.** A Gray-Mason enigma solved. [Letters]. TLS 17 S '25:600.

10833 **Stokes, Francis G.** Gray's Elegy: the fourth edition. TLS 16 D '26:935.

10834 **Toynbee, Paget J.** The text of Norton Nicholls' Reminiscences of Gray. [1843]. TLS 1 S '27:592.

10835 **Jones, T. Llechid.** First edition of Gray's Elegy: the MacGeorge copy. N&Q 154:281 Ap '28; A. Sparke; T. F. D. *ib.* 154:319–20 My '28.

10836 **Toynbee, Paget J.** An alleged holograph of Gray. [Progress of poesy]. TLS 8 N '28:834.

10837 **Whibley, Leonard.** Manuscript poems of Gray. TLS 15 N '28:859.

10838 —— Manuscripts of Thomas Gray and William Mason at York. [York cathedral library]. TLS 5 Ap '28:257.

10839 **Fukuhara, Rintaro.** Mason's edition of Gray. TLS 17 Oc '29:822; P. J. Toynbee; E. G. B. *ib.* 24 Oc '29:846: R. Martin *ib.* 31 Oc '29:874.

10840 **Williams, Aneurin.** Polyglott versions of Gray's Elegy. N&Q 156:461 Je '29; E. Bensly *ib.* 157:212 S '29.

10841 **Whibley, Leonard.** The Candidate, by mr. Gray. TLS 21 Ag '30:667–8.

10842 **Jones, William P.** Books owned by Gray. TLS 1 Je '33:380.

10843 **G., W. H.** [and **P. H. Muir**]. Gray: Odes, 1757. [Issues]. Bib N&Q 2no3:7 Ap '36; J. W. Carter *ib.* 2no4/5:4–6 My '36; S. H. N[owell-] Smith; N. Van Patten 2no7:2 Oc '36; J. W. Carter; L. Whibley 2no10:2–4 Ap '38; J. W. Carter 2no11:2–3 N '38. [Sg.: Ed.]

10844 **Stokes, Francis G.** Gray's Elegy. TLS 6 F '37:92.

10845 **Whibley, Leonard.** Notes on two manuscripts of Thomas Gray. Essays & Stud 23:52–7 '37.

   1. Chronological tables of Greek history.–2. Gray's own copy of A long story.

10846 **Eastman, James A.** Thomas Gray, in and out of the library. N.Y. Pub Lib Bull 42no10:743–9 Oc '38.

10847 **Jones, William P.** Thomas Gray's library. Mod Philol 35no3:257–78 F '38.

   'Gray's library' (p. 259–78); 'Supplementary list of Pembroke library books annotated by Gray' (p. 278)

10848 **A Strawberry** Hill forgery. [Gray's Odes]. (Sales and bibliography). TLS 30 Mr '40:164.

10849 **Rendall, Vernon.** Gray's Elegy, a restored reading. N&Q 184:102–3 F '43; sir S. Gaselee *ib.* 184:174 Mr '43; Hibernicus, *pseud.* 184:204 Mr '43; B. W. 184:237–8 Ap '43. [Sg.: V. R.]

10850 **Hazen, Allen T.** Bentley's Gray. [Designs for Poems, 1753]. TLS 3 F '45:60.

10851 **Baldi, Sergio.** A book once belonging to Gray. N&Q 192:498 N '47.

10852 **Eaves, Thomas C. D.** The second edition of Thomas Gray's Ode on the death of a favourite cat. Philol Q 28no4:512–15 Oc '49.

10853 **Cremer, R. W. Ketton-.** How Gray's Elegy came to be published. Listener 46no1167:58–9 Jl '51.

10854 **Eaves, Thomas C. D.** Further pursuit of Selima. Philol Q 30no1:91–4 Ja '51.

10855 **Hussey, Maurice.** Gray's favourite cat, additional publication. N&Q 196:498 N '51.

10856 —— An addition to Northup. [Ed. of On the death of a favourite cat]. (Note no.8). Bk Coll 1no3:192 '52.

10857 **Brown, T. Julian.** Thomas Gray, 1716–1771. (English literary autographs, VII). Bk Coll 2no3:215 '53. facsims.

10858 **Hayward, John D.** Gray's Elegy. (Query no.77). Bk Coll 5no4:384–5 '56.

10859 **Hendrickson, J. Raymond** and **H. W. Starr.** A mistaken reading in Gray's Vah, tenero. N&Q 206:55–6 F '61.

10860 **Anderson, Alan.** Gray's Elegy in Miscellaneous pieces, 1752. Library ser5 20no2:144–8 Je '65.

GRAY, WILLIAM, fl.1563

10861 **Dormer, Ernest W.** William Gray. [The fantasies of idolatry, 1563]. TLS 8 S '21:580; R. Pierpont ib. 15 S '21:596.

GREATHEAD, BERTIE, 1759–1826

10862 **Hodgkin, John E.** Arno miscellany, 1784. N&Q ser11 2:148 Ag '10; W. Scott; N. W. Hill ib. 2:234 S '10; S. Wheeler 2:293 Oc '10.

GREEN, MATTHEW, 1696–1737

10863 **Wood, Richardson K.** Matthew Green. [Bibliogr. enquiry]. TLS 5 F '25:88.

GREENAWAY, CATHERINE ('KATE'), 1846–1901

10864 **Schatzki, Walter.** Kate Greenaway's Mother Goose. [1881]. Antiqu Bkmn 8:405–6 Ag '51.

GREENE, ROBERT, 1560?–92

10865 **Bradley, Henry.** Some textual puzzles in Greene's works. Mod Lang R 1no3:208–11 Ap '06.

Repr. in The collected papers. Oxford, 1928. p. 256–7.

10866 **McKerrow, Ronald B.** Early editions of Greene's Quip for an upstart courtier, 1592. Gent Mag 300:68–71 F '06. [Sg.: R. B. McK.]

10867 **Reader, A,** *pseud.* Greene's Planetomachia. [1585]. TLS 24 Ag '16:405; sir F. G. Kenyon *ib.* 21 D '16:625; H. C. H. Candy 15 Ja '20:36.

10868 **McKerrow, Ronald B.** Greene and Gabriel Harvey. [Quip for an upstart scholar]. TLS 8 Mr '23:160.

10869 **Greene, Herbert W.** An emendation of Greene. [A looking-glass for London]. TLS 13 Mr '24:160.

10870 **Pruvost, René.** Greene's Gwydonius. TLS 6 Ag '25:521; W. Roberts *ib.* 20 Ag '25:545.

10871 **Dam, Bastiaan A. P. van.** Alleyn's player's part of Greene's Orlando furioso, and the text of the Q of 1594. Eng Stud 11no5:182–203 Oc '29; 11no6:209–20 D '29.

10872 —— R. Greene's James IV. Eng Stud 14no3:97–122 Je '32.

10873 **Pruvost, René.** Robert Greene's Notable discovery of coosenage. (Bibliographical notes). TLS 6 Oc '32:716.

10874 **Sanders, Chauncey E.** Robert Greene and his editors. Pub Mod Lang Assn 48no2:392–417 Je '33.

10875 —— and **W. A. Jackson.** A note on Robert Greene's Planetomachia, 1585. Library ser4 16no4:444–7 Mr '36.

10876 **Simpson, Evelyn M. S.** A Greene quarto. [Friar Bacon, 1594]. TLS 21 N '36:980.

10877 **Oliver, Leslie M.** The Spanish masquerado: a problem in double edition. Library ser5 2no1:14–19 Je '47. table.

10878 **Miller, Edwin H.** Deletions in Robert Greene's A quip for an upstart courtier, 1592. Huntington Lib Q 15no3:277–82 My '52.

10879 **Johnson, Francis R.** The editions of Robert Greene's three parts of Conny-catching: a bibliographical analysis. Library ser5 9no1:17–24 Mr '54.

A notable discovery of coosenage.–The second part of conny-catching.–The third and last part of conny-catching.

10880 **Miller, Edwin H.** The editions of Robert Greene's A quip for an upstart courtier, 1592. Stud Bib 6:107–16 '54. tables.

10881 —— A bestseller brought up to date: later printings of Robert Greene's A disputation between a he cony-catcher and a she cony-catcher, 1592. Pa Bib Soc Am 52:126–31 '58.

10882 **Parker, R. Brian.** Alterations in the first edition of Greene's A quip for an upstart courtier, 1592. [Cancels]. Huntington Lib Q 23no2:181–6 F '60. tables.

10883 —— A Dutch edition of Robert Greene's A quip for an upstart courtier, 1601. [Ptd. by T. Basson]. N&Q 205:130–4 Ap '60.

10884 **Shapiro, Isaac A.** The first edition of Greene's Quip for an upstart courtier. Stud Bib 14:212–18 '61.

10885 **Mukherjee, Sujit K.** The text of Greene's Orlando furioso. Indian J Eng Stud 6:102–7 '65.

10886 **Pennel, Charles A.** The authenticity of the George a Greene title-page inscriptions. [And Collier]. J Eng Germ Philol 64no4:668–76 Oc '65.

GREVILLE, SIR FULKE, 1ST BARON BROOKE, 1554–1628

10887 **Bullough, Geoffrey.** Fulk Greville's Works, 1633. TLS 15 Oc '31:802.

10888 **Ewing, S. Blaine.** A new manuscript of Greville's Life of Sidney. Mod Lang R 49no4:424–7 Oc '54.

GRIEG, JOHN, fl.1850

10889 **Corson, James C.** The Border antiquities. [Attrib. to William Mudford, but by Grieg]. Biblioth 1no1:23–6 '56.

10890 —— A supplementary note on The border antiquities. Biblioth 3no1:15–23 '60.

  1. Authorship.–2. The work in parts.–3. The editions.

GRIFFIN, BARTHOLOMEW, fl.1596

10891 **Hindle, Christopher J.** The 1815 reprint of Bartholomew Griffin's Fiedessa. [Ed. by P. Bliss]. N&Q 166:308–10 My '34.

  GRIFFITHS, RALPH, 1720–1803 *see* Book production and distribution–Printers, publishers, etc.

GRIMSTON, ELIZABETH (BERNYE), c.1563–1603

10892 **Hughey, Ruth** and **P. Hereford.** Elizabeth Grymeston and her Miscellanea. Library ser4 15no1:61–91 Je '34. facsims.

GROSART, ALEXANDER BALLOCH, 1827–99

10893 **Weber, A.** Dr. Grosart's privately printed editions. Athenæum 3319:732–3 Je '91.

10894 **Delafons, John.** A. B. Grosart, a prince of editors; tribute to a Victorian scholar. N.Y. Pub Lib Bull 60no9:444–54 S '56.

GROSSMITH, GEORGE, 1847–1912

10895 **Randall, David A.** Grossmith: The diary of a nobody. [Issues]. Bib N&Q 2no4/5:10 My '36; G. G[oodspeed] *ib.* 2no6:4 Jl '36. [Sg.: D. R.]

GROTE, JOHN, 1813–66

10896 **Scattergood, Bernard P.** The Grote manuscripts. N&Q ser8 11:208 Mr '97; C. F. S. Warren *ib.* 11:259 Mr '97.

GUTHRIE, WILLIAM, 1708–70

10897 **Lam, George L.** Note on Guthrie's History of England. N&Q 183:71–2 Ag '42.

GWINETT, AMBROSE, fl.1770?

10898 **Hayes, Gerald R.** and **L. Selden.** The Ambrose Gwynett mystery. [Works about]. Bkmns J new ser 9no29:157–8 F '24; J. Kirkby *ib.* 9no30:219–20 Mr '24.

HACKET, BP. JOHN, 1590–1670

10899 **Jones, T. Llechid.** Bishop Hacket's life of archbishop John Williams, 1693. [Scrinia reserata]. (Studies in Welsh book-land, V). Welsh Bib Soc J 6no1:28–32 Jl '43.

HADDON, WALTER, 1516–72

10900 **Ryan, Lawrence V.** An octavo edition of Poëmata by Walter Haddon, 1567. Pa Bib Soc Am 45:166–9 '51.

10901 —— Walter Haddon's Poëmata, 1592. Pa Bib Soc Am 49:68–9 '55.

HAGGARD, SIR HENRY RIDER, 1856–1925

10902 **Coykendall, Frederick.** Haggard: King Solomon's mines. [Issues]. Bib N&Q 2no10:9 Ap '38.

10903 —— [Bibliogr. note on King Solomon's mines, 1885]. Pa Bib Soc Am 34:90 '40; M. L. Parrish; F. Coykendall *ib.* 34:272–3 '40.

10904 **Scott, James E.** [Bibliogr. note on The new South Africa, by H. Rider Haggard, i.e. William Adolf Baillie-Grohman, 1900]. Pa Bib Soc Am 38:63–5 '44.

10905 **Baker, Carlos.** A great Rider Haggard accession. Princeton Univ Lib Chron 17no4:272–3 '56.

HAILES, SIR DAVID DALRYMPLE, LD., 1726–92 *see* Dalrymple, sir David, ld. Hailes, 1726–92.

HAKLUYT, RICHARD, 1552?–1616

10906 **Hakluyt's** Voyages, 1589 and 1599. (Notes on sales). TLS 15 D '32:928.

10907 **Kerr, William H.** The treatment of Drake's circumnavigation in Hakluyt's Voyages, 1589. Pa Bib Soc Am 34:281–302 '40. table.

'Census of the 1589 Hakluyt's Voyages' (p. 300–2)

10908 **Armstrong, Charles E.** The Voyage to Cadiz in the second edition of Hakluyt's Voyages. Pa Bib Soc Am 49:254–62 '55. tables.

10909 **Lindsay, Robert O.** Richard Hakluyt and Of the Russe common wealth. Pa Bib Soc Am 57:312–27 '63.

HALES, JOHN, d.1571

10910 **Feuillerat, Albert G.** Notes on old books. William Stafford and the Discourse of the commonweal of England. Library ser3 9no33:84–7 Ja '18.

HALIFAX, GEORGE SAVILE, 1ST MARQUIS OF, 1633–95 *see* Savile, George, 1st marquis of Halifax, 1633–95.

HALL, EDWARD, d.1547.

10911 **Q. V.,** *pseud.* Hall's Chronicle, Henry IV. N&Q ser11 2:368 N '10; W. Scott *ib.* 2:458 D '10.

10912 **Pollard, H. Graham.** The bibliographical history of Hall's Chronicle. Bull Inst Hist Res 10no28:12–17 Je '33. table.

10913 **Wolf, Edwin.** Edward Halle's The Vnion of the two noble and illustre famelies of Lancastre & Yorke, and its place among English Americana. Pa Bib Soc Am 33:40–54 '39.

'. . . a check-list of the earliest English Americana' (p. 49–54)

10914 **Keen, Alan.** A short account of the recently discovered copy of Edward Hall's Union of the noble houses of Lancaster and York, notable for its manuscript additions. Bull John Rylands Lib 24no2:255–62 Oc '40.

HALL, MARGUERITE RADCLYFFE, fl.1906–36

10915 **Bolton, Sheila.** A Radclyffe Hall collection. Priv Lib 2no4:50–2 Ap '59.

HALL, THOMAS, 1610–65

10916 **Vaughan, Janet E.** The authorship of Dr. Williams's library mss. 61. 1., Baxter mss. N&Q 207:380–1 Oc '62.

HALLAM, ARTHUR HENRY, 1811–33

10917 **Smith, W. J.** Tennysoniana, a book with a strange history. [Hallam's Remains]. Bkworm 6no61:31–2 D '92.

10917a **Prideaux, William F.** Poems by Arthur Hallam. [1830]. N&Q ser8 5:65 Ja '94.

10918 **McGovern, John B.** Arthur Henry Hallam. N&Q ser9 10:427–8 N '02; W. F. Prideaux *ib.* 10:510–11 D '02.

10919 **Brooks, Huxley St.J.** The bibliography of Arthur Henry Hallam's Remains. (Correspondence). London Merc 4no23:522–3 S '21.

10920 **Motter, Thomas H. V.** Hallam's Poems of 1830: a census of copies. Pa Bib Soc Am 35:277–80 '41.

10921 **Smith, Simon H. Nowell-.** A. H. Hallam's Poems, 1830. (Note 123). Bk Coll 8no4:430–1 '59; P. H. Muir *ib.* 9no1:64–5 '60.

10922 **Bond, William H.** Henry Hallam, The Times newspaper, and the Halliwell case. Library ser5 18no2:133–40 Je '63.

HALLEY, EDMOND, 1656–1742

10923 **MacPike, Eugene F.** Dr. Edmond Halley's maps, charts and plans. N&Q 170:228 Mr '36.

HALLIWELL, JAMES ORCHARD, afterwards HALLIWELL-PHILLIPPS, 1820–89 *see* Phillipps, James Orchard Halliwell-, 1820–89.

HAMILTON, EUGENE LEE-, 1845–1907

10924 **Lyon, Harvey T.** A publishing history of the writings of Eugene Lee-Hamilton. Pa Bib Soc Am 51:141–59 '57.

10925 **Pantazzi, Sybille.** Eugene Lee-Hamilton. Pa Bib Soc Am 55:231–2 '61.

10926 —— Eugene Lee-Hamilton. Pa Bib Soc Am 57:92–4 '63.

HAMILTON, JOSEPH, fl.1825

10927 **ÓCasaide, Séamus.** Joseph Hamilton. Irish Bk Lover 21no5:114 S/Oc '33; 22no2:39 Mr/Ap '34.

HAMMOND, WILLIAM, 1719–83

10928 **Wormald, Francis.** Poetical manuscripts of William Hammond. Brit Mus Q 11no1:24–6 Oc '36.

HANDEL, GEORGE FRIDERIC, 1685–1759

10929 **Streatfeild, Richard A.** The Granville collection of Handel manuscripts. Music Antiqu 2:208–24 Jl '11.

10930 **Jonas, Alfred C.** Handel's Messiah. [1st ptg.]. N&Q ser11 7:249 Mr '13.

10931 **Squire, William B.** Handel in contemporary song-books. Music Antiqu 4:103–11 Ja '13.

A. Original compositions by Handel.–B. Songs which can be identified.–C. Doubtful and spurious works.

10932 **Flower, Desmond.** Handel's publishers. Eng R 62no1:66–75 Ja '36.

10933 **A Handel** collection. [Gerald Coke]. (Private libraries, VIII). TLS 1 Oc '38:632.

Publishing methods.–The sacred oratorio.–Randall and Abel.–An author collection.

10934 **Handel** bibliography. (Bibliographical notes). TLS 18 F '39:112.

10935 **Hudson, Frederick.** Concerning the watermarks in the manuscripts and early prints of G. F. Handel. Music R 20no1:7–27 F '59. diagrs., facsims.

10936 **Stillings, Frank S.** The Arnold edition of Handel's works in the Kent State university library. Serif 1no1:15–20 Ap '64. facsim.

10937 **Picker, Martin.** Handeliana in the Rutgers university library. J Rutgers Univ Lib 29no1:1–12 D '65. facsim.

HARDIE, JAMES, 1763–1826

10938 **B., M. S.** James Hardie, 1763–1826, a failure. Aberdeen Univ Lib Bull 5no27:273–84 Je '23.

'Bibliography' (p. 280–4)

HARDINGE, GEORGE, 1744–1816

10939 **Dey, Edward M.** Essence of Malone. [1801].N&Q ser9 6:488–9 D '00; J. Radcliffe ib. 7:197 Mr '01.

HARDMAN, SIR WILLIAM, 1828–90

10940 **Cline, C. L.** Sir William Hardman's journal. (Note 267). Bk Coll 15no2:207–10 '66.

HARDY, EMMA LAVINIA (GIFFORD), d.1912

10941 **Beatty, C. J. P.** Emma Hardy's recollections. [Mss.]. TLS 1 Je '62:420; R. W. V. Gittings *ib.* 8 Je '62:429.

HARDY, THOMAS, 1840–1928

10942 **Webb, A. P.** Hardy bibliography. N&Q ser11 11:228 Mr '15.

10943 **Edwards, Ralph.** Some emendations in the poetry of mr. Hardy. TLS 18 D '19:767–8.

10944 **Hardy** manuscripts and books. (Notes on sales) TLS 9 Ag '28:584.

10945 **Hardy** and other first editions. (Notes on sales). TLS 21 F '29:148.

10946 **Purdy, Richard L.** A 1905 Dynasts. [Cancels]. TLS 14 F '29:118.

10947 **Bliss, Howard.** Thomas Hardy forgeries? (Correspondence). London Merc 21no123:255 Ja '30.

10948 **Bliss, Howard.** Thomas Hardy inscriptions. [Signed copies]. TLS 2 Ja '30:12.

10949 **Purdy, Richard L.** Thomas Hardy's works. [His bibliogr.]. TLS 19 F '31:135.

10950 —— The Thomas Hardy collection [presented by H. C. Taylor]. Yale Univ Lib Gaz 10no1:8–9 Jl '35.

10951 **Ratcliffe, Harland R.** Colby's Hardy collection outstanding. Colby Alumnus 24no5:3–6,18 Mr '35.

10952 **Adams, Frederick B.** Hardy: The distracted young preacher, 1879. [Priority of ed.]. Bib N&Q 2no2:5 F '36.

10953 **Cockerell, sir Sydney C.** Hardy's library. TLS 17 S '38:598. illus.

10954 **Hardy's** library. TLS 4 Je '38:392.

10955 **Thomas** Hardy's books. (News and notes). TLS 14 My '38:324.

10956 **Weber, Carl J.** Thomas Hardy in America. Coloph new ser 3no3:383–405 S '38; *ib.* new graphic ser 1:95–6 Mr '39; new graphic ser 4:100 Ja '40.

   I. Authorized editions.–II. Piracies.–III. Hardy's prose.–IV. Poems.–V. Manuscripts.

10957 —— Hardy's grim note in The return of the native. Pa Bib Soc Am 36:37–45 '42.

10958 —— Thomas Hardy and his New England editors. New England Q 15no4:681–99 D '42.

10959 **Purdy, Richard L.** Ms. adventures of Tess. TLS 6 Mr '43:120; 26 Je '43:307.

10960 **Weber, Carl J.** A Masquerade of noble dames. Pub Mod Lang Assn 58no2:558–63 Je '43.

10961 —— Hardy's deference to his publishers. Colby Lib Q 1no9:148–50 Ja '45.

10962 **Christensen, Glenn J.** The Thomas Hardy collection [of M. L. Parrish]. Princeton Univ Lib Chron 8no1:24–7 N '46.

10963 [**Weber, Carl J.**]. Jude from obscurity, via notoriety, to fame. Colby Lib Q 1no13:209–15 Ja '46.

10964 —— The manuscript of Hardy's Two on a tower. Pa Bib Soc Am 40no1:1–21 '46. facsims.

10965 **Adams, Frederick B.** Another man's roses. [Spurious Hardy poem, Two roses, and letter]. New Coloph 2pt6:107–12 Je '49. facsims.

10966 **Weber, Carl J.** Books from Hardy's Max gate library. Colby Lib Q 2no15:246–54 Ag '50.

10967 —— Russian translations of Hardy. Colby Lib Q ser3 15:253–6 Ag '54.

10968 **Yarmolinsky, Avraham.** Hardy behind the iron curtain. Colby Lib Q ser4 3:64–6 Ag '55.

10969 **Brown, T. Julian.** Thomas Hardy, 1840–1928. (English literary autographs, XIX). Bk Coll 5no3:249 '56. facsim.

10970 **Slack, Robert C.** The text of Hardy's Jude the obscure. Ninet Cent Fict 11no4:261–75 Mr '57.

10971 **An unrecorded** Hardy item. [An imaginative woman, trans. into French]. Colby Lib Q ser4 10:177–8 My '57.

10972 **Weber, Carl J.** Hardy's copy of Schopenhauer. Colby Lib Q ser4 11:217–24 Ag '57.

10973 **An important** Hardy manuscript. [Rough draft of The two tall men]. Colby Lib Q ser4 16:303–4 N '58.

10974 **Calhoun, Philo.** An old architect's last draft. [Line from The departure in commemoration tablet]. Colby Lib Q ser5 4:61–6 D '59.

10975 **Green, David B.** The first publication of The spectre of the real. Library ser5 15no1:60–1 Mr '60.

10976 **Bowden, Ann.** The Thomas Hardy collection. Lib Chron Univ Texas 7no2:6–14 '62. facsims.

'Desiderata' (p. 14)

10977 **Kramer, Dale.** A query concerning the handwriting in Hardy's manuscripts. Pa Bib Soc Am 57:357–60 '63.

10978 **Weber, Carl J.** Hardy's debut; how a literary career was determined one hundred years ago. [How I built myself a house, 1865]. Pa Bib Soc Am 59:319–22 '65.

10979 **Laird, John.** The manuscript of Hardy's Tess of the D'Urbervilles and what it tells us. AUMLA 25:68–82 My '66.

10980 **Schweik, Robert C.** The 'duplicate' manuscript of Hardy's Two on a tower: a correction and a comment. Pa Bib Soc Am 60:219–21 '66.

10981 —— An error in the text of Hardy's Far from the madding crowd. Colby Lib Q ser7 6:269 Je '66.

10982 **Kramer, Dale.** Two new texts of Thomas Hardy's The woodlanders. [American ed.]. Stud Bib 20:135–50 '67.

HARDYNG, JOHN, 1378–1465?

10983 **Kingsford, C. L.** The first version of Hardyng's Chronicle. Eng Hist R 27no107:462–82 Jl '12.

HARINGTON, SIR JOHN, 1561–1612

10984 **Hughs, Charles.** Sir John Harington and Nugæ antiquæ. N&Q ser10 11:161–2 F '09.

10985 **Smith, Herbert F. B. Brett-.** The Osler ms. of The schoole of Salerne. Bod Q Rec 5no60:307 Mr '29.

10986 **Kirwood, Albert E. M.** The Metamorphosis of Aiax and its sequels. Library ser4 12no2:208–34 S '31. table.

'Bibliographical appendix' (p. 231–4)

10987 **Schmutzler, Karl E.** Harington's metrical paraphrases of the seven penitential psalms: three manuscript versions. Pa Bib Soc Am 53:240–51 '59.

HARRIS, FRANK, 1856–1931

10988 **Warburton, Thomas.** Frank Harris: Mr. and mrs. Daventry, a drama. [Ever published?]. Bib N&Q 2no4/5:10 My '36.

HART, ELIZABETH ANNA (SMEDLEY), fl.1822–88

10989 **Mrs. Hart,** author of The runaway. TLS 23 N '56:xxiii.

HARVEY, CHRISTOPHER, 1597–1663

10990 **Mathews, C. Elkin.** The Synagogue, by Christopher Harvey. N&Q ser8 7:326 Ap '95; A. H. ib. 7:479 Je '95.

HARVEY, GABRIEL, 1545?–1630?

10991 **Smith, George C. Moore.** Gabriel Harvey's books. N&Q ser10 1:267 Ap '04.

10992 —— Gabriel Harvey's Letter-book. [1884; emendations]. N&Q ser11 3:261–2 Ap '11.

10993 **Gabriel** Harvey, book-collector. (Notes on sales). TLS 9 Ja '19:24.

10993a **Bennett, Josephine W.** Spenser and Gabriel Harvey's Letter-book. Mod Philol 29no2:163–86 '31. facsims., table.

10994 **Flower, Robin E. W.** Gabriel Harvey and Shakespeare. [Accession of bp. Percy's copy of Speght's Chaucer, 1598, with Harvey marginalia]. Brit Mus Q 6no2:49–50 S '31. facsim. [Sg.: R. F.]

10995 **Albright, Evelyn M.** Spenser's connections with the letters in Gabriel Harvey's Letter-book. Mod Philol 29no4:411–36 My '32.

10996 **Smith, George C. Moore.** Printed books with Gabriel Harvey's autograph or ms. notes. Mod Lang R 28no1:78–81 Ja '33; 29no1:68–70 Ja '34; 29no3:321–2 Jl '34; 30no2:209 Ap '35.

Corrections to Mod. Lang. Rev. ...–Corrections to Gabriel Harvey's Marginalia.–Additional titles.

10997 **Johnson, Francis R.** The first edition of Gabriel Harvey's Foure letters. Library ser4 15no2:212–23 S '34.

10998 **Bourland, Caroline B.** Gabriel Harvey and the modern languages. [And dictionaries]. Huntington Lib Q 4no1:85–106 Oc '40.

'Annotations and marked passages' (p. 91–106)

10999 **Johnson, Francis R.** Gabriel Harvey's Three letters: a first issue of his Foure letters. Library ser5 1no2:134–6 S '46.

11000 **Wilson, Harold S.** Gabriel Harvey's method of annotating his books. Harvard Lib Bull 2no3:344–61 '48. facsims.

11001 **Godshalk, William L.** Gabriel Harvey and Sidney's Arcadia. [Library]. Mod Lang R 59no4:497–9 Oc '64.

HARVEY, WILLIAM, 1578–1657

11002 **Kilgour, Frederick G.** Harvey manuscripts. Pa Bib Soc Am 54:177–9 '60.

'A checklist of Harvey mànuscripts' (p.178–9)

11003 **Brown, T. Julian.** William Harvey, 1578–1657. (English scientific autographs, III). Bk Coll 14no1:61 '65. facsim.

HASLEWOOD, JOSEPH, 1769–1833

11004 **Wheat, Cathleen H.** Joseph Haslewood and the Roxburghe club. Huntington Lib Q 11no1:37–49 N '47.

HAWES, STEPHEN, d.1523?

11005 **Sellers, Harry.** Two poems by Stephen Hawes and an early medical tract. Brit Mus Q 13no1:7–8 F '39. facsim.

11006 **Morgan, Alice.** The Conuercyon of swerers: another edition. Library ser5 25no1:44–50 Mr '69. facsims., table.

HAWKER, ROBERT STEPHEN, 1803–75

11007 **Marshall, Francis A.** Hawker mss. N&Q ser9 4:168–9 Ag '99; C. C. B.; A. Wallis *ib*. 4:232 S '99; J. Dallas 4:255 S '99; W. F. Prideaux 4:309–10 Oc '99; A. R. Bayley 4:400 N '99.

11008 **Gilbertson, Richard.** A variant spine label on Hawker's Ecclesia. (Note 252). Bk Coll 14no3:365 '65.

HAWKINS, SIR ANTHONY HOPE, 1863–1933 *see* Hope, Anthony, *pseud.*

HAYDON, BENJAMIN ROBERT, 1786–1846

11009 **Beckwith, Frank.** Haydon; annotated copy of Paul's letters to his kinsfolk. N&Q 182:49 Ja '42.

HAYLEY, WILLIAM, 1745–1820

11010 **Roberts, William.** Hayley's sale. [Catalogue]. N&Q ser8 10:377 N '96.

11011 **Brown, Allan R.** Hayley's Cowper, an interesting set. Bkmns J new ser 11no38:94 N '24.

11012 **Sparrow, John H. A.** Memoir of the early life of William Cowper, 1816. [Issues]. Bib N&Q 2no3:7–8 Ap '36; 2no4/5:6 My '36; J. E. Wells 2no6:3 Jl '36; J. H. A. Sparrow 2no7:2 Oc '36.

HAYWARD, SIR JOHN, 1564?–1627

11013 **Plomer, Henry R.** An examination of some existing copies of Hayward's Life and raigne of king Henrie IV. [1599]. Library ser2 3no9:13–25 Ja '02.

11014 **Dowling, Margaret.** Sir John Hayward's troubles over his Life of Henry IV. Library ser4 11no2:212–24 S '30.

11015 **Greg, sir Walter W.** Samuel Harsnett and Hayward's Henry IV. [And licensing for the press]. Library ser5 11no1:1–10 Mr '56.

Repr. in Maxwell, James C., *ed.* Collected papers. Oxford, 1966. p. [424]–36.

HAYWOOD, ELIZA (FOWLER), 1693–1756

11016 **The precursor** of Evelina. (Notes on sales). TLS 20 Ja '21:48.

HAZLITT, WILLIAM, 1778–1830

11017 **Howe, P. P.** A Hazlitt manuscript: Outlines of grammar. TLS 1 Oc '31:754.

11018 **Keynes, sir Geoffrey L.** Hazlitt's Grammar abridged. [1810]. Library ser4 13no1:97–9 Je '32. facsim.

11019 **Smith, Simon H. Nowell-.** Hazlitt: Human action, etc., 1806. [Issues]. Bib N&Q 2no7:4–5 Oc '36.

11020 **A Hazlitt** puzzle. [Essays on the principles of human action]. TLS 19 Ag '39:496.

11021 **Wilcox, Stewart C.** A manuscript addition to Hazlitt's essay On the fear of death. Mod Lang N 55no1:45–7 Ja '40.

11022 **Poston, M. L.** Hazlitt's Liber amoris. TLS 14 Ag '43:396.

11023 **Fitzgerald, Maurice H.** The text of Hazlitt. TLS 27 F '53:137; H. Tyler *ib.* 6 Mr '53:153; R. W. King 13 Mr '53:169; H. Tyler 20 Mr '53:187; R. W. King 27 Mr '53:205; H. Tyler 3 Ap '53:221; R. W. King 10 Ap '53:237; H. Tyler 17 Ap '53:253; P. G. Gates 5 Je '53:365; H. M. Sikes 12 Je '53:381.

11024 **Story, Patrick L.** William Hazlitt's The spirit of the age, third edition, 1858. [Large-paper copy sought]. (Query 206). Bk Coll 15no3:356 '66.

HEARNE, THOMAS, 1678–1735

11025 **Thomas** Hearne and Richard Gough. [Exhibition]. TLS 14 F '35:96.

11026 **Philip, Ian G.** Thomas Hearne as a publisher. Bod Lib Rec 3no31:146–55 Mr '51.

11027 —— The genesis of Thomas Hearne's Ductor historicus. [And T. Childe]. Bod Lib Rec 7no5:251–64 Jl '66.

HEATH, WILLIAM, 1795–1840 *see* Pry, Paul, *pseud.*

HENDERSON, HENRY, 1820–79

11028 **Marshall, John J.** 'Ulster Scot'. Irish Bk Lover 14no7/8:101–3 Jl/Ag '24.

HENLEY, WILLIAM ERNEST, 1849–1903

11029 **The Henley** circle. (Notes on sales). TLS 11 D '19:756.

11030 **Pennell, Elizabeth R.** William Ernest Henley, lover of the art of book-making. Coloph [2]pt5:[12p.] '31. port.

HENRY VIII, KING OF ENGLAND, 1491–1547

11031 **King** Henry VIII's prayer book [sold 6 Jl '94, from Fountaine collection]. Bkworm 7no81:261 Ag '94.

11032 **Duff, E. Gordon.** The Assertio septem sacramentorum. Library ser2 9no33:1–16 Ja '08.

HENRY FREDERICK, PRINCE OF WALES, 1594–1612

11033 **Parsons, Leila.** Prince Henry, 1594–1612, as a patron of literature. Mod Lang R 47no4:503–7 Oc '52.

HENRY THE MINSTREL (BLIND HARRY), fl.1470–92

11034 **Aldis, Harry G.** On some re-discovered fragments of an edition of Blind Harry's Wallace, printed in the types of Chepman and Myllar. Edinburgh Bib Soc Pub 9pt2:87–9 Ag '12. facsims.

HENTY, GEORGE ALFRED, 1832–1902

11035 **Quayle, Eric.** Rise and fall of Henty's empire. [Out on the pampas, 1871]. TLS 7 N '68:1251.

HERBERT, EDWARD, 1ST BARON HERBERT OF CHERBURY, 1583–1648

11036 **Williams, sir Harold H.** Lord Herbert of Cherbury's De veritate. [Ptd. abroad]. N&Q ser12 8:293–4 Ap '21.

11037 —— Lord Herbert of Cherbury's De veritate. N&Q 157:261 Oc '29.

11038 **Fordyce, C. J. and T. M. Knox.** The library of Jesus college, Oxford, with an appendix on the books bequeathed thereto by lord Herbert of Cherbury. Oxford Bib Soc Proc 5pt2:53–115 '37. illus., facsims.

'Catalogue' (p. [75]–115)

11039 **Aaron, R. I.** The autobiography of Edward, first lord Herbert of Cherbury: the original manuscript material. Mod Lang R 36no2:184–94 Ap '41.

'Appendix: The unpublished pages of draft A of the Autobiography' (p. 192–4)

11040 **Warnke, Frank J.** Two previously unnoted mss. of poems by lord Herbert of Cherbury. N&Q 199:141–2 Ap '54.

11041 **Sprott, S. E.** The Osler manuscript of Herbert's Religio laici. Library ser5 11no2:120–2 Je '56.

11042 **Rossi, Mario M.** Herbert of Cherbury's Religio laici, a bibliographical note. Edinburgh Bib Soc Trans 4pt2:43–52 '62.

HERBERT, GEORGE, 1593–1633

11043 **Cox, Edwin M.** The first edition of Herbert's Temple, 1633. Library ser3 10no37:23–5 Ja '19.

11044 **Hall, Bernard G.** The text of George Herbert. TLS 26 Oc '33:731; J. H. A. Sparrow *ib*. 14 D '33:896.

11045 **Hutchinson, F. E.** The first edition of Herbert's Temple. Oxford Bib Soc Proc 5pt3:189–97 '38.

11046 —— Missing Herbert manuscripts. TLS 15 Jl '39:421.

11047 **Gibbs, J.** An unknown poem of George Herbert. [Perigrinis almam matrem ms.]. TLS 30 D '49:857.

11048 **Akrigg, G. P. V.** George Herbert's Caller. [Ms.]. N&Q 199:17 Ja '54.

HERBERT, SIR HENRY, 1595–1673

11049 **Greg, sir Walter W.** Sir Henry Herbert's office-book. [Appeal for location of]. Gent Mag 300:72–3 F '06.

HERBERT, SIR WILLIAM, d.1593

11050 **Bond, William H.** Two ghosts: Herbert's Baripenthes and the Vaughan-Holland portrait of Sidney. Library ser4 24no3/4:175–81 D/Mr '43/4.

HERIOT, JOHN, 1760–1833

11051 **Bushnell, George H.** John Heriot as Fitz-Albion. [And The true Briton]. TLS 22 D '45:612.

HERRICK, ROBERT, 1591–1674

11052 [Phinn, C. P.]. A list of variations in three copies of the original edition of Herrick's Hesperides and Noble numbers. Library ser2 4no14:206–12 Ap '03; [Addenda, by A. W. Pollard] ib. 4no15:328–31 Jl '03.

11053 Prideaux, William F. Herrick's Hesperides, 1648. N&Q ser10 4:482–3 D '05.

11054 Lobban, J. H. Robert Herrick bibliography. Bkmn 31no186:253–4 Mr '07.

11055 Boas, Frederick S. A Herrick reading. [Hesperides]. Mod Lang R 8no1:92–3 Ja '13.

11056 Lodge, Oliver W. F. The text of Herrick. [Litany to the holy spirit]. TLS 17 Je '15:206; F. W. Moorman ib. 24 Je '15:214.

11057 Smith, George C. Moore. Some notes on Herrick. [Text]. N&Q ser12 1:205–6 Mr '16.

11058 Cox, Edwin M. Notes on the bibliography of Herrick. Library ser3 8no30:105–19 Ap '17.

11059 Hooker, Edward N. Herrick and song-books. TLS 2 Mr '33:147; N. Ault ib. 20 Ap '33:276; E. N. Hooker 1 Je '33:380; N. Ault 22 Je '33:428.

11060 Howarth, R. Guy. Attributions to Herrick. N&Q 203:249 Je '58.

11061 Crum, Margaret C. An unpublished fragment of verse by Herrick. [Ms.]. R Eng Stud new ser 11no42:186–9 My '60.

HERVIE, ROBERT, fl.1611

11062 Health in a cup of wine. [Ms.]. (Notes on sales). TLS 27 Mr '24:196.

HEWLETT, MAURICE HENRY, 1861–1923

11063 Bell, H. W. Mr. Hewlett's bibliography. [Corrections to London Merc 1no5:625–6 Mr '20]. London Merc 2no8:207 Je '20.

11064 Goodspeed, George T. Hewlett: The forest lovers, 1898. [Collation]. Bib N&Q 2no8:7 F '37. [Sg.: G. G.]

HEYLYN, PETER, 1600–62

11065 Lowther, Anthony W. G. 'A table' in Heylyn's Observations. (Query 171). Bk Coll 12no4:495 '63; Inez Williams ib. 13no3:354 '64.

11066 Hudson, J. P. Peter Heylyn's poetry notebook. Brit Mus Q 34no1/2:19–27 '69.

HEYTESBURY, WILLIAM, fl.1340

11067 **Mead, Herman R.** [Bibliogr. note on Quaedam consequentiae subtiles, c.1500]. Pa Bib Soc Am 35:155 '41.

HEYWOOD, JAMES, 1687–1776

11068 **Hughes, T. Cann.** Mr. Heywood's Letters and poems. N&Q 148:101 F '25.

HEYWOOD, JASPER, 1535–98

11069 **Greg, sir Walter W.** Notes on early plays: Seneca's Troas, translated by Jasper Heywood, 1559. Library ser4 11no2:162–73 S '30. facsims., table.

HEYWOOD, JOHN, 1497?–1580?

11070 **Greg, sir Walter W.** An unknown edition of Heywood's Play of love. [1533]. Archiv für das Studium 106hft1/2:141–3 '01.

11071 **Reed, Arthur W.** The canon of John Heywood's plays. Library ser3 9no33:27–57 Ja '18; 9no34:116–31 Ap '18.

11072 —— Heywood's Play of love, a correction. Library ser4 4no2:160 S '23.

11073 **Canzler, David G.** Quarto editions of Play of the wether. Pa Bib Soc Am 62:313–19 '68.

HEYWOOD, THOMAS, 1514?–1641

11074 **Dam, Bastiaan A. P. Van** and **C. Stoffel.** The fifth act of Thomas Heywood's Queen Elizabeth, second part. [If you know not me]. Sh Jahrb 38:153–95 '02.

11075 **Clark, Arthur M.** Thomas Heywood's Art of love, lost and found. [The scourge of venus, 1613]. Library ser4 3no3:210–22 D '22. tables.

11075a **Greg, sir Walter W.** 'The Escapes of Jupiter [ms.]' *in* Anglica; Untersuchungen zur englischen Philologie Alois Brandl. (Palaestra, 148). Leipzig, 1925. p. 211–43.

Repr. in Maxwell, James C., *ed.* Collected papers. Oxford, 1966. p.[156]–83.

11076 **Orsini, G. N. Giordano-.** The copy for If you know not me, you know no bodie. [Memorially reconstructed]. TLS 4 D '30:1037; A. W. Pollard *ib.* 11 D '30:1066.

11077 **Martin, Mary F.** If you know not me you know nobodie, and The famous historie of sir Thomas Wyat. Library ser4 13no3:272–81 D '32.

11078 **Orsini, G. N. Giordano-.** Thomas Heywood's play on 'the troubles of queen Elizabeth.' [If you know not me, 1605]. Library ser4 14no3:313–38 D '33. tables.

'Analysis of the play' (p. 324–38)

11079 **Musgrove, Sidney.** Some manuscripts of Heywood's Art of Love. Library ser5 1no2:106–12 S '46. diagr.

11080 **Brown, Arthur.** An edition of the plays of Thomas Heywood: a preliminary survey of problems. Renaiss Pa 1954:71–6 '54. facsim.

11081 —— A proof-sheet in Thomas Heywood's The iron age. Library ser5 10no4:275–8 D '55. facsims.

11082 **Davison, Peter H.** The Fair maid of the exchange. [Proofsheet]. Library ser5 13no2:119–20 Je '58. facsim.

11083 **Patrides, C. A.** Thomas Heywood and literary piracy. [The hierarchy of the blessed angels, 1635]. Philol Q 39no1:118–22 Ja '60.

11084 **Turner, Robert K.** The text of Heywood's The fair maid of the west. Library ser5 22no4:299–325 D '67. diagr., tables.

11085 **Bergeron, David M.** Two compositors in Heywood's Londons ius honorarium, 1631. Stud Bib 22:223–6 '69.

HICKES, GEORGE, 1642–1715

11086 **Hempl, George.** Hickes's additions to the runic poem. Mod Philol 1no1:135–41 Je '03. facsims.

11087 **Bennett, J. A. W.** Hickes's Thesaurus; a study in Oxford book-production. [Linguarum veterum . . . thesaurus, 1705]. Eng Stud (Essays & Stud) new ser 1:28–45 '48.

HICKES, WILLIAM, fl.1671

11088 **Smith, Courtney C.** William Hickes, compiler of drolleries. Mod Lang Q 12no3:259–66 S '51.

HILDROP, JOHN, d.1756

11089 **Rider, R. C.** A note on God's judgments upon the gentile apostatized church & A treatise of the three evils of the last times, with special reference to a volume in the library of St. Paul's cathedral, Dundee, which contains both title-pages. [Hildrop and Francis Lee]. Biblioth 3no1:31–5 '60.

'Additional note' (p. 34–5)

HILL, NICHOLAS, 1570?–1610

11090 **Jacquot, Jean.** Nicholas Hill. [Mss.]. N&Q 196:370 Ag '51.

HILTON, JAMES, 1900–54

11091 **Menhinick, E. B.** Hilton: Knight without armour, Benn, 1933. [Binding variants]. Bib N&Q 2no1:3 Ja '36.

HOBBES, THOMAS, 1588–1679

11092 **Dodd, Mary C.** The rhetorics in Molesworth's edition of Hobbes. Mod Philol 50no1:36–42 Ag '52.

11093 **Todd, William B.** The '1651' edition of Leviathan. (Note no.29). Bk Coll 3no1:68–9 '54.

11094 **Hopkins, R. H.** Annotated copies of Hobbes's Leviathan, 1651. (Query 178). Bk Coll 13no2:214 '64.

HODSON, JAMES LANSDALE, 1891–1956

11095 **Bartle, Robert.** James Lansdale Hodson, 1891–1956. Manchester R 8:221–4 '58.

'Hodson's novels in manuscript' (p. 224)

HODSON, WILLIAM, fl.1640

11096 **Hindle, Christopher J.** William Hodson. [Credo resurrectionem carnis, 1633]. TLS 16 Mr '33:184.

HOGG, JAMES, 1770–1835

11097 **Sinton, James.** The Spy [annotated by Hogg]. Scott N&Q ser2 7no6:89–91 D '05.

11098 **Alba,** *pseud.* Inedited poems by Hogg. Aberdeen J N&Q 3:311–13, 316–17 '10.

11099 **Pierce, Frederick E.** James Hogg, the Ettrick shepherd. [Colln. presented by R. B. Adam]. Yale Univ Lib Gaz 5no3:37–41 Ja '31.

11100 **Batho, Edith C.** Notes on the bibliography of James Hogg, the Ettrick shepherd. Library ser4 16no3:308–26 D '35. facsim.

11101 **The Ettrick** shepherd, a centenary exhibition. [National library, Scotland]. TLS 30 N '35:820.

11102 **Massey, Dudley.** Hogg, James: The private memoirs and confessions of a justified sinner, Longman, 1824. [Variant title]. Bib N&Q 2no8:7 F '37. [Sg.: D. M.]

11103 **Corson, James C.** Miscellaneous letters to and about James Hogg. [The domestic manners ... of Scotland, 1834]. N&Q 182:268–9 My '42; A. L. Strout *ib.* 183:187–8 S '42.

11104 **Bushnell, George H.** 'The Spy: James Hogg's adventure in journalism' *in* From papyrus to print. London, 1947. p. 147–54.

11105 **Strout, Alan L.** James Hogg's Chaldee manuscript. Pub Mod Lang Assn 65no3:695–718 S '50.

I. Introduction.–II. The background.–III. The satire.–IV. Conclusion: some unpublished letters after 1817.

11106 **Maxwell, James C.** Coleridge, a false attribution. [The cherub, by Hogg]. N&Q 208:182 My '63.

HOGG, THOMAS JEFFERSON, 1792–1862

11107 **Wright, Cyril E.** Manuscripts of T. J. Hogg and E. E. Williams. Brit Mus Q 9no3:78–81 F '35.

11108 **Babb, James T.** Hogg, Thomas Jefferson. [Memoirs of prince Alexy Haimatoff: priority of ed.]. Bib N&Q 2no11:8 N '38.

11109 —— Thomas Jefferson Hogg. [Memoirs of prince Alexy Haimatoff, 1813, 1825]. (Query no.7). Bk Coll 1no1:56–7 '52; D. Massey; W. S. Scott; J. T. Babb *ib.* 1no2:129–30 '52.

HOLBROOK, ANN CATHERINE, 1780–1837

11110 **Dodgson, Edward S.** Rebecca, a novel. N&Q ser10 3:128–9 F '05; C. F. Forshaw *ib.* 3:176–7 Mr '05; R. Thomas 3:293–4 Ap '05; E. S. Dodgson 3:435 Je '05; 5:72–3 Ja '06; C. Clarke; R. B. Douglas; F. G. Haley 5:117–18 F '06; C. Clarke 5:377 My '06; E. S. Dodgson, 7:352–3 My '07; C. Clarke 9:275 Ap '08.

HOLCROFT, THOMAS, 1745–1809

11111 **Colby, Elbridge.** Bibliography as an aid to biography. Pa Bib Soc Am 17pt1:1–11 '23.

11112 **Stallbaumer, Virgil R.** Translations by Holcroft. N&Q 173:402–5 D '37.

I. Translations falsely ascribed to Holcroft.–II. Did Holcroft translate The German hotel?

11113 **Todd, William B.** Holcroft's Follies of a day, 1785. [Two impr.]. (Note 260). Bk Coll 14no4:544 '65.

HOLINSHED, RAPHAEL, d.1580?

11114 **Moffett, S. O.** Holinshed bibliography. N&Q ser11 4:246 S '11.

11115 **Brownfield, Clarence.** Holinshed and his editors. TLS 7 Ag '37:576.

11116 **The Holinshed's** Chronicles. [Cancels and cancellanda]. Princeton Univ Lib Chron 7no2:82–3 F '46.

11117 **Scholderer, J. Victor.** The illustrations of the first edition of Holinshed. Edinburgh Bib Soc Trans 2pt4:398–403 '46. facsims., table.

11118 **Maslen, Keith I. D.** Three eighteenth-century reprints of the castrated sheets in Holinshed's Chronicles. Library scr5 13no2:120–4 Je '58. facsims.

11119 **Miller, William E.** Abraham Fleming, editor of Shakespeare's Holinshed. Texas Stud Lit & Lang 1:89–100 '59.

HOLLAND, HENRY, 1583–1650? *see under* Book production and distribution–Printers, publishers, etc.

HOLLAND, PHILEMON, 1552–1637

11120 **Menzies, Walter.** Notes on Philemon Holland's copy of Gilbertus Anglicus. Aberdeen Univ Lib Bull 7no37:1–6 Je '28. illus., facsim.

11121 **Borish, M. E.** and **W. R. Richardson.** Holland's Livy, 1600, and the 1686 version. Mod Lang N 48no7:457–9 N '33.

11122 **Goodspeed, George T.** Holland's Suetonius. [Issues]. Bib N&Q 2no8:7–8 F '37; R. S. Forsythe; Lucy E. Osborne *ib.* 2no9:2 Ja '38; J. W. Carter 2no10:4 Ap '38. [Sg.: G. G.]

HOLLAND, SIR RICHARD, fl.1450

11123 **Beattie, William.** An early printed fragment of the Buke of the Howlat. Edinburgh Bib Soc Trans 2pt4:393–7 '46. facsims.

HOLLAND, ROBERT, 1557–1622?

11124 **Davies, sir William Ll.** Robert Holland and William Perkins. (Notes, queries, and answers). Welsh Bib Soc J 2no7:273–4 D '22.

HOLME, CONSTANCE, fl.1913

11125 **A Constance** Holme typescript. [Beautiful end]. Serif 2no2:20 Je '65.

HOLT, JOHN, fl.1510

11126 **Beavan, John.** John Holt's Lac puerorum. [Antwerp, c.1500]. Bod Q Rec 3no35:247 Oc '22.

11127 **Hill, R. H.** The reconstruction of grammar. [Holt's Lac puerorum]. Bod Q Rec 3no35:247–8 Oc '22.

11128 **Fletcher, Harris F.** 'The earliest(?) printing of sir Thomas More's two epigrams to John Holt [and Lac puerorum]' *in* Allen, Don C., *ed.* Studies in honor of T. W. Baldwin. Urbana, 1958. p. 53–65. facsims.

HOLTBY, WINIFRED, 1898–1935

11129 **Taylor, Geoffrey Handley-.** Winifred Holtby. [His bibliogr.]. (Query no.50). Bk Coll 3no3:227 '54.

HOLYBAND, CLAUDE, *pseud. of* CLAUDE DE SAINLIENS, fl.1568–97

11130 **Pollard, Alfred W.** Claudius Hollyband and his French schoolmaster and French Littleton. Bib Soc Trans 13pt2:253–72 '14/15.

11131 —— [Same]: Library ser3 6no21:77–93 Ja '15.

11132 —— Claudius Hollyband and the French schoolmaster and French Littleton. Bib Soc News-sh 1–4 F '15.

HOLYOAKE, GEORGE JACOB, 1817–1906

11133 **Thomas, Ralph.** Holyoake bibliography. N&Q ser10 5:441 Je '06; C. W. F. Goss; V. G. Plarr *ib.* 5:491 Je '06; R. Thomas 6:75 Jl '06.

HOME, JOHN, 1722–1808

11134 **MacMillan, W. Dougald.** The first editions of Home's Douglas. Stud Philol 26no3:401–9 Jl '29.

11135 **Todd, William B.** Press figures and book reviews as determinants of priority; a study of Home's Douglas, 1757, and Cumberland's The brothers, 1770. Pa Bib Soc Am 45:72–6 '51. diagr., tables.

HOOD, ROBIN *see* Robin Hood.

HOOKER, RICHARD, 1554?–1600

11136 **Dunkin, Paul S.** Two notes on Richard Hooker. Pa Bib Soc Am 41:344–6 '47.

1. Date of the Ecclesiastical polity, first edition.–2. The Oxford tracts of 1612.

HOOKER, THOMAS, 1586–1647

11137 **Sheppard, Douglas H.** Thomas Hooker, 1586–1647. [The soul's humiliation, 1640]. N&Q 200:179–80 Ap '55.

HOOKES, NICHOLAS, 1628–1712

11138 **Prideaux, William F.** Hookes's Amanda. N&Q ser10 4:301–2 Oc '05.

HOOLE, CHARLES, 1610–67

11139 **Jones, Gordon W.** An unrecorded edition of a Hoole schoolbook. [Marturinus Corderius's School-colloquies, 1667]. Pa Bib Soc Am 55:226–9 '61.

HOOLE, SAMUEL, 1758–1839

11140 **Dobell, Clifford.** Samuel Hoole, translator of Leeuwenhoek's Select works. Isis 41pt2:171–80. Jl '50.

HOPE, ANTHONY, *pseud. of* SIR ANTHONY HOPE HAWKINS, 1863–1933

11141 **Muir, Percival H.** Hope: The prisoner of Zenda. [Issues]. Bib N&Q 1no3:5 Ag '35. [Sg.: P. H. M.]

HOPKINS, GERARD MANLEY, 1818–97

11142 **Gerard** Manley Hopkins. [Spicilegium poeticum, 1892]. Bib N&Q 1no1:3 Ja '35.

HOPKINS, GERARD MANLEY, 1844–89

11143 **Hardy, Robert E.** Gathorne-. Gerard Manley Hopkins. [Anthology poems]. Bib N&Q 1no3:5–6 Ag '35.

11144 **Howarth, R. Guy** [and] **A. H. House.** Hopkins, a correction. [Journal]. N&Q 193:150 Ap '48.

11145 **Bischoff, D. Anthony.** The manuscripts of Gerard Manley Hopkins. Thought (N.Y.) 26no103:551–80 '51/2.

> I. Introduction.–II. Catalogue of manuscripts. 1. The Robert Bridges collection.–2. Manuscripts at The garth, Haslemere.–3. Manuscripts at Amen house, London [O.U.P.].–4. The Arthur Hopkins manuscripts.–5. Manuscripts at Campion hall, Oxford.–6. Manuscripts at Stonyhurst college.–7. Letter at The oratory, Birmingham.–8. Letter in Balliol college library, Oxford.–9. Annotated books at 35 Lower Leeson st., Dublin.–Postscript.

11146 **Purchase** of manuscripts of Gerard Manley Hopkins. Bod Lib Rec 4no6:290 D '53.

11146a **House, A. Humphry** and **G. Storey,** *ed.* 'Catalogue of the manuscripts at Campion hall, Oxford' *in* Hopkins, Gerard M. Journals and papers. London, 1959. p. 529–35.

11147 **Brown, T. Julian.** Gerard Manley Hopkins, 1844–1889. (English literary autographs, XXXIX). Bk Coll 10no3:321 '61. facsims.

11148 **Ritz, Jean G.** 'La publication de œuvre écrite' *in* Le poète Gerard Manley Hopkins, S. J., 1844–1889: l'homme et l'œuvre. Paris [1963]. p. [21]–40.

11149 **MacKenzie, Norman H.** Hopkins mss.; old losses and new finds. TLS 18 Mr '65:220.

11150 **Thomas, Alfred.** G. M. Hopkins and the silver jubilee album. [Mss.]. Library ser5 20no2:148–52 Je '65. illus., facsim.

11151 **Gardner, W. H.** G. M. Hopkins. TLS 3 Ag '67:707; N. White *ib.* 22 Ag '68:905; N. H. MacKenzie; J. Milroy 26 S '68:1090; W. H. Gardner; N. White 31 Oc '68:1233; N. H. MacKenzie 21 N '68:1311; N. White 19 D '68:1440; R. E. Alton and P. J. Croft 23 Ja '69:87; N. MacKenzie 20 F '69:186; 13 Mr '69:272.

11152 **White, Norman** and **T. Dunne.** A Hopkins discovery ['Thee, God I come from . . .']. Library ser5 24no1:56–8 Mr '69; A. Uphill *ib.* 24no4:346 D '69.

HOPTON, SUSANNA (HARVEY), 1627–1709

11153 **Sauls, Lynn.** Whereabouts of Hopton's Collection of meditations. [Query 235). Bk Coll 18no2:225 '69.

HORNE, RICHARD HENRY (HENGIST), 1803–84

11154 **Mabbott, Thomas O.** Changes in the text of Horne's Orion. N&Q 155:441–2 D '28.

11155 **Todd, William B.** Horne, Orion: an epic poem, 1843. (Note 309). Bk Coll 18no2:219 '69.

HOSKINS, JOHN, 1566–1638

11156 **Wagner, Bernard M.** Hoskins's Directions. [Ms.]. TLS 3 Oc '36:791.

HOTTEN, JOHN CAMDEN, 1832–73 *see* Book production and distribution–Printers, publishers, etc.

HOUGHTON, RICHARD MONCKTON MILNES, 1ST BARON, 1809–85 *see* Milnes, Richard Monckton, 1st baron Houghton, 1809–85.

HOUSMAN, ALFRED EDWARD, 1859–1936

11157 **Collamore, H. B.** Housman, A. E.: Odes from the Greek dramatists, 1890. [Binding variants]. Bib N&Q 2no4/5:10 My '36; J. W. Carter *ib.* 2no6:4 Jl '36.

11158 **D., P.** Housman: Shropshire lad. [Label variants]. Bib N&Q 2no4/5:10 My '36; J. H. A. Sparrow *ib.* 2no8:2 F '37; Harriet Marlow 2no12:1 My '39.

11159 **Flower, Robin E. W.** Three poems by A. E. Housman. [Mss.]. Brit Mus Q 11no2:76–7 Mr '37.

11160 **Tillotson, Geoffrey.** The publication of A. E. Housman's comic poems. Eng 1no6:485–93 '37.

11161 **Carter, John W.** On collecting A. E. Housman. Coloph new ser 3no1:54–62 F '38.

Repr. in Books and book-collectors. London, 1956. p. 101–11.

11162 —— Two rare Housman items. [The jubilee address, 1935; The order of service, 1936]. Bib N&Q 2no9:5–6 Ja '38.

11163 **Fletcher, G. B. A.** The text of Housman's poems. TLS 3 Ag '40:375; J. W. Carter *ib.* 17 Ag '40:399; T. F. G. Richards 24 Ag '40:411.

11164 **White, William.** [Bibliogr. note on Odes from the Greek dramatists, 1890]. Pa Bib Soc Am 34:274 '40.

11165 **Richards, T. F. Grant.** Housman, 1897 1936. London, O.U.P., H. Milford; New York, O.U.P., 1941. xxii,493p. illus., ports., facsims. 22cm.

Includes I. A Shropshire lad appears.–II. The second edition.–VII. His publisher's failure.–XXII. At last a successor to A Shropshire lad! [Last poems].

11166 **Runyan, Harry J.** An emendation to A. E. Housman's translation from Euripides' Alcestis 962–1005. Mod Lang N 56no6:458 Je '41.

11167 **White, William.** [Bibliogr. note on Housman's Odes from the Greek dramatists, 1890]. Pa Bib Soc Am 35:297–8 '41.

11168 **Carter, John W.** A poem of A. E. Housman. [The sage to the young man ms.]. TLS 5 Je '43:276; 12 Je '43:288.

11169 **White, William.** [Bibliogr. note on Housman's The oracles]. Pa Bib Soc Am 37:78 '43.

11170 **Dillard, Henry B.** The manuscript poems of Alfred Edward Housman. Lib Congress Q J 5no2:7–8 F '48.

11171 **White, William.** A Shropshire lad in Shrewsbury. N&Q 196:281 Je '51.

11172 —— Two problems in A. E. Housman bibliography. Pa Bib Soc Am 45:358–9 '51.

11173 **Haber, Tom B.** A. E. Housman's notebooks. TLS 7 N '52:732.

11174 —— A. E. Housman's printer's copy of Last poems. [Grant Richards]. Pa Bib Soc Am 46:70–7 '52.

11175 **Housman, Laurence.** A. E. Housman fragments. [Mss.]. TLS 27 Je '52:421; Charles Scribner's sons, ltd.; W. White *ib.* 4 Jl '52:437; J. H. A. Sparrow 18 Jl '52:469; W. White 1 Ag '52:501.

11176 **White, William.** Editing A. E. Housman. [Collected poems]. TLS 26 S '52:629; J. W. Carter *ib.* 24 Oc '52:693.

11177 **Fletcher, G. B. A.** A. E. Housman bibliography. Library ser5 8no1:51 Mr '53.

11178 **Haber, Tom B.** Editing A. E. Housman. TLS 2 Oc '53:636; J. W. Carter *ib.* 23 Oc '53:677.

11179 **White, William.** Variant readings in Housman's Collected poems. Bk Coll 2no2:145–8 '53.

11180 —— Variant readings in Housman's More poems. (Note no.20). Bk Coll 2no1:73–7 '53.

11181 **Carter, John W.** Editing A. E. Housman. [Collected poems]. TLS 5 Mr '54:153; W. White *ib.* 14 My '54:319.

11182 **Haber, Tom B.** Housman's poetic method: his lectures and his notebooks. Pub Mod Lang Assn 69no5:1000–16 D '54.

11183 **White, William.** Housman's Collected poems. TLS 12 F '54:105.

11184 —— A Shropshire lad in process; the textual evolution of some A. E. Housman poems. Library ser5 9no4:255–64 D '54. tables.

11185 —— Variant readings in Housman's Collected poems. Bk Coll 3no2:145–8 '54.

11186 **Carter, John W.** The A. E. Housman manuscripts in the Library of Congress. [And copyright]. Bk Coll 4no2:110–14 '55.

11187 **Haber, Tom B.** The Housman dilemma. TLS 1 Jl '55:365.

11188 **White, William.** Housman's Epitaph on an army of mercenaries. (Query no.63). Bk Coll 4no2:173 '55.

11189 —— An unrecorded Housman ms. item. Pa Bib Soc Am 49:78–9 '55.

11190 **Carter, John W.** The text of Housman's poems. TLS 15 Je '56:361; Reviewer *ib.* 22 Je '56:377; T. B. Haber 20 Jl '56:435; J. W. Carter 27 Jl '56:449.

11191 **Haber, Tom B.** A unique Shropshire lad. [1903]. Pa Bib Soc Am 50:198–200 '56.

11192 **Marlow, Harriet.** Housman presentation copies. [F. B. Adams' library]. (Note no.79). Bk Coll 5no4:384 '56.

11193 **White, William.** Colophon notes for Housman collectors. Am Bk Coll 7no2:18–20 Oc '56. facsim.

A. E. Housman in French.–Housman on Stevenson.–Milton or Wolfe.

11194 —— Misprints in A Shropshire lad. Bull Bib 21no9:200 Ja/Ap '56.

11195 **Carter, John W.** A. E. Housman's contributions to an Oxford magazine. [Ye rounde table]. (Query 90). Bk Coll 6no4:404 '57.

11196 —— A variant reading in Housman's Collected poems. (Note 80). Bk Coll 6no2:182 '57.

11197 **Gow, Andrew S. F.** A Housman couplet. TLS 24 My '57:321.

11198 **White, William.** Colophon notes for Housman collectors. Am Bk Coll 7no9:3–5 Je '57.

11199 —— Misprints in Housman. Bull Bib 22no4:82 S/D '57.

11200 —— A variant reading in Housman's Collected poems. [New Year's eve, l.47–8]. (Note 80). Bk Coll 6no1:71 '57.

11201 **Lavin, J. Anthony.** A Shropshire lad. N&Q 203:89 F '58.

11202 **A. E. Housman,** a centenary exhibition. [University college, London]. TLS 4 S '59:512; J. W. Carter ib. 11 S '59:519; W. White 16 Oc '59:593.

11203 **Brown, T. Julian.** Alfred Edward Housman, 1859–1936. (English literary autographs, XXXI). Bk Coll 8no3:283 '59. facsims.

Note by John W. Carter.

11204 **Carter, John W.** Housman revised? [Complete poems, 1959]. TLS 29 My '59:321; T. B. Haber ib. 24 Jl '59:435; J. W. Carter 14 Ag '59:471.

11205 **Smith, Simon H. Nowell-.** Housman inscriptions. [Dedication in Bridges' Hopkins]. TLS 6 N '59:643.

11206 **Carter, John W.** Housman manuscripts. (Query 130). Bk Coll 9no2:204–5 '60; D. A. Randall ib. 9no4:456 '60.

11207 **Randall, David A.** A Shropshire lad with a variant title-page. (Query 135). Bk Coll 9no4:458–9 '60.

11208 **White, William.** Colophon notes for Housman collectors. Am Bk Coll 11no7:17–19 Mr '61.

11209 **Carter, John W.** Housmaniana. (Note 174). Bk Coll 11no1:84 '62.

11210 ——— Missing Housman mss. [A Shropshire lad; Last poems]. TLS 7 D '62:964.

11211 **Haber, Tom B.** A. E. Housman and Ye rounde table. J Eng Germ Philol 61no4:797–809 Oc '62.

'Housman's contributions to Ye rounde table' (p. 801–8)

11212 **Carter, John W.** Housman, Shelley and Swinburne. [Inaugural lecture, Cambridge, 1911]. TLS 6 S '63:680; 13 S '63:689.

11213 **White, William.** A. E. Housman's Collected poems. [1963]. (Note 192). Bk Coll 12no1:71 '63.

11214 ——— Emendations in Housman. (Note 234). Bk Coll 13no4:500 '64.

11215 ——— Housmaniana. Am Bk Coll 15no2:6 Oc '64.

11216 **Carter, John W.** Housmaniana. [Presentation copies]. (Note 247). Bk Coll 14no2:215–17 '65.

11217 **White, William.** Misprints in Housman's Last poems. [1922]. (Note 255). Bk Coll 14no4:540–1 '65.

11218 **Indiana. University. Lilly library.** The John Carter collection of A. E. Housman. [Bloomington, Lilly library, Indiana university, 1966]. 8p. facsim. 22cm. Covertitle.

11219 **White, William.** The text of A. E. Housman's Collected poems. [1965]. Pa Bib Soc Am 60:221–3 '66. table.

11220 ——— Henry Altemus editions of A Shropshire lad. Am Bk Coll 17no6:10 Mr '67.

11221 ——— A Shropshire lad XLIII, 1 and LXII, 31. [Text]. Serif 4no3:31–2 S '67.

11222 **Carter, John W.** A further note on A. E. Housman. TLS 14 Mr '68:278.

11223 ——— Housmaniana. (Note 247). Bk Coll 17no2:215 '68.

11224 ——— Housman's funeral hymn. [Ms. of Hymn for my funeral]. TLS 28 Mr '68:325; J. D. K. Lloyd ib. 4 Ap '68:345; J. H. H. Gaute 11 Ap '68:373.

11225 **Nosworthy, J. M.** Housman misprints. TLS 13 Je '68:628; T. B. Haber ib. 15 Ag '68:881.

11226 **White, William.** Thomas B. Mosher and A Shropshire lad. Serif 5no2:30–3 Je '68.

11227 **Carter, John W.** Misprinting Housman. [The confines of criticism]. TLS 27 N '69:1363; Audrey Jennings *ib.* 4 D '69:1405.

11228 **White, William.** Housman in Braille. Am Bk Coll 19no10:10 Je '69.

11229 —— John Lane (New York) Shropshire lads. Am Bk Coll 19no6:31 F '69.

HOWARD, HENRY, EARL OF SURREY, 1517?–47

11230 **Padelford, Frederick M.** The relation of the 1812 and 1815–1816 editions of Surrey and Wyatt. [And G. F. Knott's plagiarism]. Anglia 29:256–70 Ap '06.

11231 **Willcock, Gladys D.** A hitherto uncollated version of Surrey's translation of the fourth book of the Æneid. [Ms.]. Mod Lang R 14no2:163–72 Ap '19; 15no2:113–23 Ap '20; 17no2:131–49 Ap '22. tables.

11232 **Brooks, Cleanth J.** The history of Percy's edition of Surrey's poems. Eng Studien 68no3:424–30 F '34.

11233 **Jensen, Bent Juel-.** The poet earl of Surrey's library. (Note no.67). Bk Coll 5no2:172 '56.

11234 **Muir, Kenneth.** Surrey poems in the Blage manuscript. N&Q 205:368–70 Oc '60.

HOWARD, ROBERT, b.1597

11235 **Allison, Antony F.** Robert Howard, Franciscan. Library ser5 3no4:288–90 Mr '49.

HOYLE, EDMOND, 1672–1769

11236 **Bennett, Whitman.** Remarkable first edition of Hoyle. Pub Wkly 120no3:254–5 Jl '31. facsim.

HUDSON, WILLIAM HENRY, 1841–1922

11237 **Hudson** bibliographical discoveries. [A crystal age, 1887]. (Men and matters). Bkmns J new ser 9no27:115 D '23.

11238 **The real** first edition of Hudson's Hampshire days and other notes. Bkmns J new ser 7no18:170–1 Mr '23; E. C. Rodda; T. S. Mercer *ib.* 8no19:33 Ap '23; A. Rogers 8no23:175 Ag '23.

11239 **Waugh, Arthur.** W. H. Hudson and Henry Harford. [And Fan copyright]. TLS 19 Jl '23:488; J. M. Dent *ib.* 26 Jl '23:504; A. Waugh 2 Ag '23:520.

11240 **Wilson, George F.** A rare Hudson pamphlet. [Osprey; or, Egret and aigrettes, 1892]. Bkmns J new ser 9no29:178 F '24; F. C. Carter; G. F. Wilson *ib.* 10no31:31–2 Ap '24. [Sg.: G. F. W.]

11241 —— W. H. Hudson's Fan. Bkmns J new ser 8no23:175 Ag '23. [Sg.: G. F. W.]

11242 **W. H. Hudson:** original bindings. (Marginalia). Bkmns J ser3 16no8:461 '28.

11243 **Brooks, Philip.** W. H. Hudson's Argentine ornithology. (Marginalia). Bkmns J ser3 18no14:45–6 '30.

11244 **Sargent, George H.** ... American appreciation of W. H. Hudson. ... (American notes). Bkmns J new ser 10no35:173 Ag '34.

11245 **Hudson:** Green mansions. [Binding variants]. Bib N&Q 2no8:8 F '37; J. W. Carter *ib.* 2no11:3 N '38.

11246 **Wells, Carlton F.** The G. M. Adams–W. H. Hudson collection; an appreciation. Ann Arbor, William L. Clements library, 1943. 12p. port. 17cm. (Clements Lib Bull 39)

11247 **Hill, James J.** and **O M Brack.** First editions of William Henry Hudson. Lib Chron Univ Texas 8no1:44–6 '65. facsim.

'Desiderata' (p. 45–6)

HUEFFER, FORD MADOX (later FORD), 1873–1939 *see* Ford, Ford Madox (formerly Hueffer), 1873–1939.

HUME, ALEXANDER, 1560?–1609

11248 **Lindsay, David W.** Of the day estivall, a textual note. Stud Scot Lit 4no2:104–6 Oc '66.

HUME, DAVID, 1711–76

11249 **Chapman, Robert W.** Hume's Essays. TLS 7 Je '28:431.

11250 **Dickson, William K.** David Hume and the Advocates library. Edinburgh, W. Green, 1932. 16p. illus., facsim. 25cm.

Repr. from Juridical R 44no1:1–14 Mr '32.

11251 **Mossner, Ernest C.** A ms. fragment of Hume's Treatise, 1746. N&Q 194:520–2 N '49.

11252 —— and **H. H. Ransom.** Hume and the conspiracy of the booksellers; the publication and early fortunes of the History of England. [And Andrew Millar]. Univ Texas Stud Eng 29:162–82 '50.

11253 —— Hume's Four dissertations, an essay in biography and bibliography. Mod Philol 48no1:37–57 Ag '50.

11254 **Hume's** A treatise of human nature. Princeton Univ Lib Chron 12no2:95–6 '51.

11255 **Todd, William B.** The first printing of Hume's Life, 1777. Library ser5 6no2:123–5 S '51. tables.

11256 **Meyer, Paul H.** The manuscript of Hume's account of his dispute with Rousseau. Comp Lit 4no4:341–50 '52.

11257 **Todd, William B.** Hume Exposé succinct. (Note 97). Bk Coll 7no1:191 '58.

11258 **Nethery, Wallace.** Hume's manuscript corrections in a copy of A treatise of human nature. Pa Bib Soc Am 57:446–7 '63. table.

11259 **Gaskin, J. C. A.** Hume's suppressed dissertation, an authentic text. [Four dissertations, 1757]. Hermathena 106:54–9 '68.

HUME, JOSEPH, 1777–1855

11260 **Ravizé, A.** Hume's papers. N&Q ser10 8:268 Oc '07; W. H. Peet *ib.* 8:315 Oc '07.

HUME, TOBIAS, d.1645

11261 **Lehmuth, Marie C. F.** Song-book by Tobias Hume. [First part of ayres, 1605]. N&Q ser12 10:31 Ja '22; W. Jaggard *ib.* 10:76–7 Ja '22.

HUMPHREY, JOHN, 1621–1719

11262 **Whiting, F. Brooke.** The authorship of A proposition for the safety and happiness of the king . . . 1667. Pa Bib Soc Am 50:182–3 '56.

HUNT, JAMES HENRY LEIGH, 1784–1859

11263 **Johnson, Reginald B.** Leigh Hunt. [Books attributed to but by Thomas Powell]. Athenæum 3327:160–1 Ag '91.

11264 **Page, Frederick.** Leigh Hunt. TLS 17 F '21:108.

11265 **Teall, Gardner.** Leigh Hunt in America, 1804–1818. Bkmns J new ser 11no42:245–7 Mr '25.

11266 **Mitchell, Alexander.** Notes on the bibliography of Leigh Hunt. Bkmns J ser3 15no1:3–19 '27.

11267 **Brewer, Luther A.** The first edition of Leigh Hunt's Sir Ralph Esher. [And 2d ed.]. Bkmns J ser3 17no12:219–21 '30.

11268 **Mitchell, Alexander.** The problem of the first edition of Leigh Hunt's Sir Ralph Esher; a reply to mr. Luther A. Brewer. Bkmns J ser3 18no13:15–17 '30.

11269 **Grobel, Monica C.** Leigh Hunt and The town. Mod Lang R 26no1:80–7 Ja '31.

11270 **Bay, J. Christian.** The Leigh Hunt collection of Luther Albertus Brewer. Cedar Rapids, Iowa, Privately ptd. for the friends of the Torch pr., 1933. 38p. 18cm.

11271 **Argus book shop.** Hunt, Leigh: The palfrey, London, 1842. [Binding variants]. Bib N&Q 2no11:8–9 N '38.

11272 **Brewer, Luther A.** My Leigh Hunt library: the holograph letters. Iowa city, Iowa, University of Iowa pr. [1938]. vi,421p. facsims. 28cm.

   Rev: G. D. Stout Mod Lang N 54:393 '39; G. L. Marsh Mod Philol 36:326–8 '39.

11273 **Marchand, Leslie A.** Leigh Hunt's London journal. J Rutgers Univ Lib 6no2:45–51 Je '43.

11274 **Gates, Payson G.** Leigh Hunt's review of Shelley's Posthumous poems. Pa Bib Soc Am 42:1–40 '48.

11275 **Kaser, David.** Leigh Hunt and his Pennsylvania editor. [Samuel Adams Lee]. Pennsylvania Mag Hist & Biog 81no4:406–14 Oc '57.

11276 **Green, David B.** The first publication of Leigh Hunt's Love letters made of flowers. Pa Bib Soc Am 52:52–5 '58.

11277 —— The publication of Leigh Hunt's Imagination and fancy. Stud Bib 12:227–30 '59.

11278 **Hanlin, Frank S.** The Brewer-Leigh Hunt collection at the State university of Iowa. Keats-Sh J 8pt2:91–4 '59.

11279 **Wolfe, Joseph** and **Linda Wolfe.** An earlier version of Abou. N&Q 205:113 Mr '60.

11280 **Smith, Simon H. Nowell-.** Leigh Hunt's The descent of liberty, 1815. Library ser5 17no3:238–40 S '62.

11281 **Brewer, Luther A.** Leigh Hunt association books. Bks at Iowa 1:4–10 Oc '64.

11282 **Nicholes, E. L.** Leigh Hunt's Feast of the poets, Boston, 1813, edition. (Note 321). Bk Coll 18no4:515–18 '69.

HUNT, VIOLET, 1866–1942

11283 **Mizener, Arthur.** The lost papers of Violet Hunt. Cornell Lib J 3:1–6 '67. illus.

HUNT, WILLIAM HOLMAN, 1827–1910

11284 [**Robertson, Edward**]. The Holman Hunt papers. (Notes and news). Bull John Rylands Lib 41no1:9–11 S '58.

HUNTER, JOSEPH, 1783–1861

11285 **Carlton, William N. C.** Notes on a facsimile reproduction of Joseph Hunter's Chorus vatum Anglicanorum. Pa Bib Soc Am 11no2:43–8 Ap '17.

HUTCHINSON, LUCY (APSLEY), b.1620

11286 **Race, Sydney.** Notes on mrs. Hutchinson's manuscripts. N&Q ser13 1:3–4 Jl '23; 1:26–8 Jl '23; 1:165–6 S '23.

11287 —— Colonel Hutchinson: manuscript and printed memoirs. N&Q 199:160–3 Ap '54; 199:202–4 My '54.

HUTTON, RICHARD HOLT, 1826–97

11288 **Tener, Robert H.** R. H. Hutton's Essays theological and literary, a bibliographical note. N&Q 205:185–7 My '60.

HUXLEY, ALDOUS LEONARD, 1894–1963

11289 **Freedley, George.** Original play script and letters. [Huxley's The gioconda smile]. N.Y. Pub Lib Bull 55no9:462 S '51.

11290 **California. University. University at Los Angeles. Library.** Aldous Huxley at UCLA; a catalogue of the manuscripts in the Aldous Huxley collection ... ed. with an introduction by George Wickes. Los Angeles, 1964. 36p. illus., ports., facsims. 25cm.

11291 **Wilson, Robert H.** Versions of Brave new world. Lib Chron Univ Texas 8no4:28–41 '68. facsim.

11292 **Farmer, David.** The American edition of Huxley's Leda. (Note 312). Bk Coll 18no2:220–1 '69.

11293 —— A note on the text of Huxley's Crome yellow. Pa Bib Soc Am 63:131–3 '69. tables.

HYDE, EDWARD, EARL OF CLARENDON, 1609–74

11294 **Roper, Hugh R. Trevor-.** The copyright in Clarendon's works. [And Clarendon pr.]. TLS 17 F '50:112; J. D. Hayward *ib.* 24 F '50:121; sir A. L. P. Norrington 3 Mr '50:144; H. R. Trevor-Roper; J. D. Hayward 10 Mr '50:160; sir A. L. P. Norrington 7 Jl '50:421.

11295 **Hardacre, P. H.** Edward Hyde, earl of Clarendon, 1609–74. (Portrait of a bibliophile, I). Bk Coll 7no4:361–8 '58.

11296 **Enright, B. J.** The Ware-Clarendon manuscripts. Bod Lib Rec 6no5:586–7 Ag '60.

INGLIS, ESTHER, (MRS. B. KELLO), formerly LANGLOIS, 1571–1624

11297 **Jackson, Dorothy J.** Esther Inglis, calligrapher, 1571–1624. [With checklist of 41 mss.]. [New York, Privately ptd. at the Spiral pr., 1937]. [10]p. 17cm.

11298 **Blumenthal, Walter H.** Lady with a feathered quill; her calligraphic books now precious rarities. Am Bk Coll 14no2:7–12 Oc '63. illus., facsims.

11299 **Jackson, Dorothy J.** Esther Inglis mss. TLS 8 D '66:1160.

INGOLDSBY, THOMAS, *pseud. of* RICHARD HARRIS BARHAM, 1788–1845

11300 **Sadleir, Michael T. H.** Ingoldsby legends, 1st series. TLS 14 Ap '45:180.

11301 **Lane, William G.** The primitive muse of Thomas Ingoldsby. Harvard Lib Bull 12no1:47–83 '58; 12no2:220–41 '58. illus., facsims.

IRELAND, SAMUEL, d.1800

11302 **Murray, Edward C.** Sketch-books of Samuel Ireland. [Copy for his ptd. works]. Brit Mus Q 11no3:135–9 Je '37.

IRELAND, WILLIAM HENRY, 1777–1835

11303 **Libbis, G. Hilder.** W. H. Ireland's Chatelar and Rizzio. N&Q 148:183 Mr '25.

11304 **Bodde, Derk.** Shakspere and the Ireland forgeries. Cambridge, Mass., Harvard U.P., 1930. (Repr. Folcroft, Pa., Folcroft library editions, 1973; New York, Haskell house, 1975; Norwood, Pa., Norwood editions, 1976). 68p. 19cm. (Harvard honors theses in English, no.2)

Rev: E. J. Simmons Harvard Grad Mag 39:426–9 '31; W. Keller Sh Jahrb 67:93 '31.

11305 **Haraszti, Zoltán.** Ireland's Shakespeare forgeries; his books and letters, and several of his original forgeries, on view . . . . More Bks Boston Pub Lib Bull 9no9:333–50 N '34. facsims.

11306 —— The Shakespeare forgeries of William Henry Ireland; the story of a famous literary fraud. Boston, Mass., Trustees of the Public library, 1934. 22p. facsims. 27cm.

*Repr. from no.*11305.

11307 **Mair, John.** The fourth forger; William Ireland and the Shakespeare papers. London, Cobden-Sanderson, 1938; New York, Macmillan, 1939. (Repr. New York, Kennikat pr., 1971). xv,244p. 23cm.

1. The Ireland family.–2. The journey to Stratford.–3. The first forgeries.–4. William grows more ambitious.–5. Public opinion.–6. The historical background.–7. The mysterious gentleman.–8. Montague Talbot.–9. Negotiations for Vortigern.–10. The controversy.–11. Final preparations.–12. Edmund Malone.–13. The first night of Vortigern.–14. William loses his head.–15. Confession.–16. Anticlimax.–Appendix I: Anachronism and borrowing in the forged plays.–II. The confessions.–III. The woman with red hair.

Rev: Sylva Norman London Merc 38:465–6 '38; J. W. Carter Spectator 19 Ag '38:310; Manchester Guardian Wkly 26 Ag '38; T. James Life & Letters 19:124–5 '38; W. Stonier New Statesman new ser 16:286 '38; TLS 6 Ag '38:515; W. T. Hastings Saturday R Lit 20:16 '39; *ib*. Sh Assn Bull 14:248–51 '39; P. Hutchinson N.Y. Times Bk R 4 Je '39:2; E. W. Bowen Virginia J Education 33:201–4 '40; T. W. Baldwin Mod Lang N 55:458 '40.

11308 **Hastings, William T.** The fourth forger: a supplemental minority report. Sh Assn Bull 14no4:248–51 Oc '39.

11309 **Muir, Percival II.** The Ireland Shakespeare forgeries. (Note no.17). [Saleroom history of Ireland's mss., condensed from G. Hilder Libbis papers, now in Henry E. Huntington library]. Bk Coll 2no1:72–3 '53.

11310 **William H.** Ireland forgeries. [Acquired by Huntington and Iowa State university libraries]. Sh Q 8no1:137 '57.

IRVING, SIR JOHN HENRY BRODRIBB–, 1838–1905

11311 **Rosenberg, Marvin.** Henry Irving edition of Othello. [Sought]. N&Q 195:260 Je '50.

11312 **Rosenfeld, Sybil.** An Irving collection. [Russell-Cotes art gallery and museum, Bournemouth]. Theat Notebk 4no3:63 Ap/Je '50. [Sg.: S. R.]

JACKSON, HOLBROOK, 1874–1948

11313 **Mr.** Holbrook Jackson, (Private libraries, X). TLS 22 Oc '38:684.

Robert Burton.–Sir Henry Wotton.–Nineteenth century.–Association books.

11314 **Holbrook** Jackson in America. [Philadelphia Free library exhibition]. TLS 28 N '58:696.

11315 **Mathews, Elkin, bksllrs.,** BISHOP'S STORTFORD. The Holbrook Jackson library; a memorial catalogue, with an appreciation by sir Francis Meynell. Takeley, Bishop's Stortford, 1951. 101p. port. 22cm. (Catalogue 119)

Includes The Burton collection (p. 4–5)

JACOBS, WILLIAM WYMARK, 1863–1943

11316 **Osborne, Eric A.** Epitome of a bibliography of W. W. Jacobs. Am Bk Coll 5no7:201–4 Jl '34; 5no8/9:268–72 Ag/S '34; 5no10:286–8 Oc '34; 5no11:331–4 N '34; 5no12:358–62 D '34.

11317 **James, A. R.** W. W. Jacobs. [His bibliogr.]. TLS 20 Mr '53:187.

JAMES I, KING OF ENGLAND, 1566–1625

11318 **A prince's** school-books. [Library]. Library 2no21:352–3 S '90.

11319 **Warner, George F.** The library of James VI, 1573–1583, from a manuscript in the hand of Peter Young, his tutor, edited .... Scottish Hist Soc Misc 1:i-lxxv '93. facsim.

11320 —— The library of James VI of Scotland. Athenæum 3402:16–18 Ja '93.

Repr. in Bkworm 6no67:201–6 Je '93.

11321 **Johnston, George P.** Notice of a volume of Scots acts from the library of James VI of Scotland. Edinburgh Bib Soc Pub 6pt1:71–5 Je '04. illus., facsims.

11322 **Lyell, James P. R.** King James I and the Bodleian library catalogue of 1620. Bod Q Rec 7no79:271–83 '33. facsims.

11323 **Craigie, James.** The Basilicon doron of king James I. Library ser5 3no1:22–32 Je '48. table.

Editions in English.–Versions of Basilicon doron.–Summary of editions and versions.

11324 —— The Latin folio of king James's prose works. Edinburgh Bib Soc Trans 3pt1:19–30 '52; 3pt2:155 '54.

The three forms of the folio.–The unsigned preliminary leaves.–Table of copies examined.–Inscriptions in presentation copies of the Latin folio.–Patrick Young's letter.

JAMES I, KING OF SCOTLAND, 1394–1437

11325 **Cronin, Grover.** Two bibliographical notes on The Kingis quair. N&Q 181:341–2 D '41.

1. An unnoticed copy of David Laing's collation.–II. An addition to Geddie's Bibliography of middle Scots poets.

JAMES II, KING OF ENGLAND, 1633–1701

11326 **Randall, David A.** and **P. H. Muir.** The lost memoirs of James II and how they were found. Manuscripts 13no4:3–12 '61. facsim.

JAMES VI, KING OF SCOTLAND, 1566–1625 *see* James I, king of England, 1566–1625.

JAMES, GEORGE PAYNE RAINSFORD, 1799–1860

11327 **Frost, W. A.** Novel by G. P. R. James with three titles. [Revenge, 1852]. N&Q ser11 3:465–6 Je '11.

11328 —— The novels and short stories of G. P. R. James. N&Q ser12 2:167–8 Ag '16; C. Tearle *ib.* 2:255–6 S '16.

JAMES, HENRY, 1843–1916

11329 **Daniels, Earl.** Bibliography of Henry James. TLS 20 Ap '33:276.

11330 **Adams, John R.** At Isella: some horrible printing corrected. [In Galaxy, v.12, 1871]. Mark Twain Q 5no4:10,23 '43.

11331 **Havens, Raymond D.** A misprint in The awkward age. Mod Lang N 60no7:497 N '45.

11332 **Edel, Leon.** The texts of Henry James's unpublished plays. Harvard Lib Bull 3no3:395–406 '49. facsims.

11333 **Ferguson, Alfred R.** Some bibliographical notes on the short stories of Henry James. Am Lit 21no3:292–7 N '49.

11334 **Edel, Leon.** The promptbook of Henry James's The American. Princeton Univ Lib Chron 15no1:49 '53.

11335 **Humphreys, Susan M.** Henry James's revisions for The ambassadors. N&Q 199:397–9 S '54; L. Edel *ib.* 200:37–8 Ja '55.

11336 **Laurence, Dan H.** A bibliographical novitiate: in search of Henry James. Pa Bib Soc Am 52:23–33 '58.

11337 **Smith, Simon H. Nowell-.** Without benefit of bibliography; some notes on Henry James. Bk Coll 7no1:64–7 '58.

11338 —— Editing James. TLS 3 Jl '59:399.

11339 **Bowden, Edwin T.** In defense of a Henry James collection. Lib Chron Univ Texas 6no4:7–12 '60.

11340 **Edel, Leon.** The text of The ambassadors. Harvard Lib Bull 14no3:453–60 '60.

11341 **Donovan, Alan B.** My dear Pinker; the correspondence of Henry James with his literary agent. Yale Univ Lib Gaz 36no2:78–88 Oc '61.

11342 **Maxwell, James C.** [and] **I. Watt.** The text of The ambassadors. Essays in Crit 11no1:116–19 Ja '61; J. C. Maxwell *ib.* 11no3:370 Jl '61.

11343 **Monteiro, George.** The manuscript of The tragic muse. Am N&Q 1no5:68 Ja '63.

11344 **Maxwell, James C.** The revision of Roderick Hudson. Eng Stud 45no3:239 Je '64.

11345 **Birch, Brian.** Henry James, some bibliographical and textual matters. Library ser5 20no2:108–23 Je '65. facsims., diagr.

11346 **Rosenbaum, S. P.** [and] **B. Birch.** The editions of The ambassadors. Library ser5 21no3:248–52 S '66.

11347 —— The Spoils of Poynton, revisions and editions. Stud Bib 19:161–74 '66.

11348 **Hyde, H. Montgomery.** The Lamb house library of Henry James. Bk Coll 16no4:477–80 '67. facsim.

11349 **Kraft, James.** An unpublished review by Henry James. [Ms.]. Stud Bib 20:267–73 '67.

11350 **Gard, Roger,** *ed.* 'Appendix II: James's sales' *in* Henry James, the critical heritage. London; New York [1968]. p. 545–57.

11351 **Monteiro, George.** Addendum to Edel and Laurence: Henry James's Future of the novel. Pa Bib Soc Am 63:130 '69.

11352 **Smith, Simon H. Nowell-.** Texts of The portrait of a lady, 1881–1882, the bibliographical evidence. Pa Bib Soc Am 63:304–10 '69. diagr., table.

JAMES, MONTAGUE RHODES, 1862–1936

11353 **Millar, Eric G.** Casting the runes. [Mss.]. Brit Mus Q 11no2:81 Mr '37.

JAMES, THOMAS, 1573?–1629

11354 **Myres, J. N. L.** Thomas James Concordantiae sanctorum patrum, 1607. Bod Lib Rec 5no4:212–17 Oc '55.

11355 —— Concordantiae sanctorum patrum. Bod Lib Rec 6no5:587–8 Ag '60.

JARRY, FRANCIS, 1733–1807

11356 **Kerslake, John F.** M. de Jarry's project for an edition of the Moniteur. Library ser5 4no4:277–9 Mr '50.

JEFFERIES, JOHN RICHARD, 1848–87

11357 **A Jefferies** collation. [Land, 1896]. Bkmns J new ser 13no50:70 N '25.

11358 **Looker, Samuel J.** Richard Jefferies. TLS 27 N '37:916.

11359 —— Bibliographical discoveries in the work of Richard Jefferies. N&Q 186:91–2 F '44.

JEFFREY, FRANCIS, LD. JEFFREY, 1773–1850

11360 **Goldberg, Maxwell H.** Jeffrey, mutilator of Carlyle's Burns. Pub Mod Lang Assn 56no2:466–71 Je '41.

11361 **Agnew, L. R. C.** In search of Jeffrey. Am Bk Coll 8no5:3–11 Ja '58.

JERROLD, DOUGLAS WILLIAM, 1803–57

11362 **Owl,** *pseud.* Douglas Jerrold's dramatic works. N&Q ser8 11:211 Mr '97.

JEVON, THOMAS, 1652–88

11363 **Waller, Frederick O.** Three 1695 editions of Jevon's Devil of a wife. Stud Bib 3:255 '50/1.

11364 **Bowers, Fredson T.** Another early edition of Thomas Jevon's Devil of a wife. [1695]. Pa Bib Soc Am 49:253–4 '55.

JEWEL, BP. JOHN, 1522–71

11365 **McGovern, John B.** Bishop Jewel's library. N&Q ser11 9:401–3 My '14; 9:441–3 Je '14; 9:483–4 '14; W. D. Macray *ib.* 9:473 Je '14.

11366 —— Bishop Jewel's papers. N&Q ser11 9:505–6 Je '14.

11367 **Esdaile, Arundell J. K.** An Apology of private mass, 1562. [And Thomas Cooper]. Library ser4 1no3:161–4 D '20.

11368 **Howarth, R. Guy.** Greg's English literary autographs: a corrected reading. [Jewel's letter to Leicester, 30 Ja 1564/5, plate LXVI b]. Library ser5 16no3:214–15 S '61.

JOHN, JOHN, 1698–1770

11369 **Hipwell, Daniel.** Rev. John John, D.D., 1698–1770. [Miscellaneous observations upon authors, 1731–2]. N&Q ser8 5:205 Mr '94.

JOHN OF GADDESDEN, 1280?–1361

11370 **Finney, Byron A.** The 1516 edition of Gaddesden's Rosa Anglica. Pa Bib Soc Am 1no1:71–4 '04/5.

'Editions of Gaddesden's Rosa Anglica' (p. 74)

11371 **Dock, George.** Printed editions of the Rosa Anglica of John of Gaddesden. [n.p., Paris? 1907]. 11p. 24cm.

Repr. from Janus v.12 '07.

JOHNSON, LIONEL PIGOT, 1867–1902

11372 **Fletcher, Ian.** Amendments and additions to the Complete poems of Lionel Johnson, 1953. Vict Newsl 33:38–43 '68.

JOHNSON, RICHARD, 1734–93 *see under* Book production and distribution–Printers, publishers, etc.

JOHNSON, SAMUEL, 1709–84

11373 **Fitzgerald, Percy H.** Dr. Birkbeck Hill's edition of Johnson's Letters, examined and criticised. Part I. . . . [n.p., 1892?]. 42p. 21cm. (Not seen: NUC 174:286)

11374 **G., F.** The auction catalogue of dr. Johnson's library. Athenæum 3374:825 Je '92.

11375 **Fitzgerald, Percy H.** A critical examination of dr. G. Birkbeck Hill's Johnsonian editions issued by the Clarendon press, Oxford. London, Bliss, Sands, 1898. 86p. 26cm.

The preface and dedication.–Arrangement and laying out of the work.–The editor's editing.–Dr. B. Hill's discoveries.–Examination of the editor's notes, comments, speculations, etc.–Johnson's stay at Oxford.–Johnson's Letters and dr. Birkbeck Hill's notes.–The editor and mrs. Piozzi.–Johnsonian miscellanies.

11376 **Glover, Arnold.** A Johnson ms. [Notebook, 1775]. Athenæum 3693:191–2 Ag '98; R. McCheane *ib.* 3694:226–7 Ag '98; A. Glover 3696:291 Ag '98.

11377 **Emerson, Oliver F.** The text of Johnson's Rasselas. Anglia 22:499–509 D '99.

11378 **Hutton, Arthur W.** 'Dr. Johnson's library' *in* Johnson club, London. Johnson club papers by various hands. London; New York, 1899. p. 117–30.

11379 **Wheatley, Henry B.** Dr. Johnson as a bibliographer. Bib Soc Trans 8pt1:39–61 '04/5.

'Appendix. Johnson's letter to sir Frederic Barnard' (p. 57–61)

11380 **Axon, William E. A.** Dr. Johnson and Strahan's Virgil. N&Q ser10 12:85–6 Jl '09.

11381 **Brown, Archibald.** Johnson's poems. Athenæum 4271:267 S '09; W. H. G. Flood *ib.* 4271:269 S '09; W. Mercer; J. Lane 4272:298–9 S '09; W. H. G. Flood 4273:329–30 S '09.

11382 **Morley, Lacy Collison-.** Rasselas: the first Italian translation. N&Q ser11 1:404 My '10; R. Pierpont *ib.* 1:497 Je '10.

11383 **Nuttall, F. E.** Boswell and Johnson's Tours in the Hebrides. N&Q ser11 1:307–8 Ap '10; T. M. W.; W. Scott; E. P. Merritt *ib.* 1:377 My '10.

11384 **Bensly, Edward.** Dr. Johnson's copies of Burton's Anatomy of melancholy. N&Q ser11 6:390 N '12; 7:314 Ap '13; 10:117 Ag '14.

11385 **Courtney, William P.** Bibliography of Johnson's works. N&Q ser11 7:507–8 Je '13; W. D. Macray; E. Bensly *ib.* 8:71 Jl '13; W. E. Browning 8:155 Ag '13; E. Bensly 8:175–6 Ag '13; E. Bensly 8:292 Oc '13.

11386 **Couper, William J.** Dr. Johnson in the Hebrides, a bibliographical paper. Glasgow, Privately ptd., 1916. 23p. 20cm.

 I. Introductory.–II. Johnson's account of the tour.–III. Boswell's story of the tour.

11387 **Roberts, sir Sydney C.** Johnson's Journey to the western islands. [Text]. TLS 3 Ap '19:183–4; [R. W. Chapman] *ib.* 24 Ap '19:225; H. F. B. Brett-Smith 15 My '19:265; [R. W. Chapman] 31 Jl '19:419.

11388 **Crosse, Gordon.** Samuel Johnson and Samuel Butler. [Butler's censure of Johnson's treatment of poems which publisher had inserted in 1771 repr.]. TLS 13 My '20:203.

11389 **Millar, Eric G.** Dr. Johnson as a bibliographer. Library ser4 2no4:269–71 Mr '22. table.

11390 **Chapman, Robert W.,** *ed.* Johnson's proposals for his edition of Shakespeare, 1756, printed in type-facsimile. Oxford, O.U.P., 1923. 8[2]p. 23cm. [Sg.: R. W. C.]

11391 —— Johnson's letters. [Text]. TLS 30 Oc '24:686.

11392 **Esdaile, Arundell J. K.** Dr. Johnson the bibliographer. Contemp R 126no704:200–10 Ag '24.

 Repr. in Autolycus' pack . . . being essays. . . . London, 1940. p. 36–52.

11393 **Chapman, Robert W.** Johnson's letters. [Text]. TLS 1 Oc '25:639.

11394 —— Proposals for a new edition of Johnson's letters. Essays & Stud 12:47–62 '25. illus.

11395 **Oxford university press.** Notes on a loan collection of Johnsonian books & mss. shown at Amen house, July, 1925. [By Robert W. Chapman]. [Oxford] H. Milford, 1925. 8p. 15cm.

11396 **Chapman, Robert W.** Dr. Johnson and dr. Taylor. [Taylor's Letter to Samuel Johnson, 1787]. R Eng Stud 2no7:338–9 Jl '26.

11397 —— Johnson's Plan of a dictionary. [1747]. R Eng Stud 2no6:216–18 Ap '26.

11398 ——, *ed.* Johnson's Proposals for printing Bibliotheca Harleiana, 1742. [London, H. Milford, O.U.P., 1926]. [6]p. facsims. 42cm.

11399 **Cuming, Agnes.** A copy of Shakespeare's works which formerly belonged to dr. Johnson. R Eng Stud 3no10:208–12 Ap '27.

11400 **Manuscripts** and first editions [including Johnson's Dictionary with revisions, from Keele hall]. (Note on sales). TLS 8 D '27:940.

11401 **Powell, Lawrence F.** Johnson's part in The adventurer. R Eng Stud 3no12:420–9 Oc '27. tables.

11402 **Roberts, sir Sydney C.** Johnson's books. London Merc 16no96:615–24 Oc '27.

11403 —— On the death of dr. Robert Levet, a note on the text. R Eng Stud 3no12:442–5 Oc '27.

11404 **Dr.** Johnson's Dictionary. [Sale of proof sheets]. (Library notes and news). Bull John Rylands Lib 12no1:9–10 Ja '28; J. B. McGovern N&Q 154:62 Ja '28.

11405 **Johnson** and Boswell revised by themselves and others; three essays by David Nichol Smith, R. W. Chapman and L. F. Powell. Oxford, Clarendon pr., 1928. 66p. 16cm.

Johnson's revisions of his publications especially The rambler, Rasselas, and The idler, by David Nichol Smith.–Boswell's revises of the Life of Johnson, reprinted from the London mercury, 1927 [by R. W. Chapman].–The revision of dr. Birkbeck Hill's Boswell . . . by L. F. Powell.

Rev: TLS 24 Ja '29:65; N&Q 156:179 '29; Eng R 48:361–2 '29; A. W. Pollard Library ser4 10:111–12 '29; F. S. Boas Mod Lang R 25:354–5 '30.

11406 **Powell, Lawrence F.** Samuel Johnson: an early Friend of the Bodleian. [His donation]. Bod Q Rec 5no58:280–1 D '28.

11407 **Squire, John C.** Johnson's contributions to other people's works. London Merc 18no99:273–85 Ja '28; 18no101:575 Mr '28.

11408 **Brett, Oliver S. B., 3d viscount Esher.** A note on dr. Johnson's first editions. Life & Letters 3no17:366–8 Oc '29.

11409 **Ingpen, Roger E.** and **C. A. Stonehill.** A relic of dr. Johnson. [His copy of Bacon's Works]. London, Privately ptd. [1929]. 10p. 15cm.

11410 **Johnson** and Burns. [Letters, and mss.]. (Notes on sales). TLS 13 Je '29:480.

11411 **A unique** dr. Johnson item. [Occasional papers, by the late William Dodd, 1777]. Brit Mus Q 4no3:78–9 D '29.

11412 **Vernon, Frederick.** Johnson's Dictionary. [Prospectus, 1785 ed.]. TLS 27 Je '29:514; J. G. Hayes *ib.* 11 Jl '29:558.

11413 **Chapman, Robert W.** Johnson's works: a lost piece and a forgotten piece. [Proposal for The publisher, 1744]. London Merc 21no125:438–44 Mr '30.

11414 [——], *ed.* Proposals for The publisher, 1744, now printed in facsimile and for the first time ascribed to Samuel Johnson. London, O.U.P., H. Milford, 1930. 2l. facsim. 37cm.

11415 **McKinlay, Robert.** Some notes on dr. Johnson's Journey to the western islands. Glasgow Bib Soc Rec 8:144–50 '30.

11416 **Hill, R. H.** William Mavour. [Johnson's Memoirs of Charles Frederick, 1786]. Bod Q Rec 6no70/1:259–60 '31.

11417 **Tyson, Moses.** Unpublished manuscripts, papers and letters of dr. Johnson, mrs. Thrale and their friends, in the John Rylands library. Bull John Rylands Lib 15no2:467–88 Jl '31.

Group A. Letters to, and from, friends and acquaintances of mrs. Piozzi.–Group B. Letters to, and from, members of mrs. Piozzi's family.–Group C. Business letters and papers.–Group D. Deeds and other documents.–Group E. Mss. of works, both published and unpublished, diaries, note books, etc.

11418 **Chapman, Robert W.** Johnsonian bibliography. Coloph [3]pt12:[8p.] '32.

*See also no.*11423.

11419 —— Johnson's Journey, 1775. R Eng Stud 8no31:315–16 Jl '32.

11420 **Haight, Gordon S.** Johnson's copy of Bacon's Works. Yale Univ Lib Gaz 6no4:67–73 Ap '32.

11421 **Stiles, Robert E.** Doctor Samuel Johnson's Taxation no tyranny and its half title. Am Bk Coll 1no3:155–6 Mr '32. facsim.

11422 **Williams, Iolo A.** The elusive dr. Johnson, being the substance of part of a paper read before the Johnson club. Bk Coll Q 7:53–9 Jl/S '32.

11423 **Johnsonian** rarities. [Comments on *no.*11418]. (Bibliographical notes). TLS 5 Ja '33:12.

11424 **Tillotson, Arthur.** Dr. Johnson and the Life of Goldsmith. Mod Lang R 28no3:439–43 Jl '33.

11425 **Chapman, Robert W.** Johnsonian bibliography, 1750–1765. Coloph [4]pt16:[8p.] '34. port.

11426 **Hazen, Allen T.** A Johnson preface. [DuFresnoy's Chronological tables, 1762]. TLS 28 Je '34:460.

11427 **A Johnson** exhibition. Bod Q Rec 7no83:466–71 '34.

11428 **Rhodon,** *pseud.* Johnson's False alarm. N&Q 166:334 My '34.

11429 **Barnouw, A. J.** Rasselas in Dutch. TLS 11 Ap '35:244.

11430 **Hazen, Allen T.** Crousaz on Pope. [Trans. by Johnson). (Bibliographical notes). TLS 2 N '35:704; T. D. Cook *ib.* 9 N '35:728.

11431 **Osborn, James M.** Johnson on the sanctity of an author's text. Pub Mod Lang Assn 50no3:928–9 S '35.

11432 **Greene, Richard L.** The R. B. Adam library relating to dr. Samuel Johnson and his era. Rochester, N.Y., 1936. 11p. 19cm.

Repr. from Alumni R Univ Rochester 15no1:7–10 Oc/N '36.

11433 **Hazen, Allen T.** and **E. L. McAdam.** First editions of Samuel Johnson; an important exhibition and a discovery. Yale Univ Lib Bull 10no3:45–51 Ja '36. facsim.

11434 **McAdam, E. L.** A Johnson pamphlet. [The life of admiral Blake, 1740]. (Bibliographical notes). TLS 14 Mr '36:228.

11435 **Chapman, Robert W.** Johnson's letters. R Eng Stud 13no50:139–76 Ap '37.

11436 **Gilchrist, Donald B.** Johnsonian library in the University of Rochester. [R. B. Adam collection]. Eng Studien 71no3:436–7 Je '37.

11437 **Hart, C. W.** Dr. Johnson's 1745 Shakespeare Proposals. Mod Lang N 53no5:367–8 My '38.

11438 **Hazen, Allen T.** The Beauties of Johnson. [And George Kearsley, pub.]. Mod Philol 35no3:289–95 F '38.

11439 **Metzdorf, Robert F.** Notes on Johnson's Plan of a dictionary. Library ser4 19no2:198–201 S '38; Supplementary note *ib.* 19no3:363 D '38.

11440 **Vernon, Frederick.** Plan of a dictionary. (Bibliographical and auction notes). TLS 16 Ap '38:268.

11441 **Bradford, C. B.** Johnson's revision of The rambler. R Eng Stud 15no59:302–14 Jl '39.

11442 **Chapman, Robert W.** Dr. Johnson's letters. Notes on Boswell's text. TLS 25 F '39:128; 4 Mr '39:140; sir D'A. W. Thompson *ib.* 18 Mr '39:163.

11443 **Gove, Philip B.** Notes on serialization and competitive publishing: Johnson's and Bailey's dictionaries, 1755. Oxford Bib Soc Proc 5pt5:306–22 '39.

11444 [**Madan, Falconer**]. Cancels in Johnson's Shakespeare. Bod Lib Rec 1no3:42–3 F '39.

11445 **Chapman, Robert W.** Johnson's letters: a supplement. R Eng Stud 16no61:66–8 Ja '40.

11446 —— Johnson's letter to Taylor. [Addendum to his checklist]. R Eng Stud 16no63:317 Jl '40.

11447 **Gove, Philip B.** Dr. Johnson and the works of the bishop of Sodor and Man. R Eng Stud 16no64:455–7 Oc '40.

11448 **O'Hegarty, Patrick S.** A Dublin edition of Johnson's Poets. [1795–1802]. (Bibliographical notes). Dublin Mag new ser 15no2:68 Ap/Je '40. [Sg.: P. S. O'H.]

11449 **Hazen, Allen T.** The cancels in Johnson's Journey, 1775. R Eng Stud 17no66:201–3 Ap '41.

11450 **Chapman, Robert W.** Confusion of -t and -n. [Johnson's letters]. N&Q 183:165 S '42. [Sg.: R. W. C.]

11451 —— Emendations in Johnson's letters. N&Q 182:174–6 Mr '42; 182:201–2 Ap '42.

11452 —— Johnson's letters to Boswell. R Eng Stud 18no71:323–8 Jl '42.

11453 —— The text of Johnson's letters. TLS 26 S '42;480.

11454 **Roberts, sir Sydney C.** Dr. Johnson's library. (Bibliography). TLS 4 Jl
'42:336; Writer of the article *ib*. 11 Jl '42:343; sir S. C. Roberts 18 Jl
'42:360.

11455 **Chapman, Robert W.** Johnson as book-collector. N&Q 184:136 F '43.

11456 ——— Johnson's copy of Phillips's poems. [Not Ambrose but John
Philips]. N&Q 184:76 Ja '43. [Sg.: R. W. C.]

11457 ——— The sale of Johnson's Idler. N&Q 184:256 Ap '43. [Sg.: R. W. C.]

11458 **Gove, Phillip B.** Johnson's copy of Hammond's Elegies. [Collins's
Poetical works, 1771]. Mod Lang Q 5no4:435–8 D '44.

11459 **Chapman, Robert W.** Two centuries of Johnsonian scholarship, being the
twelfth lecture on the David Murray foundation ... 1945. Glasgow,
Jackson, 1945. 35p. 22cm.

   Rev: J. E. Butt R Eng Stud 22:241–2 '46.

11460 **Gomme, Laurence.** The Robert B. Adam library relating to dr. Samuel
Johnson and his era: a brief study. New York, Ptd. for private distribution, 1945. 9p. illus. 27cm.

11461 **Mabbott, Thomas O.** The text of dr. Johnson's dedication of Hoole's
Tasso. N&Q 189:187–8 N '45.

11462 **Liebert, Herman W.** An addition to the bibliography of Samuel Johnson.
[Lucas's Poems with a prefatory address, 1779]. Pa Bib Soc Am 41:231–8
'47. facsim.

11463 **The Adam**-Newton copy of Johnson's Dictionary. [Now in Library].
Princeton Univ Lib Chron 9no3:168 Ap '48.

11464 **Liebert, Herman W.** This harmless drudge. New Coloph 1pt2:175–83 Ap
'48.

11465 **Hyde** collection of Johnsonian manuscripts. TLS 23 S '49:624.

11466 **Chapman, Robert W.** Crousaz on Pope. [Trans. by Johnson]. R Eng Stud
new ser 1no1:57 Ja '50.

11467 **Hyde, Donald F.** and **Mary M. C. Hyde.** Johnson and journals. [Surviving
diaries]. New Coloph 3:165–97 '50. facsims.

   I. Johnson's theory of a journal.–II. Johnson's influence on others.–III. Johnson's attempts
   to keep a journal.–IV. Journals lost in the conflagration.–V. Journals which survived the
   conflagration.–VI. Conclusion.

11468 **Liebert, Herman W.** Dr. Johnson's first book. [Trans. of Lobo's Voyage
to Abyssinia]. Yale Univ Lib Gaz 25no1:23–8 Jl '50. facsim.

11469 **Hyde, Mary M. C.** The history of the Johnson papers. Pa Bib Soc Am 45:103–16 '51. facsim.

11470 **Sherbo, Arthur.** Dr. Johnson on Macbeth: 1745 and 1765. R Eng Stud new ser 2no5:40–7 Ja '51.

11471 **Rowan, D. F.** Johnson's Lives: an unrecorded variant and a new portrait. Bk Coll 1no3:174 '52. facsim.

11472 **Sherbo, Arthur.** Dr. Johnson marks a book list. N&Q 197:519 N '52.

11473 —— The proof-sheets of dr. Johnson's Preface to Shakespeare. Bull John Rylands Lib 35no1:206–10 S '52.

11474 —— The text of Johnson's Journey to the western islands of Scotland; 'Bayle' or 'Boyle'? N&Q 197:182–4 Ap '52.

11475 —— The text of The vanity of human wishes. N&Q 197:205–6 My '52.

11476 **Keast, William R.** The Preface to A dictionary of the English language: Johnson's revision and the establishment of the text. Stud Bib 5:129–46 '52/3.

11477 **Brown, T. Julian.** Samuel Johnson, 1709–1784. [English literary autographs, VI). Bk Coll 2no2:143 '53. facsims.

11478 **Keast, William R.** Some emendations in Johnson's preface to the Dictionary. R Eng Stud new ser 4no13:52–7 Ja '53.

11479 **Metzdorf, Robert F.** The first American Rasselas and its imprint. [1768]. Pa Bib Soc Am 47:374–6 '53.

11480 **Monoghan, T. J.** Johnson's additions to his Shakespeare for the edition of 1773. R Eng Stud new ser 4no15:234–48 Jl '53.

'List of Johnson's additions' (p. 247–8)

Rev: A. Sherbo Philol Q 33:283–4 '54.

11481 **Sherbo, Arthur.** The cancels in dr. Johnson's Works, Oxford, 1825. Pa Bib Soc Am 47:376–8 '53.

11482 **Thomas, Alan G.** Dr. Johnson and the book trade. ABA Ann 1953:31–7 '53.

Repr. in New Rambler 22–8 Je '61.

11483 **Todd, William B.** Concealed editions of Samuel Johnson. [The false alarm; Taxation no tyranny]. Bk Coll 2no1:59–65 '53.

11484 —— Johnson's Marmor Norfolciense. (Note no.18). Bk Coll 2no1:73 '53.

11485 **Keast, William R.** Johnson's Plan of a dictionary: a textual crux. Philol Q 33no3:341–7 Jl '54.

11486 **Kolb, Gwin J.** A note on the publication of Johnson's Proposals for printing the Harleian miscellany. Pa Bib Soc Am 48:196–8 '54.

11487 **Todd, William B.** The printing of Johnson's Journey, 1755. Stud Bib 6:247–54 '54. tables.

11488 **Kolb, Gwin J.** and **J. H. Sledd.** 'The early editions of the Dictionary' *in* Dr. Johnson's Dictionary. Chicago, 1955. p. 105–33.

11489 **Liebert, Herman W.** Proposals for Shakespeare, 1756. TLS 6 My '55:237.

11490 **Sherbo, Arthur.** Two notes on Johnson's revisions. Mod Lang R 50no3:311–15 Jl '55. table.

I. The adventurer.–II. Mrs. Master's poems.

11491 **Sledd, James H.** and **G. J. Kolb.** Dr. Johnson's Dictionary; essays in the biography of a book. [Chicago] University of Chicago pr. [1955]. viii,255p. port. 21cm.

Includes II. The composition and publication of The plan of a dictionary.–IV. The early editions of the Dictionary.

11492 **Braham, Lionel.** Johnson's edition of Roger Ascham. N&Q 201:346–7 Ag '56.

11493 **Cremer, R. W. Ketton-.** Johnson's last gifts to Windham. [Libr.] Bk Coll 5no4:354–6 '56.

11494 **Keast, William R.** Editing Johnson's Lives. New Rambler 15–29 Je '59.

11495 **Nuttall, Geoffrey F.** Johnson's fighting septuagint. [Library]. TLS 27 Mr '59:177.

11496 **Greene, Donald J.** The False alarm and Taxation no tyranny: some further observations. Stud Bib 13:223–31 '60. tables.

'Textual variants in the first four editions of Taxation no tyranny' (p. 229–31)

11497 **Kolb, Gwin J.** and **J. H. Sledd.** The history of the Sneyd-Gimbel and Pigott-British museum copies of dr. Johnson's Dictionary. Pa Bib Soc Am 54:286–9 '60.

11498 **Mahoney, John L.** Dr. Johnson at work: observations on a Columbia rare book. [Boswell presentation copy of Collins' Poems, Glasgow, 1771, with markings by Johnson]. Columbia Lib Columns 10no1:20–3 N '60.

11499 **Parish, Charles.** Johnson's books and the Birmingham library. [Books known to and used by Johnson]. New Rambler 7–21 Ja '61.

11500 **Thomas, Alan G.** Dr. Johnson and the book trade. New Rambler 22–8 Je '61.

Repr. from ABA Ann 1953:31–7 '53.

11501 **Chapple, John A. V.** A Johnson discovery. [Proposals for ptg. the History of the council of Trent, 1738]. TLS 25 My '62:373.

11502 **Eddy, Donald D.** The publication date of the first edition of Rasselas. [1759]. N&Q 207:21–2 Ja '62.

11503 —— Samuel Johnson's editions of Shakespeare, 1765. Pa Bib Soc Am 56:428–44 '62. diagr., tables.

11504 **Fleeman, J. David.** Some proofs of Johnson's Prefaces to the poets. Library ser5 17no3:213–30 S '62. tables.

'Appendix A. A tabular analysis of the changes made in these proofs' (p. 224–7); 'Appendix B. A check-list of the surviving proofs of the Prefaces' (p. 228–30)

11505 **Kolb, Gwin J.** Rasselas: purchase price, proprietors, and printings. Stud Bib 15:257–9 '62.

11506 **Chapple, John A. V.** Samuel Johnson's Proposals for printing the History of the council of Trent. [1738]. Bull John Rylands Lib 45no2:340–69 Mr '63. facsims.

I. Discovery of the Proposals.–II. Description.–III. Project.–IV. Performance.–V. Complications.–VI. Conclusion.–Appendix 1: Sarpi's Historia and its descendants.–Appendix 2: G. Walmesley, T. Birch and W. Caslon.–Appendix 3: The Sarpi 'account'.–Appendix 4: The reverend John Johnson.–Appendix 5: The reverend David Wilkins.–Appendix 6: Six sheets or twelve?

11507 **Fleeman, J. David.** The reprint of Rambler no.1. Library ser5 18no4:288–94 D '63. tables., facsims.

11508 **Kolb, Gwin J.** 'Johnson's Little pompadour: a textual crux and a hypothesis [on the publication of Rasselas]' *in* [Camden, C. Carroll.], *ed.* Restoration and eighteenth-century literature: essays in honor of Alan Dugald McKillop. [Chicago, 1963]. p. 125–42.

11509 **Powell, Lawrence F.** For Johnsonian collectors. [De historie van Rasselas, 1760]. TLS 20 S '63:712.

11510 **Bowers, Fredson T.** The text of Johnson. [The idler; The adventurer]. Mod Philol 61no4:298–309 My '64.

Repr. in Essays in bibliography, text, and editing. Charlottesville [1975]. p. [375]–91.

11511 **Fleeman, J. David.** Johnson's Journey, 1775, and its cancels. Pa Bib Soc Am 58:232–8 '64. facsims.

11512 —— Some of dr. Johnson's preparatory notes for his Dictionary, 1755. [Mss.]. Bod Lib Rec 7no4:205–10 D '64.

11513 **Hyde, Mary M. C.** ' "Not in Chapman" ' *in* Johnson, Boswell and their circle; essays presented to Lawrence Fitzroy Powell . . . . Oxford, 1965. p. [286]–319. tables.

> 1. Full letters not in Chapman.–2. Letters with Chapman numbers but without texts or full texts.–3. Defective letters.–4. Letters included by virtue of description in auction or book catalogues.–5. Letters substantiated by mention.–6. Peripheral letters.

11514 **Kendall, Lyle H.** A note on Johnson's Journey, 1775. Pa Bib Soc Am 59:317–18 '65. table.

11515 **Todd, William B.** Variants in Johnson's Dictionary, 1755. (Note 242). Bk Coll 14no2:212–13 '65. table.

> 'Table of points' (p. 213)

11516 **Allen, Robert R.** Variant readings in Johnson's London. [1738]. Pa Bib Soc Am 60:214–15 '66. table.

11517 **Howard, William J.** Dr. Johnson on abridgment, a re-examination. [Copyright]. Pa Bib Soc Am 60:215–19 '66.

11518 **Johnson** at Harvard. [Hyde collection]. TLS 17 F '66:132.

11519 **Eddy, Donald D.** Which edition did Johnson review? [An account of the conduct of Marlborough, 1742]. Cornell Lib J 2:81 '67.

11520 **Fleeman, J. David.** Hill's Johnson. [Johnsonian miscellanies, 1897]. TLS 24 Ag '67:768; R. D. Spector *ib.* 7 S '67:799.

11521 —— The making of Johnson's Life of Savage, 1744. Library ser5 22no4:346–52 D '67. tables.

11522 —— A preliminary handlist of documents & manuscripts of Samuel Johnson. Oxford, Oxford bibliographical society, 1967. 50p. 24cm.

> *Rev*: TLS 6 Je '68:602; Pa Bib Soc Am 63:64–5 '69; J. T. Boulton Library ser5 24:70–1 '69.

11523 —— Some notes on Johnson's Prayers and meditations. [Ms.]. R Eng Stud new ser 19no74:172–9 My '68.

11524 **Winans, Robert B.** Works by and about Samuel Johnson in eighteenth-century America. Pa Bib Soc Am 62:537–46 '68. table.

> 'Book catalogue listings of works by and about Johnson' (p. 546)

11525 **Greene, Donald J.** Johnson on Shakespeare. [The Yale Johnson, and methods of editing eighteenth-century texts]. TLS 17 Jl '69:779; 4 S '69:979: Your reviewer [K. Walker] *ib.* 18 S '69:1027; J. Crow 25 S '69:1079–80; A. B. Strauss 9 Oc '69:1159; D. J. Greene 6 N '69:1288.

JOHNSTON, ARTHUR, 1587–1641

11526 **Anderson, Peter J.** Arthur Johnston bibliography. N&Q ser11 10:346 Oc '14.

JONES, EDMUND, 1702–93

11527 **Williams, E. I.** A Relation of ghosts and apparitions in Wales, 1767: a lost first edition. Welsh Bib Soc J 6no3:136–44 Jl '45.

Introduction.–The title-page, 1767.–The review.–The 1780 edition.–The author's manuscript.–The ms. and the printed book compared.–Conclusion.

JONES, EDWARD, 1752–1824

11528 **Owens, B. G.** Bicentenary of Edward Jones ('Bardd y Brenin'), 1752–1824. (News and notes). Nat Lib Wales J 7no4:379 '52.

JONES, GRIFFITH, 1683–1761

11529 **Salmon, David.** A cancel in Welch piety. Welsh Bib Soc J 1no4:118–22 S '12.

11530 **Bowen, D. J.** The publication of a volume of sermons by the reverend Griffith Jones, Llandowror. (News and notes). Nat Lib Wales J 7no4:380–1 '52.

JONES, JOHN, 1792–1852

11531 **Owens, B. G.** Centenary of John Jones ('Tegid'), 1792–1852. (News and notes). Nat Lib Wales J 7no4:382 '52.

JONES, JOHN MADGWICK, 1770?–1832

11532 **Jones, Evan D.** John Madgwick Jones. [Tintern abbey, with other original poems by Clericus, 1800]. (Biographica et bibliographica). Nat Lib Wales J 14no3:367–9 '66.

JONES, OWEN, 1741–1814

11533 **Williams, G. J.** Hanes cyhoeddi'r Myvyrian archaiology. Welsh Bib Soc J 10no1:2–12 D '66.

JONES, THOMAS, 1756–1820

11534 **Jones, Idwal.** Thomas Jones o Ddinbych, Awdur a Chyhoeddwr. Welsh Bib Soc J 5no3:137–209 Jl '39. port., facsims.

Papurau Cyfrinachol Thomas Jones.–Thomas Jones fel Cyhoeddwr.–Gwasg Jones & co.–Rhestr o Gyhoeddiadau Jones & co., Mai, 1803–Medi (?) 1804.–Gwasg Rhuthyn.–Gwasg Dinbych.–Rhestr o Gyhoeddiadau Gwasg Dinbych tra'n eiddo Thomas Jones, 1809–13.–Atodiad I: Rhestr o Weithiau Thomas Jones.–Atodiad II: Thomas Jones; manuscripts at Penucha, Caerwys.

JONES, WILLIAM HENRY, fl.1889–1922

11535 **The virtue** of rarity. [A brief account of William Foxwist, 1896, in 25 copies]. (Bibliographical notes). Welsh Bib Soc J 2no1:50 Jl '16.

JONSON, BENJAMIN, 1573?–1637

11536 **Este,** *pseud.* Ben Jonson's English grammar. N&Q ser8 7:485 Je '95.

11537 **Simpson, Percy.** Field and Ben Jonson. [Volpone, 1607]. N&Q ser8 8:301 Oc '95.

11538 —— Two quartos of Ben Jonson. [Epicœne, 1612; Sejanus 1605]. N&Q ser9 4:87 Jl '99; viscount Melville *ib.* 4:152 Ag '99; P. Simpson 4:196–7 S '99.

11539 **Prideaux, W. R. B.** Ben Jonson's signature. [Library]. N&Q ser9 6:445–6 D '00.

11540 **Dam, Bastiaan A. P. Van** and **C. Stoffel.** The authority of the Ben Jonson Folio of 1616. [And Every man out of his humour]. Anglia 14:377–92 Je '03.

Rev. version of 'Een Merkwaardig Geval' *in* Herinneringsbundel Professor S. S. Rosenstein. Leiden, 1902.

11541 **Henry, Aurelia.** Ben Jonson's Epicœne. N&Q ser9 12:168–9 Ag '03.

11542 **Evans, H. A.** Ben Jonson's Works, 1616. N&Q ser10 5:7 Ja '06.

11543 **Aitken, George A.** Ben Jonson's Works. N&Q ser10 11:421–3 My '09.

11544 **Briggs, William D.** Studies in Ben Jonson. Anglia 37:463–93 D '13; 38:101–20 My '14.

I. Harl. ms. 4955.–II. The 4to and the 12mo of 1640.

11545 **Snell, Florence M.** A note on volume two of the 1640 folio of Ben Jonson's plays. Mod Lang N 30no5:158 My '15.

11546 **Hooper, Edith S.** The text of Ben Jonson. Mod Lang R 12no3:350–2 Jl '17.

11547 **Haines, C. Reginald.** Autographs of Ben Jonson. [Library]. TLS 12 Je '19:325; W. R. B. Prideaux *ib.* 19 Je '19:337; E. Brabrook, R. W. Ramsey; F. C. Wellstood 26 Je '19:349–50; W. R. B. Prideaux 10 Jl '19:378.

11548 **Greg, sir Walter W.** The first edition of Ben Jonson's Every man out of his humour. Library ser4 1no3:153–60 D '20. tables.

11549 **Hookham, George.** Ben Jonson's Timber. [Ms.]. N&Q ser12 7:311 Oc '20; E. Bensly *ib.* 7:353 Oc '20.

11550 **Greg, sir Walter W.** Notes on old books. Jonson: Every man out of his humour. [John Marston: The malcontent.] Library ser4 2no1:49–57 Je '21.

11551 **Herford, Charles H., P.** and **Evelyn M. S. Simpson.** 'Books in Jonson's library' *in* Ben Jonson. Oxford, 1925. V.I., p. [250]–71; XI (1952), p. [593]–603.

11552 **Patterson, Richard E.** Ben Jonson. [Text]. TLS 6 Ag '25:521; P. Simpson *ib.* 13 Ag '25:533.

11553 **Greg, sir Walter W.** The riddle of Jonson's chronology. Library ser4 6no4:340–7 Mr '26.

11554 **Marcham, Frank.** Thomas Walkley and the Ben Jonson Works of 1640. Library ser4 11no2:225–9 S '30; sir W. W. Greg *ib.* 11no4:461–5 Mr '31.

11555 **Tannenbaum, Samuel A.** A note on The gypsies metamorphosed. Pub Mod Lang Assn 47no3:909–10 S '32.

11556 **Whiting, George W.** The Hoe-Huntington folio of Jonson. Mod Lang N 48no8:537–8 D '33.

11557 **Dam, Bastiaan A. P. Van.** A prompt-book text of The alchemist and its important lesson. Neophilol 19no3:205–20 '34.

11558 **Greg, sir Walter W.** Text of The gypsies metamorphosed. Pub Mod Lang Assn 49no3:963 S '34.

11559 —— Was there a 1612 quarto of Epicene? Library ser4 15no3:306–15 D '34.

Repr. in Maxwell, James C., *ed.* Collected papers. Oxford, 1966. p. [314]–21.

11560 **Tannenbaum, Samuel A.** Text of the Gypsies metamorphosed. Sh Assn Bull 9no4:218–19 Oc '34.

11561 **Chester, Allan G.** Thomas Walkley and the 1640 Works of Ben Jonson. TLS 14 Mr '35:160.

11562 **Kempling, William B.** Dedicatory copies. [Jonson's The fountain of self-love]. TLS 5 D '36:1016.

11563 **Simpson, Evelyn M. S.** The folio text of Ben Jonson's Sejanus. Anglia 61:398–415 Je '37.

11564 **Simpson, Percy.** The Ben Jonson exhibition. Bod Q Rec 8no95:405–11 '37.

11565 **Vocht, Henry de.** Comments on the text of Ben Jonson's Every man out of his humour, a research about the comparative value of the quarto and the folio. Louvain, C. Uystpruyst, 1937. (Repr. Vaduz, Kraus repr., 1963). viii,167p. table. 23cm. (Materials for the study of the old English drama, v.14)

> I. The editions.–II. The dramatic division.–III. The stage-directions.–IV. The oaths.–V. The text proper.–VI. The final scenes.–VII. The press corrections.–Conclusion.–List of the variants commented upon.–Corrigenda.

> *Rev*: G. Scheurweghs Leuvensche Bijdragen, Bijbland 29:25–7 '37.

11566 **Nungezer, Edwin.** Inedited poems of Daniel. [i.e. Jonson]. N&Q 175:421 D '38.

11567 **Munsterberg, Margaret.** Ben Jonson's Art of poetry. More Bks Boston Pub Lib Bull 15no1:13 Ja '40. [Sg.: M. M.]

11568 **Wilson, Frank P.** Ben Jonson and Ralph Crane. [Jonson's Pleasure reconciled to virtue]. TLS 8 N '41:555; [facsim.] *ib.* 15 N·'41:566.

11569 **Greg, sir Walter W.** Jonson's masques; points of editorial principle and practice. [And the Herford & Simpson ed.]. R Eng Stud 18no70:144–66 Ap '42; E. M. S. Simpson *ib.* 18no71:291–300 Jl '42.

11570 **Maas, Paul.** Notes on the text of Jonson's masques. R Eng Stud 18no72:464–5 Oc '42.

11571 **McIlwraith, A. K.** The press-corrections in Jonson's The king's entertainment. Library ser4 24no3/4:181–6 D/Mr '43/4. tables.

11572 **Munsterberg, Margaret.** From the library of Ben Jonson. [Vitruvius: De architectura, 1567]. More Bks Boston Pub Lib Bull 18no5:230 My '43. [Sg.: M. M.]

11573 [**Simpson, Percy**]. 'An attack upon the Folio' *in* Herford, Charles H., P. and E. M. S. Simpson, *ed.* Ben Jonson. Volume IX: An historical survey of the text .... Oxford, 1950. (Repr. 1961). p. [74]-84.

> *Defends the 1616 F against H. de Vocht's strictures.*

11574 **Vocht, Henry de.** Comments on the text of Ben Jonson's Cynthia's revels; an investigation into the comparative value of the 1601-quarto and the 1616-folio. Louvain, Uystpruyst, 1950. (Repr. Vaduz, Kraus repr., 1963). xii,283p. table. 23cm. (Materials for the study of the old English drama, 21)

I. The quarto text.–II. Comparative study of the punctuation.–III. Comparative study of the orthography.–IV. External arrangement.–V. Alterations in the text proper.–VI. Omissions and additions of words.–VII. Passages inserted or left out.–VIII. Press corrections in the folio.–IX. Survey of the variants.–Errata [TP verso].

11575 **Nosworthy, J. M.** The Case is altered. [And H. Porter]. J Eng Germ Philol 51no1:61–70 Ja '52.

11576 **Emslie, Macdonald.** Three early settings of Jonson. [A hymn to God the father; The masque of augurs; Catiline]. N&Q 198:466–8 N '53.

11577 **Main, C. F.** Two items in the Jonson apocrypha. N&Q 199:243–5 Je '54.

11578 **Maxwell, James C.** Ben Jonson's poems. [1955 ed.]. TLS 3 Je '55:301.

11579 **Davis, Herbert J.** Note on a cancel in The alchemist, 1612. Library ser5 13no4:278–80 D.

11580 **Vocht, Henry de.** Studies on the texts of Ben Jonson's Poetaster and Seianus. Louvain, Uystpruyst, 1958. (Repr. Vaduz, Kraus repr., 1963). vii, 56p. facsims., table. 23cm. (Materials for the study of the old English drama, 27)

Studies on the text of Ben Jonson's Poetaster. 1. Its character.–2. List of variants between Q, 1602 and F, 1616.–3. Interpretation of the list.–4. The corrections at the press.–Studies on the text of Ben Jonson's Seianus. 1. Its character.–2. List of variants between Q, 1605 and F, 1616.–3. Interpretation of the list.–4. The corrections at the press.

11581 **Gerritsen, Johan.** Stansby and Jonson produce a folio; a preliminary account. Eng Stud 40no1:52–5 F '59.

11582 **Waith, Eugene M.** A misprint in Bartholomew fair. [SP 5.5.50–1]. N&Q 208:103–4 Mr '63.

11583 **Barr, C. B. L.** More books from Ben Jonson's library. (Note 223). Bk Coll 13no3:346–8 '64.

11584 **Bennett, Josephine W.** Benson's alleged piracy of Shak-speares sonnets and of some of Jonson's works. Stud Bib 21:235–48 '68.

JORDAN, THOMAS, 1612?–85

11585 **Drury, George Thorn-.** Jordan's Money is an asse, 1668. [Cancelled TP]. R Eng Stud 1no2:219–20 Ap '25.

11586 **Gourlay, James J.** Thomas Jordan. [Holograph]. TLS 17 Ag '33:549.

11587 **Elsley, Ralph C.** Thomas Jordan. [Mss.]. N&Q 196:501 N '51.

JOYCE, JAMES AUGUSTINE, 1882–1941

11588 **Roberts, R. F.** Bibliographical notes on James Joyce's Ulysses. Coloph new ser 1no4:565–79 Je '36.

> A. The Little review.–B. Shakespeare and company: first edition.–C. The Egoist press: first English edition.–D. The Egoist press: second English edition.–E. Shakespeare and company: 4th to 7th editions.–F. Shakespeare and company: 8th to 11th editions.–G. Two worlds monthly: pirated serial.–I. Pirated edition in book form.–J. The Odyssey press edition.–K. Random house: first American edition.–L. Limited editions club edition.

11589 **Corrections** of misprints in Finnegan's wake as prepared by the author after publication of the first edition. New York, Viking pr.; London, Faber & Faber, 1945. 16p. 24cm.

> *Repr. in* Finnegan's wake. London, 1945.

> *Rev:* R. E. Danielson Am Merc 176:143–5 '45.

11590 **Gilbert, Stuart.** The wanderings of Ulysses. New Coloph 2pt7:245–52 S '49. facsim.

11591 **White, William.** James Joyce: addenda to Alan Parker's bibliography. Pa Bib Soc Am 43:401–11 '49.

11592 **A James** Joyce exhibition. [Institute of contemporary arts, London]. TLS 23 Je '50:396.

11593 **Brown, T. Julian.** Finnegan's wake. [Mss.]. Brit Mus Q 17no1:4–5 Je '52.

11594 **Cahoon, Herbert.** James Joyce at Lawrence. Bks & Libs at Kansas 1no4:4–5 N '53.

11595 **Connolly, Thomas E.** The personal library of James Joyce; a descriptive bibliography. [Buffalo, N.Y.] University bookstore, University of Buffalo, 1955. 58p. 24cm. (Univ Buffalo Stud 22no1 Ap '55. Monogr in Eng 6)

> *Rev:* W. White Bull Bib 21:199 '56.

11596 **Higginson, Fred H.** Notes on the text of Finnegan's wake. J Eng Germ Philol 55no3:451–6 Jl '56.

11597 **Spoerri, James F.** The Odyssey press edition of James Joyce's Ulysses. [1932]. Pa Bib Soc Am 50:195–8 '56.

11598 **Epstein, Edmund L.** Cruxes in Ulysses: notes towards an edition and annotation. James Joyce R 1no3:25–36 S '57.

11599 **Cowie, Alfred T.** A Joyce collection. [His own]. Priv Lib Assn Q 1no5:58–62 Ja '58.

11600 **Smith, Grover.** The cryptogram in Joyce's Ulysses: a misprint. Pub Mod Lang Assn 73no4:446–7 S '58.

11601 **Hart, Clive.** Notes on the text of Finnegan's wake. J Eng Germ Philol 59no2:229–39 Ap '60.

11602 **Brown, T. Julian.** James Joyce,1882–1941. (English literary autographs, XI). Bk Coll 10no4:441 '61. facsims.

11603 **Thornton, Weldon.** Books and manuscripts by James Joyce. Lib Chron Univ Texas 7no1:18–23 '61. facsim.

'Desiderata' (p. 23)

11604 **White, William.** Press copies of Joyce's Ulysses. (Note 156). Bk Coll 10no1:72 '61.

11605 **Cohn, Alan M.** Rosenbach, Copinger and Sylvia Beach in Finnegan's wake. Pub Mod Lang Assn 77no3:342–4 Je '62.

11606 **Scholes, Robert E.** Some observations on the text of Dubliners: The dead. Stud Bib 15:191–205 '62.

'Dubliners: misprints' (p. 205)

11607 **Spielberg, Peter.** James Joyce's manuscripts & letters at the University of Buffalo, a catalogue. [New York] University of Buffalo, 1962. xxii,241p. 22cm.

Rev: C. Hart J Eng Germ Philol 63:181–3 '64.

11608 **Thornton, Weldon.** Joyce's Ulysses, 1922. [Ptg.] (Note 175). Bk Coll 11no1:84–5 '62; Herta Ryder *ib.* 11no2:214 '62.

11609 **Goldman, Arthur.** Some proposed emendations in the text of Joyce's Ulysses. N&Q 208:148–50 Ap '63.

11610 **Adams, Robert M.** Light on Joyce's Exiles? A new ms., a curious analogue, and some speculations. Stud Bib 17:83–105 '64.

11611 —— The manuscript of James Joyce's play. [Exiles]. Yale Univ Lib Gaz 31no9:30–5 Jl '64.

11612 **Anderson, Chester G.** The text of James Joyce's A portrait of the artist as a young man. Neuphilol Mitteilungen 65:160–200 '64. diagr.

11613 **Dalton, Jack P.** Hardest crux. [Finnegan's wake]. James Joyce Q 1no3:45–9 '64.

11614 **Hayman, David.** A list of corrections for the Scribbledehobble. James Joyce Q 1no2:23–9 '64.

11615 **Scholes, Robert E.** Further observations on the text of Dubliners. Stud Bib 17:108–22 '64.

11616 **Cohn, Alan M.** Joyce bibliographies, a survey. Am Bk Coll 15no10:11–16 Je '65. facsims.

11617 **Herring, Phillip F.** [and] **N. Silverstein.** Some corrections and additions to Norman Silverstein's Magic on the notesheets of the Circe episode. James Joyce Q 2no3:217–26 '65. facsims.

11618 **Kain, Richard M.** Collecting Joyce & Joyceana. Am Bk Coll 15no10:9 Je '65. facsims.

11619 **Lidderdale, J. H.** Harriet Weaver and James Joyce. [Information on ptrs. of Portrait of an artist sought]. (Query 212). Bk Coll 15no4:488–9 '66.

11620 **Tanselle, G. Thomas.** Samuel Roth's Love secrets, 1927. [Sheets of Two worlds monthly with pirated Ulysses]. (Note 282). Bk Coll 15no4:486–7 '66.

11621 **Firth, John.** Harriet Weaver's letters to James Joyce, 1915–1920. [Ulysses]. Stud Bib 20:151–88 '67.

11622 **Litz, A. Walton.** The last adventures of Ulysses. Princeton Univ Lib Chron 28no2:63–73 '67. illus., facsims.

11623 **ÓHehir, Brendan.** An unnoticed textual crux in Ulysses. James Joyce Q 5no4:297–8 '68.

11624 **Silverstein, Norman.** Toward a corrected text of Ulysses: errata of the 1934 Random house and 1960 reset Bodley head editions of the Circe episode. James Joyce Q 6no4:348–56 '69.

11625 **Thomas, Donald.** Ulysses and the attorney-general, 1936. Library ser5 24no4:343–5 D '69.

JUNIUS, *pseud.*

11626 **Rae, W. Fraser.** The Junian handwriting. Athenæum 3366:565–6 Ap '92; S. Davey *ib.* 3367:601 My '92; W. F. Rae 3372:762–3 Je '92.

11627 **Thompson, sir Edward M.** The handwriting of Junius. Athenæum 3734:627 My '09.

11628 **Read, F. W.** Junius: copy presented by sir Philip to lady Francis. N&Q 155:172 S '28.

11629 **Mitchell, C. Ainsworth.** Who wrote the letters of Junius? [Sir Philip Francis]. Discovery 10no115:217–20 Jl '29. port., facsims.

11630 **Clarkson, Paul S.** Junius, Letters of. [1st Am. ed.]. Bib N&Q 2no11:9 N '38.

11631 **Cordasco, Francesco G. M.** The first American edition of Junius. [1791]. N&Q 194:233 My '49.

11632 —— Juniana in the earl of Shelburne's library. N&Q 195:519 N '50.

11633 —— Did John Wilkes correct the ms. of Junius's Letters? A note on John Almon's edition, 1806. N&Q 196:300–1 Jl '51.

11634 **Clarkson, Paul S.** Letters of Junius. [First Am. ed., 1791 (?)]. (Query no.8). Bk Coll 1no1:57 '52; F. G. M. Cordasco ib. 1no3:194 '52.

11635 **Cordasco, Francesco G. M.** Edward Bocquet's illustrated edition of the Letters of Junius. [1811–12]. Pa Bib Soc Am 46:66–7 '52.

11636 **Spector, Robert D.** The American publication of Heron's edition of the Letters of Junius. [1804]. N&Q 197:275–6 Je '52.

11637 **Cordasco, Francesco G. M.** Junius on vellum. N&Q 204:376 Oc '59.

11638 —— The Junius collection of Francis Place. N&Q 205:76 F '60.

11639 **Evans, Gwynne B.** The missing third edition of Wheble's Junius, 1771. Stud Bib 13:235–8 '60.

11640 **Wenner, C. M.** Junius's Letters. [G. Steevens library]. N&Q 205:396 Oc '60.

11641 **Cordasco, Francesco G. M.** The Twistleton Junius: a suppressed passage of Junius restored. N&Q 206:63–4 F '61.

JUNIUS, FRANCISCUS, 1589–1677

11642 **Liddell, Mark.** Junius's edition of Chaucer. [Ms.]. Athenæum 3633:779 Je '97.

11643 **Clubb, Merrel D.** Census of extant copies of Junius's Cædmon, 1655. (Query 147). Bk Coll 11no2:218 '62.

11644 —— Junius's edition of Cædmon. Library ser5 17no2:157 Mr '62.

11645 —— Junius's edition of the Cædmon manuscript. N&Q 207:111–12 Mr '62.

11646 —— A request for assistance. Pa Bib Soc Am 56:116 '62.

KASTNER, J. CONST., fl.1853

11647 **K., L. L.** J. Const. Kastner. [Ed. of Sketches of the Hungarian struggle, 1848–51]. N&Q ser9 11:428 My '03.

KEATS, JOHN, 1795–1821

11648 **Jenks, Edward.** Keats relics. [Notebook containing holograph Pot of basil, Eve of St. Mark, and Lines on the Mermaid tavern]. Athenæum 3317:667 My '91.

11649 —— Keats relics and mss. [of The pot of basil; Lines on the Mermaid tavern; The eve of St. Mark]. Bkworm 4no44:245–6 Jl '91.

11650 **Relics** of John Keats [in Chelsea public library]. Library 3no26:59–60 F '91.

11651 **Dilke, Charles W.** Keats's copy of the Anatomy. Athenæum 3402:19 Ja '93.

11652 **Kenyon, sir Frederic G.** The new Keats ms. [in the B. M.]. Athenæum 3505:894–6 D '94. [Sg.: F. G. K.]

11653 **Livingston, Luther S.** John Keats. (The first books of some English authors, VII). Bkmn (N.Y.) 11no2:131–6 Ap '00. facsims.

11654 **Forman, Harry B.** Keats's manuscript of The cap and bells. Athenæum 3894:757 Je '02.

11655 —— Keats: some readings and notes. Athenæum 3981:210–11 F '04.

11656 **De Sélincourt, Ernest.** Recently discovered Keats mss. N&Q ser10 3:81–4 F '05.

11657 **Forman, Harry B.** Some Keats crumbs. Athenæum 4262:12–13 Jl '09.

11658 **Holman, Thomas B.** Booksellers connected with Keats. N&Q ser11 7:427 My '13.

11659 **Johnson, Robert U.** Note on some volumes now in America, once owned by Keats. Keats-Sh Memorial Bull 2:20–9 '13. facsims.

11660 **Roberts, Robert.** Fragments of Keats manuscript. Keats-Sh Memorial Bull 2:93 '13. facsims. [Sg.: R. R.]

11661 **First** editions of Keats. (Notes on sales). TLS 24 F '21:132.

11662 **John** Keats. [Exhibition]. Harvard Lib N [1no]4:78–81 Ap '21.

11663 **Sargent, George H.** Keats treasures in America. Bkmns J 3no76:434 Ap '21.

Remarkable copies of first editions.–Rare Keats letters.

11664 **Stuart, H.** A misprint in Keats. [Teignmouth]. TLS 26 My '21:341; sir S. Colvin *ib*. 9 Je '21:373.

11665 **Stout, George D.** In drear-nighted December. [1829]. TLS 14 S '22:585.

11666 **Teall, Gardner.** Keats's copy of Guzman de Alfarache. Bkmns J new ser 9no25:11–13 Oc '23.

11667 **Muirhead, James F.** The text of Keats. [In a drear-nighted December]. TLS 9 Jl '25:464; sir S. Colvin *ib*. 16 Jl '25:480; J. F. Muirhead 23 Jl '25:496.

11668 **Douglas, Noel.** A Keats replica. [Facsim. of the 1817 Poems]. TLS 23 Je '27:440; G. D. Stout *ib*. 4 Ag '27:533.

11669 **Draper, Walter A.** A literary windfall. [Ms. of La belle dame]. Am Coll 5no2:81–2 N '27.

11670 **Gohdes, Clarence.** A note on the bibliography of Keats. Mod Lang N 43no6:393 Je '28.

11671 **Roberts, John H.** Did Keats finish Hyperion? [Ms.]. Mod Lang N 44no5:285–7 My '29.

11672 **Mabbott, Thomas O.** Arcturus and Keats; an early American publication of Keat's La belle dame sans merci. Am Lit 2no4:430–2 Ja '31.

11673 **Ballman, Adele B.** On the revisions of Hyperion. [Mss.]. Mod Lang N 47no5:302–3 My '32.

11674 **Pope, Willard B.** A book of Keats's. TLS 6 Oc '32:711.

11675 **Ridley, M. R.** The text of Keats. TLS 20 Oc '32:761; W. S. Robertson *ib*. 3 N '32:815; M. R. Ridley 10 N '32:839.

11676 **Stearns, Bertha-Monica.** The first publication of two poems by Keats. TLS 4 Ag '32:557; 8 S '32:624.

11677 **Forman, Maurice B.** Letters of John Keats. [Location of]. Pub Wkly 124no25:2082 D '33.

11678 **Perry, Warren.** A bibliography of Keats. [His own]. TLS 13 D '34:895.

11679 **Finney, Claude L.** 'Bibliography of manuscript material for the study of Keats's life and poetry' *in* The evolution of Keats's poetry. Cambridge, Mass., 1936. V.2, p. [745]–77.

11680 **Page, Frederick.** The two Hyperions. [Text]. TLS 20 N '37:891.

11681 **Thorpe, Clarence D.** An unknown Keats manuscript. [I stood tip-toe.]. TLS 6 Ag '38:519; M. B. Forman *ib.* 13 Ag '38:531; 27 Ag '38:555; C. D. Thorpe 10 D '38:785–6; H. W. Garrod 24 D '38:815–16.

11682 **Rollins, Hyder E.** 'Keats's Elgin marbles sonnets' *in* Prouty, Charles T., *ed.* Studies in honor of A. H. R. Fairchild. Columbia [Miss.] 1946. p. 161–6.

11683 **Clark, Ethel B.** A manuscript of John Keats at Dumbarton Oaks. Harvard Lib Bull 1no1:90–100 '47. facsims.

11684 **Bellinger, Rossiter R.** The first publication of Ode on a Grecian urn. N&Q 194:478–9 Oc '49.

11685 **Steele, Mabel A. E.** The Woodhouse transcripts of the poems of Keats. Harvard Lib Bull 3no2:232–56 '49.

11686 **Whitley, Alvin.** The autograph of Keats's In a drear-nighted December. (Notes). Harvard Lib Bull 5no1:116–22 '51. facsims.

11687 **Ford, Newell F.** Keats's romantic seas: 'ruthless' or 'keelless'? [Ode to a nightingale, l.70]. Keats-Sh J 1:11–22 Ja '52.

11688 **Steele, Mabel A. E.** Three early manuscripts of John Keats. [Fill for me a brimming bowl; O come dearest Emma; O solitude]. Keats-Sh J 1:57–63 Ja '52. facsims.

11689 **Stull, Joseph S.** An early annotated edition of The eve of St. Agnes. [By J. W. Hales, 1892]. Pa Bib Soc Am 46:269–73 '52.

11690 **Coles, William A.** The proof sheets of Keats's Lamia. (Notes). Harvard Lib Bull 8no1:114–19 '54.

11691 **Rollins, Hyder E.** Benjamin Bailey's scrapbook. [Keats' friend]. Keats-Sh J 6:15–30 '57.

11692 **Stillinger, Jack.** Keats's Grecian urn and the evidence of transcripts. Pub Mod Lang Assn 73no4:447–8 S '58.

   Repr. in Zitner, Sheldon P., *ed.* The practice of modern literary scholarship. Glenview, Ill., 1966. p. [382]–4.

11693 **Brown, T. Julian.** John Keats, 1795–1821. (English literary autographs, XXXVI). Bk Coll 9no4:445 '60. facsims.

11694 **Patterson, Charles I.** The Keats-Hazlitt-Hunt copy of Palmerin of England in relation to Keats's poetry. J Eng Germ Philol 60no1:31–43 Ja '61.

11695 **Rogers, Neville** and **Mabel A. E. Steele.** 'I stood tip toe upon a little hill': a hitherto uncollated fragment. Keats-Sh J 10:12–13 '61. facsims.

11696 **Marchand, Leslie A.** A first edition of Endymion [acquired by Library]. J Rutgers Univ Lib 26no2:58–9 Je '63.

11697 **Stillinger, Jack.** The text of The eve of St. Agnes. Stud Bib 16:207–12 '63.

11698 **Green, David B.** An early reprinting of three poems from Keats's 1820 volume. Pa Bib Soc Am 60:363 '66.

KEBLE, JOHN, 1792–1866

11699 **Boase, George C.** John Keble and The christian year. [Ms.]. N&Q ser8 7:149 F '95.

11700 **Keble's** Christian year. (Notes on sales). TLS 14 Jl '27:492.

11701 **Peachey, George C.** The facsimile edition of the Christian year. [1877]. TLS 18 Ag '27:561.

KEELING, WILLIAM, d.1620

11702 **Foster, William.** Forged Shakespeariana. [Keeling's journal]. N&Q ser9 6:41–2 Jl '00.

11703 **Evans, Gwynne B.** The authenticity of Keeling's journal entries on Hamlet and Richard II. [And Collier]. N&Q 196:313–15 Jl '51; S. Race 196:513–15 N '51.

11704 —— The authenticity of the Keeling journal entries reasserted. N&Q 197:127–8 Mr '52; rf. J. C. Maxwell TLS 22 F '52:141; F. S. Boas 7 Mr '52:173; S. Race N&Q 197:181–2 Ap '52.

KENDALL, WILLIAM, 1768–1832

11705 **Dallas, James.** William Kendall's Poems. [1791]. N&Q ser9 3:246 Ap '99.

KENNEDY, JAMES, fl.1663

11706 **Anderson, Peter J.** Æneas Britannicus, by James Kennedy. N&Q ser10 7:388–9 My '07.

KENNEDY, JAMES, fl.1758

11707 **Kennedy, C. M.** James Kennedy. [A new description of the pictures ... Witton]. N&Q ser8 7:347 My '95; E. H. Coleman ib. 7:398 My '95.

KENRICK, WILLIAM, 1725?–79

11708 **Fussell, Paul.** William Kenrick, eighteenth century scourge and critic. J Rutgers Univ Lib 20no1:42–59 Je '57.

KICKHAM, CHARLES JOSEPH, 1826–82

11709 **O'Hegarty, Patrick S.** Kickham's novels. Irish Bk Lover 26no2:41 S/Oc '38. [Sg.: P. S. O'H.]

KILHAM, HANNAH (SPURR), 1774–1832

11710 **Hair, P. E. H.** A bibliographical note on Hannah Kilham's linguistic work. Friends' Hist Soc J 49no3:165–8 '60.

KILLIGREW, THOMAS, 1612–83

11711 **Van Lennep, William.** 'Thomas Killigrew prepares his plays for production [Author's annotated Comedies and tragedies, 1664]' *in* McManaway, James G., G. E. Dawson, and E. E. Willoughby, *ed.* Joseph Quincy Adams memorial studies. Washington, 1948. p. 803–8.

KILLIGREW, SIR WILLIAM, 1606–95

11712 **Wagner, Bernard M.** The Siege of Urbin. [Ms.] TLS 1 N '28:806.

KIMBER, EDWARD, 1719–69

11713 **Kimber, Sidney A.** The Relation of a late expedition to St. Augustine, with biographical and bibliographical notes on Isaac and Edward Kimber. Pa Bib Soc Am 28pt2:81–96 '33. facsims.

'The London magazine and the Kimbers' (p. 88–94)

KING, BP. HENRY, 1592–1669

11714 **Mason, Lawrence.** Ms. of bishop Henry King's poems. N&Q ser11 5:468 Je '12; C. E. Mathews *ib.* 6:32 Jl '12; L. Mason 7:189 Mr '13.

11715 **Simpson, Percy.** The Bodleian manuscripts of Henry King. Bod Q Rec 5no60:324–40 Mr '29. facsim.

KING, WILLIAM, 1663–1712

11716 **Esdaile, Katharine A.** The Fairy feast. TLS 12 F '31:116; sir H. H. Williams *ib.* 19 F '31:35.

11717 **Horne, Colin J.** Dr. William King's Miscellanies in prose and verse. Library ser4 25no1/2:37–45 Je/S '44.

KINGSLEY, CHARLES, 1819–75

11718 **Charles** Kingsley and Lewis Carroll. [Their libraries]. (Notes on sales). TLS 24 N '32:908.

11719 **Warburton, Thomas.** Kingsley: Glaucus. [Variant adverts. in 1st ed.]. Bib N&Q 2no3:7 Ap '36.

11720 **Thorp, Margaret F.** The Kingsley collection [of M. L. Parrish]. Princeton Univ Lib Chron 8no1:18–20 N '46.

11721 **Charles** Kingsley. [Mss. acquired for Library]. Princeton Univ Lib Chron 13no3:168 '52.

11722 **Charles** Kingsley's American notes. Princeton Univ Lib Chron 20no1:40–1 '58.

11723 **Martin, Robert B.** Manuscript sermons of Charles Kingsley. [Addition to Parrish collection]. Princeton Univ Lib Chron 23no4:181 '62.

KINGSLEY, HENRY, 1830–76

11724 **Price, H.** Two misprints [one in Kingsley's Geoffrey Hamlyn]. TLS 16 Ja '30:44.

11725 **Buckler, William E.** Henry Kingsley and The gentleman's magazine. [Mademoiselle Mathilde]. J Eng Germ Philol 50no1:90–100 Ja '51.

KIPLING, RUDYARD, 1865–1936

11726 **Livingston, Luther S.** Kipling's suppressed works. Bkmn (N.Y.) 9no1:62–3 Mr '99. facsims.

11727 —— Rudyard Kipling. (The first books of some English authors, IV). Bkmn (N.Y.) 10no4:329–37 D '99. facsims.

11728 [——]. The works of Rudyard Kipling; the description of a set of the first editions of his books in the library of a New York collector [R. F. Pick]. New York, Dodd, Mead, 1901. viii,91p. port., facsims. 26cm.

11729 **Cripps, Matthew.** Kipling in America. N&Q ser9 9:5–6 Ja '02; W. F. Prideaux ib. 9:89–91 Ja '02.

11730 **Walker, R. J.** Kipling's City of dreadful night. N&Q ser9 9:289 Ap '02; R. Pierpont ib. 11:16–17 Ja '03.

11731 **Platt, James.** Kipling in Spanish. N&Q ser10 12:448 D '09.

11732 **Young, W. Arthur.** Uncollected Kipling items. N&Q ser11 8:441–2, 464–5,485–6 D '13; P. Lewis; A. Braund *ib.* 8:515 D '13; J. H. Rivett-Carnac 9:34–5 Ja '14; W. Corfield 9:93 Ja '14; J. DeL. Ferguson 9:134–5 F '14; J. R. H. 9:309–10 Ap '14; P. Lucas; M. R. Sanborn 9:416 My '14.

11733 **Ferguson, J. DeLancey.** Rudyard Kipling's Letters of travel. N&Q ser11 9:325 Ap '14.

11734 **Monkshood, G. F.,** *pseud. of* **W. J. Clarke.** The less familiar Kipling, and Kiplingana. London, Jarrold, 1917. (2d ed. 1922; 3d ed. 1936). 167p. facsims. 22cm.

For contents see no.11764.

11735 **H., J. R.** Uncollected Kipling items. N&Q ser12 7:4 Jl '20.

11736 **Pierpont, Robert.** Stalky & co., by Rudyard Kipling. N&Q ser12 6:334 Je '20; J. R. H. *ib.* 7:57 Jl '20; D. L. Galbreath 7:118 Ag '20; J. R. H. 7:298 Oc '20.

11737 **Stevens, B. F., and Brown.** Uncollected Kipling items: With number three; Surgical and medical. N&Q ser12 6:38 F '20; C. W. Firebrace *ib.* 6:178 My '20; J. R. H. 6:258–9 My '20; 7:78 Jl '20; W. R. Power 7:136 Ag '20; J. R. H. 7:389 N '20.

11738 **Monkshood, G. F.,** *pseud. of* **W. J. Clarke.** The less familiar Kipling, and Kiplingana. New and rev. ed. London, Jarrold [1922]. (First pub. 1917; 3d ed. 1936). 190p. facsims. 22cm.

11739 **American bookman, An.** Kipling and his pirates. [Am. ed of The light that failed]. Bkmns J new ser 17no37:42 Oc '24; N. Van Patten *ib.* 11no37:43–4 Oc '24; Flora V. Livingston; H. A. Cadman 11no38:92–3 N '24.

11740 **Kipling** proofs and unknown firsts; more prices from the Bernard Buchanan MacGeorge sale. (Books in the sale rooms). Bkmns J new ser 10no36:212–13 S '24.

11741 . . . **The first** item in Kipling's bibliography [Schoolboy lyrics, 1881]; good prices for rare modern firsts. (Books in the sale rooms). Bkmns J new ser 12no48:245–7 S '25.

11742 **A new** Kipling collation. [Verses, 1897]. Bkmns J new ser 13no53:184–5 F '26.

11743 **New** Kipling fakes revealed . . . . (Marginalia). Bkmns J new ser 14no57: 101 Jl '26.

11744 **Young, W. Arthur.** Uncollected Kipling items. [Stalky]. Kipling J 3:4 Oc '27. [Sg.: Editor.]

11745 **An American** sale; high prices for rare editions. [American art association, Ja '28]. Kipling J 5:18–20 Ap '28.

11746 **A Sotheby** sale. [19 D '27]. Kipling J 4:30–1 Ja '28.

11747 **Kipling** prices current. Kipling J 6:8–9 Jl '28; 7:7–8 Oc '28; 8:14–15 Ja '29; 9:28–9 Ap '29; 10:29–30 Jl '29; 11:20–2 Oc '29; 12:17–18 Ja '30; 13:28–9 Ap '30; 15:86–8 Oc '30; 20:102–3 D '31; 21:8 Mr '32; 27:78–9 S '33; 28:129–30 D '33; 29:31 Mr '34; 30:67 Je '34; 31:92–3 S '34; 35:96–7 S '35; 40:117–18 D '36.

11748 **Reed, T. German-.** Kipling collecting. Kipling J 9:23–5 Ap '29.

11749 [**Sanderson, John**]. Kipling and his illustrators. [List of illustrators of Scribner's Outward bound ed.]. Kipling J 10:24 Jl '29.

11750 **Chandler, Lloyd H.** A Kipling problem. [Text of The light that failed]. Coloph [1]pt4:[8p.] '30.

11751 **Elwell, T. E.** Mainly bibliographical: notes on piratical issues. [American ed.]. Kipling J 15:91–2 Oc '30.

11752 **Livingston, Flora V. M.** Some notes on pirate editions. Kipling J 14:38–9 Jl '30.

11753 **In the sale room.** Kipling J 19:69–70 S '31.

11754 **Livingston, Flora V. M.** A footnote to bibliography. [Recessional]. Coloph [2]pt7:[4p.] '31. facsim.

11755 **The Kipling** society library. Kipling J 22:61 Je '32.

11756 **Martindell, Ernest W.** The Kipling birthday book, by several contributors. [1896; identification of quotations from 'uncollected matter']. Kipling J 28:123–5 D '33. [Sg.: E. W. M.]

11757 **A gift** to the Library. [The pioneer, Allahabad]. Kipling J 35:78–9 S '35.

11758 **Kipling:** Just so stories. [Binding variants]. Bib N&Q 1no3:8 Ag '35; A. Pforzheimer ib. 2no1:2 Oc '35.

11759 [**Haraszti, Zoltán**]. A Kipling exhibit in the Treasure room. (Notes and news). More Bks Boston Pub Lib Bull 11no2:37–8 F '36.

11760 [——]. Kipling first editions acquired. More Bks Boston Pub Lib Bull 11no3:100–1 Mr '36.

11761 **K., M. J.** A first edition of Kim. More Bks Boston Pub Lib Bull 11no10:454–5 D '36.

11762 **The Kipling** meeting. [Exhibition]. Univ Pennsylvania Lib Chron 4no1:18–22 Mr '36.

11763 **Millar, Eric G.** Autograph manuscripts of Rudyard Kipling. Brit Mus Q 11no1:26–7 Oc '36.

11764 **Monkshood, G. F.**, *pseud. of* **W. J. Clarke.** The less familiar Kipling, and Kiplingana. 3d rev. ed. London, Jarrolds, 1936. (First pub. 1917). 255p. facsims. 18cm.

   I. The less familiar Kipling.–II. Some less familiar Kiplingana.–III. Martindell, the master Kiplingite.–IV. The Kipling rarity and mystery, etc.

11765 **Randall, David A.** Kipling and collecting. Pub Wkly (N.Y.) 129no4:379–80 Ja '36.

11766 **Ferguson, J. DeLancey.** Two phantom Kipling books. [Mother Maturin; The book of the forty-five mornings]. Kipling J 45:7–8 Mr '38.

11767 **Caddick, A. E.** The Vampire. [Enquiry for date of pirated issue]. Kipling J 51:32 Oc '39.

11768 **Hanson, Laurence W.** and **E. G. M[illar].** The Kipling bequest. Brit Mus Q 14no4:93–5 D '40. illus.

11769 **Maitland, William G. B.** The forged letters. Kipling J 7no53:12–13 Ap '40.

11770 **Milburn, C. H.** The Song of an outsider. [Text]. Kipling J 7no54:30–1 Jl '40.

11771 **Goff, Frederick R.** [Bibliogr. note on Kipling's Departmental ditties, 1888]. Pa Bib Soc Am 36:232 '42.

11772 **A Kipling** collection. [E. A. Ballard]. (Bibliography and sales). TLS 29 Ag '42:432; 5 S '42:444.

11773 **The manuscript** of Recessional, a rare document. Kipling J 10no67:11–13 Oc '43. facsims.

11774 **Martindell, Ernest W.** The confessions of an old time Kipling collector. Bk Coll Packet 4no7:1–3 Mr '46.

   Repr. in Kipling J 13no80:5–6 D '46.

11775 **Maitland, William G. B.** This collecting game. Kipling J 13no86:15–16 Jl '48.

11776 **Naumburg, Carl T.** The Livingston Kipling collection at Harvard library. Kipling J 17no94:15 Jl '50.

11777 **C., J. P.** Kipling's first bibliographer, the late capt. E. W. Martindell. Kipling J 18no98:12 Jl '51.

11778 **Rare** specimens [in Norman Croom-Johnson collection]. Kipling J 19no101:10 Ap '52.

11779 **Yeats, Alvice W.** The Kipling collection at the University of Texas. Lib Chron Univ Texas 4no3:118–22 '52.

11780 **Maitland, William G. B.** The Wolff collection. [Echoes; Schoolboy lyrics]. (Library notes). Kipling J 21no112:13–14 D '54; 22no113:13–16 Ap '55.

11781 **Harbord, R. E.** Mulvaney: general notes for the reader's guide. Kipling J 26no130:14–17 Je '59.

11782 **Rice, Howard C.** Into the hold of remembrance; notes on the Kipling material in the Doubleday collection. Princeton Univ Lib Chron 22no3:105–18 '61. illus., facsims.

Repr. in Kipling J 28no140:19–26 D '61.

11783 —— Additions to the Doubleday collection: Kipling, T. E. Lawrence, Conrad. Princeton Univ Lib Chron 24no4:191–6 '63.

Repr. in Kipling J 28no140:19–26 D '61.

11784 **Jasenas, Michael.** Progress of the Paterson collection of Kipling. [Cornell university]. Kipling J 31no152:10–11 D '64.

Repr. from Cornell Lib Associates Occas Pa 18–19 '60/1.

11785 **Cornell, Louis L.** The authenticity of Rudyard Kipling's uncollected newspaper writings, 1882–1888. Eng Lit Transit 8no4:242–9 '65.

11786 **Naumburg, Carl T.** Pierpont library Kipling exhibition. Kipling J 33no158:19–20 Je '66.

11787 **Rice, Howard C.** A manuscript of Kipling's The light that failed. Princeton Univ Lib Chron 17no2:125–30 '66. illus.

11788 **Monteiro, George.** Rudyard Kipling: early printings in American periodicals. Pa Bib Soc Am 61:127–8 '67.

11789 **Underwood, F. A.** A small collection. [His own]. Kipling J 34no164:9–11 D '67.

11790 **The Kipling** society library [to Royal commonwealth society]. Kipling J 35no166:12–14 Je '68.

KIRBYE, GEORGE, fl.1597

11791 Arkwright, G. E. P. George Kirbye and the Triumphs of Oriana. N&Q ser8 3:207 Mr '93.

KIRK, ROBERT, 1644–92

11792 Rossi, Mario M. Text-criticism of Robert Kirk's Secret commonwealth. Edinburgh Bib Soc Trans 3pt4:253–68 '57.

Trans. by M. I. Johnston.

KIRKMAN, FRANCIS, 1632–80? *see under* Book production and distribution–Printers, publishers, etc.

KNEVET, RALPH, 1600–71

11793 Charles, Amy M. The manuscript of Ralph Knevet's Gallery to the temple, B. M. Add. ms. 27447. N&Q 204:183–5 My '59; 204:338 S '59.

KNOX, ROBERT, 1640?–1720

11794 Craster, sir H. H. Edmund. Knox's Ceylon. Bod Q Rec 1no5:116 Ap '15.

KNOX, RONALD ARBUTHNOTT, 1888–1957

11795 Carter, John W. Knox's Absolute and Abitofhell. [1913]. (Query no.21). Bk Coll 1no4:268 '52.

11796 Bede, mother M. In search of Knoxious publications. Assn Brit Theol & Philos Libs Bull 22:10–17 F '66.

KORZENIOWSKI, TEODOR JÓZEF KONRAD, 1857–1924 *see* Conrad, Joseph, *pseud.*

KYD, THOMAS, 1557?–95?

11797 Brandl, Alois. Kyd's Spanish tragedy. Acad 40:157 Ag '91; P. A. Daniel *ib.* 40:197 S '91.

11798 Brereton, J. LeGay. Notes on the text of Kydd. Eng Studien 37no1:87–99 '07.

11799 Seeberger, Alfred. Zur Entstehung der Quartoausgabe des First part of Jeronimo. Archiv für Stenographie 59hft8:236–48 Ag '08; 59hft9/12: 257–61 S/D '08.

11800 Smedley, William T. Elizabethan handwriting. [Kyd]. TLS 22 Jl '20:472.

11801 **Greg, sir Walter W.** The Spanish tragedy, a leading case? Library ser4 6no1:47–56 Je '25.

Repr. in Maxwell, James C., ed. Collected papers. Oxford, 1966. p. [149]–83.

11802 **Hazen, Allen T.** Type-facsimiles. [Facsimile ed. of Solyman and Perseda]. Mod Philol 44no4:209–17 My '47.

11803 **Freeman, Arthur.** The printing of The Spanish tragedy. Library ser5 24no3:187–99 S '69. tables.

I. Wrong-fount evidence.–II. Compositors.

LAING, DAVID, 1793–1878

11804 **Weir, John L.** David Laing's edition of Alexander Scott, 1821. [Poems]. N&Q 179:4–6 Jl '40.

LAMB, CHARLES, 1775–1834

11805 **Campbell, J. Dykes.** Lamb's John Woodvil. Athenæum 3340:583–5 Oc '91; 3342:648–9 N '91.

11806 —— An American edition of Elia. Athenæum 3482:99 Jl '94.

11807 **Harper, Francis P.** Autograph manuscript of Charles Lamb's Confessions of a drunkard. Athenæum 3481:65–6 Jl '94.

11808 **Prideaux, William F.** Charles Lamb's library. N&Q ser8 12:125 Ag '97.

11809 **Livingston, Luther S.** A literary curiosity from Charles Lamb's library; discovery of a book that has hitherto baffled Lamb students. [Lamb's copy of John Lamb's A letter to the right hon. William Windham, 1810]. Bkmn (N.Y.) 8no5:453–8 Ja '99. facsims.

11810 **P., G. H.** Lamb's Poetry for children. [1809]. Athenæum 3717:84 Ja '99; sir I. Gollancz ib. 3719:148 F '99; A. Ainger; A. T. 3720:179 F '99; sir I. Gollancz 3721:210 F '99.

11811 **Hutchinson, Thomas.** The text of Charles Lamb. Athenæum 3870:874–5 D '01.

11812 **Lucas, Edward V.** Charles Lamb as a journalist. N&Q ser9 8:60–1 Jl '01; A. Ainger ib. 8:85–6 Jl '01; Myops, pseud. 8:125–6,166–8 Ag '01.

11813 —— A new book by Charles Lamb. [The king and queen of hearts, 1809]. Athenæum 3862:596–7 N '01; W. F. Prideaux ib. 3864:664 N '01.

11814 **Potts, R. A.** An uncollected poem by Charles Lamb. [To a young lady]. Athenæum 3851:223 Ag '01.

11815 **Livingston, Luther S.** Some notes on three of Lamb's juveniles. Bibliographer 1no6:215–30 Je '02. facsims.

11816 **Bulloch, J. Malcolm.** The strange adventures of a book belonging to Charles Lamb. [Dodsley's Old plays]. Scott N&Q ser2 5no3:33 S '03. [Sg.: Ed.]

11817 **Sparke, Archibald.** Phil Elia. [Last essays of Elia]. N&Q ser10 2:527 D '04; F. A. Russell *ib*. 3:36–7 Ja '05; J. B. Wainewright 3:79 Ja '05; S. Butterworth 3:112 F '05.

11818 **Prideaux, William F.** Charles Lamb. [Elia, 1823, and his library]. N&Q ser10 4:445–6 D '05; S. Butterworth *ib*. 4:512–13,538 D '05; W. F. Prideaux 5:11–12 Ja '06.

11819 **Anderson, G. A.** Charles Lamb's folio Beaumont and Fletcher. N&Q ser12 1:267 Ap '16; W. H. Peet *ib*. 1:376 My '16.

11820–2 Cancelled.

11823 **Lamb's** King and queen of hearts. (Notes on sales). TLS 20 Je '18:292.

11824 **Anderson, G. A.** Lamb's bibliography. [Contribs. to the Annual anthology]. (Correspondence). London Merc 3no13:87–8 N '20.

11825 **A Charles** Lamb collection. [W. T. Wallace]. (Notes on sales). TLS 18 Mr '20:192.

11826 **Charles** Lamb manuscripts. (Notes on sales). TLS 29 Ja '20:72.

11827 **Turnbull, John M.** Charles Lamb's lines In the album of Catherine Orkney. TLS 25 D '24:885; T. D. Cook *ib*. 26 Mr '25:223.

11828 **Butterwick, J. C.** Lamb's King and queen of hearts. [Proofs of illus.] TLS 19 Jl '28:536.

11829 **Turnbull, John M.** Wordsworth's part in the production of Lamb's Specimens. N&Q 154:114–15 F '28.

11830 —— An unrecorded issue of Lamb's Album verses. TLS 20 Mr '30:247; DeV. Payen-Payne *ib*. 27 Mr '30:274.

11831 —— Cancels in Last essays of Elia. TLS 23 Je '32:464.

11832 **Birss, John H.** The original mss. of Elia. [1835]. N&Q 165:207 S '33.

11833 **Charles** Lamb. (Notes on sales). TLS 29 N '34:860.

11834 **McDonald, Gerald D.** Charles Lamb as a collector; memorabilia in the New York public library. N.Y. Pub Lib Bull 38no9:707–12 S '34. port.

11835 [**Griffith, Reginald H.**]. Charles Lamb ... an exhibition of books and manuscripts in the Library of the University of Texas commemorative of the centenary of his death. Austin, Tex., University of Texas, 1935. 7p. 23cm. Covertitle.

11836 **Goodspeed, George T.** Lamb: Works, 1818, 2 vols. Bib N&Q 2no9:6 Ja '36; F. Coykendall *ib.* 2no10:5 Ap '38; D. G. Wing 2no11:5 N '38. [Sg.: G. G.]

11837 **Willmett, H. James.** Charles Lamb's library. [Priced and named sale catalogue]. Bib N&Q 2no12:9 My '39.

11838 **Finch, Jeremiah S.** Charles Lamb's Companionship ... in almost solitude. Princeton Univ Lib Chron 6no4:179–99 Je '45.

'Lamb mss. in the Scribner collection' (p. 197–9)

11839 —— The Scribner Lamb collection. Princeton Univ Lib Chron 7no4:133–48 Je '46.

11840 —— Charles Lamb's copy of The history of Philip de Commines with autograph notes by Lamb and Coleridge. Princeton Univ Lib Chron 9no1:30–7 N '47.

11841 **Barnett, George L.** A critical analysis of the Lucas edition of Lamb's letters. Mod Lang Q 9no3:303–14 S '48.

11842 **French, J. Milton.** Elia. [Acquisition of 1st ed. of Elia and Last essays of Elia]. J Rutgers Univ Lib 11no2:92–4 Je '48.

11843 **Turnbull, John M.** Lamb manuscript. [Witches and other night fears]. N&Q 193:369 Ag '48. [Sg.: J. M. T.]

11844 —— An Elian make-weight. [A quaker's meeting]. N&Q 194:35–6 Ja '49.

11845 **Barnett, George L.** Corrections in the text of Lamb's letters. Huntington Lib Q 18no2:147–58 F '55.

11846 **Smith, H. G.** C. and M. Lamb's Mrs. Leicester's school. [1807 ed. sought]. (Query no.59). Bk Coll 4no1:81–2 '55.

11847 **Charles** Lamb mss. at the India office. Charles Lamb Soc Bull 133:132 N '56.

11848 **Woodring, Carl R.** Charles Lamb in the Harvard library. Harvard Lib Bull 10no2:208–39 '56; 10no3:367–401 '56. facsims.

I. First editions: 'gentleman's books'.–II. 'The old familiar faces': Lamb's friends and relations.–III. Lamb's library: 'the finest collection of shabby books'.–IV. Literary manuscripts: 'twenty guineas a sheet'?–V. Autograph letters: 'grace after meat'.

Extr. in Charles Lamb Soc Bull 136:153–4 My '57.

11849 **Davis, Bertram R.** Rare and valuable acquisition by the Society. [Poetical pieces, c.1770]. Charles Lamb Soc Bull 138:169 S '57.

11850 **Foxon, David F.** The chapbook editions of the Lambs' Tales from Shakespear. Bk Coll 6no1:41–53 '57.

11851 **Opie, Peter.** Charles Lamb and children's books; an address. [And M. J. Godwin, pub.]. Charles Lamb Soc Bull 141:194–5 Mr '58.

11852 **Charles** Lamb in the sale rooms. [Mss.]. Charles Lamb Soc Bull 150:258 N '59; 152:263–4 Ja '60.

11853 **Nethery, Wallace.** Eliana Americana, a footnote to the bibliography of Charles Lamb: Charles Lamb and America. Am Bk Coll 11no4:7–22 D '60. facsims.

11854 —— Charles Lamb in America. Am Bk Coll 12no6:7–16 F '62. illus., facsims.

11855 **Payne, Waveney R. N.** An irregular copy of Lamb's Tales from Shakespeare, 1807. (Query 155). Bk Coll 11no4:485–6 '62.

11856 **Prance, Claude A.** A Charles Lamb library. [His own]. Priv Lib 4no1:2–10 Ja '62.

   Repr. in Charles Lamb Soc Bull 166:375–8 Jl '62; 167:384–5 S '62.

11857 **Nethery, Wallace.** Charles Lamb in America to 1848. Worcester, Mass., A. J. St.Onge, 1963. 72p. port., facsims. 19cm.

11858 **Bhattacharya, S.** 'Some observations on the textual and critical study of Lamb's Dramatic specimens' *in* Hindu university, Benares. Dept. of English. Criticism and research. Varanasi, 1964. p. [22]–33.

11859 **Prance, Claude A.** Charles Lamb's illustrators, 1796–1967. Charles Lamb Soc Bull 199:600–2 Jl '68; 200:604–9 Oc '68.

LAMB, MARY ANN, 1764–1847 *see under* Lamb, Charles, 1775–1834.

LAMBARDE, WILLIAM, 1536–1601

11860 **Ward, Paul L.** Lambarde's Archeion. [Ms.]. TLS 23 Jl '54:473.

LAMPSON, FREDERICK LOCKER-, 1821–95

11861 **Roberts, William.** Mr. F. Locker-Lampson. (Bookworms of yesterday and today). Bkworm 3no27:65–71 F '90. facsims.

11862 **St.Swithin,** *pseud.* Publications of Frederick Locker-Lampson. N&Q ser12 8:307 Ap '21; R. Y. Pickering *ib.* 8:355 Ap '21.

11863 **Jameson, R.** Frederick Locker: Lyra elegantrarum. Bib N&Q 2no2:5 F
'36; J. T. Gerould; F. Coykendall *ib.* 2no3:5 Ap '36.

11864 **J., H.** Millais' portrait of Frederick Locker in Lyra elegantiarum. [Paper].
Bib N&Q 2no1:4 Ja '36.

11865 **Bates, Madison C.** 'That delightful man': a study of Frederick Locker.
Harvard Lib Bull 13no1:92–113 '59; 13no2:265–91 '59; 13no3:444–70
'59. illus., ports., facsims.

'Location of Locker material' (p. 468–70)

11866 **Cremer, R. W. Ketton-.** Locker-Lampson's Lyra elegantarum, 1867.
(Note 113). Bk Coll 8no3:296 '59.

LANCASTER, JOSEPH, 1778–1838

11867 **McGarry, Kevin.** Joseph Lancaster. N&Q 209:390 Oc '64.

LANDOR, WALTER SAVAGE, 1775–1864

11868 **Wheeler, Stephen.** An appeal for accuracy in reprints. Acad 41:330 Ap
'92. [Sg.: S. W.]

11869 —— The bibliography of Walter Savage Landor. [Letters . . . by Calvus,
1814]. Athenæum 3793:28–9 Jl '00; 3795:88 Jl '00.

11870 —— Landor bibliography. [Not author of Hebrew lyrics, 1859 or Guy's
porridge pot, 1809]. Athenæum 3773:208 F '00; R. Thomas *ib.* 3775:274
Mr '00; S. Wheeler 3777:335 Mr '00.

11871 —— Landor and his editors. [Misprints]. Athenæum 3840:694 Je '01.

11872 —— Notes on the bibliography of Walter Savage Landor. Bib Soc Trans
14pt2:135–7 '16/17.

Summary of paper read 18 D '16.

11873 —— [**Same**]: Bib Soc News-sh 3–4 Ja '17.

Report of paper read 18 D '16.

11874 —— Landor and his publishers. TLS 19 Ja '22:45.

11875 **Landor** and Conrad. (Notes on sales). TLS 21 Je '28:472.

11876 **Montagu, M. F. Ashley-.** The text of Landor. TLS 15 My '30:414; T. E.
Welby *ib.* 29 My '30:457; W. S. Landor 5 Je '30:478; T. E. Welby 12 Je
'30:496; M. F. Ashley-Montagu 12 Je '30:514.

11877 **Goodspeed, George T.** Landor: Heroic idylls, 1863. [Issues]. Bib N&Q 1no2:11 Ap '35. [Sg.: G. G.]

11878 **Payne, Denis.** A Landor ms. [A poet's dream]. TLS 30 Mr '40:159.

11879 **Metzdorf, Robert F.** Addendum: a new Landorian manuscript. [Mr. Landor's remarks on a suit]. Pub Mod Lang Assn 56no2:755–7 Je '41.

11880 **Super, Robert H.** The publication of Landor's early works. Pub Mod Lang Assn 63no2:577–603 Je '48.

> Cadell & Davies.–Sharpe of Warwick.–Slatter & Munday, Oxford.–Meyler, Bath.–Darton, London, and Valpy, London.–John Murray –Henry Colburn.

11881 **Bald, R. Cecil.** Landor's Sponsalia Polyxenae. Library ser5 4no3:211–12 D '49.

11882 **Kimmelman, Elaine.** First editions of Landor. Boston Pub Lib Q 2no4:381–3 Oc '50.

11883 **Super, Robert H.** The authorship of Guy's porridge pot and The dun cow. [By R. E. Landor]. Library ser5 5no1:55–8 Je '50.

11884 **Karlson, Marjorie.** The Walter Savage Landor collection. Yale Univ Lib Gaz 27no1:31–7 Jl '52.

> 'Desiderata' (p. 36–7)

11885 **Super, Robert H.** Notes on some obscure Landor editions. Pa Bib Soc Am 46:58–62 '52.

11886 —— Landor's American publications. Mod Lang Q 14no4:360–74 D '53.

11887 —— The publication of Landor's works. London, Bibliographical society, 1954. xi,125p. 25cm. (Bib Soc Trans Suppl 18)

> Introduction.–The early works.–Publishing from Italy.–The most prolific decade.–The last years.

> Rev: TLS 10 S '54:580; B. Dobrée R Eng Stud new ser 6:326–8 '55; H. A. Smith Mod Lang R 50:528–9 '55.

11888 **Varadi, A.** A Landor rarity. [Offerings to Buonaparte, 1814]. (Note no. 32). Bk Coll 3no1:71–3 '54.

11889 **Landor's** Imaginary conversations. [Acquisition of correspondence relating to its publication]. (Notes and news). Bull John Rylands Lib 42no2:260–1 Mr '60.

11890 **Lyde, R. G.** A Landor gift. [Library]. Brit Mus Q 22no1/2:7–8 F '60.

11891 **Smith, Simon H. Nowell-.** (Walter Savage Landor) Gebir, a poem, 1798. Library ser5 17no2:149–52 Je '62. diagrs.

11892 —— The Warwickshire talents, 1809. (Query 156). Bk Coll 11no4:486 '62.

11893 **Lohrli, Ann.** The first publication of Landor's Diana de Poictiers. N&Q 208:19–20 Ja '63.

11894 **Brumbaugh, Thomas B.** A Landor collection. [His collection, acquired by Texas]. Lib Chron Univ Texas 8no2:23–7 '66.

11895 **Prasher, A. LaVonne.** The censorship of Landor's Imaginary conversations [during publication]. Bull John Rylands Lib 49no2:427–63 '67.

LANG, ANDREW, 1844–1912

11896 **Gregory, K.** Lang, Andrew: Fairy book stories. Bib N&Q 2no7:5 Oc '36.

11897 **Green, Roger L.** Andrew Lang bibliography. [Whereabouts of C. M. Falconer's ms. bibliogr.]. TLS 31 My '41:263

11898 **Bushnell, George H.** Notes on Andrew Lang. TLS 5 Je '43:276; A. Exley *ib.* 12 Je '43:283; R. L. Green 17 Jl '43:348; 31 Jl '43:372; W. M. Parker 1 Ap '44:168.

Sources.–Biography and criticism.

11899 **Green, Roger L.** He, She and It. (Bibliography). TLS 27 My '44:264; 1 Jl '44:324.

11900 **Bushnell, George H.** 'On the bibliography of Andrew Lang' *in* From papyrus to print. London, 1947. p. 215–18.

11901 **Green, Roger L.** Collecting Andrew Lang. Priv Lib 4no8:155–60 Oc '63. illus.

11902 **Kendall, Lyle H.** Location of copies of Lang's Lines on ... the Shelley society, Meredith's Jump-to-glory Jane. (Query 237). Bk Coll 18no2:226 '69.

LANGBAINE, GERARD, 1656–92

11903 **Greg, sir Walter W.** Gerard Langbaine the younger and Nicholas Cox. Library ser4 25no1/2:67–70 Je/S '44; H. Macdonald *ib.* 25no3/4:186 D/Mr '44/5.

LANGTON, ROBERT, 1493–1524

11904 **Mitchell, R. J.** Robert Langton's Pylgrimage. Library ser5 8no1:42–5 Mr '53; E. S. de Beer *ib.* 10no1:58–9 Mr '55.

LANSDOWNE, GEORGE GRANVILLE, BARON, 1666–1735 *see* Granville, George, baron Lansdowne, 1666–1735.

LASCELLES, ROWLEY, 1771–1841

11905 **De Beer, Gavin R.** Rowley Lascelles. N&Q 193:97–9 Mr '48.

LATIMER, BP. HUGH, 1485?–1555

11906 **Talbot, William.** Latimer's Seven sermons, 1562. TLS 11 Ag '27:548; H. P. Plomer *ib*. 18 Ag '27:56].

LAUD, ARCHBP. WILLIAM, 1573–1645

11907 **Hirst, W. A.** Archibishop Laud. N&Q ser12 3:298 My '17.

11908 **Bancks, Gerard W.** Archbishop Laud's Devotions. N&Q 163:425 D '32.

11909 **Lillie, W. W.** A manuscript of Laud's. [Whereabouts]. TLS 29 F '36:184.

11910 **Oates, John C. T.** The sale of a duplicate [from Laud's library]. Bod Lib Rec 3no32:175–6 Ag '51.

11911 **Carter, Harry G.** 'Archbishop Laud and scandalous books from Holland [Smuggling of puritan books from Netherlands]' *in* [Woude, S. van der], *ed.* Studia bibliographica in honorem Herman de la Fontaine Verwey. Amstelodami, 1966 [i.e. 1968]. p. 43–55.

LAUDERDALE, RICHARD MAITLAND, 4TH EARL OF, 1653–95 *see* Maitland, Richard, 4th earl of Lauderdale, 1653–95.

LAW, JOHN, 1671–1729

11912 **Law's** Mississippi scheme. [Sale of material relating to]. (Book sales). Scott N&Q 11no1:10–11 Je '97.

11913 **Harsin, Paul.** Étude critique sur la bibliographie des œuvres de Law, avec des mémoires inédits. Liége, H. Vaillant-Carmanne; Paris, É. Champion, 1928. 126p. 25cm. (Bibliothéque de la Faculté philosophie et lettres de l'Université de Liége. Fasc. XXXIX)

LAW, WILLIAM, 1686–1761

11914 **Tennyson,** and William Law. [Sir James Knowles' library]. (Notes on sales). TLS 26 Ap '28:320.

LAWES, HENRY, 1596–1662

11915 **Shawcross, John T.** Henry Lawes's settings of songs for Milton's Comus. J Rutgers Univ Lib 28no1:22–8 D '64.

11916 **Morgan, Paula.** Henry Lawes' Ayres and dialogues. Princeton Univ Lib Chron 30no2:129–31 '69.

LAWES, WILLIAM, d.1645

11917 **Cutts, John P.** British museum additional ms. 31432; William Lawes' writing for the theatre and court. Library ser4 7no4:225–34 D '52. tables.

11918 **Crum, Margaret C.** Notes on the texts of William Lawes's songs in B.M. ms. Add. 31432. Library ser5 9no2:122–7 Je '54. tables.

LAWRENCE, DAVID HERBERT, 1885–1930

11919 **McDonald, Edward D.** Bibliography of D. H. Lawrence. [His own]. TLS 14 Ag '30:653.

11920 **James, Harold E.** Lawrence: Death of a porcupine. [English issue]. Bib N&Q 1no3:6 Ag '35; T. Warburton *ib.* 2no1:1–2 Ja '36; S. Lodge 2no3:2 Ap '36; H. E. James 2no4/5:2 My '36; 2no6:1 Jl '36.

11921 **B.** Lawrence, D. H. The white peacock, London, William Heinemann, 1911. [Issues]. Bib N&Q 2no9:6 Ja '36.

11922 **Powell, Lawrence C.,** *comp.* The manuscripts of D. H. Lawrence; a descriptive catalogue. Los Angeles, Los Angeles public library, 1937. (Repr. New York, Gordon pr., 1972). xi,79p. 23cm.

11923 **Pearce, T. M.** The unpublished Lady Chatterley's lover. New Mexico Q 8no3:171–9 Ag '38.

11924 **Tedlock, Ernest W.** The Frieda Lawrence collection of D. H. Lawrence manuscripts, a descriptive bibiliography. Alberquerque, University of New Mexico pr., 1948. xxxix,333p. facsims. 23cm.

> *Rev:* M. Geismar N.Y. Times Bk R 22 Ag '48:18; H. T. Moore Saturday R Lit 31:17–18 '48; F. J. Hoffman New Mexico Q 218:351–2 '48; R. Humphries Nation 166:724 '48; P. F. Baum South Atlantic Q 47:611 '48; C. I. Glicksberg Southw R 33:416–18 '48; W. White Pa Bib Soc Am 43:93–6 '49.

11925 **Powell, Lawrence C.** D. H. Lawrence. Bks & Libs at Kansas 1no6:1–2 My '54.

11926 **Roberts, F. Warren.** The manuscripts of D. H. Lawrence. Lib Chron Univ Texas 5no3:36–43 '55. [Sg.: Francis W. Roberts.]

11927 **Davis, Herbert.** Women in love, a corrected typescript. Univ Toronto Q 27no1:34–53 Oc '57.

11928 **Barez, Reva R.** The H. Bacon Collamore collection of D. H. Lawrence. Yale Univ Lib Gaz 34no1:16–23 Jl '59.

11929 **Roberts, F. Warren.** Collection: The D. H. Lawrence New Mexico fellowship fund collection. [With checklist of mss.]. Texas Q 3no2:211–16 '60.

11930 **Texas. University. Humanities research center.** The University of New Mexico D. H. Lawrence fellowship fund manuscript collection. Austin, 1960. 13p. port., facsims. 20cm.

11931 **Maxwell, James C.** Lady Chatterley's lover; a correction. N&Q 206:110 Mr '61; M. T. Tudsbery *ib*. 206:149 Ap '61.

11932 **Strickland, Geoffrey.** The poems of D. H. Lawrence. TLS 24 Mr '61:185; V. de S. Pinto *ib*. 31 Mr '61:201; A. Craig 14 Ap '61:233.

11933 **Gliddon, G. M.** D. H. Lawrence. TLS 6 S '63:673; P. R. Fozzard *ib*. 6 S '63:673; J. M. Newton 13 S '63:689; F. May 20 S '63:705; Jessica B. Young; F. May 4 Oc '63:787; A. Arnold 21 N '63:956; F. Carter 28 N '63:993, H. T. Moore 12 D '63:1038.

11934 **Branda, Eldon S.** Textual changes in Women in love. Texas Stud Lang & Lit 6no3:306–21 '64.

11935 **Jarvis, F. P.** A textual comparison of the first British and American editions of D. H. Lawrence's Kangaroo. Pa Bib Soc Am 59:400–24 '65. table.

'Table of substantive and semi-substantive variants' (p. 404–24)

11936 **Secker, Martin.** D. H. Lawrence. [The rainbow]. TLS 3 N '66:1012; T. J. Worthen; P. Hobsbaum *ib*. 10 N '66:1023; M. Secker 17 N '66:1052.

11937 **Dalton, Jack P.** A note on D. H. Lawrence. [Kangaroo]. Pa Bib Soc Am 61:269 '67.

11938 **Pinto, Vivian de Sola** and **F. W. Roberts.** A note on editing The complete poems. D. H. Lawrence R 1no3:213–14 '68.

11939 **Schorer, Mark.** 'David Herbert Lawrence correspondence in the Stanford university library' *in* Lawrence in the war years . . . with a check list of his correspondence in the Charlotte Ashley Felton memorial library of the Stanford university libraries. [Stanford? Calif., 1968]. p. 11–15.

11940 **Smailes, T. A.** More pansies and Last poems; variant readings derived from ms. Roberts E. 192. D. H. Lawrence R 1no3:201–13 '68. facsims.

11941 **Boulton, James T.** D. H. Lawrence's Odour of chrysanthemums, an early version. Renaiss & Mod Stud 13:5–48 '69. facsim.

11942 **Farmer, David R.** The Rainbow prosecution. [Evidence from Methuen stock ledgers]. TLS 4 S '69:979.

LAWRENCE, GEORGE ALFRED, 1827–76

11943 **Roberts, William.** G. A. Lawrence's Songs of feast, field and fray. TLS 4 Jl '35:436; M. Summers *ib.* 11 Jl '35:452; W. Roberts 18 Jl '35:464.

LAWRENCE, JAMES HENRY, 1773–1840

11944 **S., A.** Sir James Lawrence's Empire of the Nairs, 1811. N&Q ser10 3:463–4 Je '05.

LAWRENCE, THOMAS EDWARD, afterwards SHAW, 1888–1935

11945 **Reed, T. German-.** Bibliographical notes on T. E. Lawrence's Seven pillars of wisdom and The revolt in the desert. London, W. & G. Foyle, 1928. 16p. 19cm.

11946 **Hodgson, H. J.** How The seven pillars of wisdom was printed. Monotype Rec 34no2:29 '35.

11947 **Seven** pillars of wisdom [Ms.]. Bod Q Rec 8no87:106–7 '35.

11948 **An important** donation. [The seven pillars of wisdom]. Turnbull Lib Rec 2:18 Jl '40.

11949 **Bowden, Ann.** The T. E. Lawrence collection at the University of Texas. Texas Q 5no3:54–63 '62. illus., facsims.

LAWSON, JOHN, d.1712

11950 **Kirkham, E. Bruce.** The first English editions of John Lawson's Voyage to Carolina: a bibliographical study. Pa Bib Soc Am 61:258–65 '67.

LEAR, EDWARD, 1812–88

11951 **Butler, G. L.** Lear's Book of nonsense. [1846]. TLS 5 S '36:713.

11952 **Osborne, Eric A.** Edward Lear: A book of nonsense. Bib N&Q 2no12:10 My '39.

11953 **Reade, Brian.** The birds of Edward Lear. [Illus.]. Signat new ser 4:3–15 '47. facsims.

11954 **Shaw, John M.** Early American editions of Lear's A book of nonsense. (Query 151). Bk Coll 11no3:353 '62.

11955 **Nixon, Howard M.** The second lithographic edition of Lear's Book of nonsense. [1854]. Brit Mus Q 28no1/2:7–8 '64. illus.

LEE, JOHN, 1779–1859

11956 **Morton, Robert.** Principal John Lee and his Memorials for the Bible societies. Glasgow Bib Soc Rec 4pt1:12–37 '18. facsim.

'An index to principal Lee's Memorials for the Bible societies' (p. 30–7)

LEE, NATHANIEL, 1653?–92

11957 **Ghosh, J. C.** Prologue and epilogue to Lee's Constantine the great. [And Dryden and Otway]. TLS 14 Mr '29:207.

11958 **Bowers, Fredson T.** A crux in the text of Lee's Princess of Cleve, 1689, II.i. Harvard Lib Bull 4no3:409–11 '50.

11959 —— Nathaniel Lee; three probable seventeenth century piracies. Pa Bib Soc Am 44:62–6 '50. tables.

11960 —— The prologue to Nathaniel Lee's Mithridates, 1678. Pa Bib Soc Am 44:173–5 '50.

11961 **McLeod, Alan L.** Nathaniel Lee's work. TLS 1 Jl '55:365.

11962 —— The Douai ms. of Lee's Mithridates. N&Q 205:69–70 F '60.

LEE-HAMILTON, EUGENE, 1845–1905 *see* Hamilton, Eugene Lee-, 1845–1905.

LE FANU, JOSEPH SHERIDAN, 1814–73

11963 **Hibgame, Frederick T.** J. Sheridan Le Fanu's works. N&Q ser12 2:450 D '16; A. Sparke *ib.* 3:15 Ja '17; R. B. 3:59 Ja '17.

11964 **MacManus, Michael J.** Joseph Sheridan Le Fanu. [Request for information]. (Bibliographical notes). Dublin Mag new ser 7no3:57 Jl/S '32.

11965 —— Some points in the bibliography of Joseph Sheridan Le Fanu. (Bibliographical notes). Dublin Mag new ser 9no3:55–7 Jl/S '34.

Repr. in Irish Bk Lover 24no2:36–8 Mr/Ap '36.

11966 **Summers, A. Montague J-M.** A. J. S. Le Fanu. [Miss Laura Mildmay, 1871]. TLS 20 Mr '48:163; H. van Thal *ib.* 3 Ap '48:191.

11967 **Smith, Wilbur J.** Le Fanu's Ghost stories, Dublin, 1851. (Note 293). Bk Coll 17no1:78 '68.

LE GALLIENNE, RICHARD, 1866–1947

11968 **Mead, Herman R.** Richard Le Gallienne's Perseus and Andromeda. [1902]. Pa Bib Soc Am 43:399–401 '49.

11969 **Trevanion, Michael,** *pseud.* A contract of eternall bond of love, confirmed by ...? [Variants of wedding announcement]. (Query 204). Bk Coll 15no2:215 '66.

LEIGH, RICHARD, 1649–1728?

11970 **Hughes, T. Cann.** Leigh's Poems. N&Q 148:81 Ja '25; E. Bensly *ib.* 148:122 F '25.

LELAND, JOHN, 1506?–52

11971 **Clarke, Archibald L.** John Leland and king Henry VIII. Library ser3 2no6:132–49 Ap '11.

LENNOX, LD. WILLIAM PITT, 1799–1881

11972 **Whitley, Alvin.** Lord William Lennox and The tuft-hunter. [Plagiary]. (Notes). Harvard Lib Bull 6no1:125–33 '52.

LESLIE, CHARLES, 1650–1722

11973 **Joost, Nicholas.** Two American editions of Leslie's Short and easie method. N&Q 196:496–7 N '51.

11974 **Madan, Francis F.** An old error once more corrected. [The new association, 1702–3, and Sacheverell]. Library ser5 13no3:207 S '58.

L'ESTRANGE, SIR ROGER, 1616–1704

11975 **Pollard, Alfred W.** Copyright in Josephus. [1702]. Library ser3 8no30:173–6 Ap '17.

11976 **Thornton, Richard H.** The Dissenters sayings, 1685. N&Q ser12 11:172 Ag '22.

LEVER, CHARLES JAMES, 1806–72

11977 **Randall, David A.** [Bibliogr. note on Our mess, 1843–4]. Pa Bib Soc Am 34:274–6 '40.

LEWIS, BENJAMIN, 1884–1959

11978 **Roberts, Gomer M.** Nodyn ar Benjamin Lewis, Casnewydd, Mynwy. [A note on Benjamin Lewis of Casnewydd, Monmouthshire and Howell Harris]. Welsh Bib Soc J 9no4:186–7 Ap '65.

LEWIS, CLIVE STAPLES, 1898–1963

11979 **Hooper, Walter.** C. S. Lewis's mss. TLS 29 F '68:213.

LEWIS, ELLIS, fl.1661

11980 **Bowen, Geraint.** Ystyriaethau Drexelivs ar Dragywyddoldeb, Elis Lewis, Rhydychen, 1661. [Lewis's Welsh version of Ralph Winterton's tr. of Jeremias Drexelius Considerationes de aeternitate]. Welsh Bib Soc J 8no2:81–3 Jl '55.

LEWIS, MATTHEW GREGORY, 1775–1818

11981 **H., T.** The authorship of Tales of terror. [And An apology]. Acad 45:35–6 Ja '94.

11982 **Coykendall, Frederick.** A note on The monk. Coloph new ser 1no1:87–96 Jl '35. facsims.

11983 **Fletcher, Ifan W. K.** M. G. (Monk) Lewis. [Zelinda attrib. to but by Mary G. Lewis]. Bib N&Q 1no4:9 Oc '35.

11984 **Marrott, Harold V.** M. G. Lewis: The monk. [1795]. Bib N&Q 1no1:4 Ja '35; F. Coykendall ib. 1no2:4 Ap '35; 1no3:1 Ag '35.

11985 **Peck, Louis F.** Lewis's Monk. (Bibliographical notes). TLS 7 Mr '35:148; W. Roberts ib. 14 Mr '35:164; E. G. Bayford 28 Mr '35:216; F. Coykendall 25 Ap '35:276.

11986 **Sadleir, Michael T. H.** Tales of terror. [Tales of wonder, 1801]. TLS 7 Ja '39:9–10; W. Beattie ib. 14 Ja '39:26.

11987 **Peck, Louis F.** M. G. Lewis and the Larpent Catalogue. Huntington Lib Q 5no3:382–4 Ap '42.

11988 **Todd, William B.** The early editions and issues of The monk, with a bibliography. Stud Bib 2:3–24 '49.

'Bibliography' (p. 21–4)

11989 **Guthke, Karl S.** Some bibliographical errors concerning the romantic age. Pa Bib Soc Am 51:159–62 '57.

11990 **Peck, Louis F.** The publication of The monk. TLS 23 D '60:829.

11991 —— An early copy of The monk. [1796]. Pa Bib Soc Am 57:350–1 '63.

11992 —— On the date of Tales of wonder. Eng Lang N 2no1:25–7 S '64.

11993 **Lévy, Maurice.** Le manuscrit du Moine de M. G. Lewis. [In Wisbech museum and literary institute]. Caliban 3:129–31 '65.

11994 **Anderson, Howard.** The manuscript of M. G. Lewis's The monk: some preliminary notes. Pa Bib Soc Am 62:427–34 '68.

LEWYNGTON, THOMAS, fl.1503

11995 **Scholderer, J. Victor.** The Art of good lyvyng & good deyng. Brit Mus Q 7no2:41 S '32. [Sg.: V. S.]

LEYBOURN, WILLIAM, 1626–1716?

11996 **Kenney, Cyril E.** William Leybourn, 1626–1716. Library ser5 5no3:159–71 D '50. facsims.

LIDDEL, DUNCAN, 1561–1613

11997 **Anderson, Peter J.** Bibliography of theses: Duncan Liddel. N&Q ser11 7:125–6 F '13; J. R. Magrath *ib.* 7:196 Mr '13.

LIGHT, WILLIAM, 1784–1838

11998 **Steuart, A. Francis.** Col. William Light's publications. N&Q ser10 3:85–6 F '05.

LILLO, GEORGE, 1693–1739

11999 **McBurney, William H.** What George Lillo read, a speculation. Huntington Lib Q 29no3:275–86 My '66. table.

LILLY, WILLIAM, 1602–81

12000 **Roscoe, Sydney.** [Copies of Lilly's Catastrophe mundi, 1683]. (Query no.62). Bk Coll 4no2:172 '55.

LINACRE, THOMAS, 1460?–1524

12001 **Brown, T. Julian.** Thomas Linacre, 1460?–1524. (English scientific autographs, I). Bk Coll 13no3:341 '64. facsim.

LINDSAY, SIR DAVID, 1490–1555

12002 **S., A.** Rare Scottish poetical tract. [Lindsay's The convert's cordial, 1644]. N&Q ser9 8:118–19 Ag '01.

12003 **Hamer, Douglas.** The bibliography of sir David Lindsay, 1490–1555. Library ser4 10no1:1–42 Je '29. facsims., tables.

12004 **Houk, Raymond A.** Versions of Lindsay's Satire of the three estates. Pub Mod Lang Assn 55no2:396–405 Je '40.

LLOYD, DAVID, 1635–92

12005 **Jones, T. Llechid.** The reverend David Lloyd, Trawsfynydd, biographer. (Studies in Welsh book-land, IV). Welsh Bib Soc J 5no6:295–302 Jl '42.

LLOYD, THOMAS, fl.1718

12006 **G., G.** Dau lyfr Cymraeg prin. [Ffordd y gwr cyffredin, 1683; Lloyd's Siccrwydd Neu hyspysrwydd, 1718]. Welsh Bib Soc J 7no3:157–62 Jl '52.

LOCKE, JOHN, 1632–1704

12007 **Roberts, William.** Locke manuscript. N&Q ser10 5:65 Ja '06.

12008 **A Locke** exhibition. [J. & E. Bumpus, London]. (Notes on sales). TLS 5 My '32:336.

12009 **Matthews, William.** Locke's shorthand diaries. TLS 29 S '32:691.

12010 **Hughes, Helen C.** John Locke's library. Bk Coll Q 12:32–40 Oc/D '33.

12011 **MacLean, Kenneth.** John Locke, 1632–1704. [Exhibition]. Yale Univ Lib Gaz 7no3:74–5 Ja '33.

12012 **Goodspeed, George T.** Locke: Human understanding, London, 1690. [Variant imprints]. Bib N&Q 1no4:9 Oc '35; T. Warburton *ib.* 2no4/5:3 My '36; J. M. Keynes, baron Keynes 2no6:2 Jl '36; J. W. Carter 2no9:2 Ja '38; G. G. 2no10:1 Ap '38; J. W. Carter 2no12:1 My '39. [Sg.: G. G.]

12013 **Massey, Dudley.** Locke on education. (Bibliography). TLS 27 F '37:156.

12014 **Alden, John E.** [Bibliogr. note on Locke's Some thoughts concerning education, 1693]. Pa Bib Soc Am 37:309 '43.

12015 **Johnston, Charlotte S.** and **P. Laslett.** Locke's Essay; a fourth manuscript. TLS 25 Jl '52:492; M. Cranston *ib.* 8 Ag '52:517.

12016 **Laslett, Peter.** The 1690 edition of Locke's Two treatises of government: two states. Cambridge Bib Soc Trans 1pt4:341–7 '52.

12016a **Leyden, W. von.** Notes concerning papers of John Locke in the Lovelace collection. Philos Q 2no6:63–9 Ja '52.

12017 **Lough, John.** Locke's reading during his stay in France, 1675–79. Library ser5 8no4:229–58 D '53. tables.

12018 **Further** observations on Locke's Two treatises of government; three contributions by Fredson Bowers, Johan Gerritsen and Peter Laslett. Cambridge Bib Soc Trans 2pt1:63–87 '54.

12019 **Johnston, Charlotte S.** A note on an early draft of Locke's Essay in the Public record office. (VIII. Discussions). Mind 63no250:234–8 Ap '54.

12020 **Hampton, John.** Les traductions françaises de Locke au XVIIIᵉ siècle. R Litt Comparée 29no2:240–51 Av/Juin '55.

12021 **Wyllie, John C.** Locke's Two treatises of government. Library ser5 11no1:53 Mr '56.

12022 **Brown, T. Julian.** John Locke, 1632–1704. (English literary autographs, XXII). Bk Coll 6no2:171 '57. facsims.

12023 **Harrison, John R.** and **P. Laslett.** The library of John Locke. TLS 27 D '57:792.

12024 **Long, Philip.** A summary catalogue of the Lovelace collection of the papers of John Locke in the Bodleian library. Oxford, Ptd. for the [Oxford bibliographical] society at the O.U.P., 1959. xii,64p. facsim. 25cm. (Oxford Bib Soc Pubs new ser 11)

I. Journals and other personal papers.–II. Correspondence.–III. Accounts.–IV. Books.–V. Philosophy and theology.–VI. Money and coinage.–VII. Medicine.–VIII. Natural science.–IX. Trade and the colonies.–X. Miscellaneous papers.–XI. Papers of Peter King.

Rev: TLS 24 Jl '59:440.

12025 **Laslett, Peter.** John Locke's books and papers for his own university. [Oxford]. TLS 11 Mr '60:168.

12026 **Nethery, Wallace.** John Locke's essay on Humane understanding. Am Bk Coll 12no9:13–17 My '62. ports., facsims.

12027 **Long, Philip.** The Mellon donation of additional manuscripts of John Locke from the Lovelace collection. Bod Lib Rec 7no4:185–93 D '64.

'Index of the names . . . used by Locke to mount his Herbarium' (p. 190–3)

12028 **Harrison, John R.** and **P. Laslett.** The library of John Locke. [Oxford] Published for the Oxford bibliographical society by the O.U.P., 1965. (2d ed. 1971). viii,292p. illus., port., facsims. 25cm. (Oxford Bib Soc Pubs new ser XIII)

I. John Locke and his books, an essay by Peter Laslett.–II. Locke's library catalogue.–Appendixes: I. Locke's library in Christ Church, Oxford, July, 1681.–II. A. Books bearing Locke's paraph. B. Interleaved books in Locke's library. C. Books with notes and/or page lists by Locke.–III. Sources of non-Hyde entries.

Rev: J. M. Edelstein Pa Bib Soc Am 60:482–5 '66; TLS 10 F '66:112; E. S. de Beer Library ser5 21:343–7 '66; W. L. Sachse Renaiss Q 20:523–5 '67; J. Y. Yolton J Hist Philos 5:176–8 '67.

12029 **Keynes, sir Geoffrey L.** A note on Locke's library. Cambridge Bib Soc Trans 4pt4:312–13 '67. illus.

12030 **Ashcraft, Richard.** John Locke's library: portrait of an intellectual. Cambridge Bib Soc 5pt1:47–60 '69.

Religion.–Philosophy.–Science.–Politics.–Economics.–The arts.–Summary and conclusion.

12031 **Kelly, Patrick.** A note on Locke's pamphlets on money. Cambridge Bib Soc Trans 5pt1:61–73 '69.

'The list of pamphlet editions and variants' (p. 70–3)

12032 **Harrison, John R.** and **P. Laslett.** The library of John Locke. 2d ed. Oxford, Clarendon pr., 1971. (First pub. 1965). viii,313p. facsims. 26cm.

Adds appendices IV. Division of Locke's library: King-Masham lists.–V. Subject index of Locke's library.

Rev: Pa Bib Soc Am 66:91–2 '72.

LOCKER-LAMPSON, FREDERICK, 1821–95 *see* Lampson, Frederick Locker-, 1821–95.

LOCKHART, JOHN GIBSON, 1794–1854

12033 **Abrahams, Aleck.** The Ballantyne-Lockhart controversy. [Letter from Dilke concerning]. N&Q ser11 8:266 Oc '13.

12034 **Cook, T. Davidson.** Lockhart's treatment of Scott's Letters. Ninet Cent 102no607:382–98 S '27.

12035 **Chapman, Robert W.** The Bridal of Triermain, and Harold the dauntless. R Eng Stud 4no15:330–1 Jl '28.

12036 **Strout, Alan L.** John Gibson Lockhart, III. Revisions in Lockhart's novels. N&Q 175:399–404 D '38.

12037 **Carter, John W.** J. G. Lockhart: Ancient Spanish ballads, 1823. [Variant TP]. Bib N&Q 2no12:10 My '39.

12038 **Parker, W. M.** Peter's letters to his kinsfolk. [And Christopher North]. (Bibliography). TLS 22 Je '40:308; 29 Je '40:320; T. D. Cook *ib.* 6 Jl '40:327; W. M. Parker 13 Jl '40:339; J. C. Ewing 20 Jl '40:351.

Extracts in Blackwood.–Love of mystification.–Imaginary editions.–A first edition?–The Black Bull inn.–Prosecution threatened.

12039 **Hart, Francis R.** Proofreading Lockhart's Scott: the dynamics of biographical reticence. Stud Bib 14:3–22 '61.

LODGE, THOMAS, 1558?–1625

12040 **Roberts, William.** Thomas Lodge's Rosalynd. Athenæum 3883:404–5 Mr '02.

12041 **Arkle, A. H.** The Flowers of Lodowicke of Granada. N&Q ser10 5:246–7 Mr '06.

12042 **Wilson, John D.** This missing title of Thomas Lodge's reply to Gosson's School of abuse. [A defence of poetry = Honest excuses]. Mod Lang R 3no2:166–8 Ja '08.

12043 **Baskervill, Charles R.** A prompt copy of a Looking glass for London and England. Mod Philol 30no1:29–51 Ag '32. facsims.

LOFFT, CAPEL, 1751–1824

12044 **Sparrow, John H. A.** Capel Lofft. [Mss.]. TLS 14 Mr '36:224.

LONGLAND, BP. JOHN, 1473–1547

12045 **Hiscock, Walter G.** John Longland. [A sermon, 1535]. TLS 31 D '31:1053.

LONGUEVILLE, PETER, fl.1727

12046 **Esdaile, Arundell J. K.** Author and publisher in 1727: The English hermit. Library ser4 2no3:185–92 D '21.

LOVELACE, RICHARD, 1618–58

12047 **Evans, Willa McC.** Early Lovelace text. [When I by thy fair shape did swear]. Pub Mod Lang Assn 60no2:382–5 Je '45. facsims.

12048 —— Richard Lovelace's Mock-song. [Ms.]. Philol Q 24no4:317–28 Oc '45. facsims.

12049 **Cutts, John P.** John Wilson and Lovelace's The rose. [Ms.]. N&Q 198:153–4 Ap '53.

12050 **Nathan, Norman.** Lovelace's 'flie'. [To Lucasta]. N&Q 200:428–9 Oc '55.

LOWNDES, WILLIAM THOMAS, 1798?–1843

12051 **Isaacs, J. H.** On a new edition of Lowndes' Bibliographical manual. Bib Soc Trans 2pt1:14 '94.

Report of a paper read 18 D '93; *also in* Bib Soc News-sh 1:1–3 F '94.

12052 **Matthews, Albert.** Lowndes's Bibliographer's manual. N&Q ser11 6:103–4 Ag '12; W. F. Prideaux; A. Abrahams *ib.* 6:191–2 S '12; A. L. Humphreys 6:275–6 Oc '12.

12053 **Cole, George W.** W. T. Lowndes. [Bibliographer's manual]. TLS 6 N '34:604.

12054 —— Lowndes and his works. N&Q 168:245 Ap '35.

12055 —— William Thomas Lowndes. [Bibliographer's manual, pub. in parts]. Bib N&Q 1no3:8 Ag '35.

12056 **Cole, George W.** Do you know your Lowndes? A bibliographical essay on William Thomas Lowndes and incidentally on Robert Watt and Henry G. Bohn. Pa Bib Soc Am 33:1–22 '39.

LYDGATE, JOHN, 1370?–1451?

12057 **Steele, Robert.** An unknown Lydgate edition. [Governance of kings and princes, 1511]. TLS 16 F '22:109; 2 Mr '22:141.

12058 **Bühler, Curt F.** A note on Lydgate's Verses on the kings of England. [Ms.]. R Eng Stud 9no33:47–50 Ja '33.

12059 —— The British museum's fragment of Lydgate's Horse, sheep, and goose printed by William Caxton. Pa Bib Soc Am 43:397–8 '49.

12060 **Morgan, Margery M.** A specimen of early printer's copy, Rylands English ms. 2. [Lydgate's Falls of princes]. (Notes and news). Bull John Rylands Lib 33no2:194–6 Mr '51.

12061 **Bühler, Curt F.** Wynkyn de Worde's printing of Lydgate's Horse, sheep, and goose. Pa Bib Soc Am 46no4:392–3 '52.

12062 **Klinefetter, Ralph A.** Lydgate's Life of our lady and the Chetham ms. 6709. [Ms. copy of Caxton's 1484 ed.]. Pa Bib Soc Am 46:396–7 '52.

12063 **Ringler, William.** Lydgate's Serpent of division, 1559, edited by John Stow. Stud Bib 14:201–3 '61.

LYLY, JOHN, 1554?–1606

12064 **Spingarn, J. E.** Euphues. N&Q ser8 4:385–6 N '93; J. F. Palmer *ib*. 5:37 Ja '94.

12065 **Fowler, J. T.** Verses on The bee. [Ms.]. Mod Lang R 13no2:319–20 Ap '18.

LYNDSAY, SIR DAVID, 1490–1555 *see* Lindsay, sir David, 1490–1555.

LYTTLETON, GEORGE, 1ST BARON LYTTLETON, 1709–73

12066 **Todd, William B.** Variant editions of Lyttleton's To the memory of a lady lately deceased. Pa Bib Soc Am 44:274–5 '50. table.

12067 —— Multiple editions of Lyttleton's The court-secret, 1741. Pa Bib Soc Am 47:380–1 '53. tables.

12068 —— Patterns in press figures: a study of Lyttleton's Dialogues of the dead. Stud Bib 8:230–5 '56. tables.

LYTTON, EDWARD GEORGE EARLE LYTTON BULWER-, 1ST BARON LYTTON, 1803–73

12069 **Flower, Robin E. W.** The Coming race, and Marah. [Ptrs. copy]. Brit Mus Q 11no2:77–8 Mr '37.

12070 **Barnes, James J.** Edward Lytton Bulwer and the publishing firm of Harper & brothers. Am Lit 38:35–48 Mr '66. table.

'The major writings of Edward Lytton Bulwer' (p. 46–8)

LYTTON, EDWARD ROBERT BULWER, 1ST EARL OF LYTTON, 1831–91

12071 **White, Frederick C.** Lytton and his publisher. [Routledge]. N&Q 158:222 Mr '30; A. Sparke ib. 158:265 Ap '30.

12072 **Dickson, Sarah A.** The Bulwer-Lytton collection [of M. L. Parrish]. Princeton Univ Lib Chron 8no1:28–32 N '46.

12073 **Dobson, C. S. A.** By Lytton or Grenville Murray? [The press and the public service. By a distinguished writer, 1857]. (Query no.73). Bk Coll 5no3:281–2 '56.

MABBE, JAMES, 1572–1642?

12074 **Secord, Arthur W.** I. M. of the First folio Shakespeare and other Mabbe problems. J Eng Germ Philol 47no4:374–81 Oc '48.

MACARTNEY, GEORGE, 1ST EARL MACARTNEY, 1737–1806

12075 **Furber, Holden.** A preliminary report on the Macartney manuscripts. Lib Chron Univ Pennsylvania 21no2:43–50 '55.

12076 **Darwin, K.** Macartney manuscripts. N&Q 201:316 Jl '56.

12077 —— [Same]: TLS 22 Je '56:377.

12078 **Byng, J. Cranmer-.** Lord Macartney's journal. N&Q 203:87 F '58.

MACAULAY, THOMAS BABINGTON, 1ST BARON MACAULAY, 1800–59

12079 **MacKenzie, W. Douglas.** A Macaulay find? [History of England with corrections]. TLS 21 Ap '32:291.

12080 **Muir, Percival H.** Macaulay: View of the history of France. Bib N&Q 2no1:4 Ja '36; J. W. Carter *ib.* 2no3:3 Ap '36; [P. H. Muir] 2no8:1 F '37. [Sg.: P. H. M.]

12081 **Munby, Alan N. L.** Macaulay's library; being the twenty-eighth lecture in the David Murray foundation ... 1965. Glasgow, Jackson, 1966. 35p. 22cm. ([Glasgow Univ Pubs. David Murray lectures, 28])

Rev: TLS 4 Ag '66:716.

MACDONALD, GEORGE, 1824–1905

12082 **A George** MacDonald collection. [T. W. Broadley, Sheffield]. Scott N&Q ser3 8no8:151 Ag '30.

12083 **Hutton, Muriel.** The George MacDonald collection, Brander library, Huntly. [W. Will libr.]. Bk Coll 17no1:13–25 '68. illus., facsims.

MACHEN, ARTHUR LLEWELYN JONES, 1863–1947

12084 **Garland, Herbert.** Arthur Machen and his collected books. Bkmns J new ser 7no13:3–4 Oc '22. facsim.

12085 **Van Patten, Nathan.** Arthur Machen, a bibliographical note. Queen's Q 33no3:351–4 Ja/Mr '26.

12086 —— An unacknowledged work of Arthur Machen? [Tobacco talk, 1886]. Pa Bib Soc Am 20pt1/2:95–7 '26.

12087 **Thom, Ian W.** The Arthur Machen collection [in the Library]. Princeton Univ Lib Chron 26no2:113–14 '65.

MACKENZIE, HENRY, 1745–1831

12088 **Richmond, Helen M.** Mackenzie's translations from the German. Mod Lang R 17no4:412 Oc '22.

12089 **Weir, John L.** Henry Mackenzie, The man of feeling. N&Q 192:15 Ja '47.

MACKLIN, CHARLES, 1697?–1797

12090 **Matthews, William.** The piracies of Macklin's Love à-la-mode. R Eng Stud 10no39:311–18 Jl '34.

12091 **MacMillan, W. Dougald.** The censorship in the case of Macklin's The man of the world. Huntington Lib Bull 10:79–101 Oc '36.

12092 **Findlay, Robert R.** Macklin's legitimate acting version of Love à la mode. Philol Q 45no4:749–60 Oc '66.

MACKY, JOHN, d.1726

12093 **V., W. I. R.** Macky's Court characters. [Ms.]. N&Q ser9 5:165–6 Mr '00; R. A. S. Macfie *ib.* 5:364 My '00.

12094 **Trench, W. F.** and **K. B. Garratt.** On Swift's marginalia in copies of Macky's Memoirs. Library ser4 19no3:354–62 D '38.

MACLAREN, ARCHIBALD, fl.1857–74

12095 **Green, Roger L.** Burne Jones and The fairy family. TLS 26 Ag '44:420.

MACNEICE, FREDERICK LOUIS, 1907–63

12096 **Stoddard, F. G.** The Louis MacNeice collection. Lib Chron Univ Texas 8no4:50–5 '68.

'Desiderata' (p. 55)

MACNEVIN, THOMAS, fl.1845

12097 **MacGrath, Kevin.** Thomas MacNevin's copy of The nation. Irish Bk Lover 31no5:98–100 F '51.

'Index of articles written by me' (p. 99)

MACPHERSON, JAMES, 1736–96

12098 **Perrot, Francis.** Collection of poems. [An original collection of the poems of Ossian and other bards, 1816]. N&Q ser8 6:388 N '94.

12099 **S.** Ossian. N&Q 156:335 My '29; A. Sparke *ib.* 156:396–7 Je '29.

12100 **Todd, William B.** Macpherson's Fingal and Temora. (Note 122). Bk Coll 8no4:429–30 '59.

MAGINN, WILLIAM, 1793–1842

12101 **McMahon, Morgan.** Dr. Maginn's writings. N&Q ser11 1:507 Je '10; Editor, Irish Book Lover [i.e. J. S. Crone]; W. A. H.; W. Scott *ib.* 2:74–5 Jl '10.

MAITLAND, RICHARD, 4TH EARL OF LAUDERDALE, 1653–95

12102 **Boddy, Margaret P.** A manuscript of Lauderdale's Georgics. N&Q 206:433 N '61.

12103 —— Dryden-Lauderdale relationships; some bibliographical notes and a suggestion. Philol Q 42no2:267–72 Ap '63.

12104 —— The manuscripts and printed editions of the translation of Virgil made by Richard Maitland, fourth earl of Lauderdale, and the connexion with Dryden. N&Q 210:144–50 Ap '65.

MAJOR, JOHN, 1469–1550

12105 [Johnston, George P.]. John Major's History, 1521. [With illus. of ptg. pr.]. Edinburgh Bib Soc Pub 4pt1:104 Oc '00. facsim.

MALCOLME, DAVID, d.1748

12106 Phillips, D. Rhys. Malcolm's Antiquities. [Issues]. (Bibliographical notes). Welsh Bib Soc J 1no7:227–8 Ag '14. [Sg.: D. R. P.]

MALLET, DAVID, 1705?–65

12107 Sleigh, Gordon F. The authorship of William and Margaret. Library ser5 8no2:121–3 Je '53.

MALONE, EDMOND, 1741–1812

12108 Greg, sir Walter W. Editors at work and play, a glimpse of the eighteenth century. R Eng Stud 2no6:173–6 Ap '26.

12109 Jaggard, William. Malone's Inquiry. [And W. H. Ireland]. N&Q 169:103–4 Ag '35.

12110 Smith, David Nichol. Edmond Malone. Huntington Lib Q 3no1:23–36 Oc '39.

12111 Chapman, Robert W. Cancels in Malone's Dryden. [1800]. Library ser4 23no2/3:131 S/D '42.

12112 Tillotson, Arthur, ed. The correspondence of Thomas Percy & Edmond Malone. [Baton Rouge] Louisiana state U.P., 1944. xxv,302p. 23cm. (The Percy letters [1])

12113 Osborn, James M. Edmond Malone and Baratariana. [1772]. N&Q 188:35 Ja '45.

12114 Brown, Arthur. Edmond Malone and English scholarship, an inaugural lecture delivered at University college, London, 23 May, 1963. London, Published for the College by H. K. Lewis [1963]. 18p. 25cm.

Rev: S. Wells Mod Lang R 60:427–8 '65; J. K. Walton N&Q 210:36–7 '65.

12115 Osborn, James M. Edmond Malone: scholar-collector. Library ser5 19:11–37 '64. facsims., tables.

12116 Walton, James K. Edmond Malone, an Irish Shakespeare scholar. Hermathena 99:5–26 '64. port., facsims.

12117 **Sen, Sailendra K.** 'The noblest Roman of them all: Malone and Shakespearian scholarship' *in* Presidency college, Calcutta. Dept. of English. Shakespeare commemoration volume. Calcutta, 1966. p. 64–85.

MALORY, SIR THOMAS, d.1471

12118 **Oakeshott, Walter F.** The text of Malory. TLS 27 S '34:650.

12119 —— Caxton and Malory's Morte darthur. Gutenberg Jahrb 1935:112–16 '35. facsim.

12120 **Vinaver, Eugène.** A note on the earliest printed texts of Malory's Morte darthur. [Uncorrected pages show Caxton's 1485 ed. was ptd. in 8s]. Bull John Rylands Lib 23no1:102–6 Ap '39.

12121 **Gaines, Barry.** A forgotten artist: John Harris and the Rylands copy of Caxton's edition of Malory. Bull John Rylands Lib 52no1:115–28 '69.

MANDEVILLE, BERNARD, 1670?–1733

12122 **Shorter, Clement.** The Fable of the bees. N&Q ser12 8:433 My '21; W. S. B. H. *ib.* 8:499 Je '21.

MANDEVILLE, SIR JOHN, d.1372

12123 **Letts, Malcolm H. I.** Sir John Mandeville. IV. Manuscripts and printed editions. N&Q 192:134–6 Ap '47.

12124 —— The source of the woodcuts in Wynkyn de Worde's edition of Mandeville's Travels, 1499. Library ser5 6no3:154–61 D '51. table.

'Table showing de Worde's woodcuts with references to Vesler's edition of 1482 and East's edition of 1568' (p. 157–61)

12125 **Bennett, Josephine W.** The woodcut illustrations in the English editions of Mandeville's travels. Pa Bib Soc Am 47:59–69 '53.

12126 **Seymour, M. C.** The early English editions of Mandeville's travels. Library ser5 19:202–7 '64.

Pynson's edition.–De Worde's editions.–East's editions.–After East.

MANGNALL, RICHMAL, 1769–1820

12127 **Briggs, W. G.** The early editions of Mangnall's Questions. Library ser5 9no1:53–5 Mr '54.

MANLEY, MARY (DE LA RIVIÈRE), 1663–1724

12128 **Weekley, A. S.** A concealed edition? [Mrs. Manley's Secret memoirs and manners, 1709]. (Query no.33) Bk Coll 2no2:158 '53.

MANNINGHAM, JOHN, d.1622

12129 **Hotson, Leslie.** Manningham's 'mid . . .'. TLS 9 S '49:585.

12130 **Race, Sydney.** Manningham's Diary. [And Collier]. N&Q 195:218 My '50.

12131 —— Manningham's diary: the case for re-examination. [And Collier] N&Q 199:380–3 S '54.

MANSFIELD, KATHERINE, *pseud. of* **KATHLEEN (BEAUCHAMP) MURRY, 1888–1923**

12132 **Morris, Guy N.** Katherine Mansfield additions. (Bibliography and sales). TLS 13 Jl '40:344.

12133 —— Katherine Mansfield: early London days. Hist & Bib 2:102–5 Ag '48.

12134 —— Katherine Mansfield, the New Zealand period. Hist & Bib 1:28–32 Ap '48.

12135 **Taylor, Clyde R. H.** The purchase of Katherine Mansfield manuscripts. Turnbull Lib Rec 14:16–19 Mr '60. [Sg.: C. R. H. T.]

MARKHAM, GERVASE, 1568?–1637

12136 **Fussell, George E.** The farming books of Gervase Markham, 1568?–1637. N&Q 175:39–41 Jl '38.

MARLOW, JOHN, fl.1662–85

12137 **Esplin, David G.** J. M. Letters to a sick friend, 1682. (Query 132). Bk Coll 9no4:456–7 '60.

MARLOWE, CHRISTOPHER, 1564–93

12138 **Slater, J. Herbert.** Some Marlowe riddles. Athenæum 4065:411–12 S '05; J. H. Ingram *ib.* 4069:552 Oc '05; *rf.* J. LeG. Brereton 4078:868 D '05.

12139 **Smith, George C. Moore.** Marlowe's Dr. Faustus. [Emendations]. N&Q ser10 9:65 Ja '08.

12140 **Brooke, C. F. Tucker.** On the date of the first edition of Marlowe's Edward II. Mod Lang N 24no3:71–3 Mr '09.

12141 **Holthausen, F.** Zur Textkritik von Marlowe's Jew of Malta. Eng Studien 40no3:395–401 Juni '09.

12142 **Brereton, J. LeGay.** Marlowe: some textual notes. Mod Lang R 6no1:94–6 Ja '11.

12143 **Taylor, A. E.** Marlowe's Dr. Faustus. [Text]. TLS 6 D '17:597; K. Loewenfeld; P. Z. Round *ib.* 20 D '17:637.

12144 **Brooke, C. F. Tucker.** The Marlowe canon. Pub Mod Lang Assn 37no3:367–417 S '22. table.

I. The authentic works.—II. Spurious works.

12145 **Dido** queen of Carthage, 1594. (Notes on sales). TLS 22 F '23:128.

12146 **Fermor, Una M. Ellis-.** The 1592 8vo of Tamburlaine. TLS 2 My '29:362.

12147 **Brooke, C. F. Tucker.** Notes on Marlowe's Doctor Faustus. Philol Q 12no1:17–23 Ja '33.

I. Bibliographical.—II. Commentary and textual notes.

12148 **Tannenbaum, Samuel A.** 'A study of the Collier leaf [Massacre at Paris]' *in* Shaksperian scraps and other Elizabethan fragments. New York, 1933. p. 177–86.

12149 **Adams, Joseph Q.** The Massacre at Paris leaf. Library ser4 14no4:447–69 Mr '34. facsims.

'Unedited transcript of the fragment, by dr. Greg' (p. 468–9)

12150 **Dam, Bastiaan A. P. van.** The Collier leaf; a text-critical detective story. [The massacre at Paris]. Eng Stud 16no5:166–73 Oc '34.

12151 —— Marlowe's Tamburlaine. Eng Stud 16no1:1–17 F '34; 16no2:49–58 Ap '34.

12152 **Pitcher, Seymour M.** Some observations on the 1663 edition of Faustus. Mod Lang N 56no8:588–94 D '41.

12153 **Greg, sir Walter W.** The copyright of Hero and Leander. Library ser4 24no3/4:165–74 D/Mr '43/4.

12154 **Nosworthy, J. M.** The Marlowe manuscript. [Massacre at Paris]. Library ser4 26no2/3:158–71 S/D '45.

Appendix 1. A collated transcript of the fragment.–Appendix 2. The manuscript in relation to the octavo.

12155 **Kirschbaum, Leo.** The good and bad quartos of Doctor Faustus. Library ser4 26no4:272–94 Mr '46. tables.

12156 **Nosworthy, J. M.** Some textual anomalies in the 1604 Doctor Faustus. Mod Lang R 41no1:1–8 Ja '46.

12157 **Bowers, Fredson T.** The text of Marlowe's Faustus. [Review article on Greg's 1950 ed.]. Mod Philol 49no3:195–204 F '52.

12158 **Maxwell, James C.** How bad is the text of The jew of Malta? Mod Lang R 48no4:435–8 Oc '53.

12159 **Nosworthy, J. M.** Publication of Marlowe's Elegies and Davies's Epigrams. R Eng Stud new ser4:260–1 Jl '53.

See also no. 12162.

12160 **Fabian, Bernhard.** Marlowe's Doctor Faustus. [Text]. N&Q 201:56–7 F '56.

12161 **Welsh, Robert F.** Evidence of Heywood spellings in The jew of Malta. Renaiss Pa 1963:3–9 '63.

12162 **Nosworthy, J. M.** Marlowe's Ovid and Davies's Epigrams; a postscript. R Eng Stud new ser 15no60:397–8 N '64.

See also no. 12159.

12163 **Welsh, Robert F.** The printer of the 1594 octavo of Marlowe's Edward II. [Robert Robinson]. Stud Bib 17:197–8 '64.

12164 **Oliver, Harold J.** Marlowe's Massacre at Paris. TLS 11 N '65:1003.

MARMION, SHACKERLEY, 1603–39

12165 **Maxwell, Sue.** A misprint in Marmion's Holland's leaguer. Mod Lang R 39no2:179–80 Ap '44.

MARRYAT, FREDERICK, 1792–1848

12166 **J., C. P.** The bibliography of Marryat. [Peter Simple]. (Correspondence). London Merc 3no14:199 D '20.

12167 **Pierpont, Robert.** Marryat bowdlerized. N&Q 152:313–14 Ap '27.

12168 **Captain** Marryat. (Notes on sales). TLS 31 Mr '32:232.

12169 **Bader, Arno L.** Captain Marryat and the American pirates. Library ser4 16no3:327–36 D '35.

12170 **Randall, David A.** Marryat: Valerie, 1849. [Collaborator]. Bib N&Q 2no3:7 Ap '36. [Sg.: D. R.]

12171 **Sadleir, Michael T. H.** Captain Marryat: The children of the new forest, 1847. Bib N&Q 2no9:6–9 Ja '38.

MARSTON, JOHN, 1575?–1634

12172 **Brereton, J. LeGay.** Notes on the text of Marston. Eng Studien 33no2:224–38 D '03.

12173 **Brettle, Robert E.** Bibliographical notes on some Marston quartos and early collected editions. Library ser4 8no3:336–48 D '27. table.

> 1. The three states of the first edition of The malcontent, 1604.–2. The relation of the second to the first edition of The fawn, 1606.–3. The insatiate countess, 1613, 1616, 1631.–4. William Sheare's collected edition, 1633, first issue.–5. The 1652 collection.

12174 —— More bibliographical notes on Marston. Library ser4 12no2: 235–42 S '31.

> The three editions of The scourge of villanie.—Play quartos and type kept standing.

12175 **Lea, Kathleen M.** An emendation for satire X of The scourge of villanie. R Eng Stud 7no27:334–6 Jl '31.

12176 **Brettle, Robert E.** Marston bibliography; a correction. [The fawn, 1606]. Library ser4 15no2:241–2 S '34.

12177 **Halstead, W. L.** An explanation for the two editions of Marston's Fawne. Stud Philol 40no1:25–32 Ja '43.

12178 **Turner, Robert K.** The composition of The insatiate countess, Q2. Stud Bib 12:198–203 '59. tables.

12179 **Maxwell, James C.** A reading in Marston. [The fawn]. N&Q 206:195 My '61; G. Smith ib. 206:397 Oc '61.

12180 **Brettle, Robert E.** Notes on John Marston. R Eng Stud new ser 13no52:390–3 N '62.

> 1. Handwriting.–2. Life, 1605–16.

MARTIN, SARAH CATHERINE, 1768–1826

12181 **Wright, S. G.** Old mother Hubbard. Bod Q Rec 8no91:236–7 '36; 8no92:271–2 '36/7.

MARTIN, VIOLET FLORENCE, 1865–1915 *see* Ross, Martin, pseud.

MARTYN, EDWARD, 1859–1923

12182 **Miller, Liam** and **Ann Saddlemyer.** Unpublished revisions to an Edward Martyn essay. (Bibliographical notes). Irish Bk 2no3/4:130–3 '63.

MARTYN, THOMAS, 1735–1825

12183 **Henrey, Blanche.** An incorrect attribution to Thomas Martyn. [A short account of the late donation, 1713, by Richard Walker]. J Soc Bib Nat Hist 3pt1:17 D '53.

12184 **Lyle, I. F.** Thomas Martyn's The universal conchologist: an early copy and a theory. J Soc Bib Nat Hist 5pt2:141–3 Ap '69.

MARVELL, ANDREW, 1621–78

12185 **Drury, George Thorn-.** Marvell's poems, 1681. N&Q ser10 7:423–4 Je '07.

12186 **Margoliouth, Herschel M.** Marvell's Thyrsis and Dorinda. TLS 19 My '50:309.

12187 **Macdonald, Hugh.** Andrew Marvell's Miscellaneous poems, 1681. [Ms.]. TLS 13 Jl '51:444; 24 Ag '51:533.

12188 **Howarth, R. Guy.** Marvell: an emendation. [To his noble friend mr. Richard Lovelace]. N&Q 198:330 Ag '53.

12189 **Senn, G. T.** The text of Marvell's Poems. N&Q 200:302 Jl '55.

MASEFIELD, JOHN EDWARD, 1878–1967

12190 **Cooper, Guy.** Mr. Masefield's bibliography. [A young man's fancy]. (Correspondence). London Merc 2no12:728 Oc '20.

12191 **Masefield:** A poem and two plays, London, 1919. [TP cancel]. Bib N&Q 2no11:9 N '38.

12192 **Drew, Fraser B.** John Masefield in New Haven: the Sumner McKnight Crosby collection. Yale Univ Lib Gaz 32no4:151–7 Ap '58. facsim.

'John Masefield: desiderata' (p. 157)

12193 —— Some contributions to the bibliography of John Masefield. Pa Bib Soc Am 53:188–96,262–7 '59.

12194 **Tanselle, G. Thomas.** Three unrecorded issues of Masefield's Tragedy of Nan. Library ser5 23no2:145–7 Je '68.

MASON, WILLIAM, 1724–97

12195 **Gaskell, J. Philip W.** William Mason. TLS 11 My '51:293.

12196 **Todd, William B.** Duplicate editions of Mason's Musaeus, 1747. Pa Bib Soc Am 46:397–8 '52. table.

MASSINGER, PHILIP, 1583–1640

12197 **Warner, George F.** An autograph play of Philip Massinger. [Believe as you list]. Athenæum 3821:90–1 Ja '01. [Sg.: G. F. W.]

12198 **Greg, sir Walter W.** Massinger's autograph corrections in The duke of Milan, 1623. Library ser4 4no3:207–18 D '23. tables.

Repr. in Maxwell, James C., *ed.* Collected papers. Oxford, 1966. p. [110]–19.

12199 **Cruickshank, A. H.** Massinger corrections. Library ser4 5no2:175–9 S '24.

12200 **Greg, sir Walter W.** More Massinger corrections. Library ser4 5no1:59–91 Je '24. facsims., tables.

Repr. in Maxwell, James C., *ed.* Collected papers. Oxford, 1966. p. [120]–48.

12200a **Tannenbaum, Samuel A.** Corrections in the text of Believe as you list. [Arthur Symons' ed., 1889]. Pub Mod Lang Assn 42no3:777–81 S '27.

12201 **McIlwraith, A. K.** Patrons of The city-madam. [Presentation copies]. Bod Q Rec 5no58:248–9 Ag '28.

12202 **Eight** plays of Massinger. (Notes on sales). TLS 9 My '29:388.

12203 **McIlwraith, A. K.** Some bibliographical notes on Massinger. Library ser4 11no1:78–92 Je '30. tables.

12204 —— A further patron of The city-madam. [Presentation copy]. Bod Q Rec 8no85:17–18 '35.

12205 —— The printer's copy for The city-madam. Mod Lang N 50no3:173–4 Mr '35.

12206 **Gray, J. E.** Still more Massinger corrections. Library ser5 5no2:132–9 S '50. table.

12207 **McIlwraith, A. K.** The manuscript corrections in Massinger's plays. Library ser5 6no3:213–16 D '51. table.

MAUGHAM, WILLIAM SOMERSET, 1874–1965

12208 **Muir, Percival H.** William Somerset Maugham, some bibliographical observations. Bk Coll Q 9:72–84 Ja/Mr '33; 10:19–26 Ap/Je '33.

12209 **Maugham:** Liza of Lambeth. ['stomach' for 'belly']. Bib N&Q 1no1:7 Ja '35.

12210 **Maugham:** The painted veil. [States]. Bib N&Q 2no4/5:11 My '36.

12211 **Muir, Percival H.** Maugham: Cosmopolitains, 1936. [States]. Bib N&Q 2no4/5:10 My '36. [Sg.: P. H. M.]

12212 **M., G.** Maugham: Of human bondage. [Misprint, p. 257, line 4]. Bib N&Q 2no8:8 F '37.

12213 **Jonas, Klaus E.** More Maughamiana. Pa Bib Soc Am 44:378–83 '50.

12214 **Runnquist, Åbe.** Maughamiana. TLS 10 Mr '50:153.

12215 **Van Patten, Nathan.** Icelandic translations of Maugham. Pa Bib Soc Am 45:158–9 '51.

12216 **A Maugham** manuscript. [Theatre]. Princeton Univ Lib Chron 15no2:109 '54.

12217 **Wing, Donald G.** The manuscript of Somerset Maugham's On a Chinese screen [acquired]. Yale Univ Lib Gaz 29no3:126 Ja '55.

12218 **Jonas, Klaus W.** W. Somerset Maugham collections in America. Jahrb für Amerikastudien 3:205–13 '59.

12219 **Kendall, Lyle H.** The first edition of The moon and sixpence. Pa Bib Soc Am 55:242–3 '61.

12220 **Heywood, C.** Two printed texts of Somerset Maugham's Mrs. Craddock. Eng Lang N 5no1:39–46 S '67.

MAURICE, HUGH, 1775?–1825

12221 **Jones, Evan D.** Hugh Maurice (?1775–1825), a forgotten scribe. (Biographica et bibliographica). Nat Lib Wales J 1no4:230–2 '40.

MAVOR, OSBORNE HENRY, 1888–1951 *see* Bridie, James, *pseud.*

MAYER, CHARLES, fl.1894

12222 **Doughty, George W.** The Shadows of life. (Query 92). Bk Coll 7no1:77 '58.

MAYNE, JASPER, 1604–72

12223 **Greg, sir Walter W.** The printing of Mayne's plays. Oxford Bib Soc Proc 1pt4:255–62 '26.

12224 **Levinson, Harry A.** Mayne's Part of Lucian made English, 1663. [Cancels]. (Note 305). Bk Coll 18no1:90 '69.

MEDWALL, HENRY, fl.1486

12225 **Jones, Claude E.** Notes on Fulgens and Lucres. [Text]. Mod Lang N
50no8:508–9 D '35.

MELBANCKE, BRIAN, fl.1583

12226 **Maud, Ralph.** The date of Brian Melbancke's Philotimus. [1582?].
Library ser5 11no2:118–20 Je '56.

MENNES, SIR JOHN, 1599–1671

12227 **K., L. L.** Musarum deliciæ, 1656. N&Q ser 11 8:509 D '13; P. Norman; R.
Pierpont *ib.* 9:37 Ja '14.

MENNONS, JOHN, 1747–1818

12228 **Gourlay, James J.** John Mennons; an early Glasgow journalist. Glasgow
Bib Soc Rec 9:58–72 '31.

'Publications by John Mennons, so far as yet traced' (p. 72)

MERBURY, FRANCIS, fl.1579

12229 **Tannenbaum Samuel A.** Comments on The marriage of Wit and
Wisdom. Philol Q 9no4:321–40 Oc '30.

12230 **Greg, sir Walter W.** The date of Wit and Wisdom. Philol Q 11no4:410 Oc
'32; S. A. Tannenbaum *ib.* 12no1:88–90 Ja '33.

12231 **Tilley, Morris P.** Notes on The marriage of Wit and Wisdom. Sh Assn
Bull 10no1:45–57 Ja '35; 10no2:89–94 Ap '35.

12232 **Race, Sydney.** The Marriage of Wit and Wisdom. [And Collier]. N&Q
198:18–20 Ja '53.

12233 —— The Moral play of Wit and Science. [And Collier]. N&Q 198:96–9
Mr '53.

MEREDITH, GEORGE, 1828–1909

12234 **Mss.** of Meredith's novels. Athenæum 4278:493–4 Oc '09.

12235 **A Meredith** collection. [Frank Atschul]. (Notes on sales). TLS 25 Je
'31:516.

12236 **Purdy, Richard L.** The Altschul collection of George Meredith. Yale Univ
Lib Gaz 6no1:11–13 Jl '31.

12237 **Brett, Oliver S. B., 3d viscount Esher.** Meredith: Poems and lyrics, 1883.
[Issues]. Bib N&Q 2no1:4 Ja '36; P. S. O'Hegarty *ib.* 2no11:2 N '38. [Sg.:
Esher.]

12238 **Burton, Margaret.** Meredith's Poems. (Bibliographical notes). TLS 17 D '38:808.

12239 **Carter, John W.** Meredith, George: The egoist, 1879. [Variant binding]. Bib N&Q 2no10:10 Ap '38; P. S. O'Hegarty *ib.* 2no11:6 N '38.

12240 **O'Hegarty, Patrick S.** Meredith, George: Collected poems, 1912. [Variant binding]. Bib N&Q 2no11:9 N '38.

12241 **Carter, John W.** Meredith's One of our conquerors. (Sales and bibliography). TLS 27 Jl '40:368.

12242 **Smith, Simon H. Nowell-.** A Reading of life. [1901]. TLS 25 Jl '42:372.

12243 **Sadleir, Michael T. H.** The Shaving of Shagpat. [Binding variants]. (Bibliography). TLS 8 Ja '44:24.

12244 **Hudson, Richard B.** The Altschul collection of George Meredith seventeen years later. Yale Univ Lib Gaz 22no4:128–33 Ap '48.

12245 **Gettmann, Royal A.** Meredith as publisher's reader. [Chapman & Hall]. J Eng Germ Philol 48no1:45–56 Ja '49.

12246 —— Serialization and Evan Harrington. Pub Mod Lang Assn 64no4:963–75 D '49.

12247 **Hudson, Richard B.** The publishing of Meredith's Rhoda Fleming. Stud Bib 6:254–7 '54.

12248 **Bartlett, Phyllis.** George Meredith: early manuscript poems in the Berg collection. N.Y. Pub Lib Bull 61no8:396–415 Ag '57.

12249 **Cline, C. L.** The letters of George Meredith. [Texas holdings]. Lib Chron Univ Texas 6no1:30–2 '57.

12250 **Bartlett, Phyllis.** George Meredith's lost Cleopatra. Yale Univ Lib Gaz 33no2:57–62 Oc '58.

12251 **Kerpneck, Harvey.** A shorn Shagpat. [Binding]. (Note 173). Bk Coll 11no1:80–3 '62.

12252 **Beer, Gillian.** Some compositor's misreadings of The tragic comedians. N&Q 209:229–31 Je '64.

12253 **Cline, C. L.** The missing Meredith letters. [Maxse, Greenwood, Morley collections sought]. (Note 240). Bk Coll 14no1:76–8 '65.

12254 **Bartlett, Phyllis.** A copy of Meredith's Poems, 1851. [Interleaved inscribed copy sought]. (Query 208). Bk Coll 15no3:357 '66.

12255 —— A manuscript of Meredith's Modern love. Yale Univ Lib Gaz 40no4:185–7 Ap '66. facsim.

12256 **Smith, Simon H. Nowell-.** The printing of George Meredith's The amazing marriage. Library ser5 21no4:300–8 D '66. facsims.

MERES, FRANCIS, 1565–1647

12257 **Ferguson, Frederic S.** Meres's Palladis tamia. TLS 7 Je '28:430.

12258 **Unger, Emma V.** 'A note on three copies of Meres' Palladis tamia, 1598' *in* To doctor R.: essays here collected and published in honor . . . of dr. A. S. W. Rosenbach. . . . Philadelphia, 1946. p. [215]–17. facsims.

MERRETT, CHRISTOPHER, 1614–95

12259 **Gladstone, Hugh S.** Merrett's Pinax rerum, 1666. N&Q 179:388 N '40.

MERRICK, JAMES, 1720–69

12260 **McKillop, Alan D.** The Benedicite paraphrased. Pub Mod Lang Assn 58no2:582 Je '43.

MEYNELL, ALICE CHRISTIANA GERTRUDE, 1847–1922

12261 **Gibson, Strickland.** First fruits. [Ten poems, ptd. by F. Meynell, 1915]. Bod Q Rec 5no58:108–9 Ap '27.

12262 **A., R. F.** A. C. Thompson (i.e. Alice Meynell): Preludes, 1875. Bib N&Q 1no1:3–4 Ja '35; O. S. B. Brett, 3d viscount Esher; C. S. Lillicrap; C. A. W. *ib.* 1no2:3 Ap '35; 2no7:1 Oc '36.

12263 **Rogers, Arthur.** Alice Meynell: Hearts of controversy. [Binding variants]. Bib N&Q 2no1:4 Ja '36.

12264 —— Alice Meynell: Other poems. [Issues]. Bib N&Q 2no2:6 F '36.

MIDDLETON, THOMAS, 1570?–1627

12265 **Bald, R. Cecil.** A new manuscript of Middleton's Game at chesse. [Folger ms. V.a. 342]. Mod Lang R 25no4:474–8 Oc '30. table.

12266 **Tannenbaum, Samuel A.** A Middleton forgery. [In Victoria & Albert museum copy of Game at chess]. Philol Q 12no1:33–6 Ja '33; B. M. Wagner *ib.* 14no3:287–8 Jl '35.

12267 **Simpson, Percy.** Thomas Middleton's Women beware women. [1657]. Mod Lang R 33no1:45–6 Ja '38.

12268 **Greg, sir Walter W.** Some notes on Crane's manuscript of The witch. Library ser4 22no4:208–22 Mr '42. table.

'Table of variants' (p. 220–2)

12269 **Bald, R. Cecil.** An early version of Middleton's Game at chesse. [Archdall-Folger ms. by Ralph Crane]. Mod Lang R 38no3:177–80 Jl '43. table.

12270 **Shaaber, Matthias A.** The Ant and the nightingale and Father Hubburd's tales. Lib Chron Univ Pennsylvania 14no2:13–16 Oc '47.

12271 **Price, George R.** The early editions of The ant and the nightingale. Pa Bib Soc Am 43:179–90 '49. table.

12272 —— The first edition of A faire quarrell. Library ser5 4no2:137–41 S '49.

12273 —— Compositors' methods with two quartos reprinted by Augustine Matthewes. [Middleton and Rowley's A fair quarrel, and The troublesome reign of John, 1622]. Pa Bib Soc Am 44:269–74 '50.

12274 **Eberle, Gerald J.** The composition and printing of Middleton's A mad world, my masters. Stud Bib 3:246–52 '50/1. tables.

12275 **Price, George R.** The authorship and manuscript of The old law. [1656]. Huntington Lib Q 16no2:117–39 F '53.

12276 —— The first edition of Your five gallants and of Michaelmas term. Library ser5 8no1:23–9 Mr '53. tables.

12277 —— The Huntington ms. of A game at chesse. Huntington Lib Q 17no1:83–8 N '53.

12278 **Ekeblad, Inga-Stina.** A textual note on The changeling. N&Q 200:56–7 Ap '55.

12279 **Price, George R.** The manuscript and the quarto of The roaring girl. Library ser5 11no3:180–6 S '56.

12280 —— The quartos of The Spanish gypsy and their relation to The changeling. Pa Bib Soc Am 52:111–25 '58.

12281 **Lawrence, Robert G.** A bibliographical study of Middleton and Rowley's The changeling. Library ser5 16no1:37–43 Mr '61.

12282 **Price, George R.** Settings by formes in the first edition of The phoenix. Pa Bib Soc Am 56:414–27 '62.

12283 —— Dividing the copy for Michaelmas term. Pa Bib Soc Am 60:327–36 '66. table.

12284 —— The early editions of A trick to catch the old one. Library ser5 22no3:205–27 S '67; [Correction] *ib.* 23no1:57 Mr '68.

MILBOURNE, WILLIAM, fl.1638

12285 **Bald, R. Cecil.** William Milbourne, Donne, and Thomas Jackson. [Sapientia clamitans, and Donne's Sermon of valediction]. R Eng Stud 24no96:321–3 Oc '48.

MILL, JOHN STUART, 1806–73

12286 **Flower, Robin E. W.** The autograph manuscript of Mill's Logic. Brit Mus Q 3no3:76–7 D '28. [Sg.: R. F.]

12287 **John** Stuart Mill's correspondence [in the Library]. Yale Univ Lib Gaz 5no2:35 Oc '30.

12288 **Hayek, F. A.** J. S. Mill's correspondence. TLS 13 F '43:84.

Scattered letters.–Proposed publication.

12289 **Carter, John W.** J. S. Mill. [Principles of political economy, 1848]. TLS 21 Jl '50:460.

12290 **Stillinger, Jack.** The text of Mill's Autobiography. TLS 7 Ag '59:459.

12291 **The Autobiography** of John Stuart Mill. (Notes and news). Bull John Rylands Lib 42no2:262–3 Mr '60.

12292 **Stillinger, Jack.** The text of John Stuart Mill's Autobiography. Bull John Rylands Lib 43no1:220–42 S '60.

12293 **Robson, John M.** A note on Mill bibliography. Univ Toronto Q 34:93–7 Oc '64.

12294 —— Mill's mss. TLS 19 Ag '65:722.

12295 —— 'Principles and methods in the collected works of John Stuart Mill' *in* Robson, John M., *ed.* Editing nineteenth century texts; papers. . . . [Toronto, 1967]. p. [96]–122.

MILLER, JAMES, 1706–44

12296 **Stewart, Powell.** A bibliographical contribution to biography; James Miller's Seasonable reproof. Library ser5 3no4:295–8 Mr '49.

MILLER, THOMAS, 1807–74

12297 **Wright, W.** Thomas Miller. N&Q ser8 5:124 F '94; J. Pickford *ib.* 5:251 Mr '94; R. Burningham; W. Tegg; R. White; J. T. Page 5:314–15 Ap '94; W. H. Peet; R. R.; R. White; C. C. B.; Ayeahr, *pseud.* 5:372–3 My '94; W. Tegg 5:395 My '94; St. Swithin, *pseud.*; R. R. 5:474 Je '94.

MILLES, THOMAS, d.1627

12298 **Davison, Peter H.** The annotations to copies of Thomas Milles's books in the British museum and Bodleian libraries. Library ser5 16no2:33–9 Je '61. tables, facsim.

MILNES, RICHARD MONCKTON, 1ST BARON HOUGHTON, 1809–85

12299 **Wilson, Edwin G.** Edward Moxon and the first two editions of Milnes's biography of Keats. (Notes). Harvard Lib Bull 5no1:125–9 '51.

MILTON, JOHN, 1608–74

12300 **Milton's** Paradise lost. [Conditions of publication]. Bkworm 3no25:22 D '89.

12301 **Paradise** regained. [Ms. note on its publication]. Bkworm 2no16:112 Mr '89.

12302 **Ellis, Frederick S.** A chapter in the history of Paradise lost. Bkworm 7no77:141–2 Ap '94.

12303 **Lefferts, Marshall C.** Milton's Paradise lost. N&Q ser8 7:447 Je '95.

12304 **Bayne, Thomas.** A reading in Milton. [Paradise lost]. N&Q ser9 1:464 Je '98.

12305 **L., J.** An accepted emendation in Paradise regained, ii.309. Mod Q Lang & Lit 1no1:50 Mr '98.

12306 **Payne, J. F.** Milton's prose works, the folio of 1697. Athenæum 3686:791–2 Je '98.

12307 **Baxter, Wynne E.** The first edition of Paradise lost. Lib Asst 2no2:19–33 N '99. illus., port., table.

'Paradise lost, first edition: table shewing variations in one sheet of 8 pages of the text [signature L]' (p. 26)

12308 **The Milton** Bible. Athenæum 3824:177 F '01; J. Hall *ib.* 3825:213 F '01.

12309 **Payne, J. F.** A lost tract of Milton's. [The ready and easy way, 2d ed. 1660]. Athenæum 3870:877 D '01.

12310 **Baxter, Wynne E.** Early editions of Milton. Bib Soc Trans 6pt2:152–5 '01/2.

Summary of paper read 16 D '01.

12311 —— [**Same**]: Bib Soc News-sh 2–4 Ja '02.

Report of paper read 16 D '01.

12312 **Sampson, George.** Emendation in Milton's Samson. Athenæum 3872:50 Ja '02; sir W. A. Craigie *ib*. 3873:84 Ja '02.

12313 **B., C. C.** Milton's Hymn on the morning of Christ's nativity. N&Q ser9 11:88 Ja '03; W. E. Baxter; T. Bayne *ib*. 11:193–4 Mr '03; E. Yardley 11:475 Je '03; C. C. B. 12:56 Jl '03.

12314 **The manuscript** of Paradise lost. TLS 18 D '03:365.

12315 **Wright, William A.** The first edition of Paradise lost. N&Q ser9 11:107–8 F '03; E. H. Coleman *ib*. 11:191–2 Mr '03.

12316 **Hewitt, J. A.** Paradise lost of 1751. N&Q ser10 3:68–9 Ja '05; E. Heron-Allen; M. Maas *ib*. 3:133–4 F '05.

12317 **Roberts, William.** Paradise lost: original assignment. N&Q ser10 6:445 D '06.

12318 **Wright, William A.** On a passage in Lycidas. TLS 15 F '07:53.

12319 **Roberts, William.** Miltoniana in America. [Columbia university exhibition]. Athenæum 4195:354 Mr '08. [Sg.: W. R.]

12320 **Ford, Worthington C.** Paradise lost [ptd. by M Simmons, 1667]. Athenæum 4256:617 My '09.

12321 **Pollard, Alfred W.** The bibliography of Milton. Library ser2 10no37:133 Ja '09.

12322 **Lockwood, Laura E.** Milton's corrections to the minor poems. [Mss.]. Mod Lang N 25no7:201–5 N '10.

12323 **S., J. S.** Milton bibles. N&Q ser11 3:1–2 Ja '11; G. Potter; W. Roberts; P. Lucas; R. C. Bostock; J. T. Page *ib*. 3:72–3 Ja '11; W. E. Baxter 3:109–10 F '11.

12324 **Glicksman, Harry.** The editions of Milton's History of Britain. Pub Mod Lang Assn 35no1:116–22 '20.

12325 **Del Court, W.** Milton and Elzevier. N&Q ser12 9:28 Jl '21; E. Bensly *ib*. 9:116 Ag '21; W. del Court 9:158 Ag '21.

12326 **Hanford, James H.** The arrangement and dates of Milton's sonnets. [Mss.]. Mod Philol 18no9:475–83 Ja '21.

12327 **Candy, Hugh C. H.** The Milton-Ovid script. N&Q ser12 11:201–6, 221–3, 242–5, 265–9, 281–4, 305–7, 324–6, 344–6, 363–5, 387–9, 406–8, 427–9, 447–8, 463–5, 508–10, 525–7 S–D '22; 12:8–9, 28–30, 49–50, 65–6, 86–7, 105–6, 126, 158, 426–8 Ja–F, Je '23. facsims.

See also no. 12333.

12328 —— A new Milton manuscript? [The Ovid script]. TLS 26 Ja '22:60.

12329 **Rand, Edward K.** J and I in Milton's Latin script. Mod Philol 19no3:315–19 F '22.

12330 **Hanford, James H.** The Rosenbach Milton documents. Pub Mod Lang Assn 38no2:290–6 Je '23. facsim.

12331 **Madan, Francis F.** Milton, Salmasius, and Dugard. Library ser4 4no2:119–45 S '23. facsims., tables.

I. The first edition of Milton's Pro populo....–II. Dugard's deposition in the Record office.–III. Editions of the Elenchus....–IV. Editions of the Defensio regia.

12332 **Brodribb, C. W.** Ovid, Sandys, and Milton. N&Q 147:77–8 Ag '24; H. C. H. Candy *ib.* 147:122–4 Ag '24.

12333 **Candy, Hugh C. H.** Some newly discovered stanzas written by John Milton on engraved scenes illustrating Ovid's Metamorphoses. London, Nisbet [1924]. 191p. port., facsims. 21cm.

Repr. with rev. from no. 12327.

12334 **Tillyard, sir Eustace M. W.** Paragraphing in Lycidas, lines 23–24. TLS 13 N '24:731.

12335 **Figgis, Darrell.** Milton's spelling. [And editing]. TLS 25 Je '25:432; sir H. J. C. Grierson *ib.* 9 Jl '25:464.

12336 **Grierson, sir Herbert J. C.** The text of Milton. TLS 15 Ja '25:40.

12337 **Magoun, Francis P.** Miltoniana. [Harvard collections]. Harvard Lib N [2no]15:49–56 S '25.

12338 **Chapman, Robert W.** Misprints in Comus. TLS 8 Ap '26:264.

12339 **Carlton, William N. C.** The first edition of Milton's Comus, 1637. [With census of copies]. Am Coll 5no3:107–13 D '27. facsim.

12340 **Mabbott, Thomas O.** Milton's books. TLS 1 D '27:910; W. W. Vaughan *ib.* 15 D '27:961.

12341 **Stevens, David H.** The Bridgewater manuscript of Comus. [And H. Lawes]. Mod Philol 24no3:315–20 D '27.

12342 —— [**Same**]: *in* Milton papers. Chicago, Ill. [1927]. p. 14–20. facsim.

12343 **Bonnard, Georges A.** Two remarks on the text of Milton's Areopagitica. R Eng Stud 4no16:434–8 Oc '28. table.

12344 **Hanford, James H.** The manuscript of Paradise lost. Mod Philol 25no3:313–17 F '28.

12345 **Goode, James.** The Bohn edition of Milton's prose. [Text]. TLS 1 Ag '29:608.

12346 **Troxell, Gilbert McC.** Milton's Lycidas [presented to Library]. Yale Univ Lib Gaz 3no3:60 Ja '29. [Sg.: G. M. T.]

12347 **Mabbott, Thomas O.** A book of Milton's. [Gesner's Heraclides pontici, 1544]. TLS 7 Ag '30:641.

12348 **Oras, Ants.** Milton's editors and commentators from Patrick Hume to Henry John Todd, 1695–1801; a study in critical views and methods. Dorpat, Estonia, University of Tartu; London, O.U.P., 1931. (Repr. with rev. New York, Haskell house, 1967). xi,381[1]p. 24cm.

1. Introductory survey. . . .–2. Patrick Hume's commentary on Paradise lost–3. Bentley's edition of Paradise lost.–4. The reception of Bentley's edition–5. The commentary of the Richardsons.–6. Francis Peck's New memoirs.–7. James Paterson and Raymond de St.Maur.–8. John Hawkey's editions.–9. Bishop Newton and his collaborators.–10. The period between Newton's and Thomas Warton's editions, 1749–1785.–11. Thomas Warton's edition of the minor poems.–12. The commentaries between Warton and Todd.–13. Henry John Todd's editions of Milton.–Conclusion.

Rev: A. Bosker Mod Lang N 48:204–5 '33.; M. Schütt Literaturblatt für germ. und roman. Philol 55:27–8 '33.

12349 **Bradner, Leicester.** Milton's Epitaphium Damonis. TLS 18 Ag '32:581.

12350 **Candy, Hugh C. H.** Milton's autographs established. Library ser4 13no2:192–200 S '32. facsims.

12351 **Haraszti, Zoltán.** First editions of Milton. More Bks Boston Pub Lib Bull 7no9:323–35 N '32; 7no10:375–90 D '32. facsims.

12352 **Lewis, Clive S.** A note on Comus. [Mss.]. R Eng Stud 8no30:170–6 Ap '32.

12353 **Mabbott, Thomas O.** Milton's Latin poems. TLS 27 Oc '32:790.

12354 —— Notes by Milton. [His library]. TLS 17 N '32:859.

12355 **Witherspoon, Alexander M.** Exhibition of the first and rare editions of John Milton. Yale Univ Lib Gaz 7no1:10–14 Jl '32.

12356 **Darbishire, Helen.** The chronology of Milton's handwriting. Library ser4 14no2:229–35 S '33. facsims.

12357 —— The Columbia edition of Milton. R Eng Stud 9no33:61–2 Ja '33.

12358 **Grierson, sir Herbert J. C.** [and] **Helen Darbishire.** The Columbia Milton. R Eng Stud 9no35:316–19 Jl '33.

12359 **McCain, John W.** Further notes on Milton's Artis logicae. N&Q 165:56–9 Jl '33.

12360 **Candy, Hugh C. H.** Milton, N.LL., and sir Tho. Urquhart. Library ser4 14no4:470–6 Mr '34; J. W. Pendleton *ib.* 15no2:249–50 S '34; H. C. H. Candy 15no3:377–8 D '34. facsims.

12361 —— Milton's prolusio script. Library ser4 15no3:330–9 D '34. facsims.

12362 [**Haraszti, Zoltán**]. Milton's Paradise regained and Tennyson's Poems acquired by the library. More Bks Boston Pub Lib Bull 9no10:406–7 D '34.

12363 **Havens, P. S.** A tract long attributed to Milton. [J. Hall's A letter written to a gentleman, 1653]. Huntington Lib Bull 6:109–14 N '34.

12364 **Parker, William R.** A cancel in an early Milton tract. [Animadversions upon . . . Smectymnuus, 1641]. Library ser4 15no2:243–6 S '34.

12365 **Candy, Hugh C. H.** A cancel in an early Milton tract. [Smectymnuus, 1697]. Library ser4 16no1:118 Je '35.

12366 **Howard, Leon.** Early American copies of Milton. Huntington Lib Bull 7:169–79 Ap '35.

12367 **Cameron, Kenneth W.** Milton's library. (Bibliographical notes). TLS 24 Oc '36:868; M. Kelley *ib.* 19 D '36:1056.

12368 **Fletcher, Harris F.** The first edition of Milton's History of Britain. J Eng Germ Philol 35no3:405–14 Jl '36. tables.

The states of the first edition.–The text.–The portrait and current prices.

12369 **Parker, William R.** Contributions toward a Milton bibliography. Library ser4 16no4:425–38 Mr '36.

12370 —— Milton's Hobson poems: some neglected early texts. Mod Lang R 31no3:395–402 Jl '36.

12371 **Diekhoff, John S.** The text of Comus, 1634 to 1645. Pub Mod Lang Assn 52no3:705–27 S '37. facsims.

12372 **French, J. Milton.** The autographs of John Milton. Eng Lit Hist 4no4:301–30 D '37.

I. Milton's own writings.–II. Books from Milton's library.–III. Public and private documents.

12373 **Kelley, Maurice.** Milton autographs. TLS 2 Oc '37:715.

12374 —— A note on Milton's Pro populo Anglicano defensio. Library ser4 17no4:466–7 Mr '37.

12375 **Kuethe, J. Louis.** Paradise lost: 'fourteenth' and 'fifteenth' editions. N&Q 172:136 F '37.

12376 **Mabbott, Thomas O.** Milton's ms. notes. [His library]. TLS 30 Ja '37:76; 3 Jl '37:496; A. F. Scholfield ib. 17 Jl '37:528.

12377 —— and **J. M. French.** Milton's Proposalls of certaine expedients, 1659. [Lost]. N&Q 173:66–7 Jl '37.

12378 **Parker, William R.** Milton, Rothwell, and Simmons. Library ser4 18no1:89–103 Je '37.

12379 **French, J. Milton.** Milton's annotated copy of Gildas. Harvard Stud & N Philol & Lit 20:75–80 '38. facsim.

12380 —— Milton's family Bible. Pub Mod Lang Assn 53no2:363–6 Je '38.

12381 **Quare,** *pseud.* Paradise lost in Latin. [Tr. by W. Dobson, 1750–3]. N&Q 174:442–3 Je '38.

12382 **Mabbott, Thomas O.** and **J. M. French.** First supplement to the Columbia Milton. N&Q 177:329–30 N '39.

12383 **Stillman, Donald G.** Milton as proof reader. Mod Lang N 54no5:353–4 My '39.

12384 **Mabbott, Thomas O., J. M. French** and **M. Kelley.** The Columbia Milton: second supplement. N&Q 179:20–1 Jl '40.

12385 **Oldfather, W. A.** Pro Ioanne Miltono poeta populum Anglicanum iterum defendente. [= Defensio secunda, 1654]. Philol Q 19no1:88–9 Ja '40.

12386 **Darbishire, Helen.** The printing of the first edition of Paradise lost. R Eng Stud 17no17:415–27 Oc '41. tables.

12387 **Diekhoff, John S.** A note on Comus, lines 75–77. Philol Q 20no4:603–4 Oc '41.

12388 **French, J. Milton.** The burning of Milton's Defensio in France. Mod Lang N 56no4:275–7 Ap '41.

12389 **Haviland, Thomas P.** Three early Milton editions. Lib Chron Univ Pennsylvania 9no3:78–82 D '41.

12390 **Parker, William R.** Above all liberties; John Milton's relations with his earliest publishers. Princeton Univ Lib Chron 2no2:41–50 F '41. facsim.

12391 **Pershing, James H.** The different states of the first edition of Paradise lost. Library ser4 22no1:34–66 Je '41. table, facsims.

I. The title-page variants.–II. The seven extra leaves.–III. The differences in the text.

12392 **Evans, Gwynne B.** Two new manuscript versions of Milton's Hobson poems. Mod Lang N 57no3:192–4 Mr '42.

12393 **Lewis, Clarissa O.** A further note on Milton's Pro populo Anglicano defensio. Library ser4 23no1:45–7 Je '42. tables.

12394 **Maas, Paul.** Hid in, Lycidas, 1.69. R Eng Stud 19no76:397–8 Oc '43.

12395 **French, J. Milton.** Some notes on Milton. N&Q 188:52–5 F '45.

I. Milton's alleged misconduct in Italy.–II. Editions of Salmasius's Defensio regia.–III. Salmasius's reward for writing his Defensio.–IV. The burning of Milton's Defensio abroad.–V. Milton's connection with John Phillips's Responsio of 1652.–VI. Milton taunted with blindness.–VII. Effect of Milton's Defensio secunda on More.

12396 **Witherspoon, Alexander M.** A new Milton gift. [Of education, 1644, and others]. Yale Univ Lib Gaz 20no2:33–5 Oc '45.

12397 **Kelley, Maurice.** Milton's commonplace book, folio 20. Mod Lang N 62no3:192–4 Mr '47.

12398 **Parker, William R.** Fletcher's Milton: a first appraisal. [Complete poetical works in facsimile]. Pa Bib Soc Am 41:33–52 '47. tables.

12399 **Baker, C. H. Collins.** Some illustrators of Milton's Paradise lost, 1688–1850. Library ser5 3no1:1–21 Je '48; 3no2:101–19 S '48. facsims.

'Subjects illustrated in Paradise lost' (p. 117–19)

12400 **Battle, Guy A.** The box rule pattern in the first edition of Paradise lost. Pa Bib Soc Am 42:315–21 '48. table.

12401 **Fletcher, Harris F.** Milton's copy of Gesner's Heraclides, 1544. J Eng Germ Philol 47no2:182–7 Ap '48.

12402 **French, J. Milton.** The date of Milton's first Defense. Library ser5 3no1:56–8 Je '48.

12403 **Kelley, Maurice.** The annotations in Milton's family Bible. Mod Lang N 63no8:539–60 D '48.

12404 **Thorpe, James.** The presentation Paradise lost. [Spurious inscription]. New Coloph 1pt4:357–65 Oc '48. facsims.

12405 **Balston, Thomas.** Some illustrators of Milton's Paradise lost. Library ser5 4no2:146–7 S '49.

12406 **Fletcher, Harris F.** [and] **L. G. H. Horton-Smith.** Milton's copy of Orlando furioso. N&Q 194:193 Ap '49.

12407 **Fletcher, Harris F.** Milton's private library, an additional title. Philol Q 28no1:72–6 Ja '49.

12408 —— A second(?) title-page of the second edition of Paradise lost. [1674]. Pa Bib Soc Am 43:173–8 '49. facsim.

12409 **Kelley, Maurice.** 'J' and 'I' in Milton's script. Mod Lang R 44no4:545–7 Oc '49.

12410 —— Milton and the Notes on Paul Best. [Handwr.]. Library ser5 5no1:49–51 Je '50. facsims.

12411 **Mabbott, Thomas O., J. M. French,** and **M. Kelley.** The Columbia Milton: fourth supplement. N&Q 195:244–6 Je '50.

Additions.—Corrections and supplementary information

12412 **Robertson, D. S.** A copy of Milton's Eikonoklastes. TLS 15 Je '51:380; 22 Je '51:396.

12413 **Sherwin, Oscar.** Milton for the masses; John Wesley's edition of Paradise lost. Mod Lang Q 12no3:267–85 S '51.

I. Omissions.—II. Alterations.—III. Notes.

12414 **Kelley, Maurice.** Milton and Machiavelli's Discorsi. Stud Bib 4:123–7 '51/2.

12415 **French, J. Milton, M. Kelley** and **T. O. Mabbott.** The Columbia Milton: fifth supplement. N&Q 197:376–9 Ag '52.

12416 **Hughes, Merritt Y.** New evidence on the charge that Milton forged the Pamela prayer to the Eikon basilike. R Eng Stud new ser 3no10:130–40 Ap '52.

12417 **Adams, Robert M.** The text of Paradise lost: emphatic and unemphatic spellings. Mod Philol 52no1:84–91 N '54.

12418 **Miller, Sonia.** The text of the second edition of Milton's Eikonoklastes. J Eng Germ Philol 52no2:214–20 Ap '53; D. S. Robertson *ib.* 53no1:140–1 Ja 3 effl

12419 **George, J.** An entry in Milton's common-place book. [Text]. N&Q 199:383–4 S '54.

12420 **Wright, B. A.** A note on Milton's punctuation. [Paradise lost]. R Eng Stud new ser 5no18:170 Ap '54.

12421 **Evans, Robert O.** Proofreading of Paradise lost. N&Q 200:383–4 S '55.

12422 **French, J. Milton.** An unrecorded edition of Milton's Defensio secunda, 1654. Pa Bib Soc Am 49:262–8 '55. tables.

12423 **Harkness, Bruce.** The precedence of the 1676 editions of Milton's Literæ pseudo-senâtus Anglicani. Stud Bib 7:181–5 '55.

12424 **Shawcross, John T.** Milton's Fairfax sonnet. [Text]. N&Q 200:195–6 My '55.

12425 **Fletcher, Harris F.** Milton's [Index poeticus]–the Theatrum poetarum by Edward Phillips. J Eng Germ Philol 55no1:35–40 Ja '56.

12426 **Hanford, James H.** Milton among the book collectors. [Libr.]. Newberry Lib Bull 4no4:97–109 D '56.

12427 **Kelley, Maurice.** Milton's later sonnets and the Cambridge manuscript. Mod Philol 54no1:20–5 Ag '56.

12428 **Darbishire, Helen.** The text of Paradise lost. R Eng Stud new ser 8no30:173–5 My '57.

12429 **Bateson, Frederick W.** Milton for everyman. TLS 4 Jl '58:377; B. A. Wright *ib.* Jl '58:409; F. W. Bateson 25 Jl '58:423; B. A. Wright 1 Ag '58:435; J. C. Maxwell 15 Ag '58:459; P. Alexander 22 Ag '58:471.

12430 **Sirluck, Ernest.** Milton's criticism of Hall's Grammar. [Defence of the humble remonstrance, 1641]. Mod Lang N 73no1:8–9 Ja '58.

12431 **Shawcross, John T.** The date of Milton's Ad patrem. [1645]. N&Q 204:358–9 Oc '59.

12432 —— The manuscript of Arcades. N&Q 204:359–64 Oc '59.

12433 —— Notes on Milton's amanuenses. J Eng Germ Philol 58no1:29–38 Ja '59. table.

12434 **Evans, Gwynne B.** The state of Milton's text: the prose, 1643–48. [Review article]. J Eng Germ Philol 59no3:497–505 Jl '60.

12435 **Kelley, Maurice.** First editions of Milton's Literæ. TLS 29 Ap '60:273.

12436 **The Milton** collection. Turnbull Lib Rec 14:12–15 Mr '60.

12437 **Shawcross, John T.** Certain relationships of the manuscripts of Comus. Pa Bib Soc Am 54:38–56 '60; An addendum *ib.* 54:293–4 '60. table.

'Table' (p. 54–6)

12438 —— Speculations on the dating of the Trinity ms. of Milton's Poems. Mod Lang N 75no1:11–17 Ja '60.

12439 **Ayers, Robert W.** A suppressed edition of Milton's Defensio secunda, 1654. Pa Bib Soc Am 55:75–87 '61.

12440 **Parker, William R.** Notes on the text of Samson agonistes. J Eng Germ Philol 60no4:688–98 Oc '61.

Repr. in Milton studies in honor of Harris Francis Fletcher. Urbana, Ill., 1961. p. 80–90.

12441 **Shattuck, Charles H.** Macready's Comus: a promptbook study. J Eng Germ Philol 60no4:731–48 Oc '61.

'The text of Macready's Comus' (p. 747–8)

12442 **Shawcross, John T.** Division of labor in Justa Edovardo King naufrago, 1638. Lib Chron Univ Pennsylvania 27no2:176–9 '61.

12443 **Empson, William.** Milton's God. [And Eikon basilike]. TLS 2 Mr '61:137; P. L. Heyworth *ib.* 9 Mr '62:161; P. Alexander 16 Mr '62:185; W. Empson 23 Mr '62:201; B. A. Wright 30 Mr '62:217; W. Empson 27 Ap '62:281; P. Alexander 11 My '62:339; W. Empson 25 My '62:380; M. Y. Hughes 27 Jl '62:541.

12444 **Fletcher, Harris F.** The seventeenth-century separate printing of Milton's Epitaphium Damonis. [1646?]. J Eng Germ Philol 61no4:788–96 Oc '62.

12445 **French, J. Milton.** Moseley's advertisements of Milton's poems, 1650–1660. Huntington Lib Q 25no4:337–45 Ag '62.

12446 **Kelley, Maurice.** Milton's Dante-Della Casa-Varchi volume. N.Y. Pub Lib Bull 66no8:499–504 Oc '62. facsim., table.

12447 **Shawcross, John T.** Establishment of a text of Milton's poems through a study of Lycidas. Pa Bib Soc Am 56:317–31 '62.

12448 —— What we can learn from Milton's spelling. Huntington Lib Q 26no4:351–61 Ag '63.

12449 **Hinton, Percival F.** A forgotten indiscretion. [Variant illus. in Comus, 1858]. (Note 233). Bk Coll 13no4:500 '64.

12450 **Kelley, Maurice** and **S. D. Atkins.** Milton and the Harvard Pindar. [Not from Milton's library]. Stud Bib 17:77–82 '64. facsims.

12451 **Riffe, Nancy L.** Eighteenth-century translations of Milton into Latin. N&Q 210:144 Ap '65.

12452 **Shawcross, John T.** The date of the separate edition of Milton's Epitaphium Damonis. [1640?]. Stud Bib 18:262–5 '65.

12453 —— Milton's Tenure of kings and magistrates: date of composition, editions, and issues. Pa Bib Soc Am 60:1–8 '66. diagr.

12454 **Kelley, Maurice.** The recovery, printing, and reception of Milton's Christian doctrine. Huntington Lib Q 31no1:35–41 N '67.

12455 **Shawcross, John T.** A note on Milton's Hobson poems. [Mss.]. R Eng Stud new ser 18no4:433–7 N '67.

12456 **Mankin, Philip H.** Samson agonistes. [Text]. TLS 28 Ag '69:955.

12457 **Rajan, Balanchandra.** Interim Milton. [Acquisition of G. W. Stuart collection by University of Western Ontario]. TLS 17 Ap '69:415.

MIRK, JOHN, fl.1403?

12458 **Francis, sir Frank C. J.** Mirk's Liber festivalis and Quattuor sermones, Pynson, 1499. Library ser5 4no1:73 '49.

12459 **Kenyon, Lloyd Tyrell-, baron Kenyon.** Mirk's Liber festivalis and Quattuor sermones. [Pynson]. Library ser5 5no1:59–60 Je '50.

MITFORD, MARY RUSSELL, 1787–1855

12460 **King, Dorothy.** Miss Mitford and her works. N&Q ser12 3:110 F '17; A. L. Humphreys; S. L. Petty *ib.* 3:309–10 My '17.

12461 **Tremaine, George.** Miss Mitford's Our village. N&Q 146:48 Ja '24; A. Sparke *ib.* 146:90 F '24.

12462 **Coles, William A.** Magazine and other contributions by Mary Russell Mitford and Thomas Noon Talfourd. Stud Bib 12:218–26 '59.

12463 **Ewing, Douglas C.** A note on Mary Russell Mitford's Belford regis. Pa Bib Soc Am 60:473 '66.

MOLESWORTH, MARY LOUISA (STEWART), 1839–1921

12464 **Green, Roger L.** Notes on mrs. Molesworth. TLS 17 N '50:xvii.

MONTAGU, BASIL, 1770–1851

12465 **Cyril,** *pseud.* Basil Montagu's mss. N&Q ser10 4:109 Ag '05; W. Douglas *ib.* 4:156 Ag '05.

MONTAGU, LADY MARY WORTLEY (PIERREPONT), 1689–1762

12466 **Lady** Mary W. Montagu's fiction [Her library]. (Notes on sales). TLS 16 Ag '28:596.

12467 **Lang, W. J.** Unlocated British newspapers: lady Mary Wortley Montagu. [The Nonsense of common sense]. N&Q 166:423 Je '34; E. Bensly; R. T. Milford; G. W. Wright 167:32 Jl '34.

12468 **Ransom, Harry H.** Mary Wortley Montagu's newspaper. [The Nonsense of common sense]. Stud Eng Univ Texas 1947:84–9 '47.

12469 **Halsband, Robert.** Lady Mary Wortley Montagu's library. TLS 25 Ja '57:49.

MONTAGU, WALTER, 1603–77

12470 **Axon, William E. A.** The licensing of Montagu's Miscellanea spiritualia. Library ser2 2no7:269–73 Jl '01.

12471 **S. A.** Walter Montagu. N&Q ser9 11:421–2 My '03; 11:482–4 Je '03.

MONTGOMERY, HENRY RIDDELL, 1818–1904

12472 **Bigger, Francis J.** [and] **D. J. O'Donoghue.** Henry R. Montgomery. Irish Bk Lover 1no8:100–1 Mr '10.

MONTGOMERY, JAMES, 1771–1854

12473 **Bigger, Francis J.** James Montgomery. Irish Bk Lover 12no1/2:1–5 Ag/S '20. port.

MOOR, JAMES, 1712–79

12474 **P., H.** and **A. P. H.** Moore's De analogia contractionum linguae Graecae. [1753]. Biblioth 1no4:47–8 '58.

MOORE, GEORGE AUGUSTUS, 1852–1933

12475 **Newdigate, Bernard H.** Mr. George Moore and hand-printed books. (Book-production notes). London Merc 4no19:76–7 My '21.

12476 **Symons, Albert J. A.** Mr. George Moore. [Textual revisions in reissues and new ed.]. TLS 27 F '30:166.

12477 **Richter, M. C.** Moore: Modern painting. [Issues]. Bib N&Q 2no2:6 F '36; T. Warburton *ib.* 2no3:5 Ap '36.

12478 **Warburton, Thomas.** Moore, George: Ephemera critica. Bib N&Q 2no7:5 Oc '36.

12479 —— Moore, George: The untilled field. [Issues]. Bib N&Q 2no8:8 F '37.

12480 **Mott, Howard S.** [Bibliogr. note on Moore's Confessions, 1888]. Pa Bib Soc Am 36:68 '42.

12481 **Gettman, Royal A.** George Moore's revisions of The lake, The wild goose, and Esther Waters. Pub Mod Lang Assn 59no2:540–55 Je '44. table.

12482 **Munro, John M.** The survival of wickedness. [Moore's Flowers of passion, 1878]. Pa Bib Soc Am 57:356–7 '63.

MOORE, THOMAS, 1779–1852

12483 **Stevens, B. F., and Brown.** Moore ms. N&Q ser9 7:347–8 My '01.

12484 **Muir, Percival H.** Thomas Moore's Irish melodies, 1808–1834. Coloph [4]pt15:[16p.] '33.

Summary of the points of the first edition.—Dates of publication of the parts.

12485 **MacManus, Michael J.** Moore's Suppressed letters. [Issues]. Bib N&Q 1no2:12 Ap '35; O. S. B. Brett, 3d baron Esher *ib.* 1no3:3 Ag '35; P. S. O'Hegarty 2no11:1 N '38.

12486 **Moore's** Melodies and the paper maker. Irish Bk Lover 28no4:88–9 F '42.

Extr. from Whammond's Illustrated guide to Dublin and Wicklow, 1868. p. 76.

13487 **Eldridge, Herbert G.** The American republication of Thomas Moore's Epistles, odes, and other poems: an early version of the reprinting game. Pa Bib Soc Am 62:199–205 '68.

MORE, HANNAH, 1745–1833

12488 **Spinney, Gordon H.** Cheap repository tracts; Hazard and Marshall edition. Library ser4 20no3:295–340 D '39; [*cf.* TLS 30 D '39:755].

'Bibliography' (p. 312–37); 'Index of titles' (p. 338–40)

12489 **Shaver, Chester L.** The publication of Hannah More's first play. [A search after happiness, 1773]. Mod Lang N 62no5:343 My '47.

12490 **Spector, Robert D.** William Roberts' Memoirs of the life and letters of Hannah More. N&Q 197:140–1 Mr '52.

MORE, SIR THOMAS, 1478–1535

12491 **Bridgett, T. A.** Sir Thomas More's book of hours. N&Q ser8 2:121–2 Ag '92.

12492 **Roberts, William.** Old book. [A dialogue of comfort, ptd. by Tottell, 1553]. N&Q ser8 4:88 Jl '93; F. Norgate; J. Dixon *ib.* 4:139 Ag '93.

12493 **Welch, Charles.** The sir Thomas More collection at the Guildhall library. Bib Soc Trans 5pt2:177–80 '99/00.

Summary of paper read 21 My '00.

12494 —— [**Same**]: Bib Soc News-sh 2–4 Je '00.

Report of paper read 21 My '00.

12495 **Gollancz, sir Israel.** Roper's Life of sir Thomas More. [Mss.]. TLS 1 Ap '04:101.

12496 **Brooke, C. F. Tucker.** Two notes on sir Thomas More. [Mss.]. Mod Lang N 27no5:156–7 My '12.

12497 **Reed, Arthur W.** The editor of sir Thomas More's English works: William Rastell. Library ser4 4no1:25–49 Je '23.

12498 **Hitchcock, Elsie V.** Sir Thomas More. [Whereabouts of mss. of Harpsfield's Life]. TLS 19 My '27:355.

12499 **Gee, John A.** The second edition of the Utopia, Paris, 1517 [acquired by Library]. Yale Univ Lib Gaz 7no4:87–8 Ap '33.

12500 **Elkins, Kimball C.** Utopias. [F. G. Peabody collection]. Harvard Lib N 3no2:46–50 Je '35.

12501 **Teugh, Mark.** Alfred Cock, Q.C., his More collections. N&Q 168:299 Ap '35; A. F. Dauglish *ib.* 168:341 My '35.

12502 **Thomas** More and John Fisher. [Exhibitions]. (Bibliographical notes). TLS 23 My '35:336.

12503 **H., O. N.** An edition of sir Thomas More's Utopia. N&Q 172:47 Ja '37.

12504 **Peggram, Reed E.** The first French and English translations of sir Thomas More's Utopia. Mod Lang R 35no3:330–40 Jl '40.

12505 **John** Burn's More collection. (Sales). TLS 29 Ap '44:216.

12506 **Bowers, Fredson T.** Printing evidence in Wynkyn de Worde's edition of The life of Johan Picus by st. Thomas More. Pa Bib Soc Am 43:398–9 '49.

12507 **Gibson, Reginald W.** Thomas More: unlocated items. (Query 94). Bk Coll 7no2:188 '58.

12508 —— St. Thomas More's book of hours. [Present location]. (Query 126). Bk Coll 9no2:202 '60.

12509 —— The Thomas More bibliography. TLS 11 My '62:346.

12510 **Watkins, David R.** The st. Thomas More project. Yale Univ Lib Gaz 36no4:162–8 Ap '62.

12511 **Dupré, Robert.** Mss. of the Life of sir Thomas More [by Cresacre More, sought]. (Query 182). Bk Coll 13no3:356 '64.

12512 **Martz, Louis L.** and **R. S. Sylvester.** Thomas More's prayer book. Yale Univ Lib Gaz 43no2:53–80 Oc '68. facsims.

'Bibliographical description' (p. 54–9)

MORGAN, JOSEPH, fl.1739

12513 **Sirr, Harry.** J. Morgan & his Phœnix Britannicus, with notes about his other works. Margate, H. Keble, ptr., 1906. 10p. 29cm.

Repr. from Quatuor Coronati Lodge Trans 19:127–36 '06.

12514 —— J(oseph) Morgan of Phœnix Britannicus. TLS 15 D '32:963; 12 Ja '33:24.

MORISON, JAMES, 1770–1840

12515 **Bulloch, J. Malcolm.** The centenary of James Morison, the hygeist. Aberdeen Lib Bull 6no31:1–24 Je '25.

'Morison literature' (p. 11–24)

MORISON, SIR RICHARD, d.1556

12516 **Baskervill, Charles R.** Sir Richard Morison as the author of two anonymous tracts on sedition. [A lamentation . . . of seditious rebellion, 1536; A remedy for sedition, 1536]. Library ser4 17no1:83–7 Je '36.

MORLAND, GEORGE, 1763–1804

12517 **Buckley, Francis.** George Morland's sketch books and their publishers. Uppermill, Moore & Edwards, 1931. [6]p. 26cm. Covertitle.

Appendix I: Newspaper advertisements.—Appendix II: Dates of the original sketch books, with labels.

MORLAND, SIR SAMUEL, d.1695

12518 **Redgrave, Gilbert R.** Some books by sir Samuel Morland. Library ser4 1no3:165–9 D '20.

MORLEY, THOMAS, 1557–1604?

12519 **Deutsch, Otto E.** The editions of Morley's Introduction. Library ser4 23no2/3:127–9 S/D '42.

12520 **Dart, Thurston.** A suppressed dedication for Morley's four-part madrigals of 1594. Cambridge Bib Soc Trans 3pt5:401–5 '63. facsim.

MORRIS, WILLIAM, 1834–96 *see also* Book production and distribution–Printers, publishers, etc.–Kelmscott press.

12521 **B., C. C.** Mr. Morris's poems. [The defence of Guenevere, 1896]. N&Q ser8 10:334 Oc '96; R. R. *ib.* 10:419–20 N '96; C. C. B.; W. F. Prideaux 10:477 D '96.

12522 **William** Morris. [As collector]. Library ser2 2no6:113–19 Ap '01. port.

12523 **Prance, C. R.** The collected edition of William Morris. TLS 27 Ap '22:276; C. T. Jacobi *ib.* 4 My '22:292.

12524 **Bradley, Will.** William Morris: a review of his influence on the centenary of his birth. Pub Wkly 125no14:1373–6 Ap '34; W. Bentley *ib.* 125no19:1782–3 My '34. facsims.

12525 **Haraszti, Zoltán.** The centenary of William Morris; first editions of his works, and books printed by him at the Kelmscott press, on view. . . . More Bks Boston Pub Lib Bull 9no5:153–60 My '34.

12526 **Rollins, Carl P.** The works of William Morris [exhibited]. Yale Univ Lib Gaz 9no2:62–4 Oc '34.

12527 **Litzenberg, Karl.** William Morris and Scandinavian literature, a bibliographical essay. Scandinavian Stud & N 13no4:93–105 Ag '35.

12528 **Flower, Robin E. W.** The William Morris manuscripts. Brit Mus Q 14no1:8–10 Mr '40.

12529 **Green, Roger L.** William Morris's first poem. [The willow and the red cliff]. TLS 8 My '48:261.

12530 **Brown, T. Julian.** William Morris, 1834–1896. (English literary autographs, XVIII). Bk Coll 5no2:151 '56. facsims.

12531 **A William** Morris exhibition. [William Morris society]. TLS 2 Ag '57:476.

12532 **Stokes, E. E.** The Morris letters at Texas [in C. F. Murray correspondence]. J Wm Morris Soc 1no3:23–30 '63.

12533 **Philip, Ejnar.** William Morris og Alfred lord Tennyson; Maud, et melodrama, the Kelmscott press. Bogvennen 2:74–7 Juni '68. facsims.

MOTTEUX, PETER ANTHONY, 1663–1718

12534 **Bowers, Fredson T.** Motteux's Love's a jest, 1696: a running-title and presswork problem. Pa Bib Soc Am 48:268–73 '54. tables.

Repr. in Essays in bibliography, text, and editing. Charlottesville [1975]. p. [269]–76.

MOUNTCASHELL, MARGARET JANE (KINGSBOROUGH), COUNTESS OF MOUNTCASHELL, 1773–1835

12535 **Romantic** letters. TLS 4 F '65:96; E. C. McAleer *ib.* 25 Mr '65:240.

MUGGLETON, LODOWICKE, 1609–98

12536 **T., G. H.** Muggletonian writings. N&Q ser9 5:415 My '00; E. A. C.; W. D. Macray; M. N. G.; E. H. Coleman; A. J. King *ib.* 5:485 Je '00; W. F. Prideaux 6:54–5 Jl '00.

MUNDAY, ANTHONY, 1553–1633

12537 **Greg, sir Walter W.** Autograph plays by Anthony Munday. [And the play, Sir Thomas More]. Mod Lang R 8no1:89–90 Ja '13.

12538 **Thompson, sir Edward M.** The autograph manuscripts of Anthony Mundy. Bib Soc Trans 14pt2:325–53 '16/17. facsims.

12539 **Oliphant, E. H. C.** Sir Thomas More [and Munday]. J Eng Germ Philol 18no2:226–35 Ap '19.

12540 **Byrne, Muriel St.C.** Anthony Munday and his books. Library ser4 1no4:225–56 Mr '21.

12541 —— Anthony Munday's spelling as a literary clue. Library ser4 4no1: 9–23 Je '23.

12542 **Hayes, Gerald R.** Anthony Munday's romances of chivalry. Library ser4 6no1:57–81 Je '25; A postscript *ib.* 7no1:31–8 Je '26.

12543 **Bennett, R. E.** Munday's Paradoxes. [Defence of contraries, 1593]. TLS 20 Ag '31:633.

12544 **Byrne, Muriel St.C.** Bibliographical clues in collaborate plays. [The downfall of Robert earl of Huntington, and The death . . .]. Library ser4 13no1:21–48 Je '32.

12545 **Wright, Julia C. T.** Anthony Munday and the Bodenham miscellanies. Philol Q 40no4:449–61 Oc '61.

12546 **Jackson, Macdonald P.** Anthony Mundy and Sir Thomas More. N&Q 208:96 Mr '63.

12547 **Wright, Julia C. T.** Lazarus Pyott and other inventions of Anthony Mundy. Philol Q 42no4:532–41 Oc '63.

MURDOCH, JEAN IRIS (MRS. J. O. BAYLEY), 1919–

12548 **Batchelor, Billie.** Revision in Iris Murdoch's Under the net. Bks at Iowa 8:30–6 Ap '68.

12549 **Murray, William M.** A note on the Iris Murdoch manuscripts in the University of Iowa libraries. Mod Fict Stud 15no3:445–8 '69.

MURPHY, ARTHUR, 1727–1805

12550 **Caskey, J. Homer.** The first edition of Arthur Murphy's Sallust. Philol Q 13no4:404–8 Oc '34.

12551 **Trefman, Simon.** Arthur Murphy's long lost Englishman from Paris, a manuscript discovered. Theat Notebk 20no4:137–41 '66.

MURRY, KATHLEEN (BEAUCHAMP), 1888–1923 *see* Mansfield, Katherine, *pseud.*

MUSGRAVE, SIR WILLIAM, 1735–1800

12552 **Cooper, Thomson.** Sir William Musgrave. [Mss.]. N&Q ser 8 9:29 Ja '96.

12553 **Wood, D. T. B.** The Revels books; the writer of the Malone scrap. R Eng Stud 1no1:72–4 Ja '25. facsims.

NAPIER, WILLIAM, fl.1794

12554 **Archibald, Raymond C.** Napier's Scots songs, vol.iii. N&Q 171:296 Oc '36.

NASHE, THOMAS, 1567–1601

12555 **McKerrow, Ronald B.** A note on variations in certain copies of the Returne of Pasquill. Library ser2 4no16:384–91 Oc '03. table.

12556 **Greg, sir Walter W.** Was the first edition of Pierce Penniless a piracy? Library ser5 7no2:122–4 Je '52.

Repr. in Maxwell, James C., *ed.* Collected papers. Oxford, 1966. p. [402]–5.

12557 **Austin, Warren B.** Concerning a woodcut. [Have with you to Saffron-Walden, 1596]. Sh Q 8no2:245 '57.

12558 **Harlow, C. G.** Nashe's visit to the Isle of Wight and his publications of 1592–4. R Eng Stud 14no55:225–42 Ag '63.

The date of the visit.–The persecution of Nashe and the publication of Christ's tears.–The publication of The unfortunate traveller.–The publication of The terrors of the night. –Conclusion.

12559 **Sanderson, James L.** An unnoted text of Nashe's The choise of Valentines. [Ms.]. Eng Lang N 1no4:252–3 Je '64.

NEEDHAM, MARCHAMONT, 1620–78

12560 **Adams, Elizabeth L.** Three Nedham tracts in a Hollis binding. More Bks Boston Pub Lib Bull 14no5:206 My '39. [Sg.: E. L. A.]

NELSON, HORATIO, 1ST VISCOUNT NELSON, 1758–1805

12561 **Pritchard, George.** Lord Nelson. J Soc Archivists 1:8–9 Je '95. facsims.

12562 **Boulter, Walter C.** Nelson poems. N&Q ser10 4:186–7 S '05; J. A. Hewitt *ib.* 4:329 Oc '05. [Sg.: W. C. B.]

12563 **Nelson's** official manuscripts. Athenæum 4069:543 Oc '05.

12564 **Baxter, James P.** The Nelson manuscripts in the Harvard college library. Harvard Lib N [2no]22:213–20 My '29.

NEWMAN, CARD. JOHN HENRY, 1801–90

12565 **Hawkes, Arthur J.** Newman's copy of The Christian year. TLS 22 Ag '29:652.

12566 **S., J. S.** Newman. Bib N&Q 1no4:9 Oc '35; [P. H. Muir] *ib.* 2no1:2 Ja '36.

12567 **Svaglic, Martin J.** The revision of Newman's Apologia. Mod Philol 50no1:43–9 Ag '52.

12568 **Carter, John W.** J. H. Newman. The dream of Gerontius, 1866. [Binding variants]. (Note no.64). Bk Coll 5no2:171 '56.

12569 **Dessain, Stephen.** A poem wrongly ascribed to Newman. [Ornsby's The changed mother, 1845]. Bod Lib Rec 6no5:583–6 Ag '60.

12570 **Houghton, Walter E.** New articles by cardinal Newman. TLS 15 Ap '60:241.

NEWTON, SIR ISAAC, 1642–1727

12571 **Gray, George J.** Sir Isaac Newton's Principia. N&Q ser10 12:229 S '09.

12572 [**Haraszti, Zoltán**]. First edition of Newton's Principia acquired by the Library. More Bks Boston Pub Lib Bull 2no9:321–2 D '27.

12573 **Newton's** library found by a detective bookman. [De Villamil]. (Marginalia). Bkmns J ser3 15no5:282–3 '28.

12574 **De Villamil, Richard.** 'Catalogue of the library of dr. James Musgrave, rector of Chinnor, Oxon. [including Newton's library]' *in* Newton: the man. London [1931]. p. 62–103.

'Supplementary list of sir Isaac Newton's books' (p. 104–11)

12575 **MacPike, Eugene F.** Sir Isaac Newton in American libraries. N&Q 167:348–9 N '34; 168:51 Ja '35; 166:394 Je '35; 169:391–2 N '35; 171:337 N '36; 183:23 Jl '42.

12576 **Keynes, John M., 1st baron Keynes.** Newton: Principia, 1687. [Issues]. Bib N&Q 2no6:6–7 Jl '36.

12577 **The Newton** papers. (Notes on sales). TLS 18 Jl '36:604.

12578 **Schofield, B.** A Newton alchemical manuscript. Brit Mus Q 11no2:66 Mr '37.

12579 **Larson, Cedric.** Unique fiftieth anniversary gift presented to Stanford university. [F. E. Brasch's Newtoniana]. Stanford Alumni R 43no3:16–17 D '41. illus., facsim.

12580 **MacPike, Eugene F.** Sir Isaac Newton's library. N&Q 189:194 N '45; A. J. H. *ib.* 189:239 D '45; A. R. E. 189:260–1 D '45; E. F. M[acPike] 190:84 F '46; L. S. Thompson 191:263 D '46. [Sg.: E. F. M.]

12581 **Macomber, Henry P.** A comparison of the variations and errors in copies of the first edition of Newton's Principia, 1687. Isis 42pt3:230–2 Oc '51.

12582 **Munby, Alan N. L.** The two title-pages of the Principia. TLS 21 D '51:828; 28 Mr '52:228.

12583 —— The distribution of the first edition of Newton's Principia. Roy Soc N & Rec 10no1:28–39 Oc '52. facsims.

The evidence of Halley's letter to Newton of 5 July, 1687.–The publication of learned works.–The omission of the Principia from the Term catalogues.–The 'plures Bibliopolas' copies distributed first.–Part of the edition taken over by Samuel Smith.–Evidence that the Smith copies were exported.–The export and import of books.–The size of the first edition.–The value of the first edition.–Postscript.

12584 —— The Keynes collection of the works of sir Isaac Newton at King's college, Cambridge. Roy Soc N & Rec 10no1:40–50 Oc '52.

> The sale of the Portsmouth papers.–Alchemical papers.–Correspondence.–Theological papers.–Personal and miscellaneous papers.–Conduitt's memoirs.–Portraits.–Printed books.–Appendix [Ms. lot nos.].

12585 **Macomber, Henry P.** A census of the owners of copies of the 1687 first edition of Newton's Principia. Pa Bib Soc Am 47:269–92 '53. facsims.

12586 —— A census of owners of copies of the 1726 presentation issue of Newton's Principia. Pa Bib Soc Am 47:292–300 '53. facsims.

12587 **Price, Derek J. DeS.** Newton in a church tower: the discovery of an unknown book by Isaac Newton. [Not published?]. Yale Univ Lib Gaz 34no3:124–6 Ja '60.

12588 **Lyon, H. D.** More light required. [Presentation copy of Opticks, 1704]. (Query 137). Bk Coll 10no1:73 '61.

12589 **Brasch, Frederick E.** Sir Isaac Newton; an essay on sir Isaac Newton and Newtonian thought as exemplified in the Stanford collection of books. ... Published upon the occasion of an exhibition ... the Stanford university libraries ... 1962. [Stanford university, 1962]. 28p. port. 24cm.

12590 **Feisenberger, H. A.** The libraries of Newton, Hooke, and Boyle. Roy Soc N & Rec 21no1:42–55 Je '66. facsims.

> *Repr. from* Ivory hammer 3:[11] p. after p. 120 '65. facsims.

12591 **McKenzie, Donald F.** The author of Tables for purchasing leases, attributed to sir Isaac Newton. [G. Mabbot]. Cambridge Bib Soc Trans 3pt2:165–6 '66.

NIGHTINGALE, FLORENCE, 1820–1910

12592 **Carter, John W.** Florence Nightingale's Notes on nursing, 1860. [Issues]. Bib N&Q 1no4:9–10 Oc '35; C. Hopkinson *ib.* 2no1:2 Ja '36; L. L. MacKall 2no4/5:3 My '36.

NIXON, ANTHONY, fl.1602–16

12593 **Notes** on rare books. [Nixon's The foot-post of Dover]. Library ser3 10no37:18–22 Ja '19. facsims.

NOONAN, ROBERT, 1870–1911 *see* Tressell, Robert, *pseud.*

NORDEN, JOHN, 1548–1625?

12594 **Marcham, Frank.** Norden's Speculum Britanniæ. N&Q ser10 3:450 Je '05; W. J. Gadsden *ib.* 4:13 Jl '05; W. F. Prideaux; W. B. Gerish 4:75–6 Jl '05; W. F. Prideaux 4:193 S '05.

12595 **Row, Prescott.** A newly-discovered map of Surrey. [By Norden]. N&Q ser12 9:488 D '21; H. Hannen *ib.* 9:533–4 D '21.

12596 **Pollard, Alfred W.** The unity of John Norden, surveyor and religious writer. Library ser4 7no3:233–52 D '26.

12597 **Marsden, Wilfred A.** A Path-way to penitence. Brit Mus Q 13no3:96–7 S '39.

12598 **Skelton, Raleigh A.** John Norden's map of Surrey. Brit Mus Q 16no3:61–2 Oc '51.

NORTH, ROGER, 1653–1734

12599 **Almack, Edward.** Roger North's life of his brother and other seventeenth century mss. N&Q ser10 9:201–3 Mr '08.

12600 **Starr, G. A.** Roger North and the Arguments and materials for a register of estates. Brit Mus Q 31no1/2:17–19 '66.

NORTH, SIR THOMAS, 1535?–1601?

12601 **Garnett, Richard.** Misprint in North's Plutarch. Athenæum 3803:347 S '00.

12602 **Law, Roger A.** The text of Shakespeare's Plutarch. Huntington Lib Q 6no2:197–203 F '43. tables.

NORTON, THOMAS, 1532–84

12603 **Cauthen, Irby B.** Gorboduc, Ferrex and Porrex; the first two quartos. Stud Bib 15:231–3 '62.

O'CASEY, SEAN, 1880–1964

12604 **C., R. C.- and W. Partington.** A Sean O'Casey first edition unveiled. [The story of the Irish citizen army, 1919]; .... (Hints for collectors and marginalia). Bkmns J ser3 15no1:25–6 '27. [Sg.: W. P.]

12605 **O'Casey** papers acquired. N.Y. Pub Lib Bull 73no6:356–8 Je '69.

O'DALY, JOHN, fl.1878

12606 **Coleman, James.** John O'Daly. Irish Bk Lover 14no5:65–7 My '24.

O'DONOVAN, JOHN, 1809–61

12607 **[ÓLochlainn], Colm.** John ÓDonovan and the four masters. [Prospectus for his ed. of The annals of Ireland]. Irish Bk Lover 29no1:4–8 My '43; 30no2:43 F '47.

12608 —— Annals of the four masters. Irish Bk Lover 31no6:126–8 N '51.

O'DUFFY, EIMAR, 1893–1935

12609 **MacLochlainn, Alf.** Eimar O'Duffy, a bibliographical biography. Irish Bk 1no2:37–46 '59/60.

OGILBY, JOHN, 1600–76 *see under* Book production and distribution–Printers, publishers, etc.

O'HEGARTY, PATRICK SARSFIELD, 1879–1955

12610 **ÓLochlainn, Colm.** P. S. O'Hegarty. Bks & Libs at Kansas 1no13:2–3 '56.

12611 **O'Hegarty** redux. Bks & Libs at Kansas 1no21:9–10 My '59.

OLDMIXON, JOHN, 1673–1742

12612 **Rogers, J. Pat W.** A lost poem by Oldmixon. [Britannia liberata]. Pa Bib Soc Am 63:291–4 '69.

12613 —— The printing of Oldmixon's Histories. Library ser5 24no2:150–4 Je '69.

OLDYS, WILLIAM, 1696–1761

12614 **Osborn, James M.** William Oldys. (Bibliographical notes). TLS 9 Ap '38:256.

OLIPHANT, MARGARET OLIPHANT (WILSON), 1828–97

12615 **Colby, Vineta.** William Wilson, novelist. N&Q 211:60–6 F '66.

OLIVER, GEORGE, 1781–1861

12616 **Bowen, Geraint.** Collections illustrating The history of the Catholic religion, George Oliver. [Comparison of ms. draft and ptd. ed.]. (News and notes). Nat Lib Wales J 14no1:119–22 '65.

Summary in English (p. 122)

OLLIVANT, ALFRED, 1874–1927

12617 **Alfred** Ollivant's Owd Bob, 1898. [Priority of ed.]. Bib N&Q 2no9:9 Ja '38; 2no10:5 Ap '38; 2no11:5 N '38; 2no12:2 My '39.

O'MAHONY, CON., 1594–1650/6?

12618 **Conlan, J. P.** Some notes on the Disputatio apologetica. [1645]. Bib Soc Ireland Pubs 6no5:69–77 '55. facsims.

O'MOLLOY, FRANCIS, d.1677?

12619 **ÓCasaide, Séamus.** [Lucerna fidelium]. Irish Bk Lover 18no1:10–17 Ja/F '30. facsims.

12620 **MacAodhagáin, Partholán.** Two interesting copies of Grammatica Latino-Hibernica. Irish Bk Lover 32no5:101 Jl '56; P. ÓBroin *ib.* 32no6:141 S '57.

OPIE, AMELIA (ALDERSON), 1769–1853

12621 **Hibgame, Frederick T.** Amelia Opie's novels. N&Q ser9 9:267–8 Ap '02; R. A. Potts *ib.* 9:372 My '02.

ORFORD, HORACE WALPOLE, 4TH EARL OF, 1717–97 *see* Walpole, Horace, 4th earl of Orford, 1717–97.

ORRERY, ROGER BOYLE, 1ST EARL OF, 1621–79 *see* Boyle, John, 5th earl of Cork, and Orrey, 1707–62.

ORRERY, ROGER BOYLE, 1ST EARL OF, 1621–79 *see* Boyle, Roger, 1st earl of Orrery, 1621–79.

OSBORNE, DOROTHY (LADY TEMPLE), 1627–95

12622 **Smith, George C. Moore.** Dorothy Osborne's letters. [Emendations]. N&Q ser12 7:243–5 S '20; 7:263–4 Oc '20.

12623 —— New light on Dorothy Osborne's letters. TLS 28 Oc '20:704.

The text of the letters.—Conclusion.

O'SHAUGHNESSY, ARTHUR WILLIAM EDGAR, 1844–81

12624 **O'Hegarty, Patrick S.** Arthur O'Shaughnessy. An epic of women, 1870. (Bibliographical notes). Dublin Mag new ser 22no3:60 Jl/S '47.

12625 **Baum, Paull F.** Arthur O'Shaughnessy letters [acquired]. Lib N Duke Univ Lib 26:1–4 Ap '52. [Sg.: P. F. B.]

OSSIAN, *pseud., see* Macpherson, James, 1736–96.

O'SULLIVAN, TIMOTHY, fl.1795

12626 **Fiachra Eilgeach,** *pseud.* O'Sullivan's Pious miscellany. Irish Bk Lover 1no10:129–30 My '10.

OTWAY, THOMAS, 1652–85

12627 **Babcock, Robert W.** The reverend Montague Summers as editor of Otway. Pub Mod Lang Assn 48no3:948–52 S '33.

12628 **Goldberg, Homer.** The two 1692 editions of Otway's Caius Marius. Stud Bib 3:253–4 '50/1.

OUGHTRED, WILLIAM, 1575–1660

12629 **Drummond, W. J. H.** William Oughtred. N&Q 198:313 Jl '53.

12630 **Wallis, Peter J.** William Oughtred's Circles of proportion and Trigonometries. Cambridge Bib Soc Trans 4pt5:372–82 '68.

'Register of copies' (p. 382)

12631 **Hall, Trevor H.** Mathematicall recreations, an exercise in seventeenth-century bibliography. Leeds, Bibliography room, School of English, University of Leeds, 1969. 38p. 22cm. (Leeds studies in bibliography and textual criticism. Occasional paper, 1)

Rev: P. J. Wallis Library ser5 26:66–7 '71.

OUIDA, *pseud. of* MARIE LOUISE DE LA RAMÉE, 1839–1908

12632 **Sparke, Archibald.** Ouida in peridical literature. N&Q ser12 6:314 Je '20; F. J. Hytch *ib.* 6:343 Je '20.

OVERBURY, SIR THOMAS, 1581–1613

12633 **Paylor, Wilfrid J.** The editions of the Overburian characters. Library ser4 17no3:340–8 D '36.

OVERTON, RICHARD, fl.1641–63

12634 **Edwards, John.** Two anonymous tractates of the seventeenth century ascribed to Richard Overton. Glasgow Bib Soc Rec 4pt1:54–60 '18.

12635 **Zagorin, P.** The authorship of Mans mortallitie. Library ser5 5no3:179–83 D '50.

OWEN, GEORGE, 1552–1613

12636 **Charles, B. G.** Manuscripts of George Owen of Henllys. (News and notes). Nat Lib Wales J 1no4:226–7 '40.

12637 —— The second book of George Owen's Description of Penbrokeshire. [Ms.]. Nat Lib Wales J 5no4:264–85 '48. facsim.

'A fragment of the Second book' (p. 267–85)

OWEN, JOHN, 1560?–1622

12638 **Enck, John J.** John Owen's Epigrammata. (Notes). Harvard Lib Bull 3no3:431–4 '49.

12639 **Bradner, Leicester.** Musæ Anglicanæ: a supplemental list. Library ser5 22no2:93–103 Je '67.

'Appendix: The collected editions of Owen's Epigrammata' (p. 100–1)

OWEN, WILFRED EDWARD SALTER, 1893–1918

12640 **Milne, H. J. M.** The poems of Wilfred Owen. [Mss.]. Brit Mus Q 9no1:19–20 S '34.

12641 **Cohen, Joseph.** The Wilfred Owen war poetry collection. Lib Chron Univ Texas 5no3:24–35 '55.

12642 **Welland, D. S. R.** Wilfred Owen's manuscripts. TLS 15 Je '56:368; 22 Je '56:384; dame Edith Sitwell *ib.* 22 Je '56:377; J. Cohen 10 Ag '56:475; D. S. R. Welland 17 Ag '56:487.

12643 **Brown, T. Julian.** Wilfred Owen, 1893–1918. (English literary autographs, XLVIII). Bk Coll 12no4:489 '63. facsim.

12644 **Hill, James J.** The text of Wilfred Owen's Purple. [Ms]. N&Q 208:464 D '63.

OWEN, WILLIAM, 1759–1835 *see* Pughe, William Owen, formerly Owen, 1759–1835.

PALGRAVE, FRANCIS TURNER, 1824–97

12645 **B., W.** Palgrave's Golden treasury. [And Rossetti's The blessed damozel]. N&Q ser10 8:147 Ag '07; T. Bayne *ib.* 8:236 S '07; W. B. 8:351–2 N '07; W. F. Prideaux; C. C. B.; A. R. Waller; W. B. 8:393–4 N '07; W. F. Prideaux 8:454 D '07.

12646 **C., R. N.** and **W. P[artington].** The Golden treasury, its bibliography and adventure: the varying issues of the first editions. Bkmns J ser3 15no5:268–70 '28.

12647 **Bell, sir Harold I.** The original manuscript of the Golden treasury. Brit Mus Q 5no3:85–7 D '30. [Sg.: H. I. B.]

12648 **Wheeler, Hugh.** Golden treasury, 1861. Bib N&Q 1no1:2 Ja '35; J. H. A. Sparrow; A. Rogers *ib.* 1no2:1 Ap '35.

12649 **Foxon, David F.** The Golden treasury, 1861. [Publ.]. (Note no.52). Bk Coll 4no3:252–3 '55; 5no1:75 '56.

PALMER, THOMAS, fl.1553–64

12650 **Simpson, Percy.** Thomas Palmer. [Emblems]. N&Q ser8 8:243–4 S '95; ser9 1:172–3 F '98.

12651 —— Thomas Palmer's Emblems in Ashmole ms. 767. [And W. Browne]. Bod Q Rec 6no67:172–3 '30.

12652 **Tillotson, Geoffrey.** A manuscript of William Browne. [Palmer's Emblems]. R Eng Stud 6no22:187–91 Ap '30.

12653 —— Further note on Ashmole ms. 767. R Eng Stud 7no28:457–8 Oc '31.

PALTOCK, ROBERT, d.1767

12654 **Roberts, William.** Peter Wilkins. Bkworm 3no31:197–202 Je '90. facsims.

PARKER, ARCHBP. MATTHEW, 1504–75

12655 **Kershaw, S. W.** Archbishop Parker, collector and author. Library ser2 1no4:379–83 S '00.

12656 **Pearce, E. C.** Matthew Parker. [Library]. Library ser4 6no3:209–28 D '25. facsims.

12657 **Greg, sir Walter W.** Books and bookmen in the correspondence of archbishop Parker. Library ser4 16no3:234–79 D '35.

'Notes on some manuscripts in the Burghley sale catalogue, communicated by dr. M. R. James' (p. 278–9)

12658 **Wright, Cyril E.** The dispersal of the monastic libraries and the beginnings of Anglo-Saxon studies: Matthew Parker and his circle, a preliminary study. Cambridge Bib Soc Trans 1pt3:208–37 '51. facsims.

12659 **Taylor, John.** Henry Wharton and the Lambeth manuscript of the Flores historiarum. [Ed. by Parker]. N&Q 201:240–1 Je '56.

PARKYN, ROBERT, d.1570

12660 **Dickens, A. G.** Robert Parkyn's ms. books. N&Q 194:73–4 F '49.

PARNELL, THOMAS, 1679–1718

12661 **Rawson, Claude J.** Parnell on Whiston. [Ode for music on the longitude, 1727]. Pa Bib Soc Am 57:91–2 '63.

12662 —— New Parnell manuscripts. Scriblerian 1no2:1–2 '69.

PARR, SAMUEL, 1747–1825

12663 **K., L. L.** Dr. Samuel Parr's library. N&Q ser10 9:510 Je '08.

12664 **Neill, Desmond G.** Samuel Parr's Notes on Rapin's Dissertation on whigs and tories. (Note 158). Bk Coll 10no2:199–200 '61.

PARTRIDGE, JOHN, 1644–1715

12665 **Bond, Richmond P.** John Partridge and the Company of stationers. Stud Bib 16:61–80 '63.

PASSFIELD, SIDNEY JAMES WEBB, BARON, 1859–1947 *see* Webb, Sidney James, baron Passfield, 1859–1947.

PATER, WALTER HORATIO, 1839–94

12666 **Fletcher, G. B. A.** A textual error in Pater. [The myth of Demeter]. TLS 29 Ap '36:697.

12667 **Brown, Edward K.** Pater's Appreciations, a bibliographical note. Mod Lang N 65no4:247–9 Ap '50.

12668 **Chandler, Edmund.** 'The textual history of Marius the Epicurean' *in* Pater on style: an examination of the essay on Style and textual history of Marius the Epicurean. Copenhagen, 1958. p. 24–78.

PATMORE, COVENTRY KERSEY DIGHTON, 1823–96

12669 **Flower, Robin E. W.** Coventry Patmore's Odes. [And The unknown eros, I–XLVI]. Brit Mus Q 4no2:53–4 S '29. [Sg.: R. F.]

12670 **Marks, Ronald E.** Coventry Patmore's library. TLS 12 N '54:721.

12671 **Thomas, Alfred.** Coventry Patmore's literary criticism; attribution of articles. N&Q 206:229 Je '61.

PATMORE, HENRY JOHN, 1860–83

12672 **Berol, Alfred C.** Gosse and Henry Patmore's Poems. (Note 155). Bk Coll 10no1:71–2 '61.

PAYNE, HENRY THOMAS, 1759–1832

12673 **Owens, B. G.** Archdeacon Henry Thomas Payne, 1759–1832. (Biographica et bibliographica). Nat Lib Wales J 4no3/4:210–14 '46.

PEACOCK, THOMAS LOVE, 1785–1866

12674 **Young, Arthur B.** T. L. Peacock: contributions to periodicals. N&Q ser 10 8:2–3 Jl '07; W. E. A. Axon *ib.* 8:157 Ag '07.

12675 **Pierpont, Robert.** T. L. Peacock's Sir Hornbook. N&Q ser10 12:226 S '09.

12676 **Young, Arthur B.** T. L. Peacock's literary remains. [Mss.]. N&Q ser10 11:224–5 Mr '09.

12677 **Goodspeed, George T.** Peacock: Nightmare abbey, London, 1818. [Variant TP]. Bib N&Q 2no1:4 Ja '36; Quad, *pseud., ib.* 2no2:1–2 F '36; O. S. B. Brett, 3d viscount Esher 2no3:3 Ap '36. [Sg.: G. G.]

12678 **Warburton, Thomas.** Peacock: Genius of the Thames, 1810. [Cancel title-leaf]. Bib N&Q 2no6:7 Jl '36; O. S. B. Brett, 3d viscount Esher 2no8:3 F '37.

PEELE, GEORGE, 1558?–97?

12679 **Smith, George C. Moore.** George Peele. [Emendations]. N&Q ser10 9:181–2 Mr '08.

12680 —— Notes on Peele. [Emendations]. Mod Lang R 17no3:290–3 Jl '22.

12681 **Larsen, Thorlief.** George Peele. [The tale of Troy]. TLS 4 D '24:826.

12682 —— The growth of the Peele canon. Library ser4 11no3:300–11 D '30.

12683 **Sampley, Arthur M.** The text of Peele's David and Bethsabe. Pub Mod Lang Assn 46no3:659–71 S '31.

12684 **Jenkins, Harold.** Peele's Old wives tale. Mod Lang R 34no2:177–85 Ap '39.

12685 **Wilson, Robert H.** Reed and Warton on the Old wives tale. Pub Mod Lang Assn 55no2:605–8 Je '40.

12686 **Ashe, Dora J.** The text of Peele's Edward I. Stud Bib 7:153–70 '55.

12687 **Hook, Frank S.** The two compositors in the first quarto of Peele's Edward I. Stud Bib 7:170–7 '55. tables.

12688 **Cutts, John P.** Peele's Hunting of Cupid. Stud Renaiss 5:121–9 '58.

PEIRCE, SIR EDMOND, fl.1642–60

12689 **Plomer, Henry R.** An anonymous royalist writer: sir Edmond Peirce. Library ser3 2no6:164–72 Ap '11.

PENKETHMAN, JOHN, fl.1623–38

12690 **Butler, Francelia.** John Penkethman's pseudonymous plague works, 1625–1636. Stud Philol 57no3:622–33 Jl '60.

PENN, WILLIAM, 1644–1718

12691 **Mortimer, Russell S.** Penn and his printer. [John Darby]. Friends' Hist Soc J 46no2:64–5 '54. [Sg.: R. S. M.]

12692 **Goodbody, Olive C.** and **Mary Pollard.** The first edition of William Penn's Great case of liberty of conscience, 1670. Library ser5 16no2:146–9 Je '61.

PENNANT, THOMAS, 1726–98

12693 **Hancock, Thomas W.** A rare edition of Pennant's Tours in Wales. [Extra-illus. copy of Q1]. N&Q ser9 7:67–8 Ja '01.

12694 **Powell, Lawrence F.** Pennant's Tours in Scotland. (Antiquarian notes). TLS 21 My '38:360.

12695 —— The tours of Thomas Pennant. Library ser4 19no2:131–54 S '38. facsim.

'Addendum: a cancelled volume' (p. 152–4)

12696 **McAtee, W. L.** The North American birds of Thomas Pennant. J Soc Bib Nat Hist 4pt2:100–24 Ja '63. table.

12697 **Archer, H. Richard.** Thomas Pennant's copy of Kalm's Travels, 1770–71. Huntia 1:204–9 '64. facsims.

12698 **Rees, Eiluned** and **G. Walters.** Pennant and the 'pirates'. Nat Lib Wales J 15no4:423–36 '68.

'Bibliographical checklist of Dublin editions of Pennant's works and the English editions on which they were based' (p. 423–4)

PENNECUIK, ALEXANDER, d.1730

12699 **Gillis, William.** Alexander Pennecuik: two manuscripts. N&Q 202:297–8 Jl '57.

PEPYS, SAMUEL, 1633–1703

12700 **Wheatley, Henry B.** Two English bookmen, I. Samuel Pepys. Bibliographica 1pt2:155–62 '95.

12701 **Lethaby, W. R.** Pepys's London collection. London Topographical Rec 2:66–9 '03.

12702 **Savage, Ernest A.** Samuel Pepys' library. [Magdalene college, Cambridge]. Library ser2 4no15:287–91 Jl '03. facsim.

12703 **Sidgwick, Frank.** The Pepys ballads. Samuel Pepys Club Occas Pa 1:47–57 '03.

12704 **Tanner, Joseph R.** The cataloguing of the Pepysian manuscripts. Samuel Pepys Club Occas Pa 1:41–6 '03.

12705 **The Pepysian** treasures. [Magdalene college, Cambridge]. Gent Mag 300:4–11 F '06; 300:225–34 Ap '06; 300:470–8 Je '06. (Incomplete)

12706 **Pollard, Alfred W.** The Pepysian library. Library ser2 8no31:309–11 Jl '07.

12707 **Sidgwick, Frank.** Some notes on the Pepysian library. Bib Soc Trans 10pt1:7–8 '08/9.

Summary of paper read 21 D '08.

12708 —— [**Same**]: Bib Soc News-sh 3–4 Ja '09.

Report of paper read 21 D '08.

.12709 **Gaselee, sir Stephen.** Samuel Pepys' Spanish books. Library ser4 2no1:1–11 Je '21.

12710 —— The Spanish books in the library of Samuel Pepys. [Oxford] Ptd. at the O.U.P. for the Bibliographical society, 1921. 49p. 23cm. (Bib Soc Trans Suppl 2)

12711 **James, Montague R.** A descriptive catalogue of the library of Samuel Pepys. Pt.III. Mediaeval manuscripts. London, Sidgwick and Jackson, 1923. x,128p. 23cm.

Rev: Nation-Athenæum 34:17–18 '23; TLS 21 F '24:111.

12712 **Pangle, M. E.** Samuel Pepys as a bookman. Bkmns J ser3 16no8:431–6 '28.

12713 **Chappell, Edwin.** The text of Pepys. [Diary]. TLS 11 Ag '32:569; F. McD. C. Turner *ib.* 18 Ag '32:581; W. Matthews 25 Ag '32:593; F. McD. C. Turner 17 N '32:859; R. G. Howarth 26 Ja '33:59; W. Matthews 2 F '33:76.

12714 **Carlton, William J.** Samuel Pepys, his shorthand books. Library ser4 14no1:73–84 Je '33.

12715 **A Pepys** exhibition. (Notes on sales). TLS 30 N '33:860; E. Chappell *ib.* 7 D '33:878.

12716 **Birss, John H.** Books from Pepys's library. N&Q 166:370 My '34.

12717 **Chappell, Edwin.** Pepysiana. [Mss.]. TLS 14 Mr '35:160.

12718 **Matthews, William.** Pepys's transcribers. J Eng Germ Philol 34no2: 213–34 Ap '35. tables.

12719 **Gaselee, sir Stephen.** Samuel Pepys, book lover; an address . . . May 28th, 1936. [London, 1936?]. 8p. 20cm.

12720 **Sykes, W. J.** Library of Samuel Pepys. Ontario Lib R 21no1:4–5 F '37.

12721 **Dale, Donald A.** Dr. Wheatley's copy of Pepys's diary. N&Q 178:372 My '40.

12722 **Pepys** designs a book-plate. Bod Lib Rec 2no17:23 D '41.

12723 **Ladborough, R. W.** A discovery in the Pepys library. [Association copies]. (Note no.26). Bk Coll 2no4:278–9 '53.

12724 **Emslie, Macdonald.** Pepys's songs and songbooks in the Diary period. Library ser5 12no4:240–55 D '57.

12725 **Carter, Harry G.** and **B. Wolpe.** Pepys's copy of Moxon's Mechanick exercises. Library ser5 14no2:124–6 Je '59.

12726 **Emslie, Macdonald.** Two of Pepys's 'very lewd songs' in print. Library ser5 15no4:291–3 D '60.

12727 **Hughes, Garfield H.** Llyfrau Samuel Pepys. [His books of Welsh interest]. Welsh Bib Soc J 9no3:133–6 D '62.

12728 **Ladborough, R. W.** A lost Pepys-library book rediscovered. Cambridge Bib Soc Trans 3pt4:292–4 '62. facsims.

12729 **Turner, Francis McD. C.** The Pepys library. [Magdalene college, Cambridge]. Priv Lib 5no4:70–2 Oc '64.

Medieval manuscripts.–Early printed books.–Other collections.

12730 **Goldstein, Leba M.** The Pepys ballads. Library ser5 21no4:282–92 D '66. facsims.

12731 **Ladborough, R. W.** The library of Samuel Pepys. Hist Today 17no7:82 Jl '67. illus., port., facsims.

PERCEVAL, ARTHUR PHILIP, 1799–1850

12732 **Wainewright, John B.** A. P. Perceval and Tracts for the times. N&Q ser12 11:109 Ag '22; Fama, *pseud., ib.* 11:277 S '22.

PERCY, BP. THOMAS, 1729–1811

12733 **Tracts** from dr. Percy's library. Athenæum 3758:620 N '99.

12734 **Powell, Lawrence F.** Hau Kiou Choaan. R Eng Stud 2no8:446–55 Oc '26.

12735 **Reeve, C. R.** Notes on Percy's Reliques. TLS 10 Je '26:394; Alda Milner-Barry *ib.* 1 Jl '26:448; G. Gordon 8 Jl '26:464.

12736 **Powell, Lawrence F.** Percy's Reliques. Library ser4 9no2:113–37 S '28. facsim.

12737 **Thomas, P. G.** Bishop Percy and the Scottish ballads. [Reliques]. TLS 4 Jl '29:538; Marjorie Williams; C. A. Stonehill *ib.* 11 Jl '29:558; P. G. Thomas 25 Jl '29:592.

12738 **Kenyon, sir Frederic G.** The Percy manuscripts. [Libr.]. TLS 30 Jl '31:597; sir E. K. Chambers *ib.* 6 Ag '31:609.

12739 **Jones, A. Watkin-.** Bishop Percy and the Scottish ballads. Essays & Stud 18:110–21 '32.

12740 **Ogburn, Vincent H.** The Wilkinson mss. and Percy's Chinese books. [Ms. of Hau Kiou Choaan]. R Eng Stud 9no33:30–6 Ja '33.

12741 **Jones, A. Watkin-.** Percy mss. TLS 8 Mr '34:162.

12742 **Leslie, sir Shane.** The Percy library. Bk Coll Q 14:11–24 Ap/Je '34.

12743 **Shearer, Thomas** and **A. Tillotson.** Percy's relations with Cadell and Davies. Library ser4 15no2:224–36 S '34.

12744 **Churchill, Irving L.** Editions of Percy's Memoir of Goldsmith. Mod Lang N 50no7:464–5 N '35.

12745 **Munby, Alan N. L.** Cancels in Percy's Reliques. TLS 31 Oc '36:892; L. F. Powell *ib.* 7 N '36:908.

12746 **Ogburn, Vincent H.** Further notes on Thomas Percy. Pub Mod Lang Assn 51no2:449–58 Je '36.

12747 —— Thomas Percy's unfinished collection, Ancient English and Scottish poems. [Ms.]. Eng Lit Hist 3no3:183–9 S '36.

12748 **Dennis, Leah.** Gill Morice in the Reliques again. Mod Lang N 56no4:286–8 Ap '41.

12749 **Bate, Walter J.** Percy's use of his folio-manuscript. [Reliques]. J Eng Germ Philol 43no3:337–48 Jl '44.

12750 **Falconer, A. F.** Bishop Percy's annotated copy of lord Haile's Ancient Scottish poems. Edinburgh Bib Soc Trans 2pt4:432–7 '46.

12751 **Randall, David A.** Percy's Reliques and its cancel leaves. New Coloph 1pt4:404–7 Oc '48.

12752 **Baine, Rodney M.** Percy's own copies of the Reliques. (Notes). Harvard Lib Bull 5no2:246–51 '51.

12753 **Friedman, Albert B.** The first draft of Percy's Reliques. Pub Mod Lang Assn 69no5:1233–49 D '54.

12754 —— Percy's folio manuscript revalued. [Reliques]. J Eng Germ Philol 53no4:524–31 Oc '54.

12755 **Brooks, Cleanth J.** The county parson as research scholar: Thomas Percy, 1760–1770. Pa Bib Soc Am 53:219–39 '59.

12756 **Percy, bp. Thomas.** The library of Thomas Percy, 1729–1811, bishop of Dromore, editor of The reliques of ancient English poetry; removed to Caledon house, co. Tyrone, in 1812 and now sold. . . . [London] Sotheby & co. [1969]. 72p. illus., facsims. 26cm.

PERCY, WILLIAM, 1575–1648

12757 **Lawrence, William J.** Ms. plays by William Percy, 1600. N&Q ser9 8:183 Ag '01; P. Simpson *ib.* 8:227 S '01.

PERKINS, WILLIAM, 1558–1602

12758 **Dick, Hugh G.** The authorship of Foure great lyers, 1585. Library ser4 19no3:311–14 D '38.

PETERS, HUGH, 1598–1660

12759 **Williams, J. B.,** *pseud. of* **J. G. Muddiman.** Hugh Peters, post-restoration satires and portraits. N&Q ser11 10:105–6 Ag '14; G. Thorn-Drury *ib.* 10:193 S '14; J. B. Williams, *pseud.* 10:251–2 S '14.

PETTY, SIR WILLIAM, 1623–87

12760 **Hull, Charles H.** Sir William Petty. N&Q ser8 8:77 Jl '95.

PHILIPS, AMBROSE, 1674–1749

12761 **Hustvedt, S. B.** Dr. Farmer and Ambrose Philips. [Collection of old ballads, 1723–5]. TLS 6 D '23:852; M. G. Segar *ib.* 13 D '23:876.

12762 **Segar, Mary G.** Dictionary making in the early eighteenth century. [Proposals for printing an English dictionary]. R Eng Stud 7no26:210–13 Ap '31.

12763 —— A collection of ballads. TLS 3 Mr '32:154.

12764 **Griffith, Reginald H.** Persian tales. TLS 16 N '35:752; D. B. Macdonald *ib.* 14 D '35:864.

12765 **Segar, Mary G.** Ambrose Philips. (Sales and bibliography). TLS 1 F '41:60.

12766 **Cameron, William J.** Ten new poems by Ambrose Philips, 1674–1749. N&Q 202:469–70 N '57.

12767 **Jones, Claude E.** Ambrose Philips. [Armigero; ode, 1707; and Walpole's library]. N&Q 203:86–7 F '58.

PHILIPS, JOHN, 1676–1709

12768 **Todd, William B.** Philips Cyder, 1708. (Note 150). Bk Coll 10no1:68 '61; L. O. Cowgill *ib.* 19no4:526 '70.

PHILIPS, KATHERINE (FOWLER), 1631–64

12769 **Elmen, Paul.** Some manuscript poems by the matchless Orinda. Philol Q 30no1:53–7 Ja '51.

PHILLIP, JOHN, fl.1560–90

12770 **Greg, sir Walter W.** John Phillip; notes for a bibliography. Library ser3 1no3:302–28 Jl '10; 1no4:396–423 Oc '10; Further notes *ib.* 4no16:432–6 Oc '13.

PHILLIPPS, JAMES ORCHARD HALLIWELL-, 1820–89

12771 **Murray, J. A. H.** Halliwell ms. wanted. [Libr.]. N&Q ser9 12:227 S '03.

12772 **Halliwelliana.** Harvard Lib N [1no]12:255–7 D '23.

12773 **Winstanley, D. A.** Halliwell Phillipps and Trinity college library. [Book thefts]. Library ser5 2no4:250–82 Mr '48.

'Additional note, by R. W. Hunt' (p. 277–82)

12774 **J. O. Halliwell** and the Bodleian. [Book thefts]. Bod Lib Rec 2no28:237–8 F '49.

12775 **Race, Sydney.** J. O. Halliwell and Simon Forman. [And Plymouth proprietary library; Collier]. N&Q 203:315–20 Jl '58.

12776 **In the saleroom.** [Halliwell-Phillipps library]. TLS 30 Jl '64:672.

PHILLIPS, JOHN, d.1640

12777 **The Pathe** to paradise. [Ms.]. (Notes on sales). TLS 12 N '31:900.

PHILLIPS, JOHN, 1631–1706

12778 **Beaty, Frederick L.** Three versions of John Phillips' Satyr against hypocrites. (Notes). Harvard Lib Bull 6no3:380–7 '52.

12779 **Parker, William R.** The anonymous life of Milton. [And C. Skinner]. TLS 13 S '57:547; R. W. Hunt *ib.* 11 Oc '57:609; M. Kelley 27 D '57:787.

12780 **Ayers, Robert W.** The John Phillips–John Milton Angli responsio: editions and relations. Pa Bib Soc Am 56:66–72 '62. tables.

PHILLPOTTS, EDEN, 1862–1960

12781 **Trevanion, Michael,** *pseud.* Phillpotts: The three brothers, 1909. [Issues]. Bib N&Q 2no7:6 Oc '36; 2no8:5 F '37.

12782 **Hinton, Percival F.** A ghost laid. [Not the author of The ghost in the Bank of England]. (Note 226). Bk Coll 13no3:350–1 '64.

PINDAR, PETER, *pseud. of* JOHN WOLCOT, 1738–1819

12783 **Gerish, William B.** Peter Pindar's works. N&Q ser8 2:328 Oc '92; R. P. Chope; F. D. *ib.* 2:438 N '92.

12784 **Coldicott, H. Rowlands D.** Peter Pindar, dr. John Wolcot. [Mss.]. N&Q ser11 4:329 Oc '11.

PIOZZI, HESTER LYNCH (SALUSBURY), formerly MRS. THRALE, 1741–1821

12785 **Smith, Minna S.** Mrs. Piozzi's annotations to Boswell. London Merc 5no27:286–93 Ja '22; Littell's Living Age 312no4052:536–42 Mr '22.

12786 **M.** Piozzi on Boswell and Johnson. [Life of Johnson, 1816, with Piozzi notes]. Harvard Lib N [2no]17:104–11 Ap '26.

12787 **Chapman, Robert W.** A literary fraud. [Love letters of mrs. Piozzi, 1843]. London Merc 22no128:154–6 Je '30.

12788 **Letters** and papers of the Johnson circle. [Acquisition of Thrale-Piozzi papers]. (Notes and news). Bull John Rylands Lib 20no2:181–2 Jl/Ag '36.

12789 **Clifford, James L.** The printing of mrs. Piozzi's Anecdotes of dr. Johnson. Bull John Rylands Lib 20no1:157–72 Ja '36.

12790 **Chapman, Robert W.** Mrs. Thrale's letters to Johnson published by mrs. Piozzi in 1788. R Eng Stud 24no93:58–61 '48.

12791 **Finch, Jeremiah S.** Mrs. Piozzi. [Wilton Lloyd-Smith collection presented to Library]. Princeton Univ Lib Chron 14no3:161–4 '53.

12792 **Fisher, Sidney T.** The Pell copy of mrs. Piozzi's Journey. N&Q 208:72–3 F '63.

PITCAIRNE, ARCHIBALD, 1652–1713

12793 **Simpson, S. M.** An anonymous and undated Edinburgh tract. [Archimedis Epistola ad regem Gelonem, 1688]. (Note 264). Bk Coll 15no1:67 '66.

PIX, MARY (GRIFFITH), 1666–1720?

12794 **Bowers, Fredson T.** Underprinting by Mary Pix, The Spanish wives, 1696. Library ser5 9no4:248–54 D '54. tables.

PLUNKETT, EDWARD JOHN MORETON DRAX, 18th BARON DUNSANY, 1878–1957

12795 **Wilson, William.** Future and Fortune in A night at an inn. Pa Bib Soc Am 58:477–8 '64.

12796 **Stoddard, F. G.** The lord Dunsany collection. Lib Chron Univ Texas 8no3:27–32 '67.

'Desiderata' (p. 31–2).

POEL, WILLIAM, 1852–1934

12797 **Meserve, Walter J.** The William Poel collection. [Drama]. Bks & Libs at Kansas 1no19:5–7 N '58.

POLIDORI, JOHN WILLIAM, 1795–1821

12798 **Byron:** The vampyre, 1819. [Priority of ed.]. Bib N&Q 2no11:7–8 N '38; H. W. Edwards *ib.* 2no12:4 My '39.

12799 **Viets, Henry R.** The London editions of Polidori's The vampyre. Pa Bib Soc Am 63:83–103 '69.

'Bibliography' (p. 101–3)

POLYDORE VERGIL, d.1555 *see* Vergilius, Polydorus, d.1555.

POOLE, JOHN, 1787–1872

12800 **Urban,** *pseud.* John Poole, author of Paul Pry. N&Q ser8 6:308 Oc '94; A. C. W.; E. H. Coleman; J. Pickford *ib.* 6:372 N '94.

POOLE, JOSHUA, fl.1632–46

12801 **Cox, Edwin M.** Notes on rare books. [Poole's The English Parnassus, 1657]. Library ser3 9no35:215–16 Jl '18.

POPE, ALEXANDER, 1688–1744

12802 **B., W.** Pope and Thomson. N&Q ser8 12:327 Oc '97; D. C. Tovey *ib.* 12:389–91 N '97; W. B. ser9 1:23–4 Ja '98; D. C. Tovey 1:129–30 F '98; W. B. 1:193–4 Mr '98; D. C. Tovey 1:289–90,415 Ap,My '98.

12803 **Rutton, W. L.** The Basset table. [And lady M. W. Montagu]. N&Q ser9 2:141–2 Ag '98.

12804 **Aitken, George A.** Pope's Essay on man. Athenæum 4031:112 Ja '05.

12805 **O., W.** Horace, Virgil & Cicero, publishers. [Pope's Iliad and Odyssey, 1759–60]. N&Q ser10 8:70 Jl '07.

12806 **Sherborn, C. Davies.** Pope, a missing page. [Works, 1735]. Athenæum 4146:442 Ap '07.

12807 **Francis, John C.** Lord Macaulay and William John Thoms. [Dunciad]. N&Q ser10 11:165 F '09; R. Thipps *ib.* 11:215–16 Mr '09; J. S. Crone 11:293 Ap '09; W. F. Prideaux 11:354–5 My '09; 12:150–2 Ag '09.

12808 **Griffith, Reginald H.** Notes for bibliophiles. [The dunciad]. Nation (N.Y.) 93no2403:52–3 Jl '11.

12809 **Breslar, M. L. R.** Pope's Iliad; price received. N&Q ser11 6:509 D '12.

12810 **Aitken, George A.** Notes on the bibliography of Pope. Bib Soc Trans 12pt2:113–43 '12/13. facsims.

12811 —— [Same]: Bib Soc News-sh 1–4 Mr/Ap '13.

Report of paper read 17 F '13.

12812 **Griffith, Reginald H.** Some notes on the Dunciad. Mod Philol 10no2:179–96 Oc '13.

I. The new Dunciad, 1742.–II. The coronation of king Colley.–III. Two undated editions.–IV. Some unnoted variants.

12813 —— The Dunciad of 1728. Mod Philol 13no1:1–18 My '15. table.

I. The preparation of the poem for the press.–II. The preparation of the public to receive it.–III. The advertisement of the poem.–IV. The various editions.–V. Printers and publishers.–VI. The critical apparatus and the copyright.

12814 —— Alexander Pope and Popiana. N&Q ser12 4:44 F '18.

12815 **Jones, Richard F.** Another of Pope's schemes. [Bathos, 1728]. Mod Lang N 35no6:346–51 Je '20.

12816 **Loane, George G.** Some notes on Pope. [Emendations]. TLS 15 Ap '20:240; C. L. D. *ib.* 10 Je '20:369.

12817 —— Firmless in Pope. ['Stript to the naked soul ...' in Ruffhead's ed., = formless?]. TLS 10 F '21:92.

12818 **Dunciad** epics. (Notes on sales). TLS 30 Ag '23:576.

12819 **Sherburn, George.** 'Notes on the canon of Pope's works, 1714–20' *in* Manly anniversary studies in language and literature. Chicago, Ill., 1923. p. 170–9.

12820 **Loane, George G.** The new Pope. [Text of Everyman ed.]. TLS 18 D '24:871.

12821 **Pope** in the Ashley library. [And T. J. Wise]. (Notes on sales). TLS 22 My '24:328.

12822 **Case, Arthur E.** Some new poems by Pope? [In Poems on several occasions, 1717]. London Merc 10no6:614–23 Oc '24; 11no64:411–12 F '25.

12823 —— Notes on the bibliography of Pope. Mod Philol 24no3:297–313 F '27.

12824 **Osler, A. May.** Concerning Pope. [Request for whereabouts of bibliographica]. TLS 5 My '27:318.

12825 **Chandler, William K.** The first edition of the Dunciad. Mod Philol 29no1:59–72 Ag '31. tables.

1. External evidence.–2. Internal evidence.–3. The editions of 1728.

12826 **Griffith, Reginald H.** A piracy of Pope's Iliad. [1718–21]. Stud Philol 28no4:737–41 Oc '31.

12827 **Wright, S. G.** Ruffhead's Life of Pope. Bod Q Rec 7no73:12 '32. [Sg.: S. G. W.]

12828 **Babcock, Robert W.** The text of Pope's To mrs. M. B. on her birth-day. Mod Lang N 48no7:452–7 N '33.

12829 **Ault, Norman.** Pope and the miscellanies. TLS 7 D '35:838.

12830 —— Pope's lost sermon on glass-bottles. [The dignity, use and abuse of glass-bottles, 1715]. TLS 6 Je '35:360; E. Heath *ib.* 13 Je '35:380; G. Sherburn 20 Je '35:399; J. R. Sutherland 27 Je '35:416; N. Ault 4 Jl '35:432; G. Sherburn 11 Jl '35:448.

12831 **Munby, Alan N. L.** A Pope problem. [Mr. Taste's tour, c.1732]. TLS 10 Ja '35:21; H. P. Vincent *ib.* 14 F '35:92.

12832 **Flower, Desmond.** Eighteenth-century binding. [Pope's Iliad, 1720, with sheets of marbled paper]. Bib N&Q 2no2:4 F '36.

12833 **Sutherland, James R.** The Dunciad of 1729. Mod Lang R 31no3:347–53 Jl '36.

12834 **Haraszti, Zoltán.** First editions of Alexander Pope. More Bks Boston Pub Lib Bull 12no10:437–50 D '37. facsims.

12835 **Griffith, Reginald H.** The Dunciad duodecimo. Coloph new ser 3no4:569–86 D '38.

I. Premises.–II. Data.–III. The search for meanings.–Conclusion.–IV. Additional data for experiment.–Appendix.

12836 **Dobrée, Bonamy.** Pope's Horace. [Libr.]. TLS 12 Ag '39:479.

12837 **[Muir, Percival H.]**. Pope: The dunciad, 1728. [Distinction of ed.]. Bib N&Q 2no10:11 Ap '38; E. Schlengemann *ib.* 2no12:4 My '39. table.

12838 **Vincent, Howard P.** Some Dunciad litigation. [Against piracy of Dunciad]. Philol Q 18no3:285–9 Jl '39.

12839 **Root, Robert K.** Pope's contributions to the Lintot miscellanies of 1712 and 1714. Eng Lit Hist 7no4:265–71 D '40.

12840 **Sherburn, George.** Pope's letters and the Harleian library. Eng Lit Hist 7no3:177–87 S '40.

12841 **Ault, Norman.** Pope's lost poems. TLS 8 Mr '41:115.

12842 **Dearing, Vinton A.** New light on the first printing of the letters of Pope and Swift. Library ser4 24no1/2:74–80 Je/S '43.

12843 **Mack, Maynard.** Pope's Horatian poems; problems of bibliography and text. Mod Philol 41no1:33–44 Ag '43. tables.

12844 **Griffith, Reginald H.** Pope editing Pope. Univ Texas Stud Eng 1944:5–108 '44.

I. On criticism.–II. An essay on man.

12845 **Pottle, Frederick A.** The Pope collection at Colby. Colby Lib Q 1no7:106–12 Je '44.

The bicentenary exhibition.–A list of desiderata for the Pope collection.

12846 **Ratchford, Fannie E.** The Pope bicentennial exhibition. Lib Chron Univ Texas 1no1:3–9 '44. facsim.

12847 **Root, Robert K.** A Pope exhibition and an unpublished letter of Pope. Princeton Univ Lib Chron 6no1:37–40 N '44.

12848 **Mack, Maynard.** A manuscript of Pope's imitation of the First ode of the fourth book of Horace. Mod Lang N 60no3:185–8 Mr '45.

12849 **Sutherland, James.** The dull duty of an editor. [Pope and Theobald]. R Eng Stud new ser 21no83:202–15 Jl '45.

Repr. in Mack, Maynard, *ed.* Essential articles for the study of Alexander Pope. Hamden, Conn., 1964. (Rev. ed., 1968). p. 630–49.

12850 **Hagedorn, Ralph.** Pope bibliography. [Essay on criticism, 1716]. N&Q 192:388 S '47.

12851 **Rogers, Robert W.** Notes on Pope's collaboration with Warburton in preparing a final edition of the Essay on man. Philol Q 26no4:358–66 Oc '47.

12852 **Bloom, Lillian D.** Pope as textual critic: a bibliographical study of his Horatian text. J Eng Germ Philol 47no2:150–5 Ap '48. tables.

> *Repr. in* Mack, Maynard, *ed.* Essential articles for the study of Alexander Pope. Hamden, Conn., 1964. (Rev. ed., 1968). p. 495–506.

12853 **Dearing, Vinton A.** The prince of Wales's set of Pope's Works. Harvard Lib Bull 4no3:320–38 '50.

> *Repr. in* Mack, Maynard, *ed.* Essential articles for the study of Alexander Pope. Hamden, Conn., 1964. (Rev. ed., 1968). p. 368–81.

12854 —— 'The 1737 editions of Alexander Pope's Letters' *in* Essays critical and historical dedicated to Lily B. Campbell, by members of the departments of English, University of California. Berkeley, 1950. p. 185–97.

12855 **Griffith, Reginald H.** Pope's reading. N&Q 195:363–4 Ag '50.

12856 **Brown, T. Julian.** Alexander Pope, 1688–1744. (English literary autographs, IV). Bk Coll 1no4:240–3 '52. facsims.

12857 **Griffith, Reginald H.** Pope on the art Of gardening. [Rapin Of gardens, 1728]. Univ Texas Stud Eng 31:52–6 '52.

12858 **Todd, William B.** Pope: One thousand seven hundred and [thirty-] eight, dialogue II. (Note no.5). Bk Coll 1no2:127 '52.

12859 **Butt, John E.** 'Editorial problems in eighteenth-century poetry [Pope]' *in* California. University at Los Angeles. William Andrews Clark memorial library. Papers. . . . [Los Angeles, 1953]. p. 11–22.

12860 **Callan, Norman.** Pope's Iliad: a new document. [Arsenal proofsheets]. R Eng Stud new ser 4no14:109–21 Ap '53.

12861 **Dearing, Vinton A.** Pope, Theobald, and Wycherley's Posthumous works. Pub Mod Lang Assn 68no1:223–36 Mr '53.

12862 **McLeod, Alan L.** Pope and Gay: two overlooked manuscripts. N&Q 198:334–7 Ag '53; J. E. Butt *ib.* 200:23–5 Ja '55.

12863 **Butt, John E.** Pope's poetical manuscripts. (Warton lecture on English poetry). Proc Brit Acad 40:23–39 '55. facsims.

'Appendix: list of autograph manuscripts, with present locations, in approximate order of composition' (p. 38–9)

Rev: N. Callan R Eng Stud new ser 9:119 '58.

Repr. in Mack, Maynard, *ed.* Essential articles for the study of Alexander Pope. Hamden, Conn., 1964. (Rev. ed., 1968). p. 507–27.

12864 **Maurer, Oscar.** The Griffith library. [Acquisition of R. H. Griffith collection of Popiana, etc.]. Lib Chron Univ Texas 5no4:41–2 '56.

12865 **Todd, William B.** Concealed Pope editions. Bk Coll 5no1:48–52 '56; D. F. Foxon *ib.* 5no3:277–9 '56.

12866 **Dearing, Vinton A.** Two notes on the copy for Pope's letters. Pa Bib Soc Am 51:327–33 '57.

12867 **Mack, Maynard.** Some annotations in the second earl of Oxford's copies of Pope's Epistle to dr. Arbuthnot and Sober advice from Horace. R Eng Stud new ser 8no32:416–20 N '57.

12868 —— Two variant copies of Pope's Works . . . volume II: further light on some problems of authorship, bibliography, and text. Library ser5 12no1:48–53 Mr '57.

12869 **Schmitz, Robert M.** Two new holographs of Pope's birthday lines to Martha Blount. R Eng Stud new ser 8no31:234–40 Ag '57.

12870 **Boyce, Benjamin.** An annotated volume from Pope's library. [A new collection of poems relating to state affairs, 1705]. N&Q 203:55–7 F '58; W. J. Cameron *ib.* 203:291–4 Jl '58; J. A. V. Chapple 203:294 Jl '58.

12871 **Foxon, David F.** Two cruces in Pope bibliography. [Essay on man; Dunciad]. TLS 24 Ja '58:52.

12872 **Schmitz, Robert M.** The Arsenal proof sheets of Pope's Iliad: a third report. Mod Lang N 74no6:486–9 Je '59.

Repr. in Mack, Maynard, *ed.* Essential articles for the study of Alexander Pope. Hamden, Conn., 1964. (Rev. ed., 1968). p. 626–9.

12873 **Mack, Maynard.** Pope manuscripts. TLS 12 Ag '60:513.

12874 **Ryskamp, Charles.** Epigrams I more especially delight in; the receipts for Pope's Iliad. Princeton Univ Lib Chron 24no1:36–8 '62. facsims.

12875 **Halsband, Robert.** Alexander Pope at Columbia. [Ms. of Inscription on a grotto . . . at Crux-Easton]. Columbia Lib Columns 14no1:13–18 N '64. illus., port., facsim.

12876 **Eddy, Donald D.** A new note from Pope. Cornell Lib J 3:56–7 '67. facsim.

12877 **Maslen, Keith I. D.** New editions of Pope's Essay on man, 1745–48. Pa Bib Soc Am 62:177–88 '68. facsim.

'London printed editions of the Essay on man with frontispiece, 1745–48' (p. 184–8)

12878 **Dixon, Peter.** Quincunx or Arbours? A note on Pope's Epistle to Burlington. [Lines 79f.]. (Notes). Scribleriana 2no1:30 '69.

PORSON, RICHARD, 1759–1808

12879 **Sweatman, F. J.** Porson's (i.e. Southey's) Devil's walk. N&Q ser12 12:309 Ap '23.

12880 **Clarke, M. L.** Porson's edition of Aeschylus. N&Q 179:272–4 Oc '40.

POTT, CONSTANCE MARY (FEARON), (MRS. HENRY POTT), 1833–1915

12881 **Woodward, Daniel H.** A Baconian and Cervantes. (Note 146). Bk Coll 9no4:454 '60.

POTTER, HELEN BEATRIX, 1866–1943

12882 **Beatrix** Potter books. TLS 26 Ag '49:560.

12883 **Loys, mrs. Charles.** Beatrix Potter. [Appeal for bibliogr. information]. New Coloph 2pt5:82 Ja '49; D. A. Randall *ib.* 2pt6:173–4 Je '49.

12884 **Carter, John W.** Beatrix Potter: Peter Rabbit, 1900–1902. [Publ.]. (Query no.18). Bk Coll 1no3:196 '52; L. Linder; E. E. Bissell *ib.* 2no1:77 '53.

12885 **Deval, Laurie.** The bibliography of Beatrix Potter. Bk Coll 15no4:454–9 '66. illus., facsims.

POWELL, VAVASOR, 1617–70

12886 **Davies, sir William Ll.** Welsh books attributed to Vavasor Powell. (Notes, queries, and replies). Welsh Bib Soc J 2no7:272–3 D '22. [Sg.: W. Ll. D.]

POWNALL, THOMAS, 1722–1805

12887 **Guttridge, G. H.** Thomas Pownall's The administration of the colonies: the six editions. William & Mary Q ser3 26no1:31–46 Ja '69.

POWYS, THEODORE FRANCIS, 1875–1953

12888 **Powys, T. F.**: An interpretation of genesis. [1907]. Bib N&Q 2no10:12 Ap '38.

PRAED, WINTHROP MACKWORTH, 1802–39

12889 **Allott, Kenneth.** Praed's poems. TLS 1 F '52:93.

12890 —— The text of Praed's Poems. N&Q 198:118–20 Mr '53.

PRENDERGAST, JOHN PATRICK, 1808–93

12891 **Coleman, James.** John Patrick Prendergast. Irish Bk Lover 15no1:1–3 Ja '25.

PRESSICK, GEORGE, fl.1656–63

12892 **Plomer, Henry R.** George Pressick of Dublin. Irish Bk Lover 1no2:16–17 S '09.

PRICHARD, RHYS, 1579–1644

12893 **Roberts, Gomer M.** Trosiad o Ganiadau'r ficer Prichard. (Nodiadau llyfryddol). Welsh Bib Soc J 7no4:197 Jl '53.

12894 **Rees, Eiluned.** A bibliographical note on early editions of Canwyll y Cymry. Welsh Bib Soc J 10no2:96–101 Jl '68.

PRIESTLEY, JOHN BOYNTON, 1894–

12895 **Jones, L. Alun.** The first editions of J. B. Priestley. Bkmn 80no475:46 Ap '31.

12896 **Teagarden, Lucetta J.** The J. B. Priestley collection. Lib Chron Univ Texas 7no3:27–32 '68.

PRIESTLEY, JOSEPH, 1733–1804

12897 **Reid, Winifred** and **J. F. Fulton.** The bicentenary exhibition of Joseph Priestley. Yale Univ Lib Gaz 8no2:63–73 Oc '33.

I. Early biographical material.–II. Scientific works.–III. Education and history.–IV. Philosophical writings.–V. Political writings.–VI. Religious tracts.–VII. Priestley as a librarian.

12898 **Carlton, William J.** Books from Joseph Priestley's library. N&Q 166:207 Mr '34.

12899 **Fulton, John F.** and **Charlotte H. Peters.** An introduction to a bibliography of the educational and scientific works of Joseph Priestley. Pa Bib Soc Am 30pt2:150–67 '36.

'A short title list of the writings' (p. 164–7)

12900 **Chaloner, W. H.** A lost pamphlet. [On sick clubs and friendly societies]. TLS 3 Jl '48:373.

12901 **Brown, T. Julian.** Joseph Priestley, 1733–1804. (English scientific autographs, VI). Bk Coll 14no4:539 '65.

12902 Cancelled.

PRINGLE, THOMAS, 1789–1834

12903 **Robinson, George W.** A bibliography of Thomas Pringle's Afar in the desert. Pa Bib Soc Am 17pt1:21–54 '23. diagr., facsims.

'Bibliography' (p. 31–54)

PRIOR, MATTHEW, 1664–1721

12904 **Roberts, William.** Matthew Prior as a book collector. Athenæum 3634:810–11 Je '97.

12905 **Toynbee, Paget J.** Prior's Epistle to Peggy. TLS 21 Oc '15:369.

12906 **Aitken, George A.** Notes on the bibliography of Matthew Prior. Bib Soc Trans 14pt1:39–66 '15/16. facsims.

12907 **Clarke, sir Ernest.** A note on Hans Carvel and The ladle. Bib Soc Trans 14pt1:67–8 '15/16.

12908 **Aitken, George A.** Notes on the bibliography of Matthew Prior. Bib Soc News-sh 2–4 F '16.

Report of paper read 17 Ja '16: *no.*12906.

12909 **Chapman, Robert W.** Prior's Poems, 1709. R Eng Stud 3no9:76 Ja '27. [Sg.: R. W. C.]

12910 **Barrett, W. P.** A note on manuscript variants not collated in A. R. Waller's edition of Prior. R Eng Stud 9no33:63–4 Ja '33.

12911 **Chandler, William K.** Prior's Poems, 1718: a duplicate printing. Mod Philol 32no4:383–90 My '35.

12912 **Wright, H. Bunker.** Ideal copy and authoritative text: the problem of Prior's Poems on several occasions, 1718. Mod Philol 49no4:234–41 My '52. table.

12913 **Griffith, Reginald H.** Not by Prior. R Eng Stud new ser 6no21:67–9 Ja '55.

12914 **Brown, T. Julian.** Matthew Prior, 1664–1721. (English literary autographs, XXIII). Bk Coll 6no3:279 '57.

12915 **Foxon, David F.** Prior's A new collection of poems, 1724, &c. (Note 106). Bk Coll 8no1:69–70 '59.

12916 **Ellis, Frank H.** and **D. F. Foxon.** Prior's Simile. Pa Bib Soc Am 57:337–9 '63. facsims.

12917 **Godshalk, William Leigh.** Prior's copy of Spenser's Works, 1679. Pa Bib Soc Am 61:52–5 '67.

PRY, PAUL, *pseud. of* **WILLIAM HEATH, 1795–1840**

12918 **Oddities** of Paul Pry. Am Bk Coll 15no7:10–11 Mr '65.

PRYNNE, WILLIAM, 1600–69

12919 **L., R. S.** William Prynne's mss. N&Q ser10 8:168 Ag '07.

PUGHE, WILLIAM OWEN, formerly OWEN, 1759–1835

12920 **Phillips, D. Rhys.** Subscribers to W. Owen-Pughe's Welsh and English dictionary. [1793–1803]. Carmarthenshire Antiqu Soc & Field Club Trans 4pt13:46 '08/9.

12921 **Owens, B. G.** The Mysevin manuscripts. [Owen-Pughe's libr.] (News and notes). Nat Lib Wales J 2no2:90–2 '41.

12922 Cancelled.

12923 **Morgan, J. Hubert.** Coll Gwynfa: myfyrod lyfryddol ar gyfieithiad William Owen Pughe. Welsh Bib Soc J 6no3:145–57 Jl '45. facsims., table.

PURCELL, HENRY, 1659?–95

12924 **Squire, William B.** An unknown autograph of Henry Purcell. [In Gresham college]. Music Antiqu 3:15–17 Oc '11.

12925 **Purcell** and Handel exhibition. [B.M.]. TLS 15 My '59:296.

PURCHAS, SAMUEL, 1575?–1626

12926 **Dixon, Ronald.** Purchas his pilgrimes, 1625. N&Q ser9 10:109 Ag '02.

QUARLES, FRANCIS, 1592–1644

12927 **Ustick, W. Lee.** Later editions of Quarles's Enchiridion. Library ser4 9no2:184–6 S '28.

12928 **Haight, Gordon S.** The publication of Quarles' Emblems. Library ser4 15no1:97–109 Je '34.

12929 —— The sources of Quarles's Emblems. Library ser4 16no2:188–209 S '35. facsims.

12930 **Mead, Herman R.** [Bibliogr. note on Quarles' Solomon's recantation, 1645]. Pa Bib Soc Am 35:70 '41.

12931 **Munsterberg, Margaret.** First editions of Francis Quarles. More Bks Boston Pub Lib Bull 16no8:378 Oc '41. [Sg.: M. M.]

12932 **Horden, John R. B.** Francis Quarles. [Argalus and Parthenia, 1677]. TLS 6 Jl '46:319.

12933 —— Francis Quarles. N&Q 194:435 Oc '49.

12934 —— Edmund Marmion's illustrations for Francis Quarles' Argalus and Parthenia. [1629]. Cambridge Bib Soc Trans 2pt1:55–62 '54.

12935 —— Quarles's Enchiridion, 1682. (Query 95). Bk Coll 7no2:188 '58.

RADCLIFFE, ANN (WARD), 1764–1823

12936 **Sadleir, Michael T. H.** Poems by Ann Radcliffe. TLS 29 Mr '28:242.

RALEIGH, SIR WALTER, 1552?–1618

12937 **Brushfield, Thomas N.** Sir W. Ralegh and his History of the world. N&Q ser8 5:441–2 Je '94.

12938 —— Sign of the great James. [Raleigh's Judicious and select essays, 1667]. N&Q ser8 12:105 Ag '97.

12939 —— Sir W. Ralegh's library. N&Q ser8 11:109 F '97.

12940 **Wallis, Alfred.** Raleghana. [And J. P. Collier]. N&Q ser8 11:186 Mr '97.

12941 **Prideaux, W. R. B.** Ralegh's signature. [Libr.]. N&Q ser9 7:7 Ja '01.

12942 **Brushfield, Thomas N.** The History of the world, by sir Walter Ralegh, a bibliographical study. (Raleghana, pt.VI). Devonshire Assn Trans 36:181–218 '04. facsims., port., tables.

A. Text of History, 1614–1687.–B. Text of History, 1736.–C. Enumeration of later editions, abridgments, etc.

12943 **Norman, William.** Sir Walter Raleigh's Historie of the world. [1666]. N&Q ser10 3:127–8 F '05; Constance Russell; J. Radcliffe ib. 3:194–5 Mr '05; T. N. Brushfield; S. J. A. F.; W. Jaggard 3:274–5 Ap '05.

12944 **Manwaring, G. E.** Sir Walter Ralegh and John Keymer. [Keymer's Observations touching trade]. TLS 16 Jl '25:480.

12945 **Bibas, H.** Ralegh's last poem. [Ms.]. TLS 13 Oc '32:734; N. Ault ib. 27 Oc '32:789.

12946 **Sorensen, Fred.** Sir Walter Ralegh's library. N&Q 166:102–3 F '34; W. Jaggard *ib.* 166:138–9 F '34; M. 166:230 Mr '34.

12947 **Heltzel, Virgil B.** Ralegh's Even such is time. Huntington Lib Bull 10:185–8 Oc '36.

12948 **Stone, E.** Sir Walter Ralegh: History of the world, 1621. N&Q 171:352–3 N '36; W. Jaggard; A. J. H.; E. G. B.; M. *ib.* 171:394 N '36.

12949 **Bennett, Josephine W.** Early texts of two of Ralegh's poems from a Huntington library manuscript. Huntington Lib Q 4no4:469–75 Jl '41.

12950 **Starkey, Lawrence G.** and **P. Ropp.** The printing of A declaration of the demeanor and cariage of sir Walter Raleigh, 1618. Library ser5 3no2:124–34 S '48. diagrs.

12951 **Bowers, Robert H.** Raleigh's last speech; the Elms document. R Eng Stud new ser 2no7:209–16 Jl '51.

12952 **Oakeshott, Walter F.** An unknown Raleigh ms.; the working papers for The history of the world. Manuscripts 5no4:43–5 '53. facsim.

Repr. from The Times, 29 N '52.

12953 **Strathman, Ernest A.** A note on the Ralegh canon. TLS 13 Ap '56:228.

Group I mss.–Group II mss.

12954 **Lefranc, Pierre.** A miscellany of Ralegh material. [Mss.]. N&Q 202:24–6 Ja '57.

12955 **Popkin, Richard H.** A manuscript of Ralegh's The scepticke. Philol Q 36no2:253–9 Ap '57. table.

12956 **Racin, John.** The early editions of sir Walter Ralegh's The history of the world. Stud Bib 17:199–209 '64.

12957 **Oakeshott, Walter F.** Sir Walter Ralegh's library. Library ser5 23no4:285–327 D '68. facsims.

'The list' (p. 296–327)

RALPH, JAMES, 1705?–62

12958 **Abrahams, Aleck.** A Critical review of the publick buildings, &c. in London, 1734. N&Q ser11 1:189 Mr '10; W. Scott *ib.* 1:253 Mr '10; A. Matthews 1:277 Ap '10; A. Abrahams 1:374 My '10.

12959 **Shipley, John B.** A critical review of the . . . buildings, 1734. (Query 107). Bk Coll 8no1:72 '59.

12960 —— Publick buildings, TLS 8 My '59:273.

12961 —— The Touch-stone, London, 1728. (Query 145). Bk Coll 10no3:337 '61.

12962 **Shipley, John B.** Evidence of authorship [of A critical history . . . Walpole, 1743]. (Query 175). Bk Coll 13no1:71 '64.

12963 —— James Ralph's pamphlets, 1741–1744. Library ser5 19:130–46 '64.

> ('Appendix A [checklist]' [p. 138–45); 'Appendix B: The bankruptcies of Francis Cogan' (p. 145–6)

RAMÉE, MARIE LOUISE DE LA, 1839–1908 *see* Ouida, *pseud.*

RAMSAY, ALLAN, 1686–1758

12964 **W.** A curious old volume [of Ramsay's poems]. Aberdeen J N&Q 5:200–1 '12.

12965 **Chapman, Robert W.** Allan Ramsay's Poems, 1720. R Eng Stud 3no11:343–6 Jl '27. table.

12966 **Hazen, Allen T.** Ramsay's Tea-table miscellany [acquired]. Yale Univ Lib Gaz 15no2:43–4 Oc '40. [Sg.: A. H. T.]

12967 **Martin, Burns.** Two items by Allan Ramsay. TLS 28 Oc '55:639.

12968 **Farmer, Henry G.** The music to Allan Ramsay's songs. [Music for his collection, 1724]. Biblioth 2no1:34 '59.

12969 **Roy, G. Ross.** An edition of Allan Ramsay. [The gentle shepherd, 1784]. Biblioth 3no6:220–1 '62.

12970 **Pegg, M. A.** and **E. F. D. Roberts.** An unrecorded edition of Allan Ramsay. [The gentle shepherd, 1821]. Stud Scot Lit 2no1:61 Jl '64.

12971 **Yeo, Elspeth.** The manuscript of Ramsay's Gentle shepherd. Stud Scot Lit 4no1:47–8 Jl '66.

RANDOLPH, THOMAS, 1605–35

12972 **Thomas** Randolph's Poems. Bkworm 2no20:225–8 Jl '89. facsim.

12973 **Smith, George C. Moore.** A new Randolph. [Drinking academy]. TLS 4 S '30:700.

12974 **Parry, John J.** [and] **S. A. Tannenbaum.** Further comment on Randolph's text. Mod Lang N 46no8:510–12 D '31.

12975 **Tannenbaum, Samuel A.** The text of Thomas Randolph's poems. Mod Lang N 46no5:306–9 My '31.

12975a **Smith, George C. More.** The authorship of The drinking academy. [And Randolph]. R Eng Stud 8no30:212–14 Ap '32.

12976 **Bowers, Fredson T.** Problems in Thomas Randolph's Drinking academy and its manuscript. Huntington Lib Q 1no2:189–98 Ja '38. table.

12977 —— Marriot's two editions of Randolph's Aristippus. Library ser4 20no2:163–6 S '39. facsims.

12978 —— A possible Randolph holograph. Library ser4 20no2:159–62 S '39.

12979 **Forster, Leonard.** An unnoticed Latin poem by Thomas Randolph, 1633. Eng Stud 41no4:258 Ag '60.

RASTELL, JOHN, d.1536 *see* Book production and distribution –Printers, publishers, etc.

RAVENSCROFT, EDWARD, 1654?–1707

12980 **McManaway, James G.** The copy for The careless lovers. Mod Lang N 46no6:406–9 Je '31.

RAY, JOHN, 1627–1705

12981 **Gurney, J. H.** Ray's Itineraries. [Mss.]. N&Q ser10 1:468 Je '04.

12982 **Kidman, Roy** and E. Farley. Ray in Kansas. Bks & Libs at Kansas 1no9:9–10 My '55.

READ, THOMAS, d.1624 *see* Reid, Thomas, d.1624.

READE, CHARLES, 1814–84

12983 **Wheeler, C. B.** Charles Reade's note-books. N&Q ser11 11:492 Je '15.

12984 **The Cloister** and the hearth. (Notes on sales). TLS 15 Ag '29:640.

12985 **Parrish, Morris L.** Reade: Dora. [Priority of 1867 ed.]. Bib N&Q 1no4:10 Oc '35.

12986 **Birss, John H.** Charles Reade's copy of Moby-Dick. Bib N&Q 2no10:12 Ap '38.

12987 **Bond, William H.** Nance Oldfield, an unrecorded printed play. Harvard Lib Bull 1no3:386–7 '47.

12988 **Bonniwell, Ralph.** The Cloister and the hearth. New Coloph 2pt7:277 S '49; D. A. Randall *ib.* 2pt7:284–5 S '49.

12989 **Gettman, Royal A.** The serialization of Reade's A good fight. [In Once a week]. Ninet Cent Fict 6no1:21–32 Je '51.

12990 **Martin, Robert B.** The Reade collection. Princeton Univ Lib Chron 17no2:77–80 '56.

12991 —— Manuscripts and correspondence of Charles Reade [presented to Library]. Princeton Univ Lib Chron 19no2:102–3 '58. illus.

12992 **Shuman, R. Baird.** Charles Reade's contract with Fields, Osgood and co. N&Q 204:212 Je '59.

REDFORD, JOHN, fl.1535

12993 **Tannenbaum, Samuel A.** Editorial notes on Wit and Science. [Ms.]. Philol Q 14no4:307–26 Oc '35.

12994 **Brown, Arthur.** The play of Wit and Science by John Redford. [Ms.]. Philol Q 28no4:429–42 Oc '49.

REED, ISAAC, 1742–1807

12995 **Metzdorf, Robert F.** Isaac Reed and the unfortunate dr. Dodd. [Annotated Account of the life . . . of William Dodd]. (Notes). Harvard Lib Bull 6no3:393–6 '52.

REID, THOMAS, d.1624

12996 **Anderson, Peter J.** Theses by mr. secretary Thomas Reid. N&Q ser11 4:163 Ag '11; J. R. Magrath *ib.* 4:234 S '11.

REID, THOMAS MAYNE, 1818–83

12997 **Pollard, H. Graham.** Novels in newspapers: some unpublished letters of captain Mayne Reid. R Eng Stud 18no69:72–85 Ja '42.

REINOLDS, JOHN, d.1614

12998 **John** Reinolds, epigrammatist. [Prima chilias . . . epigrammatum, 1612]. Bod Lib Rec 3no29:7–8 Ja '50.

RERESBY, SIR JOHN, 1634–89

12999 **B., G. F. R.** Sir John Reresby, 1634–1689. [Mss.]. N&Q ser8 6:387–8 N '94.

REYNOLDS, BP. EDWARD, 1599–1676

13000 **Hetherington, John R.** Edward Reynolds: Three treatises, 1631. [Duplicated sheet in]. (Query no.72). Bk Coll 5no3:281 '56.

REYNOLDS, GEORGE WILLIAM MACARTHUR, 1814–79

13001 G. W. M. Reynolds and penny fiction. (Notes on sales). TLS 24 Ja '24:56.

13002 **G. W. M.** Reynolds in India. (Notes on sales). TLS 18 S '24:584.

13003 **Summers, A. Montague J-M. A.** G. W. M. Reynolds. (Bibliography). TLS 4 Jl '42:336.

Historical and domestic.–Not by Reynolds.

13004 **Stickland, Irina.** Bibliography of G. W. M. Reynolds. [Her proposed bibliogr.]. (Query 170). Bk Coll 12no3:357 '63.

REYNOLDS, JOHN HAMILTON, 1796–1852

13005 **Peck, Walter E.** Reynolds, Hunt and Keats. [To F- B-.]. TLS 11 Je '25:400.

13006 **Marsh, George L.** Newly identified writings of John Hamilton Reynolds. Keats-Sh J 1:46–55 Ja '52.

13007 **Jones, Leonidas M.** New letters, articles, and poems by John Hamilton Reynolds. Keats-Sh J 6:97–108 '57.

13008 **Kaufman, Paul.** The Leigh Browne collection at the Keats museum. Library ser5 17no3:246–50 S '62.

13009 **Riga, Frank P.** John Hamilton Reynolds, the canon. N&Q 209:151 Ap '64.

REYNOLDS, SIR JOSHUA, 1723–92

13010 **Kolb, Gwin J.** and **J. H. Sledd.** The Reynolds copy of Johnson's Dictionary. Bull John Rylands Lib 37no2:446–75 Mr '55.

13011 **Todd, William B.** Reynolds' Discourses, 1769–1791. (Note 103). Bk Coll 7no4:417–18 '58.

RICHARD DE BURY (RICHARD AUNGERVILLE), BP., 1287–1342?

13012 **Richard** de Bury. (Bookworms of yesterday and to-day). Bkworm 2no15:89–91 F '89.

13013 **Thomas, Ernest C.** Was Richard de Bury an imposter? [Libr.]. Library 1no10:335–40 Oc '89.

13014 **D., C.** The Philobiblon. N&Q ser10 9:9 Ja '08; W. A. Copinger; W. E. A. Axon; R. A. Potts; F. J. Burgoyne *ib.* 9:92–3 F '08; A. H. Arkle; J. Townshend 9:173 F '08.

13015 **McGovern, John B.** Bishop Richard of Bury's library. N&Q ser11 8:341–4 N '13; H. Maxwell *ib.* 8:397 N '13; J. B. McGovern; W. D. Macray 8:435–6 N '13; J. B. McGovern 9:17 Ja '14; ser12 2:355–6 Oc '16; 11:435 N '22.

13016 **Nelson, Axel.** Intorno al Philobiblon di Riccardo de Bury e ad alcuni nuovi codici di quell' opera. Nordisk Tidskrift för Bok- och Biblioteksväsen 16nr2/3:104–13 '29.

13017 **Reichner, Herbert.** Richard de Bury's Philobiblon. [His projected bibliogr.]. TLS 24 Mr '32:217.

13018 **Savage, Henry L.** Salutem ad Ricardum Dummelensis episcopum, Philobiblon auctorem. Princeton Univ Lib Chron 6no3:133–7 Ap '45.

13019 **Richard** de Bury's books from the abbey of St. Albans. Bod Lib Rec 3no32:177–9 Ag '51.

RICHARDS, WILLIAM, 1643–1705

13020 **Stroup, Thomas B.** The Christmas ordinary; manuscript and authorship. Pa Bib Soc Am 50:184–90 '56.

RICHARDSON, SAMUEL, 1689–1761 *see also* Book production and distribution–Printers, publishers, etc.

13021 **Jones, T. Llechid.** First edition of Clarissa Harlowe. N&Q ser11 7:250 Mr '13.

13022 **Hodgkin, John E.** Editions of Pamela. TLS 23 D '20:877.

13023 **Richardson's** illustrators. (Notes on sales). TLS 16 D '20:864.

13024 **Miller, George M.** The publisher of Pamela. [John Osborn]. TLS 31 Jl '30:628; C. J. Longman *ib.* 23 Ag '30; J. B. Whitmore 11 S '30:716.

13025 **Newbery's** edition of Pamela, 1769. (Notes on sales). TLS 6 Mr '30:196.

13026 **Sale, William M.** Sir Charles Grandison and the Dublin pirates. Yale Univ Lib Gaz 7no4:80–6 Ap '33.

13027 —— The first dramatic version of Pamela. Yale Univ Lib Gaz 9no4:83–8 Ap '35.

13028 —— Samuel Richardson and Sir William Harrington. [A. Meades' History, 1771, rev. by Richardson]. TLS 29 Ag '35:537.

13029 —— The Singer copy of Sir Charles Grandison. Univ Pennsylvania Lib Chron 3no3:42–5 Oc '35.

13030 **S. Richardson's novels.** [Ed. for children]. Bib N&Q 2no2:6 F '36; T. Warburton *ib*. 2no3:6 Ap '36.

13031 **Sale, William M.** A bibliographical note on Richardson's Clarissa. Library ser4 16no4:448–51 Mr '36. table.

13032 **Massey, Dudley.** The History of sir William Harrington, by Anna Meades, revised and corrected by Richardson: 4 volumes, 1771. [Collation]. Bib N&Q 2no10:9–10 Ap '38.

13033 **Munsterberg, Margaret.** The first edition of Clarissa. More Bks Boston Pub Lib Bull 18no6:299–300 Je '43. [Sg.: M. M.]

13034 **Eaves, Thomas C. D.** Graphic illustration of the novels of Samuel Richardson, 1740–1810. Huntington Lib Q 14no4:349–83 Ag '51. facsims.

  I. Pamela: or, Virtue rewarded.–II. Clarissa.–III. Sir Charles Grandison. IV. Conclusion.

13035 **Shipley, John B.** Samuel Richardson and Pamela. [And C. Rivington]. N&Q 199:28–9 Ja '54.

13036 **McKillop, Alan D.** Two 18th century first works. Newberry Lib Bull 4no1:10–23 N '55. facsims.

  I. Samuel Richardson's first book. [The apprentice's vade mecum, 1734].–2. James Thomson's juvenile poems [Mss.]

13037 **Weekes, M. Kinkead-.** Clarissa restored. R Eng Stud new ser 10no38:156–71 My '59.

  II. The second edition.–III. The third edition.–IV. Prefaces and postscripts.

13038 **Eaves, Thomas C. D.** and **B. D. Kimpel.** The publisher of Pamela and its first audience. [John Osborn]. N.Y. Pub Lib Bull 64no3:143–6 Mr '60.

13039 —— Richardson's revisions of Pamela. Stud Bib 20:61–88 '67.

RICHARDSON, WILLIAM, 1743–1814

13040 **Cordasco, Francesco G. M.** William Richardson's Essays on Shakespeare, 1784: a bibliographical note on the first edition. N&Q 196:148 Mr '51; H. Parsons *ib*. 196:174 Ap '51.

RIDDELL, MARIA, fl.1792

13041 **Gladstone, Hugh S.** Maria Riddell and Burns. [Ms. of The metrical miscellany]. N&Q ser11 10:50 Jl '14; 10:153 Ag '14.

13042 **Weston, John C.** The text of Maria Riddell's Sketch of Burns. [Corrected trial sheets]. Stud Scot Lit 5no3:194–7 Ja '68.

RITSON, JOSEPH, 1752–1803

13043 **Bronson, Bertrand H.** Joseph Ritson. [Whereabouts of his mss.]. TLS 5 S '29:684.

13044 —— Ritson's Bibliographica Scotica. [Ms.]. Pub Mod Lang Assn 52no1:122–59 Mr '37.

13045 **Todd, William B.** Ritson, Observations on ... the history of English poetry, 1782. [Facsimile, c.1803]. (Note 90). Bk Coll 6no4:408 '57.

ROBERTS, THOMAS FRANCIS, 1860–1919

13046 **Phillips, D. Rhys.** 'Llwynrhudol.' [Presentation copy of Roberts' Drych y prif oesoedd]. (Book notes). Welsh Bib Soc J 1no1:27 Je '10. [Sg.: D. R. P.]

ROBERTSON, ANDREW, fl.1589–91

13047 **Evans, D. Wyn.** Andrew Robertson of Aberdeen. Biblioth 4no2:81 '63.

ROBERTSON, BARTHOLOMEW, fl.1617–20

13048 **Crow, John.** A thing called Adagia. Library ser5 4no1:71–3 Je '49.

ROBERTSON, JAMES, 1714–95

13049 **Taylor, John.** Robertson family. N&Q ser8 4:68 Jl '93; W. F. Prideaux *ib.* 4:179 Ag '93; W. C. B. 4:277 S '93.

ROBERTSON, THOMAS WILLIAM, 1829–71

13050 **Savin, Maynard.** T. W. Robertson. TLS 23 Ap '49:270.

ROBIN HOOD

13051 **McGovern, John B.** Robin Hood plays. N&Q ser10 8:70 Jl '07; J. H. MacMichael *ib.* 8:295 Oc '07.

13052 **Ardagh, J.** Robin Hood bibliography. N&Q ser12 7:309 Oc '20.

13053 **Elmquist, Karl F.** Robin Hood: bibliography. [His projected bibliogr.]. N&Q 168:369 My '35; E. J. G. Forse; H. Askew *ib.* 168:428 Je '35.

ROBINSON, HENRY CRABB, 1775–1867

13054 **Baker, John M.** Crabb Robinson: bibliography. N&Q 172:387 My '37.

ROBINSON, RICHARD, fl.1576–1600

13055 [**McKerrow, Ronald B.**]. Richard Robinson's Eupolemia, Archippus, and Panoplia, 1603. (Retrospective reviews). Gent Mag 300:277–84 Ap '06.

13056 **Vogt, George McG.** Richardson Robinson's Eupolemia, 1603. [Literary earnings]. Stud Philol 21no3:629–48 Oc '24.

13057 **McKerrow, Ronald B.** Richardson Robinson's Eupolemia and the licensers. [Ms.]. Library ser4 11no2:173–8 S '30. facsim.

13058 **Greg, sir Walter W.** Richard Robinson and the Stationers' register. [Licensing]. Mod Lang R 50no4:407–13 Oc '55.

Repr. in Maxwell, James C., *ed.* Collected papers. Oxford, 1966. p. [413]–23.

ROCHESTER, JOHN WILMOT, 2D EARL OF, 1647–80 *see* Wilmot, John, 2d earl of Rochester, 1647–80.

ROGERS, CHARLES, 1863–99

13059 **Flory, Claude R.** The plays of Charles Rogers. N&Q 204:102–3 Mr '59.

ROGERS, SAMUEL, 1763–1855

13060 **Gilmour, John S. L.** The early editions of Roger's Italy. Library ser5 3no2:137–40 S '48.

13061 **Hale, J. R.** Samuel Rogers the perfectionist. Huntington Lib Q 25no1:61–7 N '61.

13062 **Yonge, Theodore.** Samuel Rogers's Poems, 1812. (Query 169). Bk Coll 12no3:356–7 '63; P. H. Hinton *ib.* 13no1:70–1 '64; J. Clements 13no3: 353 '64.

13063 **Smith, Simon H. Nowell-.** Samuel Rogers, Human life, 1819. (Note 251). Bk Coll 14no3:362–5 '65.

ROLFE, FREDERICK WILLIAM SERAFINO AUSTIN LEWIS MARY ('BARON CORVO'), 1860–1913

13064 **Mason, Stuart,** *pseud. of* **C. S. Millard.** Frederick baron Corvo. [The Weird of the wanderer, 1912]. (Correspondence). London Merc 8no48:637 Oc '23; J. Kettlewell *ib.* 9no49:78 N '23.

13065 **Spencer, Terence J. B.** Baron Corvo's Chronicles of the house of Borgia. N&Q 196:562–4 D '51.

13066 **Woolf, Cecil.** Frederick Rolfe, a bibliographical essay. Amat Bk Coll 5no9:1–5 My '55.

13067 Corvo's order of ss. Sophia. [The rule of the order, 1907]. TLS 1 N '57:664.

13068 **Weeks, Donald.** The anatomy of a Corvomaniac. Priv Lib Assn Q 1no3:30–4 '57.

13069 **Fletcher, Iain.** Two poems by Rolfe. TLS 12 D '58:721.

13070 **Andrews, Clarence A.** A baron Corvo exhibit. Bks at Iowa 1:18–27 Oc '64. facsims.

13071 **Weeks, Donald.** Hadrian VII. TLS 28 Ag '69:955.

13072 —— A second edition of Rolfe's Tarcissus. TLS 17 Jl '69:784.

ROLLAND, JOHN, fl.1560

13073 **Craigie, sir William A.** Rolland's Court of Venus. Mod Q Lang & Lit 1no1:9–16 Mr '98.

ROS, ANNA MARGARET ('AMANDA'), (McKITTRICK), d.1939

13074 **Mercer, Thomas S.** Amanda M'Kittrick Ros. (Query no.38). Bk Coll 2no3:223

ROSCOE, WILLIAM, 1753–1831

13075 **R., E. H.** William Roscoe. N&Q ser12 11:109 Ag '22; R. Stewart-Brown; A. Sparke; J. Seton-Anderson; G. F. R. B. *ib.* 11:155–6 Ag '22.

13076 **Chandler, George.** The published and unpublished poems of William Roscoe, 1753–1831. Liverpool Libs Mus & Arts Committee Bull 2no1/2: 2–27 Jl/Oc '52. facsims.

ROSENBERG, ISAAC, 1890–1918

13077 **Cohen, Joseph.** Isaac Rosenberg, the poet's progress in print. Eng Lit Transit 6no3:142–6 '63.

ROSS, ALEXANDER, 1699–1784

13078 **Wattie, Margaret.** A missing manuscript. [Ross's Helenore]. TLS 23 F '33:127.

ROSSETTI, CHRISTINA GEORGINA, 1830–94

13079 **Sparrow, John H. A.** Christina Rossetti: A pageant, 1881. [Binding variants]. Bib N&Q 2no9:10–11 Ja '38; P. S. O'Hegarty *ib.* 2no11:5 N '38.

13080 **Packer, Lona M.** Christina Rossetti's Songs in a cornfield, a misprint uncorrected. N&Q 207:97–100 Mr '62.

ROSSETTI, DANTE GABRIEL, 1828–82

13081 **Prideaux, William F.** Dante G. Rossetti; George Meredith. [Once a week]. N&Q ser8 7:233 Mr '95.

13082 **Livingston, Luther S.** Dante Gabriel and Christina G. Rossetti. (The first books of some English authors, III). Bkmn (N.Y.) 10no3:245–7 N '99. facsims.

13083 **Prideaux, William F.** Rossetti bibliography. N&Q ser10 2:464–5 D '04.

13084 **McGovern, John B.** G. Rossetti's Tre ragionamenti. N&Q ser10 5:428–9 Je '06; J. F. R.; W. M. Rossetti ib. 5:477 Je '06.

13085 **Doughty, Oswald,** ed. The letters of Dante Gabriel Rossetti to his publisher, F. S. Ellis . . . with introduction and notes. London, Scholartis pr., 1928. xlviii,150p. facsim. 22cm.

Rev: P. F. Baum Mod Lang N 44:334–6 '29.

13086 **Wallerstein, Ruth C.** The Bancroft manuscripts of Rossetti's sonnets. Mod Lang N 44no5:279–84 My '29.

13087 **Wise, Thomas J.** A Rossetti ballad. [Jan van Hunks]. TLS 12 D '29:1058; W. Marchbank ib. 27 F '30:166; G. C. M. Smith 6 Mr '30:190.

13088 **Baum, Paull F.,** ed. Dante Gabriel Rossetti; an analytical list of manuscripts in the Duke university library, with hitherto unpublished verse and prose. Durham, N.C., Duke U.P., 1931. vii,122p. facsim. 21cm.

'An analytical list of the Dante Gabriel Rossetti manuscripts in the Duke university library' (p. [1]–49)

Rev: TLS 20 Ag '31:634; S. H. Nowell-Smith ib. 10 S '31:683; N&Q 161:52 '31; H. S. V. Jones J Eng Germ Philol 31:165–6 '32; R. C. Wallerstein Mod Lang N 47:472–3 '32.

13089 **Sanford, John A.** The Morgan library manuscript of Rossetti's The blessed damozel. Stud Philol 35no3:471–86 Jl '38.

13090 **Troxell, Janet C.** The 'trial books' of Dante Gabriel Rossetti. Coloph new ser 3no2:243–58 My '38. facsim.

Repr. in Princeton Univ Lib Chron 33no3:177–92 '72.

13091 **Baum, Paull F.** The Bancroft manuscripts of Dante Gabriel Rossetti. [Now in Wilmington society of the fine arts collection]. Mod Philol 39no1:47–68 Ag '41.

13092 —— Rossetti's The white ship. [Acquisition of ms.]. Lib N Duke Univ Lib 20:2–6 Jl '48.

13093 **Metzdorf, Robert F.** The full text of Rossetti's sonnet on Sordello. (Notes). Harvard Lib Bull 7no2:239–43 '53.

13094 **Gransden, K. W.** Dante Gabriel Rossetti, 1828–82; Christina Georgina Rossetti, 1830–94. (English literary autographs, XVI). Bk Coll 4no4:309 '55. facsims.

13095 **Todd, William B.** D. G. Rossetti's Early Italian poets, 1861. [W. M. Rossetti's bibliogr. and Wise]. (Note 142). Bk Coll 9no3:329–31 '60; W. E. Fredeman *ib*. 10no2:193–8 '61; W. B. Todd 10no4:447 '61.

13096 **Fredeman, William E.** [and] **N. C. MacLeod.** D. G. Rossetti and T. J. Wise. TLS 19 My '61:309.

13097 **Bracker, Jon.** Notes on the texts of two poems by Dante Gabriel Rossetti. [Antwerp and Bruges; The carillon]. Lib Chron Univ Texas 7no3:14–16 '63.

ROSSETTI, WILLIAM MICHAEL, 1829–1919

13098 **Angeli, Helen R.** Cor cordium and Thomas J. Wise. New Coloph 2pt7:237–44 S '49.

13099 **New** W. M. Rossetti letters [acquired]. Lib N Duke Univ Lib 26:7 Ap '52.

ROWE, NICHOLAS, 1674–1718

13100 **Aitken, George A.** Shakespeare's first editor. [Rowe's library]. TLS 11 My '16:225.

13101 **Jackson, Alfred.** Rowe's edition of Shakespeare. Library ser4 10no4: 455–73 Mr '30. illus.

ROWLANDS, SAMUEL, 1570?–1630?

13102 **Waith, Eugene M.** Samuel Rowlands and Humor's antique faces. R Eng Stud 18no70:213–19 Ap '42.

13103 **Dickson, Sarah A.** The 'humours' of Samuel Rowlands. Pa Bib Soc Am 44:101–18 '50. facsims.

13104 —— The melancholy cavalier; a study in seventeenth-century plagiarism. [The melancholy knight, 1615 = J.C.'s Cavalier, 1654]. Stud Bib 5:161–3 '52/3.

RUSKIN, JOHN, 1819–1900

13105 **A Ruskin** find. [The ms. of Gold, a dialogue]. Athenæum 3347:834–5 D '91.

13106 **Schooling, J. Holt.** The handwriting of John Ruskin from 31st December, 1828 to 28th November, 1884. Strand Mag 10:669–80 '95. illus., facsims.

13107 **Cook, E. Tyas.** Ruskin and his books, an interview with his publisher. [G. Allen]. Strand Mag 24no144:709–19 D '02. illus., ports., facsims.

13108 **Copyright** and copy-wrong; the authentic and the unauthentic Ruskin. London, G. Allen, 1907. 60p. 17cm.

> *Repr. of article and correspondence in* Saturday R F '07, *with contribs. by* John Murray, G. Routledge ltd., *and* G. Allen.

13109 **Ruskin** in the auction room. (Notes on sales). TLS 9 Oc '19:552.

13110 **Madan, Falconer.** A Ruskin item. [Supplement to the Report, 1870]. TLS 15 Je '22:396.

13111 **French, Robert D.** The R. B. Adam collection of Ruskin. Yale Univ Lib Gaz 4no1:1–7 Jl '29.

13112 **Ruskin** manuscripts and books. [His library]. (Notes on sales). TLS 31 Jl '30:632.

13113 **Ruskin** portraits and manuscripts. [His library]. (Notes on sales) TLS 18 Je '31:492.

13114 **Weihe, Kenneth G.** A collection of Ruskin manuscripts. Yale Univ Lib Gaz 5no3:47–9 Ja '31.

13115 **Rhodon,** *pseud.* Ruskin's The queen's gardens. N&Q 163:225 S '32; S. J. Aldrich *ib.* 163:316 Oc '32; Rhodon, *pseud.* 163:354 N '32.

13116 **Wrentmore, Charlotte Q.,** *ed.* Letters of John Ruskin to Bernard Quaritch, 1867–1888. London, B. Quaritch, 1938. vi,125p. facsim. 20cm.

13117 **Thorp, Willard.** The Ruskin manuscripts. Princeton Univ Lib Chron 1no2:1–10 F '40.

> Early geology.–Poems, 1830.–Early prose writings, 1835–1838.–Samuel Prout, 1844 and 1879.–Essay on baptism, 1850.–Lectures on Florentine & Greek art &c, 1869–1870.–Verona and its rivers, 1870.–Notes on the Halcyon, 1872.–Notes on Frederick William, 1873.–St. Mark's rest, 1876–1877.–Deucalion.–Storm cloud of the XIXth century, 1884.–A knight's faith, 1885.–Our fathers have told us, 1880–1885, and Valle crucis, 1882.–The note books.

13118 **Hogan, Charles B.** The Yale collection of the manuscripts of John Ruskin. Yale Univ Lib Gaz 16no4:61–9 Ap '42.

13119 **Ruskin** letters and papers. [Important acquisitions]. (Notes and news). Bull John Rylands Lib 42no1:1–4 S '59; 42no2:263–4 Mr '60.

13120 **Brown, T. Julian.** John Ruskin, 1819–1900. (English literary autographs, XXXVIII). Bk Coll 10no2:185 '61. facsims.

13121 **Spence, Margaret.** The Library's Ruskin correspondence and papers. (Notes and news). Bull John Rylands Lib 44no2:273–8 Mr '62.

13122 **Dearden, James S.** John Ruskin's bookplates. Bk Coll 13no3:335–9 '64. illus.

13123 —— John Ruskin's Poems, 1850. [Copies sought]. (Query 201). Bk Coll 15no2:214 '66.

13124 **Dearden, James S.** John Ruskin, the collector, with a catalogue of the illuminated and other manuscripts formerly in his collection. Library ser5 21no2:124–54 Je '66. facsims.

'Catalogue' (p. 129–54)

13125 —— The production and distribution of John Ruskin's Poems, 1850. Bk Coll 17no2:151–67 '68. facsims.

'The present whereabouts of copies of Poems, 1850' (p. 165–7)

13126 **Landow, George P.** Ruskin's revisions of the third edition of Modern painters, volume I. [1846]. Vict Newsl 33:12–16 '68.

13127 **Dearden, James S.** John Ruskin's bookplates. (Note 303). Bk Coll 18no1:88–9 '69.

13128 —— Wise and Ruskin. Bk Coll 18no1:45–56 '69; 18no2:170–88 '69; 18no3:318–39 '69. facsims., table.

I. Authentic editions.–II. Forgeries.–III. Binary editions.–IV. Wise's editions of letters from John Ruskin.–V. Miscellanea.

RUSSEL, WILLIAM AUGUSTUS, fl.1777

13129 **Spackman, H. C.** Eighteenth-century History of England. N&Q ser9 5:127–8 F '00; H. B. Clayton; W. R. Tate; A. J. King *ib.* 5:189 Mr '00; J. T. Page 5:276–7 Ap '00; H. B. Clayton 5:398 My '00.

RUSSELL, GEORGE WILLIAM, 1867–1935 *see Æ., pseud.*

RUTHERFORD, MARK, *pseud. of* WILLIAM HALE WHITE, 1831–1913

13130 **Smith, Simon H. Nowell-.** Mark Rutherford: a correction and a query. [Catherine Furze, 1893; 'remainder']. Bib N&Q 2no1:6 Ja '36.

13131 **Bell, sir Harold I.** Autographs of Nathaniel Hawthorne and Mark Rutherford. Brit Mus Q 11no2:79–80 Mr '37.

SACHEVERELL, HENRY, 1674?–1724

13132 **Madan, Falconer.** The duplicity of duplicates and a new extension of bibliography. Bib Soc Trans 12pt1:15–24 '11/12.

13133 —— The duplicity of duplicates. Bib Soc News-sh 1–3 Ja '12.

'Note on a new extension of bibliography (p. 2–3); *report of paper read* 18 D '11.

SACKVILLE, CHARLES, 6TH EARL OF DORSET, 1638–1706

13134 **Howarth, R. Guy.** Some additions to the poems of lord Dorset. Mod Lang N 50no7:457–9 N '35.

13135 **Chapple, John A. V.** Manuscript texts of poems by the earl of Dorset and William Congreve. N&Q 209:97–100 Mr '64.

SACKVILLE, THOMAS, 1ST EARL OF DORSET, 1536–1608

13136 **Hearsey, Marguerite.** The ms. of Sackville's contribution to the Mirror for magistrates. R Eng Stud 8no31:282–90 Jl '32.

SAINLIENS, CLAUDE DE, fl.1568–97 *see* De Sainliens, Claude, fl.1568–97.

ST.ALBANS, FRANCIS BACON, BARON BERULAM AND VISCOUNT, 1561–1626 *see* Bacon, Francis, baron Verulam and viscount St. Albans, 1561–1626.

ST.GERMAN, CHRISTOPHER, 1460?–1540

13137 **Thorne, S. E.** St.Germain's Doctor and student. Library ser4 10no4:421–6 Mr '30.

13138 **Schoek, Richard J.** Christopher St.German, 1460?–1540. [Library]. N&Q 206:308–9 Ag '61.

ST.JOHN, HENRY, 1ST VISCOUNT BOLINGBROKE, 1678–1751

13139 **Barber, Giles G.** Bolingbroke, Pope, and the patriot king. Library ser5 19:67–89 '64. facsims., tables.

'Notes on the printing of the first edition of the Letters on the spirit of patriotism' (p. 86–9)

13140 **Carswell, John.** Bolingbroke Letters on history, 1738: a special copy. (Note 300). Bk Coll 17no3:351 '68.

ST.JOHN, PERCY BOLINGBROKE, 1821–89

13141 **Friend, Llerena.** Percy B. St.John in Texas. Lib Chron Univ Texas 6no3:24–8 '59.

SALA, GEORGE AUGUSTUS, 1828–96

13142 **A Sala** exhibition. [Press club, London]. TLS 31 Oc '42:540.

SALISBURY, WILLIAM, 1520?–1600?

13143 **Mathias, W. Alun.** Gweithiau William Salesbury. Welsh Bib Soc J 7no3:125–43 Jl '52.

English summary (p. 169–70)

SAMUEL, WILLIAM, fl.1551–69

13144 **Thomas, sir Henry.** Two tracts in verse by William Samuel. [The practice practised by the pope, c.1550; A warning for the city of London, c.1550]. Brit Mus Q 8no1:35–6 Jl '33. [Sg.: H. T.]

SANDYS, SIR EDWIN, 1561–1629

13145 **Rabb, Theodore K.** The editions of sir Edwin Sandys's Relation of the state of religion. Huntington Lib Q 26no4:323–36 Ag '63.

SANDYS, GEORGE, 1578–1644

13146 **Loveday, John E. T.** George Sandys. [A paraphrase upon the divine poems, 1638]. N&Q ser9 9:305 Ap '02.

13147 **Barker, Russell H.** Sandys' Metamorphoses. TLS 27 S '34:655.

13148 **Davis, Richard B.** Early editions of George Sandys's Ovid: the circumstances of production. Pa Bib Soc Am 35:255–76 '41.

13149 —— Two new manuscript items for a George Sandys bibliography. Pa Bib Soc Am 37:215–22 '43.

13150 **Bowers, Fredson T.** Two notes on running titles as bibliographical evidence. Pa Bib Soc Am 42:143–8 '48.

(1) George Sandys: 'Ovid's metamorphosis,' 1632; (2) George Sandys: 'Christ's passion,' 1640.

13151 **Davis, Richard B.** George Sandys v. William Stansby: the 1632 edition of Ovid's Metamorphosis. Library ser5 3no3:193–212 D '48.

13152 **McManaway, James G.** The first five books of Ovid's Metamorphosis, 1621, englished by master George Sandys. Stud Bib 1:71–82 '48.

Repr. in Hosley, Richard, A. C. Kirsch [and] J. W. Velz, *ed.* Studies in Shakespeare, bibliography, and theater. New York, 1969. p. [81]–91.

13153 **Davis, Richard B.** In re George Sandys' Ovid. Stud Bib 8:226–30 '56.

13154 —— Sandys's Song of Solomon: its manuscript versions and their circulation. Pa Bib Soc Am 50:328–41 '56.

13155 —— Volumes from George Sandys's library now in America. Virginia Mag Hist & Biog 65no4:450–7 Oc '57. facsims.

13156 **Schmutzler, Karl E.** Another manuscript version of Sandys' Song of Solomon. Pa Bib Soc Am 53:71–4 '59.

SAROLEA, CHARLES, 1870–1953

13157 **Griffiths, D. E.** The Sarolea papers in Edinburgh university library. Biblioth 3no1:24–31 '60.

I. Everyman papers.–II. University papers.–III. Writings by Sarolea.–IV. Correspondence and miscellaneous papers.

SAVILE, GEORGE, 1ST MARQUIS OF HALIFAX, 1633–95

13158 **Murray, John.** Halifax's Trimmer. [Ms.]. TLS 11 Ap '29:296.

13159 **Hardy, Robert Gathorne-.** Halifax's The character of a trimmer: some observations in the light of a manuscript from Ickworth. Library ser5 14no2:117–23 Je '59.

13160 **Johnson, D. W.** The authorship of A letter from a clergyman, 1688. [Probably by William Sherlock]. Bib Contribs Univ Kansas Libs 1:37–53 '69.

SAVILE, SIR HENRY, 1549–1622

13161 **Bannister, H. M.** Sir Henry Savile's concordance to the Septuagint. [By Kircher]. Bod Q Rec 2no20:197–8 Ja '19.

SCOTT, JOHN, 1710–82

13162 **Keynes, sir Geoffrey L.** Scott of Amwell's Elegy. [1769; collation]. (Note 262). Bk Coll 14no4:544–5 '65.

SCOTT, MICHAEL, 1175?–1234?

13163 **Thorndike, Lynn.** A problem as to incunabula of the Phisionomia of Michael Scot. Pa Bib Soc Am 48:411–13 '54.

SCOTT, MICHAEL, 1789–1835

13164 **Nolte, Eugene A.** Michael Scott and Blackwood's magazine: some unpublished letters. Library ser5 8no3:188–96 S '53.

SCOTT, SARAH (ROBINSON), 1723–95

13165 **Dobson, H. Austin.** Notes on old books. Millenium hall. Library ser3 8no31:283–7 Jl '17.

SCOTT, SIR WALTER, 1771–1832

13166 **Bayne, Thomas.** Carefully edited. [Scott's Border minstrelsy]. N&Q ser8 6:24–5 Jl '94; A. W. B. *ib.* 6:71 Jl '94.

13167 **Covington, W. H.** Scott bibliography. [Ancient and modern British drama, 1810]. N&Q ser8 5:148 F '94; R. R. Dees *ib.* 5:217–18 Mr '94; W. E. Wilson 5:278 Ap '94.

13168 **I.** Scott manuscripts [sold: Anne of Geierstein, and portions of Waverley and Ivanhoe]. Scott N&Q 8no3:47 Ag '94.

13169 **Thornton, Richard H.** Marmion travestied. [And Thomas Tegg]. N&Q ser8 9:328–9 Ap '96; R. R.; W. H. Peet *ib.* 9:374 My '96.

13170 **Sale** of Scott manuscripts [from collection of Francis Richardson]. Scott N&Q 11no2:28 Jl '97.

13171 **Heelis, J. Loraine.** Sir Walter Scott on Grimm's Popular stories. N&Q ser9 1:262–4 Ap '98; H. Rayment *ib.* 2:33 Jl '98; J. L. Heelis 2:93 Jl '98.

13172 **Fitzgerald, Percy H.** Early issues of the Waverley novels. N&Q ser9 5:181–2 Mr '00.

13173 **Pickford, John.** Illustrations of the Waverley novels. N&Q ser9 5:372 My '00.

13174 **Murdoch, Robert.** £101 for a Scott. [Tales of my landlord]. Scott N&Q ser2 5no8:121 F '04.

13175 **Elshie,** *pseud.* Scott's Black dwarf. [Ms.]. N&Q ser10 7:168 Mr '07; A. H. Arkle; W. Roberts *ib.* 7:295 Ap '07; A. Abrahams 7:515 Je '07.

13176 **G., E. N.** Scott illustrators. N&Q ser10 7:10 Ja '07; W. B. *ib.* 7:74 Ja '07; E. Yardley; R. L. Moreton; T. Bayne; J. Pickford 7:130–1 F '07; R. Duncan; A. Abrahams 7:176 Mr '07; A. Abrahams 9:77 Ja '08; E. N. G. 9:378 My '08.

13177 **W., L. A.** English minstrelsy. N&Q ser10 9:170 F '08; T. Hutchinson; J. T. Johnstone; T. Bayne *ib.* 9:256–7 Mr '08.

13178 **Strachan, Lionel R. M.** Variants in the text of Kenilworth. N&Q ser11 6:488 D '12; W. E. Browning; B. Rice *ib.* 7:16 Ja '13.

13179 **S., W.** Ms. of The bride of Lammermoor. N&Q ser12 2:349 Oc '16.

13180 **Blackwood, George W.** Sir Walter Scott and Blackwood's. TLS 10 My '17:225.

13181 **Crockett, W. S.** The centenary of Waverley. Glasgow Bib Soc Rec 4pt1:65–78 '18. facsims., table.

Waverley making and made.–Chief editions since 1814.–The manuscript of Waverley.

13182 **Cooke, T. Davidson.** Maturin mss. at Abbotsford. TLS 16 S '20:600.

13183 **Rait, Robert S.** Scott manuscripts. TLS 8 N '23:751. [Sg.: R. S. R.]

13184 **Scott's** Redgauntlet. [Ms.]. (Notes on sales). TLS 29 N '23:840.

13185 **Wilson, W. E.** Scott's title pages. N&Q ser12 12:353 My '23.

13186 **MacRitchie, David.** The proof sheets of Redgauntlet. TLS 11 S '24:556.

13187–8 Cancelled.

13189 **Rendall, Vernon.** Waverley poetry; a rare item. [The poetry contained in the novels, 1822]. N&Q 148:7 Ja '25; J. de B. Smith *ib*. 148:284 Ap '25.

13190 **Pottle, Frederick A.** The Scott-Croker correspondence in the Yale university library. Yale Univ Lib Gaz 2no3:33–45 Ja '28.

13191 **Moule, A. J. H.** The text of Eothen. TLS 14 N '29:926; W. Sinclair *ib*. 28 N '29:1002; G. Mackereth 12 D '29:1058; H. Gulliford 6 F '30:102.

13192 **Scott** first editions. (Notes on sales). TLS 24 Jl '30:616.

13193 **Falconer, J. A.** Two manuscripts at Abbotsford. [German trans. by Scott]. Archiv für das Studium 160hft3/4:205–12 '31.

13194 **Ruff, William.** Yale's collection of Walter Scott. Yale Univ Lib Gaz 6no2:31–2 Oc '31.

13195 **Van Antwerp, William C.** Waverley. [His intended bibliogr.]. TLS 24 S '31:730.

13196 **Cook, T. Davidson.** Scott first editions. TLS 18 Ag '32:584; R. S. Rait *ib*. 1 S '32:607; J. Curle 29 S '32:696.

13197 **A Scott** exhibition. [J. & E. Bumpus]. (Bibliographical notes). TLS 27 Oc '32:796.

13198 **Swanzy, T. Erskine.** The Lay of the last minstrel. [Text]. TLS 4 Ag '32:557; R. F. Johnston *ib*. 11 Ag '32:569.

13199 **Parsons, Coleman O.** Manuscript of Scott's Letters on demonology and witchcraft. N&Q 164:276–7 Ap '33.

13200 —— Two notes on Scott. N&Q 164:75–7 F '33.

> 1. Correct text of The shepherd's tale.

13201 **Ruff, William.** Scott's printers. TLS 7 S '33:592.

13202 **Van Antwerp, William C.** A note on Old mortality. Bk Coll Q 9:69–71 Ja/Mr '33.

13203 —— On collecting Scott. Coloph [4]pt14:[12p.] '33. port., facsims.

13204 **Rendall, Vernon.** Notes on Scott's Count Robert of Paris. N&Q 167:345–7 N '34. [Sg.: V. R.]

13205 **Batty, W. R.** Scott: Fortunes of Nigel, 1822. [Issues]. Bib N&Q 2no1:6 Ja '35.

13206 **Randall, David A.** Waverley in America. Coloph new ser 1no1:39–55 Jl '35.

13207 **Tait, John G.** The missing tenth of sir Walter Scott's journal. Edinburgh, Oliver and Boyd, 1936. 19p. facsims. 24cm. Covertitle.

> I. Errors of transcription [in David Douglas' ed.].–II. Passages omitted.–III. Arbitrary alterations. (See also no. 13213)
>
> Rev: TLS 13 Je '36:501.

13208 **Batty, W. R.** [and] **G. Worthington.** Scott, sir Walter: Chronicles of the Canongate, 2 vols., 1827. [Cancels]. Bib N&Q 2no7:6 Oc '36; W. R. Batty ib. 2no8:5 F '37.

13209 **Cook, T. Davidson.** The Waverleys in French; Scott's authorship revealed in 1822. TLS 17 Jl '37:532; F. D. Evans 24 Jl '37:548; E. B.; T. D. Cook 7 Ag '37:580. facsim.

13210 **Van Patten, Nathan.** A newly discovered issue of Scott's The vision of don Roderick. [1811]. Library ser4 18no1:109–13 Je '37. table.

13211 **Chapman, Robert W.** Scott: Lady of the lake, 1810. [Collation]. Bib N&Q 2no9:11 Ja '38; D. G. Wing ib. 2no11:5 N '38.

13212 **Mennie, D. M.** A ms. variant of sir Walter Scott's Battle of Sempach. Anglia Beibl 49:57–63 '38.

13213 **Tait, John G.** Sir Walter Scott's journal and its editor. Edinburgh, Oliver and Boyd, 1938. 35p. facsims. 24cm.

> I. Conscience in intellectual matters.–II. Deliberate alterations.–III. Lockhart's extracts.–IV. Omitted passages.–V. The reprint.–VI. An earlier pamphlet [his The missing tenth: no. 13207].–VII. Conclusion.
>
> Rev: N&Q 174:431–2 '38.

13214 **Batty, W. R.** Scott: Pirate, 1822. [Collation]. Bib N&Q 2no9:11 Ja '38; M. L. Parrish; D. G. Wing; Peveril of the peak, *pseud., ib.* 2no11:5 N '38; M. L. Parrish 2no12:2 My '39.

13215 **Lambert, Mildred** and **J. T. Hillhouse.** The Scott letters in the Huntington library. (Notes and documents). Huntington Lib Q 2no3:319–52 Ap '39.

13216 **Dobie, Marryat R.** The development of Scott's Minstrelsy: an attempt at a reconstruction. Edinburgh Bib Soc Trans 2pt1:65–87 '40.

13217 **Cook, T. Davidson.** Additions to Scott's poems. (Bibliography). TLS 15 N '41:572; 22 N '41:584; W. M. Parker *ib.* 13 D '41:636.

Scott's method.–Volume of verselets.–Additions sponsored by Lockhart.–Spurious poems.–An old song.–Captain Marjoribanks.

13218 **Ruff, William.** Interleaved copies of Scott's poems. [Mss.]. N&Q 181:176 S '41.

13219 **K., H. G. L.** The Siege of Malta. [Ms.]. N&Q 182:30–1 Ja '42; J. C. Corson *ib.* 182:108–9 F '42.

13220 **Chapman, Robert W.** Cancels in Scott's Minstrelsy. [1803]. Library ser4 23no4:198 Mr '43.

13221 —— Scott's Antiquary. R Eng Stud 19no75:295–6 Jl '43.

13222 **Poston, M. L.** Addenda to Worthington. TLS 29 My '43:264.

13223 **Stevenson, P. R.** Sir Walter Scott's diary. [Location]. TLS 15 N '47:591.

13224 **Mayo, Robert D.** The chronology of the Waverley novels; the evidence of the manuscripts. Pub Mod Lang Assn 63no3:935–49 S '48. table.

13225 **Bushnell, George H.** 'On the notices of the Christians in Peveril of the peak [attrib. to John Christian Wilks]' *in* From bricks to books. London, 1949. p. 73–80.

13226 **Todd, William B.** Twin titles in Scott's Woodstock, 1826. Pa Bib Soc Am 45:256 '51.

13227 **Cowley, John D.** Lockhart and the publication of Marmion. Philol Q 32no2:172–83 Ap '53.

13228 **Parker, W. M.** Correcting Scott's text. [Proofs]. TLS 9 D '55:752.

13229 **Cahoon, Herbert.** A Scott facsimile. [Letter, 1830]. (Query 78). Bk Coll 6no1:74 '57.

13230 **Hanford, James H.** The manuscript of Scott's The pirate [acquired by Library]. Princeton Univ Lib Chron 18no4:215–22 '57.

13231 **Kaser, David.** Waverley in America. Pa Bib Soc Am 51:163–7 '57.

13232 **Todd, William B.** The early editions and issues of Scott's Border antiquities. Stud Bib 9:244–51 '57. tables.

13233 **Dyson, Gillian.** The manuscripts and proof sheets of Scott's Waverley novels. Edinburgh Bib Soc Trans 4pt1:13–42 '60.

13234 **Corson, James C.** Scott's boyhood collection of chapbooks. Biblioth 3no6:202–18 '62.

13235 **Montgomerie, William.** William Macmath and the Scott ballad manuscripts. Stud Scot Lit 1no2:93–8 Oc '63.

13236 **Corson, James C.** Some American books at Abbotsford. Biblioth 4no2:44–65 '63; 4no5:212 '65.

13237 **Rao, Balakrishna.** Scott's proposed edition of Shakespeare. Indian J Eng Stud 6:117–19 '65.

13238 **Todd, William B.** Scott's Vision of don Frederick, 1811. [Two ed.]. (Note 261). Bk Coll 14no4:544 '65.

13239 **Parsons, Coleman O.** Chapbook versions of the Waverley novels. Stud Scot Lit 3no4:189–220 Ap '66.

13240 **Day, A. E.** The library at Abbotsford. Lib R 21no4:178–81 '67.

13241 **Parsons, Coleman O.** Scott's sixpenny public. [Chapbook condensations of the novels]. Columbia Lib Columns 16no2:13–21 F '67. facsims.

13242 **Quayle, Eric.** The ruin of sir Walter Scott. London, R. Hart-Davis, 1968. 289p. illus., ports. 21cm.

> No chapter headings or table of contents; see for Scott's relationships with A. Ballantyne, James & John Ballantyne, R. Cadell, A. Constable, Longman, Hurst, Rees and Orme, and John Murray. General biographies touching on Scott's relations with his partners and other publishers are not included in this bibliography.

> Rev:TLS 2 F '69:205.

13243 —— Scott and his printers. TLS 13 Mr '69:271; K. E. Spelman *ib*. 13 Mr '69:271; J. Carswell 20 Mr '69:299; F. C. Hood 3 Ap '69:369; E. Quayle 17 Ap '69:414; M. McLaren 24 Ap '69:440.

SEAGAR, FRANCIS, fl.1549–1611

13244 **The Album** amicorum. [Ms.]. (Notes on sales). TLS 29 Ag '18:408.

13245 **Munsterberg, Margaret.** Seagar's metrical psalter. [Certayne psalmes select out, 1553]. More Bks Boston Pub Lib Bull 14no2:51–5 F '39. facsim.

SELDEN, JOHN, 1584–1654

13246 **Pollock, Frederick.** Manuscripts of Selden's Table talk. TLS 3 F '27:76.

13247 **Sparrow, John H. A.** The earlier owners of books in John Selden's library. Bod Q Rec 6no70/1:263–71 '31.

13248 **Barratt, D. M.** The library of John Selden and its later history. Bod Lib Rec 3no31:128–42 Mr '51; 3no32:208–13 Ag '51; 3no33:256–74 D '51.

Appendixes (p. 208–13,256–74)

13249 —— The publication of John Selden's Mare clausum. Bod Lib Rec 7no4:204–5 D '64.

SETTLE, ELKANAH, 1648–1724 *see also* Book production and distribution–Printers, publishers, etc.

13250 **The first** play with illustrations. [Settle's The empress of Morocco, 1673]. Bkworm 2no17:160 Ap '89.

13251 **Fletcher, Edward G.** Bibliography of Elkanah Settle. N&Q 164:114 F '33.

13252 **Dunkin, Paul S.** Issues of The fairy queen, 1692. Library ser4 26no4:297–304 Mr '46.

SEWARD, ANNA, 1747–1809

13253 **Clifford, James L.** The authenticity of Anna Seward's published correspondence. Mod Philol 39no2:113–22 N '41.

SEWELL, ANNA, 1820–78

13254 **Carter, John W.** Sewell, Anna: Black beauty, 1877. [Binding variants]. Bib N&Q 2no11:9 N '38.

13255 **Brussel, Isidore R.** [and] **J. W. Carter.** Black Beauty's 75th anniversary. Antiqu Bkmn 10:1723–4 D '52. facsims.

SHADWELL, THOMAS, 1642?–92

13256 **Bull, A. J.** Thomas Shadwell's satire on Edward Howard. [On the British princes ms.]. R Eng Stud 6no23:312–15 Jl '30.

SHAFTESBURY, ANTHONY ASHLEY COOPER, 3D EARL, 1671–1713
see Cooper, Anthony Ashley, 3d earl of Shaftesbury, 1671–1713.

SHAKESPEARE, WILLIAM, 1564–1616

The following entries represent additions to Shakespearian bibliography and textual criticism, a bibliography (Oxford, Clarendon pr., 971) *which is complete to 1969. These entries are indexed as if they were printed there, i.e. index entries have the prefix '2'. Other items in the present two volumes which refer to Shakespeare incidentally are indexed without the prefix. The index is corrected to take account of these additions.*

GENERAL BIBLIOGRAPHIES OF AND GUIDES TO SHAKESPEARIAN LITERATURE

— PRINCIPAL PERIODICALS

3 **Shakespeare Jahrbuch.** Band 1–. Weimar, Deutsche Shakespeare-Gesellschaft, 1865–.

In 1963 the Society divided to form Deutsche Shakespeare-Gesellschaft, *and* Deutsche Shakespeare-Gesellschaft West *which pub, the following:*

3a **Shakespeare Jahrbuch.** 100, 1964; vol. numbering discontinued. Heidelberg, Deutsch Shakespeare-Gesellschaft West. 1964–.

4 **Shakespeare Newsletter.** Ed. by Louis Marder. 1no1–, Mr 1951–. New York [etc.], 1951–65; Chicago, University of Illinois at Chicago circle, 1965–.

5 **Shakespeare Quarterly.** 1no1–, Ja 1950–22no4 '71; 23no1– '72–. Bethlehem, Pa. [etc.], Shakespeare association of America, 1950–71; Washington, D.C., Folger Shakespeare library, 1972–.

6 **Shakespearean Research and Opportunities;** report of the Modern language association conference. Ed. by W. R. Elton. 1–, 1965–. Riverside, Calif., Dept. of English; New York, Graduate center, C.U.N.Y., 1965–.

8 **Shakespeare Studies,** an annual gathering of research, criticism and reviews. Ed. by J. Leeds Barroll. 1–3, 4–6, 7, 8–. [Cincinnati, Ohio] University of Cincinnati, 1965–7; Dubuque, Iowa, W. C. Brown, 1968–70; Columbia, S.C., University of South Carolina pr., 1974; New York, B. Franklin, 1975–.

—SERIAL BIBLIOGRAPHIES

24 **Barroll, J. Leeds.** 'Some articles and monographs of current interest, July, 1964–65' *then* 'Significant articles, monographs, and reviews' *in* **Shakespeare Studies.** 1–3, 4–6, 7, 8–. [Cincinnati, Ohio] University of Cincinnati, 1965–7; Dubuque, Iowa, W. C. Brown, 1968–70; Columbia, S.C., University of South Carolina pr., 1974; New York, B. Franklin, 1975–. V.1–4.

—GENERAL BIBLIOGRAPHIES AND GUIDES

34a **Finding** list of collected works of Shakespeare, and of Shakespeareana. Virginia State Lib Bull 1no4:295–308 Oc '08.

63a **Lawrence, William J.** Recent Shakespearean investigation. (Readers' bibliography). Life & Letters 2no8:71–80 Ja '29.

67 **Jaggard, William.** Shakespeare once a printer and bookman. [1934]. (Repr. New York, Haskell house, 1972; Norwood, Pa., Norwood editions, 1976)

Rev: B. H. Newdigate London Merc 30:163–4 '34.

132 **McManaway, James G.** Shakespeare in the United States. 1964.

Repr. in Hosley, Richard, A. C. Kirsch [and] J. W. Velz, *ed.* Studies in Shakespeare, bibliography, and theater. New York, 1969. p. [265]–77.

154 **Velz, John W.** Shakespeare and the classical tradition. 1968.

Rev: D. Greenwood Sh Q 24:94 '73.

156b **McManaway, James G.** Studies in Shakespeare, bibliography, and theater. Ed. by Richard Hosley, A. C. Kirsch [and] J. W. Velz. New York, Shakespeare association of America, 1969. xviii, 417p. 26cm.

Includes The cancel in the quarto of 2 Henry IV.–The two earliest promptbooks of Hamlet.–A miscalculation in the printing of the third folio.–The colophon of the second folio of Shakespeare.–Richard II at Covent Garden.–Shakespeare in the United States.–The year's contributions to Shakespearian study: Textual studies [1948–65].

Rev: E. A. J. Honigmann Library ser5 25:259–61 '70; M. Mincoff Eng Stud 53:254 '72; K. Muir Yrbk Eng Stud 1971:240–1 '72; R. Maud Coll Eng 34:1137–42 '73.

WORKS–BIBLIOGRAPHIES

175a **Brassington, W. Salt.** Hand-list of collective editions of Shakespeare's works published before the year 1800. Stratford-upon-Avon, J. Morgan, 1899. [6]p. 25cm.

175b ——Hand-list of collective editions of Shakespeare's works, 1823– . Stratford, J. Morgan, 1899. 26p. (Not seen: NUC 73:19)

178 **Cambridge. University. Trinity college. Library.** Catalogue of the books presented by Edward Capell. 1903. (Repr. Norwood, Pa., Norwood editions, 1976)

184 **Pollard, Alfred W.** Shakespeare folios and quartos. 1909. (Repr. New York, Cooper Square pub., 1970)

187 **Jaggard, William.** Shakespeare bibliography. 1911. (Repr. London, Dawsons, 1971)

Rev:[L. Marder] Sh News1 21:16 '72.

192 **Grolier club,** NEW YORK. Catalogue of an exhibition. 1916. (Repr. Folcroft, Pa., Folcroft library editions, 1973; Norwood, Pa., Norwood editions, 1976)

241 **Fisher, Sidney T.** An exhibit of Shakespeare books. 1964.

The collection is now in the University of Toronto library.

245d**New South Wales. Public library,** SYDNEY. **Shakespeare tercentenary memorial library.** An exhibition in commemoration of the 400th anniversary of the birth of William Shakespeare. Sydney, Public library of New South Wales, 1964. 30p. illus., map. 22cm.

Comp. by H. G. Caplan.

252 **Shattuck, Charles H.** The Shakespeare promptbooks: first supplement. [With index]. Theat Notebk 24no1:5–17 '69.

—COLLECTIONS AND LIBRARIES

269 **The first** editions of Shakespeare's plays. Bkworm 2no22:314–16 S '89.

Sale of colln. of Frederick Perkins.

270a **The Shakespeare** memorial library. Bkworm 7no79:205–6 Je '94.

273a **Clark, Cumberland.** The Shakespeare club: lecture. [Quartos, folios and other early editions of Shakespeare]. Sh Club (Stratford) Summary of Papers [6p.] '15/16.

Repr. from Stratford-upon-Avon Herald 24 D '15.

273b **Powell, Walter.** The Birmingham Shakespeare memorial library, a tercentenary memorial. . . . Lib Assn Rec 18no7/8:282–97 Jl/Ag '16.

Proposal for a Shakespeare library.–Other Shakespeare libraries.–Arrangement.–The catalogues.

277a **The Shakespeare** shelves. [Library's collns.]. Harvard Lib N :1no]12: 258–67 D '23.

280a **Henry** Clay Folger's love's labour. (Marginalia). Bkmns J 18no13:21 '30.

293a **Woodward, Chester.** 'Shakespeare in America [Folger Shakespeare library]' *in* Out of the blue; essays on books, art and travel. Chicago, 1939. p. 169–74. facsim.

310a **Unna, Warren.** Shakespeare folios & the Folger library. Bk Club California Q Newsl 18no4:75–80 '53.

335a **Rice, Howard C.** Salute to Shakespeare. [Report of Library's exhibition]. Princeton Univ Lib Chron 25no3:225–6 '64. [Sg.: H. C. R.]

344a **Dougan, Robert O.** The Huntington library. Bibliophilie 3:3–11 Ja '67.

—GENERAL

359 **Shakespeare's** works in the sale room. Bkworm 3no33:280 Ag '90.

360a **Wheatley, Henry B.** 'X. Prices of Shakespeare's works' *in* Prices of books, an inquiry into the changes in the price of books. . . . London, 1898. (Repr. Detroit, Mich., 1970). p. 223–40.

[First folio].–Second folio, 1632.–Third folio, 1664 (some copies dated 1663).–Fourth folio, 1685.–Separate plays.

372a **Cairncross, Andrew S.** 'Shakespeare and the staying entries' *in* Stafford, T. J., *ed.* Shakespeare in the southwest: some new directions. [El Paso] 1969. p. 80–93.

The distribution of defective or unauthorized texts was widespread. Nineteen plays owned by the King's players 'escaped to the press, and at least ten of these were corrupt' (p. 90).

373 **Dent, Robert W.** 'Reflections of a Shakespeare bibliographer' *in* McNeir, Waldo F. and Thelma N. Greenfield, *ed.* Pacific coast studies in Shakespeare. Eugene, Ore., 1966. p. 303–15.

—QUARTOS

383 **Bartlett, Henrietta C.** and **A. W. Pollard.** A census of Shakespeare's plays. 1916. (Repr. New York, Ams pr., 1971)

Rev: H. Henning Sh Jahrb West 111:201–3 '75.

418a **Unknown** Shakespearean editions. Bkmns J 1no18:351 F '20.

419a **Lawrence, William J.** The secret of the bad quartos. Criterion 10no40:446–61 Ap '31.

*Repr. in no.*424.

428 **Hart, Alfred.** Stolne and surreptitious copies. 1942. (Repr. Norwood, Pa., Norwood editions, 1976)

—FOLIOS

462p **Two** Shakespeare folios. Bkworm 7no79:224 Je '94.

F2 and F4 from libr. of Hugh G. Reid.

470g **X.Y.Z.**, *pseud*. ... America's new crop of folios. ... (Books in the salerooms—and elsewhere). Bkmns J ser3 17no9:53 '29.

John Rylands' set of 4 F; a F not in Lee sold for £10,000; and the earl of Malmesbury's F3, 1st issue.

——FIRST

498 **Ordish, T. Fairman.** The First folio Shakespeare, 1623. Bkworm 1no5:161–6 Ap '88; 1no6:206–9 My '88; 1no7:255–9 Je '88.

499 **The Dallastype** Shakespeare. Brit Bkmkr 5no3:121 N '91.

Subscription facsim. of F1 in parts, pub. by J. E. Garratt.

501a **The First** folio Shakespeare. [On various copies]. Bkworm 7no77:140 Ap '94.

506 **Lee, sir Sidney.** Some bibliographical problems connected with the Elizabethan drama. Bib Soc News-sh 2–3 My '98.

Report of paper read 21 Mr '98.

534a **H., J. R.** First folios to light the candle. Bkmns J ser3 1no14:281 Ja '20.

Mutilated copy sold at Sotheby's, c.1890.

540a **Shakespeare** folios and other treasures. ... (Books in the sale rooms). Bkmns J new ser 7no14:55 N '22; 7no15:89 D '22.

Lee XXVI.

544a **A new** and remarkable First folio. Bkmns J new ser 8no23:159 Ag '23; W. Powell *ib*. 8no24:212 S '23.

F reported by C. J. Veale in libr. of Thomason college, Roorkee, is probably a Staunton facsim.: *see no.549*.

546 **Rhodes, Raymond C.** Shakespeare's First folio. 1923. (Repr. Folcroft, Pa., Folcroft pr. [1969])

549 [**Veale, C. J.**]. A First folio in India. 1923. *See no.544a*.

550 **Shakespeare association,** London. 1623–1923: studies in the First folio. 1924. (Repr. Folcroft, Pa., Folcroft library editions, 1973; Norwood, Pa., Norwood editions, 1976)

550a **One leaf** of the Shakespeare First folio brings £70 .... (Books in the sale rooms). Bkmns J new ser 12no48:245 S '25.

Verses by L. Digges and J. M., Sotheby's, 27 Jl '25.

550f **Two** copies of the Shakespeare First folio. ... (Books in the sale rooms). Bkmns J new ser 12no46:168 Jl '25.

Defective copies, one formerly ld. Middleton's, sold 15–18 Je '25.

551a **Morgan, J. Appleton.** . . . Mrs. Shakespeare's second marriage, being an examination of a persistent theory, with an attempt to account for . . . the sources from which messrs. Jaggard and Blount obtained authority for including in the First folio of 1623 sixteen Shakespeare plays not previous[ly] printed in quarto and the text[s] from which to print them. New York, Shakespeare society of New York; Somerville, Unionist-gazette association, 1926. (Repr. New York, Ams pr. [1971]). 63p. 25cm. (N.Y. Shakespeare society. Papers, no.14)

Includes IV. Who was there at London to edit a collection of Shakespeare's plays? and was there a demand for such a collection?–V. The great First folio appears.–Appendix B [Cost of ptg. F1].

565 **Willoughby, Edwin E.** The printing of the First folio. 1932. (Repr. Norwood, Pa., Norwood editions, 1976)

574a **James, Harold E.** First folio facsimile. Bib N&Q 2no4/5:10 My '36.

Paper and the Lee facsim.

574b **Willoughby, Edwin E.** Who saved Shakespeare? The time when half the bard's plays tottered on limbo's edge. [Jaggards]. Coronet 1no6:179–82 Ap '37.

588 **Walker, Alice.** Textual problems. 1953. (Repr. High Wycombe, Bucks., Microfilms ltd. for the College of librarianship, Wales, 1972; Norwood, Pa., Norwood editions, 1976)

624 **Hinman, Charlton J. K.** 'Basic Shakespeare: steps toward an ideal text of the First folio' *in* Hinman, Charlton J. K. and F. T. Bowers. Two lectures on editing: Shakespeare and Hawthorne. [Columbus, Ohio, 1969]. p. 7–19.

Account of preparation of the Norton F facsim.

Rev: R. Knowles Sh Q 24:242 '73.

—— SECOND

640 **Smith, Robert M.** The variant issues of Shakespeare's second folio. 1928. (Repr. Norwood, Pa., Norwood editions, 1976)

650a **Nordström, Johan.** Wanderings of a second folio. N&Q ser12 11:365–6 N '22; K. Petersson *ib.* 11:413 N '22.

Copy formerly owned by P. J. Coyet, 1618–67.

650g **A newly-found** title in the Shakespeare second folio. . . . (Books in the sale rooms). Bkmns J 9no27:107 D '23.

TP variant in copy sold at Sotheby's, 20 N '23.

650m **More** variants in the Shakespeare second folio. . . . (Books in the sale rooms). Bkmns J new ser 13no49:37 Oc '25.

652p **Davies, sir William Ll.** North Wales squires and Shakespeare. (News and notes). Nat Lib Wales J 1no2:102–3 '39.

F2 formerly owned by Lewis Anwyll, d.1641.

653 **O'Hegarty, Patrick S.** Shakespeare, 1632. (Bibliographical notes). Dublin Mag new ser 14no1:70 Ja/Mr '39. [Sg.: P. S. O'H.]

Handcock copy acquired; formerly owned by rev. Thomas Butler, d.1793.

658 **McManaway, James G.** The colophon of the second folio. 1954.

Repr. in Hosley, Richard, A. C. Kirsch [and] J. W. Velz, *ed.* Studies in Shakespeare, bibliography, and theater. New York, 1969. p. [155]–6.

660 **Wilson, Larry.** On acquiring a second folio Shakespeare. Am Bk Coll 8no10:6–9 Je '58. facsims.

——THIRD

673a **Keith, Alexander.** The Library's folio Shakespeare. Aberdeen Univ Lib Bull 6no35:411–18 Je '27. facsims.

William Walker F3 perfected with leaves from F1 and F2.

676 **McManaway, James G.** A miscalculation in the printing of the third folio. 1954.

Repr. in Hosley, Richard, A. C. Kirsch [and] J. W. Velz, *ed.* Studies in Shakespeare, bibliography, and theater. New York, 1969. p. [157]–61.

—OTHER EDITIONS

700 **Furnivall, Frederick J.** Who murdered Shakespeare again, about 1730? N&Q ser8 7:9 Ja '95; W. A. Henderson *ib.* 7:95 F '95. [Sg.: F. J. F.]

Reference to Royal remarks, c.1730, taken as referring to Tate but more likely Pope's ed.

705 **Lounsbury, Thomas R.** The text of Shakespeare. 1906. (Repr. New York, Ams pr. [1970])

723a **The House** mss. destroyed. Bkmns J new ser 9no25:34 Oc '23; 9no26: 75 N '23.

Ed. of Sh's plays with annotations by H. F. House.

723b **Newdigate, Bernard H.** The printing of the Players' Shakespeare. (Book-production notes). London Merc 8no43:86–7 My '23; 9no49:86–7 N '23. facsims.

Pub. by Benn, 1923. 'The text is that of the First Folio without any emendations. Even obvious misprints are left untouched' (p. 86)

725 **Nicoll, J. R. Allardyce.** The editors of Shakespeare. 1924. (Repr. Folcroft, Pa., Folcroft library editions, 1972)

735 **McKerrow, Ronald B.** The treatment of Shakespeare's text. 1933.

Repr. in Immroth, John P., *ed.* Ronald Brunlees McKerrow, a selection of his essays. Methuchen, N.J., 1974. p. 159–88.

743a **Orcutt, William Dana.** 'From a publisher's easy chair: Sir Sidney Lee, Jean Jules Jusserand, Austin Dobson, Henry James' *in* Celebrities off parade. Chicago, 1935. (Repr. Freeport, N.Y. [1969]). p. 192–223.

On publication of the University press Shakespeare Complete works, 1907–9.

773a **Meynell, sir Francis M. W.** There's more to this than meets the eye, Horatio. Print 8no6:40–2 Ap/My '54. facsim.

On typography and design of the Nonesuch ed.

791 **Sen, Sailendra K.** Capell and Malone. 1961. (Repr. Folcroft, Pa., Folcroft pr. [1969])

811 **Filmsetting** the bard; some production and typographical facts about the new Pelican Shakespeare. Monotype Newsl 86:2–5 D '69. facsims.

TEXTUAL STUDIES

830 **Walder, Ernest.** Shaksperian criticism, textual and literary, from Dryden to the end of the eighteenth century. Bradford, T. Brear, 1895. (Repr. [Folcroft, Pa.] Folcroft library editions, 1971; [New York, Ams pr., 1972]; Norwood, Pa., Norwood editions, 1976). 135p. 24cm.

Section II. Textual criticism of Shakspere from Dryden to the end of the 18th century. 1. Relations between literary and textual criticism.–2. History of textual criticism.–3. The common-sense school.–4. The historical school.

832 **Dam, Bastiaan A. P. van** and **C. Stoffel.** William Shakespeare, prosody and text. 1900. (Repr. Ultra microfiche, Dayton, Ohio, National cash register, 1970)

843b **Bayfield, Matthew A.** A study of Shakespeare's versification, with an inquiry into the trustworthiness of the early texts, an examination of the 1616 folio of Ben Jonson's works, and appendices.... Cambridge, C.U.P., 1920. (Repr. New York, Ams pr., 1969). x,521p. 23cm.

Includes 'substance of four articles which appeared in the Literary supplement [TLS] ... on May 23 and June 6, 13, 20, 1918': *see nos.*841–2.

Includes II. The early texts.–III. Abolitions of resolutions and other abbreviations in the verse: Richard II and Richard III examined.... –IV.... the quarto plays Hamlet, Othello, and Lear examined.–V. ... the Folio plays Macbeth, The tempest, Cymbeline, Coriolanus, Antony and Cleopatra, and Julius Caesar examined.–Postscript [1616 Jonson folio] (p. 294–313)

844 **Pollard, Alfred W.** Shakespeare's fight with the pirates. 1920.

Rev: H. G[arland] Bkmns J 2:383–4 '20.

857 **Pollard, Alfred W.** The foundations of Shakespeare's text. 1923. (Repr. [New York, Haskell house, n.d.]; [Folcroft, Pa.] Folcroft pr. [1970])

860 **Kellner, Leon.** Restoring Shakespeare. 1925. (Repr. St.Claire Shores, Mich., Scholarly pr., 1972)

866 **Greg, sir Walter W.** Principles of emendation. 1928. (Repr. Norwood, Pa., Norwood editions, 1976)

921 **Williams, Philip.** New approaches to textual problems. 1956.

Repr. in Zitner, Sheldon P., *ed.* The practice of modern literary scholarship. Glenview, Ill., 1966. p. [151]–60.

937 **Bateson, Frederick W.** Shakespeare's laundry bills. 1962.

Repr. in Essays in critical dissent. [London, 1972]. p. [37]–48.

943 **Partridge, Astley C.** Orthography in Shakespeare. Lincoln, University of Nebraska pr. [1964].

951 **Honigmann, Ernst A. J.** The stability of Shakespeare's text. Lincoln, University of Nebraska pr. [1965]

Rev: J. G. McManaway Library ser5 22:161–3 '67.

962 **Waller, Frederick O.** 'The use of linguistic criteria in determining the copy and dates for Shakespeare's plays' *in* McNeir, Waldo F. and Thelma N. Greenfield, *ed.* Pacific coast studies in Shakespeare. Eugene, Ore., 1966. p. 1–19. table.

— HANDWRITING AND PALÆOGRAPHY

1000a **Nicholson, Arthur.** Shakespeare's copy of Montaigne. Gent Mag 283:349–59 Oc '97.

Argues for authenticity of markings as Sh's.

1009 **Thompson, sir Edward M.** Shakespeare's handwriting. 1916. (Repr. Norwood, Pa., Norwood editions, 1976)

1018a **A Shakespeare** forgery. Bkmns J new ser 6no7:14–15 Ap '22.

Letter 'from mie loginge at Islington', June 12.

1018k **Hjort, Greta.** Scilens. (Correspondence). London Merc 11no61:80–1 N '24; J. D. Wilson *ib*. 11no62:187 D '24.

On this spelling and its variants as a sign of Sh's hand.

1029a **Rendall, Gerald H.** Shake-speare: handwriting and spelling. [London] C. Palmer [1931]. (Repr. Norwood, Pa., Norwood editions, 1976). 55p. facsims. 20cm.

> 1. The Sir Thomas More addition.–2. Q text of the Sonnets.–3. Handwriting of Edward de Vere.–4. Q orthography and misprints.–5. Conclusions.–6. Edward de Vere extracts.–Epilogue.

— COLLECTED EMENDATIONS

1061a **D., K.** Conjectural emendations in Shakespeare. Gent Mag 302:85–7 Ja '07.

1062 **Stewart, Charles D.** Some textual difficulties. 1914. (Repr. New York, Ams pr., 1975)

1064a **Wilson, John D.** Textual points in As you like it and Twelfth night. TLS 19 Je '30:514.

INDIVIDUAL TEXTS–ANTONY AND CLEOPATRA

1092a **Wilson, John D.,** *ed.* 'Modern readings' *in* Antony and Cleopatra, by William Shakespeare; a facsimile of the First folio text. London [1929]. 4p. at end.

— — AS YOU LIKE IT

1106a **Wilson, John D.,** *ed.* 'Modern readings' *in* As you like it, by William Shakespeare; a facsimile of the First folio text. London [1929]. 2p. at end.

— — CORIOLANUS

1122b **Wilson, John D.,** *ed.* 'Modern readings' *in* Coriolanus, by William Shakespeare; a facsimile of the First folio text. London [1928]. 3p. at end.

1123m **Merchant, W. Moelwyn.** A Poussin Coriolanus in Rowe's 1709 Shakespeare. (Notes and news). Bull John Rylands Lib 37no1:13–16 S '54.

> Plate by Elisha Kirkwall after Poussin in Steevens' grangerised copy of the Johnson-Steevens 4th ed., 1793.

— — HAMLET

1144 **The first** quarto edition of Hamlet. Bkworm 1no8:270–1 Jl '88.

1145d **Vietor, Wilhelm,** *ed.* . . . Hamlet; parallel texts of the first and second quartos and the First folio. Marburg, N. G. Elwert, 1891. ii,319p. 22cm. (Shakespeare reprints, II)

> 'Corrections and notes' (p. [318]–19)

1164a **O'Donoghue, David J.** Hamlet, 1603; a Dublin discovery. Irish Bk Lover 10no9/10:81–2 Ap/My '19. [Sg.: D. J. O'D].

Discovery in Dublin in 1856 of complete copy of Q1.

1217 **Duthie, George I.** The bad quarto of Hamlet. 1941. (Repr. Norwood, Pa., Norwood editions, 1975)

1220g **Dent, Alan,** *ed.* 'Text-editing Shakespeare, with particular reference to Hamlet' *in* Hamlet, the film and the play. London, 1948. p. [6–26].

Version of text prepared for the Olivier film.

1223 **McManaway, James G.** The two earliest prompt books of Hamlet. 1949.

Repr. in Hosley, Richard, A. C. Kirsch [and] J. W. Velz, *ed.* Studies in Shakespeare, bibliography, and theater. New York 1969. p. [93]–120.

1229a **Jackson, William A.** 'Appendix B: Did Halliwell steal and mutilate the Phillipps copy of Hamlet, 1603?' *in* Munby, Alan N. L. The family affairs of sir Thomas Phillipps. Cambridge, 1952. p. 116–17.

1253f **Weiner, Albert B.,** *ed.* 'Introduction' *in* Hamlet, the first quarto, 1603. Great Neck, N.Y. [1962]. p. 1–60.

I. The early texts of Hamlet.–The discovery of Q1.–In search of the Ur-Hamlet.–The problem of Q1.–The shorthand theory.–The memorial reconstruction theory.–A comparison of stage directions in Q1, Q2, and F1.–Negative conclusions.–II. Two cruxes.–Copy for Q1.–Positive conclusions: a conjectural history of Q1.

1260 **Ferguson, W. Craig.** 'The third quarto of Hamlet' *in* Valentine Simmes, printer. . . . Charlottesville, Va., 1968. p. 90.

Q3 was not printed by Simmes.

1261 **Glick, Claris.** Hamlet in the English theater; acting texts from Betterton (1676) to Olivier (1963). Sh Q 20no1:17–35 '69.

With an account of textual alterations, and table of cuts.

1262 **Vočadlo, Otakar.** The problem of the Silesian quarto of Hamlet, an essay in suggestive hypothesis. [Acta Universitatis Carolinae Philologica 3 '69] Prague Stud Eng 13:59–75 '69.

Provenance of 2d Q 1605 in Wrocław university library.

—— 2 HENRY 4

1289 **McManaway, James G.** The cancel in the quarto of 2 Henry IV. 1946.

Repr. in Hosley, Richard, A. C. Kirsch [and] J. W. Velz, *ed.* Studies in Shakespeare, bibliography, and theater. New York, 1969. p. [67]–80.

——HENRY 5

1312 **Price, Hereward T.** the text of Henry V. 1920. (Repr. Folcroft, Pa., Folcroft library editions, 1972)

1314c **Wilson, John D.,** *ed.* 'Modern readings' *in* Henry V, by William Shakespeare; a facsimile of the First folio text. London [1931]. 4p. at end.

1328 **Leisi, Ernst.** 'Die Töchter von Harfleur; zu einer Emendation in Henry V, III.3.35' *in* Fabian, Bernhard and U. Suerbaum, *ed.* Festschrift für Edgar Mertner. München, 1969. p. 169–71.

'Deface' for 'Desire'.

—— 1 HENRY 6

1341 **Alexander, Peter.** Shakespeare's Henry VI and Richard III. 1929. (Repr. New York, Octagon, 1974)

—— 2 HENRY 6

1354 **Doran, Madeleine.** Henry VI, parts II and III. 1928. (Repr. [Folcroft, Pa., Folcroft pr., 1970?]).

——JULIUS CAESAR

1399 **Wilson, John D.,** *ed.* 'Modern readings' *in* Julius Caesar, by William Shakespeare; a facsimile of the First folio text. London [1929]. 2p. at end.

—— KING JOHN

1414 **Hayashi, Tetsumaro.** A selected bibliography of Shakespeare King John. Serif 1no3:23–7 Oc '64.

—— KING LEAR

1427 **Vietor, Wilhelm,** *ed.* . . . King Lear; parallel texts of the first quarto and the First folio. Rev. ed. Marburg, N. G. Elwert, 1892. (First pub. 1886). iv,178p. 16cm. (Shakespeare reprints, I)

1431 **Doran, Madeleine.** The text of King Lear. 1931. (Repr. New York, Ams pr., 1967)

1432c **Wilson, John D.,** *ed.* 'Modern readings' *in* King Lear, by William Shakespeare; a fascimile of the First folio text. London [1931]. 7p. at end.

1435 **Greg, sir Walter W.** The function of bibliography . . . King Lear. 1933.

Repr. in Zitner, Sheldon P., *ed.* The practice of modern literary scholarship. Glenview, Ill., 1966. p. [113]–35.

1439 **Dam, Bastiaan A. P. van.** The text of Shakespeare's Lear. 1935. (Repr. Vaduz, Kraus repr., 1935)

1449 **Bowers, Fredson T.** An examination of the . . . proof correction in Lear. 1947.

Repr. in Essays in bibliography, text, and editing. Charlottesville [1975]. p. 212–39.

1451 **Duthie, George I.** Elizabethan shorthand and the first quarto of King Lear. 1949. (Repr. Norwood, Pa., Norwood editions, 1976)

1451a **Duthie, George I.,** *ed.* 'Introduction' *in* Shakespeare's King Lear, a critical edition. Oxford, 1949. p. 1–199.

I. Preface.–II. The copy for F.–III. The copy for Q. (i) Q a reported text. (ii) Q not a stenographic report. (iii) Q a memorial reconstruction.–IV. Editorial procedure.

—— MACBETH

1508b **Wilson, John D.,** *ed.* 'Modern readings' *in* Macbeth, by William Shakespeare; a facsimile of the First folio text. London [1928]. 2p. at end.

—— MERRY WIVES OF WINDSOR

1563c **Greg, sir Walter W.,** *ed.* 'Introduction' *in* Shakespeare's Merry wives of Windsor, 1602. (Tudor & Stuart library). [Oxford] 1910. p. vii–lvi.

I. Bibliographical.–II. Critical.–Appendix I. Parallel texts (quarto 1602, Folio 1623) of the horse-stealing scene.–Appendix II. Comparative table of the main oaths and asseverations occurring in the quarto and Folio texts. 'List of irregular readings of the first quarto, together with collation of the second, and a few corrections from the First folio' (p. [95]–100)

—— OTHELLO

1610d **Schröer, M. M. Arnold,** *ed.* . . . Othello in paralleldruck nach der ersten quarto und der ersten Folio. Heidelberg, C. Winter, 1909. (Repr. 1949, mit den Lesarten der Zweiten Quarto). xvi, 211p. 25cm.

1624 **Bowers, Fredson T.** The copy for the Folio Othello. 1964.

Pt.4 (Compositor E and the Folio Othello) *repr. in* Essays in bibliography, text, and editing. Charlottesville [1975]. p. 326–58.

—— RICHARD 2

1650f **Pollard, Alfred W.,** *ed.* 'Introduction' *in* A new Shakespeare quarto: the tragedy of king Richard II, printed for the third time by Valentine Simmes in 1598. Reproduced in facsimile from the unique copy in the library of William Augustus White. London, 1916. p. [5]–102.

The first quarto.–Entered at Stationers' hall.–Not pirated.–The five editions.–The new quarto.–Its relation to the second.–Further questions.–Results to be looked for.–Elizabethan spelling.–The spelling of the quartos.–Dramatic punctuation.–Emphasis capitals.–Text.–The Cambridge Shakespeare.–First quarto errors.–Errors of hearing.–Corrections during printing.–Errors not due to copy.–First quarto errors.–Second quarto errors.–New quarto errors.–1608 quarto: its errors.–1615 quarto: its errors.–Correction of quarto errors.–Copy used for First folio.–Badness of second quarto.–Second quarto corrections.–Doubtful readings.–New quarto corrections.–Later quartos.–Later quartos lack authority.–The deposition scene.–First quarto punctuation.–Punctuation of later quartos.–Emphasis capitals.–The First folio.–Its right to its own style.–First folio errors.–First folio errors and variants.–Special corrections.–Accepted corrections.–Doubtful corrections.–Folio readings classified.–1615 quarto corrected by 1597.–Use of a prompt copy.–Lines omitted in the Folio.–History of text.–Contents of pages of the new quarto.

1659 **McManaway, James G.** Richard II at Covent Garden. 1964.

> *Repr. in* Hosley, Richard, A. C. Kirsch [and] J. W. Velz, *ed.* Studies in Shakespeare, bibliography, and theater. New York, 1969. p. [241]–63.

— — RICHARD 3

1674 **Patrick, David L.** The textual history of Richard III. 1936. (Repr. New York, Ams pr., 1967)

1690 **Smidt, Kristian,** *ed.* The tragedy of king Richard the third: parallel texts of the first quarto and the First folio, with variants of the early quartos. Oslo, Universitets forlaget; New York, Humanities pr. [1969]. 221p. 28cm.

> Texts and editorial problems.–The parallel texts.–Quarto variants.–Extant quartos and press variants: descriptive catalogue.–Press variants in the First folio.

— — ROMEO AND JULIET

1738a **Williams, George W.,** *ed.* 'Textual introduction' *in* ... The most excellent and lamentable tragedie of Romeo and Juliet, a critical edition. Durham, N. C., 1964. p. xi–xvi.

— — THE TEMPEST

1768c **Wilson, John D.,** *ed.* 'Modern readings' *in* The tempest, by William Shakespeare; a facsimile of the First folio text. London [1928]. 2p. at end.

— — TROILUS AND CRESSIDA

1829 **Greg, sir Walter W.** The printing of Shakespeare's Troilus and Cressida in the First folio. Pa Bib Soc Am 45:273–82 '51. tables.

> *Repr. in no.*147. Endorsement of A. Walker's findings (*see no.*1828) with some account of the copyright problem. [*Renumber* Williams, Philip. 1951. to 1830)

— — TWELFTH NIGHT

1839 **Wilson, John D.,** *ed.* 'Modern readings' *in* Twelfth night, by William Shakespeare, a facsimile of the First folio text. London [1928]. 3p. at end.

1843 **Yamada, Akihiro.** The textual problems of Twelfth night, 1623. Bull Liberal Arts Dept (Mie Univ) 26:57–63 '62.

— — WINTER'S TALE

1860b **Wilson, John D.**, *ed.* 'Modern readings' *in* The winter's tale, by William Shakespeare; a facsimile of the First folio. London [1929]. 3p. at end.

1861 **Tannenbaum, Samuel A.** Ralph Crane and The winter's tale. 1933. (Repr. Port Washington, Kennikat pr., [1966])

— APOCRYPHA

1886 **Pollard, Alfred W.**, *ed.* Shakespeare's hand. 1923. (Repr. Folcroft, Pa., Folcroft pr. [1969])

1918 **Clayton, Thomas S.** The Shakespearean addition in the Booke of sir Thomas Moore: some aids to scholarly and critical Shakespearean studies. Dubuque, Iowa, W. C. Brown, 1969. 119p. 27cm. (Shakespeare studies. Monogr ser 1)

General preface.–II. The Elizabethan text. i. Transcription.–ii. Orthographical indexes (a) . . . punctuation. (b) . . . speech-prefixes. (c) . . . verborum. (d) Variant spellings.–iii. Index litterarum.–III. The modern spelling texts. i. The surviving fragment of Addition IIc's original,–ii. Addition IIc.–iii. Addition III.–iv. Concordance materials for the study of Addition IIc. (a) Concordance. (b) General statistics. (c) Words of multiple occurrence in order of frequency of occurrence.–Notes.

Rev: T. H. Howard-Hill Computers & Humanities 8:338–9 '74.

— SONNETS

1978a **Carter, Albert H.** The punctuation of Shakespeare's Sonnets of 1609. Gaya Coll J 2:10–16 Ja '61. (Not seen: Sh Bib 1963:361).

SHARPE, LANCELOT, 1774–1851

13257 **Axon, William E. A.** Lancelot Sharpe, sir R. Phillips, and S. T. Coleridge. N&Q ser9 11:341–3,381–2 My '03; F. H. Retton; J. Pickford *ib.* 11:435 My '03; 11:476 Je '03.

SHARPHAM, EDWARD, fl.1607

13258 **Leech, Clifford.** The plays of Edward Sharpham: alterations accomplished and projected. R Eng Stud 11no41:69–74 Ja '35.

SHAW, CUTHBERT, 1738–71

13259 **Herrick, Alan.** 18th century verse. [The four farthing candles, 1761]. TLS 22 Je '46:295.

13260 —— Cuthbert Shaw. TLS 11 S '48:513; J. W. Hayward *ib.* 18 S '48:527.

SHAW, GEORGE BERNARD, 1856–1950

13261 **Babington, Percy L.** The bibliography of G. B. Shaw: collation of The heretics, with notes. Bkmns J new ser 12no46:165 Jl '25.

13262 **Newdigate, Bernard H.** G. B. S. and the typography of his books. (Book-production notes). London Merc 12no70:420 Ag '25; G. B. Shaw *ib.* 12no71:524 S '25; A. B. C. 12no72:639 Oc '25; B. H. Newdigate 12no72:645–6 Oc '25; G. T. Meynell; W. Maxwell 13no73:72–3 N '25; B. H. Newdigate 13no74:189 D '25.

13263 **Wells, Geoffrey H.** A further G. B. Shaw collation. [Passion, poison, and petrification, 1905]. Bkmns J new ser 13no51:112 D '25.

13264 **Holmes, sir Maurice G.** Some bibliographical notes on the novels of George Bernard Shaw. London, Dulau [1929]. 19[1]p. table. 16cm.

'Collations of the four published novels' (p. 17–[20])

13265 **Rattray, R. F.** Mystery of a Bernard Shaw pamphlet; The heretics, or The religion of the future. Bkmns J ser3 18no15:94 '30.

13266 **Brett, Oliver S. B., 3d viscount Esher.** Shaw: Socialism for millionaires. [Priority of 1901 ed.]. Bib N&Q 2no7:6 Oc '36.

13267 **Shaw, George B.** Shaw: John Bull's other island. [Priority of ed.]. Bib N&Q 2no2:7 F '36. [Sg.: G. B. S.]

13268 **The Henderson** memorial collection of Shaw. Yale Univ Lib Gaz 12no2:31–42 Oc '37. illus., facsim., port.

13269 **Loewenstein, Fritz E.** A collection of Shaviana. TLS 22 Ag '42:420; A. Wade *ib.* 5 S '42:444.

13270 **Shaw's** gift of early mss. to Dublin. [National library]. Irish Bk Lover 30no1:18 Oc '46.

> Repr. from Irish Times 7 Ja '46.

13271 **Loewenstein, Fritz E.** The autograph manuscripts of George Bernard Shaw. Bk Hndbk 1no2:85–92 '47. facsims.

13272 **Shand, James.** Author and printer: G. B. S. and R. & R. C., 1898–1948. Alphabet & Image 8:3–38 D '48. illus., facsims.

> Repr. in Bennett, Paul A., ed. Books and printing. Cleveland [1951]. p. 381–401.

13273–4 Cancelled.

13275 **Fabes, Gilbert H.** An encounter with G. B. S. [Bksllng]. Bk Hndbk 2no1:36–40 '51.

13276 **Dunlap, Joseph R.** The typographical Shaw: GBS and the revival of printing. N.Y. Pub Lib Bull 64no10:534–47 Oc '60. facsims.

13277 **Laurence, Dan H.** Shaw's War issues for Irishmen. Irish Bk 1no3:75–7 '60/1.

13278 **Brown, Alison M.** The George Bernard Shaw papers. Brit Mus Q 24no1/2:14–21 Ag '61.

13279 **Eaton, Peter.** Shaw and Shaviana. Bk Coll 11no3:349–50 '62.

13280 **Geduld, H. M.** The textual problem in Shaw. Shaw R 5no2:54–60 My '62.

13281 **Brown, T. Julian.** George Bernard Shaw, 1856–1950. (English literary autographs, L). Bk Coll 13no2:195 '64. facsim.

SHAW, THOMAS EDWARD, formerly LAWRENCE, 1888–1935 *see* Lawrence, Thomas Edward, afterwards Shaw, 1888–1935.

SHELLEY, PERCY BYSSHE, 1792–1822

13282 **The Shelley** collection in the Bodleian. Acad 44:112–3 Ag '93.

13283 **Livingston, Luther S.** Percy Bysshe Shelley. (First books of some English authors, VI). Bkmn (N.Y.) 12no4:379–83 D '00. facsim.

13284 **Sigma Tau,** *pseud.* Shelley bibliography. [Poetical works, 1870]. N&Q ser9 5:67–8 Ja '00.

13285 **Forman, Harry B.** Queen Mab and The dæmon of the world. [Text]. Athenæum 4068:507–8 Oc '05.

13286 **Vaughan, Percy.** Early Shelley pamphlets. London, Watts, 1905. (Repr. New York, Haskell house, 1972). 32p. 18cm.

Repr. from The literary guide.

I. Original poetry by Victor and Cazire.–II. Posthumous fragments of Margaret Nicholson.–III. The necessity of atheism.–IV. The Irish pamphlets.–V. A letter to lord Ellenborough.–VI. A vindication of natural diet.

13287 **Koszul, Andre H.** Notes and corrections to Shelley's History of a six weeks' tour, 1817. Mod Lang R 2no1:61–2 Oc '06.

13288 **Forman, Harry B.** Shelley's Stanzas written in dejection near Naples. [Ms.]. Athenæum 4163:155–6 Ag '07.

13289 **Grierson, sir Herbert J. C.** A Shelley ms. at Aberdeen. [The magnetic lady]. Athenæum 4172:443–4 Oc '07; W. M. Rossetti *ib.* 4174:519 Oc '07.

13290 **Lang, Andrew.** Shelley as a proof-reader. [Revolt of Islam]. Acad 72no1813:118–19 F '07; S. Haswell *ib.* 72no1814:148 F '07; T. Nicklin; F. Rhodes 72no1816:195 F '07.

13291 **Forman, Harry B.** More Shelley crumbs. Athenæum 4258:674 Je '09.

13292 **Griffith, John H. S.** Shelley's copy of abbé Barruel's work on secret societies. N&Q ser12 3:108 F '17; Madeleine H. Dodds; J. J. Mac-Sweeney; A. R. Bayley *ib.* 3:196–7 Mr '17.

13293 **Farrington, B.** The text of Shelley's translation of the Symposium of Plato. Mod Lang R 14no3:325–6 Jl '19.

13294 **Ingpen, Roger.** Shelley and his publishers; with some new letters. London Merc 1no3:291–300 Ja '20.

13295 **Gosse, sir Edmund W.** New fragments of Shelley. [Mss.]. TLS 24 F '21:126; W. E. Peck *ib.* 10 Mr '21:160.

13296 **Peck, Walter E.** Shelley's autograph corrections of The daemon of the world. TLS 23 '21:404.

13297 **Wise, Thomas J.** Shelley's Queen Mab. [1813]. TLS 30 Je '21:421.

13298 **Peck, Walter E.** Shelley's Philosophical view of reform. [Text]. TLS 6 Jl '22:444.

13299 **Sargent, George H.** Shelley treasures in America. Bkmns J new ser 6no10:101–2 Jl '22.

13300 **Shelley's** first editions. (Notes on sales). TLS 6 Jl '22:448.

13301 **Smith, Harry B.** Books and autograph letters of Shelley. Scribner's Mag 72no1:73–87 Jl '22. facsims.

13302 **Stevenson** and Shelley. (Notes on sales). TLS 20 Jl '22:480; *rf.* 3 Ag '22:512.

13303 **Marsh, sir Edward.** An emendation in Hellas. [Line 945: underlight for undelight]. (Correspondence). London Merc 9no52:413 F '24; F. Colenutt *ib.* 9no53:527 Mr '24.

13304 **Wise, Thomas J.** Two Shelley forgeries. [Adonais, 1821; Hellas, 1822]. Bkmns J new ser 9no30:219 Mr '24.

13305 —— [Same]: TLS 14 F '24:96; E. N. Adler *ib.* 21 F '24:112.

13306 **Babington, Percy L.** The errata leaf in Shelley's Posthumous poems. Library ser4 5no4:365 Mr '25.

13307 **Hill, R. H.** The 'reserved' Shelley papers in the Bodleian library. [And T. J. Wise]. Bod Q Rec 4no45:218–22 My '25; 4no46:246–50 Jl '25; *rf.* Shelleyana *ib.* 5no49:6 My '26.

13308 **Hirst, G. M.** The text of Shelley. [Recollection]. TLS 20 Ag '25:545.

13309 **Irving, R. C.** An essay by Shelley. [A true story, 1820]. TLS 12 F '25:104.

13310 **White, Newman I.** Literature and the law of libel; Shelley and the radicals of 1840–1842. [And Henry Hetherington]. Stud Philol 22no1:34–47 Ja '25.

13311 **De Ricci, Seymour M. R. R.** A bibliography of Shelley's letters, published and unpublished. [Bois-Columbes] Privately ptd., 1927. (Repr. New York, B. Franklin [1969]). 296p. facsim. 26cm.

'The "G. Byron" forgeries' (p. 293–5)

Rev: R. H. H[ill] Bod Q Rec 5:253 '28; TLS 17 My '28:384.

13312 **Pettegrove, J. P.** The text of Shelley. TLS 31 D '31:1053; N. C. Smith *ib.* 7 Ja '32:12.

13313 **Lees, George F.** Recollections of an Anglo-Parisian bibliophile: III. The great Shelley forgery. [Mss.]. Bkmn 83no493:31–3 Oc '32. facsims.

13314 **Swann, Arthur.** A rare Shelley pamphlet. [Proposals for an association of those philanthropists, 1812]. Am Bk Coll 1no6:352–6 Je '32. facsim.

13315 **Jones, Frederick L.** The revision of Laon and Cythna. [= Revolt of Islam]. J Eng Germ Philol 32no3:366–72 Jl '33.

13316 **Kessel, Marcel.** The revising of Shelley's Laon and Cyntha. TLS 7 S '33:592; H. F. B. Brett-Smith *ib.* 21 S '33:631.

13317 —— Shelley's To Constantia singing. [Text]. TLS 17 Ja '35:33; K. Glenn *ib.* 11 Ap '35:244.

13318 **Mabbot, Thomas O.** An early American printing of Shelley. [Stanzas written in dejection, 1824]. N&Q 169:242 Oc '35.

13319 **Robb, N. A.** Shelley's copy of Dante. N&Q 168:385 Je '35; T. O. Mabbott *ib.* 169:34 Jl '35.

13320 —— Shelley's Dante. TLS 30 My '35:348.

13321 **X. Y. Z.,** *pseud.* Shelley: Posthumous poems. [Issues]. Bib N&Q 1no4:10 Oc '35; J. W. Carter *ib.* 2no1:2 Ja '35; X. Y. Z., *pseud.* 2no7:1–2 Oc '36.

13322 **Cook, T. Davidson.** Sadak the wanderer, an unknown Shelley poem. TLS 16 My '36:424.

13323 **Kessel, Marcel.** The Harvard Shelley notebook. TLS 5 S '36:713; Helen Darbishire *ib.* 12 S '36:729.

13324 **Norman, Sylva.** A forged Shelley letter. TLS 20 Mr '37:222; S. de Ricci *ib.* 27 Mr '37:240; S. Norman 3 Ap '37:256; S. de Ricci 10 Ap '37:275; H. G. Pollard 17 Ap '37:292; S. de Ricci; T. D. N. Besterman 24 Ap '37:308; H. G. Pollard 8 My '37:364; M. Kessel 29 My '37:412; S. Norman 5 Je '37:428.

13325 **Booth, Bradford A.** Shelley and Mary. (Antiquarian notes). TLS 30 Ap '38:304.

13326 **Davenport, William H.** Notes on Shelley's political prose: sources, bibliography, errors in print. N&Q 177:223–5 S '39.

13327 **Goodspeed, George T.** The first American Queen Mab. Coloph new graphic ser 1:[8p.] Mr '39. facsims.

13328 **Nitchie, Elizabeth.** Shelley in Fraser's and the annuals. TLS 26 Ag '39:503.

13329 **Notopoulos, James A.** Note on the text of Shelley's translation of the Symposium. Mod Lang R 34no3:421–2 Jl '39.

13330 **G., J.** H. E. Higginbotham and the £600 Shelley. [Article in Book monthly planted by T. J. Wise?]. Am N&Q 1no6:89 S '41.

13331 **N.** Shelley's Adonais. [Illus.]. N&Q 181:218 Oc '41.

13332 **Notopoulos, James A.** Notes on the text of Shelley's translations from Plato. Mod Lang N 56no7:536–41 N '41.

13333 **Glasheen, Adaline E.** and **F. J. Glasheen.** The publication of The wandering Jew. Mod Lang R 38no1:11–17 Ja '43.

13334 **Nitchie, Elizabeth.** Variant readings in three of Shelley's poems. [Mss.]. Mod Lang N 59no4:274–7 Ap '44.

13335 **Smith, Robert M.** A chapter in The Shelley legend: the letter to Mary Shelley of December 16, 1816. [And major Byron]. Pa Bib Soc Am 38:312–34 '44. facsims.

13336 **Jones, Frederick L.** The Shelley legend. [And forgeries]. Pub Mod Lang Assn 61no3:848–90 S '46.

> A summary of The Shelley legend [by Robert M. Smith] .—An examination of The Shelley legend.

13337 **Munby, Alan N. L.** Universal suffrage, 1811. [Forgery, attrib. to Shelley]. TLS 30 N '46:596.

13338 **Thorpe, James.** A copy of Endymion owned by Haydon. N&Q 193:520–1 N '48.

13339 **Ehrsam, Theodore G.** Shelley's letter to Mary Godwin [And major Byron]. TLS 30 S '49:633; Sylva Norman *ib.* 7 Oc '49:649.

13340 **Rogers, Neville.** The Shelley-Rolls gift to the Bodleian. I. Shelley at work. [Mss.]. TLS 27 Jl '51:476.

13341 —— The Shelley-Rolls gift to the Bodleian. III. Shelley's text. TLS 10 Ag '51:508.

13342 **Brown, T. Julian.** Percy Bysshe Shelley, 1792–1822. (English literary autographs, I). Bk Coll 1no1:5 '52. facsim.

13343 **Ehrsam, Theodore G.** Concerning Shelley forgeries. Philol Q 32no2:217–19 Ap '53.

13344 **Patton, Lewis.** The Shelley-Godwin collection of lord Abinger. [With checklist of microfilmed mss.]. Lib N Duke Univ Lib 27:11–17 Ap '53.

13345 **Griffith, Ben W.** Shelley's Ginevra. TLS 15 Ja '54:41; N. Rogers *ib.* 12 F '54:112; 5 N '54:712.

13346 —— An unpublished Shelley reading list. Mod Lang N 69no4:254–5 Ap '54.

13347 **Rogers, Neville.** Four missing pages from the Shelley notebook in the Harvard college library. Keats-Sh J 3:47–53 '54. facsims.

13348 **Roth, Robert N.** The Houghton-Crewe draft of Ode to a nightingale. Pa Bib Soc Am 48:91–5 '54.

13349 **Taylor, Charles H.** The errata leaf to Shelley's Posthumous poems and some surprising relationships between the earliest collected editions. Pub Mod Lang Assn 70no3:408–16 Je '55. table.

13350 **Griffith, Ben W.** Mary Shelley's inscribed copy of Queen Mab. N&Q 200:408 S '55; The librarian, Henry E. Huntington library ib. 201:45 Ja '56.

13351 **Steadman, John M.** Errors concerning the publication date of Shelley's Ozymandias. [1818] N&Q 201:439–40 Oc '56.

13352 **Rogers, Neville.** A forged Shelley notebook. TLS 15 N '57:696; P. H. Muir ib. 29 N '57:721.

13353 **Taylor, Charles H.** The early collected editions of Shelley's poems; a study in the history and transmission of the printed text. New Haven, Yale U.P., 1958; London, O.U.P., 1959. xiv,108p. tables. 23cm. (Yale Stud Eng 140)

Part I: History of the text. 1. Posthumous poems.–2. The unauthorized editions.–3. The first edition of 1839.–Part II: Data and commentary.–4. Textual notes.–5. Supplementary textual note.–6. Bibliographical descriptions.–Appendix.

Rev: TLS 19 Je '59:376; L. J. Zillman Mod Lang Q 20:384–5 '59; D. H. Reiman J Eng Germ Philol 58:542–4 '59; S. H. Nowell-Smith Library ser5 15:73–4 '60; N. Rogers Mod Lang R 55:110–11 '60; R. H. Fogle Mod Philol 57:211 '60; P. H. Butter R Eng Stud new ser 11:338 '60; J. Crow Bk Coll 9:103–4,107–8 '60; F. T. Wood Eng Stud 41:120 '60; F. T. Bowers Keats-Shelley J 9:35–8 '60.

13354 **Zillman, Lawrence J.** Shelley's Prometheus unbound. TLS 25 S '59:545.

13355 **Massey, Irving.** Shelley's Music, when soft voices die; text and meaning. J Eng Germ Philol 59no3:430–8 Jl '60.

13356 **Matthews, G. M.** A new text of Shelley's scene for Tasso. Keats-Shelley Mem Bull 11:39–47 '60.

13357 **Carl H. Pforzheimer library,** NEW YORK. Shelley and his circle, 1773–1822. Ed. by Kenneth Neill Cameron. Cambridge, Mass., Harvard U.P., 1961–70. 4v. ports., facsims. 30cm.

Contents: I (1961): Manuscripts and essays, 1778–1809.–II (1961): Manuscripts and essays, 1809–1811.–III (1970): Manuscripts and essays, 1811–1815.–IV (1970): Manuscripts and essays, 1815–1816. Appendix I: Miscellaneous manuscripts. Appendix II: The Esdaile notebook.

13358 **Palacio, Jean de.** Shelley and Dante, an essay in textual criticism. [Convivio]. R Litt Comparée 35no1:105–12 Ja/Mr '61.

13359 **Rogers, Neville.** The Esdaile notebook. TLS 6 Jl '62:500.

13360 **Boas, Louise S.** Shelley and Mary. [Ed. by lady Jane Shelley, 1882]. TLS 14 N '63:927; Anne L. Michell *ib.* 12 D '63:1038.

13361 **Dickins, Bruce.** The U.L.C. copy of Posthumous fragments of Margaret Nicholson. Cambridge Bib Soc Trans 3pt5:423–7 '63.

13362 **Boas, Louise S.** Shelley: three unpublished lines. N&Q 209:178 My '64.

13363 **Maxwell, James C.** A Shelley letter: an unrecorded printing. N&Q 209:178–9 My '64.

13364 **Duerksen, Roland A.** Unidentified Shelley texts in Medwin's Shelley papers. [1833]. Philol Q 44no3:407–10 Jl '65.

13365 **Raben, Joseph.** Shelley's Invocation to misery, an expanded text. [Ms.]. J Eng Germ Philol 65no1:65–74 Ja '66.

13366 **Hunter, Parks C.** Textual differences in the drafts of Shelley's Una favola. Stud Romanticism 6no1:58–64 '67.

13367 **Massey, Irving.** The first edition of Shelley's Poetical works, 1839: some manuscript sources. Keats-Sh J 16:29–38 '67.

13368 **Carter, John W.** and **J. H. A. Sparrow.** Shelley, Swinburne and Housman. TLS 21 N '68:1318–19; P. S. Falla *ib.* 28 N '68:1338. facsim.

13369 **Rogers, Neville.** Shelley: texts and pretexts, the case of first editions. Keats-Sh Memorial Bull 19:41–6 '68.

13370 **Chernaik, Judith.** Shelley's To Constantia. TLS 6 Ja '69:140; N. Rogers *ib.* 13 Mr '69:159.

SHENSTONE, WILLIAM, 1714–63

13371 **Churchill, Irving L.** Shenstone's copy of M'Pherson's poems. Yale Univ Lib Gaz 6no2:40–2 Oc '31.

13372 **Fullington, James F.** Some early versions of William Shenstone's letters. Mod Philol 29no3:323–34 F '32.

13373 **Wood, Frederick T.** William Shenstone. N&Q 163:315 Oc '32; J. Sinton *ib.* 163:355 N '32.

13374 **Churchill, Irving L.** William Shenstone's share in the preparation of Percy's Reliques. Pub Mod Lang Assn 51no4:960–74 D '36.

13375 **Hardy, Robert E.** Gathorne-. William Shenstone: The schoolmistress. [Repr. 1744]. Bib N&Q 2no1:6–7 Ja '36. [Sg.: R. E. G.-H.]

13376 **Addington, Marion H.** The School mistress. (Bibliographical and auction notes). TLS 16 Ap '38:268.

13377 **Gordon, Ian A.** A Shenstone discovery. [His Miscellany]. Turnbull Lib Rec 3:11–14 Ja '41.

13378 —— Shenstone's Miscellany. R Eng Stud 23no89:43–59 Ja '47.

13379 **Sambrook, A. J.** Another early version of Shenstone's Pastoral ballad. [Ms.]. R Eng Stud new ser 18no70:169–73 My '67.

SHEPHERD, RICHARD HERNE, 1842–95

13380 **Mr.** Herne Shepherd [as editor, etc.]. Athenæum 3535:131 Jl '95.

13381 **Rotton, J. F.** Pearson's editions of Chapman's, Heywood's, and Dekker's dramatic works. [Ed. by Shepherd]. N&Q ser12 4:12 Ja '18; H. D. Sykes *ib.* 4:249 S '18.

SHERIDAN, FRANCES (CHAMBERLAINE), 1724–66

13382 **Colby, Elbridge.** A Dublin piracy. [The history of Nourjahad, 1767]. N&Q ser12 12:331–2 Ap '23; R. W. Chapman *ib.* 12:416 My '23.

SHERIDAN, RICHARD BRINSLEY, 1751–1816

13383 **Prideaux, William F.** Sheridan's Critic. Athenæum 3849:157 Ag '01.

13384 —— Sheridan's Critic. N&Q ser10 3:345 My '05.

13385 **Adams, Joseph Q.** The text of Sheridan's The rivals. Mod Lang N 25no6:171–3 Je '10.

13386 **Inquisitor,** *pseud.* Sheridan's School for scandal. N&Q ser11 7:126–7 F '13; 7:226–7 Mr '13.

13387 **Flood, W. H. Grattan.** First edition of St. Patrick's day. TLS 21 Je '23:422.

13388 **Rhodes, Raymond C.** The early editions of Sheridan. TLS 17 S '25:599; 24 S '25:617; W. Roberts *ib.* 15 Oc '25:675; G. W. Panter 15 Ap '26:283.

I. The duenna.–II. The school for scandal.

13389 —— Sheridan bibliography. [His projected bibliogr.]. TLS 17 Je '26:414.

13390 —— Sheridan, a study in theatrical bibliography. London Merc 15no88:381–90 F '27.

13391 **Hinton, Percival F.** A Sheridan pamphlet. [Authentic copy of a letter, 1789]. TLS 28 Je '28:486.

13392 **Rhodes, Raymond C.** Some aspects of Sheridan bibliography. Library ser4 9no3:233–61 D '28.

'Select bibliographical summary of early editions of Sheridan's plays and poems' (p. 260–1)

13393 **Ryan, Michael J.** The text of The school for scandal. [And long s]. TLS 22 Mr '28:212; 29 Mr '28:240; W. J. Lawrence *ib.* 5 Ap '28:257; M. J. Ryan 19 Ap '28:290; R. C. Rhodes; R. W. Chapman; V. Rendall 26 Ap '28:314; M. J. Ryan 10 My '28:358; 17 My '28:379; R. C. Rhodes; R. W. Chapman 24 My '28:396; M. J. Ryan 7 Je '28:430.

13394 **Rhodes, Raymond C.** Sheridan bibliography. TLS 10 Ja '29:28.

13395 **Bateson, Frederick W.** The text of Sheridan. [The rivals]. TLS 28 N '29:998; 5 D '29:1029; N. B. White *ib.* 5 D '29:1032; R. C. Rhodes 19 D '29:1081–2; R. L. Purdy 2 Ja '30:12; F. W. Bateson 9 Ja '30:28; R. C. Rhodes 16 Ja '30:44.

13396 **Rhodes, Raymond C.** The School for scandal. [Text]. TLS 26 D '29:1697; F. W. Bateson *ib.* 23 Ja '30:60.

13397 **Nettleton, George H.** The first edition of The school for scandal. [And Pranceriana]. TLS 11 Oc '34:695; M. J. Ryan *ib.* 25 Oc '34:735.

13398 —— The School for scandal; first edition of the authentic text. TLS 21 D '35:876; F. W. Bateson *ib.* 4 Ja '36:15.

13399 **X. Y. Z.,** *pseud.* Sheridan: The critic. [Half-title]. Bib N&Q 2no1:7 Ja '36; J. W. Carter *ib.* 2no3:3 Ap '36.

13400 **Taylor, Garland F.** The Duenna. TLS 16 Ap '38:268.

13401 **Bateson, Frederick W.** Notes on the text of two Sheridan plays. [The camp; the critic]. R Eng Stud 16no63:312–17 Jl '40.

13402 **Munsterberg, Margaret.** The first edition of The rivals. More Bks Boston Pub Lib Bull 18no6:300 Je '43. [Sg.: M. M.]

13403 **Nettleton, George H.** Sheridan's Robinson Crusoe. [1791]. TLS 23 Je '45:300; 30 Je '45:312.

13404 **Purdy, Richard L.** A gift of Sheridan manuscripts in honor of professor Nettleton. Yale Univ Lib Gaz 22no2:42–3 Oc '47. port.

13405 **Vincent, Howard P.** An attempted pirarcy of The duenna. Mod Lang N 62no4:268–70 Ap '47.

13406 **Todd, William B.** Sheridan's The critic. (Note no.68). Bk Coll 5no2:172–3 '56.

13407 **Price, Cecil J. L.** The text of the first performance of The duenna. Pa Bib Soc Am 53:268–70 '59.

13408 —— The Columbia manuscript of The school for scandal. Columbia Lib Columns 11no1:25–9 N '61. illus.

13409 —— Sheridan's doxology. [Ms.]. TLS 4 My '62:309.

13410 —— Another Crewe ms. of The school for scandal. Pa Bib Soc Am 57:79–81 '63.

13411 —— The Larpent manuscript of St. Patrick's day. Huntington Lib Q 29no2:183–9 F '66. table.

13412 —— The second Crewe ms. of The school for scandal. Pa Bib Soc Am 61:351–6 '67. tables.

SHIEL, MATTHEW PHIPPS, 1865–1947

13413 **Billings, Harold W.** Matthew Phipps Shiel: a collection and comments. Lib Chron Univ Texas 6no2:34–43 '58.

SHIRLEY, JAMES, 1596–1666

13414 **Clark, William S.** The manuscript of The generall. TLS 20 S '28:667.

13415 **Howarth, R. Guy.** A manuscript of James Shirley's Court secret. R Eng Stud 7no27:302–13 Jl '31; 8no30:203 Ap '32.

13416 **Huberman, Edward.** Bibliographical note on James Shirley's The politician. Library ser4 18no1:104–8 Je '37. table.

13417 **Jackson, William A.** [Bibliogr. note on James Shirley's The politician, 1655]. Pa Bib Soc Am 34:86 '40.

13418 **Stevenson, Allan H.** Shirley's publishers: the partnership of Crooke and Cooke. Library ser4 25no3/4:140–51 D/Mr '44/5. table.

I. William Cooke.–II. Andrew Crooke and William Cooke.–III. John Crooke and the Dublin bookshop.–IV. Richard Whitaker and after.–V. The packages from Dublin.

'Plays published by Shirley during his years in Ireland' (p. 144)

13419 **Greg, sir Walter W.** The Triumph of peace: a bibliographer's nightmare. Library ser5 1no2:113–26 S '46. facsims., table.

13420 **King, Thomas J.** Shirley's Coronation and Love will find out the way: erroneous title-pages. Stud Bib 18:265–9 '65.

13421 **Riemer, A. P.** Shirley's revisions and the date of The constant maid. R Eng Stud 17no66:141–8 My '66.

SHIRLEY, JOHN, fl.1680–1702

13422 **Magaw, Barbara L.** The work of John Shirley, an early hack writer. Pa Bib Soc Am 56:332–45 '62. table.

'Chart of titles assigned to John Shirley' (p. 344–5)

SIDNEY, SIR PHILIP, 1554–86

13423 **Plomer, Henry R.** The Edinburgh edition of Sidney's Arcadia. [1599]. Library ser2 1no2:195–205 Mr '00.

13424 **Dobell, Bertram.** Sidney's Arcadia. [Ms.]. Athenæum 4167:272 S '07; sir W. W. Greg ib. 4168:303 S '07; B. Dobell 4169:336 S '07; sir W. W. Greg 4170:368 S '07.

13425 **Flower, Robin E. W.** Elizabethan manuscripts. [Selections from Arcadia; entertainments presented to Elizabeth, 1575–92]. Brit Mus Q 2no3:69–70 D '27. [Sg.: R. F.]

13426 **Sidney's** Defence of Leicester. [Ms.]. (Notes on sales). TLS 19 My '27:360.

13427 **Rowe, Kenneth T.** The countess of Pembroke's editorship of the Arcadia. Pub Mod Lang Assn 54no1:122–38 '39.

13428 **Beese, Margaret.** Manuscripts of Sidney's Arcadia. TLS 4 My '40:224.

13429 **Eagle, Roderick L.** The Arcadia, 1593, title-page border. Library ser5 4no1:68–71 Je '49.

13430 **Ringler, William.** Poems attributed to sir Philip Sidney. Stud Philol 47no2:126–51 Ap '50.

13431 **Sir** Philip Sidney's anniversary. [Bodleian library exhibition]. TLS 10 D '54:812.

13432 **Buxton, E. John.** The Sidney exhibition. Bod Lib Rec 5no3:125–30 Jl '55.

13433 —— Sir Philip Sidney and the English renaissance. [And dedications]. Library ser5 10no4:283 D '55.

13434 **Williams, George W.** The printer of the first folio of Sidney's Arcadia. [John Windet]. Library ser5 12no4:274–5 D '57.

13435 **Buxton, E. John.** On the date of Syr P. S. his Astrophel and Stella . . . printed for Matthew Lownes. Bod Lib Rec 6no5:614–16 Ag '60.

13436 **Godshalk, William L.** A Sidney autograph. [Sig. in book from library]. (Note 211). Bk Coll 13no1:65 '64.

13437 —— Sidney's revision of the Arcadia, books III–V. Philol Q 43no2: 171–84 Ap '64.

13438 **Robertson, Jean.** Sidney and Bandello. [Sidney's library]. Library ser5 21no4:326–8 D '66. facsims.

13439 **Jensen, Bent Juel-.** Sidney's Arcadia, London, 1599: a distinguished ghost. (Note 283). Bk Coll 16no1:80 '67.

13440 —— Sir Philip Sidney's Arcadia, 1638: an unrecorded issue. Library ser5 22no1:67–9 Mr '67; rf. 22no4:355 D '67. table.

13441 **Mahl, Mary R.** A treatise of horsman shipp. [Ms. of Defence of poesy]. TLS 21 D '67:1245.

13442 **Jensen, Bent Juel-.** The Tixall manuscript of sir Philip Sidney's and the countess of Pembroke's paraphrase of the psalms. (Note 314). Bk Coll 18no2:222–3 '69.

13443 **Levy, Charles S.** A supplementary inventory of sir Philip Sidney's correspondence. Mod Philol 67no2:177–81 N '69.

SINCLAIR, MARY (MAY) AMELIA ST.CLAIR, fl.1891–1931

13444 **Boll, T. E. M.** On the May Sinclair collection. Lib Chron Univ Pennsylvania 27no1:1–15 '61.

    I. The status of May Sinclair.–II. The gift of Harold L. Sinclair, esquire.–III. Some notes on the collection.

SKELTON, JOHN, 1460?–1529

13445 **Dunbabin, R. L.** Notes on Skelton. C. Notes and emendations. Mod Lang R 12no3:257–65 Jl '17.

13446 **Edwards, H. L. R.** A Skelton emendation. [Colin Clout]. TLS 19 D '36:1052.

13447 **Dale, Donald A.** Editions of Skelton. TLS 18 F '39:106; D. Hawkins ib. 4 Mr '39:136.

13448 **Sale, Helen S.** Skelton's Heare after foloweth certain bokes. Yale Univ Lib Gaz 14no1:12 Jl '39.

13449 **Kinsman, Robert S.** The printer and date of publication of Skelton's Agaynste a comely coystrowne and Dyuers balettys. [John Rastell]. Huntington Lib Q 16no2:203–10 F '53.

13450 —— Eleanora rediviva: fragments of an edition of Skelton's Elynour Rummyng, ca.1521. Huntington Lib Q 18no4:315–27 Ag '55. table.

'Table of readings' (p. 323)

13451 —— A lamentable of kyng Edward the IIII. [Ms.]. Huntington Lib Q 29no2:95–108 F '66. diagr., tables.

SKIPPON, PHILIP, d.1660

13452 **Clouston, W. A.** A puritan book rarity. [Skippon's A pearl of price, 1649]. Bkworm 5no53:145–50 Ap '92.

SLOANE, SIR HANS, 1ST BARONET, 1660–1753

13453 **Brown, T. Julian.** Sir Hans Sloane, 1660–1753. (English scientific autographs, IV). Bk Coll 14no2:201 '65. facsim.

SMART, CHRISTOPHER, 1722–71

13454 **Spence, R. M.** Parleying with Christopher Smart, vi: an intended emendation by mr. Browning. N&Q ser9 5:124 F '00.

13455 **Williams, A. Lukyn.** Smart's Song to David. [Text]. TLS 27 Mr '24:192.

13456 **S., R. F.** Smart's Song to David. Brit Mus Q 2no2:38–9 S '27.

13457 **Jones, Claude E.** Christopher Smart, Richard Rolt, and The universal visiter. Library ser4 18no2:212–14 S '37.

13458 **Brittain, Robert E.** Christopher Smart in the magazines. Library ser4 21no3/4:320–36 D/Mr '40/1. table.

13459 —— Christopher Smart's Hymns for the amusement of children. Pa Bib Soc Am 35:61–5 '41.

13460 **Bond, William H.** Christopher Smart's Jubilate agno. Harvard Lib Bull 4no1:39–52 '50. facsims.

13461 **Callan, Norman.** Smart's poems. [Text]. TLS 3 F '50:73.

13462 **Sherbo, Arthur.** Christopher Smart and The universal visiter. Library ser5 10no3:203–5 S '55.

13463 **Williamson, Karina.** Another edition of Smart's Hymns for the amusement of children. [1772]. Library ser5 10no4:280–2 D '55.

13464 **Sherbo, Arthur.** The dating and order of the fragments of Christopher Smart's Jubilate agno. Harvard Lib Bull 10no2:201–5 '56.

13465 **Ryskamp, Charles.** Problems in the text of Smart. Library ser5 14no4:293–8 D '59.

13466 **Horrox, Reginald.** X equals —? [Jubilate agno]. TLS 12 My '61:293; W. H. Bond *ib.* 21 Jl '61:449; 10 N '61:805.

13467 **Lonsdale, Roger.** Christopher Smart's first publication in English. R Eng Stud new ser 12no48:402–4 N '61.

13468 **Price, Cecil J. L.** Books owned by Smart and Cowper. N&Q 208:221 Je '63.

13469 **Roscoe, Sydney.** The ghost of Newbery's Smart's Pope's Ode on St. Cecilia's day. (Query 205). Bk Coll 15no2:215 '66.

SMITH, ADAM, 1723–90

13470 **Marshall, Edward H.** Library of Adam Smith. N&Q ser8 7:326 Ap '95.

13471 **Bonar, James.** A catalogue of the library of Adam Smith. . . . 2d ed. Prepared for the Royal economic society. London, Macmillan, 1932. (Repr. 1966). xxxiv,218p. fold.facsims. 23cm.

First ed. 1894 attrib. to Royal economic club not seen.

Introduction.–The catalogue.–Addenda to catalogue.–Appendices. I. References made to library. . . . II. Lord Reston and his estate. III. Letter of mrs. Bannerman. . . . IV. German translation of Wealth of nations, 1776, 1778. V. Decipherment of bookplate, 1763. . . . VI. The Japanese collection.

13472 —— [Catalogue of the library of Adam Smith: addenda]. Econ J 44no174:349 Je '34.

13473 **Scott, W. R.** An early draft of part of The wealth of nations. Econ J 45no179:427–38 S '35.

13474 **Bonar, James.** Adam Smith's library. [Further additions]. Econ J 46no181:178–83 Mr '36.

13475 **Jones, Claude.** Adam Smith's library: some additions. Econ Hist (Econ J Suppl) 4no15:326–8 F '40.

13476 **Massey, Dudley.** The Wealth of nations. (Bibliographical notes). TLS 20 Jl '40:356.

13477 **Greenhill, Harold.** Adam Smith's Wealth of nations. New Coloph 1pt2:193 Ap '48; F. J. Adams *ib.* 1pt2:195–6 Ap '48.

13478 **Yanaihara, Tadao.** A full and detailed catalogue of books which belonged to Adam Smith, now in possession of the Faculty of economics, University of Tokyo. Tokyo, I. Shoten, 1951. (Repr. New York, A. M. Kelley, 1966). ix,126p, illus., facsims. 22cm.

Introduction.–Catalogue.–Appendix I. Catalogue of two books added to the library of Adam Smith after his death.–Appendix II: Catalogue of books belonging to Adam Smith esqr., 1781.

13479 **Mizuta, Hiroshi.** Adam Smith's library, a supplement to Bonar's Catalogue, with a checklist of the whole library. Cambridge, C.U.P. for the Royal economic society, 1967. xix,153p. 24cm.

Supplement to Bonar's Catalogue of the library of Adam Smith.—General checklist and index.

Rev: R. S. Howey Pa Bib Soc Am 61:396–7 '67.

SMITH, ALBERT RICHARD, 1816–60

13480 **Anderson, G. L.** Christopher Tadpole. N&Q ser12 11:290 Oc '22; R. B.; W. A. Hutchison; F. C. White; A. Sparke *ib.* 11:334–5 Oc '22.

SMITH, ALEXANDER, fl.1714–26

13481 **Secord, Arthur W.** Captain Alexander Smith. (Bibliographical notes). TLS 19 Ap '34:283.

SMITH, ALEXANDER, 1830?–67

13482 **Smith:** Dreamthorpe. [States of 1st ed.]. Bib N&Q 2no2:7 F '36.

SMITH, ALEXANDER HOWLAND ('ANTIQUE'), fl.1886–94

13483 **Roughead, William.** 'Rogues ancient and modern: II. "Antique" Smith' *in* The riddle of the Ruthvens and other studies. Edinburgh, 1919. (2d ed. 1936). p. [145]–70. facsim.

13484 **Ferguson, J. Delancey.** Antique Smith and his forgeries of Robert Burns. Coloph [4]pt13:[16p.] '33. facsims.

13485 **Roughead, William.** 'Rogues ancient and modern: II. "Antique" Smith' *in* The riddle of the Ruthvens. New ed., rev. Edinburgh, 1936. (First pub. 1919). p. 122–43.

13486 **Clarke, John S.** Forgeries of Burns manuscripts: the cause célèbre of Antique Smith. Burns Chron ser2 16:24–30 '41.

SMITH, SIR JOHN, 1534?–1607 *see* Smythe, sir John, 1534?–1607.

SMITH, JOHN, 1563–1616

13487 **Crippen, Thomas G.** Missing first edition. [John Smith's A pattern of true prayer, 1605]. Athenæum 3787:656 My '00.

SMITH, JOHN FREDERICK, 1804?–90

13488 **Anderson, Peter J.** John Frederick Smith, novelist. N&Q ser12 10:229 Mr '22; F. Jay *ib.* 20:276–7 Ap '22; W. B. H. 10:391–3 My '22; P. J. Anderson 11:56 Jl '22.

SMITH, SYDNEY, 1771–1845

13489 **Murphy, James.** Sydney Smith's contributions to the Edinburgh review. Library ser5 8no4:275–8 D '53.

SMOLLETT, TOBIAS GEORGE, 1721–71

13490 **Mayhew, A. L.** The pseudo-Smollett. [The adventures of Gil Blas; and B. H. Malkin]. Acad 42:313–14 Oc '92.

13491 **Christie, John.** Smollett's History of England. N&Q ser11 2:129 Ag '10; W. Scott *ib.* 2:213 S '10; J. Christie 2:256 S '10; N. W. Hill 2:393 N '10.

13492 **Knapp, Lewis M.** A sequel to Smollett's Humphry Clinker. [Brambleton hall, a novel, 1818]. TLS 6 Oc '32:716.

13493 —— Smollett's works as printed by William Strahan, with an unpublished letter of Smollett to Strahan. Library ser4 13no3:282–91 D '32.

13494 —— The publication of Smollett's Complete history . . . and Continuation. Library ser4 16no3:295–308 D '35.

13495 **Warburton, Thomas.** Smollett: Humphry Clinker, 1771–2. [Issues]. Bib N&Q 2no1:7 Ja '36; G. G[oodspeed]; O. S. B. Brett, 3d viscount Esher *ib.* 2no3:3 Ap '36; Luella F. Norwood 2no4/5:3 My '36.

13496 **Joliat, Eugène.** Smollett, editor of Voltaire. Mod Lang N 54no6:429–36 Je '39.

13497 **Martz, Louis L.** Tobias Smollett and the Universal history. Mod Lang N 56no1:1–14 Ja '41.

'Addenda [reviews of The modern part . . . attributed to Smollett]' (p. 12–14)

13498 **Cordasco, Francesco G. M.** J. P. Browne's edition of Smollett's works. [1872]. N&Q 19:428–9 Oc '48.

13499 —— Robert Anderson's edition of Smollett. N&Q 193:533 D '48.

13500 —— Smollett and the translation of Fénelon's Telemachus. N&Q 193:563 D '48.

13501 —— Smollett and the translation of the Don Quixote: important unpublished letters. N&Q 193:363–4 Ag '48.

13502 **Deutsch, Otto E.** Poetry preserved in music; bibliographical notes on Smollett and Oswald, Handel, and Haydn. Mod Lang N 63no2:73–88 F '48.

I. Smollett's first printed poem.—II. The lyrics of Smollett's Alceste.—Conclusion.

13503 **Cordasco, Francesco G. M.** Smollett and the translation of the Gil Blas. Mod Lang Q 10no1:68–71 Mr '49.

13504 —— An unrecorded medical translation by Smollett. [R. Dibon's Description of the veneral diseases, 1751]. N&Q 195:516 N '50.

13505 **Humphry** Clinker. New Coloph 2pt8:379–80 F '50.

13506 **Newman, Franklin B.** A consideration of the bibliographical problems connected with the first edition of Humphry Clinker. Pa Bib Soc Am 44:340–71 '50. facsims., tables.

13507 **Todd, William B.** [and] **R. G. Davis.** Texts and pretexts. [Selection of copy-text etc. for students' ed. of Humphry Clinker]. Pa Bib Soc Am 46:164–5 '52.

13508 **Knapp, Lewis M.** Forged Smollett letters. N&Q 198:163 Ap '53.

13509 —— Abridgements of Smollett for children. N&Q 199:475 N '54; 200:80–1 F '55.

13510 **Jones, Claude E.** Smollett editions in eighteenth-century Britain. N&Q 202:252 Je '57. table.

13511 **Knapp, Lewis M.** Smollett's translation of Don Quixote: data on its printing and its copyright. N&Q 202:543–4 D '57.

13512 **Scott, William.** Smollett's The tears of Scotland; a hitherto unnoticed printing and some comments on the text. R Eng Stud new ser 8no29:38–42 F '57.

13513 **Bouce, Paul-Gabriel.** Smollett's libel. [And The critical review]. TLS 30 D '65:1218.

13514 **Knapp, Lewis M.** Smollett's translation of Fenelon's Telemaque. Philol Q 44no3:405–7 Jl '65.

13515 **Brack, O M.** The bicentennial edition of the works of Tobias Smollett. Bks at Iowa 7:41–2 N '67.

13516 —— Smollett's Roderick Random, 1754. [Sought]. (Query 215). Bk Coll 16no2:225 '67.

SMYTH, AMELIA GILLESPIE, fl.1826–75

13517 **Strout, Alan L.** The anonymous works of mrs. A. Gillespie Smyth. Library ser5 10no3:208–9 S '55.

SOMERVILLE, EDITH ANNA ŒNONE, 1858–1949

13518 **Goodspeed, George T.** E. Œ. Somerville's Slipper's A B C of fox hunting. [Issues]. Bib N&Q 2no1:7 Ja '36; 2no6:2 Jl '36. [Sg.: G. G.]

13519 **Somerville** & Ross: more variant bindings. Bib N&Q 2no9:11 Ja '38.

13520 **Somerville** and Ross: In the vine country, 1893. [Variant binding]. Bib N&Q 2no7:7 Oc '36; J. W. Carter *ib.* 2no8:5 F '37.

SOMERVILLE, WILLIAM, 1675–1742

13521 **[Haraszti, Zoltán].** A poet of the chase. More Bks Boston Pub Lib Bull 14no2:72–3 F '39.

13522 **Fleeman, J. David.** William Somervile's The chace, 1735. [And William Bowyer]. Pa Bib Soc Am 58:1–7 '64. tables.

SOUTAR, WILLIAM, 1898–1943

13523 **Aitken, William R.** William Soutar: bibliographical notes and a checklist. Biblioth 1no2:3–14 '57; 1no3:46 '58.

'William Soutar, a chronological checklist' (p. 9–14)

SOUTHERNE, THOMAS, 1659–1746

13523a **Leech, Clifford.** A cancel in Southerne's The disappointment, 1684. Library ser4 13no4:395–8 Mr '33.

13523b **Hummel, Ray O.** A further note on Southerne's The disappointment. Library ser5 1no1:67–9 Je '46.

13523c **Leech, Clifford.** Southerne's The disappointment. Library ser5 2no1:64 Je '47.

13523d **Bowers, Fredson T.** The supposed cancel in Southerne's The disappointment reconsidered. Library ser5 5no2:140–9 S '50.

SOUTHEY, ROBERT, 1774–1843

13524 **Axon, William F. A.** Southey's copy of the Floresta española. Library 10no118:289–94 Oc '98.

13525 **Prideaux, William F.** Southey's Omnia, 1812. N&Q ser10 2:305 Oc '04; J. T. Curry; Greta *ib.* 2:410–11 N '04; W. F. Prideaux 2:530–1 D '04; Greta 3:92–3 F '05.

13526 **H., C.** Southey ms. [Robert Surtees, esq.]. N&Q ser11 7:30 Ja '13.

13527 **Austin, Roland.** Southey's works. N&Q ser11 10:489 D '14; T. Bayne *ib.* 11:31 Ja '15; A. L. Humphreys; T. Bayne 11:74 Ja '15.

13528 **Taylor, J. C. C.** Poet laureate and book collector. Bkmns J 4no92:221–2 Jl '21. port.

13529 **Kaufman, Paul.** The reading of Southey and Coleridge; the record of their borrowings from the Bristol library, 1793–98. Mod Philol 21no3:317–20 F '24. table.

Books borrowed by Southey.–Books borrowed by Coleridge.

13530 **Mabbott, Thomas O.** Newly identified lines by Southey. [Maria Brooks' Zóphiël, 1833, and printer's copy]. N&Q 151:26 Jl '26.

13531 **Havens, Raymond D.** Southey's contributions to the Foreign review. R Eng Stud 8no30:210–11 Ap '32.

13532 **J., B. H.** Robert Southey's library. N&Q 162:425 Je '32; H. J. B. Clements; A. H. T. *ib.* 162:465 Je '32; W. Jaggard 163:228 S '32.

13533 **Harrison, George B.** Visions of judgement. TLS 29 D '32:989; V. H. Collins *ib.* 5 Ja '33:9.

13534 **Babler, Otto F.** A book from Robert Southey's possession. N&Q 170:226 Mr '36.

13535 **Davis, Bertram R.** A Southey manuscript. [Not his]. TLS 22 Ap '44:199; Writer of the article *ib.* 27 My '44:259.

13536 **Early, Benjamin W.** Southey mss. TLS 23 Je '45:295.

13537 **Havens, Raymond D.** Southey's Specimens of the later English poets. Pub Mod Lang Assn 60no4:1066–79 D '45.

13538 —— Southey's revision of his Life of Wesley. [Ms.]. R Eng Stud 22no86:134–6 Ap '46.

13539 **Whalley, George.** The Bristol library borrowings of Southey and Coleridge, 1793–8. Library ser5 4no2:114–32 S '49.

'List of borrowings' (p. 116–26); 'Borrowings by friends of Southey and Coleridge' (p. 127–31); 'Index of Southey and Coleridge entries' (p. 132)

13540 **Curry, Kenneth.** Two new works of Robert Southey. [The geographical . . . history of Chili; 1809; An exposure of . . . mr. Marsh's review, 1813]. Stud Bib 5:197–200 '52/3.

13541 **Wright, Cyril E.** Manuscripts and papers of Robert Southey. Brit Mus Q 19no2:32–3 S '54.

13542 **Metzdorf, Robert F.** Southey manuscripts at Yale. Yale Univ Lib Gaz 30no4:157–62 Ap '56.

13543 **Curry, Kenneth.** 'The library of Robert Southey' in [Davis, Richard B. and J. L. Lievsay], ed. Studies in honor of John C. Hodges and Alwin Thaler. (Tennessee Stud Lit). Knoxville, 1961. p. 77–86.

13544 **Smith, Simon H. Nowell-.** Southey's Poems, Bristol 1797. (Note 178). Bk Coll 11no2:216 '62.

13545 —— Southey, Lamb, and Joan of Arc. [Presentation copy of 1798 ed.]. (Query 186). Bk Coll 14no1:82 '65.

13546 **Martin, Richard T.** Robert Southey's copy of Simon Browne's A defence of the religion of nature. N.Y. Pub Lib Bull 70no5:325–6 My '66.

SOUTHWELL, ROBERT, 1561?–95

13547 **Redmond, Philip.** Southwell mss. N&Q ser8 9:488 Je '96; J. deC. MacDonnell; W. I. R. V. *ib.* 10:54 Jl '96; D. M. R. 10:121 Ag '96.

13548 **Grece, Claire.** Southwell manuscripts. TLS 28 Je '34:460.

13549 **Loomis, Richard.** The Barrett version of Robert Southwell's Short rule of good life. Recus Hist 7no5:239–48 Ap '64.

SPELMAN, SIR HENRY, 1562–1641

13550 **Warren, C. F. S.** Sir Henry Spelman and the History of sacrilege. Bkworm 4no37:17–19 D '90.

13551 **Collins, A. J.** The Blackborough chartulary and the library of sir Henry Spelman. Brit Mus Q 11no2:63–5 Mr '37.

13552 **Isham, sir Gyles.** A copy of Spelman's Concilia with manuscript dedication and a poem to John Selden. Bod Lib Rec 7no2:83–6 Jl '63. port.

SPENCE, JOSEPH, 1699–1768

13553 **Davies, Godfrey.** Spence's Anecdotes. [Ms.]. TLS 29 Mr '34:229; A. Tillotson *ib.* 5 Ap '34:244.

13554 **Osborn, James M.** Joseph Spence's Collections relating to the lives of the poets. [Ms.]. Harvard Lib Bull 16no2:129–38 Ap '68.

SPENCER, HERBERT, 1820–1903

13555 **Becker, Frank C.** The final edition of Spencer's First principles, part I. J Philos Psychology & Sci Methods 3no11:287–91 My '06.

SPENSER, EDMUND, 1552?–99

13556 **Astarte,** *pseud.* Faerie queene: supplement to. [Ms.]. N&Q ser9 9:28 Ja '02.

13557 **Buck, P. M.** Add. ms. 34064 and Spenser's Ruins of time and Mother Hubberd's tale. Mod Lang N 22no2:41–6 F '07.

13558 **Plomer, Henry R.** Edmund Spenser's handwriting. Mod Philol 21no2:201–7 N '23. facsims.

13559 —— Spenser's handwriting. TLS 26 Ap '23:287.

13560 **Marsh, sir Edward.** An emendation in Spenser's Prothalamium. [Brides to Birdes]. (Correspondence). London Merc 9no51:300 Ja '24.

13561 **Davis, Bernard E. C.** The text of Spenser's Complaints. Mod Lang R 20no1:18–24 Ja '25.

13562 **Jenkins, Raymond.** Spenser's hand. [Mss.]. TLS 7 Ja '32:12.

13563 **Strathmann, Ernest A.** A manuscript copy of Spenser's Hymnes. Mod Lang N 48no4:217–21 Ap '33.

13564 **Wurtsbaugh, Jewel.** The 1758 editions of The faerie queene. Mod Lang N 48no4:228–9 Ap '33.

13565 **Andrew, Charles M.** An early edition of Spenser's Poems. [1611]. Yale Univ Lib Gaz 9no1:20–2 Jl '34.

13566 **Heffner, Ray.** The printing of John Hughes' edition of Spenser, 1715. Mod Lang N 50no3:151–3 Mr '35. table.

13567 **Jenkins, Raymond.** Newes out of Munster, a document in Spenser's hand. Stud Philol 32no2:125–30 Ap '35. facsim.

13568 **Padelford, Frederick M.** and **C. G. Osgood.** The variorum Spenser. R Eng Stud 11no41:81 Ja '35.

13569 **Wurtsbaugh, Jewel.** Thomas Edwards and the editorship of the Faerie queene. Mod Lang N 50no3:146–51 Mr '35.

13570 —— 'Improvement of the text' *in* Two centuries of Spenserian scholarship, 1609–1805. Baltimore, 1936. p. 55–70.

13571 **Bennett, Josephine W.** A bibliographical note on Mother Hubberd's tale. Eng Lit Hist 4no1:60–1 Mr '37.

13572 **Hull, Vernam.** Edmund Spenser's Mona-shul. [A view of the present state]. Pub Mod Lang Assn 56no2:578–9 Je '41.

13573 **Norton, Daniel S.** The bibliography of Spenser's Prothalamion. J Eng Germ Philol 43no3:349–53 Jl '44.

13574 **Evans, Frank B.** New evidence on the 1596 printing of the Faerie queene. Renaiss Pa 1957:4–8 '57.

13575 **Stillinger, Jack.** A note on the printing of E. K.'s glosses. Stud Bib 14:203–5 '61.

13576 **Meyer, Sam.** Spenser's Colin Clout: the poem and the book. Pa Bib Soc Am 56:397–413 '62. table.

13577 **Evans, Frank B.** The printing of Spenser's Faerie Queene in 1596. Stud Bib 18:49–67 '56. tables.

13578 **Roche, Thomas P.** The Spenser collection of Charles Grosvenor Osgood [at Princeton]. Princeton Univ Lib Chron 29no1:91–101 '67.

SQUIRE, WILLIAM, fl.1770

13579 **A., L. E.** The Squire papers. [And Cromwell]. N&Q 172:246 Ap '37; E. Bensly; E. V. Stone *ib.* 172:299 Ap '37.

STANBRIDGE, JOHN, 1463–1510

13580 **Flynn, Vincent J.** Longe parvula. [1496]. TLS 9 D '39:717.

STANHOPE, PHILIP DORMER, 4TH EARL OF CHESTERFIELD, 1694–1773

13581 **V., Q.** Lord Chesterfield's library. N&Q ser9 4:539 D '99.

13582 **Gulick, Sidney L.** The publication of Chesterfield's Letters to his son. Pub Mod Lang Assn 51no1:165–77 Mr '36.

13583 **O'Hegarty, Patrick S.** Chesterfield's Letters; Dublin edition. (Bibliographical notes). Dublin Mag new ser 14no1:70 Ja/Mr '39. [Sg.: P. S. O'H.]

13584 **Todd, William B.** The number, order, and authorship of the Hanover pamphlets attributed to Chesterfield. Pa Bib Soc Am 44:224–38 '50.

13585 **Price, Cecil J. L.** The Edinburgh edition of Chesterfield's Letters to his son. [1775]. Library ser5 5no4:271–2 Mr '51.

13586 **Brown, T. Julian.** Lord Chesterfield, 1694–1773. (English literary autographs, XXVIII). Bk Coll 7no4:397 '58. facsims.

13587 **Gulick, Sidney L.** Issued in parts: the seventh edition of Chesterfield's Letters to his son. [1776]. Pa Bib Soc Am 60:159–65 '66. tables.

STANLEY, CHARLES, 8TH EARL OF DERBY, fl.1669

13588 **Lord** Derby's Jesuites policy, 1678. (Notes on sales). TLS 8 Mr '23:164.

STANLEY, THOMAS, 1625–78

13589 **Wright, Lyle H.** Bibliographical note [on Poems and translations, by Thomas Stanley, esquire, 1647]. Huntington Lib Q 2no2:231–2 Ja '39.

13590 **Crump, Galbraith M.** A Thomas Stanley ms. TLS 26 Jl '57:457.

13591 —— Thomas Stanley's manuscript of his Poems and translations. Cambridge Bib Soc Trans 2pt5:359–65 '58.

STANLEY, WILLIAM, 6TH EARL OF DERBY, c.1561–1642

13592 **Greg, sir Walter W.** Derby his hand, and soul. [Handwriting]. Library ser4 7no1:39–45 Je '26. facsims.

STAPYLTON, SIR ROBERT, d.1669

13593 **Bowers, Fredson T.** The first editions of sir Robert Stapylton's The slighted maid, 1663, and The step-mother, 1664. Pa Bib Soc Am 45:143–8 '51.

STEDMAN, JOHN, fl.1782

13594 **Doyle, Paul A.** A rare copy of John Stedman's Laelius and Hortensia. [And W. Melmoth]. Pa Bib Soc Am 51:241–4 '57.

STEELE, SIR RICHARD, 1672–1729

13595 **Steele** and The ladies library. Bkworm 1no2:49–52 Ja '88.

13596 **Aitken, George A.** Steele's Ladies library. Bkworm 2no14:62–3 Ja '89.

13597 —— Steele's Conscious lovers and the publishers. Athenæum 3345:771 D '91.

13598 **Blanchard, Rae.** Steele's Christian hero and the errata in The tatler. R Eng Stud 6no22:183–5 Ap '30.

13599 **Baine, Rodney M.** The publication of Steele's Conscious lovers. Stud Bib 2:169–73 '49.

13600 **Foxon, David F.** A piracy of Steele's The lying lover. [1732]. Library ser5 10no2:127–9 Je '55.

13601 **Brown, T. Julian.** Richard Steele, 1672–1729. Joseph Addison, 1672–1719. (English literary autographs, XXV). Bk Coll 7no1:63 '58. facsims.

13602 **Kenny, Shirley S.** Two scenes by Addison in Steele's Tender husband. Stud Bib 19:217–26 '66.

13603 **Bloom, Edward A.** and **Lillian D. Bloom.** Steele in 1719: additions to the canon. Huntington Lib Q 31no2:123–51 F '68.

13604 **Kenny, Shirley S.** Eighteenth-century editions of Steele's Conscious lovers. Stud Bib 21:253–61 '68. tables.

STEEVENS, GEORGE, 1736–1800

13605 **Abraham, Aleck.** Upper heath, Hampstead. N&Q ser12 11:102–3 Ag '22.

STEPHENS, HENRY, fl.1693–1732

13606 **Joost, Nicholas.** Henry Stephens; a bibliographical and biographical note. N&Q 194:379–80 S '49.

STEPHENS, JAMES, 1882–1950

13607 **Solomons, Bethel.** Bibliographies of modern authors. [Corrections]. (Correspondence). London Merc 4no21:411 Ag '21.

13608 **Sargent, George H.** . . . James Stephens 'hoists the sale' [at the Chandler sale, American art galleries, 6 F '25]. (American notes). Bkmns J new ser 12no43:27 Ap '25.

13609 **Saul, George B.** James Stephens' contributions to The Irish review. Pa Bib Soc Am 46:398–9 '52.

13610 **McFate, Patricia.** A holograph notebook and the publication of its contents; a bibliographical note on James Stephens. Pa Bib Soc Am 57:226 '63.

13611 **McFate, Patricia.** The publication of James Stephens' short stories in The nation. Pa Bib Soc Am 58:476–7 '64.

13612 **The James** Stephens papers, a catalogue: Serif 2no2:29–32 Je '65.

STERN, GLADYS BERTHA, 1890–1973

13612q **Gregory, K.** A. B. Stern: Tents of Israel. [Variant bindings]. Bib N&Q 2no7:7 Oc '36.

STERNE, LAURENCE, 1713–68

13613 **Bromley, James.** Tristram Shandy. Athenæum 3958:316 S '03.

13614 **Ryan, Michael J.** An edition of Sterne. [Works, 1773]. TLS 16 S '26:616.

13615 **Sellers, Harry.** A Sterne problem [in Tristram Shandy, London, D. Lynch, 1760]. TLS 21 Oc '26:722; C. Wanklyn *ib.* 4 N '26:770.

13616 **Tristram** Shandy, first edition. Brit Mus Q 1no4:101 Mr '27.

13617 **Curtis, Lewis P.** The printer of Sterne's Political romance. [C. Ward, York]. TLS 28 F '29:163.

13618 **Whibley, Charles,** *ed.* A facsimile reproduction of a unique catalogue of Laurence Sterne's library; with a preface. London, J. Tregaskis; New York, E. H. Wells, 1930. 14,94p. 23cm.

   Rev: Oxford Mag 13 Mr '30:620; Library ser4 15:390–1 '30; G. M. Troxell Saturday R Lit 6:812 '30.

13619 **Curtis, Lewis P.** The first printer of Tristram Shandy. [A. Ward, York]. Pub Mod Lang Assn 47no3:777–89 S '32.

   Typography.–Watermarks.–Press numbers.–Signatures.

13620 —— Sterne's letters and mss. N&Q 162:63 Ja '32.

13621 **Points** in Tristram Shandy. (Bibliographical notes). TLS 22 F '34:132.

13622 **Curtis, Lewis P.** Forged letters of Laurence Sterne. Pub Mod Lang Assn 50no4:1076–106 D '35. tables.

13623 **Laurence** Sterne. [Illus. by Lewis Stern in Poems of Michael Wodhull, 1772]. Bib N&Q 2no2:7 F '36.

13624 **S.** Sterne: Tristram Shandy. [Binding wrappers]. Bib N&Q 2no1:7–8 Ja '36; S. H. Nowell-Smith *ib.* 2no2:2 F '36.

13625 **Marlow, Harriet.** Sterne: Sentimental journey, first edition. [Collation]. Bib N&Q 2no11:9 N '38; D. Massey *ib.* 2no12:5 My '39.

13626 **Yoklavich, John M.** Notes on the early editions of Tristram Shandy. Pub Mod Lang Assn 63no2:508–19 Je '48.

13627 **Monk, Samuel H.** Laurence Sterne at Princeton, [Letters]. Princeton Univ Lib Chron 10no3:137–9 Ap '49.

13628 **Thompson, Karl F.** The authorship of Yorick's Sentimental journey continued. [Anon, 1769]. N&Q 195:318–19 Jl '50.

13629 **A., R. F.** Sterne: Sentimental journey, first edition. (Query no.9). Bk Coll 1no1:57 '52.

13630 **Oates, John C. T.** On collecting Sterne. Bk Coll 1no4:247–58 '52. facsims.

13631 **Benson, Carolyn.** The advertisement in The sentimental journey. (Query no.9). Bk Coll 2no2:157 '53.

13632 **Oates, John C. T.** Notes on the bibliography of Sterne. Cambridge Bib Soc Trans 2pt2:155–69 '55. facsims., table.

I. Letters from Eliza to Yorick, 1775 [Forgery].–II. Letters from Yorick to Eliza, 1775.–Priority of editions and dates of publication.

13633 **Brown, T. Julian.** Laurence Sterne, 1713–1768. (English literary autographs, XXVII). Bk Coll 7no3:285 '58. facsim.

13634 **Kaufman, Paul.** Mr. Yorick and the Minster library. N&Q 205:308–10 Ag '60.

Repr. in Libraries and their users. London, 1969. p. 90–2.

13635 **Monkman, Kenneth.** Early editions of Tristram Shandy. [Sought]. (Query 217). Bk Coll 16no3:377 '67.

13636 **Oates, John C. T.** Shandyism and sentiment, 1760–1800. Cambridge, Ptd. for the Cambridge bibliographical society and sold by the Laurence Sterne trust, 1968. 31p. facsim. 18cm.

Rev: TLS 31 Jl '69:864; Pa Bib Soc Am 63:59 '69; R. Lonsdale Library ser5 24:352–3 '69.

13637 **Rousseau, G. S.** Harvard's holdings on Laurence Sterne. Harvard Lib Bull 16no4:400–1 Oc '68.

STEVENSON, JOSEPH, 1806–95

13638 **H., F.** Church historians of England. N&Q ser11 3:308 Ap '11; Seeley and co. ltd.; R. Pierpont; A. R. Bayley; W. Scott *ib.* 3:373 My '11; R. B—r 4:58 Jl '11; W. Scott; R. Pierpont 4:117 Ag '11; R. B—r 4:154 Ag '11; R. Pierpont 4:253–4 S '11; 6:296–7 Oc '12.

STEVENSON, ROBERT LOUIS, 1850–94

13639 **Livingston, Luther S.** Robert Louis Stevenson. (The first books of some English authors, V). Bkmn (N.Y.) 10no5:437–40 Ja '00. facsims.

13640 **Prideaux, William F.** Stevenson's New Arabian nights. N&Q ser10 5:107 F '06.

13641 —— The Widener-Stevenson collection. N&Q ser11 9:301–2 Ap '14.

13642 **Stevenson** in the auction room. (Notes on sales). TLS 4 D '19:720.

13643 **Newdigate, Bernard H.** A Stevenson trifle. [The bandbox]. (Book-production notes). London Merc 4no21:297–8 Jl '21.

13644 **Balfour, Graham.** Misprints of R. L. Stevenson. TLS 2 F '22:77; E. W. White; R. L. B. *ib.* 9 F '22:92; sir D. W. Thompson 23 F '22:125; B. 2 Mr '22:141; J. P. MacLeod 22 Je '22:413.

13645 **A rare** Stevenson item collated. [Confessions of a Unionist, 1921]. Bkmns J new ser 7no13:11 Oc '22.

13646 **Colvin, sir Sidney.** The Vailima Stevenson. [Text of collected works]. TLS 28 Je '23:440; 12 Jl '23:472.

13647 **Kebler, Leonard.** The first edition of Kidnapped. TLS 26 Je '24:404.

13648 **Moncrieff, Charles K. S.** Textual errors in Stevenson. TLS 29 Ap '26:323; J. D. Hamilton; A. J. Bird *ib.* 20 My '26:339; R. A. S. Macalister 5 Ag '26:525; C. H. Dick 19 Ag '26:549.

13649 **Stevenson's** Records of a family of engineers. [Ms.]. (Notes on sales). TLS 4 Ag '27:536.

13650 **Lockett, W. G.** R. L. S. and Mrs. MacMorland. [Text]. TLS 29 Ag '29: 668; G. S. Pringle *ib.* 26 D '29:1097; W. G. Lockett 30 Ja '30:78; 31 Jl '30:628.

13651 **Pearson, T. S.** R. L. S.'s New poems and variant readings. TLS 6 F '30:102.

13652 **Wright, Herbert G.** Textual errors in Stevenson. TLS 21 Ag '30:668.

13653 **Hellman, George S.** Stevenson's annotated set of Wordsworth. Coloph [2]pt7:1–8 '31. facsim.

13654 **Hills, Gertrude.** Three letters from Robert Louis Stevenson, a bibliographical note. [Essex house pr.]. Am Bk Coll 2no4:209–11 Oc '32.

13655 —— Stevenson: The charity bazaar. Bib N&Q 1no3:6 Ag '35. [Sg.: G. H.]

13656 **Heron, Flodden W.** Stevenson: Treasure island. [Drawing for 1st ed.]. Bib N&Q 2no1:8 Ja '36.

13657 **Carter, John W.** The Hanging judge acquitted. Coloph new ser 3no2:238–42 My '38.

13658 **Stevenson, R. L.** [Macaire, 1885: variant imprints]. Bib N&Q 2no11:10 N '38; M. L. Parrish *ib.* 2no12:5 My '38.

13659 **Carter, John W.** Stevenson, R. L.: New Arabian nights, 1882. [Issues]. Bib N&Q 2no11:9 N '38; D. Massey; C. W. Trapp *ib.* 2no12:5 My '39.

13660 **A Stevenson** exhibition. Colby Lib Q 1no9:139–41 Ja '45.

13661 **Bushnell, George H.** 'R. L. S. and "Henderson's weekly"' *in* From papyrus to print. London, 1947. p. 190–8.

13662 **Beinecke, E. J.** Stevenson, Wise. [Ticonderoga, 1887, a Wise forgery?]. New Coloph 2pt5:82,85–7 Ja '49.

13663 **Stevenson** manuscripts. [C. Glidden Osborne library]. TLS 1 Jl '49:436.

13664 **Balfour, M. L. G.** In defense of The hanging judge. New Coloph 3:75–7 '50.

13665 **Smith, Janet A.** Stevenson's poems. [Mss.]. TLS 17 F '50:112.

13666 **Robert** Louis Stevenson. [Mss. acquired for Library]. Princeton Univ Lib Chron 13no3:167–8 '52.

13667 **Robert** Louis Stevenson. [Additions to collection]. Princeton Univ Lib Chron 14no2:105 '53.

13668 **Wynne, Marjorie G.** R. L. Stevenson manuscripts at Yale. Autogr Coll J 5no2:2–8,51 '53. facsims.

13669 **Robert** Louis Stevenson. [Additions to collection]. Princeton Univ Lib Chron 15no2:107 '54.

13670 **Robert** Louis Stevenson. [Acquisition of mss. and association items]. Princeton Univ Lib Chron 16no2:100–1 '55.

13671 **Randall, David A.** The Stevenson collection. Princeton Univ Lib Chron 17no2:92–5 '56.

13672 **Robert** Louis Stevenson. [Further donations by Henry E. Gerstley]. Princeton Univ Lib Chron 17no2:105–7 '56.

13673 **Caldwell, Elsie N.** Requiem: gem of archives; who deleted the middle stanza from this much-quoted poem . . .? Manuscripts 13no3:13–17 '61. facsim.

13674 **Mehew, Ernest.** A Stevenson manuscript. [Travels with a donkey: Preface]. TLS 14 Jl '61:433.

13675 **McKay, George L.** Note on R. L. Stevenson's Requiem. Yale Univ Lib Gaz 36no3:122–5 Ja '62.

13676 **Hart, James D.** The private press ventures of Samuel Lloyd Osbourne and R.L.S., with facsimiles of their publications. [San Francisco] Book club of California, 1966. 49p. illus., port., facsims. 26cm.

STIRLING, SIR WILLIAM ALEXANDER, EARL OF, 1567?–1640
see Alexander, sir William, earl of Stirling, 1567?–1640.

STOKER, ABRAHAM, 1847–1912

13677 **Logs,** *pseud.* Stoker, Dracula, 1897. [Issues]. Bib N&Q 2no9:11 Ja '38; P. Seyboldt *ib.* 2no11:5–6 N '38.

STOW, JOHN, 1525?–1605

13678 **Clark, R.** Stow's London. N&Q ser8 5:308 Ap '94.

13679 —— Proposal for reprinting Stow's Survey of London. [1708]. N&Q ser8 7:268 Ap '95; E. H. Coleman *ib.* 7:351 My '95.

13680 **Abrahams, Aleck.** The 1618 edition of Stow's Survey. N&Q ser11 10:248 S '14.

13681 **Ringler, William.** John Stow's editions of Skelton's Workes and of Certaine worthye manuscript poems. Stud Bib 8:215–17 '56.

13682 **Martin, Mary F.** Stow's Annals and The famous historie of sir Thomas Wyat. Mod Lang R 53no1:75–7 Ja '58.

STRACHEY, GILES LYTTON, 1880–1932

13683 **Sanders, Charles R.** Lytton Strachey's revisions in Books and characters. Mod Lang N 60no4:226–34 Ap '45. table.

13684 **Stratford, A. Jenny L.** Eminent Victorians. [Acquisition of drafts, notebooks and other mss.]. Brit Mus Q 32no3/4:93–6 '68.

STRACHEY, WILLIAM, fl.1609–18

13685 **Lang, Andrew.** A point in bibliography. [Strachey's use of materials of William Simmons]. Athenæum 3719:148 F '99.

STRODE, WILLIAM, 1602–45

13686 **Crum, Margaret C.** William Fulman and an autograph manuscript of the poet Strode. Bod Lib Rec 4no6:324–35 D '53. facsims.

STUBBES, HENRY, 1632–76

13687 **Jones, Harold W.** Stubbe and Wotton. [Copies of their books sought]. (Note no.63). Bk Coll 5no1:78 '56; C. S. Bliss *ib.* 5no3:276 '56.

13688 **Main, C. F.** Henry Stubbe and the first English book on chocolate. [The Indian nectar, 1662]. J Rutgers Univ Lib 23no2:33–47 Je '60.

13689 **Jones, Harold W.** An unexplained 17th-century cancel. [Henry Stubbes' Legends, no histories, 1670]. (Query 129). Bk Coll 9no2:203–4 '60; C. S. Bliss *ib.* 10no1:72 '61; R. J. F. Carnon 11no3:351–2 '62.

STUBBES, PHILIP, fl.1583–91

13690 **Pearson, Terry P.** Phillip Stubbes. N&Q 202:406–7 S '57.

13691 —— The composition and development of Phillip Stubbes' Anatomie of abuses. Mod Lang R 56no3:321–2 Jl '61.

'Supplementary note' (p. 331–2)

STUKELEY, SIR LEWIS, d.1620

13692 **Brushfield, Thomas N.** Sir Lewis Stukeley's Petition. [1618]. N&Q ser10 3:428 Je '05.

STURGIS, HOWARD OVERING, fl.1891–1906

13693 **Carter, John W.** A binding variant. Howard Overing Sturgis. Belchamber. Constable, 1904. (Query no.13). Bk Coll 1no2:130 '52.

SUCKLING, SIR JOHN, 1609–41

13694 **Goodspeed, George T.** Suckling: Fragmenta aurea, 1646. [Collation]. Bib N&Q 2no9:11–12 Ja '38; J. H. Pershing *ib.* 2no11:6 N '38. [Sg.: G. G.]

13695 **Wyllie, John C.** The printer of a 1641 Suckling pamphlet. [John Dawson and Copy of a lettter]. Pa Bib Soc Am 47:70 '53.

13696 **Beaurline, Lester A.** The canon of sir John Suckling's poems. Stud Philol 57no3:492–518 Jl '60.

13697 —— An editorial experiment: Suckling's A sessions of the poets. [Ms.]. Stud Bib 16:43–60 '63. diagrs., tables.

13698 **Armitage, C. M.** Identification of New York public library manuscript Suckling collection and of Huntington manuscript 198. [And Joseph Haslewood]. Stud Bib 19:215–16 '66.

SUMMERS, ALPHONSE MONTAGUE JOSEPH-MARY AUGUSTUS, 1880–1948

13699 **Smith, Timothy d'A.** A Montague Summers collection. [His]. Bks (J Nat Bk League) 354:129–33 Jl/Ag '64.

SURREY, HENRY HOWARD, EARL OF, 1517?–47 *see* Howard, Henry, earl of Surrey, 1517?–47.

SURTEES, ROBERT SMITH, 1805–64

13700 **Grant, R. G.** A Surtees point. [Analysis of the hunting field, 1846]. (Sales and bibliography). TLS 13 Mr '37:192.

13701 **Marlow, Harriet.** Surtees, R. S.: The horseman's manual, 1831. [TP variants]. Bib N&Q 2no11:10 N '38.

13702 **Richards, Gertrude R. B.** The sporting novels of Robert Smith Surtees. More Bks Boston Pub Lib Bull 19no9:363–4 N '44. [Sg.: G. R. B. R.]

13703 **Steedman, J. W.** R. S. Surtees: The horseman's manual, 1831. Which issue was the earlier? (Query 231). Bk Coll 17no4:492 '68.

SWIFT, JONATHAN, 1667–1745

13704 **Dean** Swift's library. Bkworm 2no23:343–4 Oc '89.

13705 **Swiftiana** in The gentleman's magazine. Bkworm 2no14:39–42 Ja '89.

> Isaac Bickerstaff.–A new session of the poets.–Gulliver's travels.–Irish woollen manufactures, 1731.–Epitaph on the duke of Schomberg.–Delany's riddle to lady Carteret.

13706 **Waller, W. F.** Aldine Swift, 1833. N&Q ser8 3:28 Ja '93.

13707 **Wise, Charles.** Swift's works. [Miscellanies, 1751]. N&Q ser8 5:248 Mr '94.

13708 **C., J. G.** Swift's letters to Motte. N&Q ser8 10:215 S '96.

13709 **G., F.** A pamphlet by Swift. [The present miserable state of Ireland, 1721]. Athenæum 3567:314 Mr '96.

13710 **LeFanu, T. P.** Dean Swift's library. Roy Soc Antiqu Ireland J ser5 6pt2:113–21 '96.

13711 **Scott, Temple,** *pseud. of* **J. H. Isaacs.** The Tale of a tub. N&Q ser8 10:337 Oc '96.

13712 **Dennis, G. R.** Gulliver's travels. Athenæum 3666:153–4 Ja '98; G. A. Aitken 3668:215–16 F '98; F. H. Evans 3670:279 F '98.

13713 **Aitken, George A.** Swift's church pamphlets. [Project for the advancement]. Athenæum 3712:867 D '98.

13714 **White, Newport J. D.** Swiftiana in Marsh's library. Hermathena 27:369–81 '01.

Repr. in An account of archbishop Marsh's library, Dublin. Dublin, 1926.

13715 **Dowden, Edward.** Jonathan Swift: a text recovered. [A letter . . . concerning the sacramental test, 1708]. Bibliographer 2no2:103–6 F '03.

13716 **Robbins, Alfred F.** Swift and Temple's letters. N&Q ser10 8:21–2 Jl '07.

13717 **Guthkelch, Adolph C. L.** Swift's Tale of a tub. Mod Lang R 8no3:301–13 Jl '13; Addendum *ib.* 9no1:100 Ja '14.

Includes 'The history of Martin' (p. 310–13)

13718 **James, Montague R.** Swift's copy of Dampier. TLS 26 F '25:138.

13719 **Williams, sir Harold H.** The Motte editions of Gulliver's travels. Library ser4 6no3:229–63 D '25. port., facsims., table.

'Some variations of the Motte editions' (p. 236–7)

13720 **Doane, Gilbert H.** Swift's Tale of a tub. [With autogr. notes]. TLS 23 S '26:632; sir H. H. Williams *ib.* 30 S '26:654.

13721 **Gulliver's** travels. (Notes on sales). TLS 11 N '26:804.

13722 **Le Fanu, T. P.** Catalogue of dean Swift's library in 1715 with an inventory of his personal property in 1742. Roy Irish Acad Proc 37secCno13:263–75 Jl '27.

'A catalogue of books belonging to dr. Jonathan Swift . . . Aug. 19th 1715' (p. 269–73)

13723 **A misplaced** paragraph in Gulliver's travels. (Notes on sales). TLS 30 Je '27:460; sir H. H. Williams *ib.* 28 Jl '27:520.

13724 **Williams, sir Harold H.** Gulliver's travels: further notes. Library ser4 9no2:187–96 S '28.

13725 —— A sentence of Gulliver's travels in Swift's hand. TLS 10 Ja '29:28.

13726 **Leslie, sir Shane.** Swift's handwriting. TLS 24 Jl '30:611.

13727 **Smyth, J. deLacy.** A book from dean Swift's library. [Ælianus: Historical anecdotes, 1668]. Irish Bk Lover 18no6:158–61 N/D '30.

13728 **Williams, sir Harold H.** A Hue and cry after dismal. R Eng Stud 6no22:195–6 Ap '30.

13729 —— Stella's handwriting. TLS 5 Je '30:475.

13730 **Davis, Herbert J.** Verses on the death of dr. Swift. Bk Coll Q 2:57–73 Mr '31.

13731 **Williams, sir Harold H.** Dean Swift's library, with a facsimile of the original catalogue and some account of two manuscript lists of his books. Cambridge, C.U.P.; New York, Macmillan, 1932. viii,93p. + 16p. facsims. 21cm.

Early purchases.–Manuscript lists and the sale catalogue.–The Abbotsford manuscript.–The sale catalogue and dr. Wilson.–The Abbotsford manuscript.–The sale catalogue. –Theology.–Classics.–The starred books.–Annotated books not in the sale catalogue. –French books.–English books.–The Battle of the books.–A Tale of a tub.–Gulliver's travels.–Facsimile of the sale catalogue.

Rev: TLS 4 Ag '32:555; H. C. Hutchins R Eng Stud 9:488–94 '33; R. P. Bond Virginia Q R 10:302–7 '34.

13732 **Birss, John H.** A volume from Swift's library. N&Q 163:404 D '32; 164:334 My '33.

13733 **Dix, Ernest R. McC.** A new specimen of early Limerick printing: the Drapier letter. [2d Drapier letter, ptd. 1724]. Irish Bk Lover 21no5:110 S/Oc '33.

13734 **ÓCasaide, Séamus.** A priced copy of dean Swift's auction catalogue. Irish Bk Lover 21no4:85–7 Jl/Ag '33.

13735 **Higgins, T. F.** More Swiftiana. [Ptg.]. TLS 13 D '34:895.

13736 **King, William.** Dean Swift's library. Bk Coll Q 13:76–80 Ja/Mr '34.

13737 **Kirkpatrick, T. Percy C.** Faulkner's edition of Swift. [1735]. TLS 12 Ap '34:262.

13738 **Leslie, sir Shane.** The script of Jonathan Swift and other essays. Philadelphia, University of Pennsylvania pr.; London, H. Milford, O.U.P., 1935. 97p. facsims. 24cm. (A. S. W. Rosenbach Fellowship in bibliography)

I. The script of Jonathan Swift.–II. The rarest Irish books.–III. Saint Patrick's purgatory.

Rev: TLS 20 Je '35:398; W. King Spectator 155:196 '35.

13739 **Williams, sir Harold H.** The Drapier's letters. TLS 6 Je '35:364.

13740 —— [and] **H. J. Davis.** Jonathan Swift and the Four last years of the queen. Library ser4 16no1:61–90 Je '35; 16no3:343–6 D '35. facsims.

13741 [**Haraszti, Zoltán**]. Two imitations of Jonathan Swift. [Memoirs of the court of Lilliput; A complete key to the Tale of a tub]. More Bks Boston Pub Lib Bull 13no5:202 My '38.

13742 **Mr. Harold Williams.** (Private libraries, V). TLS 27 Ag '38:560.

The Swift collection.–Editions of Gulliver.–The poetry canon.–The editor's task.

13743 **Rothschild, N. M. Victor, baron Rothschild.** The publication of the first Drapier letter. Library ser4 19no1:107–15 Je '38. tables.

13744 **Cornu, D.** Swift, Motte and the copyright struggle: two unnoticed documents. Mod Lang N 54no2:114–24 F '39.

13745 **Mack, Maynard.** The first printing of the letters of Pope and Swift. Library ser4 19no4:465–85 Mr '39.

13746 **O'Hegarty, Patrick S.** Some bibliographical notes on Dublin editions of Swift: Faulkner's 1735–8 edition. (Bibliographical notes). Dublin Mag new ser 14no1:67–70 Ja/Mr '39. [Sg.: P. S. O'H.]

13747 **Williams, sir Harold H.** and **N. M. V. Rothschild, baron Rothschild.** The Grand question debated. [Ms.]. R Eng Stud 15no59:328–30 Jl '39.

13748 **Williams, sir Harold H.** Swift: Miscellanies in prose and verse. Second edition, 1713. [Reset]. Bib N&Q 2no11:10 N '38; D. G. Wing *ib.* 2no12:6 My '39.

13749 **Brooks, E. St.John.** A poem of Swift's. [On the little house]. TLS 10 Jl '43:331.

13750 **Davis, Herbert J.** The canon of Swift. Eng Inst Ann 1942:119–32 '43.

13751 **Bracher, Frederick.** The maps in Gulliver's travels. Huntington Lib Q 8no1:59–74 N '44.

13752 **Davies, Godfrey.** A new edition of Swift's The story of the injured lady. [And Charles Lucas]. Huntington Lib Q 8no4:388–92 Ag '45.

13753 **Williams, sir Harold H.** Swift exhibition at Cambridge. TLS 20 Oc '45:504.

13754 **Case, Arthur E.** 'The text of Gulliver's travels' *in* Four essays on Gulliver's travels. Princeton, 1945; London, 1947. p. 1–49.

13755 **Wiley, Autrey N.** Jonathan Swift, a bicentennial exhibition, Oct-ober–December, 1945. Lib Chron Univ Texas 2no1:17–20 '46.

13756 **Griffith, Reginald H.** Swift's Contests, 1701: two editions. N&Q 192:114–17 Mr '47. tables.

Table I. Some distinguishing marks.–Table II. Printing by forms.

13757 **Hennig, John.** Swift in Switzerland. [Rare Swiftiana exhibited]. Irish Bk Lover 30no3:54–5 N '47.

13758 **MacManus, Michael J.** An unrecorded Swift item. [A defence of English commodities, Dublin, 1720]. Irish Bk Lover 30no3:52–4 N '47.

13759 **Teerink, Herman.** The publication of Gulliver's travels. Dublin Mag new ser 23no1:14–27 Ja/Mr '48.

13760 **Wiley, Autrey N.** A probable source of the text of Sheridan's Inventory as printed in the Cheltenham journal. [Inventory of dean Swift's goods]. N&Q 193:186–7 My '48.

13761 —— Unrecorded printings of Thomas Sheridan's Inventory of dean Swift's goods at Laracor. N&Q 193:56–7 F '48.

13762 **Davis, Herbert J.** 'The manuscript of Swift's Sermon on brotherly love' *in* Clifford, James L. and L. A. Landa, *ed.* Pope and his contemporaries; essays presented to George Sherburn. Oxford, 1949. p. 147–58.

13763 **Teerink, Herman.** A source-book for A tale of a tub from Swift's own library. [De Mezeray's Abrégé chronologique de l'histoire de France, 1696]. Irish Bk Lover 31no3:59–62 Oc '49.

13764 —— Swift's Cadenus and Vanessa. (Notes). Harvard Lib Bull 2no2:254–7 '48; 3no3:435–6 '49.

13765 —— Swift's Discourse . . . contests . . . Athens and Rome, 1701. Library ser5 4no3:201–5 D '49. table.

13766 **A book** from Swift's library. Bod Lib Rec 3no32:180–1 Ag '51.

13767 **Todd, William B.** Another attribution to Swift. [Rollin's Taste, 1732]. Pa Bib Soc Am 45:82–3 '51.

13768 **Teerink, Herman.** Swift's Verses on the death of doctor Swift. [Ptg.]. Stud Bib 4:183–8 '51/2. tables.

*See also no.*13778.

13769 **Griffith, Reginald H.** and **Edna L. Steeves.** 'Bibliographical notes on The last volume of Motte's Miscellanies, 1727' *in* Steeves, Edna L., *ed.* The art of sinking in poetry. New York, 1952. p. [195]–207.

13770 **Williams, sir Harold H.** The text of Gulliver's travels. Cambridge, Cambridge U.P., 1952. vii,94p. 20cm. (Sandars lectures in bibliography, 1950)

> I. The publication of Gulliver's travels.–II. Swift's part in the revision of the 1735 text of Gulliver's travels.–III. Swift's autograph corrections of the Miscellanies, 1727–32.
>
> *Rev*: TLS 19 D '52:844; sir H. H. Williams *ib.* 9 Ja '53:25; N&Q 19:134–5 '53; L. A. Landa R Eng Stud new ser 6:322–3 '55.

13771 **Sherburn, George.** The Swift-Pope Miscellanies of 1732. (Notes). Harvard Lib Bull 6no3:387–90 '52; Corrigendum *ib.* 7no2:248 '53.

13772 **Brown, T. Julian.** Jonathan Swift, 1667–1745. (English literary autographs, V). Bk Coll 2no1:69 '53. facsims.

13773 **Ehrenpreis, Irvin.** Swift's April fool for a bibliophile. [Advert for spurious auction, 1709]. Bk Coll 2no3:205–8 '53.

13774 **Davis, Herbert J.** 'The manuscripts of Swift's Directions to servants' *in* Miner, Dorothy E., *ed.* Studies in art and literature for Belle da Costa Greene. Princeton, N. J., 1954. p. 433–44. facsims.

13775 **Leslie, sir Shane.** 'The Swift manuscripts in the Morgan library' *in* Miner, Dorothy E., *ed.* Studies in art and literature for Belle da Costa Greene. Princeton, N.J., 1954. p. 445–8. facsim.

13776 **Mayhew, George P.** A draft of ten lines from Swift's poems to John Gay. Bull John Rylands Lib 37no1:257–62 S '54.

13777 —— Swift's manuscript version of On his own deafness. (Notes and documents). Huntington Lib Q 18no1:85–7 N '54.

13778 **Teerink, Herman.** Addenda: Verses on the death of doctor Swift again. Stud Bib 7:238–9 '54.

13779 **Todd, William B.** The text of Gulliver's travels. Library ser5 9no2:135–6 Je '54; sir H. H. Williams *ib.* 9no4:270 D '54.

13780 **Ehrenpreis, Irvin** and **J. L. Clifford.** Swiftiana in Rylands English ms. 659 and related documents. Bull John Rylands Lib 37no2:368–92 Mr '55.

13781 **Maxwell, James C.** The text of A tale of a tub. Eng Stud 36no2:64–6 Ap '55.

13782 **Scouten, Arthur H.** Materials for the study of Swift at the University of Pennsylvania. Lib Chron Univ Pennsylvania 23no2:47–52 '57. facsims.

13783 **McCue, Daniel L.** A newly discovered broadsheet of Swift's Last speech and dying words of Ebenezor Elliston. Harvard Lib Bull 13no3:369–400 '59. facsims.

13784 **Mayhew, George P.** A missing leaf from Swift's Holyhead journal. [In B.M.]. Bull John Rylands Lib 41no2:388–413 Mr '59.

13785 **Rossi, Mario M.** Notes on the eighteenth-century German translations of Swift's Gulliver's travels. Lib Chron Univ Pennsylvania 25no2:84–8 '59.

The 1761 translation.–The original of the 1761 translation.

13786 **Danchin, Pierre.** The text of Gulliver's travels. Texas Stud Lang & Lit 2no2:233–50 '60.

13787 **Dustin, John E.** The 1735 Dublin edition of Swift's Poems. Pa Bib Soc Am 54:57–60 '60. table.

'Foliation, date, and pagination for those pages on which the poem's title and date are printed' (p. 60)

13788 **Mayhew, George P.** Rage or raillery: Swift's Epistle to a lady and On poetry, a rhapsody. Huntington Lib Q 23no2:159–80 F '60.

13789 **Eby, Cecil D.** When Swift first employed George Faulkner. Pa Bib Soc Am 56:354–6 '62.

13790 **Scouten, Arthur H.** The earliest London printings of Verses on the death of doctor Swift. Stud Bib 15:243–7 '62. tables.

13791 **Slepian, Barry.** The publication history of Faulkner's edition of Gulliver's travels. Pa Bib Soc Am 57:219–21 '63.

13792 **Eddy, Donald D.** Jonathan Swift's copy of the Comoediae sex of Terence. [In Library]. Cornell Lib J 1:40–1 '66. [Sg.: D. D. E.]

13793 **Halsband, Robert.** Jonathan Swift and Swiftiana at Columbia. Columbia Lib Columns 16no3:19–23 My '67. port., facsim.

13794 **Mayhew, George P.** 'Appendix: A brief description of the Swift manuscripts at the Huntington library' *in* Rage or raillery: the Swift manuscripts at the Huntington library. San Marino, Calif., 1967. p. [157]–83.

13795 **Weedon, Margaret J. P.** An uncancelled copy of the first collected edition of Swift's poems. [Faulkner's ed.]. Library ser5 22no1:44–56 Mr '67.

'Summary table of cancellations' (p. 46–7)

13796 **Aden, John M.** Swift, Pope, and the sin of wit. Pa Bib Soc Am 62:80–5 '68.

13797 **Jenkins, Clauston.** The Ford changes and the text of Gulliver's travels. Pa Bib Soc Am 62:1–23 '68.

13798 **Potter, Lee H.** The text of Scott's edition of Swift. Stud Bib 22:240–55 '69.

13799 **Wolf, Edwin** and **J. Freehafer.** Scriblerian [Swift and Pope] publications at the Library company of Philadelphia. (Notes). Scribleriana 2no1:30–1 '69.

SWINBURNE, ALGERNON CHARLES, 1837–1909

13800 **Black, William G.** Swinburne bibliography. N&Q ser8 9:126 F '96.

13801 **Wontner, Rupert.** Swinburne translations. N&Q ser10 9:250 Mr '08; E. Bensly *ib.* 9:375 My '08.

13802 **Chatto and Windus, ltd.** Swinburne copyrights. TLS 5 Ap '17:166.

13803 **Gosse, sir Edmund W.** The first draft of Swinburne's Anactoria. Mod Lang R 14no3:271–7 Jl '19.

Repr. in Aspects and impressions. London, 1922. (2d ed. 1928). p. 87–95.

13804 **Livingston, Flora V. M.** Swinburne's proof sheets and American first editions; bibliographical data relating to a few of the publications of Algernon Charles Swinburne, with notes on the priority of certain claimants to the distinction of editio princeps. Cambridge, Mass., Privately ptd., 1921. 30p. facsims. 21cm.

13805 **Ratchford, Fannie E.** The first draft of Swinburne's Hertha. Mod Lang N 39no1:22–6 Ja '24.

13806 **Lafourcade, Georges.** Swinburne manuscripts. TLS 18 Mr '26:218.

13807 **Swinburne's** Under the microscope [with both cancellandum and cancellanda, 1872]. (Marginalia). Bkmns J ser3 15no5:277 '28.

13808 **Praz, Mario.** Il manoscritto dell'Atalanta in Calydon. (Ricerche di filologia moderna). La Cultura (Rome-Florence) 8:405–15 Jl '29.

13809 **Duffy, James O. G.** The first American Atalanta. [1866]. TLS 5 F '31:99.

13810 **Symons, Arthur. W.** Notes on two manuscripts. [Swinburne's final copy of Cleopatra; Rossetti's original ms. of Eden bower]. Eng R 54:514–20 My '32.

13811 **[Haraszti, Zoltán].** The library's copy of Swinburne's Sienna. More Bks Boston Pub Lib Bull 9no10:407–8 D '34.

13812 **A Swinburne** exhibition. [Bodleian library]. TLS 10 Ap '37:280.

13813 O'Hegarty, Patrick S. Swinburne, A. C.: Love's cross currents. [Mosher piracy, 1901, is 1st ed.]. Bib N&Q 2no11:10 N '38.

13814 Hughes, Randolph. A Swinburne ms. [The chronicle of Tebaldeo Tebaldei]. TLS 24 F '40:99.

13815 Knickerbocker, Kenneth L. Browning and Swinburne: an episode. [Publ.]. Mod Lang N 62no4:240–4 Ap '47.

13816 Hughes, Randolph. Swinburne's Lesbia Brandon. [Seeks missing leaves of ms.]. Am N&Q 8no7:106 Oc '48.

13817 A Swinburne ms. [Ave atque vale]. TLS 4 S '48:504.

13818 Hughes, Randolph. Swinburne: Lesbia Brandon. [Ms.]. N&Q 194:39 Ja '49.

13819 Noyes, Alfred. Lesbia Brandon. [Proofs, and T. J. Wise]. TLS 10 Oc '52:661; R. Hughes ib. 17 Oc '52:677; A. Noyes 24 Oc '52:693; R. Hughes 31 Oc '52:709; C. Y. Lang 31 Oc '52:716; A. Whitehouse 7 N '52:725; R. Hughes 28 N '52:784.

13820 Lang, Cecil Y. The first chorus of Swinburne's Atalanta. Yale Univ Lib Gaz 27no3:119–22 Ja '53.

13821 Baum, Paull F. A Swinburne manuscript. [The queen's pleasance]. Lib N Duke Univ Lib 29:11–19 Ap '54. facsim.

13822 Bissell, E. E. Swinburne problems. (Query no.51). Bk Coll 3no3:227–8 '54.

13823 Lang, Cecil Y. Some Swinburne manuscripts. J Rutgers Univ Lib 18no1:1–11 D '54. facsim.

13824 Mayfield, John S. Swinburne's Atalanta in Calydon. [Copies sought]. (Note no.39). Bk Coll 3no4:307 '54.

13825 —— A Swinburne puzzle. [Provenance of Atalanta, 1865, and T. J. Wise]. (Note no.42). Bk Coll 4no1:74–8 '55. facsims.

13826 —— Two presentation copies of Swinburne's Atalanta in Calydon. [And C. A. Howell]. Pa Bib Soc Am 49:360–5 '55.

13827 Rogers, Arthur. The first edition of Atalanta in Calydon. [Size of ed.]. (Query no.71). Bk Coll 5no3:281 '56.

13828 Lang, Cecil Y. A manuscript, a mare's nest, and a mystery. [The triumph of time; A leave-taking]. Yale Univ Lib Gaz 31no4:163–71 Ap '57.

13829 **Henry, Anne W.** A reconstructed Swinburne ballad. [Duriesdyke]. Harvard Lib Bull 12no3:354–62 '58.

13830 **Baum, Paull F.** The Fitzwilliam manuscript of Swinburne's Atalanta, verses 1038–1204. Mod Lang R 54no2:161–78 Ap '59.

13831 **Paden, W. D.** Footnote to a footnote. [Swinburne's A word for the navy, and T. J. Wise]. TLS 23 Oc '59:616; A. R. Redway *ib.* 20 N '59:677; Janet C. Troxell 4 D '59:709.

13832 **Todd, William B.** Collection: Swinburne manuscripts at Texas. Texas Q 2no3:152–63 '59.

'Checklist of Swinburne mss.' (p. 157–63)

13833 **Brown, T. Julian.** Algernon Charles Swinburne, 1837–1909. (English literary autographs, XXXVII). Bk Coll 10no1:57 '61. facsims.

13834 **Lang, Cecil Y.** Atalanta in manuscript. Yale Univ Lib Gaz 37no1:19–24 Jl '62.

13835 **Ehrenpreis, Anne H.** Swinburne's edition of popular ballads. [Ms. of Ballads of the English border]. Pub Mod Lang Assn 78no5:559–71 D '63.

13836 **Smith, Simon H. Nowell-.** Swinburne's The queen-mother [and] Rosamond, 1860. [Publishing history]. (Query 184). Bk Coll 13no3:357–9 '64.

13837 **Powell, Everett G.** The manuscript of Swinburne's Off shore. Lib Chron Univ Texas 8no2:8–22 '66. facsim.

13838 **A rare** find. [Parts of two chapters of Lesbia Brandon]. Am Bk Coll 17no7:6 Mr '67.

13839 **Two** leaves of Swinburne's manuscript of Lesbia Brandon. Courier 27:1–5 '67. facsim.

13840 **Swinburne's** Autumn in Cornwall. [Ms.]. Courier 29:2–5 '68. facsim.

13841 **Burnett, T. A. J.** Swinburne's The ballad of Bulgarie. Mod Lang R 64no2:276–82 Ap '69.

13842 **Greenberg, Robert A.** Swinburne's Heptalogia improved. Stud Bib 22:258–66 '69.

13843 **Todd, William B.** An unrecorded Wiseian issue. [Dead love]. (Note 318). Bk Coll 18no4:385–6 '69.

SYMONDS, JOHN ADDINGTON, 1840–93

13844 **Symons, Albert J. A.** J. A. Symonds' books. TLS 29 Ap '26:323.

13845 **Mack, James D.** Symonds's Renaissance in Italy. New Coloph 1pt2:193–4 Ap '48.

13846 **Smith, Timothy d'A.** John Addington Symonds: the 'peccant' pamphlets. [Privately ptd.]. (Note 215). Bk Coll 13no1:68–70 '64; Elkin Mathews, ltd. *ib.* 13no2:206–7 '64.

SYMONS, ARTHUR WILLIAM, 1865–1945

13847 **Arthur** Symons. [Acquisition of A. E. Gallatin collection]. Princeton Univ Lib Chron 12no2:92–3 '51.

SYNGE, JOHN MILLINGTON, 1871–1909

13848 **Greene, David H.** John Millington Synge: mss. N&Q 175:441 D '38.

13849 —— An adequate text of J. M. Synge. Mod Lang N 61no7:466–7 N '46.

13850 **O'Hegarty, Patrick S.** J. M. Synge. The Aran islands. [1906]. (Bibliographical notes). Dublin Mag new ser 23no1:45–6 Ja/Mr '48.

13851 **John** Millington Synge at Colby. Colby Lib Q ser4 9:157–8 F '57.

13852 **Black, Hester M.** J. M. Synge. Bks & Libs at Kansas 1no21:10–11 My '59.

13853 **MacPhail, Ian S.** John Millington Synge, some bibliographical notes. Irish Bk 1no1:3–10 '59. port.

13854 **Synge** in translation: Italian. (Bibliographical notes). Irish Bk 1no2:49 '59/60.

13855 **Synge** in translation: Polish. (Bibliographical notes). Irish Bk 1no2:50 '59/60.

13856 **Synge** in translation: Scots-Gaelic. (Bibliographical notes). Irish Bk 1no2:49 '59/60.

13857 **Synge** in translation: German. (Bibliographical entries). Irish Bk 3no1:38 '64.

13858 **Synge** in translation: Hebrew. (Bibliographical entries). Irish Bk 3no1:38 '64.

TALON, NICHOLAS, 1605–91

13859 **Workman, D. Hansard.** The Holy history, by Nicholas Talon. [And Henry, baron Arundell's, library]. N&Q ser12 6:89 Ap '20.

TANNER, BP. THOMAS, 1674–1735

13860 **Hindle, Christopher J.** Bicentenary of the accident to bishop Tanner's books. Bod Q Rec 6no72:295–6 '31.

13861 **Davies, William T.** Thomas Tanner and his Bibliotheca. TLS 14 D '35:856.

13862 **Hunt, Richard W.** Tanner's Bibliotheca Britannico-Hibernica. Bod Lib Rec 2no28:249–58 F '49.

'Tanner's proposal for the Bibliotheca' (p. 257–8)

TATE, NAHUM, 1652–1715

13863 **[Haraszti, Zoltán].** The poems of Nahum Tate. More Bks Boston Pub Lib Bull 13no4:152 Ap '38.

13864 **Astor, Stuart L.** The laureate as huckster: Nahum Tate and an early eighteenth century example of publisher's advertising. Stud Bib 21:261–6 '68.

TAYLOR, MISS, fl.1832

13865 **Roberts, William.** Fatherless Fanny. [Novel by 'miss Taylor', 1832.] TLS 17 Ja '35:33.

TAYLOR, BP. JEREMY, 1613–67

13866 **White, Newport B.** Bibliography of Jeremy Taylor. TLS 25 S '30:758; R. Gathorne-Hardy *ib.* 2 Oc '30:782; sir G. L. Keynes 9 Oc '30:810.

13867 **Bone, Gavin.** Jeremy Taylor and Elizabeth Grymeston. Library ser4 15no2:247–8 S '34.

13868 **Stranks, Charles J.** Sermons by Jeremy Taylor. [Mss.]. TLS 27 S '34:655.

13869 **Hardy, Robert Gathorne-.** The bibliography of Jeremy Taylor. Library ser5 3no1:66 Je '48.

13870 —— Some notes on the bibliography of Jeremy Taylor. Library ser5 2no4:233–49 Mr '48. facsims.

13871 —— Jeremy Taylor and Christian consolations. TLS 20 Ap '51:245.

13872 **Brown, W. J.** Jeremy Taylor's sermons. [Mss.]. TLS 11 Ja '52:25.

13873 **Hardy, Robert Gathorne-.** Jeremy Taylor and Hatton's Psalter of David. TLS 18 F '55:112.

TAYLOR, JOHN, 1578–1653

13874 **T., J. B.** The thumb Bible. Aberdeen J N&Q 2:30–1 '09.

13875 **Smith, G. C. Moore.** John Taylor, the water-poet. N&Q ser11 6:226–7 S '12.

13876 **Rushforth, Marjorie.** Two John Taylor manuscripts at Leonard Lichfield's press. [Printer's copy]. Library ser4 11no2:179–92 S '30. facsims.

13877 **Carter, John W.** John Taylor's Booke of martyrs, 1633. (Note no.49). Bk Coll 4no2:171–2 '55; W. A. Jackson *ib.* 4no4:327 '55.

13878 **Jensen, Bent Juel-.** Isaac Oliver's portrait of prince Henry and Poly-olbion, a footnote. [Taylor's Great Britain all in black]. Library ser5 10no3:206–7 S '55. facsim.

13879 **Kendall, Lyle H.** Two unrecorded editions of John Taylor's Verbum sempiternum. Library ser5 12no1:46–8 Mr '57.

13880 **Freeman, Arthur.** Octavo nonce collections of John Taylor. Library ser5 18no1:51–7 Mr '63.

13881 **Kendall, Lyle H.** John Taylor's piracy of The pack-mans paternoster. [Sempill's Pasternoster pub. as A pedlar and a romish priest, 1641]. Pa Bib Soc Am 57:201–10 '63.

TAYLOR, JOHN, 1781–1864 *see under* Book production and distribution–Printers, publishers, etc.

TAYLOR, THOMAS, 1758–1835

13882 **Axon, William E. A.** Thomas Taylor the platonist. Library 2no19:245–50 Jl '90; 2no20:292–300 Ag '90.

TAYLOR, TOM, 1817–80

13883 **Rayner, Colin** and **J. Reading.** Tom Taylor: manuscript plays. Theat Notebk 19no3:83–9 '65.

TEMPLE, SIR WILLIAM, 1628–99

13884 **Cronin, Margaret.** The library at Moor park. N&Q 159:9 Jl '30; E. Bensly *ib.* 159:48 Jl '30.

13885 **Hanson, Laurence W.** Sir William Temple, pamphleteer. [Lettre d'un marchand de Londres, 1666]. TLS 15 Ja '44:36.

13886 **Roberts, William.** Sir William Temple on Orinda: neglected publications. Pa Bib Soc Am 57:328–36 '63. facsim.

TENNYSON, ALFRED, 1ST BARON TENNYSON, 1809–92

13887 **Cattle, Frederic.** Some less-known Tennysoniana. Bkworm 2no21:263–4 Ag '89.

13888 **Wilcock, A. B.** Tennyson's earlier poems. [The poet; The poet's mind; The mystic]. Bkworm 3no34:317–19 S '90.

13889 **The songs** in The princess. Athenæum 3327:161 Ag '91; G. Grove *ib.* 3328:194 Ag '91.

13890 **Tennysoniana** [at Sotheby's, 4 Mr '91]. Bkworm 4no41:143–4 Ap '91; 4no46:311–12 S '91.

13891 **C.** Tennysoniana. [Publication of The lover's tale]. Athenæum 3390:517 Oc '92.

13892 **First** editions of Tennyson. [Puttick and Simpson's sale]. Bkworm 6no61:26 D '92.

13893 **Gray, George J.** Tennysoniana. [Timbucktoo]. N&Q ser8 3:206 Mr '93.

13894 **The ms.** of Poems by two brothers. Bkworm 6no62:51 Ja '93; *cf. ib.* 6no63:69 F '93; 6no66:183 My '93.

13895 **Watts, Theodore.** Tennysoniana. [On the price paid for copyright of Poems by two brothers]. Athenæum 3406:154 F '93.

13896 **Gray, George J.** Tennysoniana: the manuscript of Poems by two brothers, 1827. N&Q ser8 3:426 Je '93; A. M. Handy; A. H. *ib.* 4:218 S '93; G. J. Gray 5:385 My '94.

13897 **J., R. B.** Tennysoniana. [Latin trans. of In memoriam, 1861]. Athenæum 3497:606 N '94; C. Walters *ib.* 3498:644 N '94; W. S. Sonnenschein 3499:677 N '94.

13898 **Layard, George S.** Tennyson and his pre-Raphaelite illustrators, a book about a book. London, E. Stock; Boston, Copeland and Day, 1894. (Repr. Folcroft, Pa., Folcroft pr. [1969]; Norwood, Pa., Norwood editions, 1976). 68p. illus. 23cm.

I. Introductory.–II. As to the origin of 'P.R.B.'.–III. Millais.–IV.–Holman Hunt.–V. Rossetti.

13899 **N., P. E.** Tennysoniana. [Idylls of the king; Poems, 1849]. Acad 45:57–8, 81 Ja '94.

13900 **Poems,** chiefly lyrical [with Poems by Arthur Hallam, esquire]. Bkworm 7no74:48 Ja '94.

13901 **A valuable** copy of Lyrical poems. Bkworm 7no77:157 Ap '94.

13902 **Prideaux, William F.** Tennyson bibliography. Athenæum 3631:715 My '97. [Sg.: W. F. P.]

13903 **Proctor, Robert G. C.** Sir Galahad. Athenæum 3665:118 Ja '98.

13904 **Livingston, Luther S.** The Tennysons. (The first books of some English authors, II). Bkmn (N.Y.) 10no2:123–7 Oc '99. facsims.

13905 **Spence, R. M.** Tennyson's The ancient sage. N&Q ser9 3:248 Ap '99.

13906 **Hardie, Martin.** The Moxon Tennyson, 1857. [Illustrated]. Bk-Lover's Mag 7pt2:45–51 '07. illus.

13907 **Haney, John L.** Tennyson bibliography. N&Q ser10 11:322 Ap '09.

13908 **Roberts, William.** Poems by two brothers, by the Tennysons. Athenæum 4237:44 Ja '09.

   Repr. in Bk Auc Rec 6:viii–ix '09.

13908a **Quaritch, Bernard.** Description of an important collection of holograph manuscript poems by lord Tennyson, also the holograph manuscript of Sardanapalus by lord Byron, in the possession of. . . . London, 1914. [24]p. facsims. 25cm.

13909 **Gosse, sir Edmund W.** Tennyson's manuscripts. TLS 12 Je '19:325.

13910 **Ratchford, Fannie E.** The Tennyson collection in the Wrenn library. Southwest R 7:95–105 Ja '22.

13911 **Lindimp,** *pseud.* Tennyson songs. N&Q 149:171 S '25; J. H. H.; J. C. *ib.* 149:213 S '25.

13912 **Tennyson** manuscripts. (Notes on sales). TLS 17 Jl '30:596.

13913 **Wise, Thomas J.** An apocryphal Tennyson poem. [By sir Joseph Arnould]. TLS 27 Mr '30:274; W. B. Kempling; A. Rogers *ib.* 3 Ap '30:298.

13914 **Osborne, Eric A.** Tennyson's Holy grail. (Bibliographical notes). TLS 25 Ag '32:596.

13915 **Adkins, Nelson F.** Tennyson's Charge of the heavy brigade: a bibliographical note. · N&Q 167:189–90 S '34; Olybrius, *pseud., ib.* 167:266 Oc '34.

13916 **Pollard, H. Graham.** Tennyson's A welcome, 1863. TLS 15 F '34:112; T. J. Wise *ib.* 8 Mr '34:168; H. G. Pollard 15 Mr '34:200.

13917 **Brett, Oliver S. B., 3d viscount Esher.** Tennyson: Enoch Arden. [Issues]. Bib N&Q 1no1:6–7 Ja '35; I. A. Williams; C. A. W.; J. W. Haines *ib.* 1no2:5–6 Ap '35. [Sg.: Esher.]

13918 —— Tennyson: Maud. [Advertisements in]. Bib N&Q 1no1:5–6 Ja '35; J. H. A. Sparrow; I. A. Williams; [P. H. Muir] *ib.* 1no2:5 Ap '35; D. A. Randall 1no3:1 Ag '35. [Sg.: Esher.]

13919 **Wells, John E.** [and] **P. H. Muir.** Tennyson: In memoriam. [Issues]. Bib N&Q 2no3:8 Ap '36.

13920 **Munsterberg, Margaret.** Rare editions of Tennyson. More Bks Boston Pub Lib Bull 13no4:157–8 Ap '38. [Sg.: M. M.]

13921 **Bay, J. Christian.** A Tennyson-Browning association book. [Maud]. [Cedar Rapids, Iowa] Ptd. for the friends of Walter M. Hill, 1940. 16p. facsim. 20cm.

Repr. in no.2344.

13922 **Twenty-nine** Tennyson letters [acquired]. Lib N Duke Univ Lib 10:6 My '41.

13923 **A Tennyson** exhibition. Colby Lib Q 1no1:3–5 Ja '43.

13924 **Munsterberg, Margaret.** From Tennyson's library. More Bks Boston Pub Lib Bull 19no2:71 F '44. [Sg.: M. M.]

13925 **Carter, John W.** Tennyson's Carmen saeculare, 1887. [And T. J. Wise]. Library ser5 2no2/3:200–2 S/D '47.

13926 **Shannon, Edgar F.** The proofs of Gareth and Lynette in the Widener collection. Pa Bib Soc Am 41:321–40 '47.

'Appendix [transcripts]' (p. 336–40)

13927 **Friedman, Albert B.** The Tennyson of 1857. [Poems]. More Bks Boston Pub Lib Q 23no1:15–22 Ja '48.

13928 **Bowman, Mary V.** The Hallam-Tennyson Poems, 1830. Stud Bib 1:193–9 '48/9.

13929 **Evans, Charles.** Victorian writers and the Great exhibition. [Tennyson mss.]. N&Q 197:60 F '52.

13930 **Paden, W. D.** A note on the variants of In memoriam and Lucretius. Library ser5 8no4:259–73 D '53. table.

13931 **Buckler, William E.** Tennyson's Lucretius bowdlerized. R Eng Stud new ser 5no19:269–71 Jl '54.

13932 **Gransden, K. W.** Some uncatalogued manuscripts of Tennyson. Bk Coll 4no2:159–62 '55. facsim.

13933 **Shannon, Edgar F.** and **W. H. Bond.** Literary manuscripts of Alfred Tennyson in the Harvard college library. Harvard Lib Bull 10no2:254–74 '56. facsim.

'Index of titles' (p. 264–8); 'Index of first lines' (p. 268–74)

13934 **B., A. C.** Extant copies of Tennyson's Timbuctoo, 1829. (Query 101). Bk Coll 7no3:296 '58.

13935 **Elliott, Philip L.** Another manuscript version of To the queen. N&Q 203:82–3 F '58.

13936 —— Tennyson's To Virgil. N&Q 204:147–8 Ap '59.

13937 **Hartman, Joan E.** The manuscript of Tennyson's Gareth and Lynette. Harvard Lib Bull 13no2:239–64 '59. facsim.

13938. **Marshall George O.** Textual changes in a presentation copy of Tennyson's Poems, 1833. Lib Chron Univ Texas 6no3:16–19 '59.

13939 **Shannon, Edgar F.** The history of a poem: Tennyson's Ode on the death of the duke of Wellington. Stud Bib 13:149–77 '60.

'Appendix: the development of the text' (p. 167–77)

13940 **Smith, Simon H. Nowell-.** Tennyson's In memoriam 1850. (Note 129). Bk Coll 9no1:76–7 '60.

13941 **Paden, W. D.** Twenty new poems attributed to Tennyson, Praed, and Landor. Vict Stud 4no3:195–218 Mr '61; 4no4:291–314 Je '61.

13942 **Collins, Rowland L.** Tennyson's original issue of poems, reviews, etc., 1842–1886; a compilation by Henry Van Dyke. Princeton Univ Lib Chron 24no1:39–50 '62.

13943 **Smith, Simon H. Nowell-.** (Tennyson, A., C., & F.). Poems by two brothers, 1827. (Note 172). Bk Coll 11no1:80 '62.

13944 **Brown, T. Julian.** Lord Tennyson, 1809–1892. (English literary autographs, XLV). Bk Coll 12no1:61 '63. facsim.

13945 **Hall, P. E.** A Latin translation of Tennyson's In memoriam. [By O. A. Smith, 1861]. (Note 207). Bk Coll 12no4:490–2 '63.

13946 **Ricks, Christopher.** The variants of In memoriam. Library ser5 18no1:64 '63.

13947 **Smith, Simon H. Nowell-.** The Tennysons' Poems by two brothers, 1827. (Note 172). Bk Coll 12no1:68 '63.

13948 **Taylor, John R.** The Hotten piracy of Tennyson's Poems, MDCCCXXX–MDCCCXXXIII. [And T. J. Wise]. (Note 208). Bk Coll 12no4:492–3 '63.

13949 **Paden, W. D.** The Tennysons' Poems by two brothers, 1827, reconsidered. Library ser5 19:147–61 '64. facsim., table.

13950 **Ricks, Christopher.** Tennyson's Hail, Briton! and Tithon: some corrections. [Ms.]. R Eng Stud new ser 15no57:52–5 F '64.

13951 **Todd, William B.** Wise, Wrenn, and Tennyson's Enoch Arden, 1864. (Note 214) Bk Coll 13no1:67–8 '64.

13952 **Hardie, William.** The light brigade. [Ms.]. TLS 3 Je '65:455; sir C R. L. Tennyson *ib.* 15 Jl '65:597.

13953 **Hinton, Percival F.** The 'green' Tennysons. [Points]. (Note 246). Bk Coll 14no2:215 '65.

13954 **Paden, W. D.** Tennyson's The lover's tale, R. H. Shepherd, and T. J. Wise. [Forgery]. Stud Bib 18:111–45 '65. tables.

13955 **Ricks, Christopher.** A note on Tennyson's Ode on the death of the duke of Wellington. Stud Bib 18:282 '65.

13956 —— Tennyson's Lucretius. Library ser5 20no1:63–4 Mr '65.

13957 **Ryals, Clyde deL.** A nonexistent variant in Tennyson's Poems chiefly lyrical, 1830. (Note 245). Bk Coll 14no2:214–15 '65.

13958 **Bartlett, Phyllis.** A copy of Tennyson's The princess, 1848. [Inscribed copy sought]. (Query 207). Bk Coll 15no3:356–7 '66.

13959 **Carter, John W.** and **H. G. Pollard.** An enquiry [on whereabouts of doubtful (Wisean) copies of The cup and The promise of May]. TLS 30 Je '66:584.

13960 —— The forgeries of Tennyson's plays. Oxford, Distributed for the authors by B. H. Blackwell, 1967. 21p. 22cm. (Working paper, no.2)

The falcon.–The cup.–The promise of May.–Summary.–Annexe: dossier for Becket.

13961 —— Precis of Paden on The sources of The new Timon. Oxford, Distributed for the authors by B. H. Blackwell, 1967. 24p. facsims. 22cm. (Working papers, 1)

The forgeries of the piracies.–The sales record of the forgeries.–The Quaritch records. –Wise's description of Shepherd's piracies. (*See no.* 13954)

Rev: TLS 1 Je '67:496.

13962 **Hall, P. E.** A Latin translation of In memoriam. [Other trans. by O. A. Smith]. (Note 207). Bk Coll 17no1:78 '68.

13963 —— Tennyson's Idylls of the King and The holy grail. (Query 222). Bk Coll 17no2:218–19 '68; M. Trevanion, *pseud., ib.* 17no4:490–1 '68.

13964 **Smith, Simon H. Nowell-.** Tennyson's In memoriam, 1850. (Note 129). Bk Coll 17no3:350–1 '68.

13965 **Bishop, Morchard** [and] **A. Closs.** Tennyson mss. [Napoleon's retreat from Moscow]. TLS 28 Ag '69:954; C. Ricks *ib.* 11 S '69:1002; J. P. W. Gaskell 18 S '69:1026.

13966 **Smith, Simon H. Nowell-.** Tennyson's Tiresias, 1885. Library ser5 24no1:55–6 Mr '69.

TENNYSON, FREDERICK, 1807–98

13967 **Fall, Christine.** An index of the letters from papers of Frederick Tennyson. Texas Stud Eng 36:155–63 '57.

13968 **Collins, Rowland L.** The Frederick Tennyson collection. [Bibliogr. of mss. in Lilly library, Indiana university]. Vict Stud Suppl 7:57–76 D '63. facsims.

THACKERAY, WILLIAM MAKEPEACE, 1811–63

13969 **Sabin, Frank T.** Thackerayana. [Illus. in C. G. Addison's Damascus and Palmyra, 1838]. Athenæum 3327:160 Ag '91.

13970 **Thackeray** letters and mss. [from colln. of J. F. Boyes]. Bkworm 4no38:49–50 Ja '91.

13971 **Owen, Hugh.** Thackeray. [Ms.]. N&Q ser8 7:247 Mr '95.

13972 **Hebb, John.** Thackeray's contributions to Punch. N&Q ser9 6:149–50 Ag '00.

13973 **Livingston, Luther S.** William Makepeace Thackeray. (The first books of some English authors, VI). Bkmn (N.Y.) 11no1:26–30 Mr '00. facsims.

13974 **Clayton, Herbert B.** Thackeray's early writings. [The exquisites, 1839]. N&Q ser9 8:383 N '01.

13975 **H., M.** Thackeray and Damascus and Palmyra. N&Q ser9 12:446 D '03.

13976 **Harrap, George G.** Thackeray's poem of Catherine Hayes. [As illustrator of C. E. Addison's poem]. N&Q ser9 12:446 D '03; R. B. *ib.* 12:494 D '03.

13977 **Kitton, Frederic G.** More hints on etiquette: was Thackeray the author? [No; 1836]. Athenæum 3943:656–7 My '03.

13978 **Slater, J. Herbert.** Early editions of Thackeray. Biblioph 2no8:90–7 Oc '08. facsims.

13979 **Thackeray's** notebook for Henry Esmond. N.Y. Pub Lib Bull 18no12:1463–4 D '14. facsims.

13980 **Terry, Astley.** Vanity fair. N&Q ser12 1:467 Je '16; A. Sparke *ib.* 2:13 Jl '16; F. S. Dickson 2:355 Oc '16.

13981 **Smythe, H. Gerald.** A misprint in Esmond. TLS 26 S '18:457.

13982 **Troxell, Gilbert McC.** The Ganson Goodyear Depew memorial collection. [Thackeray and Kipling]. Yale Univ Lib Gaz 1no4:53–5 Ap '27. [Sg.: G. M. T.]

13983 **Wells, John E.** On a sheet of Thackeray manuscript. ['The notch on the axe']. Cornhill Mag new ser 74:34–44 Ja '33.

13984 **Wormald, Francis.** A Thackeray autograph. [The second funeral of Napoleon, 1841; printer's copy]. Brit Mus Q 9no1:17–18 S '34.

13985 **Bruce, R. F. D.** Thackeray's Four Georges. [Foreign ed.]. TLS 14 Mr '36:228; Sotheby and co. *ib.* 21 Mr '36:244.

13986 **Marlow, Harriet.** Thackeray: The rose and the ring, 1855. [Presentation leaf]. Bib N&Q 2no11:10 N '38.

13987 **Waynflete, George,** *pseud.* Thackeray, W. M.: Pendennis. Bib N&Q 2no12:10 My '39.

13988 **Randall, David A.** [Bibliogr. note on Vanity Fair, 1847–8]. Pa Bib Soc Am 34:276–8 '40.

13989 **Cline, C. L.** A Thackeray forgery. [Letter, 1854–62]. Lib Chron Univ Texas 2no4:187–9 '47.

13990 **Weitenkampf, Frank.** Thackeray, illustrator. N.Y. Pub Lib Bull 51no11:640–3 N '47.

13991 **Randall, David A.** Notes towards a correct collation of the first edition of Vanity fair. Pa Bib Soc Am 42:95–119 '48. facsims., table.

'Vanity fair textual variations' (p. 105–9)

13992 **Brown, T. Julian.** William Makepeace Thackeray, 1811–63. (English literary autographs, II). Bk Coll 1no2:96–7 '52. facsim.

13993 **Waynflete, George,** *pseud.* Thackeray: Pendennis. (Query no.3). Bk Coll 1no1:54 '52.

13994 **W., C.** Thackeray: The rose and the ring. [Presentation copies]. (Query no.10). Bk Coll 1no1:57–8 '52; J. D. Gordan *ib.* 2no1:77 '53.

13995 **Metzdorf, Robert F.** M. L. Parrish and William Makepeace Thackeray. Princeton Univ Lib Chron 17no2:68–70 '56.

13996 **Swenson, Paul B.** Thackeray drawings in the Print department. Boston Pub Lib Q 10no2:101–5 Ap '58. facsim.

13997 **Stevens, Joan.** A note on photography: the ms. of Vanity fair. [Dangers of photographic reproductions]. AUMLA 21:84–8 My '64.

13998 —— 'The relevance of Thackeray's illustrations' *in* Australasian universities' languages and literature association. Congress, 9th. Proceedings, ed. by Marion Adams. Melbourne, 1964. p. 60.

13999 —— Thackeray's Vanity fair. [Illustrations]. R Eng Lit 6no1:19–38 Ja '65.

14000 **White, Edward M.** Thackeray's contributions to Fraser's magazine. Stud Bib 19:67–84 '66.

'Disallowed attributions' (p. 74–8); 'Thackeray's contributions to Fraser's' (p. 78–84)

THELWALL, JOHN, 1764–1834

14001 **Gibbs, Warren E.** John Thelwall and the Panoramic miscellany. N&Q 155:386 D '28.

THOMAS, DAVID RICHARD, 1833–1916

14002 **Owens, B. G.** Archdeacon David Richard Thomas, 1833–1916. (Biographica et bibliographica). Nat Lib Wales J 4no3/4:214–16 '46.

THOMAS, DYLAN MARLAIS, 1914–53

14003 **Gransden, K. W.** Early poems of Dylan Thomas. [Mss.]. Brit Mus Q 19no3:50–1 S '54.

14004 **Sinclair, T. A.** Dylan Thomas. [Text of Twenty-five poems, 1936]. TLS 10 S '54:573.

14005 **Campbell, James.** Issues of Dylan Thomas's The map of love. (Note 82). Bk Coll 6no1:73–4 '57.

14006 **Todd, William B.** The bibliography of Dylan Thomas. (Note 81). Bk Coll 6no1:71–3 '57.

14007 **White, William.** Dylan Thomas and A. E. Housman. [Mss.] Pa Bib Soc Am 52:309–10 '58.

14008 **Manley, Frank.** The text of Dylan Thomas' Under Milk wood. Emory Univ Q 20no2:131–44 '64.

14009 **Smith, Timothy d'A.** The second edition of Dylan Thomas's 18 Poems. [3 impr., 1942, 1946, 1954]. (Note 227). Bk Coll 13no3:351–2 '64; [Correction] *ib.* 13no4:503 '64.

14010 **White, William.** Dylan Thomas, mr. Rolph, and John O'London's weekly. [Dare I, 1934]. Pa Bib Soc Am 60:370–2 '66.

14011 **Cleverdon, Douglas.** Under Milk wood. [Ms.]. TLS 18 Jl '68:761.

14011a —— The growth of Milk wood with the textual variants of Under Milk wood by Dylan Thomas. London, J. M. Dent [1969]. x,124p. 22cm.

> History of the text.–Stage I: Botteghe oscure.–II: New York, May, 1953.–III: The manuscript.–IV: New York, October, 1953.–V: The BBC production.–VI: The published texts.–Summary of versions cited.–Analysis of textual variants.

THOMAS, PHILIP EDWARD, 1878–1917

14012 **Guthrie, James J.** The bibliography of Edward Thomas. [Six poems]. (Correspondence). London Merc 3no15:314 Ja '21.

14013 **Eckert, Robert P.** Edward Thomas. Bib N&Q 1no1:7 Ja '35; [Oliver S. B. Brett, 3d viscount] Esher; J. W. Haines *ib.* 1no2:6 Ap '35.

14014 **Bell, sir Harold I.** Autograph poems of Edward Thomas. Brit Mus Q 12no1:11–13 Ja '38.

14015 **Robson, W. W.** Edward Thomas's Roads. TLS 23 Mr '62:208.

14016 **Prance, Claude A.** An Edward Thomas collection. [His own]. Priv Lib 6no4:66–72 Oc '65.

THOMAS, SIMON, fl.1718

14017 **P.** Hanes y Byd a'r Amseroedd. (Bibliographical notes). Welsh Bib Soc J 2no1:52–5 Jl '16.

THOMPSON, EDWARD, 1738?–86

14018 **Bleackley, Horace W.** Capt. Edward Thompson's poems. N&Q ser10 12:46 Jl '09.

THOMPSON, FRANCIS JOSEPH, 1859–1907

14019 **Connolly, Terence L.** An account of books and manuscripts of Francis Thompson. Chestnut Hill, Mass., Boston college [1937]. 79p. port. 23cm.

Includes The story of the Seymour Adelman collection, by S. Adelman.

14020 —— Francis Thompson's 'chatter'. [Hound of heaven]. TLS 9 S '60:577.

THOMS, WILLIAM JOHN, 1803–85

14021 **Race, Sydney.** Harleian ms. 6395 and its editor. N&Q 202:77–9 F '57.

THOMSON, MRS., fl.1787–1818

14022 **Rhodes, Dennis E.** Mrs. Thomson and Miss Pigott. (Note 86). Bk Coll 6no3:293–6 '57; H. W. Edwards *ib.* 6no4:405 '57; D. E. Rhodes 7no1: 77–8 '58.

THOMSON, JAMES, 1700–48

14023 **Tovey, D. C.** An interleaved copy of Thomson's Seasons. [And Pope]. Athenæum 3433:131–2 Jl '94.

14024 **W., T. M.** Rule Britannia: variant reading. N&Q ser10 8:188 S '07; W. B. *ib.* 8:258 S '07; W. H. Cummings 8:313 Oc '07.

14025 **Thiefes, P.** Catalogue of the poet Thomson's library. N&Q ser11 9:110 F '14.

14026 **Cook, T. Davidson.** Thomson's Scottish airs. N&Q ser12 10:371 My '22.

14027 **Chapman, Robert W.** The Castle of indolence. R Eng Stud 3no12:456 Oc '27.

14028 **Whiting, George W.** James Thomson, editor of Areopagitica. N&Q 164:457 Jl '33.

14029 **Fletcher, Edward G.** Notes on two poems by James Thomson. [Ms.]. N&Q 168:274–5 Ap '35.

14030 **Wells, John E.** Manuscripts of Thomson's poems to Amanda and elegy on Aikman. Philol Q 15no4:405–8 Oc '36.

14031 **Wells, John E.** [and] **I. A. Williams.** Thomson's (?) A poem to the memory of mr. Congreve. TLS 3 Oc '36:791.

14032 **Wells, John E.** Variants in the 1746 edition of Thomson's Seasons. Library ser4 17no2:214–20 S '36.

14033 **Hamilton, Horace E.** James Thomson. [Sale catalogue of his library]. (Bibliographical notes). TLS 19 Mr '38:192.

14034 —— Sale catalogue of James Thomson's, 1700–1748, library. N&Q 174: 188 Mr '38.

14035 **Wells, John E.** James Thomson's poem On the death of his mother. Mod Lang R 33no1:46–50 Ja '38.

14036 ——Thomson's Seasons, 1744; an unnoticed edition. Eng Studien 72no2:221–6 Ag '38.

14037 **Taylor, Eric S.** James Thomson's library. [The sale catalogue]. TLS 5 Jl '41:323.

14038 **Wells, John E.** Thomson's subscription Seasons, 1730. N&Q 180:350 My '41.

14039 **James** Thomson's library. TLS 20 Je '42:312; E. H. W. Meyerstein *ib.* 4 Jl '42:336.

The poet's workshop.–Travel and science.–Literature.–The arts.

14040 **Wells, John E.** Thomson's Agamemnon and Edward and Eleonora; first printings. R Eng Stud 18no72:478–86 Oc '42.

14041 —— Thomson's Britannia: issues, attribution, date, variants. Mod Philol 40no1:43–56 Ag '42.

14042 —— Thomson's Spring: early editions true and false. Library ser4 22no4:223–43 Mr '42.

14043 **Munsterberg, Margaret.** The Castle of indolence. More Bks Boston Pub Lib Bull 18no1:28–9 Ja '43. [Sg.: M. M.]

14044 **Wells, John E.** James Thomson's minor poems; more manuscripts. Philol Q 22no1:69–71 Ja '43.

14045 —— Thomson's Seasons 'Corrected and amended.' [Works, 1750]. J Eng Germ Philol 42no1:104–14 Ja '43.

14046 **Todd, William B.** The 1748 editions of The castle of indolence. (Note no.9). Bk Coll 1no3:192–3 '52.

14047 —— Unauthorized readings in the first edition of Thomson's Coriolanus. Pa Bib Soc Am 46:62–6 '52. table.

14048 —— The text of The castle of indolence. Eng Stud 34no3:117–21 Je '53. table.

'Collation of variants' (p. 120–1)

14049 **Francis, T. R.** The quarto edition of James Thomson's Works, 1762. N&Q 201:211–12 My '56.

14050 —— A variant issue of Thomson's Summer, 1727. Bk Coll 5no4:383 '56.

14051 **McKillop, A. Dugald.** Thomson and the licensers of the stage. Philol Q 37no4:448–53 Oc '58.

14052 **Foxon, David F.** 'Oh! Sophonisba! Sophonisba! Oh!' Stud Bib 12:204–13 '59. tables.

14053 **Francis, T. R.** James Thomson's Tancred and Sigismunda. (Note 109). Bk Coll 8no2:181–2 '59; C. J. Stratman *ib.* 9no2:188 '60.

THOMSON, WILLIAM, fl.1733

14054 **Jolley, Leonard J.** William Thomson's Orpheus Caledonius [1733]. Biblioth 1no2:26–7 '57.

THRALE, Hester LYNCH (SALUSBURY), 1741–1821 *see* Piozzi, Hester Lynch (Salusbury), formerly mrs. Thrale, 1741–1821.

TICKELL, THOMAS, 1686–1740

14055 **Butt, John E.** Notes for a bibliography of Thomas Tickell. Bod Q Rec 5no59:299–302 D '27.

14056 —— A first edition of Tickell's Colin and Lucy. Bod Q Rec 6no65:103–4 '30.

14057 **Thomas** Tickell and Thersites. [Horn-book]. Bod Lib Rec 4no6:291 D '53.

TIGHE, MRS. GEORGE WILLIAM, 1773–1835 *see* Mountcashell, Margaret Jane (Kingsborough), countess of Mountcashell, 1773–1835

TIGHE, MARY (BLACHFORD), 1772–1810

14058 **Dix, Ernest R. McC.** The first edition of mrs. Tighe's Psyche. Irish Bk Lover 3no9:141–3 Ap '12.

14059 **Henchy, Patrick.** The works of Mary Tighe, published and unpublished. Dublin, Sign of the three candles, 1957. 14p. 22cm. (Bib Soc Ireland Pubs 7no6)

14060 **Smith, Simon H. Nowell-.** A ghost of Psyche? [1795?]. (Query 193). Bk Coll 14no4:545 '65.

TILLOTSON, ARCHBP. JOHN, 1630–94

14061 **Brown, David D.** The text of John Tillotson's sermons. Library ser5 13no1:18–36 Mr '58.

14062 **Brown, David D.** The dean's dilemma: a further note on a Tillotson passage. [The protestant religion vindicated, 1680]. Library ser5 14no4:282–7 D '59. diagr., facsims.

TILNEY, EDMUND, d.1610

14063 **Bassett, J. G. Tilney-.** Edmund Tilney's The flower of friendshippe. [Duties in marriage]. Library ser4 26no2/3:175–81 S/D '45. facsims.

TIMBERLAKE, HENRY, d.1626

14064 **Redgrave, Gilbert R.** An ancient pilgrimage to the holy land. [A true . . . discourse of the travails of two English pilgrims]. Library ser3 10no38:69–72 Ap '19.

TOFT, MARY, 1701?–63

14065 **Griffiths, E. F.** Mary Toft; bibliographical query. N&Q 181:188–9 Oc '41; D. A. H. Moses *ib.* 181:223 Oc '41.

TOMKIS, THOMAS, fl.1604–15

14066 **The comedy** of Albumazar. (Notes on sales). TLS 28 Ag '19:464.

14067 **Dick, Hugh G.** Presentation copy of Tomkis's Albumazar. N&Q 178:10 Ja '40.

14068 **Turner, Robert K.** Standing type in Tomkis's Albumazar. Library ser5 13no3:175–85 S '58. tables.

TOMLINSON, HENRY MAJOR, 1873–1958

14069 **W., V.** Tomlinson: The sea and the jungle, 1912. Bib N&Q 1no1:3 Ja '35; 1no2:3 Ap '35.

14070 **McCord, David.** Misprints in Tomlinson. Bull Bib 22no5:111 Ja/Ap '58.

14071 **Haack, Peter R.** H. M. Tomlinson's A bluebell at Thiepval. (Query 149). Bk Coll 11no2:219 '62.

TONE, THEOBALD WOLFE, 1763–98

14072 **O'Kelley, Francis.** Wolfe Tone's novel. [Belmont castle, 1790]. Irish Bk Lover 23no2:47–8 Mr/Ap '35.

14073 **O'Hegarty, Patrick S.** Wolfe Tone. An argument on behalf of the Catholics of Ireland, 1791. (Bibliographical notes). Dublin Mag new ser 22no3:60 Jl/S '47.

TOTTELL, RICHARD, d.1594 *see* Book production and distribution—Printers, publishers, etc.

TOURNEUR, CYRIL, 1575?–1626

14074 **Maxwell, James C.** Two notes on The revenger's tragedy. Mod Lang R 44no4:545 Oc '49.

14075 **Price, George R.** The authorship and bibliography of The revenger's tragedy. Library ser5 15no4:262–77 D '60. tables.

14076 **Murray, Peter B.** The authorship of The revenger's tragedy. Pa Bib Soc Am 56:195–218 '62. tables.

TOWNSHEND, AURELIAN, fl.1601–43

14077 **Veevers, Erica.** Albions triumph, a further corrected state of the text. Library ser5 16no4:294–9 D '61.

'List of variant readings' (p. 295–8)

TOWNSHEND, GEORGE, 1ST MARQUIS, 1724–1807

14078 **Ehrman, Albert.** Correspondence. [Enquiry about Miscellaneous poetry upon various subjects ... by Townshend, Printed by Ann marchioness Townshend, 1791 and 1807]. Bk Coll Q 8:93 Oc/D '32.

TRAHERNE, THOMAS, 1637–74

14079 **Wade, Gladys I.** The manuscripts of the poems of Thomas Traherne. Mod Lang R 26no4:401–7 Oc '31.

14080 **Marks, Carol L.** Traherne's Christian ethicks. N&Q 208:270 Jl '63.

14081 —— Thomas Traherne's commonplace book. Pa Bib Soc Am 58:458–65 '64.

14082 **Osborn, James M.** A new Traherne manuscript. [Select meditations]. TLS 8 Oc '64:928.

14083 **Marks, Carol L.** Traherne's Church's year-book. [Ms.]. Pa Bib Soc Am 60:31–72 '66.

14084 **Sauls, Lynn.** The careless compositor for Christian ethicks. Pa Bib Soc Am 63:123–6 '69.

14085 —— Whereabouts of books owned by Traherne, Hopton, Bridgemon. (Query 236). Bk Coll 18no2:225–6 '69.

14086 **Sicherman, Carol L. M.** Traherne's Ficino notebook. Pa Bib Soc Am 63:73–81 '69.

TRESSELL, ROBERT, *pseud of* **ROBERT NOONAN, 1870–1911**

14087 **Slater, Montagu.** Robert Tressell's novel. [Ms. of The ragged trousered philanthropists]. TLS 11 Ap '52:251; J. W. Harper *ib.* 25 Ap '52:281; J. MacGibbon 2 My '52:297.

TROLLOPE, ANTHONY, 1815–82

14088 **Marsh, sir Edward.** An emendation [to Dr. Thorne]. (Correspondence). London Merc 4no22:411–12 Ag '21.

See also no. 14110.

14089 **Sadleir, Michael T. H.** Anthony Trollope and his publishers; a chapter in the history of nineteenth-century authorship. Library ser4 5no3:215–42 D '24.

14090 ... **Some** Anthony Trollope firsts among the moderns. (Books in the sale rooms). Bkmns J new ser 13no50:76–7 N '25.

14091 **Bell, sir Harold I.** Anthony Trollope's Autobiography. [Printer's copy]. Brit Mus Q 7no3:72 D '32. [Sg.: H. I. B.]

14092 **Hollings, Frank.** Trollope: The Eustace diamonds. [Binding variants]. Bib N&Q 1no3:6–7 Ag '35; M. T. H. Sadleir *ib.* 2no4/5:2 My '35.

14093 **Wilson, Carroll A.** Cancel leaf in Framley parsonage. Bib N&Q 1no1:10–11 Ja '35; [O. S. B. Brett, 3d viscount] Esher *ib.* 1no2:8 Ap '35.

14094 **Chapman, Robert W.** The text of Phineas redux. (Notes and queries). Coloph new ser 3no3:460–1 S '38; Correction *ib.* 3no4:608 D '38.

14095 **Tinker, Chauncey B.** The Trollope manuscripts. Yale Univ Lib Gaz 14no4:64 Ap '40.

14096 **Chapman, Robert W.** The text of Trollope. TLS 25 Ja '41:48; 22 Mr '41:144; S. H. Nowell-Smith *ib.* 8 F '41:72; R. W. Chapman 1 Mr '41:108.

14097 —— The text of Trollope's Autobiography. [Ms.]. R Eng Stud 17no65:90–4 Ja '41.

14098 —— The text of Trollope's novels. R Eng Stud 17no67:322–31 Jl '41. table.

I. Statistics.–II. An attempt at classification.–Summary of classified errors.

14099 —— The text of Trollope's Phineas redux. R Eng Stud 17no66:184–92 Ap '41; G. Bone *ib* 17no68:452–8 Oc '41.

14100 —— Trollope's Autobiography. [Ms.]. N&Q 181:245 N '41.

14101 —— The text of Trollope's Ayala's angel. Mod Philol 39no3:287–94 F '42.

14102 **Sadleir, Michael T. H.** A new Trollope item. [History of the Post office in Ireland, 1857]. TLS 25 Jl '42:372; C. Clay *ib.* 8 Ag '42:396; M. T. H. Sadleir 29 Ag '42:432.

14103 **Tinker, Chauncey B.** [and] **R. W. Chapman.** The text of Trollope's Phineas redux. R Eng Stud 18no69:86–92 Ja '42.

14104 **Wade, Allan** [and] **R. W. Chapman.** The text of Trollope. [Framley parsonage]. TLS 10 Ja '42:24.

14105 **Chapman, Robert W.** The text of Phineas Finn. TLS 25 Mr '44:156; S. H. Nowell-Smith *ib.* 15 Ap '44:192; R. L. Purdy 29 Jl '44:372.

14106 —— The text of Trollope's Sir Harry Hotspur. N&Q 186:2–3 Ja '44. [Sg.: R. W. C.]

14107 **D., T. C.** Victorian editors and Victorian delicacy. [Is he Popenjoy, 1877–8, and All the year round]. N&Q 187:251–3 D '44.

14108 **Booth, Bradford A.** The Parrish Trollope collection. Trollopian 1no1:11–19 '45.

I. Printed books.–II. Autograph letters.

14109 **Chapman, Robert W.** Textual criticism: a provisional bibliography. Trollopian 1no1:45 '45.

14110 **Guttridge, George H.** Sir Edward Marsh's emendation. [Dr. Thorne, chapt. 26]. (Notes and queries). Trollopian 1no2:49 '45.

*See also no.*14088.

14111 **Wilson, Carroll A.** Morris L. Parrish, Trollope collector. Trollopian 1no1:5–10 '45.

14112 **[Booth, Bradford A.].** Trollope manuscripts. [A census]. (Notes and queries). Trollopian 1no1:47 '45; 1no3:57–8 S '46.

14113 [——]. Trollope's library. [Catalogue found]. (Notes and queries). Trollopian 1no1:47–8 Mr '46.

14114 **Taylor, Robert H.** The Trollope collection [of M. L. Parrish]. Princeton Univ Lib Chron 8no1:33–7 N '46.

14115 **Chapman, Robert W.** Trollope's copy of Browning. (Notes and queries). Trollopian 2no2:119 S '47.

14116 **Taylor, Robert H.** The manuscript of Trollope's The American senator, collated with the first edition. Pa Bib Soc Am 41:123–39 '47. table.

14117 **Chapman, Robert W.** The text of Miss Mackenzie. Trollopian 3no4:305–8 Mr '49.

14118 **Tingay, Lance O.** Trollope's library. N&Q 195:476–8 Oc '50.

14119 **Sadleir, Michael T. H.** Orley farm, an underline variant. (Query no.16). Bk Coll 1no3:195 '52; F. R. Powell *ib.* 1no4:267 '52; Gladys Green 2no2:157 '53.

14120 **Green, Gladys.** Can you forgive her? [Illustrators]. (Query no.35). Bk Coll 2no2:158 '53.

14121 **Trollope's** Did he steal it? [Acquired by Library]. Princeton Univ Lib Chron 17no1:47 '55.

14122 **Anthony** Trollope. [Ms. of Life of Cicero presented]. Princeton Univ Lib Chron 17no2:106–7 '56.

14123 **Tingay, Lance O.** The publication of Trollope's first novel. [The Macdermots of Ballycloran]. TLS 30 Mr '56:200; Sylva Norman *ib.* 6 Ap '56:207; J. Hagan 4 My '56:269.

14124 **Bićanić, Sonia.** A missing page of The Claverings. Studia Romanica et Anglica Zagrabiensia 8:13–15 D '59.

14125 **Ekeblad, Inga-Stina.** Anthony Trollope's copy of the 1647 Beaumont and Fletcher folio. N&Q 204:153–5 Ap '59.

14126 **Carter, John W.** Trollope's La vendée, London, Colburn, 1850. (Note 152). Bk Coll 10no1:69–70 '61.

14127 **Booth, Bradford A.** Author to publisher: Anthony Trollope and William Isbister. Princeton Univ Lib Chron 24no1:51–67 '62.

14128 **Goldman, Arnold.** Trollope's North America. TLS 28 N '68:1338; R. Mason; J. A. Cochrane *ib.* 5 D '68:1385; A. Goldman 14 D '68:1409; 19 D '68:1433.

TROLLOPE, FRANCES (MILTON), 1780–1863

14129 **Smalley, Donald.** Frances Trollope's Domestic manners of the Americans: notebooks and rough draft. [Acquired by Library]. Indiana Q Bkmn 4no2/3:39–52 Jl '48.

TROTTER, WILFRED BATTEN LEWIS, 1872–1939

14130 **Wilfred** Trotter's Instincts of the herd. [Ms.]. Bod Lib Rec 2no19/20:56 Ap/Je '42.

TRUSSELL, JOHN, fl.1595–1642

14131 **Trussel's** Rape of faire Helen. (Notes on sales). TLS 9 Jl '31:552; S. C. Wilson; N. B. White *ib*. 16 Jl '31:564.

TURBERVILLE, GEORGE, 1540?–1610?

14132 **Turberville's** Hunting and hawking. (Notes on sales). TLS 1 S '21:568.

14133 **Munsterberg, Margaret.** The Booke of falconrie. More Bks Boston Pub Lib Bull 18no9:427 N '43. [Sg.: M. M.]

14134 **Berry, Lloyd E.** Richard Hakluyt and Turberville's poems on Russia. Pa Bib Soc Am 61:350–1 '67.

TURPIN, RICHARD, 1706–39

14135 **Parks, Joseph.** Dick Turpin literature. Coll Misc new ser 4:67–8 My/Jl '33; 5:89–90 Ag/S '33; B. Ono; F. Thorpe *ib*. 6:105–7,111 Oc/N '33. illus.

TWEEDSMUIR, JOHN BUCHAN, BARON, 1875–1940 *see* Buchan, John, baron Tweedsmuir, 1875–1940.

TYNDALE, WILLIAM, d.1536

14136 **Munsterberg, Margaret.** Tyndale's Parable of the wicked mammon. More Bks Boston Pub Lib Bull 16no8:384 Oc '41. [Sg.: M. M.]

TYRIE, JAMES, 1543–97

14137 **Law, Thomas G.** Note on some writings attributed to father James Tyrie, S.J., 1594–5. Edinburgh Bib Soc Pubs 3pt3:137–40 Mr '99.

UDALL, NICHOLAS, 1505–56

14138 **Larkey, Sanford V.** The Vesalian compendium of Geminus and Nicholas Udall's translation; their relation to Vesalius, Caius, Vicary and de Mondeville. Library ser4 14no4:367–94 Mr '33. facsims., diagr., tables.

'The English translation by Nicholas Udall, 1553' (p. 374–91); 'Bibliography' (p. 391–4)

14139 **Sullivan, Frank.** Ralph Roister Doister, an immaculate copy. N&Q 178:263 Ap '40.

14140 **Goff, Frederick R.** [Bibliogr. note on Udall's Flowers . . . gathered out of Terence, 1572]. Pa Bib Soc Am 35:294 '41.

14141 **Craik, T. W.** The text of Respublica: a conjecture. N&Q 198:279 Jl '53.

14142 **Starr, G. A.** Notes on Respublica. N&Q 206:290–2 Ag '61.

UPCOTT, WILLIAM, 1779–1845

14143 **Abrahams, Aleck.** William Upcott. [Mss.]. N&Q ser9 12:389 N '03.

VAUGHAN, HENRY, 1622–95

14144 **Martin, Burns.** Vaughan's The world. [Text]. TLS 3 Ag '33:525.

14145 **Parker, William R.** Henry Vaughan and his publishers. Library ser4 20no4:401–11 Mr '40.

14146 **Hutchinson, F. E.** The strange case of Olor Iscanus. R Eng Stud 18no71:320–1 Jl '42.

14147 **Muusterberg, Margaret.** The swan of Usk. [Olor Iscanus]. More Bks Boston Pub Lib Bull 18no7:341 S '43. [Sg.: M. M.]

14148 **Marilla, Esmond L.** 'The publisher is the reader' of Olor Iscanus. R Eng Stud 24no93:36–41 Ja '48.

14149 **Martin, Leonard C.** Henry Vaughan and The chymists key. TLS 11 D '53:801.

14150 **Wolf, Edwin.** Some books of early English provenance in the Library company of Philadelphia. Bk Coll 9no3:275–84 '60. facsims.

Checklist of 14 books formerly owned by Henry Vaughan (p. 283–4)

14151 **Simmonds, James D.** The publication of Olor Iscanus. Mod Lang N 76no5:404–8 My '61.

VAUGHAN, ROWLAND, fl.1629–58

14152 **Davies, sir William Ll.** Rowland Vaughan, Caergai, and a law-suit [concerning his trans. of Bayley's Practice of piety]. (Notes, queries and replies). Welsh Bib Soc J 2no7:271 D '22. [Sg.: W. Ll. D.]

14153 **Williams, William.** Rowland Vaughan, a further note. (Notes, queries, and replies). Welsh Bib Soc J 2no8:317–18 Ag '23. [Sg.: W. W.]

VAUGHAN, THOMAS, 1622–66

14154 **Rudrum, A. W.** Some errors in A. E. Waite's transcription of Thomas Vaughan's manuscript notebook. N&Q 211:258–9 Jl '66.

VENNAR, RICHARD, d.1615?

14155 **Shaw, Phillip.** Richard Vennar and The double PP. [And Thomas Dekker]. Pa Bib Soc Am 43:199–202 '49.

VERGILIUS, POLYDORUS, d.1555

14156 **Payne, William,** Polydore Vergil's History of England. N&Q ser8 4:248 S '93; W. C. B. *ib.* 4:315 Oc '93; J. P. Stilwell 4:357 Oc '93.

14157 **Hay, Denys.** Corrections in a Bodleian copy of Polydore Vergil. [Hologr. notes in Adagia and De inventoribus rerum]. Bod Q Rec 8no96:457–8 '37/8.

14158 **Simpson, S. M.** A Pleasant and compendious history of the first inventers: the 1685 edition a ghost. (Note 288). Bk Coll 16no2:224 '67.

VINCENT, AUGUSTINE, 1584?–1626

14159 **Wood, Edward R.** A Discoverie of errours in The case of William Jaggard, 1619. N&Q 202:62–3 F '57.

14160 —— Cancels and corrections in A discovery of errors, 1622. Library ser5 13no2:124–7 Je '58.

VITZETELLY, HENRY RICHARD, 1820–94 *see* Book production and distribution–Printers, publishers, etc.

WAGSTAFFE, WILLIAM, 1685–1725

14161 **Dearing, Vinton A.** Jonathan Swift or William Wagstaffe. [Miscellaneous works]. (Notes). Harvard Lib Bull 7no1:121–30 '53.

WAKE, ARCHBP. WILLIAM, 1657–1737

14162 **Mayor, John E. B.** Archbishop Wake. N&Q ser8 8:121–2 Ag '95.

WALEY, ARTHUR DAVID, 1889–1966

14163 **Johns, Francis A.** The privately printed Chinese poems, 1916. (Query 136). Bk Coll 9no4:458 '60, G. F. Sims *ib.* 10no1:72 '61.

14164 —— Arthur Waley's Chinese poems, 1916. (Note 210). Bk Coll 12no4:494 '63.

14165 **Waley, Alison.** Arthur Waley's mss. TLS 2 N '67:1036; 'Commentary' *ib.* 2 N '67:1043; D. Hawkes 9 N '67:1061; A. C. Scott 30 N '67:1167; P. Eaton 14 D '67:1215; Alison Waley 21 D '67:1239; 14 Mr '68:278; A. C. Scott 15 F '68:157; P. Eaton 22 F '68:181; I. Morris 14 Mr '68:278.

WALFORD, EDWARD, 1823–97

14166 **Buckler, William E.** Edward Walford: a distressed editor. [And Once a week]. N&Q 198:536–8 D '53.

WALKER, HENRY, fl.1641–60

14167 **Williams, J. B.,** *pseud. of* **Joseph G. Muddiman.** The literary frauds of Henry Walker the ironmonger. N&Q ser11 10:441–2, 462–3, 483–4, 503–4 D '14; 11:2–4, 22–4, 42–3, 62–3 Ja '15.

WALKINGHAME, FRANCIS, fl.1747–85

14168 **Wallis, Peter J.** Francis Walking(h)am(e) and The tutor's assistant. N&Q 201:258–61 Je '56.

WALLACE, JAMES, d.1688

14169 **Grant, Ian R.** James Wallace's An account of the islands of Orkney, London, 1700. Biblioth 4no1:36–8 '63.

WALLACE, RICHARD HORATIO EDGAR, 1875–1932

14170 **Morland, Nigel.** Edgar Wallace bibliography. [Proposed]. TLS 3 My '33:322.

WALLER, EDMUND, 1606–87

14171 **A Waller** find. [Ms. of Upon the present war with Spain]. Athenæum 3524:610 My '95; G. T. Drury; H. B. Forman *ib.* 3526:675 My '95.

14172 **Ham, Roswell G.** Manuscripts of Waller. TLS 8 S '32:624.

WALMESLEY, BP. CHARLES, 1722–97

14173 **Ferrar, M. L.** Pastorini's prophecy. [Walmesley's General history of the Christian church]. N&Q ser12 8:251 Mr '21; D. A. Cruse *ib.* 8:313 Ap '21; F. J. Bigger; Editor, I. B. L. [i.e. J. S. Crone] 8:396 My '21.

WALPOLE, HORACE, 4TH EARL OF ORFORD, 1717–97 *see also* Book production and distribution–Printers, publishers, etc.–Strawberry Hill press, Twickenham, 1757–97.

14174 **L.** The dispersion of the treasures collected by Horace Walpole at Strawberry Hill. [Library]. Bkplate Ann & Armorial Yrbk 3:11–22 '96. illus.

14175 **Prideaux, William F.** Walpoliana. N&Q ser9 2:287–8 Oc '98.

14176 **Rotton, J. F.** Horace Walpole's letters to Mann. N&Q ser9 7:229–30 Mr '01.

14177 **Merritt, Edward P.** The Strawberry Hill catalogue. N&Q ser10 7:461–2 Je
'07; F. A. Russell *ib.* 7:517 Je '07; A. Abrahams 12:216–17 S '09; W.
Roberts 12:294–5,353 Oc '09; E. P. Merritt 12:430–2 N '09; A. Abrahams; Curious, *pseud.* 12:491–2 D '09; L. A. W. ser11 1:34 Ja '10; E. P.
Merritt 1:214–15 Mr '10.

14178 —— Strawberry Hill, Description of the villa, 1774. N&Q ser11 4:207 S
'11; W. F. Prideaux *ib.* 4:251–2 S '11.

14179 **Sargeaunt, John.** The text of Walpole's and Gray's letters. TLS 13 My
'20:302; P. J. Toynbee *ib.* 20 My '20:320; S. G. S. Sackville 27 My '20:335;
J. Sargeaunt; F. 10 Je '20:368; R. L. Antrobus 24 Je '20:403.

14180 **From** mr. Horatio Walpole's library. Harvard Lib N [2no]14:23–9 Mr
'25.

14181 **Chapman, Robert W.** Walpole's Anecdotes of painting. [Position of
plates]. Bod Q R 5no51:55–6 Oc '26.

14182 **Carlton, William N. C.** Horace Walpole's edition of DeGrammont's
Memoires. Am Coll 4no6:206–8 S '27.

14183 **Partington, Wilfred G.** Hugh Walpole's library of affections. Bkmns J
ser3 17no10:59–66 '29.

14184 **Lewis, Wilmarth S.** A library dedicated to the life and works of Horace
Walpole. Coloph[1]pt3:[12p.] '30. illus.

14185 **Needham, Francis R. D.** A Strawberry Hill North Briton. [Fragments,
1763]. TLS 27 N '30:1014; J. C. Fox *ib.* 11 D '30:1066.

14186 **Lewis, Wilmarth S.** Walpole's Anecdotes. [Advertisement to Anecdotes,
1780]. TLS 7 My '31:367.

14187 **[Haraszti, Zoltán].** A great Walpole collection at Harvard. More Bks
Boston Pub Lib Bull 10no7:265–6 S '35.

14188 **Lewis, Wilmarth S.** Horace Walpole. [Contribs. to Old England, and The
remembrancer). TLS 24 Ja '35:48.

14189 **Tucker, Mildred M.** The Merritt Walpole collection. Harvard Lib N
3no2:41–5 Je '35.

14190 **Perkinson, Richard H.** Walpole and a Dublin pirate. [The mysterious
mother, 1791]. Philol Q 15no4:391–400 Oc '36.

14191 **Gaselee, sir Stephen.** The Walpole letters. [or, On benefactions to the
great libraries]. TLS 13 N '37:871; Your reviewer *ib.* 20 N '37:891.

14192 **Hazen, Allen T.** Strawberry Hill sale catalogues, 1842. N&Q 192:33–5 Ja '47.

14193 **Lewis, Wilmarth S.** The books at Strawberry Hill. Atlantic Mnthly 180no3:109–13 S '47.

14194 —— Horace Walpole's library. Library ser5 2no1:45–52 Je '47.

14195 —— Collector's progress. [Includes account of formation of Walpole collection]. New York, A. A. Knopf, 1951; London, Constable; Toronto, Longmans, 1952. xix,253,viiip. illus., facsims. 21cm.

> *Rev:* E. Weeks Atlantic Mag Ag '51:79–80; G. F. Whicher Am Scholar 21:118–22 '51; D. Ferguson N.Y. Times Bk R 1 Jl '51:9; F. B. Adams Yale R 41:125–7 '51; A. B. Shepperson Virginia Q R 27:608–11 '51; S. C. Chew N.Y. Herald Tribune Bk R 22 Jl '52:6; TLS 9 My '52:320; C. Connolly Sunday Times 15 Je '52:11; R. W. Chapman Listener 48:148–9 '52; R. Fedden Observer 25 My '52:7.

14196 **Bennett, Charles H.** The text of Horace Walpole's correspondence with Hannah More. R Eng Stud new ser 3no12:341–5 Oc '52.

14197 **Brown, T. Julian.** Horace Walpole, 1717–1797. (English literary autographs, VIII). Bk Coll 2no4:275 '53. facsims.

14198 **Ilchester, The earl of** [i.e. **Giles S. H. Fox-Strangeways**]. 'Some pages torn from the last journals of Horace Walpole *in* Miner, Dorothy E., *ed*. Studies in art and literature for Belle da Costa Green. Princeton, N.J., 1954. p. 449–58.

14199 **Horace** Walpole library. TLS 17 My '57:312.

14200 **Lewis, Wilmarth S.** Horace Walpole's library. Cambridge, C.U.P., 1958. x,74p. illus., facsims. 19cm. (Sandars lecture, 1957)

> I. The books.–II. Walpole's reading.–III. The dispersal of the library.

> *Repr. with rev. in* Hazen, Allen T., *ed*. A catalogue of Horace Walpole's library. New Haven, 1969. V.1, p. xlvii–xci. *See also no.*14204.

> *Rev:* Jane E. Norton Library ser5 13:212–13 '58; TLS 31 Ja '58:68; R. W. Ketton-Cremer Bk Coll 7:200 '58; J. C. Wyllie Pa Bib Soc Am 52:223 '58; F. W. Hilles Yale R 47:599–600 '58; E. A. Bloom Mod Lang R 54:94–5 '59; F. K. Stanzel Anglia 77:363 '59; D. M. Low R Eng Stud new ser 11:120–1 '60.

14201 **Gerson, J. H. C.** The 1796 edition of Walpole's Anecdotes: a fifth volume. (Note 279). Bk Coll 15no4:484 '66.

14202 **Hazen, Allen T.** 'The earlier owners of Walpole's books' *in* Smith, Warren H., *ed*. Horace Walpole, writer, politician, and connoisseur: essays. . . . New Haven, 1967. p. 167–79.

14203 —— A catalogue of Horace Walpole's library. With Horace Walpole's library, by Wilmarth Sheldon Lewis. New Haven, Yale U.P., 1969. 3v. illus., facsims. 26cm.

> V. 1. The main library.–V. 2. The main library, cont.– The glass closet.–The library in the offices.–V. 3. The library in the offices, cont.–The Round tower.–Appendix 1: False attributions.–Appendix 2: Books given away by Walpole.–Appendix 3. Books owned by Walpole when at Eton and Cambridge.–Index of binders.–Index of owners. (*See also no.*14204)

> *Rev*: Johnsonian Newsl 29:1–2 '69; H. H. Campbell Pa Bib Soc Am 64:471–4 '69; TLS 4 S '70:980; R. J. Roberts Library ser5 26:280–2 '71; G. S. Rousseau Stud Burke 12:1910–20 '71; J. D. Fleeman Bk Coll 21:275–9 '72.

14204 —— and **W. S. Lewis.** The introduction to A catalogue of Horace Walpole's library . . . and Horace Walpole's library. [n.p., New Haven] 1969. 90p. illus., facsims., plan. 25cm. (Sandars lectures, 1957)

> Introduction. I. Walpole's collecting methods.–II. Walpole's collection and his use of it.–III. The housing of the books.–IV. The main library.–V. The library in the offices.–VI. The print room in the Round tower.–VII. Press-marks, bookplates, and Walpolian provenance.–VIII. The sale in 1842: the catalogues and their problems.–IX. The arrangement of the present catalogue.–X. Acknowledgements.–Horace Walpole's library, by Wilmarth Sheldon Lewis. I. The books.–II. Walpole's reading.–III. The dispersal of the library.

WALPOLE, SIR HUGH SEYMOUR, 1884–1941

14205 **Muir, Percival H.** Walpole: The dark forest, 1916. [Binding variants]. Bib N&Q 2no1:8 Ja '36; Katherine deB. Parsons *ib*. 2no4/5:3 My '36; J. W. Carter 2no10:1–2 Ap '38. [Sg.: Ed.]

14206 **Sir** Hugh Walpole. (Private libraries, III). TLS 30 Jl '38:512.

> The manuscript collection.–Fiction in English.–The nineties.–Baron Corvo.

14207 **Sir** Hugh Walpole's nineties collection. Bod Lib Rec 2no18:40–1 F '42.

14208 **Sir** Hugh Walpole's books. TLS 9 Mr '46:120.

14209 **Muir, Percival H.** Sir Hugh Walpole. (Bibliomanes, II). Bk Coll 4no3:217–28 '55; 4no4:299–307 '55; 5no1:38–47 '56.

WALTON, IZAAK, 1593–1683

14210 **Walton's** Complete angler. Bkworm 4no43:222–3 Je '91.

14211 **Marston, Robert B.** Walton and some earlier writings on fish and fishing. London, E. Stock, 1894. xxv,264p. 16cm. (Book-lover's library)

14212 **Bright, Allan H.** Izaac Walton, Samuel Woodford, and Charles Beale. [Presentation copy Reliquiæ Wottonianæ, 1672]. N&Q ser9 1:284 Ap '98.

14213 **Lang, Andrew.** Walton's books. [In Salisbury cathedral library].
Athenæum 3816:793 D '00; R. B. Marston; A. W. Pollard *ib.* 3817:826 D
'00.

14214 **Dobson, H. Austin.** On certain quotations in Walton's Angler. Library
ser2 2no5:4–11 Ja '01.

14215 **Dale, P. T.** Walton's Lives; Matthew Kendrick. [Presentation copy]. N&Q
147:120 Ag '24; W. C. Forman; H. J. B. Clements *ib.* 147:157–8 Ag '24;
147:230–1 S '24.

14216 **Butt, John E.** Izaak Walton's copy of Pembroke and Ruddier's Poems.
Bod Q Rec 7no76:140 '32.

14217 —— Walton's copy of Donne's Letters, 1651. R Eng Stud 8no29:72–4 Ja
'32.

14218 —— Izaak Walton's collections for Fulman's Life of John Hales. [Mss.].
Mod Lang R 29no3:267–73 Jl '34.

14219 **The Compleat** angler. (The sale room). TLS 9 N '35:728.

14220 **Coon, Arthur M.** Izaak Walton a stationer? Mod Lang N 56no5:363–6
My '41.

See also no.14223.

14221 **Exley, Arthur.** The Complete angler. TLS 14 Mr '42:132.

14222 **Brooke, C. F. Tucker.** The Lambert Walton-Cotton collection. Yale Univ
Lib Gaz 17no4:61–5 Ap '43.

14223 **Pettit, Henry J.** Izaak Walton a stationer? Mod Lang N 58no5:410 My
'43.

See also no.14220.

14224 **Silver, Louis H.** The first edition of Walton's Life of Herbert. (Notes).
Harvard Lib Bull 5no3:371–2 '51.

14225 **Wing, D. W.** Izaak Walton. [Library]. TLS 13 Jl '51:437.

14226 **Howarth, R. Guy.** Prowett's edition of the Life of Walton. N&Q
198:339–40 Ag '53; 199:39 Ja '54; I. A. Shapiro *ib.* 199:500 N '54.

WANLEY, HUMFREY, 1672–1726

14227 **Barwick, George F.** Humfrey Wanley and the Harleian library. Library
ser2 3no9:24–35 Ja '02, 3no11:243–55 Jl '02.

14228 **Wright, Cyril E.** Humfrey Wanley: Saxonist and library-keeper. (Sir Israel Gollancz memorial lecture). Proc Brit Acad 46:99–129 '60. port.

14229 **'Some** observations concerning the invention and progress of printing, to the year 1465'. Bod Lib Rec 6no6:634–5 S '61.

14230 **Bennett, J. A. W.** Wanley's Life of Wolsey. [By Cavendish]. Bod Lib Rec 7no1:50–2 Je '62.

WARD, EDWARD, 1667–1731

14231 **Eddy, William A.** Ned Ward and Lilliput. [Gulliver's travels]. N&Q 158:148–9 Mr '30.

14232 **Millar, Nola L.** Ned Ward, the brewing poet. [Library's holdings]. Turnbull Lib Rec 4:9–10 Jl/D '41.

WARE, SIR JAMES, 1594–1666

14233 **Wilson, Philip.** The writings of sir James Ware and the forgeries of Robert Ware. Bib Soc Trans 15pt1:83–94 '17/18.

14234 ——— [**Same**] Bib Soc News-sh 1–3 Ja '18.

Report of paper read 17 D '17.

14235 **Ware's** Annals annotated [by author]. Irish Bk Lover 28no3:69 S '14.

14236 **Bourke, Francis S.** Harris' Ware. [History of bishops of Ireland]. Irish Bk Lover 32no2:39–40 Jl '53.

WARTON, JOSEPH, 1722–1800

14237 **MacClintock, William D.** Joseph Warton's Essay on Pope; a history of the five editions. Chapel Hill, University of North Carolina pr.; London, H. Milford, O.U.P., 1933. xii,74p. facsims. 24cm.

I. Warton's Essay on Pope: origin, significance, reception.–II. A history of the five editions.–III. Summary of the changes made in the five editions.–Appendices: Biographical note on Joseph Wharton. A list of Warton's literary works. A bibliographical note.

Rev: G. Putt R Eng Stud 10:480–1 '34; R. H. Griffith Mod Lang N 50:69 '35.

14238 **Kinsley, James.** The publication of Warton's Essay on Pope. Mod Lang R 44no1:91–3 Ja '49.

14239 **Schick, George B.** Delay in publication of the second volume of Joseph Warton's Essay on Pope. N&Q 200:67–9 F '55.

14240 **Pittock, Joan.** Joseph and his second volume of the Essay on Pope. R Eng Stud new ser 18no71:264–73 Ag '67.

WARTON, THOMAS, 1728–90

14241 **Lee, A. Collingwood** and **J. Pickford.** The Oxford sausage. [Ed. by Wharton]. N&Q ser10 2:227 S '04; H. C.; H. L. Wainewright; E. H. Coleman *ib.* 2:376 N '04.

14242 **Wecter, Dixon.** Thomas Warton's Poems. TLS 14 Je '28:450; P. F. Hinton *ib.* 12 Jl '28:520; 24 Ap '30:352.

14243 **Vincent, Howard P.** Warton's last words on the Rowley papers. Mod Lang R 34no4:572–5 Oc '39.

14244 **Tillotson, Geoffrey.** Warton on the Rowley papers. Mod Lang R 35no1:62 Ja '40.

14245 **Smith, David Nichol.** Thomas Warton's miscellany: The union. R Eng Stud 19no75:263–75 Jl '43.

14246 **Blakiston, Jack M. G.** A Dublin reprint of Thomas Warton's History of English poetry. Library ser5 1no1:69–70 Je '46.

WARWICK, ARTHUR, 1604–33

14247 **Höltgen, Karl J.** and **J. R. B. Horden.** Arthur Warwick, 1603/4–1633, the author of Spare minutes. Library ser5 21no3:223–30 S '66. facsims.

WATSON, JAMES, 1664?–1722 *see* Book production and distribution—Printers, publishers, etc.

WATSON, JOHN, 1725–83

14248 **Anderton, Henry P. J. Ince-.** Watson's Earls of Warren and Surrey. N&Q 168:298 Ap '35; 168:355–6 My '55; 168:411 Je '35. [Sg.: H. I. A.]

14249 **Hanson, Thomas W.** The subscribers to Watson's Halifax. [And proposal]. Halifax Antiqu Soc Trans 41–8 '50.

WATSON, SIR JOHN WILLIAM, 1858–1935

14250 **Swayze, Walter E.** The sir William Watson collection. Yale Univ Lib Gaz 27no2:71–6 Oc '52.

WATSON, WILLIAM DAVY, 1811–88

14251 **Green, David B.** William Davy Watson, author of Trevor, or The new saint Francis. Pa Bib Soc Am 59:55–7 '65.

WATT, ROBERT, 1774–1819

14252 **[Mason, Thomas].** A bibliographical martyr; dr. Robert Watt, author of the Bibliotheca Britannica. Library 1no2:56–63 F '89.

14253 **Cole, George W.** Robert Watt: Bibliotheca Britannica. [Pub. in parts]. Bib N&Q 1no3:8 Ag '35.

14254 —— Robert Watt's Bibliotheca Britannica. N&Q 168:244–5 Ap '35; J. Ardagh *ib.* 168:282 Ap '35.

WATTS, ISAAC, 1674–1748

14255 **Isaac** Watts' family Bible. Congreg Hist Soc J Trans 1no4:275–7 Mr '01.

14256 **Ward, James.** Notes on a unique copy of dr. Isaac Watts's Divine songs lately in the possession of James Ward. Nottingham, Printed for private circulation at the Thoroton pr., 1902. 23p. illus., port., facsims. 22cm.

WATTS-DUNTON, WALTER THEODORE, 1832–1914 *see* Dunton, Walter Theodore Watts-, 1832–1914.

WAUGH, EVELYN ARTHUR ST. JOHN, 1903–66

14257 **Davis, Robert M.** Some textual variants in Scoop. Evelyn Waugh Newsl 1no2:1–3 '67.

14257a **Doyle, Paul A.** Decline and fall: two versions. [1928 and 1962]. Evelyn Waugh Newsl 1no2:4–5 '67.

14257b **Davis, Robert M.** Notes toward a variorum Brideshead. Evelyn Waugh Newsl 2no3:4–6 '68; A. Clodd *ib.* 3no1:5–6 '69.

14257c —— Textual problems in the novels of Evelyn Waugh. Pa Bib Soc Am 62:259–63 '68; 63:41–6 '69.

14258 —— The serial version of Brideshead revisited. Twent Cent Lit 15no1:35–43 Ap '69.

14258a **Doyle, Paul A.** and **A. Clodd.** A British Pinfold and an American Pinfold. Evelyn Waugh Newsl 3no3:1–5 '69.

WEALE, WILLIAM HENRY JAMES, 1832–1917

14259 **Brockwell, Maurice W.** W. H. James Weale, the pioneer. Library ser5 6no34:200–11 D '51.

WEBB, MARY GLADYS, 1881–1927

14260 **Stone, P. M.** Webb, Mary: Short stories. Bib N&Q 2no6:8 Jl '36. [Sg.: P. M. S.]

14261 **Barratt, Bruce.** Webb, Mary: Precious bane. [Binding variants]. Bib N&Q 2no6:7–8 Jl '36; F. B. Adams *ib.* 2no8:4 F '37.

14262 **Stone, P. M.** Mary Webb's House in Dormer forest and Seven for a secret. [Binding variants]. Bib N&Q 2no9:12 Ja '38; T. Warburton *ib*. 2no10:6 Ap '38.

WEBB, SIDNEY JAMES, BARON PASSFIELD, 1859–1947

14263 **D., R. E.** Webb, S. and B.: Soviet communism. [Advance ptg?]. Bib N&Q 2no6:8 Jl '36; D. A. Randall *ib*. 2no8:4 F '37.

WEBBE, JOSEPH, fl.1612–33

14264 **Salmon, Vivian.** An ambitious printing project of the early seventeenth century. [Patented method of teaching language, and ptg. costs]. Library ser5 16no3:190–6 S '61.

WEBSTER, JOHN, 1580?–1625?

14265 **Watson, Foster.** John Webster. [Signature in The writing schoolmaster in Cambridge university library]. (Correspondence). London Mercury 3no15:308 Ja '21; M. L. Sparkman *ib*. 3no17:540 Mr '21; F. Watson 3no18:652 Ap '21.

14266 **Lucas, Frank L.** Some notes on the text of Webster. N&Q 150:183–6 Mr '26; S. *ib*. 150:232 Mr '26.

14267 **Maxwell, James C.** A correction in Webster. [Duchess of Malfi]. N&Q 193:302 Jl '48.

14268 **Brown, John R.** The printing of John Webster's plays, I. Stud Bib 6:117–40 '54.

14269 —— The printing of John Webster's plays, II. Stud Bib 8:113–27 '56. tables.

14270 —— The printing of John Webster's plays, III: The duchess of Malfi. Stud Bib 15:57–69 '62. tables.

14271 **Freeman, Arthur.** The White devil, I.ii.295: an emendation. N&Q 208:101–2 Mr '63.

WEEVER, JOHN, 1576–1632

14272 **Weever's** Faunus and Melliflora. (Notes on sales). TLS 12 Je '24:376.

14273 **Armstrong A.** Weever's Faunus and Melliflora. Library ser5 5no1:59 Je '50.

14274 **Jensen, Bent Juel-.** [Note no.49. John Weever's An agnus dei, 1601, a miniature book]. Bk Coll 4no4:327 '55.

WELCH, DENTON, 1915–48

14275 **Gransden, K. W.** Denton Welch's Maiden voyage. [Mss.]. Brit Mus Q 21no2:31–2 Jl '57.

WELDON, SIR ANTHONY, d.1649?

14276 **White, Beatrice.** Anthony Weldon. [Ms. of Court and character of James I]. (Antiquarian notes). TLS 14 My '38:344.

WELLS, HERBERT GEORGE, 1866–1946

14277 **Brett, Oliver S. B., 3d viscount Esher.** Wells: In the days of the comet, 1906. [Issue dated 5:5:'06]. Bib N&Q 2no2:8 F '36. [Sg.: Esher.]

14278 **Naumburg, Edward.** Wells, H. G.: Love and mr. Lewisham. [Am. ed., 1899]. Bib N&Q 2no6:8 Jl '36.

14279 **O'Hegarty, Patrick S.** Wells, H. G.: Tales of space and time. [New York, 1899]. Bib N&Q 2no11:10–11 N '38; 2no12:6 My '39.

14280 **H. G.** Wells manuscripts go to Illinois. Manuscripts 6no3:159 '54.

14281 **Bergonzi, Bernard.** The publication of The time machine, 1894–5. R Eng Stud new ser 11no41:42–51 F '60.

14282 **Ray, Gordon N.** H. G. Well's contributions to the Saturday review. Library ser5 16no1:29–36 Mr '61.

14283 **Timko, Michael.** H. G. Wells's dramatic criticism for the Pall mall gazette. Library ser5 17no2:138–45 Je '62.

WESLEY, JOHN, 1703–91

14284 **Hipwell, Daniel.** Wesley mss. N&Q ser8 11:166 F '97.

14285 **Jackson, F. M.** A bibliographical catalogue of books mentioned in John Wesley's journals. Wesley Hist Soc Proc 4pt1:17–19 '03; 4pt2:47–51 '03; 4pt3:74–81 '03; 4pt4:107–11 '03; 4pt5:134–40 '03; 4pt6:173–6 '04; 4pt7:203–10 '04; 4pt8:232–8 '04.

14286 **Tew, E. L. H.** Wesley journals. N&Q ser11 4:369 N '11.

14287 **Brown, William.** John Wesley's first publication. [The Christian's pattern, 1735]. N&Q ser12 10:9 Ja '22.

14288 **Jackson, George.** John Wesley as a bookman. London Q & Holborn R 160:294–305 Jl '35.

14289 **Ingram, W. G.** John Wesley's books. TLS 14 Ag '37:592.

14290 **Herbert, Thomas W.** John Wesley as editor and author. Princeton, N.J., Princeton U.P.; London, H. Milford, O.U.P., 1940. vii,146p. 23cm. (Princeton Stud Eng 17)

14291 **Noyes, Gertrude.** John Wesley's Complete English dictionary. [1753]. N&Q 187:103 Ag '44; T. Murgatroyd *ib.* 187:172 Oc '44; H. Ll. Davis 187:238–9 N '44. [Sg.: G. N.]

14292 Cancelled.

14293 **Baker, Frank.** The Frank Baker collection, an autobiographical analysis. Lib N Duke Univ Lib 36:1–9 D '62.

WESLEY, SAMUEL, 1691–1739

14294 **Williams, Iolo A.** S. Wesley: Poems on several occasions. [1736]. Bib N&Q 2no1:8 Ja '36.

WEST, DAME REBECCA, *pseud. of* **CICILY ISABEL (FAIRFIELD) ANDREWS, 1892–**

14295 **Warburton, Thomas.** West, Rebecca: The return of the soldier, London, 1918. [States]. Bib N&Q 2no7:7 Oc '36; C. S. Lillicrap *ib.* 2no8:5 F '37.

WESTMORLAND, MILDMAY FANE, 2D EARL OF, d.1666 *see* Fane, Mildmay, 2d earl of Westmorland, d.1666.

WHATELY, ARCHBP. RICHARD, 1787–1863

14296 **M., F.** Archbishop Whately's Logic. N&Q ser9 7:69 Ja '01; F. H. Coleman *ib.* 7:177 Mr '01.

WHITE, GILBERT, 1720–93

14297 **R., M. U. H.** Chandos classics: illustrations to White's Selborne. [1879]. N&Q 173:443 D '37; Frederick Warne & co. ltd.; H. S. Gladstone *ib.* 174:34 Ja '38.

14298 **Brown, T. Julian.** Gilbert White, 1720–1793. (English literary autographs, XXIX). Bk Coll 8no1:51 '59. facsims.

WHITE, WILLIAM HALE, 1831–1913 *see* Rutherford, Mark, *pseud.*

WHITEFIELD, GEORGE, 1714–70

14299 **J., H. E. H.** Whitefield's Hymns; first edition. N&Q ser9 10:109 Ag '02.

14300 **Lam, George L.** and **W. H. Smith.** Two rival editions of George Whitefield's Journal, London, 1738. [Piracy]. Stud Philol 41no1:86–93 Ja '44.

WHITEHEAD, PAUL, 1710–74

14301 **Chapman, Robert W.** Paul Whitehead's State dunces. Bod Q Rec 5no50:27–8 Jl '26.

14302 —— Whitehead's State dunces, 1733. (Note 135). Bk Coll 9no2:195 '60.

WHITEHEAD, WILLIAM, 1715–85

14303 **Todd, William B.** A hidden edition of Whitehead's Variety, 1776. Pa Bib Soc Am 45:357–8 '51. table.

WHITGIFT, ARCHBP. JOHN, 1530?–1604

14304 **Munsterberg, Margaret.** Answer to a puritan manifesto. [An answer to . . . An admonition . . . , 1572]. More Bks Boston Pub Lib Bull 16no6:297 Je '41. [Sg.: M. M.]

14305 **O'Sullivan, William.** Archbishop Whitgift's library catalogue. TLS 3 Ag '56:468.

WHITING, JOHN, 1656–1722

14306 **Tolles, Frederick B.** Some unpublished works of John Whiting. Friends' Hist Soc J 47no2:52–6 '55.

WHITNEY, GEOFFREY, 1548?–1601?

14307 **Craster, sir H. H. Edmund.** The first draft of Geoffrey Whitney's Emblems (Ms. Rawlinson poetry 56). Bod Q Rec 6no67:172–3 '30.

14308 **Muir, Percival H.** Whitney's Choice of emblems, 1586. TLS 9 Ja '43:19.

WHITTINTON, ROBERT, d.1554

14309 **Bromley, James.** Wynkyn de Worde. [Whittinton's Tully's Offices, 1534]. Athenæum 3449:80 D '93.

14310 **White, Beatrice.** An early Tudor grammarian. Mod Lang R 30no3:344–7 Jl '35.

WILD, ROBERT, 1609–79

14311 **Pirie, Robert.** Two editions of Iter boreale, 1668. (Note 196). Bk Coll 12no2:204–5 '63.

WILDE, JANE FRANCESCA (ELGEE), LADY, 1826–96

14312 **Higham, Charles.** Speranza and Swedenborg. N&Q ser9 7:287 Ap '01.

WILDE, OSCAR O'FLAHERTIE WILLS, 1856–1900

14313 **B., C.** Oscar Wilde's De profundis. N&Q ser10 4:168 Ag '05; W. F. Prideaux; S. Mason, *pseud.*; E. Menken *ib.* 4:233 S '05.

14314 **Mason, Stuart,** *pseud. of* **C. S. Millard.** Oscar Wilde bibliography. N&Q ser10 4:266 S '05; S. J. A. F. *ib.* 5:12 Ja '06; S. J. A. F.; W. P. Courtney 5:133 F '06; C. Clarke 5:176–7 Mr '06; S. Mason 5:238–9,313 Mr,Ap '06; T. Bayne; S. Mason 5:355 My '06; 6:296–7 Oc '06; 7:13 Ja '07; 11:254 Mr '09.

14315 **Ross, Robert.** An American edition of Oscar Wilde's works. [Complete works]. TLS 28 Je '07:206; R. Le Gallienne *ib.* 3 Oc '07:299; R. Ross 10 Oc '07:307.

14316 **Mason, Stuart,** *pseud. of* **C. S. Millard.** The Stetson collection of Oscar Wilde. TLS 13 My '20:303.

14317 **Hutchison, W. A.** Oscar Wilde's Salome. [1907]. N&Q ser12 10:329 Ap '22.

14318 **Millard, Christopher S.** [and] **Lagos,** *pseud.* Wilde: The picture of Dorian Gray. [Undated ed.]. Bib N&Q 2no2:8 F '36. [Sg.: C. S. M.]

14319 **Wilde:** Picture of Dorian Gray, New York, 1890. [Variant states]. Bib N&Q 2no9·12 Ja '38; I. R. B[russel] *ib.* 2no12:2–3 My '39.

14320 **Horodisch, Abraham.** Oscar Wilde's Ballad of Reading gaol, a chapter in bibliographie raisonée. Folium 2no5/6:113–35 '52 facsims.

See also no.14323.

14321 **Wing, Donald G.** The Katherine S. Dreier collection of Oscar Wilde. Yale Univ Lib Gaz 28no2:82–7 Oc '53. facsim.

14322 **Horodisch, Abraham.** Oscar Wilde's Ballad of Reading gaol, a bibliographical study. New York, Aldus, 1954. 126p. illus., facsims. 25cm.

I. The translations.–II. The illustrated editions.–III. The American editions.

14323 —— Oscar Wilde's Ballad of Reading gaol, a chapter in bibliographie raisonnée, II. Folium 3no1/2:1–37 '54. facsims.

14324 **California. University. University at Los Angeles. William Andrews Clark memorial library.** Oscar Wilde and his literary circle; a catalog of manuscripts and letters in the William Andrews Clark memorial library. Comp. by John Charles Finzi. Berkeley, Published for the Library by the University of California pr.; London, C.U.P., 1957. [xvi,262p.] illus., ports., facsims. 26cm. (Reproduced from typewriting)

14325 **Sims, George.** Who wrote For love of the king? [Mrs. Chan Toon]. Bk Coll 7no3:269–77 '58.

14326 **Wyndham, Horace.** 'Edited by Oscar Wilde.' [The woman's world]. Twent Cent 163no975:435–40 My '58.

14327 **Ryals, Clyde deL.** Oscar Wilde's Salome. [Ms.]. N&Q 204:56–7 F '59.

14328 **Pinhorn, Malcolm.** An Oscar Wilde collection. [His own]. Priv Lib 3no1:2–5 Ja '60.

'Periodical and paper back publications' (p. 4–5)

14329 **Houdard, G. E.** Dorian Gray. [Ms.]. TLS 23 Je '61:387.

WILKES, JOHN, 1727–97

14330 **Bleackley, Horace W.** Wilkes's Essay on woman. N&Q ser10 9:442–3 Je '08; D. *ib.* 9:492 Je '08; W. F. Prideaux 10:90–1 Ag '08; H. W. Bleackley 11:493–4 Je '09.

14331 **Watson, Eric E.** John Wilkes and The essay on woman. [Ms.]. N&Q ser11 9:121–3, 143–5, 162–4, 183–5, 203–5, 222–3, 241–2 F, Mr '14.

14332 **McCracken, George.** John Wilkes. [Ed. of Catullus, 1788; and his library]. Philol Q 11no2:108–34 Ap '32. table.

14333 **Liebert, Herman W.** Ex libris John Wilkes. Yale Univ Lib Gaz 31no1:53 Jl '56. [Sg.: H. W. L.]

WILKINS, GEORGE, fl.1607

14334 **Blayney, Glenn H.** Variants in the first quarto of The miseries of inforst mariage. Library ser5 9no3:176–84 S '54. table.

14335 —— Wilkins's revisions in The miseries of inforst mariage. J Eng Germ Philol 56no1:23–41 Ja '57. table.

'Appendix: compositor analysis; evidence of running titles' (p. 39–41)

WILKINSON, ROBERT, fl.1607

14336 **Cordasco, Francesco G. M.** An eighteenth-century forgery of Robert Wilkinson's Merchant royall, 1607. Library ser5 5no4:274 Mr '51.

WILLIAMS, SIR CHARLES HANBURY, 1708–59

14337 **Todd, William B.** Three notes on Charles Hanbury Williams. Pa Bib Soc Am 47:159–60 '53. tables.

WILLIAMS, THOMAS, 1550?–1622?

14338 **Bowen, Geraint.** 'Lhyuran or Sacrauen o Benyd', Thomas Wiliems o Drefriu, un o weithiau defosiynol reciwsantiaid Cymru. [A short treatise of the sacrament of penance, the original of his lost translation]. (Biographica et bibliographica). Nat Lib Wales J 13no3:300–5 '64.

Summary in English (p. 305).

WILLIAMS, WILLIAM ('PANTYCELYN'), 1717–91

14339 **Davies, John H.** The printed works of Williams, Pantycelyn. Calvinistic Methodist Hist Soc J 3no2:59–66 D '17. [Sg.: J. H. D.]

14340 **Edwards, Huw.** Un o lyfrau Pantycelyn a'r cysylltiadau. [One of his books and its associations]. Calvinistic Methodist Hist Soc J 16no3:122–6 Medi '31.

14341 **Roberts, Gomer M.** Williams Pantycelyn ac Aleluja, 1744. [And John Morgan, ptr.]. Welsh Bib Soc J 6no3:113–25 Jl '45.

Resumé in English (p. 165–6)

14342 —— 'Atodiad IV: Llyfrgell Pantycelyn [William Williams' library]' *in* Y Per Ganiedydd Pantycelyn. Cyfrol I: Trem ar ei fywyd. Aberystwyth, 1949. p. [230]–1.

14343 —— Dau o Lyfrau Pantycelyn. (Nodiadau llyfryddol). Welsh Bib Soc J 7no4:196–7 Jl '53.

WILLIAMSON, HENRY, 1895–

14344 **Williamson,** Henry. Tarka the other. TLS 29 N '28:938.

14345 **Girvan, I. Waveney.** Henry Williamson. [Intended bibliogr.]. TLS 2 Ap '31:271.

WILMOT, JOHN, 2D EARL OF ROCHESTER, 1647–80

14346 **Harris, Brice.** Rochester's Remains and an old manuscript. N&Q 163:170–1 S '32.

14347 —— A Satyr on the court ladies. [Attrib. to Rochester and by G. Wharton]. TLS 20 Ag '31:633; G. Bullough *ib.* 18 F '32:112.

14348 **Wilkinson, Cyril H.** Lord Rochester. [Poems in The triumph of wit, 1688]. TLS 11 Jl '35:448.

14349 **Dale, Donald A.** Antwerpen editions of Rochester. N&Q 172:137 F '37; 172:206–7 Mr '37; 172:332 My '37.

14350 **Gray, Philip H.** Rochester's Poems on several occasions: new light on the dated and undated editions, 1680. Library ser4 19no2:185–97 S '38. facsims.

'Bibliography' (p. 196–7)

14351 **Pinto, Vivian de Sola** [and] **D. Dale.** The 1680 Antwerp edition of Rochester's Poems. Library ser4 20no1:105–6 Je '39.

14352 **Thorpe, James.** The earliest edition of Rochester's Poems. [1680]. Princeton Univ Lib Chron 8no4:172–6 Je '47. facsim.

14353 —— Rochester's Poems on several occasions. Princeton Univ Lib Chron 12no1:42–3 '50.

14354 **Hayward, John D.** Rochester rarities. Bk Coll 2no3:224 '53.

14355 **Paden, W. D.** Rochester's Satyr! Bks & Libs at Kansas 1no3:8–11 Ap '53.

14356 **A Rochester** poem. [Artemisa to Cloe, 1679]. Bod Lib Rec 4no4:183–4 Ap '53.

14357 **Todd, William B.** The 1680 editions of Rochester's Poems, with notes on earlier texts. Pa Bib Soc Am 47:43–58 '53. diagr., tables.

'Check-list of separate texts in the British museum and Bodleian libraries' (p. 50–6); 'Collation of variants' (p. 56–8)

14357a **Pinto, Vivian de Sola.** A poem attributed to Rochester. [Ms. of Directions for a minister of state]. TLS 5 N '54:705.

14358 **Hook, Lucyle.** The publication date of Rochester's Valentinian. Huntington Lib Q 19no4:401–7 Ag '56.

14359 **Vieth, David M.** The text of Rochester and the editions of 1680. Pa Bib Soc Am 50:243–63 '56. diagr., table.

14360 —— Two Rochester songs. N&Q 201:338–9 Ag '56.

14361 —— Order of contents as evidence of authorship: Rochester's Poems of 1680. Pa Bib Soc Am 53:293–308 '59. table.

14362 —— A textual paradox: Rochester's To a lady in a letter. [Ms.]. Pa Bib Soc Am 54:147–62 '60.

14363 —— An unsuspected cancel in Tonson's 1691 Rochester. [Poems, &c. on several occasions]. Pa Bib Soc Am 55:130–3 '61. diagr.

14364 **Thomas, D. S.** Prosecutions of Sodom: or, The quintessence of debauchery, and Poems on several occasions by the E of R, 1689–1690 and 1693. Library ser5 24no1:51–5 Mr '69.

WILSON, ANGUS FRANK JOHNSTONE, 1913–

14365 **McDowell, Frederick P. W.** The Angus Wilson collection. Bks at Iowa 10:9–23 Ap '69. facsim.

14366 —— and **E. Sharon Graves.** The Angus Wilson manuscripts in the University of Iowa libraries. Iowa City, Friends of the University of Iowa libraries, 1969. 16p. facsims. 23cm. Covertitle.

Rev: TLS 11 S '69:1008; Pa Bib Soc Am 67:95 '73

WILSON, ARTHUR, 1595–1652

14367 **Roberts, William.** Arthur Wilson's play The Swisser. [Ms.]. Athenæum 3929:219–20 F '03. [Sg.: W. R.]

14368 **Bald, R. Cecil.** Arthur Wilson's The inconstant lady. [Mss.]. Library ser4 18no3:287–313 D '37. facsims.

WILSON, JOHN, 1595–1674

14369 **Crum, Margaret C.** A manuscript of John Wilson's songs. Library ser5 10no1:55–7 Mr '55.

WILSON, JOHN, 1799–1870

14370 **G., A. B.** John Wilson mss. N&Q ser11 1:464–5 Je '10.

WILSON, ROBERT, d.1600

14371 **Mann, Irene.** A political cancel in The coblers prophesie. Library ser4 23no2/3:94–100 S/D '42. table.

14372 —— The copy for the 1592 quarto of The three ladies of London. Philol Q 23no1:86–9 Ja '44.

14373 —— The Dibelius edition of The coblers prophesie. N&Q 189:48–50 Ag '45.

14374 —— Notes on the Malone society reprint of The cobler's prophecy. Library ser4 26no2/3:181–9 S/D '45. tables.

14375 **Nathanson, Leonard.** Variants in Robert Wilson's The three lords. Library ser5 13no1:57–9 Mr '58.

14376 **Mithal, H. S. D.** The variants in Robert Wilson's The three lords of London. Library ser5 18no2:142–4 Je '63. tables.

WILSON, THOMAS, 1525?–81

14377 **Wagner, Russell H.** The text and editions of Wilson's Arte of rhetorique. Mod Lang N 44no7:421–8 N '29.

WINCHILSEA, ANNE FINCH, COUNTESS OF, 1661–1720 *see* Finch, Anne, countess of Winchilsea, 1661–1720.

WISE, THOMAS JAMES, 1859–1937

14378 **A book** hunter's spoils. [Wise's libr.]. Bkworm 5no59:329–33 Oc '92.

14379 **Kingsland, William G.** Privately printed books. Bkworm 7no82:289–93 S '94.

14380 **Roberts, William.** Mr. Thomas J. Wise. (Book collectors of to-day). Bkworm 7no79:193–200 Je '94. facsims. [Sg.: W. R.]

14381 **Wheeler, Harold F. B.** The Ashley library. (Notable private collections, no.1). Biblioph 3no13:3–17 Mr '09. port., facsims.

14382 **Sermones,** *pseud.* Mr. Thomas J. Wise. (Books and the man, no.22). Bkmns J 3no69:289 F '21. port.

14383 **Olla** podrida . . . First problems. [Swinburne and Wise]. Bkmns J new ser 8no20:49 My '23.

14384 **Gibson, Strickland.** The Ashley library. Bod Q Rec 4no40:75–6 Ja '24.

14385 **Bay, J. Christian.** The minority's opinion. [On the Carter-Pollard disclosures]. Am Bk Coll 5no10:297–8 Oc '34.

14386 **Carter** discovery stirs bibliographical world. Pub Wkly 125no22:2069 Je '34.

14387 **Carter, John W.** and **H. G. Pollard.** An enquiry into the nature of certain nineteenth century pamphlets. London, Constable; New York, C. Scribner's; Toronto, Macmillan, 1934. (Repr. New York, Haskell house, 1971). xii,400p. illus., facsims. 23cm.

> Part I: Deduction. The origin and early stages of the investigation.–The Sonnets from the Portuguese.–The need for positive evidence.–The analysis of the paper.–The typographical evidence.–Further tests.–Summary of proved conclusions.–Part II: Reconstruction. The modern first edition market, 1885–1895.–The forger's method.–Establishing the pedigrees.–Marketing the forgeries.–Part III: Dossiers. Matthew Arnold.–Elizabeth Barrett Browning.–Robert Browning.–Charles Dickens.–George Eliot.–Rudyard Kipling.–William Morris.–Dante Gabriel Rossetti.–John Ruskin.–Robert Louis Stevenson.–Algernon Charles Swinburne.–Alfred, lord Tennyson.–W. M. Thackeray.–William Wordsworth.–Edmund Yates.–Appendix I. Census of copies of the Reading Sonnets.–Appendix II. Mr. Griffin's purchases.–Stop-press.

> *Rev*: TLS 5 Jl '34:472; T. J. Wise *ib.* 12 Jl '34:492; H. E. Gorfin; J. D. Hayward; J. H. Stonehouse 19 Jl '34:511; J. W. Carter 26 Jl '34; lord Esher 23 Ag '34:577; F. L. Wise 30 Ag '34:589; J. H. A. Sparrow Spectator 153:20 '34; S. Mitchell New Eng Q 7:602–6 '34; D. A. Randall Pub Wkly 126:54–6 '34; A. W. P[ollard] Library ser4 15:379–84 '34; C. B. Tinker Saturday R Lit 11:45–6 '34; M. J. MacManus Dublin Mag 9:52 '34; A. J. A. Symons Bk Coll Q 15:1–16 '34; M. D. Zabel Mod Philol 32:335–6 '35.

14388 **The greatest** rare book sensation. Am Bk Coll 5no8/9:241–4 Ag/S '34.

14389 [**Haraszti, Zoltán**]. The biggest fraud in the history of book collecting. More Bks Boston Pub Lib Bull 9no7:268–71 S '34.

14390 —— A check list of the forged 19th century pamphlets in American libraries. [T. W. Koch: compilation in preparation]. More Bks Boston Pub Lib Bull 9no10:407 D '34.

14391 —— The forged nineteenth-century pamphlets. More Bks Boston Pub Lib Bull 9no8:310–11 Oc '34.

14392 **Nineteenth-**century pamphlets. (Notes on sales). TLS 2 Ag '34:544.

14393 **Symons, Albert J. A.** The nineteenth century forgeries. Bk Coll Q 15:1–16 Jl/S '34.

14394 **Wells, Gabriel.** The Carter-Pollard disclosures. Garden City, N.Y., Doubleday, Doran, 1934. 13p. + tipped-in 'Postscript'. 22cm.

14395 **Wise, Frances L.** Mr. T. J. Wise. [Terminates following correspondence]. TLS 30 Ag '34:589.

14396 **Wise, Thomas J.** Nineteenth-century forgeries. TLS 12 Jl '34:492; H. E. Gorfin; J. W. Carter; J. H. Stonehouse *ib.* 9 Jl '34:511; J. W. Carter 26 Jl '34:528; [O. S. B. Brett], viscount Esher 23 Ag '34:577.

14397 **Carter, John W.** The 19th century pamphlet forgeries, an early reference. Pub Wkly 127no6:719–21 F '35.

14398 [**Haraszti, Zoltán**]. Who is the villain of the pamphlet forgeries? [Largely quotes McKerrow's Library rev. of *no.*14387]. More Bks Boston Pub Lib Bull 10no2:65–6 F '35.

14399 **Hopkins, Frederick M.** Victorian forged pamphlets. [Rev. of Baughman's Some Victorian forged rarities]. Pub Wkly 130no3:200–3 Jl '36.

Kernless letters f and j.–Other new suspects.–Alaric at Rome.

14400 **The Ashley** library. [Acquired by B.M.]. TLS 18 S '37:680.

14401 **Ashley** library for the nation. (Notes and news). Bull John Rylands Lib 21no2:307–9 Oc '37.

14402 **Carter, John W.** The puzzle of Thomas J. Wise. (Old & rare books). Pub Wkly 131no22:2213–14 My '37.

14403 **Simpson, Percy.** The late T. J. Wise. Bod Q Rec 8no94:375–6 '37.

14404 **Grant, Julius.** Analytical methods in the dating of books and documents. [Mainly in relation to Wise forgeries]. Nature 142no3588:239–41 Ag '38.

14405 **Marsden, Wilfred A.** The Ashley library. Brit Mus Q 12no1:20–1 Ja '38.

14406 **Partington, Wilfred G.** Forging ahead; the true story of the upward progress of Thomas James Wise, prince of book collectors, bibliographer extraordinary and otherwise. New York, G. P. Putnam's [1939]. xv,315p. ports., facsims. 23cm.

1. Introducing the secret emperor of book forgers and some of his forerunners.–2. Early and eventful years.–3. Robert Browning, his Pauline and other affairs.–4. Wordsworth adventures and a new fake revealed.–5. Shelley stories: the pirate in full sail.–6. Revelations of the contemporary diary of mr. Y.Z.–7. Women, wine, & friends; the roles of Buxton Forman and Edmund Gosse.–8. Marriage, secret publishing, and Ruskin ruses.–9. Three men and a boy.–10. Ruskin's romance and the archivist's disillusion.–11. Remarriage, and the writing on the wall.–12. The trio at The pines and the secrets of the Vatican Venus.–13. Threats, counter-threats, and more mysteries illumined.–14. Paying off old scores and finding a scapegoat.–15. Revelations grave and gay.–16. War and exploitation.–17. Portrait of a dictator.–18. Firsts and super-firsts.–19. Byron romantics.–20. A revised story about mrs. Browning's love sonnets.–21. The exposure and some surprising sequels.–22. Why were the forgeries done?–Appendix: The bibliography of the bibliographer.

Rev: J. W. Carter Pub Wkly 136:1974–5 '39; F. B. Adams N.Y. Times Bk R 29 Oc '39:10.

14407 **Ratchford, Fannie E.** The Wise forgeries. Southwest R 25no4:363–77 Jl '40.

14408 —— Thomas J. Wise to John Henry Wrenn on nineteenth-century bibliography. Pa Bib Soc Am 36:215–28 '42.

14409 ——, *ed.* Letters of Thomas J. Wise to John Henry Wrenn, a further inquiry into the guilt of certain nineteenth-century forgers. New York, A. A. Knopf, 1944. xiv,591,xvip. ports., facsims. 24cm.

A further inquiry. . . . : The Wrenn library comes to Texas.–Wise's letters follow, and are sealed by their writer.–Thomas J. Wise, collector and publisher.–The Wise–Wrenn friendship.–Letters read.–Carter and Pollard's exposé.–Thomas J. Wise convicted as forger.–Wise's defence.–Letters re-read.–Wise's accomplices and confederates.–The Wrenn library evaluated.–A selection from Thomas J. Wise's letters to John Henry Wrenn.–Appendixes: I. A list of the forgeries in the Wrenn library, with purported sources and dates of acquisition.–II. Idylls of the hearth, reprinted from the Southwest review.

Rev: D. A. Randall N.Y. Times Bk R 17 D '44:3; R. M. Smith Pub Wkly 146:2385–8 '44; W. A. Jackson Pa Bib Soc Am 39:169–71 '45; C. J. Weber Mod Lang N 60:347–8 '45; D. G. Wing Yale R 33:757–9 '45; G. T. Goodspeed Am Merc 175:137 '45; L. Trilling Nation 160:47–8 '45; A. Sampley Sewanee R 30:203–5 '45; TLS 28 Apr '45:200; E. P. Goldschmidt *ib.* 12 My '45:223; J. W. Carter and H. G. Pollard 14 Jl '45:331; F. E. Ratchford 21 Jl '45:343.

14410 **Carter, John W.** Thomas J. Wise and his forgeries. Atlantic Mnthly 175no2:93–100 F '45; [Summary] Pub Wkly 147:948 F '45.

14411 **Goldschmidt, Ernst P.** The Wise forgeries. TLS 12 My '45:223; J. W. Carter and H. G. Pollard *ib.* 14 Jl '45:331; Fannie E. Ratchford 21 Jl '45:343.

14412 **Raymond, William O.** The forgeries of Thomas J. Wise and their aftermath. J Eng Germ Philol 44no3:229–38 Jl '45.

> Repr. in his The infinite moment and other essays. [Toronto, 1950]. (2d ed. 1965). p. [176]–92.

14413 **Ratchford, Fannie E.** A review of reviews. Univ Texas Lib Chron 1no4:3–32 '45; 2no1:21–55 '46. facsims.

14414 **Blunden, Edmund C.** Book forgeries: An enquiry re-read. TLS 28 S '46:472; A. Smith ib. 19 Oc '46:507; W. O. Raymond 14 D '46:620.

14415 **Carter, John W.** and **H. G. Pollard.** T. J. Wise and H. Buxton Forman; further light on the 19th-century pamphlets. TLS 1 Je '46:264. facsim.

14416 **Fletcher, Edward G.** The proof that Forman knew. Lib Chron Univ Texas 2no3:136–55 '46.

14417 **Partington, Wilfred G.** Thomas J. Wise in the original cloth; the life and record of the forger of the nineteenth-century pamphlets. With an appendix by George Bernard Shaw. London, R. Hale, 1946. (Repr. London, Dawsons, 1974). 372p. illus., ports. 23cm.

> 1. Introducing the secret emperor of book forgers and some of his forerunners.–2. Early and eventful years.–3. Robert Browning, his Pauline, and other affairs.–4. The Lake poets: Lyrical ballads faked.–5. Shelley stories: the pirate in full sail.–6. Revelations of the contemporary diary of mr. Y.Z.–7. The roles of Harry Buxton Forman and sir Edmund Gosse.–8. Marriage, secret publishing, and Ruskin ruses.–9. Three men and a boy.–10. Endings sweet & bitter: first doubts of certain XIXth century pamphlets.–11. Re-marriage, and the writing on the wall.–12. The two Swinburnes: surprises in the poet's study.–13. Watts-Dunton's surrender: more secrets of The Pines Venus.–14. Paying off old scores and finding a scapegoat.–15. Revelations grave and gay.–16. Joseph Conrad: Wise takes a *Chance*.–17. Portrait of a dictator.–18. His Magnum opus, super-firsts, and high honours.–19. Byron romantics.–20. The pretty tangle of mrs. Browning's love sonnets untangled.–21. The exposure and some surprising sequels. 22. Why the forgeries were done.–Appendix I: Notes by George Bernard Shaw, with the author's footnote replies.–Appendix II: The bibliography of the bibliographer.–Appendix III: Necrology.

> Rev: P. H. Muir Sunday Times 21 D '47:3; B. C. Cambridge J 1:321–2 '48; TLS 14 F '48:94; sir F. C. Francis Library ser5 3:152–4 '48; F. E. Ratchford Southwest R 33:304–10 '48.

14418 **Frey, Ellen F.** Thomas James Wise, friend of Duke university library: passages from his correspondence with professor Newman I. White, compiled. . . . Lib N Duke Univ Lib 18:3–15 Jl '47. facsims.

14419 **Ratchford, Fannie E.,** ed. Between the lines; letters and memoranda interchanged by H. Buxton Forman and Thomas J. Wise. Austin, University of Texas pr., 1947. xii,38p. + 2 fold.facsims. facsims. 24cm.

> The introductory essay.–The packet opened.–Part I. Holograph manuscript of The building of the idylls by H. Buxton Forman.–Part II. Galley-proof . . .–Part III. Page-proof. . . .–Part IV. Letters and memoranda interchanged.–Part V. Forman's penciled notes on . . . The true and the false. Proof of Wise's contribution to Tennysoniana. Two sets of the published sheets of The building of the idylls.

> Rev: N&Q 192:22 '47.

14420 **Carter, John W.** and **H. G. Pollard.** The firm of Charles Ottley, Landon & co.; footnote to An enquiry. London, R. Hart-Davis; New York, C. Scribner's, 1948. 95p. facsims. 18cm.

> Introduction.–1. The four pamphlets.–2. The official story examined.–3. The Redway editions of A word for the navy.–4. Wise and the Redway editions.–5. Conclusion.– Chronology.

14421 —— [**Same**]: Corrections & additions, 1967. 4p. 18cm.

> *Rev*: Sir F. C. Francis Library ser5 3:152–4 '48; P. Brooks N.Y. Times Bk R 3 Jl '49:14; H. G. Dick Ninet Cent Fict 3:243 '49; J. E. Morpurgo Observer 20 Mr '49:3.

14422 **Draper, John W.** [and] **Fannie E. Ratchford.** Thomas J. Wise and the Wrenn Catalogue. Mod Lang N 63no2:135–9 F '48.

14423 **Partington, Wilfred G.** Follies of the Wise. TLS 6 Mr '48:135; W. R. Rutland *ib*. 20 Mr '48:163; W. G. Partington 10 Ap '48:205; V. Baddeley 17 Ap '48:219; W. G. Partington 22 My '48:289.

14424 **Referee,** *pseud.* Mr. T. J. Wise. Hist & Bib 1:47–9 Ap '48.

14425 **Tragedy** and twitter: mr. T. J. Wise. Hist & Bib 2:122–7 Ag '48.

14426 **Altick, Richard D.** 'The case of the curious bibliographers' *in* The scholar adventurers. New York, 1950. [And in reprs.]. p. 37–64.

14427 **Clemens, Cyril.** Thomas James Wise: master literary forger. Hobbies 56no6:127–8 Ag '51.

14428 **Carter, John W.** Thomas J. Wise's Verses, 1882 & 1883. (Query no.36). Bk Coll 2no2:158–9 '53; sir M. P. Pariser *ib*. 2no4:283 '53.

14429 **Baughman, Roland.** The peccancies of T. J. Wise, et al.; some aftermaths of the exposure. Columbia Lib Columns 3no3:12–28 My '54. illus., facsim.

14430 **Doughty, Oswald.** T. J. Wise again. TLS 2 N '56:649.

14431 **Foxon, David F.** Another skeleton in Thomas J. Wise's cupboard. [Mutilation of B.M. copies of early plays]. TLS 19 Oc '56:624.

14432 **Alden, John E.** T. J. Wise and Tales of the wild and the wonderful. (Query 104). Bk Coll 8no3:300–3 '59; J. Rubinstein *ib*. 8no3:303–6 '59.

14433 **Bissell, E. E.** Gosse, Wise and Swinburne. (Note 115). Bk Coll 8no3:297–9 '59.

14434 **Carter, John W.** Thomas J. Wise and 'Richard Gullible'. [R. Jennings]. (Note 110). Bk Coll 8no2:182–3 '59.

14435 **Foxon, David F.** Thomas J. Wise and the pre-restoration drama; a study in theft and sophistication. London, Bibliographical society, 1959. viii,41p. facsims. 25cm. (Bib Soc Pubs Suppl 19)

Thomas J. Wise and the pre-restoration drama.–Plays with stolen leaves.–Appendix I: Stolen leaves still untraced.–Appendix II: Other made-up Ashley plays. (*See also no.*14440)

Rev: TLS 5 Je '59:344; M. Linton Theat Notebk 14:31 '59; H. G. Pollard Bk Coll 8:319–23 '59.

14436 **Todd, William B.,** *ed.* Thomas J. Wise; centenary studies. Essays by John Carter, Graham Pollard, William B. Todd. Austin, University of Texas pr.; Edinburgh, T. Nelson [1959]. 128p. port., facsim., table. 24cm. (Texas Quarterly. Supplement)

Thomas J. Wise in perspective; an address given at the University of Texas on All fools' day, 1959, by John Carter.–Thomas J. Wise: Letters to J. E. Cornish 30 April–22 August, 1894, on various Morris, Rossetti, Ruskin, and Swinburne forgeries. With commentary by William B. Todd.–Thomas J. Wise: Letter to sir Edmund Gosse, 16 February, 1897, on a number of Tennyson forgeries. With commentary by Graham Pollard.–The case of The devil's due; another Swinburne pamphlet condemned as a forgery, by Graham Pollard.–Thomas J. Wise: Introduction to the Browning library, 1929; The master concocts a tale. With commentary by William B. Todd.–The scope for further typographical analysis, by Graham Pollard.–A handlist of Thomas J. Wise, by William B. Todd.

Rev: W. White Am Bk Coll 11:4 '60; A. N. L. Munby New Statesman 60:621 '60; TLS 14 Oc '60:667; R. Baughman Bk Coll 9:232,235–6 '60.

14437 **Mayfield, John S.** New crimes of Thomas James Wise. Am Bk Coll 10no8:17–18 Ap '60.

14438 **Rogers, Neville.** Thomas Wise and R. W. Chapman. TLS 28 Oc '60:693; 25 N '60:759.

14439 **Adams, Donald K.** 'A certain 4to Elegy'. Pa Bib Soc Am 55:229–31 '61.

14440 **Foxon, David F.** and **W. B. Todd.** Thomas J. Wise and the pre-restoration drama: a supplement. Library ser5 16no4:287–93 D '61.

14441 **Re-shuffle** or declare? TLS 3 F '61:73; D. F. Foxon *ib.* 17 F '61:105; W. B. Todd 3 Mr '61:137.

14442 **Singer, George C.** Who was mr. Y. Z.? (Query 152). Bk Coll 11no3:353 '62; J. W. Carter *ib.* 11no4:484 '62.

14443 —— T. J. Wise and the technique of promotion. [And J. C. Thomson]. (Note 184). Bk Coll 11no3:347–8 '62; J. W. Carter *ib.* 11no4:480–2 '62; M. Trevanion, *pseud.* 12no1:74 '63; J. W. Carter 12no2:202 '63.

14444 **The case** against Wise. TLS 21 D '62:996; R. Binfield *ib.* 1 F '63:77.

14445 **Carter, John W.** Thomas J. Wise's descriptive formula. (Query 181). Bk Coll 13no2:214–15 '64; M. Trevanion, *pseud., ib.* 13no3:355–6 '64.

14446 —— Wise after the event. [Pariser collection exhibited at Manchester]. TLS 5 Mr '64:195; D. I. Colley *ib.* 27 Ag '64:771.

14447 **Davison, J. A.** Wise on show. [Pariser collection exhibited at Manchester]. TLS 24 S '64:886; sir M. P. Pariser *ib.* 1 Oc '64:899.

14448 **Moran, James.** Thomas J. Wise and his printers. Black Art 3no3:67–80 '64/5. facsim., map.

14449 **Pariser, sir Maurice P.** H. Buxton Forman and T. J. Wise. TLS 23 Jl '64:649; J. W. Carter and H. G. Pollard *ib.* 18 Mr '65:220.

14449a **Pedley, Katherine G.** Moriarty in the stacks; the nefarious adventures of Thomas J. Wise. Berkeley, Calif., Peacock pr., 1966. 27p. port. 19cm.

14450 **Gullible, Richard,** *pseud. of* **R. Jennings.** An enquiry into An enquiry. Bk Coll 16no2:186–93 '67.

14451 **Kendall, Lyle H.** The not-so-gentle art of puffing: William G. Kingsland and Thomas J. Wise. Pa Bib Soc Am 62:25–37 '68.

14452 **Todd, William B.** Some Wiseian ascriptions in the Wrenn catalogue. Library ser5 23no2:95–107 Je '68. tables.

14453 **Carter, John W.** Wise forgeries in Doves bindings. (Query 226). Bk Coll 17no3:352–3 '68.

14454 **Barnes, Warner.** Wiseana: correspondence between Thomas J. Wise and A. J. Armstrong. . . . (Notes and queries). Browning Newsl 2:34 Ap '69.

14455 **Carter, John W.** Thomas J. Wise's Verses, 1882/1883. Library ser5 24no3:246–9 S '69.

14456 **Moran, James.** How T. J. Wise was able to deceive his printers. Gutenberg Jahrb 1969:161–7 '69. map.

14457 **Smith, Simon H. Nowell-.** T. J. Wise as bibliographer. Library ser5 24no2:129–41 Je '69.

14458 —— Wise, Smart & Moody. (Note 319). Bk Coll 18no4:386–7 '69.

WISHART, BP. GEORGE, 1599–1671

14459 **Weir, John L.** Mark Napier on Montrose. [Wishart's . . . De rebus . . . Caroli. . .]. N&Q 191:56 Ag '46; R. C. Jarvis *ib.* 191:171–2 Oc '46; J. L. Weir 192:39–40 Ja '47.

14460 **MacKenna, R. O.** Memoirs of James, marquis of Montrose. [The genesis of a ghost]. Biblioth 1no1:27–8 '56.

WITHER, GEORGE, 1588–1667

14461 **Eames, Wilberforce.** The first American edition of Wither's poems and Bacon's Essays. Bibliographer 1no1:11–21 Ja '02. facsims.

14462 **Simpson, Percy.** Walkley's piracy of Wither's poems in 1620. Library ser4 6no3:271–7 D '25.

14463 **Haines, J. W.** George Wither: Poems, in 3 vols. [Date of facsimile repr.]. Bib N&Q 2no1:8 Ja '36.

14464 **Kirschbaum, Leo.** Walkley's supposed piracy of Wither's Workes in 1620. Library ser4 19no3:339–46 D '38.

14465 **Templeman, William D.** Some commendatory verses by George Wither. N&Q 183:365–6 D '42.

14466 **Kendall, Lyle H.** Notes on some works attributed to George Wither. R Eng Stud new ser 5no20:390–4 Oc '54.

Genuine works by Wither.–A probable Wither item.–Works composed by other hands.

14467 —— George Wither's Three private meditations. (Note 87). Bk Coll 6no4:405–6 '57.

14468 —— An unrecorded prose pamphlet by George Wither. [A declaration of major George Wither, 1661–3]. Huntington Lib Q 20no1:190–5 F '57.

14469 **French, J. Milton.** Thorn-Drury's notes on George Wither. Huntington Lib Q 23no4:379–88 Ag '60.

Autographs.–Manuscripts.–Unique(?) copies.–A poem by Wither.–A poem to Wither.

14470 **Pritchard, Allan.** George Wither's quarrel with the stationers; an anonymous reply to The schollers purgatory. Stud Bib 16:27–42 '63.

14471 —— A manuscript of George Wither's Psalms. Huntington Lib Q 27no1:73–7 N '63.

14472 **Carlson, Norman E.** Wither and the stationers. Stud Bib 19:210–15 '66.

WODEHOUSE, SIR PELHAM GRENVILLE, 1881–1975

14473 **Magee, David B.** On collecting P. G. Wodehouse. Bk Club California Q Newsl 29no2:29–35 '64.

14474 **Lewis, A. Jenny** [i.e. **Stratford**]. Brinkmanship at Blandings. [Ms.]. Brit Mus Q 30no3/4:98–9 '66.

WOLCOT, JOHN, 1738–1819 *see* Pindar, Peter, *pseud.*

WOLFE, CHARLES, 1791–1823

14475 **Bayne, Thomas.** The burial of sir John Moore. N&Q ser9 4:21–2 Jl '99; 4:177 Ag '99.

WOOD, ELLEN (PRICE), (MRS. HENRY WOOD), 1814–87

14476 **Sadleir, Michael T. H.** Bindings of mrs. Henry Wood's novels. (Bibliographical notes). TLS 8 F '36:120.

WOOD, JOHN GEORGE, 1827–89

14477 **Leston, D.** J. G. Wood. [His projected bibliogr.]. TLS 13 Mr '53:176.

WOOD, ROBERT, 1717?–71

14478 **Davison, J. A.** Robert Wood's essay on Homer. [Essay on the original genius of Homer]. TLS 18 Ap '52:265; C. B. Oldman; L. W. Hanson *ib.* 2 My '52:297.

WOODES, NATHANIEL, fl.1581

14479 **Jackson, William A.** Woodes's Conflict of conscience. TLS 7 S '33:592; sir W. W. Greg *ib.* 26 Oc '33:732; Celesta Wine 23 N '33:840.

WOODFORD, SAMUEL, 1636–1700

14480 **The Woodforde** family. [Exhibition]. (Notes on sales). TLS 2 Mr '33:152.

WOODWARD, HEZEKIAH, 1590–1675

14481 **Rhodes, Dennis E.** The authorship of The life and death of William Lawd, 1645. Library ser5 16no2:140–1 Je '61.

WOODWARD, PHILIP, c.1557–1610

14482 **Fr.** Philip Woodward. [St. Gregory's Dialogues]. Bod Lib Rec 2no16:3 Oc '41.

14483 **Allison, Antony F.** Notes on the authorship of three works against Thomas Bell. Library ser5 2no4:286–9 Mr '48.

14484 **Russell, G. H.** Philip Woodward: Elizabethan pamphleteer and translator. Library ser5 4no1:14–24 Je '49.

'Appendix . . . works discussed in the above paper' (p. 23–4)

WOOLF, ADELINE VIRGINIA (STEPHEN), 1882–1941

14485 **Brett, Oliver S. B., 3d viscount Esher.** Woolf: Common reader, first series. [Binding variants]. Bib N&Q 1no3:8 Ag '35. [Sg.: Esher.]

14486 **Lewis, A. Jenny** [i.e. **Stratford**]. From The hours to Mrs. Dalloway. [Ms.]. Brit Mus Q 28no1/2:15–18 '64.

WORDSWORTH, CHRISTOPHER, 1774–1846

14487 **Wordsworth, Jonathan.** Wordsworth letters. [Checklist]. TLS 8 My '59:273.

WORDSWORTH, WILLIAM, 1770–1850

14488 **Hutchinson, Thomas.** Notes on two recent editions of Wordsworth's poems. Acad 44:170–3 Ag '93; 44:211–14 S '93; 44:340–3 Oc '93; 44:391–2 N '93; 44:486–8 D '93.

I. The chronology of Wordsworth poems.–II. The collation of the text.

14489 **Campbell, James D.** The Philadelphia reprint of the Lyrical ballads. [1802]. Athenæum 3460:213–24 F '94. [Sg.: J. D. C.]

14490 **Hutchinson, Thomas.** The Eversley Wordsworth: errata in vol. II. Athenæum 3576:620 My '96; W. Knight; G. L. Craik ib. 3578:681–2 My '96; T. Hutchinson 3580:746 Je '96; 3584:35–6 Jl '96.

14491 **Roberts, William.** Books from Wordsworth's library. Athenæum 3579:714 My '96. [Sg.: W. R.]

14492 **White, W. Hale,** ed. A description of the Wordsworth & Coleridge manuscripts in the possession of mr. T. Norton Longman. London, Longmans, Green, 1897. (Repr. Norwood, Pa., Norwood editions, 1976). iv,72p. facsims. 32cm.

14493 **Potts, R. A.** Lyrical ballads, 1798. Athenæum 3716:51 Ja '99.

14494 —— The editio princeps of The convict, by W. Wordsworth. Athenæum 4007:209 Ag '04; 4009:272 Ag '04.

14495 **Prideaux, William F.** Lyrical ballads, 1798. N&Q ser10 2:228 S '04.

14496 **Cooper, Lane.** Wordsworth: variant readings. N&Q ser11 2:222–3 S '10; T. Bayne; C. C. B. ib. 2:294–5 Oc '10; L. Cooper 2:416 N '10; T. Bayne 2:476 D '10.

14497 **Simpson, Percy.** Wordsworth's punctuation. [The convention of Cintra]. TLS 6 Ja '16:9; The reviewer ib. 13 Ja '16:21; sir W. Raleigh; 'Stanley Hutton' 20 Ja '16:33; P. H. Wicksteed 27 Ja '16:45; C. Wordsworth 3 F '16:57; G. G. Wordsworth; A. C. Taylor 10 F '16:69.

14498 **Garrod, H. W.** A misprint in the text of Wordsworth. [Prelude, bk. XI]. TLS 1 My '19:238.

14499 **Wordsworth** as a book collector. (Notes on sales). TLS 27 My '20:340.

14500 **Morley, Edith J.** A manuscript poem of Wordsworth. [To the moon]. Mod Lang R 19no2:211–14 Ap '24.

14501 **De Sélincourt, Ernest.** The composition of The prelude. TLS 19 Mr '25:196.

14502 —— Notes in correction of the text of Wordworth's Prelude. R Eng Stud 1no2:151–8 Ap '25. (Repr. Norwood, Pa., Norwood editions, 1976)

14503 **Winship, George P.** Oxford vs. Harvard. [Assessment of Wordsworth holdings]. Harvard Lib N [2no]14:33–7 Mr '25. [Sg.: G. P. W.]

14504 **Hughes, Helen S.** Two Wordsworthian chapbooks. Mod Philol 25no2:207–10 N '27.

14505 **Hughes, T. Cann.** Wordsworth's library. N&Q 153:243–4 Oc '27.

14506 **De Sélincourt, Ernest.** Wordsworth's Prelude. TLS 23 Ag '28:605.

14507 **Bell, sir Harold I.** Wordsworth and Coleridge manuscripts. [Lyrical ballads, 1800, mss.]. Brit Mus Q 6no3:74–5 D '31. [Sg: H. I. B.]

14508 **De Sélincourt, Ernest.** Early readings in The prelude. [Mss.]. TLS 12 N '31:886.

14509 **Hall, Bernard G.** Wordsworth emendations. TLS 21 My '31:408.

14510 **The Bristol** Lyrical ballads. [1798]. (Notes on sales). TLS 28 Ap '32:316.

14511 **Chapman, Robert W.** Lyrical ballads, 1800. Bk Coll Q 6:25–6 Ap/Je '32.

14512 **Macdonald, Hugh.** Lyrical ballads. TLS 17 Mr '32:202.

14513 **Wells, John E.** De Quincey's punctuation of Wordsworth's Cintra. [1809]. TLS 3 N '32:815.

14514 —— Variants in the Lyrical ballads of 1798. TLS 23 Je '32:464.

14515 **Broughton, Leslie N.,** *ed.* Wordsworth and Reed; the poet's correspondence with his American editor, 1836–1850. Ithaca, N.Y., Cornell U.P.; London, H. Milford, O.U.P., 1933. xviii,288p. illus., port. 22cm.

   Rev: TLS 14 S '33:606; F. S. Arnold Am Church Mnthly 34:174–7 '33; N.Y. Times Bk R 4 Je '33:10; Birmingham Post 25 Jl '33; P. S. A. Union Alumni Mnthly 22:234 '33; G. R. B. R. Boston Transcript 1 Jl '33; Living Church 16 D '33.

14516 **McAdam, Edward L.** The publication of the Lyrical ballads, 1800. Yale Univ Lib Gaz 8no1:43–6 Jl '33.

14517 **Wells, John E.** Lyrical ballads, a variant? [1798]. R Eng Stud 9no34: 199–201 Ap '33.

14518 **McMaster, Helen.** Wordsworth's copy of Vaughan. TLS 12 Ap '34:262.

14519 **Evans, Benjamin I., baron Evans of Hungershall.** Variants in Wordsworth's Poems, 1807. TLS 13 Je '36:494.

14520 **Morris, Joseph E.** Wordsworth's copy of Modern painters. N&Q 173:366 N '37; L. R. M. Strachan *ib.* 173:409 D '37.

14521 **Whicher, George F.** Notes on a Wordsworth collection. [Amherst]. Coloph new ser 2no3:367–80 Jl '37.

14522 **Christensen, Francis.** The date of Wordworth's The birth of love. [1802]. Mod Lang N 53no4:280–2 Ap '38.

14523 **Daniel, Robert W.** The publication of the Lyrical ballads. [1798]. Mod Lang R 33no4:406–10 Jl '38.

14524 **L., R.** Lyrical ballads, 1800. N&Q 174:349 My '38.

14525 **Connecticut college for women,** NEW LONDON. **Palmer library.** An exhibition of first and other early editions of the works of William Wordsworth . . . lent from . . . John Edwin Wells . . . New London, Conn., 1938. 8l. 29cm. (Reproduced from typewriting)

14526 **Wells, John E.** Lyrical ballads, 1800: cancel leaves. Pub Mod Lang Assn 53no1:207–29 Mr '38.

14527 —— Wordsworth's Lyrical ballads, 1820. Philol Q 17no4:398–402 Oc '38.

14528 —— Lyrical ballads 1800: a paste-in. Library ser4 19no4:486–91 Mr '39.

14529 **Meyerstein, Edward H. W.** Wordsworth and Coleridge. [Beauty and moonlight ms.]. TLS 29 N '41:596; 6 D '41:611; J. R. Sutherland *ib.* 6 D '41:611; E. de Sélincourt 20 D '41:643.

14530 **Simpson, Percy.** An emendation in the text of Wordsworth. [The excursion]. R Eng Stud 18no70:228 Ap '42.

14631 **Wells, John E.** Lyrical ballads, 1798. TLS 17 Ja '42:36.

14532 —— Wordsworth's To the queen, 1846. Philol Q 21no4:415–19 Oc '42.

14533 **Noyes, Russell.** The Oscar L. Watkins Wordsworth–Coleridge collection. Indiana Q Bkmn 1no1:18–26 Ja '45. illus.

14534 **Meyerstein, Edward H. W.** Wordsworth's Ode. [Text]. TLS 12 Oc '46:500.

14535 **Peacock, Markham.** Variants to the Preface to Lyrical ballads. Mod Lang N 61no3:175–7 Mr '46.

14536 **Bond, William H.** Wordsworth's Thanksgiving ode, an unpublished postscript. Harvard Lib Bull 1no1:115–16 '47.

14537 **Wynne, Marjorie G.** Commemoration of the one-hundredth anniversary of the death of William Wordsworth. [Exhibition]. Yale Univ Lib Gaz 25no1:38–9 Jl '50. [Sg.: M. G. W.]

14538 **Zall, Paul M.** Wordsworth and copyright. TLS 16 Oc '53:668; J. J. Auchmuty *ib.* 20 N '53:743.

14539 **Foxon, David F.** The printing of Lyrical ballads, 1798. Library ser5 9no4:221–41 D '54. facsims., diagrs.

14540 **Brown, T. Julian.** Wordsworth and his amanuenses. (English literary autographs, XIII). Bk Coll 4no1:49–50 '55. facsims.

14541 **Owen, W. J. B.** The text of Wordsworth's prose. N&Q 200:37 Ja '55.

14542 **Raysor, Thomas M.** Wordsworth's early drafts of The ruined cottage in 1797–98. J Eng Germ Philol 55no1:1–7 Ja '55.

14543 **Todd, F. M.** Wordsworth's monody of Lamb; another copy. [Written after the death of Charles Lamb, 1836]. Mod Lang R 50no1:48–50 Ja '55.

14544 **Zall, Paul M.** Wordsworth and the Copyright act of 1842. Pub Mod Lang Assn 70no1:132–44 Mr '55.

See also no. 14549.

14545 **Owen, W. J. B.** The text of Wordsworth's Essay upon epitaphs. N&Q 201:214–15 My '56.

14546 **Schulze, Fritz W.** 'Wordsworthian and Coleridgian texts, 1784–1822, mostly unidentified or displaced' *in* Strena Anglica; [Festschrift für] Otto Ritter. Halle, 1956. p. [225]–58.

The Dirge and Collins' Odes.–Orpheus and Eurydice and the Aeneid translation.–Synthetic anacreontics.–Lewti.—The mss. of the Mathew elegies and Address to the scholars. . . .–Away away it is the air and The thorn.–The text history of The forsaken Indian woman.–Some notes on The ancyent marinere.–The Florentine sonnets.

14547 **Owen, W. J. B.** Costs, sales and profits of Longman's editions of Wordsworth. Library ser5 12no2:93–107 Je '57.

14548 [——]. Manuscript variants of Wordsworth's poems. N&Q 203:308–10 Jl '58.

14549 **Noyes, Russell.** Wordsworth and the Copyright act of 1842: addendum. Pub Mod Lang Assn 76no4:380–3 S '61.

14550 **Woof, R. S.** A misreading. [And C. Wordsworth's Address to silence]. TLS 6 Jl '62:493.

14551 **Crawford, Walter B.** A three-decker novel in Wordsworth's library, 1802. N&Q 209:16–17 Ja '64.

14552 **Little, G. L.** Wordsworth, Lockhart, Barron Field and the Copyright act. [1842]. N&Q 210:411–13 N '65.

14553 **Pottle, Frederick A.** An important addition to Yale's Wordsworth–Coleridge collection. [Duplicate of the second volume of the printer's copy for Lyrical ballads, 1802]. Yale Univ Lib Gaz 41no2:45–59 Oc '66. facsims.

WOTTON, SIR HENRY, 1568–1639

14554 **Conway, Agnes.** A new stanza to You meaner beauties of the night. TLS 4 S '24:540; G. E. Manwaring; Mabel E. Wotton *ib.* 25 S '24:596; A. E. H. Swaen 9 Oc '24:631; A. Conway 30 Oc '24:686; T. D. Cook; G. E. Manwaring 6 N '24:709–10; A. Conway 11 D '24:850; G. B. Verity 26 F '25:138.

14555 **Jackson, Holbrook.** The Reliquiæ Wottonianæ. Bibliophile's Almanack 1927:4–12 '27. facsim.

14556 **Leishman, J. B.** You meaner beauties of the night; a study in transmission and transmogrification. Library ser4 26no2/3:99–121 S/D '45. diagr.

14557 **Wolf, Edwin.** If shadows be a picture's excellence: an experiment in critical bibliography. Pub Mod Lang Assn 63no3:831–57 S '48. tables.

The poem.–The sources of the text.–The text of the poem and its variants.–Analysis of the text.–The interrelationship of the texts.–The cause of variants.

14558 **Main, C. F.** Wotton's The character of a happy life. [Mss.]. Library ser5 10no4:270–4 D '55.

14559 **FitzGerald, Maurice H.** Emendations to Wotton. TLS 23 D '60:829; C. O. Fox *ib.* 10 F '61:89.

WRANGHAM, FRANCIS, 1769–1842

14560 **Plomer, Henry R.** Bibliography. N&Q ser9 3:425–6 Je '99; W. C. B. *ib.* 3:492 Je '99.

14561 **Sadleir, Michael T. H.** Archdeacon Francis Wrangham, 1769–1842, and his books. Library ser4 17no2:129–30 S '36.

14562 —— 'The collector of books' *in* Archdeacon Francis Wrangham, 1769–1842. (Bib Soc Trans Suppl 12). [Oxford] 1937. p. 42–9. facsim.

14563 —— Archdeacon Francis Wrangham: a supplement. Library ser4 19no4:422–61 Mr '39.

14564 **Shelley, Philip A.** Archdeacon Wrangham's Poems. Library ser5 4no3:205–11 D '49.

14565 **Bloomfield, Barry C.** An unrecorded pamphlet by archdeacon Wrangham. [The life . . . of John . . . Lonsdale, n.d.]. (Note 203). Bk Coll 12no3:355 '63; C. B. L. Barr *ib.* 13no1:64–5 '64; 13no2:206 '64.

WRATISLAW, THEODORE, 1871–1933

14566 **Smith, Timothy d'A.** Theodore Wratislaw's Caprices, 1893. (Note 306). Bk Coll 18no1:90–2 '69.

WYATT, SIR THOMAS, 1503?–42

14567 **Utley, Francis L.** Wyatt as a Scottish poet. [Ms.]. Mod Lang N 60no2:106–11 F '45. tables.

14567a **Muir, Kenneth.** Wyatt's poems in Add. ms. 17492. N&Q 193:53–4 F '48; 193:124–5 Mr '48.

14567b **Harrier, Richard C.** Notes on the text and interpretation of sir Thomas Wyatt's poetry. N&Q 198:234–6 Je '53; K. Muir *ib.* 198:236 Je '53; J. C. Maxwell 198:361 Ag '53.

14568 **Hoeniger, F. David.** A Wyatt manuscript. N&Q 202:103–4 Mr '57. table.

14569 **Muir, Kenneth.** An unrecorded Wyatt manuscript. TLS 20 My '60:328; R. Southall *ib.* 27 My '60:337; K. Muir 3 Je '60:353; R. Southall 10 Je '60:369.

14570 **Tydeman, William M.** Wyatt's poems and the Blage manuscript; verbal resemblances. N&Q 208:293–4 Ag '63.

14571 **Huttar, Charles A.** Wyatt and the several editions of The court of Venus. Stud Bib 19:181–95 '66.

WYCHERLEY, WILLIAM, 1640?–1716

14572 **Haraszti, Zoltán.** Early editions of Wycherley's comedies. More Bks Boston Pub Lib Bull 9no2:45–58 F '34. facsim.

14573 **Vincent, Howard P.** William Wycherley's Miscellany poems. Philol Q 16no2:145–8 Ap '37.

14574 —— William Wycherley's Posthumous works. [Ed. by Theobald, 1728]. N&Q 185:12–13 Jl '43.

14575 **Megaw, Robert N. E.** The two 1695 editions of Wycherley's Country-wife. Stub Bib 3:252–3 '50/1.

14576 **Brown, T. Julian.** William Wycherley, 1640?–1716; sir John Vanburgh, 1664–1726. (English literary autographs, XLI). Bk Coll 11no1:63 '62. facsims.

WYNNE, THOMAS, 1627–92

14577 **Morgan, J. Hubert.** Nodiadau llyfryddol: Gwaith Thomas Wynne y Crynwer. Welsh Bib Soc J 3no7:290–9 Jl '30.

YATES, EDMUND, 1831–94

14578 **Carter, John W.** Edmund Yates: Mr. Thackeray, mr. Yates and the Garrick club. [4° ed., 1859?]. Bib N&Q 2no11:11 N '38; E. Schlengemann *ib.* 2no12:6 My '39.

YEATS, WILLIAM BUTLER, 1865–1939

14579 **MacKay, W. MacDonald.** Bibliography of W. B. Yeats. [Corrections to Bibliographies of modern authors]. (Correspondence). London Merc 2no10:463 Ag '20.

14580 **Alspach, Russell K.** Yeats's first two published poems. Mod Lang N 58no7:555–7 N '43.

14581 —— Two songs of Yeats's. [Red Hanrahan's song about Ireland; The song of wandering Aengus]. Mod Lang N 61no6:395–400 Je '46.

14582 **Freyer, Grattan.** W. B. Yeats. [Misprints]. TLS 20 Ap '46:187.

14583 **Auty, R. A.** Byzantium. [Text]. TLS 11 Ag '50:501; Gwendolen Murphy *ib.* 25 Ag '50:533; R. Murphy; M. Craig 1 S '50:549; Gwendolen Murphy; J. Christopherson 15 S '50:581; V. Watkins; B. Dobrée 22 S '50:597; Gwendolen Murphy 3 N '50:693.

14584 **Saul, George B.** Yeats and his poems. TLS 31 Mr '50:208; A. Wade *ib.* 7 Ap '50:215.

14585 **Friends of the Wellesley college library.** William Butler Yeats at Wellesley. [n.p., Wellesley] 1952. 22p. 23cm. (Bulletin, no.10). Covertitle.

14586 **Wit, Marion.** W. B. Yeats. [Additions to Wade's bibliography]. TLS 11 Ap '52:251.

14587 **Rubenstein, Jerome S.** Three misprints in Yeat's Collected poems. [1951]. Mod Lang N 70no3:184–7 Mr '55.

14588 **Books** and manuscripts of W. B. Yeats. [Exhibition in Trinity college, Dublin]. TLS 4 My '56:276.

14589 **Adams, Hazard.** The William Butler Yeats collection at Texas. Lib Chron Univ Texas 6no1:33–8 '57.

'Desiderata' (p. 37–8)

14590 **Alspach, Russell K.** Some textual problems in Yeats. Stud Bib 9:51–67 '57.

14591 **Saul, George B.** Prolegomena to the study of Yeats's poems. Philadelphia, University of Pennsylvania pr.; London, O.U.P., 1957. (Repr. New York, Octagon books, 1973). 196p. 21cm.

A note to which attention is solicited.–I. Divisions of Collected poems, 1951.—II. The individual poems.

Rev: T. J. B. Spencer Mod Lang R 53:626–7 '58; TLS 16 My '58:270; D. Donoghue Stud 48:106–7 '59; P. Ure R Eng Stud new ser 11:113–14 '60.

14592 —— Prolegomena to the study of Yeats's plays. Philadelphia, University of Pennsylvania pr. [1958]. (Repr. New York, Octagon books, 1971). 106p. 21cm.

'Corrigenda' *tipped in after TP.*

Prefatory note.–[Individual plays].–Appendix I: Notes on uncollected or unpublished drama.–Appendix II: Note on first American printing of definitive Collected plays.

Rev: Sarah Youngblood Bks Abroad 33:218–20 '58; TLS 24 Ap '59:239.

14593 —— W. B. Yeats: corrigenda. [To his Prolegomena]. N&Q 205:302–3 Ag '60.

14594 **Sidnell, M. J.** Manuscript versions of Yeats's The countess Cathleen. Pa Bib Soc Am 56:79–103 '62. tables.

14595 **Skelton, Robin.** Images of a poet: W. B. Yeats. A note on the exhibition held . . . 3 May to 3 June, 1961 . . . . Irish Bk 1no4:89–97 '62.

14596 **Mayhew, George P.** A corrected typescript of Yeats's Easter 1916. Huntington Lib Q 27no1:53–71 N '63.

14597 **Saddlemyer, Ann.** On Paragraphs from Samhain and some additional Yeats letters. (Bibliographical notes). Irish Bk 2no3/4:127–8 '63.

14598 **Skelton, Robin.** The first printing of W. B. Yeats's What then? (Bibliographical notes). Irish Bk 2no3/4:129–30 '63.

14599 **Brown, T. Julian.** William Butler Yeats, 1865–1939. (English literary autographs, XLIX). Bk Coll 13no1:53 '64. facsim.

14600 **Mortenson, Robert.** Yeats's Vision and The two trees. Stud Bib 17:220–2 '64.

14601 **Bradford, Curtis B.** Yeats at work. Carbondale, Southern Illinois U.P. [1965]. xix,407p. 24cm.

Preface.–Part one: Poems, an introduction.–Part two: Plays, an introduction.–Part three: Prose, an introduction.

Rev: J. Stallworthy R Eng Stud new ser 18:225–7 '67.

14602 **Monteiro, George.** Unrecorded variants in two Yeats poems. Pa Bib Soc Am 60:367–8 '66. tables.

14603 **Sidnell, M. J.** Manuscript versions of Yeat's The shadowy waters: an abbreviated description and chronology of the papers relating to the play in the National library of Ireland. Pa Bib Soc Am 62:39–57 '68; Lola L. Szladits Addenda *ib*. 62:614–17 '68. tables.

14604 **Lister, Raymond.** W. B. Yeats as an editor of William Blake. Blake Stud 1no2:123–38 '69.

YOSY, ANN, fl.1815–33

14605 **De Beer, G. R.** Mrs. Ann Yosy and her books. N&Q 194:61–2 F '49.

YOUNGER, ARTHUR, 1741–1820

14606 **Bauer, Harry C.** Annals of agriculture, or, Arthur Young, completer of sets. Bull Bib 20no10:240–2 Ja/Ap '53.

YOUNG, EDWARD, 1683–1765

14607 **Chapman, Robert W.** Young's Night thoughts. R Eng Stud 4no15:330 Jl '28. [Sg.: R. W. C.]

14608 **Sherburn, George.** Edward Young and book advertising. R Eng Stud 4no16:414–17 Oc '28.

14609 **Boas, Frederick S.** A manuscript copy of Edward Young's Busiris. TLS 22 My '30:434.

14610 **Chapman, Robert W.** Young's Night thoughts. (Bibliographical notes). TLS 28 Mr '36:284.

14611 **Pettit, Henry J.** The dating of Young's Night-thoughts. [1742–6]. Mod Lang N 55no3:194–5 Mr '40.

14612 **Chapman, Robert W.** Young's Naval lyrick. [Imperium pelagi]. N&Q 183:343–4 D '42. [Sg.: R. W. C.]

14613 **Pettit, Henry J.** The text of Edward Young's letters to Samuel Richardson. [And mrs. Barbauld]. Mod Lang N 57no8:668–70 D '42. table.

14614 —— 'Preface to a bibliography of Young's Night-thoughts' *in* Elizabethan studies and other essays in honor of George F. Reynolds. Boulder, Col., 1945. p. 215–22.

Anonymity.–Serialization.–Printers and booksellers.–Paper.

14615 —— Young's Night-thoughts re-examined. Library ser5 3no4:299–301 Mr '49.

14616 **Leek, Helen.** The Edward Young–Edmund Curll quarrel: a review. Pa Bib Soc Am 62:321–35 '68. facsim.

[The true count of items is 15156].